LANDLORD AND TENANT LAW

AUSTRALIA
LBC Information Services Ltd
Sydney

CANADA and **USA**
Carswell
Toronto

NEW ZEALAND
Brooker's
Auckland

SINGAPORE and **MALAYSIA**
Thomson Information (S.E. Asia)
Singapore

LANDLORD AND TENANT LAW

Sweet & Maxwell's Textbook Series

By Martin Davey, LL.B

Senior Lecturer in Law, University of Manchester

LONDON
SWEET & MAXWELL
1999

Published in 1999 by
Sweet & Maxwell Limited of
100 Avenue Road, London NW3 3PF
(http://www.smlawpub.co.uk)
Typeset by Tradespools Ltd, Frome, Somerset
Printed in England by
Clays Ltd, St. Ives plc

No natural forests were destroyed to make this product;
only farmed timber was used and replanted

A C.I.P. catalogue record for this book is available from the British Library

ISBN 0-421-556 706

PREFACE

In many universities today a one year, or even two year, land law course with a large landlord and tenant component is a fond memory, at least for land law teachers if not for students. Modular structured degree programmes cannot afford such luxuries and it is more than likely that a modern single module land law course will only be able to deal in brief with the law of landlord and tenant. But quite apart from such curricula developments, a proper treatment of the modern law of landlord and tenant requires a separate module. Leasehold tenure is a widespread feature of the property market and hence of British society and as such the fundamental principles of the relevant law need to be understood by many present and prospective lawyers.

This book is designed to provide a textual basis for such a course. It is of necessity selective to some degree and in places reflects the academic and practical interests of the writer. The law of landlord and tenant is a mixture of contract law and land law but these common law principles and rules are heavily overladen by extensive schemes of statutory regulation. The text seeks to build upon a student's prior knowledge of those two bodies of substantive law by providing an exposition of how their frequently divergent approaches to landlord and tenant problems are synthesised by the law.

The law of landlord and tenant broadly covers three different sectors of the property market; the residential, the commercial-industrial and the agricultural sectors. The fundamental principles of the basic common law of landlord and tenant govern all three areas and therefore the first part of the book contains an examination of the general law concerning the essential characteristics of tenancies, their formal requirements, major common terms and the effect of alienation of the landlord or tenant's interest in the property on the enforceability of those terms. It concludes with a chapter on the termination of leases at common law including statutory protection for tenants and certain other occupiers by way of laws dealing with harassment and unlawful eviction. The remainder of the book comprises an exposition and analysis of the principal statutory regimes which regulate the residential and commercial sectors of the leasehold property market. The omission of any treatment of the special codes which apply to tenancies of agricultural land and dwellings is not meant to denigrate its significance. It is done partly because of length constraints and partly because it is a less commonly encountered area of practice which in any event makes some use of concepts and mechanisms to be found in the other statutory codes.

Despite the prolonged and still far from complete phasing out of the Rent Acts since 1989, a relatively extensive examination of that code is offered not least because of its historical significance and the importance of the principles at stake. Academic debates in the United Kingdom and the United States have raged between the laissez faire and interventionist protagonists. But quite apart from these issues, which are social, economic and political in nature, there is the very practical consideration that many of the concepts and devices employed by other codes (such as that in the Housing Act 1988 governing assured tenancies and the secure tenancy regime of the Housing Act 1985) are derived from the Rent Act regime.

The law of landlord and tenant is at present in a state of flux. The body of case law continues to grow at an alarming rate and the original Law Commission programme to codify the law of landlord and tenant has been only partially fulfilled so far. A number of the Commission's Reports on landlord and tenant law reform have now been gathering dust for some years. One measure of reform which might reach the statute book in the not too distant future is the introduction of a new commonhold tenure to deal with some of the outstanding criticisms of the long leasehold system of tenure. If so readers can anticipate a complex measure no less challenging than other statutory attempts, such as the Landlord and Tenant Act 1987, to deal with these intractable problems in recent decades.

In an effort to make some sense of the current legal position the book examines the present law of landlord and tenant with an eye to possible reforms. It also seeks to demonstrate to student readers the important influence which practitioners and powerful client groups can have on the shape of the law. My intention is not only to make students aware of this factor but to draw attention generally to the issues of legal policy at stake when considering the present law and reform proposals.

Sweet & Maxwell have excelled themselves in dealing with the manuscript more expeditiously than any author could reasonably expect and I would like to offer the editorial staff my sincere thanks for their boundless patience. Finally and not least I owe an immense debt of gratitude to my family. Despite the inroads which the task of writing has made on family life they have borne my absences and tolerated my occasional ill humour with understanding and loving support for which I am truly grateful.

I have tried to state the law as at September 1 1998.

Martin Davey

October 1998

TABLE OF CONTENTS

F.   Premiums

G.   Housing Association Tenancies

H.   Restricted Contracts

11   Secure Tenancies

A.   Grounds on Which the Court may Order Possession if it Considers it Reasonable

B.   Grounds on Which the Court may Order Possession if Suitable Alternative Accommodation is Available

C.   Grounds on Which the Court may Order Possession if it Considers it Reasonable, and Suitable Alternative Accommodation is Available

TABLE OF CASES

TABLE OF UK STATUTES

TABLE OF STATUTORY INSTRUMENTS

Chapter 1

INTRODUCTION: NATURE AND TYPES OF LEASES

Definition and terminology

The relationship of landlord and tenant is normally created when a person with a freehold or leasehold estate in land, known as the landlord, confers on another person, known as the tenant, the right to exclusive possession of that land for a term. That right is known as a tenancy. It will be either a legal or equitable estate or interest. (See below for the formalities governing legal and equitable tenancies.) A word of warning as to the appropriate legal language is in order here. Alternative terms for "landlord", "tenant" and "tenancy", such as "lessor", "lessee" and "lease", respectively, are often used—most frequently by lawyers. This alternative terminology is, as a matter of practice, frequently reserved for more formally created longer fixed-term interests, whilst the terms "landlord", "tenant" and "tenancy" are reserved for shorter, less formal fixed-term or periodic interests. However, this is simply a matter of practice and the relevant terms are often used interchangeably, at least by persons other than lawyers.

It is a source of further confusion that the term "lease" can be used not only as a noun, to describe the interest granted by the landlord to the tenant, but also as a verb, to describe the act of letting a property to another. (Where a lease/tenancy has been created by deed (as to which, see below) the word "lease" is also frequently used to describe that deed.) To avoid confusion, the terms "landlord", "tenant" and "tenancy" will, wherever possible, be used throughout this book. Indeed an important recent statute, the Landlord and Tenant (Covenants) Act 1995, also adopts this approach. More ancient terms, such as "demise", meaning to let or to lease or indeed the estate created, will be avoided altogether.

Although it is not an essential requirement for a tenancy to arise, as confirmed by the Court of Appeal in *Ashburn Anstalt v. Arnold* [1989] Ch. 1, the additional element of consideration will also be present, save in exceptional cases. Thus tenancies are usually granted in consideration of either a capital sum, often referred to as a premium, or for periodic payments—rent, or sometimes for a combination of the two.

Essential elements of a tenancy

The definition of a tenancy offered above contains two essential requirements. First, that "exclusive possession" be granted to the occupier, and second that it be "for a term". In this context the expression "for a term" means that the occupier is granted a right for a definite fixed period—however short or long—or on a periodic basis (*e.g.* from week to week, or year to year, until determined by notice given by either party). This requirement is dealt with separately below, when the natures of the two different types of tenancy are examined. Before then we need to consider carefully the significance of the requirement of exclusive possession.

Exclusive occupation licences

As we have seen above, a tenancy is a legal or equitable interest in land which is capable of binding third-party successors in title of the landlord. But not all arrangements for the occupation of land by another give rise to a tenancy. Of course, if an arrangement for the occupation of land does not involve the grant of exclusive possession, then there can be no question of a tenancy having been created, and in such a case a licence or some other right will be found to have been created. In contrast to a tenancy, a licence is an arrangement whereby a person is given the personal right to occupy land belonging to another, but without creating any estate or interest in the land (see *Radaich v. Smith* (1959) 101 C.L.R. 209 at 222 *per* Windeyer J.; see further, J. Stevens and R.A.Pearce, *Land Law*, (Sweet & Maxwell 1997), chap. 12 for an account of the law governing licences for the use of land).

In general, licences, whether gratuitous or contractual, are not proprietary rights and therefore they are not capable of binding third party successors in title of the licensor. (For an account of the failed attempt by Lord Denning to elevate the contractual licence to the status of an (equitable) interest in land in a series of judgments in the Court of Appeal, see *Ashburn Anstalt v. Arnold* [1989] Ch. 1, where there is also a discussion of the limited exceptional circumstances in which such a licence might bind a third-party purchaser from the licensor through the medium of a constructive trust).

Until the twentieth century it was clearly established that where an occupier was granted exclusive possession for a term at a rent, this would automatically give rise to a tenancy. As long as this principle was good law there was no scope for the argument that such a grant could be equally consistent with the creation of a licence. However, from 1920 onwards most residential tenants, but not licensees, were afforded the twin benefits of rent control and security of tenure. The latter prevented landlords from recovering possession at the end of the contractual tenancy save in exceptional circumstances. Furthermore, valuable succession rights could arise on the death of a protected tenant. (From 1946, furnished licensees with exclusive possession were subject to a form of rent regulation and afforded a more limited form of security of tenure under a separate statutory code.) The relevant legislation was popularly known as "the Rent Acts" and introduced an important new dimension to the thorny issue of how a tenancy was to be distinguished from a licence, and a body of case law soon emerged. At this point a subtle shift of reasoning occurred. Whilst exclusive possession remained an essential requirement of a tenancy, the courts began to focus their attention on the "intention of the parties".

In practice, cases fell into one or both of two categories. The first was where, despite the grant of exclusive possession for a term, there were certain factors present which, in the court's view, would negative the intention to create a tenancy. An example would be where an owner, as an act of generosity, granted a person exclusive possession on a temporary basis without either of the parties intending to create a tenancy. It was quite clear in such cases that the court's finding that the parties had no "intention to create a tenancy" was a legal fiction to justify the court labelling the arrangement in such a way as to prevent the landlord being saddled with a Rent Act protected tenant, where the court considered that to be an unjust outcome. The main difficulty faced by the courts in these cases was that of determining what special factors would negative the intention to create a tenancy. The fictional nature of the requisite intention became obvious in those cases where the parties had probably never even addressed their minds to the legal status of their arrangement.

The second group of cases was more difficult. These were cases where there were no special circumstances, but where the agreement actually declared that, despite the grant of exclusive possession, the parties had no intention to create a tenancy. Both strands of authority raised difficulties. In the second group of cases the court had to decide whether it was possible to go behind the wording of the agreement to overturn the expressed intentions of the parties. This created a conflict between two judicial lines of reasoning. On the one hand there was a desire by some judges to give effect to the terms of the expressed bargain, perhaps motivated by a sneaking sympathy for landlords seeking to avoid the Rent Acts. On the other hand there was also some judicial reluctance to permit landlords to dress up as a "licence" what in substance was a tenancy, for the sole purpose of avoiding the special statutory regimes. There was of course a logical difficulty here. How could the court determine what was in substance a tenancy if this turned upon the intention of the parties?

How to distinguish a tenancy from a licence

The nature of the dilemma faced by the courts was well highlighted by Denning L.J. in *Facchini v. Bryson* [1952] 1 T.L.R. 1386, who, having noted that—

> "In all the cases where an occupier has been held to be a licensee there has been something in the circumstances, such as a family arrangement or an act of friendship or generosity, or such like to negative any intention to create a tenancy"

went on to say that, in the absence of such special circumstances where, as in that case, a person had been allowed into (exclusive) occupation of a house at a rent in consideration of a weekly payment, that arrangement had all the hallmarks of a tenancy:

> "and the parties cannot by the mere words of their contract turn it into something else. Their relationship is determined by law and not by the label which they choose to put on it."

(See also *Addiscombe Garden Estates Ltd v. Crabbe* [1958] 1 Q.B. 513).

Despite this robust defence of the traditional test for distinguishing between a tenancy and a licence, the emerging tendency in other cases to state the test for distinguishing between a tenancy and a licence in terms of the "intention of the parties" persuaded landlords that they would be able to avoid the application of Rent Act protections by framing agreements so as to deny any intention of creating a tenancy. Indeed, in *Abbeyfield Society Ltd v. Woods* [1968] 1 W.L.R. 374, Lord Denning M.R. himself said that—

> "The modern cases show that a man may be a licensee even though he has exclusive possession, even though the word 'rent' is used, and even though the word 'tenancy' is used. The court must look at the agreement as a whole and see whether a tenancy really was intended."

Landlords could also take comfort from the words of McNair J. in *Murray Bull and Co Ltd v. Murray* [1953] 1 Q.B. 211, holding that—

"both parties intended that the relationship should be that of licensee and no more...The primary consideration on both sides was that the defendant, as occupier of the flat, should not be a controlled tenant."

This conflict of approach was thrown into relief in 1985 when the leading case of *Street v. Mountford* reached the House of Lords ([1985] A.C. 809, HL).

The defendant, Wendy Mountford, was given the right to occupy two rooms in a house for a weekly payment, under a written agreement with the owner, Roger Street (a Bournemouth solicitor). Mr Street knew his case law and the agreement contained a number of terms including one which described it as a personal non-assignable licence. At the bottom of the agreement, Mrs Mountford had signed an undertaking which stated that 'I understand and accept that a licence in the above form does not and is not intended to give me a tenancy protected under the Rent Acts.' Mrs Mountford subsequently had a fair rent determined under the Rent Act 1977 on the basis that in law she had a regulated tenancy within the meaning of that Act. Mr Street argued that she had a licence which was not within the ambit of the fair rent scheme, which applied only to tenancies.

Mr Street was clearly relying on the proposition, discussed above, that whilst the grant of exclusive possession by an estate owner to the other party for a fixed or periodic term at a rent was a necessary condition for the creation of a tenancy, a clear statement manifesting an intention not to create a tenancy would negative any finding of such an interest. In similar vein, Slade L.J., in *Street v. Mountford*, stated that—

"it seems to me that if Mrs Mountford is to displace the express statement of intention embodied in the declaration, she must show that the declaration was a deliberate sham or at least an inaccurate statement of what was the true substance of the real agreement between the parties. (1985) 49 P.& C.R. 324, 330"

In other words, Mrs Mountford would need to have shown that the parties had agreed a tenancy which had been dressed up as a licence. This meaning of the term "sham" was derived from the definition afforded by Diplock L.J. in *Snook v. London & West Riding Investments Ltd* [1967] 2 Q.B. 786,802 where he stated that it means—

"acts or documents executed by the parties to the 'sham' which are intended by them to give to third parties or to the court the appearance of creating between the parties legal rights and obligations different from the actual legal rights and obligations (if any) which the parties intended to create."

Because Mrs Mountford was unable to establish such a common intention on the part of herself and Mr Street, the Court found that she was a licensee and not a tenant.

Undaunted, Mrs Mountford appealed to the House of Lords (despite having been offered a five-year assured shorthold tenancy at £14 per week—the rent which the rent officer had determined for her regulated tenancy—in return for an undertaking to abandon her appeal). The House reversed the decision of the Court of Appeal and reasserted the traditional rule that the grant of exclusive possession for a fixed or periodic term at a rent automatically creates a tenancy unless it appears from the surrounding circumstances either that there was no intention to create a legal relationship at all or that the right to exclusive possession is referable to a legal relationship other than a tenancy. Although at first sight it looked as though Lord Templeman was stating that the element of rent was an essential characteristic of a tenancy, it has since been made clear by the Court of Appeal that this is not so (see *Ashburn Anstalt v. Arnold* [1989] Ch. 1, above). However, it is strongly arguable that the absence of provision for payment in that and similar cases should have severely weakened the finding of a tenancy, in the absence of any express intention by the parties to create such an interest (see [1988] Conv. 201 M. Thompson).

Because it was conceded by Mr Street that Mrs Mountford had exclusive possession, and none of the exceptional circumstances indicated by Lord Templeman were present, it followed that the parties had created a tenancy and the express statement of the parties that this was not what they intended was irrelevant. As Lord Templeman memorably observed—

> "the consequences in law of the agreement, once concluded, can only be determined by consideration of the effect of the agreement. If the agreement satisfied all the requirements of a tenancy, then the agreement produced a tenancy and the parties cannot alter the effect of the agreement by insisting that they only created a licence. The manufacture of a five pronged implement for manual digging results in a fork even if the manufacturer, unfamiliar with the English language, insists that he intended to make and has made a spade. ([1985] A.C. 809 at 819, HL.)"

The context of *Street v. Mountford* is all-important. It came at a time when the use of "licence agreements" to avoid the Rent Acts had become a widespread practice, and in the words of Lord Templeman—

> "Although the Rent Acts must not be allowed to alter or influence the construction of an agreement, the court should in my opinion be astute to detect and frustrate sham devices and artificial transactions whose only object is to disguise the grant of a tenancy and to evade the Rent Acts. [1985] A.C. 809, 825, H.L."

It is difficult to believe that, despite the opening words of this sentence, the Rent Act avoidance nature of the transaction in *Street v. Mountford* did not play a significant part in the decision of the House of Lords. (An interesting postscript to this landmark case is that the litigation cost the landlord £40,000—to which the Small Landlords Association contributed £5,000—while Mrs Mountford eventually left in return for £1,800!) (see (1985) 129 S.J. 852).

The meaning of exclusive possession

After the decision of the House of Lords in *Street v. Mountford*, those landlords who wished to avoid the Rent Acts were forced either to create tenancies which fell within certain specified exceptions to the Rent Act regime catered for by the Act itself (*e.g.* a tenancy where "board" was provided), or to attempt to circumvent the decision in some other way.

In *Street v. Mountford* the grant of exclusive possession was not disputed:

> "In the present case it is clear that exclusive possession was granted and so much was conceded. In these circumstances it is unnecessary to analyse minutely the detailed rights and obligations contained in the agreement. [1985] A.C. 809, 823 per Lord Templeman"

Exclusive possession is a legal concept. It means the right of the occupier to exclude all others, including the landlord, save for the exercise of any express, implied or statutory right of entry. Thus, by agreement, a person might as a *matter of fact* be in exclusive *occupation* on a day-to-day basis of land belonging to another, in circumstances where the owner has retained a sufficient degree of management and control sufficient to deprive the occupier of exclusive *possession* in law.

> "In *Shell Mex & BP Ltd v. Manchester Garages* [1971] 1 W.L.R. 612, CA a licence agreement for the use of the plaintiff's petrol filling station was granted to the defendant company solely for the purpose of selling the plaintiff company's petrol. The defendants agreed not to impede the plaintiffs in exercising their rights of possession of the premises and to facilitate any alterations that the plaintiff's might wish to carry out. The Court of Appeal considered the rights of control which remained vested in the plaintiff company to be inconsistent with a grant of exclusive possession to the defendants and therefore rejected the defendant's claim, made when the plaintiffs purported to terminate the licence, that they had a tenancy protected by Part II of the Landlord and Tenant Act 1954 (which does not apply to licences)."

This decision was approved of in *Street v. Mountford* and for a while afterwards landlords of residential property sought to avoid the creation of a tenancy by exploiting this distinction between exclusive occupation (a matter of fact) and exclusive possession (a matter of law). Indeed, landlords were able to obtain succour in this respect from Lord Templeman's speech in *Street v. Mountford* because, after stating that "the only intention which is relevant is the intention demonstrated by the agreement to grant exclusive possession for a term at a rent", his Lordship also observed that "Sometimes it may be difficult to discover whether, on the true construction of an agreement, exclusive possession is conferred." Indeed, as noted above, Lord Templeman had already acknowledged that the intention to grant exclusive possession was one demonstrated by the agreement.

Exclusive possession denied

The case of *Antoniades v. Villiers* [1990] 1 A.C. 417 HL is a classic example of the shift in focus from the consequences of exclusive possession to the denial of exclusive possession.

> The landlord entered into separate 'licence' agreements with a young couple to occupy an attic flat. The couple had applied together for the flat. Each agreement emphasised that the 'licensee' occupier was not to have exclusive possession and that the intention of the parties was to create a licence outside the Rent Act. The agreements also provided that 'The licensor shall be entitled at any time to use the rooms together with the licensee and permit other persons to use all of the rooms together with the licensee.'

The House of Lords held that a joint tenancy had been created. Lord Templeman reasoned that because the couple applied to rent the flat jointly and to enjoy exclusive occupation, which they subsequently enjoyed in fact, a tenancy was thereby created. Consequently the clause which reserved power to the landlord to deprive them of exclusive occupation was an ineffective attempt to contract out of the Rent Act indirectly (there already being a tenancy by virtue of the exclusive occupation). Lord Templeman here seemed to treat the terms "exclusive occupation" and "exclusive possession" as synonymous, suggesting that if exclusive occupation is in fact afforded to the occupier, then save in those exceptional cases referred to in *Street v. Mountford* (above), he will have a tenancy and it is then too late to provide that it is anything other than a tenancy. Thus the wording used becomes unimportant and irrelevant. This gloss upon the notion of the construction of the agreement referred to in *Street v. Mountford* clearly placed even bigger obstacles in the way of landlords with a mind to avoid the Rent Acts.

Furthermore, in *Antoniades v. Villiers*, Lord Templeman also considered that in any event the sharing clause was a "pretence" intended only to deprive the occupiers of Rent Act protection. By contrast, Lord Oliver was of the opinion that on the terms of the documents the occupiers did not have exclusive possession in law because of the rights reserved to the owner. Nevertheless he went on to conclude that a joint tenancy had been created, but only on the basis that the arrangement was a "sham". All the evidence, including the actual conduct of the parties and the fact that sharing with another or others was hardly consistent with the size and physical layout of the premises, showed that the "licences" were artificial transactions designed to evade the Rent Act. They were sham documents designed to disguise the true intention of the parties, that is that the occupiers should enjoy together exclusive occupation. There was no intention by either landlord or occupiers to operate the sharing clause.

This decision of the House of Lords effectively overruled the earlier pre-*Street v. Mountford* decisions of the Court of Appeal which had given the green light to avoidance mechanisms of the kind employed in *Antoniades v. Villiers* (*viz, Somma v. Hazelhurst* [1978] 1 W.L.R. 1014; *Aldrington Garages v. Fielder* (1978) 37 P.& C.R. 461 and *Sturolson v. Weniz* (1984) 17 H.L.R. 140. *cf. Demuren v. Seal Estates* (1978) 7 H.L.R. 83, CA and *O'Malley v. Seymour* (1978) 250 E.G. 1083, CA where non-exclusive occupation licence agreements were found not to reflect the true intentions of the parties).

Shams and pretences

The principle established in *Antoniades v. Villiers* was subsequently applied by the Court of Appeal in *Aslan v. Murphy; and Wynne v. Duke* [1990] 1 W.L.R. 766; and *Nicolaou v. Pitt* [1989] 21 E.G. 71. In the former the Court subtly distinguished between two types of case. The first is where the whole agreement is dressed up by both parties as a licence by the use of misleading terminology (see *Snook v. London & West Riding Investments Ltd* [1967] 2 Q.B. 786, 802 above). The second is where the agreement is not a sham as such but nevertheless contains provisions which, if taken at their face value, would prevent a tenancy arising. An example would be a "sharing clause" of the kind discussed above. In such a case, if those provisions are in reality pretences and do not form part of the true bargain between the parties, they can be disregarded.

> In *Aslan v. Murphy* the defendant entered into occupation of a single room under an agreement which stated that 'the licensor is not willing to grant the licensee exclusive possession of any part of the room.' The agreement further provided that the licensee had a licence to use the room between the hours of midnight and 10.30 a.m. and between noon and midnight each day, and that the landlord should retain keys to the room and have an absolute right of entry at all times. It also contained a 'sharing clause'. The Court held that, save for the retention of keys clause, these provisions were a pretence and to be disregarded, whilst the retention of keys was not in the circumstances inconsistent with a tenancy. A tenancy was also found in *Duke v. Wynne* where the court disregarded a sharing clause in a licence agreement with a married couple to occupy a three-room flat. Although sharing was physically possible in that case, there was no evidence of any serious intention for the sharing clause to be operative.

The same conclusion was reached in *Nicolaou v. Pitt* (above) where three friends signed a joint "licence agreement" of a two-bedroom flat. On the departure of two of them the remaining occupier and a new occupier (a friend whom she subsequently married) each signed a non-exclusive occupation agreement. The Court of Appeal could see no reason to disturb the finding of the county court judge that the occupiers jointly had exclusive possession and hence a tenancy.

Exclusive possession legitimately denied

To be contrasted with this line of authority, which is clearly concerned to strike down blatant attempts to evade the Rent Act, is a different strand of authority which permits effect to be given to flat or house-sharing agreements where a joint tenancy was clearly and genuinely not intended by the parties. In these cases the parties could not be said to have joint exclusive possession of the premises.

In *A.G. Securities Ltd v. Vaughan* [1990] 1 A.C. 417, HL a flat was occupied by four occupiers, all of them initially strangers to each other, who each entered into a separate licence agreement with the owner. Each agreement stated that the licensee was not to have exclusive possession of the flat or any part of it and was to enjoy occupation in common with the other occupiers. The agreements were entered into on different occasions and were for differing amounts. The occupiers arranged amongst themselves for each to occupy a separate bedroom and to have shared use of the remainder of the flat. When one left, the landlord decided upon a new occupier. There was no provision for sharing occupation with the landlord. The House of Lords held that they were in occupation under separate licences. It could not be said that they enjoyed exclusive possession sufficient to make them joint tenants.

The decision was applied by the Court of Appeal in *Stribling v. Wickham* (1989) 2 E.G. L.R. 1353, CA where three separate identical licence agreements for the occupation of a flat were granted on the same day to three individuals who already knew each other. All three had originally entered into occupation at different times under earlier agreements. The flat was suitable for use by a multiple and shifting population of occupiers. Each was made liable to pay for his own use and occupation only and the landlord reserved the right to select any replacement occupiers. Notwithstanding the additional presence of the notorious sharing clause of the type outlawed by the House of Lords in *Antoniades v. Villiers*, the Court was satisfied that in the light of all the circumstances the agreements represented the realities of the transactions and a genuine and sensible arrangement for the benefit of both sides. (Of course, in all flat-sharing cases if, as is not uncommon in student houses, the landlord has granted each of the occupiers exclusive possession of a part of the premises (*e.g.* a bedroom), with shared use of the remainder, each occupier might be found to be tenant of that part of which he or she has exclusive possession).

Arguably more surprising was the decision of the Court of Appeal in *Mikeover v. Brady* [1989] 3 All E.R. 618, CA, where a couple who occupied a two-room flat under separate licence agreements were held jointly to have exclusive possession but nevertheless to be licensees because they were not jointly and severally liable for the total rent, each being liable for his or her share only, thereby precluding a finding of a joint tenancy on the basis that there was no unity of interest. The decision would seem to have opened the way for a landlord to avoid the creation of a tenancy simply by providing for each occupier to be responsible only for his share of the rent. In the light of the law established by the House of Lords, the decision is difficult to justify. In *Antoniades v. Villiers* Lord Templeman had stated that if the landlord chose to require each of the tenants to pay half the rent, this did not by itself negative a finding of a joint tenancy. The distinguishing of the decision in *Antoniades v. Villiers* on the basis that there was a sham sharing clause in that case seems highly questionable.

However, it was not long before the House of Lords was to have another opportunity to return to the issue in a case involving a local authority landlord.

> In *Westminster City Council v. Clarke* [1992] 2 A.C. 288 the House of Lords upheld as genuine a licence agreement whereby a man was permitted to occupy a room in single men's hostel run by the council. A resident warden was employed to look after the building, assist residents and enter rooms with a duplicate key where necessary. The agreement also contained a "sharing clause" and provided that the occupier could be required to remove to a different room on request. There were also restrictions on visitors. The House of Lords held that the agreement and the special nature of the hostel indicated that the council had retained such a degree of control over the room that in law the occupier did not have exclusive possession and therefore did not have a secure tenancy. The Court further held, overruling on this point *Family Housing Association v. Jones* [1990] 1 W.L.R. 779, CA, that although, by section 79(3) of the Housing Act 1985, a licensee can enjoy the protections afforded to a secure tenant this is only the case where he has exclusive possession.

In reaching the conclusion that the occupier was a licensee who did not have exclusive possession Lord Templeman stated—

> "I take into account the object of the council, namely the provision of temporary accommodation for vulnerable homeless persons, the necessity for the council to retain possession of all the rooms in order to make and administer arrangements for the suitable accommodation off all the occupiers and the need for the council to retain possession of every room not only in the interests of the council as the owners of the hostel but also for the purpose of providing for the occupier supervision and assistance. (p.301)"

Lord Templeman also made it clear that the decision was a very special case which turned on the peculiar nature of the hostel maintained by the council, the use of the hostel by the council, the totality, immediacy and objectives of the powers exercised by the council and the restrictions imposed on Mr Clarke. He went on to warn that the decision in the case will not allow a landlord, public or private to free himself from the Rent Acts or from the restrictions of a secure tenancy merely by adopting or adapting the language of a licence to occupy (p.302).

Of course the court was able to come to the conclusion that there was no tenancy because of the absence of exclusive possession in the light of all the circumstances. By contrast, this avenue was not open to the Court of Appeal in *Family Housing Association v. Jones* (a decision overruled by the House of Lords on another point; see above). The Court there held that where a housing association (to which the local authority had licensed the property) granted an occupier exclusive possession under a licence agreement, a tenancy was created. This was so notwithstanding that the agreement was for a temporary licence pending enquiry by the local authority as to whether it owed any more extensive duties to the applicant under the homelessness provisions in Part III of the Housing Act 1985. However such a tenancy only becomes secure if the tenancy is not terminated within 12 months, and this mitigates to a considerable degree the problems which might otherwise have been caused to hard-pressed local authorities seeking to carry out their statutory duties to the homeless by making optimal use of their housing stock. (But contrast the Court of Appeal decision in *Bruton v. London and Quadrant Housing Trust* [1997] 4 All E.R. 970 CA).

It follows from the above discussion that in the absence of a sham the distinction between exclusive occupation and exclusive possession can still be vital. This was critical in the *Clarke* case because by section 79(3) of the Housing Act 1985 the protection afforded to secure tenants also applies to a licence to occupy a dwelling-house. Although the Court of Appeal had earlier held that this meant that any licensee would be protected, (the House of Lords, in *Clarke*, ruled that this would only be the case where the licensee had exclusive possession and Mr Clarke did not have exclusive possession (see above).

Lodgers

In *Street v. Mountford* Lord Templeman made it clear that a lodger does not have exclusive possession and therefore there can be no question of a tenancy arising in such a case. The lodger is only a licensee—

> "The occupier is a lodger if the landlord supplies attendance or services which require the landlord or his servants to exercise unrestricted access to and use of the premises. A lodger is entitled to live in the premises but cannot call the place his own."

In *Monmouth Borough Council v. Marlog* (1995) 27 H.L.R. 30, CA the Court of Appeal found that where a council tenant had allowed the defendant occupier and her two children to have the use of two of the three bedrooms and the shared use of the kitchen, bathroom and living accommodation, she became no more than his lodger and did not have a sub-tenancy (which would have been binding on the council on whom the tenant had served notice to quit terminating his tenancy). It was not clear in this case whether the landlord/tenant supplied attendance or services, but it was clear that he could enter the defendant's room if he wished for reasonable purposes. Whatever the technical niceties of the landlord/lodger relationship the Court was clearly influenced by what Nourse L.J. described as "the entirely informal nature of the relationship" which was such that "it would be simply ludicrous to suggest that there had been an intention between these two persons to create the relationship of landlord and tenant" (at p.242). To this extent the case looks very much like one affected by the "generosity factor" discussed above.

To be contrasted with these cases are more formal arrangements but where the circumstances are such that the occupier, although possibly enjoying exclusive *occupation* does not enjoy exclusive *possession*. Pre-*Street v. Mountford* examples, which are still good law, are provided by *Abbeyfield Society Ltd v. Woods* [1968] 1 W.L.R. 374 and *Marchant v. Charters* [1977] 1 W.L.R. 1181. In the former case a charitable society rented an unfurnished room in an old people's home to the defendant, the society providing food, heating, light and a housekeeper. The agreement, which provided that the society reserved the right to recover possession on one month's notice where absolutely necessary in the interests of himself and other residents, was held to have created a licence. Thus the society, who had done everything they could to arrange more suitable accommodation for Mr Woods where he could be looked after, were able to recover possession when Mr Woods was no longer capable of looking after himself. The Court of Appeal held that the agreement was too personal in nature to amount to a tenancy. In *Street v. Mountford* Lord Templeman treated this as a finding that Mr Woods was a lodger. In *Marchant v. Charters* an arrangement for occupation for a rent of a room in a house, where there was a resident housekeeper who cleaned the rooms daily and provided a weekly change of linen, gave rise to a licence only. While disapproving of Lord Denning's test, in that case, of determining the nature and quality of the occupancy from the intention of the parties, Lord Templeman approved of the actual decision on the basis that the occupier was a lodger and therefore did not have exclusive possession. (See also *Appah v. Parncliffe Investments Ltd*

[1964]1 W.L.R. 1064 and *Luganda v. Service Hotels Ltd* [1969] 2 Ch. 209). But the courts will be astute to detect attempts to exploit this category of exceptional cases. Thus in *Crancour v. De Silvaesa* (1986) 18 H.L.R. 265 a six-month licence agreement not only purported to exclude the licensees from occupation of the premises between 10.30 a.m. and noon, but also gave the licensor power to move the licensee to another flat of comparable size in the same building. It further provided for possession, management and control of the flat to remain vested in the licensor at all times and gave him unrestricted access for various purposes including the provision of service requiring attendance. The Court of Appeal suspected a possible sham, stating that if it is shown that the cleaning of the room never took place and that other services did not in fact require unrestricted access then it might be open to the court to conclude that the true agreement between the parties did not provide that they were lodgers rather than tenants.

In all the cases where a person is found to be a lodger, it is because the landlord or his servants have the right to unrestricted access for the purpose of providing services. This does not mean that there cannot be a tenancy in other cases where although personal services are provided, the landlord does not have unrestricted access for this purpose. Indeed, the Rent Act 1977, s.7(1) specifically excludes from protected tenancy status a tenancy where there is payment in respect of "attendance" (defined in *Palser v. Grinling* [1948] A.C. 291, 310, HL as "the provision of services which are personal to the tenant, and performed by an attendant provided by the landlord"). This therefore presupposes that such attendance does not automatically prevent the occupier having exclusive possession and therefore a tenancy. Nevertheless the consequences for the private sector occupier being found to be a licensee are less dramatic than before January 15, 1989 because, as noted below, the Rent Act 1977 is for the most part confined to tenancies created before that date.

However, the wide meaning afforded to the term "lodger" by the House of Lords in *Street v. Mountford* suggests that for sound practical reasons the courts consider the licence to be a more appropriate and flexible tool for regulating the occupation of old people's homes, boarding houses and single person's hostels run by charitable or public sector organisations (see *Westminster City Council v. Clarke*, above).

Parliament to the rescue of private landlords?

Many of the cases outlined above are examples of attempts by landlords to frame agreements which avoid the application of the Rent Acts. In most of the cases the attempt failed. However, since January 15, 1989 (when the relevant parts of the Housing Act 1988 came into force) it has not been necessary for landlords to resort to licence agreements, sham or otherwise, to avoid the Rent Act protection afforded to tenants. This is because since that date, save for certain transitional cases, it has not been possible to create new Rent Act protected tenancies.

Although the Housing Act provided for most tenancies created on or after the operative date to take effect automatically as "assured tenancies", which are afforded a degree of security modelled broadly on the Rent Act scheme, an alternative type of assured tenancy was also made available. The Act permitted the creation of what is termed an assured shorthold tenancy. This was a tenancy which originally had to be for a fixed term of at least six months and was subject to certain pre-tenancy formal notice requirements (as well as a bar on any break clause being exercised by the landlord within the first six months). However, there was no security of tenure to speak of because it was a relatively simple matter for the landlord to obtain possession following determination of the fixed term, provided he served the requisite statutory notice. Furthermore, if at the end of a shorthold tenancy the landlord granted the tenant at that time a new tenancy, then that tenancy, irrespective of length, would automatically be a shorthold tenancy to which the notice formalities did not apply. In the light of these provisions it came as no surprise to discover that for the most part, private sector landlords preferred the assured shorthold tenancy to the fully assured version. Indeed the fully assured tenancy was so little favoured that the Housing Act 1996 reversed the position by providing that, save in a number of specified cases, assured tenancies created on or after February 28, 1997 now take effect automatically as assured shorthold tenancies unless the parties agree to create a fully assured tenancy. Thus the need for a statutory pre-tenancy notice, a minimum fixed term and the prohibition on the operation of a landlord's break clause are all abolished in the case of such tenancies, although a court order for possession cannot be made so as to take effect within a period of six months from the beginning of the tenancy.

Shorthold tenancies have the added attraction for landlords that the rent is determined by agreement between the parties and can be challenged only in very limited circumstances, and then only to have a market rent determined. In such circumstances it is hardly surprising that since 1989 the private sector non-exclusive occupation licence agreement has become an extinct species and is now rarely if ever encountered in practice.

Continued importance of the lease/licence distinction

The enactment of the Housing Act 1988 does not mean that the lease/licence distinction is no longer of any significance. It can still be most important to determine whether an arrangement for the use and occupation of private residential accommodation amounts to a tenancy or not. Most tenants (and licensees with exclusive possession) of local authorities or certain housing associations are protected as "secure tenants" by the Housing Act 1985, whilst many business tenants have the protections afforded to them by Part II of the Landlord and Tenant Act 1954. Furthermore, while few private sector landlords will go out of their way expressly to create a licence agreement rather than an assured shorthold tenancy, there will be other cases where the parties have not come to any written agreement and yet where, for good reasons, the landlord would wish to establish that, despite exclusive occupation by the occupier, the arrangement does not create a tenancy, even an assured shorthold tenancy (see *Gray v. Taylor, The Times,* April 24, 1998, which charitable trustees of an almshouse created a license).

These circumstances were outlined in *Street v. Mountford (above)* by Lord Templeman, who said that—

> "Sometimes it may appear from the surrounding circumstances that there was no intention to create legal relationships. Sometimes it may appear from the surrounding circum- stances that the right to exclusive possession is referable to a legal relationship other than a tenancy. Legal relationships to which the grant of exclusive possession might be referable and which would or might negative the grant of an estate or interest in the land include occupancy under a contract for the sale of the land, occupancy pursuant to a contract of employment or occupancy referable to the holding of an office. [1985] A.C. 809, 826"

Each of these cases is examined below in the light of post-*Street v. Mountford* developments.

The generosity cases—no intention to create legal relations

In *Booker v. Palmer* [1942] 2 All E.R. 674, in 1940 the owner of a cottage agreed to allow a friend, Mrs Goldsmith, to install an evacuee, Mrs Palmer, in the cottage rent-free for the duration of the war. The agricultural land on which the cottage was situated was later leased to a third party who required possession for the accommodation of an agricultural labourer. The Court of Appeal held that the arrangement between the landowner and Mrs Goldsmith was not intended to create legal relations at all. Thus despite the fact that Mrs Palmer had exclusive occupation of the property, she did not have a tenancy. The only intention was for an informal non-contractual licence for Mrs Palmer to live in the cottage and therefore the purchaser was entitled to seek and obtain possession of the cottage. (See p.18 below as to the validity of tenancies for the duration of the war).

Similarly in *Heslop v. Burns* [1974] 1 W.L.R. 1241, where an owner of a cottage, as an act of generosity, permitted a family, with whom he was friends, to occupy the property rent-free, indefinitely, the Court of Appeal held that there was no intention to create a legal relationship. (See also the family arrangement in *Cobb v. Lane* [1952] 1 All E.R. 1199, CA where the Court of Appeal found that a sister who permitted her brother to live in a house owned (but not occupied by her) had only created a gratuitous revocable licence.) Although the decisions on the facts in both of the last two cases were approved of by the House of Lords in *Street v. Mountford*, it should be noted that they are no longer good authorities for the proposition that the relevant test for distinguishing between a lease and a licence where there is exclusive possession is the intention of the parties.

The dividing line between tenancy and licence is clearly very thin in these cases, and the fact that there is a family relationship between the parties will not necessarily be sufficient to exclude a finding of a tenancy where appropriate. In *Nunn v. Dalrymple* (1989) 21 H.L.R. 569, a couple gave up their tenancy of a council house in order, by agreement, to move into a cottage, owned (on a lease) by their daughter's father-in-law, where they stayed for nine years in return for a weekly payment. The Court of Appeal held that this arrangement gave rise to a tenancy. As Stocker L.J. observed (at p.578), "The proposition that it is possible, even where there is exclusive possession coupled with rent, to negative the conclusion of a tenancy by reason of family relationship does not itself mean that because of the family relationship that conclusion is negatived." Similarly in *Ward v. Warnke* (1990) 22 H.L.R. 496 a man who permitted his daughter and son-in-law to occupy a cottage, a second home which he had brought as a prospective retirement residence, at a rent was held to have created a tenancy. The payment of rent was treated as important in both cases.

In both *Heslop v. Burns* and *Cobb v. Lane*, where no rent was paid, any tenancy would have been a tenancy at will which as the law then stood would have terminated automatically after one year without payment of rent, thereby allowing the tenant to acquire title to the freehold by adverse possession after a further 12 years. (See now Limitation Act 1980, s.15 (6)). This consequence was one clearly viewed with some horror by the court in each case and neatly avoided by the finding of a licence, thereby precluding any claim to title by adverse possession.

The "generosity factor" was also crucial in *Marcroft Wagons v. Smith* [1951] 2 K.B. 496 where the daughter of a deceased tenant claimed to be the statutory tenant by succession under the Rent Act (see further p.263 *et seq* below). The landlord disputed the daughter's claim to a statutory tenancy (a legal creature described by Lord Evershed M.R. as a *monstrum horrendum*) but in the meantime allowed her to remain in occupation in return for an agreed payment. This occupation lasted six months before the landlord sought possession. The Court was clearly reluctant in the circumstances to find an intention to create a new contractual periodic tenancy and considered it to be a very different case from one where a landlord allows a new occupant into possession at a rent. The defendant had lost her mother, and the landlord, who disputed her right to succeed to a statutory tenancy, had allowed her to stay temporarily at the old rent whilst he considered his position. As Lord Evershed M.R. observed (at p.501)—

> "It seems to me that it would be quite shocking if, because a landlord allowed a condition of affairs to remain undisturbed for some short period of time, the law would have to infer therefrom that a relationship had arisen which made it impossible thereafter for the landlord to recover possession of the property when, admittedly, by taking proper measures from the start he could have got possession."

The Court observed that the longer such a state of affairs is allowed to continue the greater the risk to the landlord that the court will infer the grant of a new tenancy. In *Street v. Mountford*, Lord Templeman treated *Marcroft Wagons v. Smith* as a case of no intention to contract at all, despite the presence of consideration, leaving it to take effect, by default, as a revocable licence.

Difficulties can also arise where an owner who is seeking to sell his property permits another to occupy the property on a temporary basis pending sale with vacant possession. The Court of Appeal held in one such case that despite an agreement for exclusive possession for a (periodic) term at a rent, with provision for a month's notice, and therefore all the indicia of a tenancy, the parties had only created a temporary licence. The Court held that the arrangement fell within the exceptional circumstances to the general rule envisaged in *Street v. Mountford*, without specifying on what particular ground (*Sharp v. McArthur and Sharp* (1987) 19 H.L.R. 364. Contrast *Bretherton v. Paton* (1986) 18 H.L.R. 257, where an owner who wanted to sell his property, orally permitted a prospective purchaser, who agreed to pay the rates, to enter into possession in return for a weekly payment to cover a contribution to the insurance. When no sale materialised and the owner wished to remove the occupier it was held by the Court of Appeal that having granted the occupier exclusive possession in return for a periodic rental payment the owner had, whether he realised it or not, created a tenancy.)

This category of cases highlights the dilemma created by *Street v. Mountford*. On the one hand the law is anxious to outlaw blatant avoidance mechanisms by way of so-called "licence" agreements whilst reserving the licence category for those cases where the court is convinced that in substance neither party envisaged the creation of a tenancy with all that such an act entails. In these circumstances the licence is the fall-back category provided by law for characterising the relationship of the parties. Thus it is not so much a case of no intention to create legal relations, for a licence is a legal relationship, but simply one of no intention to create a tenancy. To this extent "the intention of the parties" to be ascertained in the light of all the circumstances is still a relevant factor.

Service occupiers

If an employee has exclusive possession of a dwelling-house belonging to his employer then ordinarily he will be a (service) tenant and it will not matter that he came into possession as a result of being an employee of the landlord (*Torbett v. Faulkner* [1952] 2 T.L.R. 659, CA; *Facchini v. Bryson* [1952] 1 T.L.R. 1386, CA). A service tenancy may be a protected tenancy under the Rent Act 1977 or an assured tenancy under the Housing Act 1988, although in both cases there is a discretionary ground for possession (Rent Act 1977, Sched.15, case 8: Housing Act 1988, Sched. 2, ground 16). See further Chapters 9 and 10 below.

By contrast, if the occupier/employee is required to occupy the premises for the more convenient, that is efficient, performance of his or her duties, he or she will have a service occupancy which will be no more than a licence whether or not he has exclusive occupation. (*Glasgow Corporation v. Johnstone* [1965] A.C. 609, HL; *Fox v. Dalby* (1874) L.R. 10 C.P. 285, DC; *Thompsons (Funeral Furnishers) v. Phillips* [1945] 2 All E.R. 49, CA; *Street v. Mountford*, above). A service occupier with exclusive occupation does not have a tenancy because the occupation is deemed to be that of the employer (see *Smith v. Seghill Overseers* (1875) L.R. 10 Q.B. 422 at 428, cited by Lord Templeman in *Street v. Mountford*). A tenancy would similarly not be created where the occupancy is referable to the holding of an office (*Street v. Mountford*, above).

In *Norris v. Checkfield* [1991] 1 W.L.R. 1241 an employee who worked as a semi-skilled mechanic was invited to move into a property owned by the employer in order better to perform the duties of a coach driver for the employer once he had applied for and obtained a PSV licence. The occupational licence agreement which he signed made it clear that occupation of the property was a condition of his employment and that on termination of the employment the licence would cease. It so happened that unknown to the employer (and possibly the employee at that time), the employee was disqualified from driving. When the employer subsequently terminated his employment the employee argued that because occupation was not required for the better performance of the duties carried out at the time the licence to occupy was granted, it could not be a service occupancy. The Court of Appeal rejected this argument and held that a service occupancy will arise where the employee went into occupation in anticipation that at some time in the future that occupation would be beneficial to the occupier's employment by the landlord. There was a sufficient factual nexus between occupation of the premises and the employment.

It will also be very unlikely that the court will be willing to find a tenancy where the arrangement comes to an end but as an act of generosity the occupier is permitted to remain temporarily, in return for periodic payments (*Burns v. Hammond* (1952) 159 E.G. 602, CA; *Thompsons (Funeral Furnishers) v. Phillips* (above)). On the other hand a tenancy arose in *Postcastle Properties v. Perridge* (1986) 18 H.L.R. 100 where following termination of a service licensee's employment the property was sold to a purchaser who did not seek possession but accepted rent from the occupier who was told to "carry on as usual". The court held that this was insufficient to rebut the presumption that a tenancy arose by virtue of exclusive possession coupled with periodical rental payments.

A tenancy was also held to have arisen in *Royal Philanthropic Society v. County* (1986) 18 H.L.R. 83 where a school houseparent who had a service licence of accommodation within the school building for the better performance of his duties got married and moved into a house two miles away which was owned by his employer. Because he had exclusive possession and the house was not required to be occupied for the better performance of his duties, he became a tenant and not a licensee.

Business licences

Although, as discussed above, the incentive for landlords in the private residential sector to create licences, in order to avoid the consequences of creating a tenancy, has diminished since the advent of the Housing Act 1988, the same cannot necessarily be said to be the case with regard to the commercial sector. Business tenants still enjoy the extensive protection of Part II of the Landlord and Tenant Act 1954, which does not extend to licensees, and although it is open to both landlord and tenant to make an application to court for exemption from the statutory protection in the case of a term of years, certain landlords might be tempted to avoid the necessity of such an application by relying on a licence agreement instead. Even before

Street v. Mountford the courts were astute to detect pretences where exclusive possession was granted to an occupier under an agreement for the use of some tennis courts containing many of the usual provisions one would expect to find in a business tenancy, save that the terminology had been altered so as to describe the arrangement as a licence. (See *Addiscombe Garden Estates Ltd v. Crabbe* [1958] 1 Q.B. 513). This approach was endorsed in *Street v. Mountford*, where it was made clear that the principles established by the House of Lords are just as applicable to business premises as they are to residential accommodation. Thus in *University of Reading v. Johnson-Houghton* [1985] 2 E.G.L.R. 113, a grant of a right, described as a licence, to occupy land for the purpose of training and exercising racehorses, which gave the occupier the right to exclude all persons, including the owner, from the area, was held to have created a tenancy. *Street v. Mountford* was also applied in *London & Associated Investment Trust plc v. Calow* (1987) 53 P.& C.R. 340 where a firm of solicitors had by agreement been given exclusive occupation of the plaintiff's premises in anticipation of obtaining a sub-tenancy or an assignment of the plaintiff's tenancy. This did not happen, and when the defendants subsequently left on very short notice it was held that they were tenants and not licensees, and therefore remained liable to pay rent (see also *Bretherton v. Paton*, above). Furthermore, as in the case of residential lettings, where the occupier has exclusive occupation the courts will be astute to reject any provision in an agreement which purports to deny exclusive possession by providing for the retention of possessory rights for the owner where such rights are patently not intended to be exercised. (See *Dellneed Ltd v. Chin* (1986) 53 P.& C.R. 172, where an agreement for the use of a Chinese restaurant was held to give rise to a tenancy). But where such rights are genuine they will be effective to deprive the occupier of exclusive possession and therefore negate any claim to a tenancy.

> In *Esso Petroleum Co Ltd v. Fumegrange Ltd* [1994] 46 E.G. 99 a licence agreement for the occupation of a service station contained terms whereby the owners retained an extensive degree of control and management of the site, including the right to make alterations, to install a car wash and to change the layout of the shop. The Court of Appeal held that the cumulative effect of these rights was to give the owners such a degree of control as to be inconsistent with any right to exclusive possession by the occupiers, who claimed to be tenants. (See also *Shell Mex & BP Ltd v. Manchester Garages* [1971] 1 W.L.R. 612, CA.)

The court was also unable to detect a sham in *Dresden Estates Ltd v. Collinson* (1988) 55 P.& C.R.47, CA. In that case, where the premises used by a scaffolder for storing his equipment consisted of a unit in industrial premises (a former pottery), a licence agreement not only denied any intention to grant exclusive possession and stated that it was personal to the licensees, but also gave the owner the right to relocate the occupier to other premises owned by the licensor. The court was satisfied that this clause was both genuine and appropriate in the circumstances. (See also *Smith v. Northside Developments Ltd* (1987) 55 P.& C.R. 164.)

Despite the fact that the courts have in general emphasised that the principles in *Street v. Mountford* are equally applicable to agreements for the occupation of business premises they have been more willing to recognise as valid, agreements that might have been expected to come under more sceptical scrutiny had they involved residential accommodation. Thus in *Camden LBC v. Shortlife Community Housing Ltd* (1992) 25 H.L.R. 330 the court was prepared to uphold a licence agreement whereby short life property which was destined for redevelopment was made available by the local authority to a tenants' co-operative which granted sub-licences to individual occupiers. The court held that on the construction of the agreement, exclusive possession had not been granted to the co-operative. (See also *Essex Plan Ltd v. Broadminster* (1988) 56 P.& C.R. 353.)

What does seem clear is that even in business arrangements it will no longer suffice to prevent a tenancy arising where all the *Street v. Mountford* indicia are present simply to state that the parties do no intend to create a tenancy. (In this light the earlier decision in *Euston Centre Properties Ltd v. H & J Wilson* (1982) 262 E.G. 1079 is difficult to sustain.)

A. TYPES OF LEASES

Legal leases

A lease is one of the two estates which are capable of taking effect as a legal estate by virtue of section 1(1) of the Law of Property Act LPA 1925. (The other is the fee simple absolute in possession commonly referred to, albeit technically inaccurately, as the freehold). However, not all leases are legal estates. To take effect as such the lease must be a "term of years absolute", as defined in LPA 1925, s.205(1)(xxvii). This is widely drafted to cover all leases for a fixed period, however long or short. It also includes periodic tenancies (whether weekly, monthly, quarterly or yearly). (See p.19 below as to types of tenancy). The fact that, as is commonly the case, a lease is determinable by notice or by forfeiture or by operation of law does not prevent it from being a legal estate. However, it is important to note that whilst the need to comply with the definition of a term of years absolute is a necessary requirement for the lease to take effect as a legal estate, it is not by itself a sufficient requirement. There is also the need for the lease to be created in accordance with the appropriate formalities, that is by way of a deed, where they are applicable. (See p.22 below for formalities and the consequences of failure to comply with them).

The statutory definition of the term of years absolute does not require that the lease take effect in possession. Thus in principle a lease which is expressed to take effect at a date subsequent to that of its creation can still be a legal lease and is referred to as a reversionary lease. The only qualification to this general rule is that by LPA 1925, s.149(3) a lease, at a rent or granted in consideration of a fine, to take effect more than 21 years from the date of the instrument purporting to create it is void. Similarly a contract to create such a lease (*i.e.* one which when granted would infringe s.149(3)) is also void. Thus a contract on January 1, 1998 to create a lease on January 1, 1999, the lease to take effect from January 1, 2022, would be void because it is a contract to create a term which would, when granted, infringe the provision. By contrast, an option in a lease for 25 years granted on January 1, 1998 for renewal of the lease at the end of the term for a further 25 years is not struck down by s.149(3). This is because the option contract relates to a term which when granted will not itself infringe the provision (*Re Strand & Savoy Properties Ltd* [1960] Ch. 582. But note that a contract to renew a term for more than 60 years is void by virtue of LPA 1922, Sched. XV para. 7(3)).

Section 149(3) expressly provides that it does not apply to leases taking effect under a settlement.

Broadly speaking, most tenancies fall into one of two categories. They are either for a fixed term or periodic.

Fixed-term tenancies

A fixed-term tenancy is created expressly. It is a tenancy for any period, the start and maximum duration of which is either (a) certain when the tenancy is created or (b) capable of being rendered certain by the time the tenancy takes effect in possession. Most tenancies will fall within (a) An example of a tenancy that would fall within (b) is a tenancy granted for "whatever fixed period X shall name".

The main problem with regard to the validity of a fixed-term tenancy is likely to turn upon the need for certainty of duration.

> In *Lace v. Chantler* [1944] K.B. 368 a tenancy was purportedly granted for the duration of the Second World War. The Court of Appeal held that this failed to create a fixed-term tenancy because the maximum duration of the term was uncertain at the outset. It was not known how long the war would last.

Note that the rule requires that the maximum duration of the term be certain. Thus it appears that a tenancy granted for 10 years but determinable on the ending of the war would have been perfectly valid. Indeed, because of the large number of tenancies granted during the Second World War which fell foul of the rule, Parliament enacted the Validation of Wartime Leases Act 1944, which saved such tenancy by deeming them to be for a 10-year term determinable by notice after the end of the war. It should also be noted that if the tenant has entered into possession and paid rent on a periodic basis, then quite irrespective of the invalidity of the fixed term, an implied periodic tenancy will arise at law (see *Lace and Chantler* (above); and see further p.19 below). This would of course ordinarily be determinable by a notice to quit served by either party. (For any statutory protection that might be available, see Chapters 9 and 10 below.)

The decision in *Lace v. Chantler* was endorsed almost 50 years later by the House of Lords in *Prudential Assurance Co Ltd v. London Residuary Body* [1992] 3 W.L.R. 279 where it was confirmed that the rule of certainty of duration applies to all tenancies including a periodic tenancy (as to which, see below).

Tenancies for life

It follows from the above rule that a tenancy for the life of the tenant (or indeed any other person) would be invalid for uncertainty at common law. However, by statute special provision is made for (a) leases granted for a life or lives (whether or not that of the tenant) or for a term of years determinable with life or lives and (b) leases granted for a term of years determinable on the marriage of the tenant. (Note that a lease for a term of years determinable *by notice* after death of the tenant during the term is valid at common law and does not need any special statutory saving: *Bass Holdings Ltd v. Lewis* [1986] 2 E.G.L.R. 40).

Section 149(6) of the Law of Property Act 1925, provides that—

> "Any lease...at a rent or in consideration of a fine...for life...or for any term of years determinable with life...or on the marriage of the..lessee...shall take effect as...a lease for a term of ninety years determinable after the death or marriage as the case may be of the original lessee...by at least one month's notice in writing given to determine the same by one of the quarter days applicable to the tenancy...."

The notice can be given by either the lessor or the lessee for the time being. If the life in question is that of a person other than the lessee, the lease will become determinable (in accordance with the above provision) on the death of that person. Where the determining lives are of more than one person (whether or not including the tenant), the operative event is the death of the survivor. Section 149(6) specifically extends to underleases and contracts for leases.

A modern example of this provision in operation is provided by *Skipton Building Society v.*

Clayton (1993) 66 P.& C.R. 263 where a purported "licence to occupy for life" at a premium was construed as a lease within s.149(6). (For the construction of "licences" as leases, see p.3 *et seq* above.)

It will be observed that section 149(6) does not affect leases taking effect in equity under a settlement. Hence the requirement of a rent or a fine in the case of those leases to which the special statutory rule applies.

Perpetually renewable leases

If a lease for a term of years specifically permits perpetual renewal of the term at the tenant's option, this will create what is termed in law a perpetually renewable lease. In order to discourage such leases and for the sake of simplicity it is provided that such a lease (whether created before or after January 1, 1926) is automatically converted into a 2,000-year term with a right for the tenant, by notice, to terminate it on one of the dates on which the tenancy would otherwise have determined (LPA 1922, s.145 and Sched. xv).

This is of course a Draconian consequence for landlords and it is difficult to imagine that a landlord would want to create such a term without inserting appropriate provisions, such as a rent review clause, in the lease. (See the powerful reasoning of Sachs L.J. in his judgment in *Caerphilly Concrete Products v. Owen* [1972] 1 W.L.R. 372, below.) In practice the greatest danger is that a landlord will be held to have created such a term unwittingly. For example, suppose that a grant of a five-year lease contains an option to renew on the same terms and conditions as contained in the original lease. If construed literally, this would mean that one of those terms would be the option itself, thereby permitting renewal on the same terms (including the option to renew for a further five-year term) *ad infinitum*. The courts have rejected such a literal interpretation and held that such a lease permits only one renewal. But should it make a difference if the original lease permits a renewal on the same terms and conditions, including the option to renew? Does this mean one more renewal and no more, or does it have the effect of permitting a renewal every five years? In *Caerphilly Concrete Products v. Owen* above it was held that such a provision can only be intended to create a perpetually renewable lease. The court was unable to distinguish the earlier authority of *Parkus v. Greenwood* [1950] Ch. 644. (But see the judgment of Sachs L.J. who only followed the earlier decision with the greatest reluctance, and contrast the approach to construction adopted by the court in *Marjorie Burnett Ltd v. Barclay* (1980) 125 S.J. 99. See further Wilkinson, "Renewable Leases" (1981) 131 N.L.J. 683.)

In practice, such unintended outcomes should be avoided by making it clear in the original lease how many renewals, if more than one, are contemplated by the parties.

Periodic tenancies

A periodic tenancy, such as a yearly, monthly or weekly tenancy, is one that will run continuously from period to period until terminated by notice given by one of the parties. It arises either expressly or impliedly. It will arise impliedly when a person goes into exclusive possession and pays rent calculated on a periodic basis and where there is nothing (such as an express agreement to the contrary) to negative the implication of a periodic tenancy.

The periodic tenancy is anomalous in the sense that in principle it is a tenancy for an indeterminate period determinable by notice. As such it ought to fall foul of the rule requiring certainty of duration, unless it is accepted that for practical and common-sense purposes that rule does not apply to periodic tenancies. On the other hand it could be analysed as amounting to a succession of fixed terms. Thus a yearly tenancy, for example, could be treated as a definite term for one year followed by another year and so on as long as no determining notice was served. This is the analysis which from the sixteenth century onwards commended itself to the courts, and was confirmed by the House of Lords as recently as 1992 in *Prudential Assurance Co. Ltd v. London Residuary Body* [1992] 2 A.C. 386.

> In 1930 the predecessor in title of the appellant landlord granted a lease of a strip of land to the predecessor in title of the respondent tenant at a rent of £30 per annum. The lease was expressed to continue until the land was required by the landlord for road-widening purposes, at which point it could be determined by two months' notice by the landlord. In proceedings to determine the validity of a notice to quit, served at a time when the land was admittedly not required by the landlord for road widening purposes, the House of Lords held that the purported lease was void for uncertainty of duration (see above). It was then held that in accordance with settled principles, an implied yearly tenancy had arisen when the tenant entered into possession and paid the rent. Such a tenancy is ordinarily determinable by six months' notice to quit by either party (see below) and in the meantime contains all the terms of the defective lease in so far as is consistent with a yearly tenancy. However, in this case the House of Lords held that the fetter on the landlord giving notice was not so incorporated because it was inconsistent with the nature of a yearly tenancy.

By this decision the House of Lords (overruling the Court of Appeal decisions in *Charles Clay & Sons Ltd v. British Railways Board* [1971] Ch. 725 and *Ashburn Anstalt v. Arnold* [1989] Ch. 1) confirmed that the freely agreed contractual fetter on the landlord's right to serve notice to quit was subordinated to what in his speech Lord Browne-Wilkinson referred to as "an ancient and technical rule of property law which requires the maximum duration of a term of years to be ascertainable from the outset." The sole reason for perpetuating the rule seems to have been a familiar unwillingness on the part of the judiciary to upset long-established titles by abolishing property law rules of long standing, leaving any such decision to the legislature. This despite the fact that, in the words of Lord Browne-Wilkinson, "No one has produced any satisfactory rationale for the genesis of the rule...[or]been able to point to any useful purpose that it serves at the present day." Lords Griffiths, Mustill and Browne-Wilkinson all expressed the hope that the Law Commission would consider whether there was any good reason for maintaining the rule. (For a plea in favour of a contractual-based approach to such fetters in any reforming measure, see S. Bright, "Uncertainty in Leases – is it a Vice?" (1993) 13 L.S. 38.

The way in which the decision in *Prudential* was calculated to defeat the intentions of the parties was illustrated by Lord Browne-Wilkinson. He explained that the original lease had been created as part of a sale and leaseback transaction whereby the owner of shop premises had sold and leased back a strip of land to the local highway authority for road-widening. Since then the remainder, along with the strip, had been used as retail premises with frontage onto the road. However, after the House of Lords' decision the shop premises would be left without a road frontage whilst the landlords would be left with a strip of land useless by itself (but presumably of great ransom value to them!).

Despite these serious reservations about the usefulness of the rule it has been argued that it provides an opportunity to rewrite bargains which have become improvident in the light of changed circumstances. After all, the tenancy in the *Prudential* case was clearly only intended to be a short-term arrangement and the rent of £30 per annum was now grossly out of line with the agreed current market rental value of £10,000 per annum (see, *e.g.* Sparkes, "Certainty of Leasehold Terms" (1993) 109 L.Q.R. 93).

(For a case where the Court of Appeal struck down a fetter on the landlord under a periodic tenancy serving a notice to quit which was contained in an agreement collateral to the tenancy, see *Cheshire Lines Committee v. Lewis & Co.* (1880) 50 L.J.Q.B. 121, and for an invalid fetter preventing the landlord from ever serving a notice to quit, see *Centaploy Ltd v. Matlodge* [1974] Ch. 1; *c.f. Breams Property Investment Ltd v. Stroulger* [1948] 2 K.B. 1, where a fetter for a maximum of three years was upheld).

Tenancies at will

Since medieval times a tenancy at will has been held to arise where a person is let into possession of land by the owner but has not been granted any certain term. A tenancy at will is a precarious right because it can be determined at any time by the will of either party. Indeed the use of the word "tenancy" is misleading, because the tenant does not have any estate or interest in the property beyond a purely personal right which will not survive either an assignment by or the death of either party. Nor can the tenant pray in aid the statutory scheme of protection for business tenants, contained in Part II of the Landlord and Tenant Act 1954. It has been held as a matter of construction that the Act does not apply to such a "tenancy" arising impliedly at common law (*Wheeler v. Mercer* [1957] A.C. 416, HL). Nor does it apply to an expressly created tenancy at will, although here the courts will look very carefully at the agreement to ensure that it is not an attempt by the landlord to circumvent the statutory scheme by dressing up what is in reality a periodic tenancy as a tenancy at will *Hagee (London) Ltd v. A B Erikson and Larsen (a firm) and others* [1976] 1 Q.B. 209). In coming to its decision in *Hagee* the Court of Appeal was influenced by the fact that it is possible to contract out of the 1954 Act scheme with the approval of the county court, which will invariably grant approval to an agreement drawn up by two business people properly advised by their lawyers.

It is clear from the above cases that a tenancy at will can arise impliedly or expressly, whether or not rent is being paid. But we have already seen that where a property owner allows another into possession of his (the owner's) land in return for rent without the parties coming to an express agreement as to the nature of the transaction, the normal presumption in such circumstances is that the parties intended to create a periodic tenancy. How is this apparent conflict of presumptions to be resolved? The answer lies in the need for intention to create a periodic tenancy. This intention will be presumed from exclusive possession combined with payment and acceptance of rent on a periodic basis. But it will not be presumed if those features when combined with any other relevant circumstances indicate that the correct inference to draw is that the parties had no such intention. This is illustrated by *Javad v. Aquil* [1991] 1 W.L.R. 1007.

> The defendant was allowed into possession of business premises by the owner pending negotiation of a 10-year lease. The defendant paid rent on a periodic basis. When the negotiations broke down he argued that he had a periodic tenancy protected by Part II of the Landlord and Tenant Act 1954. The Court of Appeal held that the true inference to be drawn from all the circumstances was that the parties did not intend to create such a tenancy and therefore the defendant was in possession merely as a tenant at will. (See also the comment of Scarman L.J. in *Hagee (London) Ltd v. A B Erikson and Larsen (a firm) and others* (above) that "entry into possession while negotiations proceed is one of the classic circumstances in which a tenancy at will may exist"). The Court considered it very material that in the present case the occupier had been allowed into possession in anticipation of terms being agreed, such agreement never in fact having been concluded.

Thus the implied tenancy at will still seems to have a role to play at least as a legal mechanism to protect an occupier during a period of transition (see *Heslop v. Burns* [1974] 1 W.L.R. 1241 at 1243, *per* Scarman L.J.). To this end the courts have also been reluctant to find an intention to create a new (periodic) tenancy where a land owner accepts rent from an occupier who holds over after the termination of an earlier tenancy (*Longrigg Burrough & Trounson v. Smith* (1979) 251 E.G. 847), although in modern times this is more likely to be construed as having created a licence of some kind rather than a tenancy at will. In practice it will probably make very little difference save that termination of the licence might require some period of notice.

B. FORMALITIES FOR LEASES

For evidential and ritual reasons, the law has long prescribed formalities which must be complied with for the creation or transfer of a legal estate in land. Subject to a few exceptions, the most important being a lease for less than three years at a rent equal to two-thirds or more of real value, the Statute of Frauds 1677 provided that a written instrument was essential for the conveyance or creation of a legal estate. The Real Property Act of 1845 strengthened these formalities by prescribing that thereafter the writing had to be by way of deed. This requirement was retained by the Law of Property Act 1925 (section 52), below) which is still in force today.

The Statute of Frauds also introduced the need for formalities to be complied with for a contract to convey or create a legal estate or interest in land to be enforceable by action. Such contracts were formerly actionable even if made orally. The relevant provisions of the Statute of Frauds were eventually replaced by the Law of Property Act 1925, s.40 which provided that the contract would be unenforceable by action unless it was in writing or evidenced in writing by a note or memorandum of the contract which was signed by the party (or his authorised agent) to be charged.

Whilst the need for a deed to convey or create a legal estate has proved to be relatively uncontroversial, the formalities governing land contracts have proved to be contentious and the relevant law was reformed as recently as 1989. In their Report on *Formalities for Contracts of Sale etc. of Land* (Law Com. No. 164, 1987) the Law Commission examined the rationale for formalities and came down in favour of their retention for four principal reasons: (a) to prevent the likelihood of contracts for the sale or other disposition of land becoming binding before the parties have obtained legal advice in what is likely to be a major transaction for them (a "consumer protection" function); (b) because of their evidential value in promoting certainty, minimising the risks of litigation and preventing fraud; (c) to enable such contracts to be classified and subject to standardised routine forms (a "channelling function"); and (d) because most other jurisdictions prescribe formalities for such contracts.

Agreements for leases

In the case of most (real) property sales the parties will first enter into a formal contract for sale, to be followed at some subsequent stage by a deed of conveyance, at which point the purchaser will become the legal owner (section 52 LPA 1925). Where title to the land is registered under the Land Registration Acts 1925–1996 the legal estate will not actually pass until, in pursuance of the transfer, the buyer is registered as proprietor (Land Registration Act (LRA) 1925, s.20 (freeholds) and s.23 (leaseholds)).

By contrast, many prospective landlords and tenants, especially in the case of short-term residential lettings, will often dispense with the first stage and simply create a legal tenancy in accordance with the requirements set out below. (The distinction between contract and tenancy is frequently obscured by inconsistent use of terminology. Thus short-term residential lettings are sometimes referred to as tenancy agreements when in fact they are legal tenancies).

Nevertheless in a number of cases, particularly in the case of complex tenancies of commercial property, the parties may begin with a contract. The point is important because if an enforceable contract has been created, failure to comply with its terms will amount to a breach of contract, giving the other party the right to claim damages or if appropriate a decree of specific performance. Furthermore, if the parties have only reached the contract stage and the landlord disposes of the property to a third party before any tenancy is granted, a question will arise as to whether the contract for the tenancy is enforceable against that person. (Thus to be absolutely safe the prospective tenant, where title to the land is unregistered, should register the agreement as an estate contract—Class C(iv)—under the Land Charges Act (LCA) 1972 (s.2(1),(4)) otherwise it will be void against a purchaser of a legal estate in the land for money or money's worth (LCA 1972, s.4(6)). If, as will frequently be the case, title to the land is registered under the Land Registration Acts 1925–1996, the contract should be protected by entry of a caution in the register of title (under section 53—caution against first registration—or section 54—caution against dealings—as the case may be). In the event that the tenant has been allowed into possession before completion, his contract will be protected as an overriding interest under section 70(1)(g) LRA 1925 (see *e.g. Woolwich Equitable B.S. v. Marshall* [1952] Ch. 1).

To amount to a valid contract the agreement must first identify: (a) the parties, (b) the subject matter of the lease; (c) the commencement and duration of the term; (d) the rent or consideration to be paid; and (e) any other terms agreed. Secondly, it must comply with the formalities as to writing, set out below.

As noted above, after 1925 the position with regard to the validity and enforceability of contracts to convey or create a legal estate (thus including legal tenancies) was governed by section 40 LPA 1925. This provided that such a contract was enforceable by action only if it, or some note or memorandum thereof, was in writing and signed by the party to be charged or his agent. Note first that the contract was not invalid for failure to comply with these requirements, but was unenforceable by action. This meant that it could be relied upon for other purposes such as forfeiture by the seller of a deposit paid by a buyer who subsequently failed to complete the purchase in breach of contract (see, *e.g. Monnickendam v. Leanse* (1929) 39 T.L.R. 445). The second point to note is that the contract itself did not have to be in writing to be enforceable by action, provided there was a satisfactory memorandum of its essential terms. The complexity of this provision and the body of case law which grew up around it was legendary. Equally notorious was the equitable doctrine of part performance which enabled a party to a contract which did not comply with the formalities of section 40 to obtain specific performance on the basis of having partly performed his side of the contract. (See, for example, *Rawlinson v. Ames* [1925] Ch. 96 where, following an oral contract to let, the landlord had carried out alterations to the property at the request of and under the supervision of the prospective tenant. The landlord was able to enforce the contract). Happily this was all swept away by the Law of Property (Miscellaneous Provisions) Act 1989 which was enacted in the wake of the Law Commission *Report on Formalities for Contracts of Sale etc. of Land* (Law Com. No. 164, 1987). The 1989 Act repealed section 40 LPA 1925 (and with it the doctrine of part performance) for contracts created on or after September 27, 1989 and replaced both with a more modern set of statutory requirements. However, it is of interest to note that the legislation did not follow in every respect the Law Commission's draft Bill.

Thus it is now provided that:

(1) A contract for the sale or other disposition of an interest in land can only be made in writing and only by incorporating all the terms which the parties have expressly agreed in one document, or where contracts are exchanged, in each. The reference to exchange is to cover the traditional method of preparing a contract in two parts, one to be signed by the buyer (or tenant) and the other by the seller (or landlord) following which the parties exchange their parts (s.2(1)).

(2) The terms may be incorporated in a document either by being set out in it or by reference to some other document (s.2(2)).

(3) The document incorporating the terms or, where contracts are exchanged, one of the documents incorporating them (but not necessarily the same one) must be signed by or on behalf of each party to the contract (s.2(3): on the meaning of "signed" in this context, see *First Post Homes Ltd. v. Johnson* [1996] 13 E.G. 125).

An important exception to the above requirements is provided by section 2(5)(a) in the case of a contract to grant a lease governed by section 54(2) LPA 1925. As will be seen below, section 54(2) exempts a lease taking effect in possession for a term not exceeding three years, at the best rent reasonably obtainable without taking a fine, from the general requirement (in section 52 LPA 1925) that a lease must be created by deed for it to take effect a legal estate. Accordingly section 2(5)(a) affords a contract to create such a lease a parallel exemption from the formalities of the 1989 Act governing contracts to create leases. (There was no such exemption from the formalities for contracts entered into before September 27, 1989).

A thorny issue which troubled practitioners from the moment the 1989 Act reforms came into force is the effect of the revised formal requirements on what are commonly referred to as "side letters". These are agreements between the parties which relate to some aspect of the transaction in question, possibly by way of amendment or variation of the formal contract or indeed by way of collateral or supplementary terms which, for whatever reason, the parties wish not to appear on the face of the formal contract. There are two main difficulties with such arrangements. The first problem is that if they amount in themselves to a contract for the sale or other disposition of an interest in land, they will need to comply with section 2. If not they will constitute a void transaction. The second problem is that if they are treated as part of the main contract there is a danger that that contract will be void because, unless the terms of the supplemental agreement have been incorporated by reference, all the terms of "the contract" will not be contained in a document signed by both parties. As we have seen, the formal requirements introduced in 1989 were considerably stricter than those hitherto prevailing and this created a very real fear that parties would seek to avoid contracts by raising technical defences in the hope that the courts would adopt a very literal interpretation of the statutory requirements. These fears have happily proved to be on the whole unfounded.

In *Record v. Bell* [1991] 1 W.L.R. 853 a contract of sale, by way of formal exchange, was accompanied by an exchange of letters between buyer and seller whereby the parties agreed that the sale was conditional on the satisfaction of certain conditions relating to the vendor's title. These conditions were in due course satisfied, but the purchaser sought to escape from the sale and refused to complete, pleading that because the main contract neither contained the terms of, nor referred to, the terms of the ancillary agreement, that contract thereby failed to satisfy the requirements of section 2. The court, perhaps not surprisingly, rejected this plea and found that although the terms of the ancillary agreement had not been incorporated by reference into the principal contract, this was not fatal to the seller's case. This was because the court treated that secondary agreement as an independent collateral contract, not amounting to a contract for the sale, etc., of land, but entered into simply in order to induce the purchaser to exchange contracts. Therefore it neither needed to comply with section 2 nor invalidated the main contract.

A different but not unrelated problem arose in *Tootal Clothing Ltd v. Guinea Properties Management Ltd* [1992] 41 E.G. 117.

> A prospective landlord and tenant of shop premises exchanged contracts for the grant of a 25-year lease. It was expressly stated that the document 'sets out the entire agreement of the parties'. It was a term of the contract that the tenant would carry out some shopfitting works within a period of 12 weeks. On the same date they also entered into a second agreement (which recited the lease agreement) that the landlord would pay the tenant £30,000 for the shopfitting works and that the 12-week fitting out period would be rent-free. (Such agreements are often kept secret because the landlord does not want others, such as potential tenants of other premises, to know about such financial inducements). The lease was subsequently granted and the tenant carried out the works, but the landlord refused to pay for them. The landlord argued that the terms of the second agreement were an integral element of the total bargain and because they had not been incorporated in the lease agreement or the lease there was a failure to comply with section 2 of the 1989 Act which requires all the terms to be contained in the same document.

Once again, as in *Record v. Bell* (above) the court was clearly anxious to reject a technical defence which was otherwise devoid of any merit. In the instant case the court did so by holding that section 2 was concerned with the enforceability of executory contracts. Once an agreement had been executed (as in this case by the grant of the lease) it did not matter whether or not the contract would have been void for lack of compliance with section 2. Thus the second agreement stood by itself as a collateral agreement not governed by s.2 and therefore there was no bar to its enforcement. Scott L.J. was in any event of the opinion that even had the contract for the lease not been executed when a dispute arose the second agreement would have been treated as a collateral contract unaffected by section 2. (Parker L.J. was of the opinion that even if the second agreement had been a land contract it would have complied with section 2 by virtue of having incorporated the main contract and/or the lease by reference). See further, *Lotteryking Ltd v. AMEC Properties Ltd* [1995] 28 E.G. 100 where, prior to the grant of leases of two shop units and following discovery of damp in the units, the landlord gave a collateral undertaking that certain repairs would be carried out over a period of time during which the tenant was to enjoy a reduced rent in respect of one of the units and a rent-free period in respect of the other. The court held that these undertakings were simply modifying or supplementing the terms of the leases themselves and were not contracts for the disposal of an interest in land. They were not therefore required to comply with section 2 of the 1989 Act.

To be distinguished from the above cases is the position where a dispute arises over the terms of an agreement to vary a contract for the sale, etc., of land before completion. In *McAusland v. Duncan Lawrie Ltd* [1996] 4 All E.R. 995, CA the parties had entered into a perfectly valid contract of sale for a property which complied with the requirements of section 2 of the 1989 Act. However, it was subsequently realised that the specified completion date was a Sunday and therefore by an exchange of letters it was agreed that the date should be brought forward by two days. The Court of Appeal observed that the 1989 Act was intended to bring about a radical change in the law by introducing new and strict requirements as to the formalities to be observed for the creation of a valid contract for the disposition of an interest in land. In particular it required all the terms to be contained in one document signed by both parties. (Note that this can be by incorporation. See section 2(2) and *First Post Homes Ltd v. Johnson and Others* [1996] 13 E.G. 125.) With this in mind the Court held that the variation in this case was invalid because section 2 has to be applied to the contract as varied, which was a new contract. The Court, however, also made it clear that the ineffective variation did not taint the original contract, leaving the parties bound by that agreement. (The moral of the tale is for the variation to be embodied in one document, signed by both parties, which incorporates the original terms subject to the variation).

What happens where the parties have agreed terms but they have not all been reduced to the necessary written contractual document? Are the omitted terms unenforceable? The answer is normally yes. (*Enfield LBC v. Arajah and others* [1995] E.G.C.S. 164). But, in an appropriate case the court may be willing to rectify the contract on the basis that the document has failed to state what it was intended it should. (See *Wright v. Leonard Robert Developments Ltd* [1994] E.G.C.S. 69 for a case where a contract for the purchase of a long lease of a show flat on a development failed to make reference to the agreement of the parties that the price should include carpets, curtains, furniture and appliances *in situ*. The court was unsurprisingly not sympathetic to the developer who had removed the furniture and appliances two days before completion. It was held that the written agreement would be rectified to supply the omitted terms, thereby producing a valid enforceable contract. On the role of rectification in this context see further Law Com. No. 164, (above) p.20).

Conclusion

The judicial emphasis on the reforming nature of section 2 of the Law Reform (Miscellaneous Provisions) Act 1989 is to be welcomed. Equally welcome is a robust common-sense approach on the part of the courts to the recognition of conveyancing practice, a prime example being the willingness to find a collateral contract where appropriate. The aim of the law should be to promote, and not to undermine, justice by acknowledging a sufficient degree of flexibility to be exercised when applying the formal requirements in order to protect parties against ignorance, mistake and sharp practice. So far the courts seem to be measuring up to this task.

C. CREATION OF LEASES

The general rule

Section 52 of the Law of Property Act 1925 provides that to take effect as a legal estate a lease must be created by deed. It is important to note that, in any area of compulsory registration of title, the grant of a term of years absolute for more than 21 years from the date of delivery of the grant is void on the expiration of two months from that date—or any authorised extension of that period—so far as regards the grant of the legal estate is concerned, unless the lessee has in the meantime applied to be registered as proprietor of that estate (section 123(1) LRA 1925). Areas were designated as areas of compulsory registration on a piecemeal basis until on December 1, 1990, since when the whole of England and Wales has been so designated (Registration of Title Order 1989: S.I. 1989 No. 1347).

Until it was reformed in 1989, the law governing the execution of deeds, which was formulated in very different times, was susceptible to critical comment. One writer described it as "confused, highly technical, often ignored in practice and capable of producing unexpected results"—*Barnsley's Conveyancing Law and Practice* (3rd ed.), p.402. For these reasons the

Law Commission examined the law and in 1987 it produced a Report (Law Commission Report on Deeds and Escrows: Law Com. No. 163) which contained a number of proposals for reform. These recommendations were subsequently implemented by the Law of Property (Miscellaneous Provisions) Act (LP (MP) A) 1989. The new rules apply to deeds executed after July 30, 1990. The old rules still apply to documents executed as deeds on or before that date. These old rules will be considered briefly before the new rules are examined. (For further discussion, see Law Com. No. 163.)

Deeds executed by an individual before July 31, 1990

The document must be:

(1) Signed (although it will suffice to make a "mark" instead): section 73(1) LPA 1925 (repealed for deeds executed on or after the operative date—see below). Although, unlike a will, there is no formal requirement at common law for a witness to such deeds, it had long been common practice for a deed to be attested by an independent witness, who then signed the deed as such.

(2) Sealed. The rationale of this requirement, which originated in times of general illiteracy as a means of authenticating a document, has long since disappeared and the courts have held it to be satisfied by a wafer seal or even a printed circle containing the letters L.S. (*locus sigilli*—the place of the seal): *First National Securities v. Jones* [1978] 2 All E.R. 221.

(3) Delivered. This is an express or, more usually, implied acknowledgment by the person making the deed which shows that the document is intended to be finally executed and hence binding on him. It is now usually inferred from signing and sealing. A document can be delivered unconditionally, in which case it takes effect immediately, or conditionally. If it is made conditionally it becomes operative when the condition is fulfilled as from the date of its original delivery. (See *Alan Estates Ltd v. W.G. Stores Ltd* [1982] Ch. 551).

Deeds executed by a corporation before July 31, 1990

A deed executed before the operative date will be deemed to have been properly executed if the corporate seal has been affixed in the presence of and attested by two witnesses, namely the "clerk, secretary or other permanent officer or his deputy" and "a member of the board of directors, council or other governing body of the corporation" (section 74 LPA 1925). In the absence of such it would be necessary to establish, in the absence of any contractual stipulation to the contrary, that the deed of a corporation was executed in accordance with the formalities required by its memorandum, articles of association or charter.

Deeds executed after July 30, 1990

As stated above, the law was modified for deeds executed after the coming into force of section 1 of the Law of Property (Miscellaneous Provisions) Act 1989.

It is now provided that an instrument shall not be a deed unless:

(1) it makes it clear on its face that it is intended to be a deed by the person making it. Although the Act did not adopt the Law Commission proposal that the phrase

"signed as a deed" be compulsory, it makes sense either to state this or otherwise to describe the document as a deed;

(2) it is validly executed as a deed by that person.

Valid execution by an individual

To be validly executed as a deed by an individual the document will be validly executed as a deed if and only if:

(1) it is signed (which includes making a mark)—

    (a) by him in the presence of a witness who attests the signature; or

    (b) by somebody else in his presence and by his direction and in the presence also of two witnesses who each attest the signature; and

(2) it is delivered as a deed by him or some other person (*e.g.* a solicitor) authorised to do so on his behalf.

Thus, for deeds executed on or after the operative date, the obsolete need for a seal has been abolished, whilst the requirement of delivery has been retained. This is because it fixes the date from which the deed takes effect. The need for, but obviously not the practice of, attestation by a witness is a change from the former law.

Execution of deeds by a company

It should be noted that section 36A Companies Act 1985 (added by section 130(2) Companies Act 1989) provides for an alternative form of execution by a company to that of affixing its common seal (see above).

Since July 31, 1990 a document signed by two directors or by a director and a secretary of the company and expressed (in whatever form of words) to be executed by the company will have the same effect as if it were under the company seal. Such a document which is intended to be a deed and which makes it clear on its face that it is so intended by the persons making it has effect upon delivery as a deed. It is presumed, unless a contrary intention is proved, to be delivered on its being so executed. (*Cf.* section 1 LP(MP)A 1989 which allows an agent to deliver a deed on someone else's behalf.)

In practice, where a lease is made by deed it is usual for one copy (the lease) to be executed by the landlord alone and for another (the counterpart) to be executed by the tenant. These are then exchanged. It does not follow, however, that when the lease is executed it is to be treated as delivered in escrow (*i.e.* conditional on exchange of lease and counterpart): *Longman v. Viscount Chelsea* (1989) 58 P.& C.R. 189, CA.

Where a lease does not specify a commencement date it will be operative from the date of delivery (*Marshall v. Berridge* (1881) 19 Ch. D 233). By contrast, an agreement for a lease which omits the commencement date will not take effect as a valid contract (*Harvey v. Pratt* [1965] 1 W.L.R. 1025).

An exception to the need for a deed

Despite the general rule that a deed is necessary for the creation of a legal lease, there is an important statutory exception to that rule. (See also section 52(1)(d) LPA 1925).This exception is contained in section 54(2) LPA 1925 which provides that a lease can still take effect as a legal estate, under the following conditions.

(a) Provided that it takes effect in possession. This means that the term must come into effect immediately from the date of the instrument creating it.

> In *Long v. Tower Hamlets LBC* [1996] 3 W.L.R. 317 a landlord (through his agents) wrote a letter dated September 4, 1975 to a prospective tenant offering a quarterly tenancy to commence on September 29, 1975. On September 8 the prospective tenant endorsed a copy of the letter agreeing to the terms as set out in the agent's letter. He later entered into possession on September 29. A dispute subsequently arose in which it became necessary to determine whether the exchange of letters amounted to the express grant of a (legal) period tenancy or whether the tenant occupied under an implied periodic tenancy which arose when he entered into possession and paid rent. The court held that the exchange of letters did not create a legal tenancy because it did not take effect in possession immediately (for the purposes of section 54(2) LPA 1925, and therefore not being made by deed fell foul of section 52 LPA 1925. (Such a lease is classified as a reversionary lease p.17 above.) The only valid legal lease therefore was the periodic tenancy which arose when the tenant entered into possession and paid rent. (See also S. Bright [1998] Conv. 229)

The important practical point at issue in this case was that for the purposes of a claim to the land by way of limitation following prolonged non-payment of rent, time may exceptionally run in favour of a tenant under an oral periodic tenancy from the date of last payment of the rent whereas in the case of a periodic tenancy in writing time only runs from the end of the tenancy, which will usually be on the expiry of a notice to quit (Limitation Act 1980, s.15 and Sched. 1 para. 5(1)).

(b) For a term not exceeding three years (see below).

(c) At the best rent which can reasonably be obtained without taking a fine. (The statutory definition of a fine—contained in LPA 1925, s.205(1)(xxiii)—as including "a premium or foregift and any payment consideration or benefit in the nature of a fine, premium or foregift" serves to obscure rather than illuminate. This quaint term is more simply understood in this context as a capital payment or other like benefit in kind as opposed to periodic rental payments. A difficult question is whether capitalised rent is a premium. In principle it should not be. In *Grace Rymer Investments Ltd v. Waite* [1958] Ch. 831 where there was a weekly periodic tenancy which provided for three years' rent in advance. The Court of Appeal held that such a payment was not a fine; *c.f. Hughes v. Waite* [1957] 1 W.L.R. 713, *per* Harman J).

The purpose of this exception is to preserve the status of a tenancy as a legal estate for the multitude of commonly created short-term tenancies which are invariably created by informal writing or indeed orally. These tenancies will thus automatically bind third parties (such as a new landlord) either by virtue of being a legal estate (where title to the land is unregistered) or as an overriding interest under section 70(1)(k) of the Land Registration Act 1925 where title to the land is registered. Since the Land Registration Act 1986 came into force para. (k) of section 70 applies to a tenancy granted (*i.e.* as a legal estate: *City Permanent Building Soc. v. Miller* [1952] Ch. 840) for a term not exceeding 21 years. Before that date it only applied to such a tenancy if granted at a rent without taking a fine).

In many respects the rule in section 54(2) is a generous one and specifically extends to a tenancy which includes a power on behalf of the tenant to extend it (even if the exercise of such an option would take the extended term beyond the three-year limit; see *Hand v. Hall* (1877) 2 Ex. D. 355). But on the other hand it does not apply to a tenancy for more than three years, which gives the tenant an option to determine the tenancy at the end of any year; *Kushner v. Law Society* [1952] 1 K.B. 264. Of course it does sensibly apply to all periodic tenancies, whether express or implied, because such tenancies automatically renew themselves at the end of each period until determined by one or both of the parties; see *Prudential Assurance Co Ltd v. London Residuary Body* [1992] 2 A.C. 386 see p.20 above. Thus, even though the cumulative periods of such a tenancy might last beyond three years, the exception in section 54(2) is still applicable: *Re Knight, ex parte Voisey* (1882) 21 Ch D 442. It is unclear how the requirement of a deed affects a lease for a discontinuous period. For example does a lease for one month a year for four years need to be created by deed? See *Cottage Holiday Associates Ltd v. Customs & Excise Commissioners* [1983] Q.B. 735).

It should be noted that, although tenancies within section 54(2) can be *created* informally as legal leases, the legal estate can only be *disposed of* to a third party by way of a formal deed of assignment because this is governed by section 52(1), which applies to all leases: *Crago v. Julian* [1992] 1 W.L.R. 372 (where the Court of Appeal confirmed that an oral periodic tenancy could only be legally assigned by a deed of assignment). There appears to be a curious exception covered by section 52(2)(g) which provides that the need for a deed does not apply to "conveyances taking effect by way of operation of law". Thus in *Milmo v. Carreras* [1946] K.B. 306 the Court of Appeal (*obiter*) expressed the opinion that in circumstances where a tenant, by writing not taking effect as a deed, purports to sub-let for a period longer than the term vested in him, the legal estate still passes because by law this operates as a deemed assignment (see Chapter 4 for assignment of tenancies).

If a lease is professionally drafted it can be expected that the solicitor will be aware of the need for compliance with the above formalities. But not all leases are so drafted, and there is a danger that a transaction will not take effect as a legal lease for the relevant period for want of compliance with the formal requirement for a deed. However, even if the lease is defective for want of a deed, a periodic tenancy will still arise by implication at common law if the tenant enters into possession and pays rent on a periodic basis. This tenancy will incorporate all the terms of the otherwise ineffective lease in so far as they are compatible with a periodic tenancy. Of course a periodic tenancy is determinable by notice and in the absence of statutory protection may offer very limited security to the tenant. But all may not be lost, because there is an important equitable doctrine which states that, to all intents and purposes, equity will treat a specifically enforceable contract to create a lease as if it were as good as a legal lease (*Walsh v. Lonsdale* (1882) 21 Ch D 9). But suppose there is no express contract? This will not matter because equity has long permitted a lease which is void for the purpose of creating a legal estate to take effect in equity instead as a contract to create a legal lease of which specific performance can be granted assuming that there is no bar to such: *Parker v. Taswell* (1858) 2 De G.&F. 559. (See also *Milmo v. Carreras* (above) where the deemed assignment was treated as a specifically enforceable contract to assign the legal estate). It should be noted that writing is required for a valid equitable assignment: section 53(1)(a) LPA 1925.

Of course, to be a valid contract, the agreement must comply with the writing requirements contained in section 2 of the Law of Property (Miscellaneous Provisions) Act 1989 (discussed above): It has been argued (by Jean Howell at [1990] Conv. 441), where it is subtly argued that an informal lease which fails to comply with section 52 LPA 1925 can no longer be treated as a valid contract because section 2 requires *the contract* to be in writing, and a lease which fails for lack of formality cannot itself amount to the deemed contract because this confuses contract and (albeit defective) lease. The argument is that before section 2 came into force a contract only had to be in writing or evidenced in writing—section 40 LPA 1925—thus enabling the defective lease to be treated as the necessary evidence of the deemed contract. This forceful argument, although intellectually tenable, is unlikely to find favour with the courts, who would not be expected to find that a long-established equitable doctrine has been swept away by a side-wind.

If for some reason the contract is not specifically enforceable or it is void against a purchaser for non-registration, the tenant may still fall back on the periodic tenancy implied at common law. (See *Coatsworth v. Johnson* (1885) 55 L.J.Q.B. 220, CA where the tenant was not entitled to specific performance because he was in breach of the proposed covenants in the lease.)

Chapter 2

COVENANTS IN LEASES

Introduction

As a general rule, a tenancy is both an estate or interest in land and a contract. It is created either expressly or impliedly. (See Chapter 1 above). As such, it is governed both by the ordinary rules of contract law—although those rules are sometimes modified in their application to the landlord and tenant relationship—and special property law based rules. Furthermore, although it is true to say that a tenancy is a contract, it is an executed contract, and it would be more accurate to state that it is one which entails a bundle of obligations, some of which fall on the landlord and some on the tenant. These obligations, which are commonly referred to as covenants whether or not the tenancy has been created by deed, will differ according to the type of tenancy. They take the form of either express or implied terms or obligations. Express terms are those terms which the parties have agreed between themselves, whilst implied terms are terms which are implied either at common law or by statute. In the case of some statutory terms it is provided that any attempt by the parties to exclude or vary those terms will be void. (See for example the statutory repairing obligations in sections 11–16 of the Landlord and Tenant Act 1985 (examined in Chapter 3 below), which are imposed on landlords of residential tenancies for less than seven years.

The remedy for breach of an obligation will depend on the nature of the obligation. Breach of a covenant will usually give rise to an action for damages, although a serious breach could be so serious as to amount to a repudiatory breach, which would give the other party a right to elect to treat the tenancy as at an end and sue for damages (see p.132 below). However, the limits of this doctrine, in so far as it applies to covenants and other obligations in leases, have yet to be fully explored. (See further *Chartered Trust plc v. Davies* [1997] 49 E.G. 135). Where an obligation is by way of an implied "condition", then breach will certainly permit the tenant to treat the tenancy as having been repudiated by the landlord and to accept that repudiation. Damages for breach of a repairing obligation by the tenant are subject to special rules. Other remedies that might be available where appropriate for breach of covenants in tenancies are the equitable remedies of specific performance and injunction, either to compel a party to carry out an obligation or to prevent a party from breaching or continuing to breach an obligation respectively. (But see *Co-operative Insurance Society Ltd v. Argyll (Holdings) Ltd* [1996] Ch. 286 where the House of Lords held that a "keep open covenant" (whereby the tenant agrees to continue trading from the leased premises) cannot be enforced by a decree of specific performance but only by a claim for damages; (as to which, see *Costain Property Development Ltd v. Finlay Ltd* [1989] 1 E.G.L.R. 237 and *Transworld Land Co. Ltd v. J. Sainsbury plc* [1990] 2 E.G.L.R. 255. See further P.Luxton [1998] Conv.396 and M.Barclay and P.Marco, [1997] 25 E.G. 128.)

In addition, if the tenancy contains a right of entry and forfeiture for breach of a tenant's covenant, the landlord can exercise that right and forfeit the tenancy as well as sue for damages, although the tenant may be able to seek and obtain relief against forfeiture (see Chapter 6 below).

Implied terms

Where the parties simply enter into a tenancy and, save for agreement as to the rent and period of the tenancy, do not address the issue of the terms of that tenancy, the position will be governed entirely by any implied common law terms coupled with any statutory obligations that might be imposed on the parties to the particular type of tenancy in question. The terms implied at common law are very limited.

(a) Landlord's obligations

    (1)   A covenant for quiet enjoyment (see below).
    (2)   An obligation not to derogate from his grant (see below).
    (3)   Certain limited obligations as to fitness and repair (see Chapter 3 below).

(b) Tenant's obligations

    (1)   To pay rent.
    (2)   To pay any local taxes (such as council tax) and water rates.
    (3)   Certain limited obligations with regard to the use and condition of the property (see Chapter 3 below).
    (4)   To permit the landlord to enter in order to view the state of repair and to carry out any repairs where the landlord is under an express or implied obligation to repair. Even if the landlord is not obliged to repair, he will have a similar right of entry where he has an express right to carry out any repairs. Otherwise a landlord will have no right of entry, save that in the case of a weekly tenancy of a dwelling-house the landlord has a right to enter for the purpose of remedying any defects which may cause personal injury to the tenant or his visitors (*Mint v. Good* [1951] 1 K.B. 517).

Despite the above limited obligations, which are implied at commom law, there are a number of statutory provisions which give rights to and/or impose obligations on landlord and tenants, depending on the type of tenancy. The more important of these are dealt with in subsequent chapters (see Chapter 3 and 4 below).

The "usual covenants"

If the tenancy has been preceded by an open contract to create a tenancy, the courts will imply into the tenancy what are referred to as "the usual covenants", even if the agreement is silent on the matter (*Propert v. Parker* (1832) 3 My.&K. 280). These covenants will also apply where the parties have expressly agreed to include "the usual covenants".

The covenants, which were set out in the decision in *Hampshire v. Wickens* (1878) 7 Ch D 555, are:

    (1)   on the part of the landlord—
          a qualified covenant for quiet enjoyment;

   (2)   on the part of the tenant—

        (a)   to pay the rent;

        (b)   to pay tenant's rates and taxes (*i.e.* all those not imposed by law on the landlord);

        (c)   to keep the premises in repair and deliver them up in repair at the end of the term;

        (d)   (if the landlord has covenanted to repair) a covenant to permit the landlord to enter and view the state of repair;

        (e)   a condition of re-entry for non-payment of rent but not for breach of any other covenant.

Quite apart from the above "usual" covenants, it is always possible to show as a matter of fact that the inclusion of a particular covenant is "usual" according to local custom or commercial usage in the sense that it is invariably included in a tenancy of the particular type in question (*Flexman v. Corbett* [1930] 1 Ch. 672). But of course this does not mean that covenants which are invariably found in most tenancies (see below) will be found to be usual in the technical sense and therefore automatically incorporated. Thus in *Hampshire v. Wickens* (above) it was held that a covenant against assignment without the consent of the landlord was not a usual covenant, despite its common usage. As to when a covenant, will be included it has been said that—

> "it is a question of fact to be determined by the court, not necessarily on the view of conveyancing counsel but by looking at the nature of the premises,their situation, the purpose for which they are being let, the length of the term, the evidence of conveyancers and the books of precedents. (*Chester v. Buckingham Travel Ltd* [1981] 1 W.L.R. 96 at 101, *per* Foster J.)"

In that case the court held that in the circumstances a number of tenant's covenants, in a tenancy of garage workshops let for 14 years in 1971 in Chelsea, London, would be accepted as usual; *viz.* qualified covenants against alterations to, and change of use of the premises, along with covenants not to obstruct windows, or to cause a nuisance, annoyance or disturbance.

Express terms

The parties to a tenancy will not usually be content to rely upon the limited obligations and rights implied by law and will make express provision for a host of matters including those obligations which would ordinarily be implied. Not surprisingly these express terms will vary widely according to the presence or absence of any of a number of relevant factors. These include: (a) the type of property which has been let (*e.g.* whether it is agricultural, commercial, industrial or residential); (b) the physical nature of the property (such as whether it is a separate building or part of a building); (c) the length of the term (which can vary from say a weekly tenancy to a 999-year fixed term granted for a premium and a low ground rent). In these days of sophisticated precedents, compact disk or on-line tenancies can be tailor-made to suit any set of circumstances. One writer for practitioners has observed that—

> "The advent of new technology, in particular the word processor, has made a significant impact on drafting practice. Office precedents can be easily updated, and the reproduction of lengthy drafts becomes painless. The result has tended to be longer documents, and a

modern commercial lease, together with its schedules can easily run to 60 pages or more. (S. Tromans, *Commercial Leases*, (2nd ed., 1996) p.4.)"

Of course, whilst precise draftsmanship to clear up any difficult points is admirable, there is always a potential danger in professionally drawn up leases of the draftsman getting carried away with himself or herself and producing unnecessarily long and unwieldy documents which seek to cater for very conceivable contingency. In so doing he or she may perhaps unwittingly lay the parties open to litigation over some arcane point of construction. Thus slavish and unquestioning adherence to precedents should be eschewed—

> "Precedents stored electronically have a tendency to accumulate further provisions over the years, rather like barnacles on the hull of a man-of-war. A provision may be entirely appropriate when added in the context of a particualr transaction, but it should not necessarily always be applied thereafter. (*Ibid.*)"

Typical terms that one might expect to find in most tenancies include:

(1) by the tenant, an obligation to pay the rent, not to assign or sub-let or part with possession, not to use the premises for particular purposes or other than for a specific purpose, to repair;

(2) by the landlord, liability to repair, and to afford the tenant quiet enjoyment of the premises.

Occasionally the tenancy will include a covenant by the landlord that at the tenant's option he will renew the tenancy or sell the landlord's interest to the tenant on specified terms.

A written tenancy will also almost certainly include a right on the part of the landlord to re-enter and forfeit the tenancy for breach of covenant by the tenant.

Residential tenancies of flats will often contain provisions governing the provision of services by the landlord and a reciprocal obligation by the tenant to pay a service charge, and similar arrangements are likely to be found in commercial tenancies of parts of a building or of units on an industrial estate or a commercial development such as a shopping centre. (See the *"Guide to Good Practice for Service Charges in Commercial Properties"* (1995), agreed to by the main organisations representing commercial landlords and tenants.) Provisions governing the repair of common parts may also be dealt with through a service charge (see Chapter 3 below. See also [1998] 24 E.G. 120).

In a general text of this kind it is not appropriate to consider all these possibilities, and therefore emphasis will be placed on the most important types of term usually found in tenancies. These will be dealt with in some depth. There are also various statutory codes which govern particular types of tenancy and which deal, *inter alia*, with certain obligations in the tenancy. A number of these codes are dealt with separately later in the book where the relevant provisions are considered in the appropriate place.

Rent

At this point it would be appropriate to mention one particular obligation on the part of the tenant. This is the obligation to pay rent. As far as residential tenancies in the private sector are concerned the matter of rent regulation or the lack of it is dealt with elsewhere in the book see Chapters 9 and 10 below. With regard to commercial leases the main issue concerns the use of rent review clauses. If a tenancy is granted for any length of time, over which there is likely to be a significant change in the value of money (as in the case of the traditional 25-year business tenancy), the landlord will want to protect himself by including a rent review clause which provides machinery whereby the rent can be increased at periodic intervals. These intervals have tended to become shorter in recent decades, particularly in times of relatively high inflation.

Landlords will also be concerned not only with inflation but with changing property values arising from other causes (*e.g.* nearby development or a new motorway) which will affect the capital value of their property and hence its rental value. Tenants who wish to resist the inclusion of a rent review clause will only be able to do so at the expense of a shorter tenancy which may not suit their needs, although in recent years commercial tenancies have been getting shorter as recession has swung the balance of bargaining power further towards tenants. Alternatively tenants under longer leases (*e.g.* 25 years) have managed to negotiate break clauses which permit them to threaten to determine the tenancy prematurely if they are not happy with a prospective rent increase brought about by the operation of a rent review clause (see Chapter 6 below).

Over time, therefore, the use of rent review clauses has become commonplace and since around 1970 it has been virtually unknown for a tenancy of over five years of commercial premises not to have included a rent review clause. These clauses will provide for disputes to be dealt with by arbitration. Nevertheless they have been much litigated, thereby producing a vast body of case law. As a result, rent review clauses have been fine-tuned and exhibit increasingly higher levels of sophistication. (For the increasing use, and advantages of, "turnover rents" whereby the tenant pays a basic rent plus a percentage of trading profits, see [1998] 12 E.G. 127.) The most commonly used type of clause simply aims to ensure that rents are maintained in line with the current open market rental value of the premises, although this is more easily stated than achieved. Professional valuers will need to be used and disputes resolved. This can prove to be a lengthy and expensive process. The drafting and operation of rent review clauses and their mechanisms to deal with such matters has therefore not surprisingly become an industry in itself. For details, reference should be made to the major practitioners' works on landlord and tenant (*e.g. Woodfall; Hill & Redman* and *Emmett on Title*, along with other titles such as Murray Ross, *The Drafting and Negotiation of Commercial Leases* (4th ed., 1994); R. Bernstein and K. Reynolds, *Essentials of Rent Review* (1995); J.E.Adams and D.N.Clarke, *Rent Reviews and Variable Rents* (3rd ed., 1991); S.Tromans, *Commercial Leases*, (2nd ed., 1996), Chap. 6).

Two obligations in particular are dealt with in the remainder of this chapter; that is on the part of the landlord: (1) a covenant for quiet enjoyment, and (2) an obligation not to derogate from grant.

COVENANT FOR QUIET ENJOYMENT

The covenant

There is implied automatically into every legal tenancy, whether oral, by writing or by deed, an undertaking on the part of the landlord that the tenant shall have the property unfettered by the assertion of any right which interferes with its ordinary and lawful enjoyment (*Budd-Scott v. Daniel* [1902] 2 K.B. 351). Such a term is also implied into a specifically enforceable contract for a tenancy (*Markham v. Paget* [1908] 1 Ch. 697). In *Smith v. Nottinghamshire County Council, The Times*, November 13, 1981 the court even found an equivalent term to be implied into a contractual licence of student accommodation, thereby enabling the student licensees to obtain an injunction to stop building work being carried out by their landlord which was interfering with their revision for examinations.

The covenant contains two limbs. First that the tenant must be given possession at the outset, and second that he be given peaceable enjoyment thereafter. (See further M.J. Russell (1976) 40 Conv. 418). Despite the use of the word "quiet", this does not refer as such to freedom from acoustic interference. It simply means that the tenant, who has exclusive possession, shall enjoy the property without interference (*Jenkins v. Jackson* (1888) 40 Ch. D 71). Nevertheless, there can be a breach of the covenant if in the circumstances the noise complained of is of such a nature and degree that it amounts to interference with the tenant's lawful enjoyment of his property (see below).

The implied covenant will be displaced by an express covenant where, as is common, such a covenant is included in the tenancy (*Miller v. Emcer Products* [1956] Ch. 304).

For whose acts is the landlord responsible

The covenant affords the tenant a remedy where his lawful enjoyment of the property is interfered with by the lawful or unlawful acts of the landlord or the lawful acts of a person claiming under him. In this context a "lawful" act is one which the person, or the person on whose behalf it is performed, is permitted to do apart from the covenant.

It follows that for the landlord to be liable for the acts of those claiming under him, such as a tenant of an adjoining property, the act complained of should be lawful in the sense that it is permitted by the tenancy, and is not tortious. If an act is tortious the tenant adversely affected would have a remedy in tort against the perpetrator, but if it were not tortious the only remedy open to the tenant would be an action against the landlord on the covenant for quiet enjoyment. This is because it is by the landlord's action in permitting the conduct complained of that the tenant's enjoyment of his property has been interfered with (*Wallis v. Hands* [1893] 2 Ch. 75). *Sanderson v. Berwick on Tweed Corporation* (1994) 13 Q.B.D. 549 is a good illustration of the operation of this principle. The defendant local authority had made a drainage system in the district by which several farms were drained by underground drains, whereby water passed through all the farms. The defendant let farm A to the plaintiff with a covenant for quiet enjoyment. He had already let farms B and C to farmers who were permitted to use the drains which passed through the plaintiff's farm so far as they were adequate to carry the neighbouring farms' water. Eventually the plaintiff's farm was flooded as a result of (a) the excessive use by the tenant of farm B of a perfectly good drain and (b) by the proper use of a defective drain by the tenant of farm C. In an action by the plaintiff against the defendants for breach of the covenant for quiet enjoyment, it was held that they were liable for the second type of damage, because farmer C's proper use of the drain was a lawful act, whereas they were not liable for the loss which came about as a result of farmer B's unlawul actions which amounted to a nuisance.

However, a landlord can become liable under the covenant for quiet enjoyment in respect of an unlawful act of an adjoining occupier who claims under him if he has authorised that act. This occurred in *Sampson v. Hodgson-Pressinger* [1981] 3 All E.R. 710 (*cf. Toff v. McDowell* (1993) 25 H.L.R. 650). The plaintiff tenant occupied a lower flat in a building. The first defendant was the tenant of the flat above, which had a terrace above the ceiling of the plaintiff's living room. When this was walked on it created an intolerable noise in the plaintiff's flat. The court accepted that ordinarily use of the terrace would have been lawful, but in the circumstances it was not, because as constructed it was not fit to be used in the normal way without causing a nuisance. Thus in letting it in that state, whereby its use would be unlawful (*i.e.* the tort of nuisance) the (second defendant) landlord was in breach of the covenant for quiet enjoyment even though he had not actually constructed the roof terrace in that way. (The claim against the first defendant was withdrawn, but the court stated that had it not been the first defendant would have been entitled to a complete indemnity from the landlord). The landlord was further held to be liable in nuisance because he was authorising the nuisance committed by the tenant of the flat above. A local authority landlord has also been held capable of being liable for breach of the covenant for quiet enjoyment where the subject flat was inadequately insulated and as a result all the noises of everyday living could be heard from adjoining flats (*Baxter v. Camden LBC* [1998] 30 H.L.R. 507, CA applied in *Southwark LBC v. Mills and others* [1998] 22 E.G. 151). This is an important development because it is now clear that a landlord might have to improve a defectively insulated property by bringing it up to modern standards of insulation in order to remedy the breach of a covenant for quiet enjoyment. This could have serious financial implications for both local authority and private sector landlords. In the *Mills* case above, counsel for the local authority landlord pleaded (to no effect) that to impose liability on the council would have serious implications for the housing budget not only of that authority but of many others. The above decisions can be contrasted with that in *Jenkins v. Jackson* (above) where the landlord was held not to be responsible for a nuisance caused to the tenant by a dancing school in the flat above which was also let by the landlord).

In *Sampson v. Hodgson-Pressinger* (above) the landlord was automatically authorising the nuisance because he was responsible for the conditions which brought about that nuisance. But in the absence of such he will not be liable in tort for the acts of others claiming under him unless he has actually authorised those acts.

The traditional rule is that to be liable for the third party's unlawful acts it is not sufficient for the landlord merely to suffer those acts. It must be shown that he has authorised them.

In *Malzy v. Eicholz* [1916] 2 K.B. 308 a tenant of property adjoining that let by the same landlord to the plaintiff broke a covenant in his tenancy by licensing another person to carry out mock auctions on the premises. The landlord was not liable to the plaintiff for this interference with his use and enjoyment of his property because he had not authorised it nor was the letting to the tenant for a purpose which necessarily involved a nuisance. (See also *Matania v. National Provincial Bank* [1936] 2 All E.R. 633).

In *Jaeger v. Mansions Consolidated* (1903) 87 L.T. 690 a flat was let to the plaintiffs with a covenant for quiet enjoyment by the landlord and a covenant by the tenant not to use or permit the premises to be used for immoral purposes. The plaintiffs subsequently claimed that a tenant of an adjoining property was in breach of the immoral user covenant in her tenancy agreement and that this amounted to a breach of the covenant for quiet enjoyment by the landlord. The Court of Appeal disagreed, finding that what had occurred was merely a nuisance. Collins M.R. stated (at p.696) that it was not enough that the nuisance was committed with the landlord's knowledge and consent unless "the acts of the persons using these flats for immoral purposes could be construed to be the acts of the defendant in the sense that they authorised them—not merely that that they did not stop them but that they were in effect party to them."

An attempt to impose liability on a landlord also failed in *O'Leary v. Islington LBC* (1983) 9 H.L.R. 61 (approved in *Hussain v. Lancaster CC*, *The Times*, May 27, 1998, CA) where it was held that a failure to enforce a "no nuisance" covenant in the tenancy of the person whose actions are complained of does not by itself make the landlord liable to another tenant either in tort or contract. (See also *Smith v. Scott* [1973] Ch. 314, where the court rejected an analogous duty of care to tenants with regard to the selection of neighbouring tenants. Reference should also be made to Chapter 11 where there is a discussion of the much stronger powers available to landlords, since the Housing Act 1996, to evict unruly neighbours).

The above authorities show that it can be difficult to establish that a landlord has authorised the unlawful actions of another tenant by mere inaction. But other recent authorities have shown that this will not be impossible. In *Hilton v. James Smith & Sons (Norwood) Ltd* [1979] 2 E.G.L.R. 44 a tenant was granted a right of way over a roadway which had been retained by the landlords. The roadway was seriously obstructed by parked vehicles which the landlords could have done something about by enforcing covenants in the tenancies of the persons causing the obstruction. They did not and the tenant obtained an injunction against permitting the continuance of the obstruction on the basis of breach of the covenant for quiet enjoyment, nuisance and non-derogation from grant. (See also *Chartered Trust plc v. Davies* [1997] 49 E.G. 135 below).

Scope of the covenant

The implied covenant for quiet enjoyment does not operate so as to impose liability on the landlord for the acts of a person claiming by title paramount (*Jones v. Lavington* [1903] 1 K.B. 253). In *Kelly v. Rogers* [1892] 1 Q.B. 910, CA the covenant for quiet enjoyment in a sub-tenancy was limited to the acts of the landlord or any person claiming under him. When the head tenancy was forfeited for non-payment of rent and breach of covenant by the head tenant (thereby destroying the sub-tenancy: see p.149 below) the sub-tenant was unable to sustain a succesful action against the head tenant for breach of the covenant for quiet enjoyment given by the head tenant in the sub-tenancy. The interference with the sub-tenant's right to possession came about as a result of the actions of a person (the head landlord) claiming by title paramount and not somebody claiming by, through or under the landlord covenantor. It follows that a sub-tenant, who does not have a right to see the head tenancy, should take care to obtain a covenant from his landlord that the landlord will observe all the covenants in the head tenancy. (See also Law of Property Act 1925, s.146(4) for a sub-tenant's right to seek relief against forfeiture in an action for forfeiture of a head tenancy).

A landlord will be liable on his covenant for quiet enjoyment if he has expressly covenanted to be responsible for the acts of a person claiming by title paramount. This happened in *Queensway Marketing Ltd v. Associated Restaurants Ltd* [1998] 32 E.G. 41 where the Norwich Union let premises to the defendants, Associated Restaurants, for 20 years. In turn the premises were sub-let by the defendants to the plaintiff sub-tenants under a tenancy for 20 years less 10 days. The sub-tenancy contained a covenant for quiet enjoyment which defined the term "landlord" as including any superior landlords without naming them as such. This was sufficient to make the landlord responsible for the acts of the superior landlord, Norwich Union, who had erected scaffolding outside the premises which had allegedly interfered with the plaintiff's business.

The qualified nature of the implied covenant for quiet enjoyment means that the landlord is also not responsible for the acts of a predecessor in title as in *Celsteel Ltd v. Alton House Holdings Ltd (No. 2)* [1986] 1 W.L.R. 512, CA where the landlord granted a tenancy to X, whose use of the property was interfered with by Y who had a right of way over X's property. Y held a tenancy of the same landlord but it had been granted along with the right of way by that landlord's predecessor in title, from whom the present landlord had acquired the reversion. The landlord was not liable for the inteference caused by the lawful exercise of the right of way by Y because it had not been created by him and Y was therefore not "claiming under him" when using that right of way.

What acts constitute a breach of the covenant?

"But it appears to us to be in every case a question of fact whether the quiet enjoyment of the land has or has not been interrupted; and where the ordinary and lawful enjoyment of the demised land is substantially interfered with by the acts of the lessor, or those lawfully claiming under him the covenant appears to be broken. (*Sanderson v. Berwick on Tweed Corporation* (above) at p. 551, *per* Fry L.J.)"

The cases are not in full agreement as to what constitutes a breach of the covenant. Traditionally it was held that some physical interference with the enjoyment of the plaintiff's premises was required. (See *Lavendar v. Betts* [1942] 2 All E.R. 72, where the landlord removed the tenant's doors and windows). In *Browne v. Flower* [1991] 1 Ch. 219 the landlord of tenant A consented to the erection of an open iron staircase to A's upper floor flat which passed in front of the window of the ground floor flat which had been let to the plantiff, tenant B, by that landlord. It was held that this did not amount to a breach of the covenant for quiet enjoyment because there was no physical interference with the plaintiff tenant's premises. He was really complaining of a breach of privacy, which is a right not recognised by English law.

The question was not settled in *Owen v. Gadd* [1956] 2 Q.B. 99 where the landlord had erected scaffolding outside the plaintiff tenant's shop, causing a loss of business. The landlord was held liable for breach of the covenant for quiet enjoyment because although there was no actual physical contact with the plaintiff tenant's premises by the scaffolding, there was a substantial interference with the use of the premises sufficient to amount to a breach of covenant. Romer L.J. spoke of the need for the interference complained of to be physical *or* direct, whilst Evershed M.R. referred to physical *and* direct interference.

In *Kenny v. Preen* [1962] 3 All E.R. 814, CA a change of emphasis can be detected. The plaintiff was the the tenant of a two-room flat let to her by the defendant landlord who lived in the same building. The landlord served a purported notice to quit on the footing that the premises were furnished, although this was a matter of dispute. Eighteen months later he began to write offensive letters to the plaintiff and bang on her door from time for time for a period of a year, despite the fact that her solicitors had written to the landlord at the beginning of the year claiming that she had an unfurnished tenancy protected by the Rent Acts. The Court of Appeal held that the landlord's conduct amounted to a breach of the covenant for quiet enjoyment. They described it as a course of intimidation which seriously interfered with the tenant's freedom of action in exercising her right to possession and which tended to deprive her of the full benefit of that right. There was some difference of opinion on the direct/physical point, with some indication that this was not actually necessary for there to be a breach of the covenant, but in any event it was certainly present in that case because of the banging on the door of the plaintiff's flat. The decision in this case seemed to favour the proposition that there will be a breach of the covenant if there is a substantial or intolerable interference, provided it was intended or reasonably forseeable that it would interfere with the tenant's freedom of action in exercising his or her right to possession. (See also *Sampson v. Floyd* [1989] 2 E.G.L.R. 49). This modified test, which concentrates on the effects of the acts complained of on the tenant, is clearly of great importance in those cases where a landlord has been responsible for intimidatory acts done with the intention of causing the tenant to leave. (See for example *Perera v. Vandiyar* [1953] 1 W.L.R. 672 where a disconnection of the tenant's gas and electricity supplies was held to amount to a breach of the covenant). However, because of the measure of damages available for breach of the covenant, the value of the covenant to a harassed tenant is severely limited. This issue is discussed further in Chapter 5.

The measure of damages for breach of the covenant for quiet enjoyment was discussed in *Mira and Others v. Aylmer Square Investments Ltd and Others* [1990] 22 E.G. 61 where the landlords had begun work under a scheme for the construction of penthouse flats on the top of four blocks of flats which they had acquired. The scheme proved to be disastrous and many tennats suffered from dust, noise, dirt, etc. whilst some top floor flats had suffered water penetration. The issue before the court was whether tenants, who had long leases and had left their flats, but were unable to sub-let because of the state of the property, could recover damages for what they might have obtained by sub-letting had that been possible. The Court of Appeal held that they could—

> "if a tenant is driven out of possession by reason of breaches of a repairing covenant or breach of the covenant for quiet enjoyment, he can recover the costs of alternative accommodation. If the tenant happens to own other accommodation which he is driven to use, through the landlord's breach, he ought to be able to recover the loss which he actually sustains because he is unable to sublet the flat in question during the time that it is rendered uninhabitable. In my judgment...loss was within the contemplation of the parties within the first rule of *Hadley v. Baxendale* (1854) 9 Exch 341 it was not unusual and it was readily forseeable. (Stuart-Smith L.J. at p.64.)"

Mutual lettings schemes

A tenant whose enjoyment of his property is interfered with by the actions of a neighbouring tenant of the same landlord may, as an alternative to relying on the covenant for quiet enjoyment, seek an injunction directly against the tenant complained of if the plaintiff can establish the existence of a mutual lettings scheme. The essence of such a scheme is that there is a common development comprising a number of dwelling-houses which are let off on tenancies, each one containing restrictive user covenants. These covenants are entered into on the footing that each tenant will have the reciprocal benefit of the identical covenants restricting the use of the other dwelling-houses. If the court finds that such a scheme exists then any tenant may restrain the landlord or any other tenant from using any other part of the development for purposes inconsistent with the scheme. This was accepted in *Newman v. Real Estate Debenture Corporation* (1940) 162 L.T. 183 where it was also observed that a purchaser from the landlord with notice of the scheme would also be bound. The requirements of a mutual lettings scheme mirror those of a building scheme for the purpose of enforcing restrictive covenants affecting freehold land (see Stevens & Pearce, *Land Law* (1998) Chapter 10). It will therefore be necessary to prove all the requirements of such a scheme, the essence of which is a common intention that the tenants will be subject to mutual reciprocal obligations enforceable *inter se*. (See *Elliston v. Reacher* [1908] 2 Ch. 365; *Baxter v. Four Oaks Properties Ltd* [1965] 1 Ch. 816 and *Re Dolphin's Conveyance* [1970] Ch. 654). In *Kelly v. Battershell* [1949] 2 All E.R. 830, where the Court of Appeal refused to imply a scheme affecting flats in one building, *Newman* was described by Cohen L.J. as the "high water mark" of lettings scheme cases.

Non-derogation from grant

It is a general principle applicable to all grants and not just tenancies that a grantor may not give rights on the one hand and then on the other hand derogate from that grant by taking those rights away by some means or other. The principle is based on broad notions of equity—

"The expression 'derogation from grant' conjures up images of parchment and sealing wax, of copperplate handwriting and fusty title deeds. But the principle is not based on some ancient technicality of real property. As Younger L.J. observed, in *Harmer v. Jumbil (Nigeria) Tin Areas Ltd* [1921] 1 Ch. 200, it is a principle which embodies in a legal maxim a rule of common honesty. It was imposed in the interests of fair dealing. (*Johnston & Sons Ltd v. Holland* [1988] 1 E.G.L.R. 264, 267 *per* Nicholls L.J.)"

The principle of non-derogation from grant applies to a tenancy where the premises are let to the tenant for a particular purpose (known to the landlord at that time: *Robinson v. Kilvert* (1889) 41 Ch. 88) which is then interfered with by the actions of the landlord or those claiming under him. It also embodies an implied undertaking that the landlord will not use adjoining property for purposes inconsistent with the tenant's lawful use of his property such as to amount to a substantial interference with that use. Thus even though there may not have been a breach of the covenant for quiet enjoyment by the landlord, he may be restrained from engaging in conduct which interferes with the tenant's particular use of the property. But to amount to a breach of this principle the conduct complained of must render the tenant's premises less fit or materially less fit to be used for the purposes for which they were let. A breach of privacy will not be such an interference with an ordinary residential tenancy (*Browne v. Flower*, above). It is comfort rather than use which is interfered with in such a case. There was also found to be insubstantial interference in *Kelly v. Battershell* (above), where part of the premises were incorporated into a hotel by the landlord.

In *Aldin v. Latimer Clark, Muirhead & Co* [1894] 2 Ch. 437 the landlord had let premises to be used as drying sheds for timber. It was held that he could not therefore build on his adjoining land in such a way as to interfere with the free flow of air to the sheds, because this would amount to a derogation from his grant—

"where a landlord demises part of his property for carrying on a particular business, he is bound to abstain from doing anything on the remaining portion which would render the demised premises unfit for carrying on such business in the way in which it is ordinarily carried on. (Per Sterling J. at p.444.)"

The principle was applied in *Lend Lease Development Pty Ltd v. Zemlicka* (1985) 3 N.S.W.L.R. 207, where landlords were held to have derogated from their grant by demolishing buildings on their retained land which had adjoined the tenant's kangaroo skins warehouse. This action had rendered the tenant's premises more vulnerable to theft. A breach also occurred in *Harmer v. Jumbil* (above) where a tenant with an explosive store on his land was granted an injunction against an adjoining tenant of the same landlord to prevent him building on that land with the landlord's permission. If the building had gone ahead the tenant's store would need to have been closed because of the terms of a licence governing the proximity of other buildings to explosive stores.

The principle of non-derogation of grant does not mean that the landlord or another tenant cannot conduct a competing business on adjoining land (*Romulus Trading Property Ltd v. Comet Properties Ltd* [1996] 2 E.G.L.R. 70). Its purpose is not to protect the tenant from mere economic loss.

The decision of the Court of Appeal in *Chartered Trust plc v. Davies* [1997] 49 E.G. 135 (above) has opened up an interesting line of argument and is a novel variation on the letting scheme line of cases (see above). The tenant in that case was granted a tenancy of a shop in a shopping mall. Three years later in 1992 at the height of recession the landlord granted a tenancy of another shop in the mall to a pawnbroker, the light from whose windows onto a common passageway was obscured by potential customers who blocked the passage. All this had a depressing effect on the plaintiff's trade (the sale of puzzles and executive toys), whose business was substantially interfered with by the pawnbroker's use of her premises, which amounted to a nuisance. It was clear that simply letting adjoining premises, to a pawnbroker was not a breach of the covenant for quiet enjoyment nor a derogation from grant by the landlord. But the conduct complained of here was the nuisance actually caused by the conduct of the pawnbroker's business. The crucial issue was whether by their inaction the landlord could be said to have authorised the nuisance. For Henry L.J. the answer to this question turned upon whether the landlord had a duty to do something. Despite the line of authority (discussed above) suggesting that a landlord cannot be held to have authorised a nuisance committed by another of his tenants simply by failing to enforce a covenant against the offending conduct in that tenant's lease, the judge found that the landlord did have a duty to act in this case. On the facts of the case, "the nature of the grant to a large measure depended upon proper management of the shopping mall and the common parts thereof. . .If a landlord was never required to take action to protect what he had granted to his tenant, he could render valueless the protection of his tenant's business seemingly built in to the letting scheme he was marketing. That would offend the principle of fair dealing." In a passage which gets to the heart of the issue, his Lordship continued—

"Where a landlord is granting leases in his shopping mall, over which he has maintained control, and charged a service charge therefor, it is is simply no answer to say that a tenant's sole protection is his own ability and willingness to bring his individual action. Litigation is too expensive, too uncertain and offers no protection against, say trespassing or threatening members of the public [a reference to the persons who gathered outside the pawnbrokers in that case]. The duty to act lies with the landlord (p.140)."

The court went on to hold that the landlord's failure to act amounted to an authorisation of the continuance of the nuisance and to be a derogation from his grant to the tenant. As to the remedy, the Court of Appeal was not prepared to interfere with the decision of the judge that the tenant was justified in treating the tenancy as repudiated. The decision in this case is of considerable interest not only because it applies the principles of adoption of a nuisance by inactivity in a landlord and tenant context, but also in permitting the tenant to treat the tenancy as repudiated (see Chapter 6 below for termination of tenancies by repudiation).

Chapter 3

REPAIRING OBLIGATIONS

Introduction

(a) Residential lettings

The poor condition of a large proportion of the housing stock in England and Wales is well documented. Having analysed information contained in the *English House Condition Survey 1991* (Department of the Environment (1993) and the *1993 Welsh House Condition Survey* (Welsh Office 1994) the Law Commission concluded in 1996 that "of all private rented properties, more than one fifth of those in England and more than a quarter of those in Wales are unfit" (Law Commission No. 238 "Landlord and Tenant: Responsibility for State and Condition of Property" (1996), para. 8.7). Although the incidence of unfit property is primarily concentrated in older stock in the private rented sector, there is still a significant amount of public sector housing that is unfit. Public sector housing comprises approximately 20 per cent of all occupied property in England and Wales, of which 6.9 per cent in England and 15.8 per cent in Wales is statutorily unfit (*ibid.*).

It is clear therefore that landlords and tenants are falling down on their repairing obligations. In practice, for the most part this means landlords because, as will be seen below, most repairing obligations, in the case of periodic tenancies, fall by agreement or (more often) by statute upon the landlord. This makes sense, because such tenants have no capital stake in the premises. So the question which arises is why are so many landlords not honouring their obligations? The traditional landlord response has been that rent controls and security of tenure imposed by the Rent Acts since 1915 (See Chapter 8 below) have meant that the economic returns were not sufficient to permit the landlord to expend the necessary sums on repairs, and that many landlords were themselves relatively poor elderly people with only one or two houses, usually inherited. This is undoubtedly true in some cases although it does not satisfactorily explain why the properties in disrepair include those managed by professional landlords who have often bought the property with a sitting tenant at a price substantially discounted from the vacant possession value of the property. It remains to be seen whether the "deregulation" of the private rented sector by the Housing Act 1988 (as accelerated by the Housing Act 1996) will make a difference. Most private sector tenancies created since January 15, 1989 are assured shorthold tenancies where the tenant is obliged to negotiate a market rent with the landlord in return for a tenancy with no statutory security of tenure. Landlords should therefore now be in receipt of rents which permit them to comply with their repairing obligations. Indeed it would make sense to make a property as attractive as possible, in order to command the higher rents now obtainable in law. We must wait for appropriate research findings and see whether this has proved to be the case; because, despite the reintroduction of market rents, many tenants in the private rented sector are dependent on housing benefit in order to pay the whole or part of their rent and landlords frequently protest that the regulations which govern housing benefit are framed in such a way as to deny landlords a full market rate of return on their investment.

In the past, some amelioration of the state of repair of the nation's housing stock has been achieved through the availability of various forms of state-funded improvement grants but these tend to dry up as Governments embark on public expenditure efficiency drives. This is a complex area of housing law which is not within the scope of this book but it is worth mentioning here that until recently certain grants (*i.e.* renovation grants, disabled grants and minor works grants—the last now replaced by "home repairs grants") were compulsory. They have since been made discretionary by the Housing Grants, Construction and Regeneration Act 1996, although landlords may be eligible for mandatory grants in "renewal areas".

A residential tenant who occupies property on a relatively short-term or periodic basis, who is dissatisfied with the state of repair or condition of the property and who has appealed without success to the landlord will need to consider (a) whether the landlord is in breach of covenant, and if so what private law remedies might be available in respect of that breach, and (b) whether there is any other course of action that might be taken under public law powers in order to compel the landlord to comply with his obligations.

(b) Business tenancies

Different considerations apply to commercial lettings. This is an area of landlord and tenant law where traditionally there has been minimal interference with the freedom of the parties to allocate repairing responsibilities between themselves by agreement. The form of such agreements will depend on many factors, including the value of the property, the length of the tenancy and the respective bargaining power of the parties in the light of prevailing market conditions. Thus tenants can expect to be able to drive harder bargains when the market is in recession and operating in their favour. A tenant who is able to bargain for a shorter lease may, for example, be able to persuade the landlord to undertake more extensive repairing obligations than he would in the case of a longer lease.

Most landlords of business premises normally seek to impose all repairing obligations on the tenant, a position referred to in practice as a "clear lease". This is particularly so in the case of an "institutional lease" where the landlord is an investment institution such as an insurance company or a pension fund which holds the premises as an investment and wishes to maximise rental returns and minimise their outgoings. Whilst this sort of arrangement is suitable for the letting of a single building, commercial tenancies are often of parts of a building or of units on an estate or in a commercial centre. In such cases it is more practical for the landlord to undertake repairs to the structure and common parts but to charge the costs to the tenants through a service charge. (See, *e.g. Postel Properties Ltd v. Boots the Chemist Ltd* [1996] 2 E.G.L.R. 60; and *New England Properties v. Portsmouth New Shops* [1993] 23 E.G. 130.)

It can be seen that the issue of responsibility for repairs in a tenancy will differ according to the nature of the property, such as whether it is residential or commercial or both (as in the case of a shop with a flat above), a house or a flat, a shop or a factory; the length of the tenancy, be it an oral weekly tenancy of a house, or a 25-year lease of an office in a block; the value of the property and a multitude of other factors. But in all cases the same basic common law principles of landlord and tenant law will apply, subject to any express or statutory provision to the contrary to deal with particular types of tenancies. Thus the remainder of this chapter will consider those general principles and the relevant statutory provisions.

It will first examine the position as to repair in the absence of express agreement between the parties and then look at express repairing obligations, before dealing with the nature and efficacy of the remedies available to landlord and tenant where the other party is in breach of a repairing obligation. The chapter will conclude with a section on proposals for law reform governing responsibility for the state and condition of leased property.

A. THE POSITION AT COMMON LAW

General rule—No implied liability

In the absence of express agreement there is in general, apart from statute, no obligation on either the landlord or the tenant to repair the premises. The position of the landlord was made clear in *Sleafer v. Lambeth BC* [1960] 1 Q.B. 43—

> "It is well established that, in the absence of agreement to the contrary, the law imposes no obligations on a landlord to keep the demised premises in repair" (p.62 *per* Willmer L.J. See also *Tennant Radiant Heat Ltd v. Warrington Development Corporation* [1988] 1 E.G.L.R. 41,43),

whilst it has been said in similar terms that "apart from express contract, a tenant owes no duty to the landlord to keep the premises in repair" (*Warren v. Keen* [1954] 1 Q.B. 15, 20 per Denning L.J.).

The general rule qualified?

(a) Tenants

Waste   The ancient law of waste which affords the (original) landlord a (non-assignable) remedy in tort in respect of acts which alter the nature of the property, still technically applies to tenancies, although it rarely features in modern litigation because the matters which it covers are usually governed by the express or implied terms of the tenancy. As Dillon L.J. has observed, "Waste is a somewhat archaic subject now seldom mentioned." (*Mancetter Developments Ltd v. Garmanston Ltd* [1986] Q.B. 1212, 1218.) The principal types of waste are "voluntary waste" and "permissive waste". The law of voluntary waste, which applies to all tenancies, makes the tenant liable for any damage to, or alteration to the character of, the property which has diminished its value (*Marsden v. Edward Heyes Ltd* [1927] 2 K.B. 1). Permissive waste, by contrast, was described by Blackstone with reference to a house as "a matter of omission only, as by suffering it to fall for want of reparations" (2 *Commentaries*, p.281). But what is the nature and extent of this obligation? The Law Commission has stated that—

> "Authorities on a tenant's liability for permissive waste are not easy to find, not least because of uncertainties as to when it is applicable. It is also remarkably difficult to ascertain the content of this liability. If the tenant is liable should he allow the property to fall down, that implies that he is under a positive obligation to take steps to prevent such an occurrence. However it is far from clear how far he can be regarded as being under a positive duty to repair or maintain the property. (Law Com. No. 238 'Landlord and Tenant: Responsibility for State and Condition of Property' (1996), para. 10.19.)"

Quite apart from the law of waste, every tenant is under an implied duty to use the premises in a tenant-like manner. The nature and extent of this obligation has been explained by Denning L.J. (as he then was) as follows:

> "The tenant must take proper care of the place. He must if he is going away for the winter, turn off the water and empty the boiler. He must clean the chimney, when necessary, and also the windows. He must unstop the sink when it is blocked by his waste. In short he must do the little jobs about the place which a reasonable tenant would do. In addition, he must, of course, not damage the house wilfully or negligently; and must see that his family and guests do not damage it: and if they do, he must repair it. But apart from such things, if the house falls into disrepair through fair wear and tear or lapse of time, or for any reason not caused by him, then the tenant is not liable to repair it. (*Warren v. Keen* [1953] 1 Q.B. 15, 20, CA.)"

This would certainly seem to be true of a weekly tenant, as in *Warren v. Keen* (above) although Somervell L.J. assumed, without deciding the point, that a yearly tenant might be liable to do minor repairs to keep the premises wind- and water-tight, fair wear and tear excepted. (See also *Wedd v. Porter* [1916] 2 K.B. 91.) The qualification with regard to disrepair arising from fair wear and tear exempts the tenant from any liability for disrepair coming about from the reasonable use of the premises and the ordinary operation of natural forces (*Haskell v. Marlow* [1928] 2 K.B. 45, 59 *per* Talbot L.J.; and *Regis Property Co. Ltd v. Dudley* [1959] A.C. 370). The same fair wear and tear qualification also applies to the doctrine of permissive waste (*Manchester Bonded Warehouse Company Ltd v. Carr* (1880) 5 C.P.D. 507).

The ambit of the obligation to use the premises in a tenant-like manner was at issue in *Wycombe Area Health Authority v. Barnett* (1982) 47 P.& C.R. 384, CA). A monthly tenant who failed to lag the water pipes, including the rising main, or to drain the system and switch off the water at the main tap when she went away for a day, but stayed an extra day, in February, was held not to be in breach of this obligation when the pipes froze and a burst occurred. The Court held that the extent of the tenant's obligations depended on all the circumstances. Clearly it could be a different matter if the tenant went away for some time when to her knowledge a very cold spell was likely.

In any event, like the law of waste, the obligation to use the premises in a tenant-like manner does not place a positive repairing obligation on the tenant. "They are obligations as to his conduct, and user of the premises, and so long as they are fulfilled as they ought to be no question of repair arises" (*Regis Property Co Ltd v. Dudley* [1959] A.C. 370, 407 *per* Lord Denning).

(b) Landlords

Furnished houses As we have seen above the general rule is that a landlord will be contractually liable to the tenant only where he has expressly undertaken an obligation to repair or maintain the property. By contrast, in *Wettern Electric v. Welsh Development Agency* [1983] 2 All E.R. 629, the court was willing to imply a fitness for purpose term into a contractual licence for the occupation of factory premises in order to give business efficacy to the contract. Thus the licensee was able to recover for loss of production, and the cost of removal and general disruption when it had to relocate because of serious structural faults in the building. A licence to occupy would thus seem to be governed by different commercial principles than a tenancy which is subject to very long-standing special rules which are confined to the landlord and tenant relationship.

Similarly, there is no term implied by law in a tenancy that the premises should be fit for the purpose for which they are let (*Hart v. Windsor* (1843) 12 M.&W. 68, 88; 152 E.R. 1114, 1122 *per* Parke B.). But this is qualified by the rule in *Smith v. Marrable* (1843) 11 M.&W. 5; 152 E.R. 693 to the effect that there is a common law implied condition that a furnished house will be fit for habitation when let. (See also *Wilson v. Finch Hatton* (1877) 2 Ex. D. 336.) The rule is based on the dubious rationale that the hire of the furniture is a central component of the tenancy bargain thereby dictating a more consumer protection orientated approach.

Where the implied condition applies it is subject to the normal contractual rule governing conditions, that if it is broken the tenant will be entitled to repudiate the tenancy (*Collins v. Hopkins* [1923] 2 K.B. 617). But the ambit of the condition is limited. Not only does it seem to be confined to health hazards such as an infestation of bugs (as in *Smith v. Marrable* itself) or the recent presence of a person with an infectious disease (*Bird v. Lord Greville* (1884) Cab. & El. 317 (measles); it also does not extend to unfurnished lettings of houses (*Hart v. Windsor* (1844) 12 M.&W. 8, 152 E.R. 1114) or flats (*Cruse v. Mount* [1933] Ch. 278, Maugham J.).

Furthermore it is limited to the condition of the property when let and does not extend throughout the tenancy (*Sarson v. Roberts* [1895] 2 Q.B. 395). So even if the obligation does apply, it does not oblige the landlord to *keep* the premises fit throughout the tenancy.

Common parts

The House of Lords has recognised that where the tenancy does not make express provision dealing with the question of liability, it is necessary to imply a term on the part of the landlord of a high-rise block of flats in multiple occupation to take reasonable care to maintain the common parts and facilities (including stairs, lifts and rubbish chutes) in a state of reasonable repair and usability (*Liverpool City Council v. Irwin* [1977] A.C. 239, HL). The test which governs the implication of this term is one of necessity. In the *Irwin* case, which involved a 15-storey block of local authority flats, life in the dwellings as a tenant would have been impossible without the rubbish chutes, lifts and staircases. In those circumstances

"The subject matter of the lease [high rise blocks] and the relationship created by the tenancy demand, of their nature, some contractual obligations on the landlord" (*per* Lord Wilberforce at p.254). It should be noted that the duty on the part of the landlord is qualified rather than absolute, and on the facts of the *Irwin* case the duty had been complied with by the landlord authority, which had done its best to combat the vandalism in the block which was the root cause of the breakdown and poor state of the facilities in question.

It is important to appreciate the limits of this implied term. Simply because a tenant has an easement over land retained by the landlord does not mean that the landlord is under a duty of repair with regard to the part retained. Consequently the term was not extended to impose liability on a landlord for the repair of a drain on land retained by him, which served adjoining property let to the tenant, and over which that tenant had an easement (*Duke of Westminster v. Guild* [1985] Q.B. 688). The easement carried with it the right to enter the landlord's property and repair the drain, and in the absence of express provision the court would not impose a repairing obligation on the landlord. Similarly, a landlord of individual flats in a block of flats will not be liable, in the absence of an express covenant, for repairs to the structure of the building in which the flats are located, expecially where such matters were covered by an insurance policy taken out by the landlord and to which the tenants were required to contribute (*Adami v. Lincoln Grange Management Ltd* [1998] 17 E.G. 148, CA). On the other hand an implied obligation was held to arise so as to make a local authority landlord of a terraced house on an estate liable to repair the side and rear access path to the subject property (*King v. South*

Northamptonshire DC [1992] 06 E.G. 152, CA). Because of the layout of the estate the rear access was essential for deliveries and the removal of refuse and as such the houses could not be enjoyed or function in accordance with their design without that access. Accordingly an implied repairing obligation on the part of the landlord was considered to be necessary in the circumstances.

Correlative obligation

The Court of Appeal has also implied an obligation on the part of a landlord to repair the exterior of a house where the tenancy agreement imposed liability for repair of the interior of the property on the tenant. This was for the simple reason that sooner or later the tenant's covenant would not be capable of being complied with unless the outside had been kept in repair. (Water penetration, for example, could render internal decoration useless.) In the absence of any express provision in the tenancy for repair of the exterior it made business sense to place that obligation on the landlord (*Barrett v. Lounova (1982) Ltd* [1990] 1 Q.B. 348; CA, where the tenancy began in 1941. But note the very special circumstances beyond which such an obligation will not be implied. See *Adami v. Lincoln Grange Management Ltd* (above.) In the case of most short-term and periodic residential tenancies created since October 24, 1961 there is now a statutory repairing obligation on the landlord to repair, *inter alia*, the exterior (see below).

It does not follow, however, that the courts will always imply a term as to repair on one of the parties where the tenancy is silent on the matter—

> "it is a phenomenon, certainly known at common law, that there may be situations in which there is no repairing obligation imposed either expressly or impliedly on anyone in relation to a lease (*Demetriou v. Robert Andrews (Estate Agencies) Ltd* (1990) 62 P.& C.R. 536, 544–545, *per* Stuart-Smith L.J.)."

It can be seen from the above review that there is no coherent set of principles governing implied repairing obligations on the part of either the landlord or the tenant. The present law is based on a laissez-faire approach modified by case law in a piecemeal fashion by the development of rules of limited application and uncertain scope. However, before attempting any overview it is necessary to examine a number of statutory rules governing repairing obligations in leases which overlay and frequently supersede the position at common law as outlined above.

B. IMPLIED STATUTORY REPAIRING OBLIGATIONS

Landlord and Tenant Act 1985, sections 11–16

The most important obligations which are imposed on certain landlords by statute are those contained in what is now section 11 of the Landlord and Tenant Act 1985. (The 1985 Act is a consolidating Act. These obligations were first introduced by the Housing Act 1961, ss. 32 and 33 in the case of leases granted on or after October 24, 1961. Thus references below to the provisions of the 1985 Act should where relevant be treated as encompassing the equivalent earlier provisions which were in force at the relevant time). They are frequently invoked in practice and constitute an important exception to the absence at common law of any repairing obligation on the part of the landlord. They were described by Judge Colyer Q.C. in advice to the Law Commission as "of enormous social significance" (Law Com. No. 238 "Landlord and Tenant: Responsibility for State and Condition of Property" (1996), para. 5.12). For a critical account of the interpretation afforded by the courts to the statutory covenants as to fitness (see below) and repair see J.I. Reynolds (1974) 37 M.L.R. and for a rejoinder see M. Robinson (1976) 39 MLR 43.

(a) Leases to which the Act applies

Subject to the exceptions below, the implied repairing covenant under section 11 applies to a lease of a dwelling-house granted for a term of less than seven years (Landlord and Tenant Act 1985, s.13(1)). (In *Brikom Investments Ltd v. Seaford* [1981] 2 All E.R. 783 the lease was for seven years but the landlord was estopped from denying that section 11 applied because a fair rent had been registered by the rent officer on a number of occasions on the erroneous assumption that the lease was for less than seven years.) For this purpose, a lease of a dwelling-house means a lease by which a building or part of a building is let wholly or mainly as a private residence (*ibid.* s.16(b)).

There are a number of provisions designed to prevent landlords attempting to avoid the Act.

(1)   If the landlord purports to grant a lease for more than seven years but backdates its commencement, any part of the term which falls before the grant is disregarded (s. 13(2)(a)). Thus a lease for 10 years granted in 1999 but expressed to commence in 1995 will be treated as a lease for six years for the purposes of section 11.

(2)   A lease which is determinable at the option of the lessor before the expiration of seven years from its commencement falls within section 11(1) (s.13(2)(b). By contrast, a lease which gives the tenant the option for renewal which, when taken with the original term, amounts to more than seven years, is outside section 11(1) (s.13(2)(c)). Thus a lease for five-years with an option to renew for a further five year term will be outside section 11 from the outset.

The specific exceptions to section 11 (as to which see section 14) are:

(1)   a new lease granted to a tenant whose previous lease was outside section 11;

(2)   a lease of a dwelling-house which is a tenancy of an agricultural holding within the meaning of the Agricultural Holdings Act 1986 or to a farm business tenancy within the meaning of the Agricultural Tenancies Act 1995;

(3)   a lease granted on or after October 3, 1980 to local authorities and certain other public or publicly funded bodies including a registered housing association and an educational body as specified by regulations for the purposes of section 8 of the Rent Act 1977 or sched. 1 para. 8 of the Housing Act 1988 (See Chapters 9 and 10 below). This last exemption is designed to encourage private sector landlords to let properties to universities etc. who will sub-let to students. It means that whilst the university will be liable under section 11 to the sub-tenants, the landlord will not in turn be liable to the university;

(4)   a lease granted on or after October 3, 1980 to the Crown (but not the Crown Estates Commissioners) or a government department.

(b) The obligation

Lease created on or after October 24, 1961 and before January 15, 1989 In those leases to which it is applicable (see above) section 11(1) implies a covenant by the landlord—

> "(a) to keep in repair the structure and exterior of the dwelling-house (including drains, gutters and external pipes) and
>
> (b) to keep in repair and proper working order the installations in the dwelling-house for—
>
> > (i) the supply of water, gas and electricity and for sanitation (including basins, sinks, baths, and sanitary fittings, but not other fixtures,fittings and appliances for making use of the supply of water, gas or electricity) and
> >
> > (ii) space heating and heating water."

Where the section 11 covenant is implied there is also implied a covenant by the tenant that the landlord, or any person authorised by him in writing, may at reasonable times of the day and on giving 24 hours' notice in writing to the occupier, enter the premises comprised in the tenancy for the purpose of viewing their condition and state of repair (s.11(6)).

Structural and exterior repairs "Keep in repair" means "put and keep in repair", thus obliging the landlord to rectify any defects existing at the time the tenancy began as well as those arising during the tenancy (see *Proudfoot v. Hart* (1890) 25 Q.B.D. 42 and *Liverpool City Council v. Irwin* (above).

With regard to the "structure" it has been said that it "consists of those elements of the overall dwelling-house which gives it its essential appearance, stability and shape. The expression does not extend to the many and varied ways in which the dwelling-house will be fitted out, equipped decorated and generally made to be habitable" (*Irvine v. Moran* (1992) 24 H.L.R. 1, 5). Thus it was held in *Irvine v. Moran* that external windows along with their frames and sashes were part of the structure, but that internal plaster was not. (But contrast *Staves v. Leeds City Council* [1992] 29 E.G. 119, CA, below, where it was conceded that plaster was part of the structure).

The reference to the "exterior" of the property has been construed as extending to means of access to the premises, such as front steps leading up to the house (*Brown v. Liverpool Corporation* [1969] 3 All E.R. 1345) but not to a rear and non-essential means of access (*Hopwood v. Cannock Chase DC* [1975] 1 W.L.R. 373, CA. See also *King v. South Northamptonshire DC* [1992] 06 E.G. 152, CA, (p.50 above) where the court implied a repairing obligation at common law, on the *Irwin* principle, with regard to a rear access path which was not covered by section 11 because it was not part of the "exterior" of the dwelling-house).

Section 11(1) was restrictively construed by the Court of Appeal in *Campden Hill Towers Ltd v. Gardner* [1977] Q.B. 823 where it was held not to apply to (a) the structure and exterior of a block of flats in relation to a tenancy of one of the flats in the block, nor to (b) an installation, such as a common boiler located in the basement of the building, which was not in the physical confines of the flat. "Dwelling-house" was held to mean the premises leased, not the building of which those premises formed a part or any other part of that building. On this basis the roof of the block would not normally be a physical part of a flat in the block (see

Rapid Results College v. Angell [1986] 1 E.G.L.R. 53, a case of an express repairing covenant) although it could be in the case of a top-floor flat (as in *Douglas-Scott v. Scorgie* [1984] 1 W.L.R. 716), whether or not it was expressly included within the subject matter of the tennancy. On the other hand, repair of the exterior wall of an individual flat was held to be within the landlord's obligation even if (as in *Gardner*) it was expressly stated by the lease not to be within the subject matter of the tenancy. The crucial test was whether as a matter of fact it formed part of the structure of the flat. On that test it was held that in the case of a flat, the exterior would extend to the outer walls of the flat, the outside of inner party walls of the flat, the outer sides of the horizontal divisions between the flat and those above and below and the structural framework and beams directly supporting the floor, ceilings and walls of the flat. A term of the tenancy which excluded any such part from the property let did not make any difference.

The landlord in *Wycombe Area Health Authority v. Barnett* (1982) 47 P.& C.R. 384, CA (see p.48 above) was held not to be in breach of the statutory obligation to keep installations etc. in proper working order when he failed to lag cold the water pipes which froze in extremely cold water causing a burst and consequential damage. His only obligation was to keep the pipes in good mechanical condition.

Leases created on or after January 15, 1989 Because of the restricted scope of section 11 as originally enacted (and as revealed by *Campden Hill Towers Ltd v. Gardner* (above) it was amended by the Housing Act 1988, s.116(1) which added sections 11(1A), 11(1B) and 11(3A) to the Landlord and Tenant Act 1985, but only in respect of tenancies entered into on or after January 15, 1989.

Section 11(1A) provides that, in the case of such tenancies, where the premises let form part of a building—

(1) the obligation to repair the structure and exterior of the dwelling-house also extends to any part of the building in which the landlord has an estate or interest (provided the disrepair is such as to affect the tenant's enjoyment of the dwelling-house or of any common parts which he is entitled to use (s.11(1B));

(2) the obligation in relation to installations applies also to those installations which directly or indirectly serve the dwelling-house and which either (i) form part of the building in which the landlord has an estate or interest or (ii) are owned by him or are under his control.

This effectively overrules *Campden Hill Towers Ltd v. Gardner* (above) in the case of leases granted on or after January 15, 1989.

To deal with the position in cases where the landlord does not have access to other parts of the building (because, for example, he has let them to another tenant without reserving any right of access to enable him to undertake repairs or works that affect other parts of the building) it is provided (by s.11(3A) that it will be a defence to an action by the tenant which is based on s.11(1A) for the landlord to establish—

(1) that he does not have a sufficient right in the part of the building or installation concerned to enable him to carry out the required works or repairs; and

(2) that he unsuccessfully used all reasonable endeavours to obtain such rights as would be adequate to enable him to carry out the required works or repairs.

Obligations outside section 11

The obligations in section 11 of the Landlord and Tenant Act 1985 specifically do not apply (by virtue of section 11(2)) so as to make the landlord liable—

(1)   to carry out works or repairs for which the tenant is liable under his obligation to use the premises in a tenant like manner (see p.47 above for the scope of that obligation) or under a contractual obligation in respect of any matters within that obligation;

(2)   to reinstate the premises in the case of destruction or damage by fire, tempest, flood or other inevitable accident;

(3)   to keep in repair or maintain anything which the lessee is entitled to remove from the dwelling-house. (This is a reference to what are known as "tenants' fixtures". These are certain categories of fixtures (*e.g.* ornamental) that the tenant has attached to the premises during the lease and which he is entitled to remove within a reasonable period after the expiry of the lease).

No contracting out

Unless it has been authorised by the county court (see below), any agreement is void in so far as it purports—

(1)   to exclude or limit the obligations of the landlord or the immunities of the tenant under section 11; or

(2)   to authorise any forfeiture, or impose on the tenant any penalty, disability or obligation on a tenant who seeks to enforce or rely upon those obligations or immunities (s.12(1)).

The county court may, by an order consented to by both parties, authorise an agreement in the lease or elsewhere which excludes or modifies the provisions of section 11 if it appears to the court to be reasonable to do so in the circumstances (s.12(2)).

It is also provided that in so far as any covenant in a lease purports to make the tenant liable for obligations which are imposed on the landlord by section 11, it shall be of no effect (s.11(4)). Thus if the tenant has covenanted to repair the interior and exterior of the property he will only be liable for those repairs which are outside the landlord's statutory obligation under section 11. (See above for the extent of that obligation, and see *Irvine v. Moran* (above) where a tenant's covenant to paint the exterior was to that extent of no effect). In any event if the landlord is liable to repair, this will involve making good any consequential damage to decorations even if the tenant is obliged by an express term of the tenancy to carry out internal decoration (*McGreal v. Wake* (1984) 13 H.L.R. 107, CA; *Bradley v. Chorley BC* (1985) 83 L.G.R. 623, CA. See further below as to consequential losses).

It is clear from section 11(1) that the landlord is obliged to keep in repair and proper working order any gas fires that are provided for the tenant as well as a central heating system. In practice many landlords charge the tenant, by way of a "service charge", for the cost of an annual inspection of these items. This is a dubious practice which would appear to fall foul of section 11(4). (For the landlord's obligations with regard to gas applicances, see also S.I. 1994 No. 1886, reg. 35 as amended).

Extent of the obligation

The obligation to repair which is imposed on a landlord by section 11 is by way of an implied covenant to "put and keep in repair". This means that if the disrepair is to the demised premises or an installation therein, the landlord is not liable until he has notice of the disrepair and has failed to repair within a reasonable time thereafter. The tenant should clearly state what is required—it is not sufficient simply to tell the landlord that the property is in need of repair and that more details will be provided and then fail to provide those further details (*Al Hassani v. Merrigan* [1988] 03 E.G. 88). This requirement can have harsh consequences. In *O'Brian v. Robinson* [1973] A.C. 912, HL the tenant and his wife were in bed when the ceiling collapsed as a result of a latent defect of which neither the landlord nor the tenant had been aware up to that point. The House of Lords held that the landlord could not be liable for the consequential damage (including the personal injury) caused by the collapse because he did not have notice at that time. He was of course liable to repair the damage to the property of which he now had notice. (For liability in tort for consequential damage, possibly even in the absence of notice, see below). By notice is meant "information about the existence of a defect such as would put a reasonable landlord on enquiry as to whether works of repair are needed" (*British Telecommunications plc v. Sun Life Assurance Soc. plc* [1996] Ch. 69, 74 *per* Nourse L.J. It was made clear in this case that where the disrepair is of a part of the building which is under the landlord's control, liability, at least under a covenant "to keep in repair", arises immediately the disrepair occurs).

Notice can be direct or indirect. In *Dinefwr BC v. Jones* (1987) 19 H.L.R. 445, CA it was sufficient to fix the local authority landlord with knowledge of the disrepair that it had been seen by an officer from the environmental health department of the authority. Furthermore, notice was also deemed to have been obtained in that case by virtue of the chief executive having received a valuation report in connection with a right to buy application in respect of the property which had listed the relevant defects. (See also *Hall v. Howard* (1988) 20 H.L.R. 566, CA and *McGreal v. Wake* above). Thus whether notice has been acquired by the landlord will be a question of fact in every case. In *Sheldon v. West Bromwich Corpn.* (1973) 13 H.L.R. 23 the landlord's plumbers had visited the property on at least six occasions to investigate reports of discoloration of water in, and noises from, the water tank. This was sufficient to give the landlord authority knowledge of the need for repair and so it was held liable for damage caused when the tank subsequently burst.

A further serious obstacle in the way of tenants is graphically illustrated by the decision of the Court of Appeal in *Quick v. Taff Ely BC* [1986] Q.B. 809. The Law Commission drew attention to the plight of the tenant in that case in the opening paragraph of their Report on "Landlord and Tenant: Responsibility for State and Condition of Property", Law Com. No. 208, (1996), para. 1.1—

> "An unemployed council house tenant in Pontypridd found that his council house was virtually uninhabitable because of condensation. This was attributable to a defect in the design of the property. The tenant's furniture, carpets, curtains and decorations were ruined by the damp. Although the landlord was under an implied statutory obligation to repair the structure and exterior of the premises, it was not liable for the tenant's loss, nor could it be compelled to remedy the defect."

The reason the landlord was not liable was because the inherent design defect did not amount to disrepair of an item covered by section 11, that is the structure or exterior. This is because, as the Court of Appeal subsequently made clear in *Post Office v. Aquarius Properties Ltd* [1987] 1

All E.R. 1055, CA, a state of disrepair connotes a deterioration from some previous physical condition. Thus if, as in *Quick*, what is complained of is a design defect which does not cause disrepair to any part of the structure of exterior of the dwelling or an installation therein, the landlord will not be liable for the consequences of the defect even if that defect makes the property virtually uninhabitable. (See also *McNerny v. Lambeth LBC* [1989] 1 E.G.L.R. 81 and *Palmer v. Sandwell MBC* [1987] 2 E.G.L.R. 79.) Happily, it was possible to distinguish *Quick* in a number of subsequent cases where the tenant was able to point to some relevant item of physical disrepair brought about by the design defect. Thus in *Staves v. Leeds City Council* [1992] 29 E.G. 119, CA, condensation which was caused by a design defect saturated the plaster on the walls to such a degree that it needed replacing. This was conceded to be sufficiently part of the "structure" as to amount to disrepair for which the landlord was liable (cf. *Irvine v. Moran*, p.54 above). Liability was also imposed on the landlord in *Stent v. Monmouth DC* (1987) 19 H.L.R. 269, where a badly designed front door to a house on an exposed site, built in 1953 to lower standards than those permitted at the time of the action, let in water which caused the door to rot. The water also caused damage to the tenant's carpets. The defective door needed repeated repairs over many years. The damage to the door was held to be disrepair to the structure for which the landlord was held liable. The only effective remedy was to replace the door with a weather-proof door, which indeed the landlord had eventually done, thereby eliminating the defect. (By contrast, in *Murray v. Birmingham City Council* [1987] 2 E.G.L.R. 53 it was found as a fact that it was not necessary to rectify a defective roof by replacing it with a new roof). It is quite clear from these cases that the courts will confine the unfortunate decision in *Quick* to those circumstances where no disrepair can be found.

Also to be contrasted with design defects which do not cause disrepair to the fabric of the building is the case of a defectively designed installation. In *Liverpool City Council v. Irwin* [1977] A.C. 239, HL the plaintiff tenant complained of a lavatory cistern which flooded the floor every time it was used. The House of Lords held that the landlords were liable to put the matter right. An inherently defective cistern could hardly be kept in "proper working order" without putting the defect right in the first place, whether that defect had been there from the beginning or not.

It can be seen that in many of the cases on section 11 referred to above, the landlord is a local authority. The significance of this is that the cases are often test cases which are but the tip of the iceberg. Success for the tenant in such cases would inevitably entail extensive liability by the defendant landlord in respect of hundreds or thousands of similar defects throughout their stock, and the same would apply to other local authorities. It emerged during the trial in *Quick* that had the defendant local authority lost, they would have been required to spend some £9 million on rectifying the same defect in a large number of houses within their stock. The fact that such cases are fought in expensive court actions is some indication of the sums at stake and a sad reflection on the financial plight of many authorities whose housing stock contains accommodation some of which is in a very poor state of repair.

A related issue concerning the extent of the landlord's obligation under section 11 is the distinction between repair and renewal or improvement. The landlord is only under an obligation to repair that which was let to the tenant initially. He is not liable to provide something different. That would be an improvement as distinct from repair (see below). Thus in *Wainwright v. Leeds City Council* (1984) 13 H.L.R. 117, where a house suffered from rising damp, the landlord was not obliged to deal with the problem by installing a damp proof course (that is a barrier to protect against rising damp) when the house did not have one in the first place. To have required them to do so would have imposed on the landlord an obligation to give back a different property to that let. (See also *Pembery v. Lamdin* [1940] 2 All E.R. 434). The fact that the landlord was a local authority did not impose any wider obligation on them than that which is imposed by section 11 on a private landlord. (See further *McDougall v. Easington DC* (1989) 58 P.& C.R. 201). Whether the necessary remedial works amount to a "repair" or an "improvement" can be a difficult matter (see further below). In *Elmcroft Developments v. Tankersley-Sawyer* (1984) 15 H.L.R. 63 a landlord who had covenanted to repair was held liable to replace a defective slate damp proof course in a flat, in a high-class fashionable area of central London, with a more modern silicone injection course to prevent a recurrence of rising damp. It follows therefore that a delicate line is to be drawn between, on the one hand, a repair which involves a necessary degree of betterment and, on the other hand, an improvement which would not be within an ordinary repairing obligation. It would seem that in section 11 cases the courts might be more likely to sanction a patching-up operation, rather than a more extensive longer-lasting solution (see *Trustees of the Dame Margaret Hungerford Charity v. Beazley* (1994) 26 H.L.R. 269, CA and *Murray v. Birmingham City Council*, above).

Because the obligation imposed by section 11 is by way of an implied covenant, the way is paved for an argument that a serious failure to comply with the statute will permit the tenant to elect to treat the tenancy as terminated on the basis of the ordinary contractual doctrine of repudiation and sue for damages for loss caused by the breach (*Hussein v. Mehlman* [1992] 2 E.G.L.R. 87; see p.132 below. See further Susan Bright, *"Repudiating a Lease—Contract Rules"* [1993] Conv. 71; Charles Harpum, *"Leases as Contracts"* [1993] C.L.J. 212).

Standard of repair

Section 11(3) provides that "in determining the standard of repair required by the lessor's repairing covenant, regard shall be had to the age, character and prospective life of the dwelling-house and the locality in which it is situated." Save as to the reference to the prospective life of the property, this is an enactment of the common law rule as to the standard of repair in express repairing obligations (see below). In practice the prospective life of the dwelling-house will be an important consideration where short life property (that is property in a poor condition which has been earmarked for redevelopment) has been let at a low rent. A much lower-grade obligation will be imposed on the landlord in such circumstances. Thus in *Newham London Borough Council v. Patel* (1978) 13 H.L.R. 77, CA a house which had actually been found by the local authority to be unfit for human habitation was let at a low rent pending demolition. The tenant's counterclaim for breach of the statutory repairing obligation was dismissed. (But contrast *McClean v. Liverpool City Council* (1988) 20 H.L.R. 25 where a house let at a low rent would only have cost £1200 to repair and where it was not near the end of its life. It could not be assumed that the landlord would have no duty to repair in that case).

Statutory implied terms as to fitness for habitation

Many of the difficulties faced by a tenant whose house is all but unfit for habitation and yet technically not in a state of disrepair would disappear if there were an adequate implied term with regard to fitness for habitation. Whilst there is at present a statutory implied term it is far from adequate. In a re-enactment of a provision which first appeared in a more limited format in the Housing of the Working Classes Act 1885, it is provided by the Landlord and Tenant Act 1985, s.8 that in the case of certain contracts for the letting of a house for human habitation there is implied, notwithstanding any stipulation to the contrary—

(1)   a *condition* that the house is fit for human habitation at the commencement of the tenancy, and

(2)   an undertaking that the house will be kept by the landlord fit for human habitation throughout the tenancy.

Meaning of unfit The Act requires that in determining for this purpose whether a house is unfit for human habitation, regard must be had to its condition in respect of the following matters:

- repair;
- stability;
- freedom from damp;
- internal arrangement;
- natural lighting;
- ventilation;
- water supply;
- drainage and sanitary conveniences;
- facilities for preparation and cooking of food and for the disposal of waste water.

The house is to be regarded as unfit for human habitation if, and only if, it is so far defective in one or more of the above matters that it is not reasonably suitable for occupation in that condition (s.10). In this respect it has been held that—

"If the state of repair of a house is such that by ordinary use damage may naturally be caused to the occupier , either in respect of personal injury to life or limb or injury to health, then the house is not in all respects reasonably fit for human habitation". (*Morgan v. Liverpool Corporation* [1927] 2 K.B. 131, CA *per* Atkin L.J. adopted by the House of Lords in *Summers v. Salford Corporation* [1943] A.C. 283 where on the facts a broken sash cord which jammed a bedroom window was held to render the whole house unfit for human habitation.)

It has been held that, as in the case of the implied repairing covenant in section 11, the landlord will not become liable unless and until he has had notice of the need for repair and failed to remedy the defect within a reasonable time thereafter (*McCarrick v. Liverpool Corporation* [1947] A.C. 219).

Landlord's right of entry

By section 8(2) the landlord, or a person authorised by him in writing, may at reasonable times of the day, on giving 24 hours' notice in writing to the tenant or occupier, enter the premises comprised in the tenancy for the purpose of viewing their condition and state of repair.

Repudiatory breach

If the landlord is in breach of his obligation under section 8, the tenant can sue for damages and/or treat the tenancy as repudiated: (*Walker v. Hobbs & Co.* (1889) 23 Q.B.D. 458; cf. *Hussein v. Mehlmann* (above) because it is an implied condition (that is a serious contractual term, breach of which entitles the victim to treat the contract as at an end).

Rent limits

Unfortunately, the section 8 implied condition as to fitness for purpose is a dead letter because it only applies where the rent payable per annum does not exceed a certain limit. (See the critical comments in *Quick v. Taff Ely BC* (above). Those limits, which vary according to the date of the contract and the location of the property, are as follows.

Date of contract	Location	Rent limit (per annum)
Before July 31, 1923	In London	£40
	Elsewhere	£26 (or £16 where the borough population was below 50,000)
On or after July 31, 1923	In London	£40
and before July 6, 1957	Elsewhere	£26
On or after July 6, 1957	In London	£80
	Elsewhere	£52

It can be seen that this statutory implied term, which specifically does not apply where a house is let for three years or more upon terms that the tenant is to put the premises in a condition fit for human habitation (s.8(5)), is of no value to most tenants. Furthermore, because there is such a term the courts have shied away from implying a term in all residential tenancies that a dwelling-house is, and will be kept, fit for human habitation (see *McNerny v. Lambeth LBC*, above). The matter has been left to Parliament, which has proved to be conspicuously unresponsive to the judicial invitation to breathe new life into section 8 of the Landlord and Tenant Act 1985 by updating the rental limits. The present position has been strongly criticised by the Law Commission, which has recommended a new statutory implied term of fitness for habitation (both at the beginning and throughout the tenancy) to be applicable, save in exceptional cases, to all new residential tenancies for less than seven years (see below). It is also recommended that the landlord should not be liable if the property cannot be made fit for human habitation at reasonable expense. Indeed the courts have already placed this gloss on section 8 of the Landlord and Tenant Act 1985 (*Buswell v. Goodwin* [1971] 1 W.L.R. 92).

Liability in tort

The rule at common law was that a landlord is liable in contract only to the tenant(s) for breach of a repairing covenant. If a third party, such as a member of the tenant's family or a visitor, was injured because of the failure to repair, the landlord incurred no liability in contract or tort towards that person (*Cavalier v. Pope* [1906] A.C. 428). This common law position with regard to liability in tort has now been reversed by section 4 of the Defective Premises Act 1972, in circumstances where the landlord is under an express, implied or statutory repairing obligation (or is deemed to be so obliged, for the purposes of the 1972 Act) with regard to the demised premises. But it remains the case that, save where section 4 of the Defective Premises Act 1972 imposes a duty of care on him, the landlord will not be liable in negligence for injury or other loss either to the tenant or a third party arising from a defect in the state of the premises. (For the background to the Defective Premises Act 1972 see Law Com. No. 40 (1970) *"Civil Liability for Defective Premises"*. Section 4 of the Defective Premises Act 1972 replaces the Occupiers' Liability Act 1957, s 4. which was more limited in scope).

By section 4(1)—

"Where premises are let under a tenancy which puts on the landlord an obligation to the tenant for the maintenance or repair of the premises, the landlord owes to all persons who might reasonably be expected to be affected by defects in the state of the premises a duty to take such care as is reasonable in all the circumstances to see that they are reasonably safe from personal injury or from damage to their property caused by a relevant defect."

It is important to appreciate that this provision does not as such place any repairing obligation on a landlord. It imposes tortious liability on a landlord who is already under an express, implied or statutory repairing obligation (*e.g.* under section 11 of the Landlord and Tenant Act 1985 above. See section 4(5)). However, it is further provided that, even in those cases where the landlord is not *obliged* to repair, if he has an express or implied *right* to enter to repair he will be treated as being under an obligation to repair for the purposes of section 4(1) of the Defective Premises Act 1972 (s.4(4)). In such a case therefore, although not obliged to repair, the landlord will be responsible for personal injury to, or damage to the property of, a person within the ambit of the section, that is caused by a relevant defect.

The point is neatly illustrated by the facts of *Smith v. Bradford MBC* (1982) 44 P.& C.R. 171. The tenant occupied a council house which had a paved area to the rear beyond which was a concrete yard called a "patio" (described by Donaldson L.J. as an area of "very crazy paving") leading to a grassed area in front of the back fence. The patio (which had been built by a former tenant) fell into a potentially dangerous state and was in need of repair, as the council were aware. Later that year the concrete crumbled whilst the tenant was hanging out washing. He slipped and suffered a fractured leg. By the terms of the tenancy the council had reserved the right to repair the premises, which were widely defined as extending beyond the house to include any garage, outbuilding, garden or yard. This was sufficient to embrace the patio and therefore impose liability on the council under section 4 of the Defective Premises Act 1972.

The same conclusion was reached in *McCauley v. Bristol City Council* [1992] 1 Q.B. 134, where the landlord had an implied right to enter. The weekly tenancy agreement expressly obliged the tenant "to give the council's agents and workmen all reasonable facilities for entering upon the premises at all reasonable hours for any purposes which may from time to time be required by the council." It was held that this was sufficient to imply a right to enter for the purpose of carrying out repairs not just to the dwelling-house (which they had expressly covenanted to do), but to the whole property let, including the garden. Thus the landlord owed a duty of care in respect of a defective garden step on which the tenant had slipped and suffered injury. It was a defect which exposed the tenant and any lawful visitors to significant risk of injury. Therefore the court implied a right in the council to carry out repairs for the removal of that risk of injury notwithstanding the absence of any express, implied or statutory obligation on the council actually to do the repair. (See also *Mint v. Good* [1951] 1 K.B. 517).

Of course in such cases landlords are effectively under an indirect repairing obligation, because otherwise if injury or loss is caused by a defect they will be liable in tort. It is therefore necessary to carry out such repairs if tortious liability is to be avoided.

The landlord's duty is owed if he "knows (whether as the result of being notified by the tenant or otherwise) or if he ought in all the circumstances to have known of the relevant defect" (s.4(2)). A "relevant defect" is a defect in the state of the premises which arises from, or continues because of, an act or omission by the landlord which is either a failure by him to carry out his obligation to the tenant for the maintenance or repair of the premises, or would have been if he had had notice of the defect (s.4(3)). The defect must exist at or after the time when (i) the tenancy commences; or (ii) the tenancy agreement is entered into; or (iii) possession is taken of the premises in contemplation of the letting—whichever is the earliest (s.4(3)(b)). In the case of tenancies entered into before January 1, 1974 the duty is owed in respect of defects in existence on or after that date.

It is important to note that section 4 only applies to defects in the premises let, and not to other parts of the property which the landlord might be liable to repair (*e.g.* under the Landlord and Tenant Act 1985, s.11(1A) or by way of an implied term, as in *King v. South Northamptonshire DC*, above).

For the purposes of section 4, "tenancy" includes an agreement for a lease or a tenancy agreement, as well as a tenancy at will or sufferance (Defective Premises Act 1972, s. 6(1)). It also includes a right of occupation given by contract or any enactment that does not amount to a tenancy: *ibid.*, s. 4(6). It will apply accordingly to premises occupied by virtue of a contractual licence.

Section 4 is important because it affords a remedy not only to the tenant (see *Smith v. Bradford MBC*, above) but also to certain third parties who have suffered personal injury or damage to their property as a result of a relevant defect. Furthermore, it applies whether the landlord knew or *ought to have known* of the defect. This means that it will not necessarily be a defence for the landlord to establish that he had not been given notice of the need for repair. If he ought to have known of a defect, for example because he failed to make regular inspections of the premises, then he can still be liable.

In *Clarke v. Taff Ely BC* (1984) 10 H.L.R. 44 employees of the landlord local authority had visited the premises to carry out certain repairs. Subsequently the tenant's sister-in-law, who was visiting her sister and her husband to help redecorate the property, was injured when she stood on a table which slipped because a rotted floor gave way. The landlord was held liable because when the workmen had carried out the earlier repairs it would have been reasonable for them to have inspected the state of the floor because of the nature of its construction. (The house was in an area prone to damp and there was no under-floor ventilation). Thus its defective state was something which they ought reasonably to have known about, and this was sufficient for liability to be imposed. It was reasonably foreseeable that a visitor such as the plaintiff might be injured by the defective floor.

Liability of landlord as builder and/or designer of the premises

Where the landlord has been responsible for the design/and or construction of the property he is under a duty to take reasonable steps to ensure that the premises are reasonably safe and habitable. In *Targett v. Torfaen BC* [1992] 3 All E.R. 27 a local authority had designed and built a council house, access to which was down two flight of stone steps which were not lit; nor was there a handrail to the lower steps. The council was held liable in negligence to the tenant when he fell down the steps. The Court of Appeal held that the landlord was under a duty to take reasonable care to ensure that the property was free from defect likely to cause injury to any person whom they ought reasonably to have in contemplation as likely to be affected by such a defect. Although the tenant had knowledge of the danger, this was not sufficient to negate the landlord's liability because it was not reasonable in the circumstances for the tenant to remove or avoid the danger (although he was held to be 25 per cent contributorily negligent). (See also *Rimmer v. Liverpool City Council* [1985] Q.B. 1 where a tenant slipped on a child's toy and was seriously injured when his hand went through an internal glass panel which was of insufficient thickness. The house had been designed and built by the council landlord, which was held liable for the tenant's injuries).

Liability in respect of adjoining premises

In contrast to the landlord's common law immunity from liability in negligence for defects in the property let to the tenant, it has been long established that the landlord can be liable in negligence for damage caused to persons or property by a building retained by the landlord (*Cunard v. Antifyre Ltd* [1933] 1 K.B. 551).

Furthermore a landlord, who is under an obligation to repair, can also incur liability in nuisance to third parties in respect of the leased premises where they have fallen into such a state of disrepair as to constitute a nuisance. (See *Wringe v. Cohen* [1940] 1 K.B. 229, where the landlord was held liable to a neighbouring shop-owner whose property was damaged when a defective wall on the landlord's adjoining property collapsed).

C. EXPRESS REPAIRING OBLIGATIONS

Introduction

We have seen above that where the parties do not deal in whole or in part with the issue of repair, the gaps may be filled by terms implied either at common law or by statute in certain circumstances. Of course in many tenancies, particularly professionally drafted business tenancies, the issue of repair is dealt with expressly by the terms of the agreement.

As already noted above, in so far as the matter is not conclusively settled by statute, the form of such obligations will turn on many factors, including the value of the property, the length of the tenancy and the respective bargaining power of the parties in the light of prevailing market conditions.

Most professionally drafted, or standard form, residential tenancy agreements actually mirror the statutory position by including an express covenant in identical terms to that which would be imposed in any event by the Landlord and Tenant Act 1985, s.11.

As noted at the beginning of this chapter, professionally drafted business tenancies will usually seek to impose repairing obligations on the tenant, save in the case of buildings or developments (*e.g.* a shopping centre) where the tenant is taking a tenancy of only part of the building or development. In such a case the landlord will usually be made repsonsible for repairs but be able to recoup the costs from tenants by means of a service charge.

A central issue when construing repairing obligations in such cases involves the nature and extent of those obligations. To avoid problems as to the precise scope of the landlord's covenants a practice is sometimes adopted, in the case of a tenancy of part of a building, for the landlord to let to the tenant the space enclosed by the surrounding walls, floors and ceilings, along with the internal surface areas of those boundaries and any landlord's fixtures and services exclusively serving the leased premises. The tenant's repairing covenant can then be confined to the premises let, leaving the landlord responsible for the remainder. (See, *e.g. City Offices (Regent Street) Ltd v. Europa Acceptance Group* [1990] 5 E.G. 71).

The extent of the covenant

There is a subtle but important distinction which has to be appreciated between a covenant "to repair" and a covenant "to keep in repair". The former obliges the covenantor to rectify any disrepair that might occur after the commencement of the tenancy, whereas the latter includes an obligation to put the premises into repair if they are not in a state of repair at the commencement of the tenancy (*Proudfoot v. Hart* [1890] 25 Q.B.D. 42, CA). The premises can only be *kept* in repair if they are in that state in the first place. Alternatively or additionally a repairing covenant might oblige the tenant to leave the premises in repair at the end of the tenancy. In such a case the landlord will draw up a schedule of dilapidations, detailing any works of repair that are needed, towards the end of the tenancy. This is often an occasion for protracted and expensive arguments between the parties as to what, if anything, is required by way of works of repair.

The meaning of repair

A vast body of case law has built up on the meaning of the term "repair". In a leading case, decided in 1911, it was said that—

"Repair is restoration by renewal or replacement of subsidiary parts of a whole. Renewal, as distinguished from repair, is reconstruction of the entirety, meaning by the entirety not necessarily the whole but substantially the whole subject matter under discussion. I agree that if repair of the whole subject matter has become impossible a covenant to repair does not carry an obligation to renew or replace. But if that which I have said is accurate it follows that the question of repair is in every case one of degree, and the test is whether the act to be done is one which in substance is the renewal or replacement of defective parts, or the renewal or replacement of substantially the whole. (*Lurcott v. Wakeley & Wheeler* [1911] 1 K.B. 920, 924 per Buckley L.J. See also *Brew Bros v. Snax (Ross) Ltd* [1970] 1 Q.B. 612.)"

In *McDougall v. Easington DC* (1989) 21 H.L.R. 310, 316 it was said that in determining the difference between repair and renewal, three different tests can be distilled from the authorities—

"which may be applied separately or concurrently as the circumstances of the individual case may demand, but all to be approached in the light of the nature and age of the premises, their condition when the tenant went into occupation, and the other express terms of the tenancy:

    (i)   whether the alterations went to the whole or substantially the whole of the structure or to only a subsidiary part;
   (ii) whether the effect of the alterations was to produce a building of a wholly different character from that which had been let;
  (iii) what was the costs of the works in relation to the previous value of the building, and what was their effect on the value and lifespan of the building."

Thus an obligation to repair will not extend to replacement of the whole (see also *Lister v. Lane* [1893] 2 Q.B. 212). Despite the fact that the above passage from *Lurcott v. Wakeley & Wheeler* draws a distinction between repair and renewal it has been held that a covenant to "repair and renew" will not by itself make the tenant liable for renewal of the whole. Much clearer words than this will be necessary (*Collins v. Flynn* [1963] 2 All E.R. 1068).

But this is qualified by the rule that a repairing covenant by the tenant will oblige him to replace a building which has been destroyed by fire or some other exceptional cause. (See

Manchester Bonded Warehouse Co v. Carr (1880) 5 C.P.D. 507 at 513 and *Redmond v. Dainton* [1920] 2 K.B. 256 where the tenant had covenanted "to substantially repair, uphold, support, sustain and maintain the dwelling-house". The house was destroyed by an enemy bomb and the tenant was held liable to replace the dwelling which was substantially standing).

Because of the limits of an ordinary repairing covenant, tenants are sometimes placed under a far more onerous obligation to maintain the property. An example of such a clause is provided by *Norwich Union Life Assurance Society v. British Railways Board* [1987] 283 E.G. 846 where the tenant's repairing covenant was "To keep the demised premises in good and substantial repair and condition and when necessary to rebuild, reconstruct or replace the same and in such repair and condition to yield up the same at the expiration or sooner determination of the said lease." It was held that whilst this extended the tenant's obligations beyond that of a mere obligation to repair, it was so onerous that the tenant was entitled to a 27.5 per cent rent reduction on the occasion of a rent review, to reflect the depressing effect it would have on the value of the lease. (See also *New England Properties v. Portsmouth New Shops* [1993] 23 E.G. 130 where it was made clear that an obligation to renew can clearly involve an element of improvement where work involves substantial structural and design changes. Indeed the court was of the view that in any event the necessary remedial work fell within the meaning of "repair").

Another example is provided by *Credit Suisse v. Beegas Nominees* [1994] 4 All E.R. 80 where the landlord had covenanted "to maintain repair amend renew cleanse repaint and decorate and otherwise keep in good and tenantable condition". The clause also provided that the landlords would not be liable for any defect or want of repair unless they had received notice of the need for repair. It was held that the wording was such that liability beyond a mere repairing obligation was being undertaken and therefore the covenant embraced the need to replace the total cladding of the building, an undertaking which in the circumstances went beyond "repair". (See also *Plough Investments Ltd v. Manchester City Council* [1989] 1 E.G.L.R. 244). The tenants were thus able to recover consequential loss, including the lost chance of an assignment, and a sum representing their liabilities under the lease (of which they would otherwise have been able to dispose). Although this loss would be offset by rents received from sub-lettings, those rents were much reduced because of the economic recession at that time.

Repair is also sometimes contrasted with "improvement", which again is a question of fact and degree. A covenantor is clearly not liable to improve what was let in the first place, although sometimes it is inevitable that a repair will involve a degree of betterment, as where a worn out item (*e.g.* a boiler) is replaced by a modern equivalent (see *Morcom v. Campbell Johnson* [1956] 1 Q.B. 106, 115 per Denning L.J.).

As we have already seen above, repairing covenants are sometimes qualified by the expression "fair wear and tear excepted". This will relieve the tenant from liability in respect of disrepair which has come about from the reasonable use of the premises coupled with the ordinary operation of natural forces. But the benefit of this qualification is reduced by the rule that it will not preclude liability in respect of any consequential damage, such as that caused by water penetration which has come about as a result of a missing roof slate (*Regis Property Ltd v. Dudley* [1959] A.C. 370, HL).

Inherent defects

In recent decades there has been much litigation over whether a repairing obligation extends to an inherent defect in the building. The starting point was the decision of Forbes J. in *Ravenseft Properties v. Davstone (Holdings) Ltd* [1980] Q.B. 12. The subject property was a 16-storey block of flats (Campden Hill Towers), which was constructed between 1958 and 1960 with a reinforced concrete frame with stone cladding. The tenant of the building covenanted to repair the structure, including the walls. In 1973 the building became unsafe partly as a result of bad design and partly by reason of bad workmanship. The main problem was that the stone cladding was coming away from the walls because of the absence of expansion joints which would have prevented this. Despite the fact that the absence of such joints amounted to an inherent design defect, it was held to be still within the tenant's repairing obligation because the cost of rectifying the fault (£55,000) was trivial compared to the value of the building at that time (£3 million). The insertion of the necessary expansion joints would not change the character of the building so as to amount to an improvement as opposed to a repair. Forbes J. held that—

> "It is always a question of degree whether that which the tenant is being asked to do can properly be described as repair, or whether on the contrary it would involve giving back to the landlord a wholly different thing from that which he demised ([1980] Q.B. 12, 21)."

By contrast to *Ravenseft* a tenant was not held liable to rebuild an inherently defective "jerry built" wall which formed the exterior of a covered utility room which had been constructed in what was an exterior yard. It was a very relevant factor that the cost of rebuilding the utility room would have been greater than one third of the cost of rebuilding the whole (*Halliard Property Co Ltd v. Nicholas Clarke Investments Ltd* (1984) 269 E.G. 1257. See also *Holding and Management v. Property Holding & Investment Trust* [1990] 1 E.G.L.R. 65).

Of course, in many of these cases the outcome will turn on the precise wording of the covenant, and thus their use as precedents is accordingly of limited value. In *Smedley v. Chumley & Hawke Ltd and Another* (1981) 44 P.& C.R. 50, defects developed as a result of design faults in the foundations of a restaurant. The landlord was held to be in breach of his covenant "to keep the main walls and roof in good structural repair and condition...and to promptly make good all defects due to faulty materials or workmanship in the construction of the premises." This was sufficiently wide to make the landlord liable for the defects which had come about even though the remedy of the defects would give the tenant a substantially different property to that let. The lease had put an unqualified obligation on the landlord and the remedy of the defects would only be giving the tenant the premises in the condition which both parties contemplated at the time of the lease.

In all the above cases there was disrepair. But if the inherent defect does not cause disrepair as opposed to lack of amenity, the covenantor will not be liable. This is why the landlord was not liable in *Quick v. Taff Ely BC* (above) where a design defect had caused intolerable condensation damp in the house let to the tenant but had not caused physical disrepair to the structure of exterior or the property which the landlord had covenanted to repair. (But contrast *Stent v. Monmouth DC* (1987) 19 H.L.R. 269 (p.56 above). The point was illustrated in *Post Office v. Aquarius Properties Ltd* [1987] 1 All E.R. 1055, CA where there was a tenant's repairing covenant in respect of a commercial property. Because of a design defect in the foundational structure the basement was prone to flooding, although no physical disrepair was caused to the fabric of the building. Because any remedial work would have involved structural alterations or improvements to the building it was held that this did not come within the ambit of a covenant to repair. Disrepair connoted a "deterioration from some previous condition".

A contractual claim against builders and architects' etc.

In very limited circumstances, a tenant who has entered into a repairing covenant in respect of a defective building might be able to compel the landlord to sue the builder where the landlord has a contractual claim against that person. The fact that the loss is suffered by the tenant will not matter for this purpose (*Linden Gardens Trust Ltd v. Lenesta Sludge Disposals Ltd* [1994] A.C. 85). Any damages obtained by the landlord would be passed on to the tenant or set off against the tenant's repairing liability. Alternatively, a tenant of a new building can seek to obtain an independent collateral warranty from the builder and other professionals such as architects and structural engineers who were involved in its design and construction, although the value of such a warranty will depend on the solvency of the individual defendant in question. (See Tromans, *Commercial Leases* (2nd ed.), p.141).

Where the tenant is aggrieved by the defective state of the building, any claim by him in tort against the builder or other person whose negligence has led to the building being defective will be precluded by the House of Lords' decision in *Murphy v. Brentwood District Council* [1991] 1 A.C. 398) which confines any recoverable loss in a negligence claim to that sustained by way of personal injury or damage to property other than the building itself.

Standard of repair

The obligation of a covenantor under a repairing covenant is to keep the property in—

> "such repair as, having regard to the age, character, and locality of the house, would make it reasonably fit for the occupation of a reasonably minded tenant of the class who would be likely to take it (*Proudfoot v. Hart* [1890] 25 Q.B.D. 42,52 CA)."

In applying this test, and leaving aside any discomfort caused, in these less class-conscious times, by the reference to the class of occupier, regard must be had to the circumstances as at the time of the letting. Thus the standard should not be reduced merely because the area in which the property is located has deteriorated (*Calthorpe v. McOscar* [1924] 1 K.B. 716, CA).

Need for notice

The general rule is that a landlord covenantor will be liable for breach of a covenant to keep in repair as soon as the disrepair occurs. This was confirmed in *British Telecommunications plc v. Sun Life Assurance Soc. plc* [1995] 3 W.L.R. 622 where the landlord who had let to the tenant the sixth and seventh floors of an office block had covenanted to keep in repair the demised premises and the outside walls of the building. The disrepair complained of stemmed from a bulge in the wall at fifth-floor level. It was held that the landlords were liable as soon as the bulge appeared and not just after they had had a reasonable time to remedy the defect. The Court of Appeal left open the issue of whether the same rule applies to a covenant "to repair" as opposed to a covenant to "keep in repair". (Aldous J. at first instance considered that liability would only arise following notice of the need for repair in such a case—(see below). However, the better opinion is that there should be no distinction between the two forms of covenant. What is clear is that if the disrepair relates solely to the demised premises the landlord does not become liable until he has had notice of the need for repair and has failed to do so within a reasonable time thereafter (see, for example, *O'Brien v. Robinson* [1973] A.C. 912, HL and p.55 above.

Remedies for breach of repairing covenant

1. Tenant's covenant

(a) Damages

A special rule Special rules govern a claim for damages in the case of certain tenancies which are governed by the Leasehold Property (Repairs) Act 1938. The Act applies to a tenancy for a term of seven years or more, of which three or more are unexpired when an action for damages is begun. Before any such claim can be made the landlord must serve on the tenant a notice of not less than one month under section 146 of the Law of Property Act 1925 which (in characters not less conspicuous than those used in any other part of the notice—as to which, see *Middlegate Properties Ltd v. Messimeris* [1973] 1 W.L.R. 168, CA) informs the tenant that he may serve a counter notice claiming the benefit of the 1938 Act. (A section 146 notice is the notice required as a preliminary to forfeiture proceedings for breach of covenant, and in that notice the landlord must specify the breach complained of, require it to be remedied (if capable of remedy) and require compensation in money for the breach. See Chapter 6 below.)

Once the tenant has served a counter-notice under the 1938 Act the landlord is not permitted to proceed with his action for damages (or indeed any forfeiture claim) without the leave of the court, which can only be granted if the landlord proves (on the balance of probabilities— *Associated British Ports v. CH Bailey plc* [1990] 2 A.C. 703) that one of the following grounds exists:

(1) that the immediate remedying of the breach is required in order to prevent a substantial diminution in the value of the landlord's reversion or that the value of that reversion has been substantially diminished by the breach;

(2) that it is necessary for the breach to be remedied immediately in order to comply with a requirement imposed by virtue of a statute or byelaw or a court order;

(3) where the tenant is not in occupation of the whole or part of the premises, that the immediate remedying of the breach is required in the interest of the occupier of the whole or part of the premises;

(4) that the costs of remedying the breach would be relatively little expense compared to the expense that would probably be occasioned by postponing the work;

(5) that there are special circumstances which in the opinion of the court make it just and equitable that leave should be ordered.

It can be seen that, where it is applicable, the 1938 Act places a formidable obstacle in the way of a landlord who seeks to enforce a repairing obligation during the currency of the tenancy. It was designed to prevent landlords buying up reversions and threatening the tenants with forfeiture or a claim for substantial damages in a lengthy schedule of dilapidations, in the hope that the tenant would be persuaded to give up possession.

The Act also contains a number of less obvious pitfalls for landlords. Thus if the landlord goes ahead and carries out the repairs himself he will not be able to sue the tenant for damages because, as noted above, service of a section 146 notice is an essential prerequisite to such a claim and this cannot be done if the breach has already been rectified, albeit by the landlord. (*Sedac Investments Ltd v. Tanner* [1982] 1 W.L.R. 1342; see [1983] Conv. 72).

This difficulty is usually avoided by the inclusion in the tenancy of a provision whereby if the tenant, after notice from the landlord, fails to comply with his repairing obligations the landlord reserves the right to enter and carry out the necessary repairs himself and to recoup the expenditure from the tenant. (Where the landlord under a Rent Act protected or statutory tenancy has an entitlement to do repairs, it is a condition of the tenancy that the tenant shall afford to the landlord access to the dwelling-house and all reasonable facilities for executing those repairs: Rent Act 1977, s.3(1) (statutory tenancy), s.148 (protected tenancy). There is an identical term implied into all assured tenancies (Housing Act 1988, s.16).)

The advantage of such a provision for the landlord is that his claim for the expenditure which he has incurred when exercising his right is not an action on the repairing covenant but an action in debt and as such it is immune from the strictures of the 1938 Act. This was settled by the Court of Appeal in *Jervis v. Harris* [1996] 1 All E.R. 303 (approving of *Hamilton v. Martell Securities Ltd* [1984] Ch. 226 and *Colchester Estates (Cardiff) v. Carlton Industries plc* [1986] Ch. 80 and overruling *Swallow Securities Ltd v. Brand* (1981) 45 P.& C.R. 328).

Measure of damages Section 18 of the Landlord and Tenant Act 1927 places a statutory limit on the amount of damages that a landlord can recover for breach of a tenant's repairing covenant. It provides that damages for breach of a covenant to keep or put premises in repair during the currency of the tenancy, or to leave or put premises in repair at the end of the tenancy, must not exceed the amount by which the reversion is diminished as a result of the breach of covenant. This means the difference in value between the reversion with the premises in their present state of disrepair and the value it would have if the covenant had been complied with. No discount is to be made for the fact that if the landlord is also forfeiting the tenancy he will acquire the reversion earlier than would otherwise have been the case (*Hansom v. Newman* [1934] Ch. 298). But section 18 goes on to provide that if it is established that the premises are to be pulled down or to be structurally altered such as to render the repairs valueless, then no damages are recoverable. (This means a decision by the landlord to demolish or alter, and therefore section 18 does not preclude a claim for damages in the unusual circumstances of the tenant being a local authority which intends to demolish the property under its slum clearance powers: *Hibernian Property Co. Ltd v. Liverpool Corporation* [1973] 2 All E.R. 1117).

Otherwise, where the tenancy has, or is about to, come to an end the normal rule will be that the landlord's loss (the diminution in value of the reversion) is measured by the cost of the repairs, provided those repairs have been or will be carried out. For this purpose it does not matter that they will be carried out by an incoming tenant (*Haviland v. Long* [1952] 2 Q.B. 80). But this would clearly not be an appropriate measure of damages if the lease has a considerable period of time to run even where the repairs are to be carried out. The effect of the disrepair on the value of the reversion in such a case may be minimal.

(b) Specific performance

Until recently it had been believed (following *Hill v. Barclay* (1810)16 Ves. 102) that specific performance of a tenant's repairing obligation would never be ordered by a court. However, in *Rainbow Estates v. Tokenhold Ltd* [1998] 2 All E.R. 860 (see also *Joyce v. Liverpool City Council* [1995] 3 All E.R. 11) it was held by Mr Laurence Collins Q.C. (sitting as a deputy High Court judge) that, subject to the overriding need to avoid injustice or oppression, there was no reason in principle why specific performance should not be decreed where it was an appropriate remedy, although the judge acknowledged that this would only be in rare cases. This could be because in the circumstances of the case (as in *Rainbow Estates v. Tokenhold Ltd*) the landlord might not have any right of access to enter and carry out repairs or indeed to forfeit the tenancy. The reference to injustice or oppression is particularly relevant in those cases where the landlord's right to seek damages or forfeiture would be constrained by the terms of the Leasehold Property (Repairs) Act 1938 (above). The Act does not apply to the remedy of specific performance and therefore the court should be astute in such a claim to ensure that the landlord is not seeking to circumvent the provisions of that Act. Given that most tenancies are drafted so as to be determinable by forfeiture for breach of covenant or subject to a right on the part of the landlord to enter and do the repairs at the tenant's expense (see above), the award of a decree of specific performance for breach of a tenant's repairing covenant can be expected to be a rare occurrence.

(c) Forfeiture

If the tenancy contains a forfeiture clause which permits the landlord to forfeit the lease and re-enter for breach of covenant by the tenant, the landlord may choose to exercise this right, although the tenant may seek relief against forfeiture. (This issue is dealt with fully at Chapter 6, to which reference should be made.)

2. Landlord's covenant

(a) Damages

The normal contractual rules as to recovery of damages will apply where the landlord is in breach of his covenant to repair (see *Hadley v. Baxendale* (1854) 9 Exch. 341; *Victoria Laundry (Windsor) Ltd v. Newman Industries Ltd* [1949] 2 K.B. 528; *Ruxley Electronics and Constructions Ltd v. Forsyth* [1995] 3 W.L.R. 118). "The object of awarding damages against a landlord for breach of his covenant to repair is not to punish the landlord but, so far as money can, to restore the tenant to the position he would have been in had there been no breach" (*Calabar Properties Ltd v. Stitcher* [1983] 1 All E.R. 759, 768 *per* Griffiths L.J.). The tenant will be able to recover not only the cost of the repairs but also any consequential redecoration (see also *McGreal v. Wake* (above); *Bradley v. Chorley BC* (above); *Davies v. Peterson* (1988) 21 H.L.R. 63; and *Chiodi v. De Marnay* [1988] 41 E.G. 80). If it is reasonable for the tenant to move out of the property as a result of the disrepair, it will also be possible to recover the reasonable cost of the alternative accommodation and damages for any "disappointment, discomfort, loss of enjoyment, and bouts of ill health which the tenant has suffered from living in the defective property" (*Calabar Properties Ltd v. Stitcher* (above), where disrepair had caused water penetration to the flat which led to the tenant suffering from bronchitis and pleurisy see also *Wallace v. Manchester City Council* [1998] 41 E.G. 223, CA.

Reference can also be made to *Marshall v. Rubypoint Ltd* [1997] 25 E.G. 142, CA where, because of the landlord's failure properly to repair the front door of the building in which the tenant's flat was located, the tenant suffered physical assault from burglars who also stole his property. The loss was not considered to be too remote and the landlord was liable. See also *Morris v. Liverpool City Council* [1988] 14 E.G. 59.

One limitation of a claim for damages is that the loss is measured from the date when the landlord became liable (see above), up to the date when the writ is served. Thus future loss will be excluded from such a claim, which is why the tenant might wish to consider seeking in addition a mandatory injunction or order for specific performance.

(b) Specific Performance or mandatory injunction

Despite earlier doubts it has been held that in principle a landlord's repairing covenant can in an appropriate case be enforced, at the court's discretion, by way of a decree of specific performance, although (by way of analogy with specific enforcement of building contracts) this is only likely in a case where damages would not be an adequate remedy (perhaps because an emergency repair is required or the loss is difficult to quantify in money terms) and the repair is capable of easy supervision. (Specific performance was awarded in *Jeune v. Queens Cross Properties Ltd* [1974] Ch. 97 where the disrepair affected a balcony to a flat which had not been included within the property let (thereby precluding the tenant from doing the repairs and suing for damages). See also *Francis v. Cowcliffe Ltd* (1976) 33 P.& C.R. 368 (where the landlord's financial inability to supply and maintain a lift in accordance with his covenant was held to be no defence to a claim by the tenant for specific performance) and *Peninsular Maritime Ltd v. Padseal Ltd* (1981) 259 E.G. 860). However, in *Gordon v. Selico and Co Ltd* [1985] 2 E.G.L.R. 79 the power of the court to order specific performance of a covenant within the tenancy as opposed to the contract of tenancy itself was queried by Goulding J. at first instance, when he observed that the jurisdiction of a court of equity is to enforce specifically the performance of contracts, not of particular stipulations therein.

Quite apart from any general equitable jurisdiction to award specific performance, the court has a statutory power, in the case of a tenancy of a dwelling-house, to grant specific performance where proceedings are brought in respect of a breach of a landlord's covenant to repair any part of the property in which the dwelling-house is comprised, whether or not the breach relates to the part of the premises let to the tenant (section 17 Landlord and Tenant Act 1985 replacing with amendments Housing Act 1974, s.125). For this purpose "repair" is widely defined as including a covenant to "repair, maintain, renew, construct or replace any property": *ibid.*, s.17(2)(d).

Apart from specific performance, the court might choose to grant a mandatory injunction instead. One apparent advantage of this remedy, which is identical in effect to that of a decree of specific performance, is that unlike the latter it can (albeit in rare cases) be granted by way of interlocutory relief in cases of urgency and hardship. (See *Parker v. Camden LBC* [1986] Ch. 162 where elderly tenants in local authority sheltered accommodation were without heating in severely cold weather because the boilers had broken down and the council heating engineers were on strike. The landlords were ordered to allow access to an expert inspector to determine what remedial work to the boilers was necessary). It is important to appreciate the very limited scope of the injunction granted in this case and it is only ever likely to be used where the required work is very simple.

The Law Commission gave the issue of specific performance as a remedy for breach of repairing obligations extensive consideration in Part IX of their Report No. 238 "Landlord and Tenant: Responsibility for State and Condition of Property" (1996) where it was recommended that a court should at its discretion have power to decree specific performance of a repairing obligation imposed on the landlord or tenant in any tenancy.

(c) Appointment of a receiver

The court has power to appoint a receiver in all cases in which it appears to the court to be just and equitable to do so (Supreme Court Act 1981, s.37(1); County Courts Act 1984, s.38). This might be an appropriate remedy where, for example, a landlord of a block of flats is not carrying out his repairing obligations. (But it is not available against a local authority landlord it being considered inappropriate to use this remedy in respect of a statutory body of this kind: see *Parker v. Camden LBC*, above). If appointed, a receiver could collect any rents and service charges and discharge them in carrying out any necessary repairs or improvements in accordance with the terms of the tenancy (*Daiches v. Bluelake Investments Ltd* [1985] 2 E.G.L.R. 67, following *Hart v. Emelkirk Ltd* [1983] 1 W.L.R. 1289). But the costs of appointing the receiver are nor recoverable from the landlord (*Evans v. Clayhope Properties Ltd* [1987] 1 W.L.R. 225).

(d) Appointment of a manager

It is provided that, save in the exceptional cases specified below, where the premises consist of the whole or part of a building and the building or part contains two or more flats, a leasehold valuation tribunal is empowered, on application, to appoint a manager in certain circumstances. (Landlord and Tenant Act 1987, ss. 21–24B, as amended by the Housing Act 1996, s.86). The exceptional cases where the jurisdiction does not apply are (a) tenancies with a public sector landlord (b) resident landlord tenancies and (c) business tenancies within Part II of the Landlord and Tenant Act 1954.

The circumstances in which the tribunal can appoint a manager include the position where the landlord is in breach of any obligation owed by him to the tenant under his tenancy and the tribunal considers it to be just and convenient to do so in all the circumstances of the case (LTA 1987, s.24(2)). It therefore includes breach of a repairing obligation. If appointed, the manager will be required to carry out such functions in connection with the management of the premises or such functions of a receiver or both as the tribunal thinks fit (s.24(1)).

Where the statutory code of the Landlord and Tenant Act 1987 applies (see Chapter 12 below) the general jurisdiction to appoint a manager or a receiver is inapplicable (s.21(7)).

(e) Set-off and deduction from rent

Faced with an intransigent landlord who will not perform his repairing obligations, a tenant might prefer to carry out the repairs himself and seek a declaration from the court permitting him to deduct the cost from future rental payments. This would seem to be feasible if the landlord has been given notice of the tenant's intentions after having been given an opportunity to carry out the repairs (*Lee-Parker v. Izzet* [1971] 3 All E.R. 1099). Tenants who exercise this right need to take care. Thus it will be important to obtain more than one estimate and for these to be sent to the landlord before any work is carried out.

Alternatively, if a tenant ceases to pay rent and is sued by the landlord for non-payment of rent, he may set off against the unpaid rent a counterclaim for unliquidated damages for breach of the landlord's covenant to repair (*British Anzani (Felixstowe) Ltd v. International Marine Management (UK) Ltd* [1980] Q.B. 137; see also *Melville v. Grapelodge Developments Ltd* (1978) 39 P.& C.R. 179 and *Asco Developments and Newman v. Lowes, Lewis and Gordon* (1978) 248 E.G. 683 (where it was arrears of rent that were set off against a claim in respect of disrepair by the tenant). In *Sturolson v. Mauroux* (1988) 20 H.L.R. 332 a tenant successfully counterclaimed for breach of the landlord's repairing covenant. The landlord argued that because the rent officer had registered a fair rent which would have taken into account the state of disrepair at the time, the tenant had therefore not suffered any loss because he would have been compensated by a lower rent than would otherwise have been the case. The court rejected the argument on the basis that it was wrong to assume that the rent officer when assessing a fair rent would have ignored the value to the tenant of the landlord's covenant.

A similar right of set-off exists where the landlord seeks to levy distress on the tenant's goods in respect of unpaid rent (*Eller v. Grovecrest Investments Ltd* [1994] 4 All E.R. 845).

A landlord who wishes to prevent this equitable right to set off should make clear provision to that effect in the tenancy. Such a provision will not fall foul of the Unfair Contract Terms Act 1977, which does not apply to "any contract so far as it relates to the creation or transfer of an interest in land" (Sched. 1, para. 1(b)) (*Electricity Supplies Nominees v. IAF Group Ltd* [1993] 37 E.G. 155), although it has been suggested that it might be vulnerable to challenge under the Unfair Terms in Consumer Contracts Regulations 1994 (S.I. 1994 No. 3159, which came into force on July 1, 1995—see Butterworths' *Landlord and Tenant Guide* para 4.69; , *Cf.* (1995) 58 H.L.R. 696). It will not be sufficient to exclude the right of set-off for the tenant to covenant to pay the rent "without deduction". Much more explicit wording will be required (*Connaught*

Restaurants Ltd v. Indoor Leisure Ltd [1994] 1 W.L.R. 501).

If the tenant is able to set off a claim in respect of breach of covenant by the landlord this may be a complete defence and it will therefore also preclude any claim for forfeiture by the landlord for breach of the covenant to pay rent.

Secure tenants of a local authority landlord also have the benefit of a scheme (applicable in the case of certain specified defects) whereby if, following service by the tenant on the landlord of a repair notice, the landlord fails to carry out necessary repairs within a prescribed period, the tenant is entitled to compensation subject to a maximum of £50 (see Housing Act 1985, s.96 as amended and S.I. 1994 No. 844).

Public health and housing legislation—fitness for habitation

Local housing authorities have a wide range of statutory mechanisms at their disposal to deal with unfit housing either on an area or individual basis. They also have extensive powers of control over houses in multiple occupation (HMOs). (The relevant provisions are mainly in Parts VI to XII of the Housing Act 1985, as amended.) A detailed examination of these powers is beyond the scope of this book but it should be appreciated that they include the ability to deal both with individual dwelling-houses or HMOs which are unfit for human habitation and those which, although not unfit for human habitation, are in need of substantial repairs in order to bring them up to an appropriate standard. Each of these two situations is examined briefly below. A knowledge of these powers is important because they can be a useful alternative route to that of a civil action in the courts. Indeed where no such cause of action exists (as in *Quick v. Taff Ely BC*, above) they are likely to be the only source of relief to a tenant seeking relief from conditions brought about by a seriously unfit property (see further D. Hughes and S. Lowe *Social Housing Law and Policy* (1995) and J. Morgan *Housing Law* (1998).

Unfit housing

Where a local housing authority is satisfied that a dwelling-house (the term covers both flats and houses) or a house in multiple occupation is statutorily unfit for human habitation it must serve a repair notice (which requires specified works of repair and/or improvement) on the person having control of the property if satisfied, in accordance with section 604A, that that is the most satisfactory course of action (s.189(1)). This duty also extends to a dwelling-house which is a flat or a flat in multiple occupation where the unfit state relates to the common parts. In such a case the notice is to be served on the person having control of the part of the building in question (s.189(1A)). In the case of an HMO the notice may be served on the manager instead (s.189(1B)). The definition of unfit for this purpose is contained in section 604 and is examined below. Despite the mandatory terms of section 189, it is further provided that if the authority is also satisfied that a group repair scheme is to be prepared in the following 12 months the section 189 duty will be inapplicable in as much as it relates to works to be included in that scheme (s.190). But it will revive if the works are not in fact carried out under that scheme or if the scheme is abandoned or does not receive government approval.

The matter will come to the authority's attention either because of a report from the responsible local authority officer either on his own volition (s.606(1)) or following a complaint from a justice of the peace or a parish council in the area (s.606(2)) or as a result of the annual review of unfit housing in the area which the authority are obliged to conduct under section 605.

Otherwise when deciding whether a section 189 repair notice is the most satisfactory course of action the authority will consider alternative responses. These include making a closing order (s.264(1)), or a demolition order (s.265(1)), or including the property in a clearance area (s.289). Finally it could choose to defer any action (under the Housing Grants etc. Act 1996, s.81). The choice as to which course of action to take will be made by having regard to the guiding criteria given under section 604A (see DoE Circular 17/96 Annex B). The guidance is heavily in favour of a solution to unfit housing being sought in an area, rather than individual, response to the problem.

The current fitness standard which is in Housing Act 1985, s.604 was introduced by the Local Government and Housing Act 1989. A dwelling-house (which may be a house or part of a house, *i.e.* a flat) will not be fit for human habitation if in the opinion of the authority it is not reasonably suitable for occupation because it fails to meet one or more of the following requirements. They relate to—

(a) structural stability;
(b) freedom from serious disrepair;
(c) freedom from dampness prejudicial to the health of the occupants;
(d) adequate provision for lighting, heating and ventilation;
(e) adequate piped supply of wholesome water;
(f) satisfactory facilities for the preparation of food including a sink with a satisfactory supply of hot and cold water;
(g) a suitably located WC;
(h) a suitably located fixed bath or shower and wash hand basin, each with a satisfactory supply of hot and cold water;
(i) an effective system for the draining of foul waste and surface water.

As indicated above there is also a second limb to the fitness standard which additionally applies to flats. Thus even if a flat meets the above standards it can still be deemed unfit for habitation if the building, or a part of the building outside the flat, fails to meet one or more of the following requirements—

(a) the building or part is structurally stable;
(b) it is free from serious disrepair;
(c) it is free from dampness;
(d) it has adequate provision for ventilation;
(e) it has an effective system for the draining of foul waste and surface water;

and by reason of that the flat is not reasonably suitable for occupation (s.604(2)).

The "person having control" is the person who receives the rack rent (a rent of not less than two-thirds the net annual (or rateable) value) (s.207), although in the case of a flat where the unfitness affects common parts (see s.604(2)) above) it is the owner of the common parts.

A drawback of the section 189 procedure is that it cannot be used by the local authority against itself (*R. v. Cardiff City Council, ex parte. Cross* (1982) 6 H.L.R. 1, CA). The provision is thereby deprived of effect as far as local authority tenants are concerned.

Housing which is not statutorily unfit but still in need of repair

If a local housing authority is satisfied that—

(1) a house or HMO is in such a state of disrepair that although not unfit for human habitation (as to which, see above) substantial repairs are necessary to bring it up to a reasonable standard having regard to its age, character and locality; or

(2) whether on a representation made by an occupying tenant or otherwise that a dwelling-house or HMO is in such a state of disrepair that although not unfit for human habitation its condition is such as to interfere materially with the personal comfort of the occupying tenant or in the case of an HMO the persons occupying it as tenants or licensees

it may (under HA 1985, s.190) serve a repair notice on the person having control (usually the freeholder or a long lessee with a lease of more than 21 years) of the dwelling-house or HMO. Similar rules as are contained in section 189(1A) with regard to flats and the state of common parts apply here also where the disrepair is of the common parts (s.1901A)).

The person on whom the notice is served must then execute the works within a reasonable time (s.190(2), otherwise the local authority can do the works itself and recover the cost from that person (s.190(3)). This power, which was first introduced by the Housing Act 1969, was designed to prevent a landlord permitting a property to fall into such a state that it is unfit for habitation thus enabling him to evict a protected tenant, do the property up and sell it. (See *Kenny v. Kingston upon Thames Royal LBC* (1985) 17 H.L.R. 344).

It is still an open point as to whether the courts will apply a test on the lines of whether the house is repairable at reasonable expense. The courts certainly did so before section 190 was amended by the Local Government and Housing Act 1989 at a time when the decision whether to use section 189 or one of the alternative courses of action was expressly subject to a "reasonable expense test" in section 206. (See *Kenny v. Kingston upon Thames Royal LBC* (above) and *Hillbank Properties Ltd v. Hackney LBC* [1978] 3 All E.R. 343). But that test is no longer applicable to section 189 since the 1989 Act amendments to sections 189 and 190 and the repeal of section 206. It remains to be seen whether it will be resurrected for the purposes of section 190 or whether the local authority's discretion will be governed instead by the guidance in Circular 6/90 (above).

Statutory nuisances

A local authority is under a duty to inspect its area in order to detect statutory nuisances and to take such steps as are practicable to investigate any complaint of such a nuisance (Environmental Protection Act 1990, s.79(1)).

The list of statutory nuisances includes "any premises in such a state as to be prejudicial to health or a nuisance" (s.79(1)(a)). "Prejudicial to health" is defined as "injurious or likely to cause injury to health" (s.79(7)) and in this context is most likely to arise from dampness, as in *Salford City Council v. McNally* [1976] A.C. 379, for its limits see *R. v. Bristol City Council ex. parte Everett* [1998] 3 All E.R. 603 where it was held not to cover premises in a state likely to lead to an accident causing personal injury.

The two limbs of section 79(1)(a) are to be read disjunctively (*Salford City Council v. McNally*, above) and "nuisance" for this purpose means either a private or public nuisance as understood at common law. This means that the nuisance must emanate from premises other than those from which the complaint is made. It follows that a nuisance "cannot arise if what has taken place affects only the person or persons occupying the premises where the nuisance is said to have taken place" (*National Coal Board v. Thorne* [1976] 1 W.L.R. 543, 547 per Natkins J.).

Where a local authority is satisfied that a statutory nuisance exists or is likely to occur or recur in its area it must serve a notice requiring all or any of the following—

(1) the abatement of the nuisance or prohibiting or restricting its occurrence or recurrence;

(2) the execution of such works and the taking of such other steps as may be necessary for any of these purposes (EPA 1990, s.80(1)).

Failure to comply is a criminal offence punishable by a fine of up to £5,000 (Criminal Justice Act 1988, s.37) (EPA 1990 s.80(4)–(6)). It is a defence that the best practicable means were used to prevent or counteract the effects of the nuisance (s.80(7)). A compensation order (of up to £5,000) may also be made where such an offence is committed (Powers of Criminal Courts Act 1973, s.35 and Magistrates Courts Act 1987, s.40). (See *Herbert v. Lambeth Borough Council* (1991) 24 H.L.R. 299, where the court emphasised that this power should only be exercised in simple and straightforward cases and was inappropriate where substantial compensation was sought for matters which should be the subject of a civil action).

If the local authority considers that the circumstances are such that the above nuisance procedure would entail unnecessary delay it may serve a notice on the person responsible, stating that it intends to remedy the defect and specify what the defects are that will be remedied (Building Act 1984, s.76(1)).

The drawback of the above provsions is that the initiative in instigating proceedings lies with the local authority. A more powerful alternative course of action is for the tenant to take advantage of the following provision.

A person aggrieved by a statutory nuisance may give notice to the person responsible that he intends to bring proceedings by way of complaint to a magistrates court (s.82(6)). The court may then make an order for either or both of the purposes for which the local authority could have served a notice (s.82(1), (2)). Non-compliance is a criminal offence punishable with a fine (s.82(8)). It is again a defence that the best practicable means were used to prevent or counteract the effects of the nuisance (s.82(9)). A compensation order may also be made where such an offence is committed (Powers of Criminal Courts Act 1973, s.35 and Magistrates' Courts Act 1980 s.40), even if the landlord is willing to comply with the nuisance order (*Botross v. Hammersmith and Fulham LBC* (1995) 16 Cr.App.R. (S.) 622, QBD).

It has been established that a person guilty of an offence under section 80(4) does not thereby become liable in a civil suit for breach of statutory duty to a person who has suffered loss or damage (*Issa v. Hackney LBC* [1997] 1 W.L.R. 956). This was a case where the defendants were a local authority whose property was so badly affected by condensation and mould growth as to amount to a statutory nuisance. The Court of Appeal's decision that there was no consequential civil cause of action thus closed the door to a possible way round the decision in *Quick v. Taff Ely BC* (above) in cases where a tenant suffers ill health or damage to his personal property by way of condensation and/or mould growth. It further highlights the need for the swift implementation of the recommendation of the Law Commission (see below) that provision for a new implied term as to fitness for habitation in certain tenancies be enacted.*Issa v. Hackney LBC* does, however, demonstrate that the statutory nuisance provisions in the EPA 1990 are applicable to local authorities, against whom there have been many complaints in respect of condensation and mould growth. *Birmingham DC v. Kelly* (1985) 17 H.L.R. 572 was such a case. Condensation in a council flat led to mould growth which was found to be prejudicial to the health of the occupiers. The Divisional Court dismissed an appeal from the decision of a magistrate who had made a nuisance order in the terms agreed by the parties, which included the provision of double glazing, improved ventilation and the provision of full central heating. However, the court stressed in this case that the terms of the order were agreed and it should not be considered a precedent. In the ordinary case it would require compelling evidence to require such extensive works to abate a nuisance, and even where the terms are agreed the magistrates must consider for themselves whether they are reasonably necessary.

The local authority was also at fault in *GLC v. Tower Hamlets LBC* (1983) 15 H.L.R. 54 where because of the design and construction of a flat it was unusually exposed to the elements on three sides. The inadequate form of heating provided by the landlord combined with a lack of provision for adequate ventilation or insulation led to condensation damp and mould growth which was held to amount to a statutory nuisance.

But condensation will not always be held to have been caused by the landlord. In *Dover DC v. Farrar* (1980) 2 H.L.R. 32 the local authority had constructed dwellings with electrical heating systems intended as background heating downstairs and to maintain the structure of the house at an adequate temperature but which would require to be supplemented by other systems. In some cases dampness by condensation had occurred so as to be prejudicial to health and the tenants issued proceedings under the statutory nuisance procedure. The court held that the reason condensation had occurred was because the tenants had failed to use the system provided, on the ground of cost, and had used other systems which led to condensation. In those circumstances the landlord had not committed an offence.

It is not possible for a group of tenants in a block, each of whom is aggrieved by a statutory nuisance in his or her flat, to complain about the building as a whole (*Birmingham DC v. McMahon* (1987) 19 H.L.R. 452). The tenant can only complain in respect of his or her own particular flat.

Law reform

The Law Commission has long been concerned with the uncertainties and injustices inherent in the present law governing the rights and liabilities of landlord and tenant with regard to the state and condition of leased property. (see *e.g.* Law Com. No. 67, "Report on Obligations of Landlords and Tenants" (1975); Law Com. No. 123, "Landlord and Tenant: Responsibility for State and Condition of Property, Consultation Paper" (1992). See further P.F. Smith, "Repairing Obligations: A case against radical reform", [1994] Conv. 186. The most recent and comprehensive examination of the present law and its shortcomings is contained in Law Com. No. 208 "Landlord and Tenant: Responsibility of State and Condition of Property", (1996). For a critical examination of this report, see S. Bridge, "Putting it right? The Law Commission and the condition of tenanted property" [1996] Conv. 342.

The principal weaknesses in the present law which were identified in the Law Commission's Report No. 208 were as follows.

(1) The absence of a satisfactory standard which has to be met by leased premises.
    We have seen above that the fitness for habitation condition contained in ss. 8–10 of the Landlord and Tenant Act 1985 is obsolete because of the unrealistic rental limits.

(2) The possibility of tenancies where neither party is responsible for repair (*i.e.* where there are no express or implied repairing obligations). Although technically possible, this scenario is less likely these days because in most cases there will be express, implied or statutory obligations which deal to a greater or lesser degree with the issue of responsibility for the state of the property. (But for a case where nobody was required to repair the structure of a building containing maisonettes which were let to tenants on long leases for a capital sum and a nominal rent, see *Adami v. Lincoln Grange Management Ltd*, *The Times*, December 22, 1997, CA)

(3) The ineffectiveness of remedies, such as the limited availability of specific performance and uncertainty as to the scope of self-help remedies.

(4) The piecemeal development of common law and statutory rules has led to confusion and overlap and an absence of logic about repairing obligations and remedies.

A solution to the problem?

The Law Commission recommend a new statutory framework to govern the position as to responsibility for repairs as between landlord and tenant. It proposes—

(1) That there be an implied obligation on the landlord to keep in repair. This would be implied in all new tenancies (*i.e.* both residential and business). Where the leased premises are part only of a building, the landlord would be under a similar obligation with regard to any other parts which are within his ownership (subject to similar qualifications (as to accessibility etc.) as apply at present under the current repairing obligation in the Landlord and Tenant Act 1985, s.11(1A) (above). The implied obligations would be subject to the following exceptions—

    (a) tenancies of dwellings for less than seven years; (these would remain subject to section 11 of the Landlord and Tenant Act 1985);

    (b) oral tenancies;

    (c) agricultural tenancies (*i.e.* a lease of an agricultural holding or a farm business tenancy).

As in the case of the repairing obligation placed on landlords by the Landlord and Tenant Act 1985, s. 11, the landlord should not be required to undertake any of the following matters—

    (a) any work of repairs that the tenant is obliged to carry out under his implied covenant to take proper care of the premises;

    (b) the rebuilding or reinstatement of the premises in whole or in part if they are destroyed by inevitable accident; and

    (c) the repair of any tenant's fixtures.

The standard of repair should be that which is appropriate having regard to the age, character and prospective life of the premises and to their locality.

The obligation would not apply where the parties have made express provision for repairing obligations. The aim of this proposal is to ensure that the parties direct their minds to the need to cater for repairing obligations otherwise the implied term would apply by default. The parties would also be free to modify the implied obligation or to exclude it in whole or in part.

(2) That there be an implied covenant by the landlord of a dwelling-house let for a term of less than seven years (on a new lease) that the dwelling-house is fit for human habitation when let and that it will be kept fit throughout the lease. (For a discussion of this proposal see P.F. Smith, "*A Case for Abrogation: The No-Liability for Unfitness Principle*" [1998] Conv. 189). The aim of this proposal is to provide a correlative effective fitness condition alongside the statutory repairing obligation implied in leases for less than seven years by Landlord and Tenant Act 1985, s. 11. It would ensure a remedy for tenants such as the plaintiff in *Quick v. Taff Ely BC*

(p.55 above) where a design defect had caused intolerable condensation damp in the house let to the tenant but had not caused physical disrepair to the structure or exterior of the property which the landlord had covenanted to repair. There would be no low rent limit.

The obligation would not apply to certain leases. The proposed exceptions are modelled on those applicable in the case of the section 11 LTA 1985 repairing covenant but also extend to leases where the land is held by a public body (*e.g.* a council) for development and has been temporarily let pending development.

The landlord should not be liable if the property cannot be made fit for human habitation at reasonable expense. This would incorporate the judicial limitation which has been placed on the existing (obsolete) fitness condition in Landlord and Tenant Act 1985, s. 8. (See *Buswell v. Goodwin* [1971] 1 W.L.R. 92, CA.)

The fitness standard would be measured by the same criteria as those applied in section 604 of the Housing Act 1985 (see p.73 above).

(3)   That a court should have power (at its discretion) to grant a decree of specific performance of a repairing obligation (widely defined to mean a covenant to repair, maintain, renew, construct or replace any property) in any tenancy. The remedy would extend to the fitness for habitation obligation. This would significantly extend the range of remedies available and clear up any existing uncertainty as to the extent of the courts' powers to grant specific performance for breach of a repairing or fitness obligation, whether imposed on the landlord or the tenant.

(4)   That the tort of waste be abolished along with the obligation of a tenant to use the premises in a "tenantlike" manner. These would be replaced by an obligation on tenants and contractual licensees (a) to take proper care of the premises and common parts, (b) to make good wilful damage by the tenant or any other lawful occupier or visitor and (c) not to carry out alterations or other works which will, or are likely to destroy or alter the character of the whole or any part of the premises to the detriment of the landlord or licensor.

Although the Law Commission has had a better record in recent years with regard to the legislative implementation of its proposals for law reform, it has to be said that the prospects for the successful adoption of this latest set of proposals do not look good. It is clear that as far as public sector landlords are concerned, stricter more extensive contractual obligations would lead to a massive strain on local government finances which could not be sustained without a substantial cash injection from central government. It would also need political acceptance of the fact that the imposition of more exacting standards on private sector landlords would lead to any extra expenditure being placed on tenants through rent increases, a significant portion of which would fall upon the social security budget in the form of increased housing benefit expenditure. (One commentator has questioned whether, even if implemented, the reforms would have much impact on residential tenants (save for the extended availability of specific performance) and suggests that it would be a brave assured shorthold tenant who sought to enforce any extended rights against the landlord, given the precarious position of such tenants in the absence of any security of tenure: S.Bridge [1996] Conv. 342.)

Chapter 4

ALIENATION COVENANTS

Introduction (See generally L.Crabb, *Leases, Covenants and Consents* (Sweet & Maxwell, 1991).)

As we have seen (save for a tenancy at will) a tenancy, whether periodic or for a fixed term, is both a contract and a property right, taking effect either at law as a legal estate or in equity as an equitable interest. This means that in the absence of any express or statutory provision to the contrary, the tenant has the right to deal with that estate or interest as he or she chooses (*Doe & Mitchinson v. Carter* (1798) 8 Term Rep. 57 at 60, 61). By contrast, a tenancy at will comes to an end as soon as the landlord has notice of any assignment (*Doe & Daines v. Thomas* (1851) 6 Excts., 854, 857; *Pinhom v. Souster* (1853) 8 Excts., 763, 762).

> "It is of the nature of the creation of a term of years that the owner of the term is capable of dealing with it as a piece of property. The only way that can be prevented or hampered is by virtue of the common form clause that he covenants not to do it and there may be a forfeiture of the term if he does it. (*Old Grovebury Manor Farm Ltd v. W Seymour (Plant Sales & Hire) Ltd (No. 2)* [1979] 3 All E.R. 504 at 506 *per* Lord Russell. See also *Leith Properties Ltd v. Byrne* [1983] 2 W.L.R. 67 at 71 *per* Slade L.J.)."

In the same way the landlord is free to deal with the reversion. Even where the tenant is prevented by contract from assigning or otherwise dealing with the tenancy, it does not follow that any prohibited disposition which the tenant might make will be ineffective. It simply gives the landlord the opportunity to forfeit the tenancy (if there is a forfeiture clause in the tenancy) or to sue for damages. In *Hemingway Securities Ltd v. Dunraven* [1995] 9 E.G. 322 a further remedy was recognised where there was an unlawful sub-letting. At the request of the head landlord the court issued a mandatory injunction which required the surrender of the sub-tenancy, which had been created in breach of covenant. (See further p.186 below for the exceptional circumstances in which a head landlord can enforce covenants against a sub-tenant).

The present chapter is devoted primarily to contractual and statutory restrictions on the tenant's power of disposition, but before the relevant law is examined it is necessary to consider the wide variety of ways in which dealings with the tenancy can occur. The main instances are as follows.

1. Assignment

An assignment occurs where the tenant's interest in the whole or part of the property leased to him passes to another, such as where the tenant sells and conveys or gives away his interest to a person known as the assignee. Thus if in 1996 L granted T a 10-year legal tenancy of Blackacre and in 1998 T wishes to dispose of the residue of that tenancy to a purchaser A, he will execute a legal assignment of his term of years. This will have the effect of passing the legal estate to A, who will now step into the shoes of T and become the tenant under that tenancy. T will no longer have any estate or interest in the property assigned, although this will not necessarily mean that he ceases to be contractually liable in respect of post-assignment breaches of covenant by an assignee (The liability of original parties and assignees of the tenancy and the reversion is dealt with in Chapter 7).

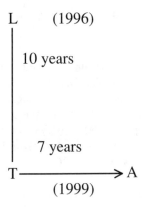

The point at which the legal estate will pass depends upon whether or not title to the lease is registered under the Land Registration Act 1925. If title to the lease is not registered it is necessary for the assignment to be by way of deed for the legal estate to pass to the assignee (Law of Property Act 1925, s.52). This requirement applies to any term of years absolute, however long or short the tenancy and, perhaps surprisingly, even if a deed was not necessary for the creation of the tenancy (*i.e.* certain tenancies not exceeding three years; see LPA 1925, s.54(2); see p.30 above). Thus whether the tenancy is an oral weekly tenancy or a 999-year term, a deed is necessary in both cases to pass the legal estate by way of assignment (*Crago v. Julian* [1992] 1 All E.R. 744). In practice, of course, when legal advice might not be sought, tenants of short-term or periodic oral tenancies will rarely use a deed of assignment and it may be necessary to rely on the landlord having accepted the "assignee" as a tenant, thereby creating a new tenancy between them. (This was not the case in *Crago v. Julian* (above) because the landlord terminated the tenancy on learning of the original tenant's departure). If a deed is not used, a purported assignment in writing can operate as a contract to convey the legal estate provided it complies with the Law of Property (Miscellaneous Provisions) Act 1989, s.2 (see p.30 above).

If title to the lease is registered at HM Land Registry, under the Land Registration Act 1925, a legal assignment will be way of a registrable transfer. The transaction will be completed by the registrar entering the transferee (*i.e.* the assignee) on the register as the new owner of the leasehold estate transferred. Until that time the transferor will remain the legal owner (Land Registration Act 1925, ss.21–23). This crucial difference in the rules governing the passing of the legal estate on a transfer of registered land, whereby the legal estate does not pass until registration, produced dramatic consequences in *Brown & Root Technology Ltd v. Sun Alliance & London Assurance Co. Ltd* [1997] 1 E.G.L.R. 39. The landlord had granted a tenancy which contained a break clause exercisable by the original tenant. In December 1993 the tenant company assigned the lease to its parent company but the assignee was never registered as the new tenant. Following a dramatic fall in the rental value of the property (£1.3 million p.a.) the original tenant sought to exercise the break clause. The court held that this was still possible because the legal estate had never passed to the assignee. The result can fairly be described as at the very least unfortunate for the landlord, and the case is yet another example of where the machinery of the Land Registration Act 1925 has produced a difference in the substantive law from the position where title to the land is unregistered.

In the cases mentioned below an assignment of a lease, title to which is not registered under the Land Registration Act 1925, will give rise to the need for first registration of title to that lease under the Act. In this connection it should be noted that a lease is not eligible for registration with its own title unless there are more than 21 years unexpired at the time of the application (Land Registration Act 1925, s.8(1)).

The cases referred to are every assignment (whether by way of gift, or for valuable or other consideration, or in pursuance of a court order) of a lease with more than 21 years to run from the date of assignment (LRA 1925, s.123(1)(c)). Failure by the assignee to apply within two months of that date for registration will mean that the legal estate will revert to the assignor and the transaction will take effect only as a contract to assign the legal estate (LRA 1925, s.123(5)(A)).

As stated above, an assignment can be of the tenant's interest in the whole of the property or of part. In the case of an assignment of part, the tenant will of course remain tenant of that part of the property which has been retained.

Assignments can also occur involuntarily. The two most important instances in practice are, first, where the tenant is adjudicated bankrupt, as a result of which his interest in the tenancy will automatically vest by law in the trustee in bankruptcy (Insolvency Act 1986, s.306). The second, described by a former Lord Chancellor (Lord Thurlow) as "alienation by Act of God" (*Seers v. Hinds* (1791) 1 Ves. 294), is where the tenant dies as a result of which his leasehold interest vests either in his executors or, where there are no executors appointed by will, in the Public Trustee pending appointment of administrators (Administration of Estates Act 1925, ss. 1 and 9).

2. Sub-letting

A sub-tenancy is created by the tenant granting a tenancy for a period at least one day less than that under which he holds. The sub-tenant can in turn create a further sub-tenancy, and so on. The creation of a sub-tenancy by a tenant does not create any legal relationship between the tenant's landlord and the sub-tenant because there is no contractual relationship between them, nor do they stand in the relationship of landlord and tenant with regard to the same estate in land. The estate held by the sub-tenant is a quite different estate to that retained by the tenant. The estate retained by the tenant is sometimes referred to, particularly in the case of longer leases, as the leasehold reversion.

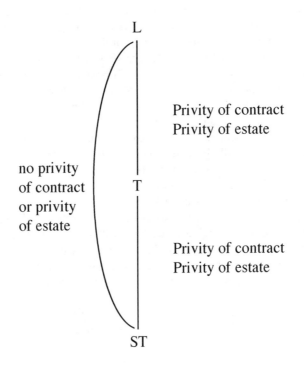

The distinction between an assignment of a tenancy and the creation of a sub-tenancy is thus that in the case of the former the tenant disposes of his whole interest in the property assigned and the assignee steps into his shoes as the new tenant. In the case of a sub-letting the tenant remains a tenant under his tenancy and also becomes a landlord under the sub-tenancy, which is a new and separate estate in the land. Of course if the tenant purports to sub-let for a period which is the same as or longer than the residue of the tenancy which he holds at that time, this cannot create a sub-tenancy. It will take effect instead as an assignment at law (*Milmo v. Carreras* [1946] K.B. 306). Thus if a tenant with five years remaining of his tenancy purports to sub-let for six years, this will operate as an assignment of the residue of the term. The tenant will no longer have an estate in the property and the "sub-tenant" will in fact take the tenancy as an assignee of the term.

Covenants against alienation

As we have seen above, a leasehold estate is freely alienable either by way of assignment or sub-letting. For this reason it is necessary for a prospective landlord who wishes to restrain the tenant's freedom to deal with his tenancy as he wishes to ensure that the lease contains a provision which will enable him to achieve that objective. Whether such a provision will be included in a particular tenancy, and if so the form it will take, will depend on a number of factors. These include the length of the tenancy, the nature of the property and the relative bargaining strength of the parties. Virtually all tenancies in writing will contain a provision governing alienation which will invariably operate to place some form of restraint on the tenant's freedom of disposition . As will be seen below, restraints can take a number of forms, from the mildest to the most Draconian. Nevertheless, it must be appreciated, particularly in the case of commercial tenancies, that extensive control over the tenant's freedom of action can have a significant effect on what the landlord can expect to obtain by way of a premium or rent, either on granting the tenancy or on the occasion of a subsequent rent review. Furthermore, because every covenant against alienation effectively curtails the tenant's common law freedom to deal with his estate as he wishes, it will be construed strictly against the landlord in a case of ambiguity.

Finally, it should be noted that special rules concerning alienation apply to certain tenancies governed by one of the special statutory regimes which regulate residential tenancies. These rules are dealt with at the end of this chapter after the discussion of the general principles of law.

Covenants against assignment

A simple covenant against assignment will prohibit the tenant from legally assigning the residue of the tenancy in the whole of the premises by way of assignment. If the landlord also wishes to prohibit an assignment of part of the premises the wording of the covenant should be extended accordingly. Otherwise, only an assignment of the whole will be prohibited. In any event a covenant against assignment, whether extending to the whole or part of the premises, will not prevent a lawful sub-letting of either the whole or part of the premises comprised in the tenancy. If the landlord wants to prohibit sub-letting, the covenant must be further extended accordingly (see below).

It seems to be tolerably clear that an involuntary assignment by operation of law such as that occurring on bankruptcy or on a deceased tenant's property vesting in his personal representatives will not be a breach of the covenant against assignment. (See, *e.g. Re Riggs* [1901] 2 K.B. 16 where the tenant was adjudicated bankrupt on his own petition). Indeed a personal representative stands in the shoes of the deceased tenant. However, the covenant does bind a personal representative and can as a matter of construction bind a trustee in bankruptcy. Therefore any voluntary disposition by either person will be governed by the covenant. (In *Re Wright* [1949] Ch. 729, a trustee in bankruptcy was bound by a covenant against assignment which was expressed to be binding on the tenant and his successors in title. In the case of covenants entered into from 1926 onwards, successors in title will always be bound, unless the contrary is expressed in the tenancy (LPA 1925, s.79(1)). For a discussion of the position generally on the death of the tenant see Barnsley 27 Conv. 159.

In practice it is common to avoid such difficulties by providing for a right of forfeiture and re-entry exercisable by the landlord upon the tenant's insolvency (see p.134 below).

Nothing less than a legal assignment for the entire residue of the tenancy will be a breach of the covenant. Thus mortgaging the tenancy by way of a charge by way of legal mortgage will not be a breach of the covenant. For the same reason a declaration of trust of the tenancy will also not amount to a breach of the covenant because the legal estate does not pass (*Gentle v. Faulkner* [1900] 2 Q.B. 267). It has been suggested that it would be sensible for alienation covenants to be drafted so as to prohibit an equitable as well as a legal assignment (see P. Walter [1996] Conv. 432)

Where the landlord brings forfeiture proceedings following breach of a covenant against assignment the defendant will be the assignee because he will be the person with the legal estate. As we saw above, a covenant against assignment does not invalidate an unlawful assignment but merely affords the landlord remedies in respect of the breach (*Old Grovebury Manor Farm Ltd v. W. Seymour Plant Sales & Hire Ltd* [1979] 1 W.L.R. 1397, CA).

Covenants against sub-letting

A simple covenant against sub-letting will prohibit a sub-letting of the whole, but not part, of the premises within the tenancy (*Wilson v. Rosenthal* (1906) 22 T.L.R. 233). Hence a sub-letting of part would not be a breach of such a covenant unless the sub-tenant had already sub-let the rest and the effect of the most recent sub-letting was that the whole was now sub-let (*Chatterton v. Terrell* [1923] A.C. 578). Thus if the landlord wants to prohibit a sub-letting of part he should ensure that the covenant is so drafted (*e.g.* "the tenant shall not sub-let the whole or any part of the premises"). By contrast it has been held that a covenant which merely prohibits the sub-letting of any part of the premises will also be breached by a sub-letting of the whole, because a disposal of the whole necessarily involves a disposition of part (*Field v. Barkworth* [1986] 1 All E.R. 362, followed in *Troop v. Gibson* (1986) 277 E.G. 1134. The same principle applies in respect of the assignment of part of the premises).

The issue of whether a covenant against subletting is broken by an assignment was left open by the Court of Appeal in *Marks v. Warren* [1979] 1 All E.R. 29. There is Irish authority that it would not be a breach (*Re Doyle and O'Hara's Contract* [1899] I.R. 113).

A mortgage by way of creating a sub-tenancy in favour of the mortgagee would certainly be a breach of a covenant against sub-letting (*Serjeant v. Nash, Field & Co.* [1903] 2 K.B. 304). (For this method of creating a mortgage, see Law of Property Act 1925 s.86(1).) But if the tenancy provides that the tenant may, subject to the landlord's consent, create a mortgage by way of sub-tenancy, it is provided by statute that such consent must not to be unreasonably withheld; LPA 1925, s.86(1).) By contrast, it would seem that a mortgage by way of legal charge would not be a breach of a covenant against subletting because the mortgagee does not actually obtain a sub-tenancy even though he is given the same rights and remedies as if he had a sub-tenancy (see LPA 1925, s.87(1) and *Grand Junction Canal Co Ltd v. Bates* [1954] 2 Q.B. 160 at 168). It would be sensible therefore to require the landlord's consent to the creation of a charge by way of legal mortgage over the tenancy, such consent not to be unreasonably withheld. (See also Landlord and Tenant Act 1927, s.19 below.)

Covenants against parting with possession

A covenant against assignment or sub-letting will not prevent the tenant dealing with his property in such a way that he parts with possession of the whole or part of the property by way of an arrangement falling short of an assignment or sub-lease. An example would be the creation of a licence to occupy. (Although it should be recalled that a "licence" granting the "licensee" exclusive possession might be construed as a tenancy: see *Street v. Mountford* [1985] A.C. 809 and p.2 *et seq* above). Consequently it is not uncommon in practice to encounter covenants framed so as to prohibit a parting with possession of the whole or any part of the premises. However, if the tenant grants another a licence to occupy the premises, this will not amount to a breach of the covenant "unless his agreement with his licensee wholly ousts him from the legal possession. . .nothing short of a complete exclusion of the grantor or licensor from the legal possession for all purposes amounts to a parting with possession." (*Stenning v. Abrahams* [1931] 1 Ch. 470 at 473.) Whether this has occurred will depend on all the circumstances of the case. In *Lam Kee Ying Sdn Bhd v. Lam Shes Tong* [1975] A.C. 247 it was accepted by the Privy Council that "A covenant which forbids a parting with possession is not broken by a lessee who in law retains the possession even though he allows another to use and occupy the premises" (at p.256 *per* Sir Harry Gibbs). In that particular case the tenant partners who ran a business from the leased premises dissolved the partnership and formed a company which thereafter used the premises for its business purposes. It was held that in the circumstances there had actually been a parting with legal possession. It follows that in order to avoid evasion of the covenant by the creation of an arrangement for occupation by a third party under an agreement which does not involve the tenant parting with legal possession, it would be necessary to frame the alienation covenant in sufficiently wide terms to catch any such licence. Indeed in an appropriate case a tenancy might include a covenant which also prohibits any sharing of the use and occupation of the premises by the tenant with a third party, although it is usual practice to permit a sharing of occupation with companies in the same group as the tenant company.

Finally it can be noted that a covenant against parting with possession will by itself be effective to prohibit not only a parting with legal possession by way of a licence arrangement but also by way of an assignment or subletting even if the tenancy does not expressly forbid those types of disposition. Dispositions by way of assignment or subletting necessarily involve a parting with possession. Thus in *Marks v. Warren* (above) an assignment was held to be a breach of a covenant not to sublet or part with possession of the premises.

Absolute and qualified covenants

The degree to which a tenant is prohibited from dealing with the property depends on how strictly the covenant is drawn. The traditional distinction is between absolute and qualified covenants against alienation. An absolute covenant, which forbids the prohibited act completely, is very onerous for a tenant. Although a landlord who has the benefit of such a covenant can if asked choose to permit a disposition which would otherwise amount to a breach of covenant, he cannot be compelled so to do. The landlord may similarly choose to waive a breach of the covenant. Otherwise, the only qualification to the operation of an absolute covenant is where the landlord's objection to a proposed dealing is on the basis of racial or sexual discrimination against the proposed assignee or subtenant , or is discrimination based on the disability of that person (Sex Discrimination Act 1975, s.31; Race Relations Act 1976, s.24; Disability Discrimination Act 1995, s.22). In such cases the covenant will be treated as a fully qualified covenant. (The Law Commission recommended that, save for specified exceptional cases, absolute disposition covenants should be prohibited. See Law Com. No.141, 1985.)

It is common in practice to prohibit the absolute assignment of part of the premises in the case of business tenancies.

By contrast to an absolute covenant, a qualified covenant against assigning etc. is a covenant not to assign etc. *without the consent of the landlord.* Such a covenant usually adds the words "such consent not to be unreasonably withheld", thereby turning the qualified covenant into what is sometimes referred to as a fully qualified covenant. Indeed even if this proviso is not included it will be implied by statute (Landlord and Tenant Act 1927, s.19(1)(a)) in all leases save mining leases, leases of agricultural holdings to which the Agricultural Holdings Act 1986 applies, and farm business tenancies within the Agricultural Tenancies Act 1995 (LTA 1927, s.19(4)). The statutory proviso expressly does not preclude the landlord from requiring the payment of a reasonable sum in respect of any legal or other expenses incurred in connection with such licence or consent. It is also provided that if a mortgagee of a lease seeks to dispose of the lease in exercise of an express or statutory power of sale, the landlord's consent to the proposed sale, where there is a qualified covenant against assignment, must not be unreasonably withheld (LPA 1925, s.89(1)).

The Landlord and Tenant Act 1927, s.19(1)(b) goes even further than s.19(1)(a) by additionally providing that where the qualified covenant is contained in a building lease for more than 40 years (under which the landlord is not a Government Department or local authority or other specified public body or utility) the landlord's consent to a disposition is not required where there are more than seven years of the lease left at that time, provided that notice in writing of the disposition is given to the landlord within six months after the transaction. This does not prevent the landlord imposing other restrictions, by way of preconditions, in the lease. Thus in *Vaux Group plc v. Lilley* [1991] 4 E.G. 136 the obligation under the tenancy for the tenant to obtain an acceptable guarantor for the assignee's performance of the obligations under the tenancy and to procure a direct covenant by the assignee with the landlord to observe the covenants in the lease was held not to contravene section 19(1)(b). It is important to note that section 19(1)(b) does not apply in relation to the assignment of a lease which is a qualifying lease for the purpose of the Landlord and Tenant (Covenants) Act 1995 (see below for the significance of the 1995 Act in this context).

If a qualified covenant against alienation states that the landlord will not refuse consent in the case of a respectable and responsible person, this will curtail his freedom to that extent. It follows therefore that if the proposed assignee meets those criteria the landlord will not be able to withhold consent on any other ground, whether or not he could be said to be reasonable in refusing consent on the ground(s) relied upon (*Moat v. Martin* [1950] 1 K.B. 175).

Despite the presence of a qualified covenant in a tenancy it is important that the tenant requests permission of the landlord even if in the circumstances the landlord could not reasonably refuse consent to the proposed assignee or sub-tenant, etc. Thus in *Barrow v. Isaacs* [1891] 1 Q.B. 417 where there was a covenant that consent to a proposed assignment would not be withheld in the case of a respectable and responsible person, it was still held to be a breach of covenant when through mere forgetfulness the tenant forgot to obtain the landlord's consent even though the landlord could not have reasonably refused had he been asked. The court refused to grant equitable relief against forfeiture on the basis that to grant relief would be to ignore the obligation to seek consent and to encourage carelessness on the part of tenants (see also *Eastern Telegraph Co Ltd v. Dent* [1899] 1 Q.B. 835). However, since the statutory jurisdiction to grant relief against forfeiture (see p.146 below) was extended to covenants against alienation by the Law of Property Act 1925, the courts have on rare occasions, and in special circumstances, been willing to grant relief against forfeiture for an inadvertent breach of the covenant. (See *Scala House Ltd v. Forbes* [1973] 3 W.L.R. 14, CA: see p.148 below).

No "fine" payable for consent

Unless the tenancy provides to the contrary, there is a statutory proviso that, where there is a covenant against disposition without the licence or consent of the landlord, "no fine or sum of money in the nature of a fine" shall be payable for or in respect of any consent. But this does not preclude the right to require the payment of a reasonable sum in respect of any legal or other expenses in relation to the licence or consent (LPA 1925, s.144). "Fine" is widely defined to include "a premium or foregift and any payment, consideration or benefit in the nature of a fine, premium or foregift" (LPA 1925, s.205(1)(xxiii)).

There is some dispute about the scope of section 144. In *Waite v. Jennings* [1906] 2 K.B. 11 the Court of Appeal doubted whether a demand by the landlord that the proposed assignee enter into a direct covenant with the landlord to pay the rent and observe the covenants in the lease would amount to a request for a fine (see further p.168 below). In practice such demands are common. On the other hand, a demand for an increase in the rent payable under the tenancy would seem to be prohibited (*Jenkins v. Price* [1907] 2 Ch. 229). A demand that an assignee publican enter into a covenant with the landlord brewer that the premises should be a tied house for the remainder of the term was also held to be illegal (*Gardner v. Cone* [1928] 1 Ch. 955), as was a demand for an amendment to the tenancy to incorporate a landlord's break clause (*Barclays Bank plc v. Daejan Investments* [1995] 18 E.G. 117—a decision on the parallel prohibition on fines in the Landlord and Tenant Act 1927, s.19(3) dealing with covenants against change of user. (See p.119 below for break clauses). However, once a fine has been paid there is no provision for its recovery (*Andrew v. Bridgman* [1908] 1 K.B. 596).

In practice landlords should deal with all such matters by making provision in the tenancy because it is expressly permissible to contract out of the provisos in LTA 1927, s. 19(1)(1)(a) and LPA 1925, s.144.

A tenant who seeks consent of the landlord under a qualified covenant against assignment may go ahead and assign if the landlord unreasonably withholds consent (*Treloar v. Bigge* (1874) L.R. 9 Ex. 151). The problem with this, however, is that the tenant and assignee may be unwilling to risk the possibility of a forfeiture action by the landlord whose refusal is subsequently found to be reasonable by the court. Furthermore, at common law the landlord was under no obligation to give the reasons for withholding consent. To be safe therefore the tenant would need to go to court for a declaration that the landlord was unreasonably withholding consent. In practice, time and expense might make this unfeasible. At one time tenants also faced the problem that the landlord who was asked for consent to a proposed disposition might simply delay communicating his decision for so long that the transaction would fail to proceed. To deal with some of these difficulties the Landlord and Tenant Act 1988 was enacted following Law Commission Report No. 141, "Covenants Restricting Dispositions, Alteration and User" (1985) and Law Commission Report No. 161, "Leasehold Conveyancing" (1987).

The Act applies to all leases (except Housing Act 1985 secure tenancies), whether entered into before or after the Act came into force (September 29, 1988), containing (either expressly or by statutory implication) a fully qualified covenant against assigning, sub-letting, charging or parting with possession of the whole or any part of the leased premises.

It provides that—

(1) Where the tenant by writing has sought the landlord's consent to a proposed disposition, the landlord must, within a reasonable time, give consent unless it is reasonable not to give consent (s.1(3)(a)). Giving consent subject to an unreasonable condition will not satisfy this duty (s.1(4)). Nor will it be satisfied if the tenancy includes a *Moat v. Martin* clause (see above) and the landlord refuses consent, despite the proposed assignee being a respectable and responsible person (s.1(5)). In such circumstances the tenant is free to go ahead and assign. (A similar duty is owed by the landlord to a sub-tenant where the tenant has covenanted not to give permission for a sub-tenant to assign, sub-let, charge or part with possession without (the tenant) first obtaining the landlord's consent which is not to be unreasonably withheld). The duty arises once the tenant has given the landlord written application for approval or has passed on to the landlord a written request for approval made to the tenant by the sub-tenant (s.2).

What is a reasonable time is a matter for the court. (The original Law Commission proposal had suggested 28 days). In *Midland Bank plc v. Chart Enterprises* [1990] 45 E.G. 68 the tenant's application was made on February 15, 1989 and the landlord's decision was given on May 5, 1989. It was held that this was unreasonable delay. Popplewell J. accepted that if the landlord suspected that there had been a breach of covenant by the tenant he would need time to enquire into this. However, in that particular case this issue had been raised with the tenant in an affidavit in November 1989 long after the giving of the conditional consent on May 5, thereby robbing the landlord's argument of any force. (See further below on undisclosed reasons). A related issue considered in *Dong Bang Minerva (UK) Ltd v. Davina Ltd* [1996] 31 E.G. 87, CA is when time begins to run.

In July 1993, the tenant of a lease sought consent to a proposed sub-letting and in return the landlord trust company sought an undertaking from the tenant as to costs. In other words, the landlord was seeking to protect itself against wasted costs if the transaction were not to go ahead. The tenant company refused to give such an undertaking because it considered that the estimated costs (£4,500) were unreasonable. The tenant sued for damages for breach of s.1(3) and a declaration that the landlords were unreasonably withholding consent. It was agreed by both sides in the Court of Appeal that the reasonable period within which the landlord is required to come to a decision and inform the tenant would be suspended until the undertaking was received, but only where the undertaking requested was for a reasonable sum. The court held that on the facts the defendant was in breach of its statutory duty because the sum requested was in excess of the landlord's reasonable costs. Therefore the landlord should have reached a decision by August 8, 1993 at the latest.

(2)   The landlord must serve on the tenant written notice of his decision whether or not to give consent. If he is giving consent subject to conditions, the notice must specify the conditions. If consent is withheld the notice must state the reasons for that decision (s.1(3)(b)) (see *Norwich Union Life Assurance Society v. Shopmoor Ltd* [1998] All E.R. 32.
      The common law onus of proof on these matters is reversed by the Act. It is for the landlord to prove that where he gave consent he did so within a reasonable time. If in a case where he gave conditional consent the issue of the reasonableness of that consent arises, the onus is upon the landlord to show that it was reasonable. If he did not consent it is for the landlord to show that it was reasonable for him to refuse consent (s.1(6)).

(3)   The landlord must within a reasonable time pass on an application to others from whom it is believed consent is required (s.2). The most usual circumstances where this will apply is where there is a superior landlord whose consent is necessary. Thus if a sub-tenant wishes to assign or further sub-let he will frequently require the consent not only of his landlord—the tenant—but also that of the head landlord.

The effect of these statutory obligations is that the landlord in default will be liable in tort for breach of statutory duty (s.4). Thus the tenant should be able to recover losses suffered from a proposed transaction having failed to proceed as a result of the landlord's breach of duty.

A thorny issue is whether a landlord can subsequently rely on reasons which were not disclosed to the tenant at the time the landlord's decision was given. It was accepted (before the Landlord and Tenant Act 1988 that) this was possible, by Slade L.J. in an *obiter dictum* in *Bromley Park Garden Estates Ltd v. Moss* [1982] 1 W.L.R. 1019. However, the judge considered that this would only be so where the reasons were ones which influenced the landlord at the time of the refusal. This was applied in the post-1988 Act case of *C.I.N Properties v. Gill* [1993] 37 E.G. 152. However, more recently it has been held that if a landlord refuses consent and does not give his reasons in writing within a reasonable time of the request for consent he cannot later rely on those reasons in court. *(Footwear Corp. Ltd v. Amplight Properties Ltd* [1998] 3 All E.R. 52).

What is reasonable?

A substantial body of case law has developed with regard to the issue of when a refusal of consent to an assignment would be reasonable or not. The leading case is the decision of the Court of Appeal in *International Drilling Fluids Ltd v. Louisville Investments (Uxbridge) Ltd* [1986] Ch. 513, in which Balcombe L.J. (with whom the rest of the Court agreed) sought to distil the relevant principles from that mass of case law. He set them out in the following series of propositions.

(1) The purpose of a fully qualified covenant against assignment is to protect the landlord from having his premises used or occupied in an undesirable way or by an undesirable assignee *(per* Smith L.J. in *Bates v. Donaldson* [1896] 2 Q.B. 241 at 247, as approved by the Court of Appeal in *Houlder Brothers & Co v. Gibbs* [1925] Ch. 575).

(2) As a corollary to (1) above a landlord is not entitled to refuse his consent to an assignment on grounds which have nothing whatever to do with the relationship of landlord and tenant in regard to the subject matter of the tenancy. Thus it was unreasonable for the landlord to refuse consent in *Houlder Brothers & Co v. Gibbs* (above) on the basis that the proposed assignee was a tenant of other premises held of the same landlord which the tenant would probably give up and the landlord would then have to go to the trouble of reletting, which could be very difficult given the recession at the time. The court considered that this had nothing to do with the subject premises or the personality of the assignee.

It was for this reason that the landlord was held also to have unreasonably refused consent to a proposed assignment in *Bromley Park Garden Estates v. Moss* (above). (See also *Roux Restaurants Ltd v. Jaison Property Development Co. Ltd* [1997] 74 P& C.R. 357, CA). More recently in *Norwich Union Life Insurance Society v. Shopmoor Ltd* (above) the court expressed the view that it would not be reasonable for a landlord to refuse consent to a proposed sub-letting simply because he believed that (because of the rent to be payable) it would have an adverse effect on future rent levels of other properties in the area in which the landlord had an interest.

The plaintiffs in *Moss* had purchased an estate of 50 properties including a two-storey building used as a restaurant on the ground floor which was let to X and a top floor flat let to Y. The lease of the flat contained a fully qualified covenant against assignment and when Y sought permission to assign to the defendants the landlord refused, saying that it was not company policy to permit assignments and stating that if she wished to leave she should surrender her tenancy. At the hearing the landlord argued that in the interests of estate management it was not their policy to permit multiple lets of buildings because it reduced their investment value. (They had in fact arranged to grant X a lease of the whole building with a full repairing covenant by the tenant). The court held that the landlords had unreasonably withheld consent because even if their decision was in the interest of good estate management it was an attempt to obtain an uncovenanted for collateral advantage.

As Cumming-Bruce L.J. observed in *Bromley Park Garden Estates v. Moss* (above), in all the cases where the landlord was held to have reasonably withheld consent it was because the prospective use of the premises after assignment would be detrimental to the landlord's own interest under the lease. Even though such detriment might be suffered by him in connection with his other property, the fact is that he would have been in a worse position after assignment than before. When the landlords in that case bought the building it was subject to two separate leases. If they could recover possession they would be able to let the building on one lease, which they could not do before.

However, it has been held reasonable for a landlord to refuse consent to a proposed assignment where the assignee would acquire statutory rights which are unavailable to the assignor tenant.

In *Bickel v. Duke of Westminster* [1977] Q.B. 517, tenants of a dwelling-house who had sublet requested consent to assign the nine year residue of the 37-year lease to the sub-tenant. The lease was a long tenancy at a low rent (as defined) for the purposes of the Leasehold Reform Act 1967 which permits an occupier under such a lease to compel the landlord to sell him or her the freehold reversion at a discounted price (see Chapter 12 below). However, in the present case the tenants did not qualify under the Act because they were not in occupation. The sub-tenant did not qualify because her sub-tenancy was not at a low rent. Thus she was willing to pay a premium for the lease in order to be able to exercise the right to buy the freehold under the LRA 1967 after five years' occupation as a tenant (since reduced to three years). It was held reasonable for the landlord (the Grosvenor Estates) to refuse consent to an assignment which would otherwise give them a tenant with extensive rights to which the original tenant was not entitled.

There is also a line of authority to the effect that a landlord might reasonably object to a proposed disposition, the effect of which is to enable the new tenant to obtain security of tenure under the Rent Acts, contrary to the purpose of the letting. (See, *e.g. Lee v. K Carter Ltd* [1949] 1 K.B. 85 where a company proposed assigning to a director who would as an individual be able to qualify as a statutory tenant (see p.262 below); *West Layton Ltd v. Ford* [1979] Q.B. 593 where the landlord was held to have reasonably refused consent to a furnished sub-letting to respectable and responsible sub-tenants on the basis that since the tenancy had been granted the Rent Act 1974 had been enacted, which gave retrospective full Rent Act protection to furnished tenancies. See further *Leeward Securities Ltd v. Lilyheath Properties Ltd* (1984) 271 E.G. 279). However, unless in the case of an assignment the tenancy was granted before January 15, 1989, this is no longer a problem because it has not been possible to create new Rent Act protected tenancies since January 15, 1989 (see p.249 below). Thus a sub-tenancy would be outside the Rent Act and it might not be reasonable in those circumstances for the landlord to refuse consent (see also *Deverall v. Wyndham* (1988) 58 P.& C.R. 12). Furthermore, because most private sector residential tenancies created on or after February 28, 1997 will take effect as assured shorthold tenancies under the Housing Act 1988, at market rents with no statutory security of tenure, it cannot be argued that the landlord's interests will be damaged if it is proposed to assign premises to such a tenant where the existing tenancy (which was created on or after January 15, 1989) is outside the 1988 Act (for example, because the tenant is a company—*i.e.* not an individual for the purposes of Housing Act 1988, s.1 (see Chapter 10 below re: assured and assured shorthold tenancies).

(3) The onus of proving that consent that been unreasonably withheld is on the tenant As noted above, this has since been overturned by the Landlord and Tenant Act 1988 which obliges the landlord to show that his refusal was reasonable (s.1(6)(c)).

(4) It is not necessary for the landlord to prove that the conclusions which led him to refuse consent were justified, if they were conclusions which might be reached by a reasonable man in the circumstances (*Pimms v. Tallow Chandlers Co.* [1964] 2 Q.B. 547 at 564). In that case the landlord refused consent to a proposed assignment to a developer of the short residue of a lease of a restaurant in an area to be redeveloped. The landlord's fears that the assignee would use the nuisance value of the lease to be admitted to the redevelopment scheme, thereby reducing the profit to the landlord, was held to have been reasonably entertained. The court considered that this was a case where the reason related to the personality of the assignee. This proposition of law was applied in *Air India v. Balabel* [1993] 2 E.G.L.R. 66 which confirmed that it is not affected by the Landlord and Tenant Act 1988. Thus the landlord was not required to justify its belief that a proposed assignee (of a lease of premises to be used as a nightclub) was a thoroughly unsuitable person. It was a belief that a reasonable man might have come to in the circumstances.

(5) It may be reasonable for the landlord to refuse his consent to an assignment on the ground of the purpose for which the proposed assignee intends to use the premises even though that purpose is not forbidden by the lease (*Bates v. Donaldson* above, at 244) The proposed user by the assignee is a common ground of objection by landlords. If by a user covenant use is restricted to a particular purpose or purposes, it will not necessarily be reasonable for the landlord to refuse consent to a proposed assignment even where he anticipates a breach of the user covenant by the assignee. He must wait and see whether a breach of the user covenant does occur and if so, pursue his appropriate remedy. This is particularly so where the user covenant is a fully qualified covenant under which the assignee might seek permission for a change of user. (*In Killick v. Second Covent Garden Property Co. Ltd* [1973] 2 All E.R. 337 there was a qualified user covenant that the premises should not be used other than for the purposes of the business of printer. The assignees proposed to use the premises as offices. This was held not to be a reasonable ground for objecting to the proposed assignment. Even if the assignment were to go ahead, it did not follow that the landlord would be able to oppose successfully the proposed change of use. Indeed the court considered that it would not have made a difference even if the covenant had been unqualified, because the landlord could still wait and see whether a breach occurred and pursue his appropriate remedies. The decision in *Killick* was applied in *British Bakeries (Midlands) Ltd v. Michael Testler and Co. Ltd* [1986] 1 E.G.L.R. 64, although in that case the landlord was held to have reasonably refused consent to a proposed assignment on the basis that the assignee had not provided sufficient evidence of his financial viability.

By contrast, refusal by the landlord to grant consent may not be reasonable where the intended user would involve a breach of a positive covenant (*e.g.* a "keep-open covenant" whereby a commercial tenant has covenanted to continue trading from the premises in a shopping centre). Thus in *F.W. Woolworth plc v. Charlwood Alliance Properties Ltd* (1986) 282 E.G. 585 the retailer tenant had ceased trading in a store, in breach of covenant, and refused to say whether the assignee would resume trading. The landlord had good reason for anticipating that if the breach continued the effect would be detrimental to other properties in the centre let from the landlord, and hence to the landlord's interests. In these circumstances it was held that the landlord was not unreasonably withholding consent to a proposed assignment. (Whilst a keep-open covenant can be enforced by way of an action for damages, the court will not, save in exceptional circumstances, grant specific performance. See *Co-operative Insurance Society Ltd v. Argyll Stores (Holdings) Ltd* [1997] 2 W.L.R. 898, HL.) In similar vein it has also been held that it was reasonable for a landlord to refuse consent to an assignment where there were outstanding breaches of a repairing covenant and it was likely that such breaches would continue (*Orlando Investments Ltd v. Grosvenor Estates Belgravia* (1989) 59 P.& C.R. 21).

It might be thought that if the proposed use was not prohibited by the lease, the landlord could not reasonably object on the ground of that proposed use. However, as Balcombe L.J. indicates in proposition (5) (above) the landlord may be reasonable in refusing consent in such a case in appropriate circumstances. In *International Drilling Fluids Ltd v. Louisville*

Investments (Uxbridge) Ltd (above) where the user clause permitted only one type of user it was held that the landlord could not reasonably object where the assignee proposed to use the premises for that very purpose and where the consequence of a refusal was that the property would lie empty.

Although it has been held that it is legitimate for the landlord to refuse consent on the basis that the proposed use would compete with the use of nearby premises occupied by the landlord (*Whiteminster Estates Ltd v. Hodges Menswear* (1974) 232 E.G. 7715) or another tenant of his (*Premier Confectionery (London) Co. v. London Commercial Sale Rooms Ltd* [1933] Ch. 904) it has been suggested by Balcombe L.J. (*International Drilling Fluids*) that this should only be so where protection from competition was a purpose of the relevant provisions. Otherwise the landlord would be seeking an unwarranted uncovenanted advantage by his refusal (as to which see *Bromley Park Garden Estates v. Moss* (above). See also S. Tromans, *Commercial Leases* (2nd ed.) p.193).

(6) A landlord need normally only consider his own relevant interests when deciding whether to refuse or give consent, but there may be cases where there is such a disproportion between the benefit to the landlord and the detriment to the tenant if the landlord refuses consent that it is unreasonable for the landlord to refuse consent.

(7) Subject to the above propositions it is a question of fact in each case depending on all the circumstances whether the landlord's consent is being unreasonably withheld. In *International Drilling Fluids Ltd v. Louisville Investments (Uxbridge) Ltd* (above) the lease restricted the use of the property to use as offices with ancillary showrooms. There was a fully qualified covenant against assignment. The tenants sought consent to assign to a person who wanted to use the building for the provision of "serviced accommodation" (that is, the business of providing clients, who wanted office facilities on a short-term basis, with fully furnished offices with all ancillary support services such as receptionist, telephonist, typist, photocopiers, fax machines, etc.). The landlord refused on the basis that this would be detrimental to the investment value of the landlord's reversion because of the proposed use. The judge, whose decision was endorsed by the Court of Appeal, considered that any such diminution in the value of the reversion was a "paper one" only because there was no immediate prospect of that interest being sold or fully mortgaged and therefore it could not be a ground for a reasonable apprehension of damage to the landlord's property interest. A refusal of consent would cause grossly disproportionate harm to the tenant. (Cf. *Ponderosa International Development Inc v. Pengap Securities (Bristol) Ltd* [1986] 1 E.G.L.R. 66 where the landlord planned to sell the reversion in the near future and it was reasonably considered that the assignment would create an unfavourable market reaction to the value of the landlord's interest).

This principle was considered by Neuberger J. in *Blockbuster Entertainment Ltd v. Leakcliff Properties Ltd* [1997] 08 E.G. 139 where the 15-year lease (granted at a rent of £115,000 a year) contained a fully qualified covenant against sub-letting and provided that any sub-lease had to be at a market rental value to be approved by the landlord. The tenant sought consent to sub-let to Byte Computer Stores at an initial rent of £75,000 p.a., and the landlord refused. One of the grounds of objection was based on the landlord's belief that this would be damaging to the value of their reversion, which they planned to sell. The judge found that this was not justified on the evidence, which in fact indicated quite the opposite; *i.e.* that the reversion would be increased in value by the proposed sub-letting. He also rejected the landlord's argument that it was reasonable to require the tenant to postpone any sub-letting until the market improved, when a higher rent could be obtained. If permitted, this would effectively deprive the tenant of the right to sub-let for the foreseeable future.

By contrast it can be reasonable for a landlord to refuse consent to a sub-letting which provided for a high premium and a low rent, because of the potentially damaging effect of such a transaction on the value of the reversion (*Re Town Investments Ltd's Underlease* [1954] Ch. 301).

In *Straudley Investments Ltd v. Mount Eden Land Ltd* (1996) 74 P.& C.R. 306, Phillips L.J. suggested that two further propositions might be added to those set out in *International Drilling Fluids Ltd v. Louisville Investments (Uxbridge) Ltd* (above). They are, first, that it would normally be considered reasonable for a landlord to refuse consent or impose a condition if this is necessary to prevent his contractual rights under the head lease being prejudiced by the proposed assignment or sublease, and secondly that it will normally be considered unreasonable for the landlord to seek to impose a condition which would increase or enhance the control which the landlord was able to exercise under the terms of the head lease. The court therefore held in that case that it was not reasonable for the landlord to give consent to a proposed sub-letting on the condition that the sub-tenant paid a deposit (to be held in the joint names of the landlord and the head tenant) where the head tenancy did not provide for such. If permitted, it would have given the landlord a further safeguard over and above the rights which he already enjoyed to control sub-lettings.

Specifying grounds and conditions in advance

The general rule is that it is not possible to circumvent section 19(1)(a) of the Landlord and Tenant Act 1927 by specifying in the lease or elsewhere what would be a reasonable ground for refusing consent to a proposed disposition of a tenancy containing a fully qualified covenant against assignment (*Re Smith's Lease* [1951] 1 All E.R. 346, where the covenant contained a proviso that it would be deemed reasonable for the landlord to offer to take a surrender of the lease should the tenant request consent to an assignment). Landlords have therefore sought to circumvent this obstacle by a drafting device.

Pre-conditions

The device took the form of a provision that where a tenancy contains a qualified covenant against alienation and the tenant wishes to assign, he must, before seeking the licence or consent of the landlord, first offer the landlord a surrender of the lease. The main advantage to the landlord of such a precondition would seem to be to permit him, rather than the tenant, to benefit from any increase in property values which has occurred since the lease was granted. If exercised it would enable the landlord to obtain possession and re-let, possibly to the proposed assignee, at a higher rent or premium than that payable by the outgoing tenant. Whether this would be worthwhile would depend of course on what provision is made for calculating the surrender value (if any) of the tenancy, which has to be paid to the tenant for the surrender, (see *Greene v. Church Commissioners* [1974] 3 All E.R. 609, 611 *per* Lord Denning M.R.) If a landlord does permit an assignment without compelling the tenant to offer a surrender, the obligation to offer a surrender will not be enforceable against the assignee if he subsequently decides to assign unless it was protected as an estate contract under the Land Charges Act 1972 (or, if title to the land was registered under the Land Registration Act 1925, as a minor interest) when the tenancy was legally assigned (*Greene v. Church Commissioners for England*, above).

In *Bocardo SA v. S & M Hotels Ltd* [1980] 1 W.L.R. 17 it was held that such a precondition did not offend section 19(1) of the Landlord and Tenant Act 1927 because it was drafted as an independent prerequisite for the covenant against assignment to come into operation, rather than as an attempt to stipulate when a refusal of consent by the landlord would be reasonable.

The latter is generally outlawed by section 19 although, as will be seen below, it is now possible, in the case of certain qualifying tenancies granted on or after January 1, 1996, for landlord and tenant to agree on (a) the circumstances in which a landlord can withhold consent and/or (b) any conditions on which consent may be granted by the landlord (LTA 1927, s.19(1A) added by Landlord and Tenant (Covenants) Act 1995, s.22).

There is a further difficulty with offer to surrender clauses of the *Bocardo* type. This is because it has been held that if such an offer is made and accepted, the resulting contract is void under the Landlord and Tenant Act 1954 (*Allnatt Properties Ltd v. Newton* [1981] 2 All E.R. 290, Megarry V.-C. affirmed at [1984] 1 All E.R. 423, CA). In the latter case, the Court held that the contract was caught by section 38(1) of the Landlord and Tenant Act 1954, which provides that any agreement relating to a tenancy to which Part II of that Act applies (*i.e.* a business tenancy) is void in so far as it purports to preclude the tenant from making an application or request (*e.g.* for a new tenancy) under that Act. Thus if the tenant agrees to surrender his tenancy he will (arguably) be precluded from making such an application. This is an unsatisfactory decision, (a) because it ignores the fact that section 24 of the Landlord and Tenant Act 1954 permits a tenant to terminate a lease falling within Part II of the Act by surrender (see the letter at (1983) 127 S.J. 855) and (b) because it means that if, as in the *Bocardo* case, the clause requiring the tenant to offer a surrender says that the tenant can only seek permission to assign if he has made an offer which the landlord has rejected, it follows that the tenant will not be free to proceed where he has made such an offer which the landlord has accepted, despite the fact that the resulting agreement to surrender is void (see Blake [1983] Conv. 158). Thus there would be stalemate whereby neither a surrender nor an assignment would be possible.

Whilst the legal position as outlined above is still of importance in the case of tenancies granted before January 1, 1996, it must now be considered in the light of the Landlord and Tenant (Covenants) Act 1995 in the case of tenancies (known as "new tenancies") granted on or after that date. Section 22 of the 1995 Act has made important amendments to section 19 of the Landlord and Tenant Act 1927 by the addition of subsections (1A) to (1E). These additional provisions permit the landlord and tenant under a "qualifying lease" to agree as to (a) the circumstances in which the landlord may withhold his licence or consent to an assignment of the whole or part of the leased premises or (b) any conditions subject to which any such licence or consent may be granted by the landlord.

If there is such an agreement and the landlord subsequently refuses consent to an assignment on any of the grounds specified in the agreement, he is not to be regarded as unreasonably withholding consent. In like manner, if the landlord gives consent subject to one of the agreed conditions, he is not to be regarded as giving it subject to unreasonable conditions (s.19(1A)).

Any such agreement by the parties can be contained in the tenancy or be made at any other time up to the tenant's application for consent (s.19(1B)).

A qualifying lease means a new tenancy for the purposes of section 1 of the Landlord and Tenant (Covenants) Act 1995, other than a residential lease (see further Chapter 7 below). A residential lease is defined as a lease by which a building or part of a building is let wholly or mainly as a private residence (s.19(1E)). Thus a business letting of a building which is then sub-let to individual residential occupiers would still be a qualifying lease, because this would not be a letting as *a* private residence.

Protection for the tenant is provided by a stipulation that any circumstances or conditions specified in the agreement must not be framed by reference to any matter falling to be determined by the landlord or any other person (for example the landlord's agent) for the purposes of the agreement unless—

(1)   that person's power to determine that matter is required to be exercised reasonably; or

(2)   the tenant is given an unrestricted right to have the matter determined by an independent person whose identity is ascertainable from the agreement and whose decision is final (s.19(1C)).

Thus if for example the tenancy states that any proposed assignee must in the landlord's opinion be of equivalent financial standing to that of the tenant, this would be void because it provides that the power to determine whether that is the case is entirely within the landlord's discretion and there is no requirement that the discretion be exercised reasonably. On the other hand, if the agreement stated that permission to assign would not be granted by the landlord unless the proposed assignee had net profits of £x p.a. for the last three years, this would be perfectly legitimate.

The background to this provision is more fully explained elsewhere (see Chapter 7 below). For the moment we can simply observe that its inclusion in the Landlord and Tenant (Covenants) Act 1995 was the political price which the major commercial tenants' interest group (the British Retail Consortium) had to pay to obtain abolition of the privity of contract principle by that Act. Without that concession the Act would have been sabotaged at Bill stage by the British Property Federation, a powerful institutional landlords pressure group. The privity of contract principle provided that a tenant is bound by the covenants throughout the term notwithstanding an assignment and therefore liable for a breach of covenant committed by an assignee. It is now abolished by the 1995 Act in the case of qualifying leases granted on or after January 1, 1996.

Landlords feared that with the abolition of privity of contract liability they could possibly be faced with assignees of progressively weakening reliability over whose identity and economic strength they would have no effective control. If such an assignee defaulted, landlords would no longer be able to sue the original tenant whom they had chosen. Without a specific statutory power to impose conditions on assignment to preserve covenant strength, such as the provision of guarantors, or stringent financial criteria to be met by assignees, landlords feared that any attempt to do so would be struck down as in violation of section 19 as it then stood. They would then have to resort to absolute covenants against assignment to protect themselves, with the danger that in a tenant's market this would prove difficult or would have a depressing effect on the rent obtainable originally or on the subsequent operation of a rent review clause. This is why section 19 was amended as above by section 22 of the 1995 Act. That provision, which was introduced into the Bill at the eleventh hour, proved to be the most intractable in the Bill. It was printed only two days before the Committee stage in the House of Lords.

It will be appreciated that as amended, section 19 of the Landlord and Tenant Act 1927 gives landlords considerable power (at least where market circumstances are favourable to them) to impose onerous conditions, including the need for a guarantor, rent deposits and financial guarantees by the assignees. Of course landlords will need to avoid making these requirements so onerous that in substance the qualified covenant against disposition becomes an absolute covenant, with adverse consequences on rent review and the possibility that tenants will seek to sub-let instead because a qualified covenant against sub-letting is not affected by the amendments to section 19. (For a critique of the recommended draft assignment clauses published by the Association of British Insurers for the benefit of institutional landlords, see D.Sands [1996] E.G. 51 and for an examination of post-1995 Act practice see S. Fogel (Blundell Memorial Lectures) [1996] E.G. 64. These lectures suggest that in practice, landlords tend to opt for a simple assignment regime designed to ensure that the assignee is in the reasonable opinion of the landlord of sufficient financial standing and that the assignor give an authorised guarantee agreement guaranteeing the performance of covenants in the tenancy by the assignor's immediate assignee: (see p.180 below for authorised guarantee agreements). See further R.Porter and J.Vivian [1996] E.G. 154. For a more critical view suggesting that in practice tenants have suffered badly (through onerous alienation covenants) as a result of an Act originally designed to help them, G. Acheson see [1997] 03 E.G. 132.

It has been argued that offers to surrender agreements made after 1995 will be caught by the anti-avoidance provision in section 25 LTCA 1995 (Fancourt *Enforceability of Landlord and Tenants Covenants*, 1997, p.256).

SPECIAL STATUTORY REGIMES

The general rules governing alienation of leases are subject to a number of special statutory schemes which apply to particular types of tenancy. These are examined below.

1. Rent Act 1977

Effect of assignment and sub-letting

(a) **Protected tenancy** A protected tenant can lawfully assign or sub-let the whole or part of the premises in the same way as any other contractual tenancy, unless of course the relevant transaction is prohibited by the terms of the lease (see above). An unlawful assignment will be a breach of covenant (unless waived) and may give rise to possession proceedings on the basis of the discretionary ground for possession in the Rent Act 1977, Sched. 15, case 1 (see p.275 below).

Furthermore, even if the assignment is not in breach of covenant, case 6 provides a discretionary ground for possession where the tenant has since December 8, 1965 (or certain other dates for tenancies which became regulated by legislation subsequent to the Rent Act 1965) assigned the whole of the dwelling-house, (or sub-let part, the remainder having already been sub-let), without the consent of the landlord (see, *e.g. Regional Properties Co. Ltd v. Frankenschwerth* [1951] 1 All E.R. 178, CA). It should be noted though that, because in these circumstances the assignment (or sub-letting) will not have been in breach of covenant, the landlord will need to be able independently to determine the contractual tenancy before seeking possession of the dwelling-house. If it has become a statutory tenancy, however, this will not be necessary and the landlord will be able to rely on the assignment during the contractual term (see *Leith Properties v. Springer* [1982] 3 All E.R. 731 and *Pazgate Ltd v. McGrath* (1984) 272 E.G. 1069, CA).

(b) **Statutory tenancy** If a statutory tenant purports to assign or sub-let the whole dwelling-house and goes out of occupation the tenancy will cease to be a statutory tenancy because the tenant will no longer be occupying the dwelling-house as a residence for the purposes of Rent Act 1977, s.2. On the other hand, a lawful sub-letting of part may be possible without the tenant losing his status as a statutory tenant. (See below for the position of the sub-tenant).

Furthermore, the Rent Act 1977, s.3(5) and Sched. 1, Part II, expressly permits a transmission of the statutory tenancy *inter vivos* in certain circumstances whereby the transferee will become the statutory tenant.

(c) **Protection of sub-tenants** Where the sub-landlord is a protected or statutory tenant and that tenancy comes to an end (for whatever reason), the sub-tenant will then be deemed to hold as a tenant directly of the head landlord as if the tenant's statutorily protected tenancy (whether it be contractual or statutory) had continued (Rent Act 1977, s.137(2)(4)). Thus the sub-tenant will replace the tenant on the same terms under which the latter formerly held. A possession order against the tenant will not give the landlord an automatic right to recover possession as against the sub-tenant (s.137(1)). However, if the sub-letting, albeit not in breach of covenant, did not have the landlord's consent then case 6 (above) can be used not only against the tenant but also the sub-tenant. Otherwise it would in practice be useless to landlords (*Leith Properties Ltd v. Byrne* [1983] Q.B. 433).

2. Housing Act 1988 Assured tenancies

(a) **Assignment, etc. of assured tenancies.** It is an implied term of every assured tenancy which is a *statutory* periodic tenancy that, except with the consent of the landlord, the tenant shall not—

- (a)   assign the tenancy in whole or in part; or
- (b)   sub-let or part with possession of the whole or any part of the dwelling-house let on the tenancy (s.15(1)).

Section 19 of the Landlord and Tenant Act 1927 (which provides that in the case of a qualified covenant against alienation the landlord's consent shall not be unreasonably withheld; see above) does not apply to such an implied term (s.15(2)). Thus consent can be withheld on any ground, whether reasonable or not.

The same implied term also applies (a) to a *contractual* (*i.e.* not statutory) assured periodic tenancy which does not expressly make provision permitting or prohibiting assignment, etc. and (b) in the unusual circumstances of the tenancy providing for a premium to be payable on the grant or renewal of the tenancy (s.15(1)(3)). Thus a contractual assured periodic tenancy can make its own provision for assignment etc., otherwise the statutory implied term will apply.

A fixed-term assured tenancy will be subject to the same rules as any other fixed-term tenancy (see above).

(b) Sub-tenancies

If an assured tenant has lawfully created a sub-tenancy and the head tenancy subsequently comes to an end the sub-tenant will thereafter hold directly of the landlord on an assured tenancy provided his new landlord is not disqualified from being a landlord under an assured tenancy (s.18).

3. Housing Act 1985 Secure tenancies

(a) **Assignment** The general rule is that a secure tenancy which is either a periodic tenancy or a fixed-term tenancy created on or after November 5, 1982 is not capable of being assigned (Housing Act 1985, s.91(1)) except in one of the three exceptional cases set out below.

Furthermore, although a fixed-term tenancy created before November 5, 1982 can be assigned, this will result in permanent loss of secure status save in one of those three exceptional cases (s.91(2))—the cases are;

(1)   an assignment by exchange under section 92;
(2)   an assignment in pursuance of a court order under section 24 of the Matrimonial Causes Act 1973;
(3)   an assignment to a potential statutory successor on death (s.91(3)).

In each exceptional case, therefore, the assignment is perfectly effective and the assignee can become a secure tenant even if there is an absolute prohibition on assignment in the tenancy (*Governors of the Peabody Donation Fund v. Higgins* [1983] 1 W.L.R. 1091. But see section 84 and Ground 1 of schedule 2 for recovery of possession by the landlord - **cross ref**).

The right to exchange in section 92 provides that a secure tenant may exchange his or her tenancy with another secure tenant with the written consent of their landlord(s), such consent not to be unreasonably withheld except on one of the grounds set out in Schedule 3 (s.92(1)(2)). The landlord can only rely on such a ground where he has notified the tenant of the ground and the relevant particulars within 42 days of the tenant's application for consent (s.92(4)). If consent is withheld on any other ground, it is deemed to have been granted (s.92(3)).

The landlord can give consent conditionally where there are rent arrears or there is some other outstanding breach of covenant or obligation of the tenancy. The condition is that the tenant pay the outstanding arrears or rectify the breach, as the case may be (s.92(5)). Any other condition is to be disregarded (s.92(6)).

Thus secure tenants can exchange even if they have different landlords. Exchange may also take place with an assured tenant whose landlord is a registered housing association (or the Housing Corporation, Housing For Wales or a charitable housing trust)(s.92(2A)).

Whether a court will exercise its powers under MCA 1973, s.24 will probably depend on the attitude of the local authority especially if there is a prohibition on assignment in the tenancy agreement (*Thompson v. Thompson* [1976] Fam. 25). The court also has power to transfer a secure tenancy under Family Law Act 1996, Sched. 7.

(b) Sub-letting Section 93(1) provides that it is a term of every secure tenancy that the tenant (a) may take in lodgers (see, *e.g. Monmouth BC v. Marlog* (1994) 27 H.L.R. 30, CA p.10 above) but (b) may not, without the written consent of the landlord sub-let or part with possession of part of the dwelling-house. (Note that the Landlord and Tenant Act 1988 (above) does not apply to a secure tenancy).

Consent to a sub-letting (which may be given retrospectively: s.94(4)) must not be unreasonably withheld (and if unreasonably withheld is to be treated as given: s.94(2)). The onus is on the landlord to show that consent was withheld reasonably (s.94(2)). Conditional consent is not permitted and if conditions are imposed is to be treated as given and the conditions can be ignored (s.95(5)).

A failure to respond to a request for consent within a reasonable time is to be taken as a refusal of consent (s.94(6)(b)). If consent is requested in writing the landlord must give written reasons to the tenant where consent is refused (s.94(6)(a)).

If the secure tenant parts with possession, or sub-lets the whole (including sub-letting part and then the remainder), the tenancy ceases to be a secure tenancy and cannot become a secure tenancy again (s.93(2)). This would permit the landlord to end the tenancy by a notice to quit.

A tenancy which ceases to be secure because the tenant condition in section 81 (occupation by the tenant) ceases to be satisfied remains subject to the restrictions in sections 91 and 93 above.

Chapter 5

HARASSMENT AND UNLAWFUL EVICTION

Introduction

Despite the legal rules governing the termination of residential tenancies, a small minority of landlords will always be tempted to resort to self-help measures in order to persuade tenants or other occupiers to leave the premises which they occupy. Such conduct will of course frequently give rise to a civil cause of action for breach of contract. Peremptory eviction or harassment of tenants will usually constitute a breach of the covenant for quiet enjoyment which is implied into all leases, if not expressly included (see p.37 above). This will entitle the tenant victim to claim damages and/or an injunction. The landlord's conduct might also give rise at common law to liability in tort (such as trespass to land or interference with goods or even nuisance where the landlord is operating from neighbouring property). Quite apart from any civil liability which the landlord might incur, his conduct could also amount to a crime, such as assault, for which he could be prosecuted in the criminal courts. But the criminal law has gone even further since 1964 when, following the Rachman scandal of the early 1960s (see p.192 below) the newly elected Labour Government came into office pledged to strengthen the position of the unlawfully evicted or harassed residential occupier. The Government acted swiftly and introduced the temporary Protection From Eviction Act 1964. This was soon replaced by the Rent Act 1965 which, as will be seen, (Chapter 8 below) reimposed controls on residential tenancies by way of rent regulation and security of tenure, thereby increasing the temptation for landlords and others to resort to unlawful measures of eviction in order to recover possession and sell. Part III of the Rent Act 1965 accordingly created new criminal offences of unlawful eviction and harassment of residential occupiers. The relevant provisions were later consolidated in the Protection From Eviction Act (PEA) 1977 which was itself the subject of important amendments by the Housing Act 1988. (As will be seen below, the 1988 Act also extended the range of civil remedies by creating a new statutory tort of unlawful eviction). The changes brought about by the 1988 Act were prompted by a fear that some landlords would otherwise be tempted to evict Rent Act protected tenants who enjoyed a fair rent in order to re-let at market rents on assured shorthold tenancies under the 1988 Act (see p.198 below).

Quite apart from the offences contained in the Protection from Eviction Act 1977, the Criminal Law Act 1977, s.6, makes it an offence for any person, without lawful authority, to use or threaten violence for the purpose of securing entry into any premises for himself or for any other person provided that there is someone present on the premises who is opposed to the entry and the person using or threatening violence knows that to be the case. The violence can be directed towards either the property or the person. The maximum penalty on conviction is a fine not exceeding £5,000 or six months' imprisonment or both (Criminal Justice Act 1982, s.37). The reference to lawful authority is designed to protect from liability persons such as a court officer who evicts an occupier by executing a warrant for possession issued by the court.

Although the possibility of tough criminal penalties will be a deterrent to some landlords who would otherwise be minded to take the law into their own hands, its limits are well recognised. Indeed one major problem is that many landlords are unaware that their conduct is criminal. They often believe that it is legitimate to resort to some of the strategies which are in fact outlawed, usually because there has been a breach of covenant by the occupier (*e.g.* non-payment of rent or nuisance or annoyance). This is particularly so in those cases where a landlord and a tenant are living in close proximity in the same building. (Indeed it is of interest to note that in such cases the occupier will have little or no security of tenure (see below) and could be legitimately removed relatively quickly, although for some landlords this is not quick enough, given the need to go to court and the possibility of delayed possession orders. (See further Rauta and Pickering, *Private Renting in England 1990*, (1992), Table 7.12.)

The tenancy relations officers employed by local authorities to investigate allegations of unlawful conduct by landlords and others are only too aware of the fact that the merits are not always on one side. They frequently seek to conciliate the parties with a view to achieving an agreed resolution of the problem, rather than bringing the full weight of the criminal law to bear on the alleged offender. In serious cases they will prosecute, although this outcome is sometimes affected by diminishing financial resources. Local authorities are empowered to prosecute by PEA 1977, s.6.

The table below shows the number of defendants prosecuted at the magistrates courts and convicted at all courts under the Protection from Eviction Act 1977 (Home Office).

England and Wales
Unlawful eviction
(Section 1(2) Protection from Eviction Act 1977))

	Prosecutions	Convictions
1992	131	77
1993	123	48
1994	99	61
1995	87	45
1996	66	31

Unlawful harassment
(Section 1(3) Protection from Eviction Act 1977)

	Prosecutions	Convictions
1992	88	37
1993	67	36
1994	68	45
1995	62	32
1996	53	23

It seems quite clear from the statistical evidence that few cases of alleged unlawful eviction and/or harassment proceed to trial, and only approximately 50 per cent of those result in a conviction. Furthermore, the number of prosections and convictions is falling, year on year.

There is a widespread belief amongst those critical of the efficacy of the criminal justice system in this area, that when the police become involved in landlord and tenant disputes they do not treat it with sufficient seriousness. They will only prosecute where the conduct complained of amounts to some offence under the criminal law other than those created by the Protection from Eviction Act 1977. Rebuke has also often been levelled at the courts, particularly magistrates' courts, for imposing derisory penalties on convicted offenders. Indeed as long ago as 1971 it was observed by the Francis Committee (*Report of the Committee on the Rent Acts*, Cmnd.4609) that there was—

> "a residue of offences committed by landlords who know or suspect that they are breaking the law and who are undeterred by warnings. This is the group most likely to commit the true 'Rachmanite' offence of harassment and illegal eviction for gain, and it is also unfortunately the group perhaps least likely to be deterred by prosecution while sentences remain light. (p.105.)"

Researchers who have investigated the role of the criminal law in this area go so far as to suggest that the penalties imposed send a message out to landlords that "crime can pay". (See, e.g. Jew, *Law and Order in Private Rented Housing: Tackling Harassment and Unlawful Eviction* (Campaign for Bedsit Rights, 1994) quoted in Bright and Gilbert, *Landlord and Tenant Law, The Nature of Tenancies* (OUP, 1995). See Bright and Gilbert (*op. cit.*) p.625–629 for a discussion of research findings on the operation of the criminal law governing harassment and unlawful eviction.)

It seems hard to deny from the research evidence available that there is considerable force in the view that the criminal law is a poor deterrent to a determined landlord. By contrast, the enactment of a statutory tort of unlawful eviction where damages are measured by the profits to be gained by the landlord is potentially a much more powerful deterrent, at least in those cases where the conduct complained of goes so far as to amount to an unlawful eviction. The relevant provisions of the criminal and civil law governing unlawful eviction and harassment are dealt with below, but it is first necessary to examine the circumstances in which a court order is needed for a landlord to be able to recover possession of his property lawfully from a residential occupier.

Need for a court order to recover possession

(a) Tenants protected by special regimes

The general rule is that unless prohibited by statute, a landlord can recover possession without the need for a court order. However, most residential tenants are governed by one of the special statutory codes examined elsewhere in this book which afford the tenant a greater or lesser degree of security of tenure, depending on the code (see Chapters 8–11 below). Thus, a landlord cannot recover possession of premises let on a protected or statutory tenancy under the Rent Act 1977 without obtaining a court order, having first established a ground for possession under Schedule 15 to that Act (see p.273 below). The same need for a court order applies in the case of an assured tenancy, whether shorthold or not, under the Housing Act 1988 (s.5) and a secure tenancy under the Housing Act 1985 (s.82(1)).

(b) Other tenancies and licences

In the case of certain other tenancies and licences which are not protected by one of those regimes, it will similarly be necessary for the landlord to bring court proceedings in order to recover possession if an occupier refuses to leave when the tenancy or licence comes to an end.

Section 3(1) of the Protection from Eviction Act 1977 provides that where any premises have been let as a dwelling under a tenancy which has come to an end and the occupier continues to reside in the premises, or part of them, it is unlawful for the owner to enforce against the occupier, other than by proceedings in court, his right to recover possession of the premises. A landlord who enforces his right in some other way runs the risk of incurring civil or criminal liability (see below).

The term "occupier" is widely defined to mean any person lawfully residing in the premises or part of them at the termination of the former tenancy (s.3(2)). Thus it covers not only tenants, and family members but also sub-tenants or indeed anyone else lawfully living there. Unlawful occupiers are not covered (*e.g.* a lodger where the tenancy prohibits the taking of lodgers).

Section 3 not only applies to tenancies but also to—

(1) a licence, created on or after November 28, 1980, which amounts to a restricted contract (s.3(2A)). (There are very few restricted contracts in existence today because the Housing Act 1988 prohibited the creation of new restricted contracts on or after January 15, 1989 and most of those created before that date have since come to an end (see p.301 below);

(2) any premises occupied as a dwelling under any other licence, other than an "excluded licence" (see below) whenever it was created (s.3(2)(B)).

Furthermore, it is provided that a person who, under the terms of his employment, had exclusive possession of any premises other than as a tenant shall be deemed to have been a tenant (s.8(2)). Thus service occupiers (*i.e.* licensees) are included. (See, *e.g. Warder v. Cooper* [1970] Ch. 495 where Stamp J. held that a failure to comply with section 3 would incur liability in tort for breach of statutory duty).

(c) Statutorily protected tenancies excluded

It should be noted that section 3 does not apply to two classes of tenancy or licence. The first is what is referred to as a "statutorily protected " tenancy. Such a tenancy is not covered by section 3 because as we have seen above it will have the benefit of one of the separate statutory codes of protection which prevent the landlord from lawfully recovering possession without the benefit of a court order. This category comprises—

(1) A protected tenancy within the meaning of the Rent Act 1977 (see Chapter 10 below) or a tenancy to which Part I of the Landlord and Tenant Act 1954 applies; (the latter governs certain long tenancies at a low rent created before January 15, 1989 - see Chapter 12 below). From January 1, 1999 such tenancies will be governed by the Local Government and Housing Act 1989 (see (7) below).

It is of interest to note that, for whatever reason, the definition does not extend to a statutory tenancy, nor indeed to a secure tenancy under the Housing Act 1985. Section 3 will thus apply in such cases. In *Haniff v. Robinson* [1993] 1 All E.R. 185, CA a statutory tenancy was ended by a court order, against which the tenant appealed. Despite knowing this the landlord went ahead and applied for execution. But, rather than wait for possession to be recovered by the bailiff the landlord forcibly ejected the tenant on Christmas Eve. The tenant's appeal to set aside the possession order was successful. Furthermore, because she remained protected by the Protection from Eviction Act, s.3, the landlord had committed the tort of unlawful eviction under the Housing Act 1988, s.27 (see p.110 below).

(2) A protected occupancy or statutory tenancy as defined in the Rent (Agriculture) Act 1976 (*i.e.* agricultural workers, or former agricultural workers occupying under a service licence, who are protected by a regime analogous to that applicable to protected or statutory tenants under the Rent Act 1977).

(3) A tenancy to which Part II of the Landlord and Tenant Act 1954 applies (*i.e.* certain business tenancies (see Chapter 13 below).

(4) A farm business tenancy within the meaning of the Agricultural Tenancies Act 1985,

(5) A tenancy of an agricultural holding governed by the Agricultural Holdings Act 1986.

(6) An assured tenancy or assured agricultural occupancy under Part I of the Housing Act 1988 (see Chapter 9 below).

(7) A tenancy to which Schedule 10 to the Local Government and Housing Act 1989 applies (*i.e.* certain long tenancies at a low rent granted on or after January 15, 1989, or such tenancies granted before that date which are still in existence on January 1, 1999 (see Chapter 12 below).

(d) Excluded tenancies and licences

The second category of tenancies and licences to which section 3 does not apply are referred to as "excluded tenancies and licences". These exceptions were introduced by the Housing Act 1988 (s.31). They comprise—

(1) Tenancies or licences where a resident landlord/licensor shared accommodation with the tenant/licensee at the end of the tenancy; provided that immediately before the tenancy/licence began the landlord/licensor occupied as his only or principal home premises of which the whole or part of the shared accommodation formed part. For this purpose "shared accommodation" does not include areas used for storage, nor a staircase, passage, corridor or other means of access. Presumably sharing a WC would suffice. (*Cf.* Rent Act 1977, ss. 21, 22 and Housing Act 1988, s.3.) The rationale would seem to be to exclude arrangements where the parties have lived in close proximity to each other. It is the same rationale which motivated the resident landlord exceptions to assured tenancy status under Part I of the Housing Act 1988 and protected tenancy status under the Rent Act 1977 (see pp.219 and 257 below).
The same rule applies where the sharing is with a member of the landlord/licensor's family, who satisfies the same conditions, provided the landlord/licensor also occupied as his only or principal home premises in the same building as the shared accommodation and that building is not a purpose-built block of flats (as defined in Part III Sched. 1 Housing Act 1988).

(2) A tenancy or licence granted as a temporary expedient to a person who had entered the premises in question as a trespasser.

(3) A tenancy or licence granted for the purposes only of a holiday.

(4) A gratuitous tenancy or licence.

(5) A licence to occupy a hostel provided by a local authority or certain other specified public or publicly funded bodies (including a housing association). Occupiers of such accommodation are unlikely to be tenants—*Westminster City Council v. Clarke* [1992] 2 A.C. 288 see p. 309 below). Furthermore, in *Mohamed v. Manek and the Royal Borough of Kensington & Chelsea* (1995) 27 H.L.R. 439, CA it was held that an occupier of hotel or hostel accommodation under a temporary licence, granted whilst the local authority made enquiries as to the licensee's statutory

entitlement to accommodation as a homeless person, could not be said to "occupy a dwelling under a licence" for the purposes of section 3 and therefore the issue of the present exclusion did not arise in that case. It did not matter for this purpose whether the accommodation was provided directly by the local authority or as in that case via a third party. The court considered that such provision of accommodation was not intended to be governed by section 3.

It can be seen from the above that to be an excluded tenancy, and therefore outside the ambit of section 3, the tenancy must have been entered into on or after January 15, 1989 unless in pursuance of a contract entered into before that date. But, if a tenancy was created before January 15, 1989 and the terms are varied on or after that date so as to affect the rent payable, a new post-1988 Act tenancy will be deemed to have been entered into. By contrast the retrospective extension of the protection of section 3 to all licences (whether created before or after November 28, 1980) from January 15, 1989, does not apply to an excluded licence whenever it was created.

Forfeiture proceedings

Section 2 of the Protection from Eviction Act 1977 provides that where premises are let as a dwelling on a tenancy which is subject to a right of re-entry or forfeiture, it is unlawful to enforce that right other then by proceedings in court while any person is lawfully residing in the premises or part of them. (see p.136 below for forfeiture by peaceable re-entry)

Offences of unlawful eviction and harassment

(a) General

Section 1 of the Protection from Eviction Act creates three criminal offences in connection with the unlawful eviction and/or harassment of a "residential occupier" of any premises. The maximum penalties for conviction of an offence under section 1 are on summary conviction a fine not exceeding £5,000 or imprisonment for a term of six months or both and on conviction on indictment to a fine (unlimited) or to imprisonment for a term not exceeding two years or both (PEA 1977, s.1(4)). As we have seen above, it is rare for the maximum penalties to be imposed on convicted offenders, although reported cases show that in serious cases imprisonment will be appropriate. (See for example *R. v. Brennan and Brennan* [1979] Crim. L.R. 603 where a sentence of three months' imprisonment was imposed on a landlord who used the services "of a very large man and an alsatian dog" to evict unlawfully a group of students). Although seemingly rarely used, the criminal court also has power on conviction of an offender to make compensatory awards up to a maximum of £5,000 (Powers of Criminal Courts Act 1973, s.35). An example of this remedy is *R. v. Bokhari* (1974) 59 Cr. App. R. 303 where the landlord was sent to prison for two years and was ordered to pay £1,600 compensation to the tenant. A compensatory award may be given as an alternative to the imposition of a fine. Furthermore if an award is made, it will be deducted from any damages (in respect of the same loss) that are subsequently awarded in any civil proceedings (Powers of Criminal Courts Act 1973, s.38). This would not prevent recovery of other damages representing other types of loss (*e.g.* stress, loss of the right to occupy, etc., as to which see below). It has been suggested that in practice, exercise of the power is likely to be restricted to such losses as the cost of emergency accommodation or the value of damaged or destroyed belongings (Arden and Partington, *Quiet Enjoyment* (4th ed.), p.93).

(b) Residential occupier

For the purposes of the section 1 offences, "residential occupier" is defined as—

"a person occupying the premises as a residence , whether under a contract or by virtue of any enactment or rule of law giving him the right to remain in occupation or restricting the right of any other person to recover possession of the premises (s.1(2))."

The wide terms of this definition make it clear that these provisions cover a wide range of occupiers, including—

(1) tenants who are protected by one of the statutory regimes which requires a court order for the recovery of possession by the landlord. They will thus extend, *inter alia*, to protected or statutory tenants under the Rent Act 1977 and assured tenants (including assured shorthold tenants) under the Housing Act 1988.

(2) Unprotected tenants (but not an unprotected tenant who had an excluded tenancy (see above) granted on or after January 15, 1989 which has come to an end).

(3) Contractual licensees (including an ex-licensee who has remained in occupation if that person's licence was not an excluded licence for the purposes of section 3 of the PEA 1977). In the case of the latter this is because section 3 stipulates that a court order is required to obtain possession from the occupier (see above). An ex-licensee under an excluded licence becomes a trespasser on termination of the licence and is thus excluded from being a "residential occupier" for the purposes of the PEA 1977 (see *R. v. Blankley* [1979] Crim. L.R. 166).

(c) Unlawful eviction

The first offence created by section 1 of the PEA 1977 is that of unlawful eviction. It is committed where any person unlawfully deprives the residential occupier of any premises of his occupation of the premises, or any part thereof, or attempts to do so unless he proves that he believed, and had reasonable cause to believe, that the residential occupier had ceased to reside in the premises (s.1(2)).

We have seen above, that as a general rule it is unlawful to recover possession from a residential occupier other than under a court order (ss. 2 and 3). Thus the use of self-help is likely to amount to an offence under section 1, although it has been held that the acts in question, while not limited to a permanent deprivation of occupation, must be in the nature of an eviction. Thus an offence under s.1(2) was held not to have been committed in *R. v. Yuthiwattana* (1985) 80 Cr. App. R. 55 where the occupier was deprived of occupation for a day and a night by the landlord's refusal to replace a missing door key.

"Premises" is a wide term and may consist of a single room (*Thurrock DC v. Shina* (1972) 23 P. & C.R. 205, DC) or a fixed caravan (*Norton v. Knowles* [1969] 1 Q.B. 572).

Problems can arise as to when a deprivation actually takes place. In *R. v. Davidson-Acres* [1980] Crim. L.R. 50, CA a couple occupied a flat in the defendant landlord's house. While they were away for a short period the landlord changed the locks on the front door and when the tenants returned after 10 days he refused them entry. The landlord relied on the "reasonable belief" defence (see above). But is it crucial that he holds this belief at the time of the acts in question or when the occupiers are effectively deprived (*i.e.* on their return)? The Court of Appeal held that this was a decision for the jury and not the judge.

(d) Harassment with intent

The first offence of harassment is created by PEA 1977, s.1(3) and is committed—

"If any person with intent to cause the residential occupier of any premises—"

(a)   to give up the occupation of the premises or any part thereof; or
(b)   to refrain from exercising any right or pursuing any remedy in respect of the premises or part thereof:

does acts likely to interfere with the peace or comfort of the residential occupier or members of his household, or persistently withdraws or withholds services reasonably required for the occupation of the premises as a residence, he shall be guilty of an offence."

It should be noted seen that the substitution of the word "likely" for the original "calculated" (by the Housing Act 1988, s.29(1)) was designed to make it easier to secure a conviction.

The acts in question do not have to be in breach of the occupier's rights in civil law. Thus in *R. v. Burke* [1991] 1 A.C. 135 the landlord's conviction of an offence under section 1(3) was upheld by the House of Lords. The landlord had prevented the tenants using the lavatories nearest their rooms by padlocking the door, and had disconnected the front door bell. The court held that the conduct of the landlord, although not a breach of contract, was still criminal if done with intent to cause the tenants to leave. (Lord Griffiths pointed out that the offence can be committed by anyone, not just the landlord and therefore a contractual relationship cannot be essential). See also *R. v. Yuthiwattana* (above) where the landlord's failure to replace the occupier's lost key was held to be an offence under section 1(3)). In *Westminster City Council v. Peart* (1968) 19 P.& C.R. 737 the question of whether a failure by the landlord to pay bills leading to the cutting off of the supply of utilities to the tenant's premises can amount to the offence of harassment under section 1(3) was left open (see also *McCall v. Abelesz* [1976] Q.B. 585).

Although no statutory defence is provided, the mens rea of the defendant must be established. The offence is not one of strict liability. Thus if the defendant argues that he honestly believed that the person harassed was not a residential occupier this will need to be disproved by the prosecution. (See *R. v. Pekhoo* [1981] 3 All E.R. 84, where the conviction of the defendant who threatened harm to two men whom he believed to be squatters was quashed).

(e) Non-intentional harassment

A second offence of harassment, which was created by an amendment introduced by the Housing Act 1988, is similar to the first save that it does not require proof of specific intent, that a defence of "reasonable grounds" is available and that it can only be committed by the landlord or an agent of the landlord of a residential occupier. (By contrast the offence under section 1(3) (above) can be committed by "any person"). Section 1(3A) thus provides that a landlord or agent is guilty of an offence if—

(a)   he does acts likely to interfere with the peace or comfort of the residential occupier or members of his household; or
(b)   persistently withdraws or withholds services reasonably required for the occupation of the premises in question as a residence

and (in either case) he knows or has reasonable cause to believe that the conduct is likely to cause the residential occupier to give up the occupation of the whole or part of the premises or to refrain from exercising any right or pursuing any remedy in respect of the whole or part of the premises. (s.1(3A).)" A person is not guilty of this offence if he proves that he had reasonable grounds for doing the acts or withdrawing the services in question (s.1(3B)).

Civil remedies

(a) General

Although the above provisions in the PEA 1977 create criminal offences, they do not prejudice any liability or remedy to which a person guilty of an offence may be subject in civil proceedings. Thus the offending conduct will not only be a criminal offence but can also form the basis of a civil action for damages and or an injunction. The basis of such an action will usually be for breach of a covenant or other obligation under the tenancy (*e.g.* the covenant for quiet enjoyment or the obligation of the landlord not to derogate from his grant) or, where appropriate, in tort (*e.g.* trespass or nuisance).

Furthermore, although in *Warder v. Cooper* [1970] Ch. 495 breach of section 3 was sufficient to give rise to an action in tort for breach of statutory duty, thereby enabling the evicted occupier to be reinstated by way of an injunction, the Court of Appeal held in *McCall v. Abelesz* [1976] Q.B. 585 that the mere fact that a criminal offence is committed under PEA 1977, s.1 does not of itself afford the victim a remedy in tort for breach of statutory duty. (In that particular case the landlord had failed to pay utility bills which were outstanding when he bought the property, with the result that the gas supply was turned off by the gas board. Electricity and water supplies were also cut off). A civil remedy will thus need to be sought elsewhere either by way of an action for breach of contract or in tort or both. The nature of any claim and the remedy sought will depend on all the circumstances. A victim who wishes to bring a civil action must choose his cause of action carefully, depending on a host of factors. Each of the principal civil causes of action will be examined in turn.

(b) Breach of the covenant for quiet enjoyment

This is a covenant, which if not express, is implied into all tenancies. Its effect is that the landlord covenants that the tenant shall have the property unfettered by the assertion of any right, by the landlord or by persons claiming through or under the landlord, which interferes with its ordinary and lawful enjoyment (see p.37 above).

The remedy is damages for breach of contract. However, exemplary damages cannot be awarded if the conduct complained of amounts solely to a breach of this covenant and does not also involve commission of a tort. The limitations of this remedy are revealed by a number of well known cases where, despite despicable behaviour on the part of the landlord, only negligible compensation was recovered by the victim (although an injunction was also obtained).

In *Kenny v. Preen* [1963] 1 Q.B. 499 the plaintiff tenant established a breach of covenant when the landlord, who had served a defective notice to quit on the tenant, sought to persuade her to leave, despite her legal right to remain, by a number of acts of intimidation. These included banging on her door and shouting threats at her, sending offensive letters and threatening to evict her and throw her goods out on to the street. Nevertheless, because she had not suffered any actual pecuniary or material damage she was awarded only nominal damages of £2. A similar outcome occurred in *Perera v. Vandiyar* [1953] 1 W.L.R. 672 where, with the intention of persuading the tenant to leave, the landlord turned off the supply of gas and electricity to the premises. Following two days of discomfort, the tenant was forced to leave for five days before returning after the supplies were restored following an interlocutory injunction granted by the county court. The tenant sued for breach of the covenant for quiet enjoyment and the landlord was ordered to pay special damages of £3.50 and general damages, for discomfort, of £25. The Court of Appeal overturned an award of exemplary damages by the judge, on the basis that no tort was established.

Furthermore, damages are not in general recoverable in contract for distress by way of injury to feelings suffered by the victim (*Addis v. Gramophone Co. Ltd* [1909] A.C. 488). Only in exceptional cases are such damages recoverable in contract. One such instance is where the contract in question is one the purpose of which is to provide pleasure, relaxation, peace of mind or freedom from molestation. (See, *e.g. Jarvis v. Swann's Tours* [1973] Q.B. 233 (breach of a contract to provide a better holiday than that provided) and *Heywood v. Wellers* [1976] Q.B. 446 where solicitors, in breach of their contractual duty of care, failed to gain an injunction for the plaintiff client to stop molestation by her former boyfriend). In *Branchett v. Beaney* [1992] 3 All E.R. 910 the Court of Appeal held that a contract of tenancy is not in that exceptional category of cases where damages can be recovered for injury to feelings.

Thus the remedy by way of an action on the covenant for quiet enjoyment suffers from a number of defects, not the least of which is that such an action precludes a claim for damages for injured feelings. Such a claim must be based in tort, where the courts have traditionally been more sympathetic to claims by plaintiffs who allege that they have suffered mental distress and injury to feelings. Liability in tort is therefore examined below. (It should be noted that the Law Commission has recommended that statute should provide that aggravated damages be confined to cases of compensation for mental distress and that the expression "aggravated damages" should be replaced by "damages for mental distress" (Law Com. No. 247 "Aggravated, Exemplary and Restitutionary Damages" 1997)).

(c) Action in tort at common law

Before examining these cases it is necessary to distinguish between exemplary and aggravated damages, although the courts do not always make this distinction. Exemplary (or punitive) damages are damages awarded to punish the defendant for his wrongful conduct. On the other hand, aggravated damages are, in the words of the Law Commission, damages which "compensate the victim of a wrong for mental distress (or 'injury to feelings') in circumstances in which that injury has been caused or increased by the manner in which the defendant committed the wrong, or by the defendant's conduct subsequent to the wrong" (Law Com. No. 247 "Aggravated, Exemplary and Restitutionary Damages" (1997). This would not seem to prevent an award of general damages being made to compensate for distress and inconvenience where, for example, exemplary or aggravated damages are not sought, for whatever reason. (See *Millington v. Duffy* (1984) 17 H.L.R. 232).

It is a controversial issue as to whether exemplary damages are a proper function of the law of tort, whose primary aim is to compensate plaintiffs and not to punish defendants. Nevertheless there is authority which supports the award of exemplary damages in tort claims based on an unlawful eviction. Before examining that law it can be observed that if a court is minded to award exemplary damages in tort any fine that might have been levied on the defendant in earlier criminal proceedings should be taken into account (*Ashgar v. Ahmed* (1985) 17 H.L.R. 25). (See also the Powers of Criminal Courts Act 1973, s.38 (above) with regard to the need for a court to set off a compensation award under that Act against damages awarded by the court in subsequent civil proceedings).

In *Drane v. Evangelou* [1978] 1 W.L.R. 455 the Court of Appeal upheld an award of £1,000 by way of exemplary damages for the tort of trespass where the tenant had been unlawfully evicted by the landlord, whose associates had changed the locks on the premises and thrown the tenant's belongings out into the street. (The landlord's conduct appeared to have been in retaliation for a successful application by the tenant for registration by the rent officer of a fair rent that was lower than the contractual rent. See p.288 below for fair rent regulation). The tenant only regained possession 10 weeks later after a series of court hearings. The Court observed that the landlord was motivated to gain a benefit at the expense of the tenant. This was a category of case where it was still possible to have an award of exemplary damages in tort. The Court cited in support Lord Devlin's statement in *Rookes v. Barnard* [1964] A.C. 1129 at 1227 that "exemplary damages can be awarded whenever it is necessary to teach a wrongdoer that tort does not pay." Goff and Lawton L.J. J. also made the point that the award could also be justified in whole or in part on the basis of a claim for aggravated damages—

> "It seems to me that my task here is to look at the facts and to start by asking the question what sort of sum would it have been proper to award for aggravated damages in this case, which was undoubtedly one for aggravated damages. . .. To deprive a man of a roof over his head is, in my judgment, one of the worst torts which can be committed. It causes stress, worry and anxiety. It brings the law into disrepute if people like the landlord can act with impunity in the way that he did. . .If ever there was a case where a landlord like this landlord should be taught a lesson, it is this case." ([1978] 1 W.L.R. 455 at 461 *Per* Lawton L.J.)."

The decision was followed in *Guppy's (Bridport) Ltd v. Brookling* (1983) 14 H.L.R. 1 where landlords wanted to convert a house in multiple occupation and having failed to persuade all the tenants to leave, carried out major works with two tenants in occupation. The electricity and water supplies were disconnected, toilet facilities interfered with and rooms demolished. Once again the Court of Appeal upheld an award of £1,000 exemplary damages for the torts of trespass and nuisance.

Both of these cases illustrate the superior nature, in an appropriate case, of a claim in tort which enables the victim to recover either aggravated damages to compensate for distress and humiliation, or exemplary damages where it is an appropriate case to teach the wrongdoer that tort does not pay, or if appropriate both types of damages. Thus in *McMillan v. Singh* (1984) 17 H.L.R. 120 an award of both aggravated and exemplary damages was made against a landlord who had physically ejected the tenant and thrown his belongings out of the property. (See also *Ashgar v. Ahmed* above).

(d) A statutory tort—Housing Act 1988

As already noted above, the hand of the victim was further strengthened by the Housing Act 1988, s.27, which created a new civil remedy by way of an action for damages in tort.

The Government was prompted to strengthen the law in this way because of a fear that the "deregulation" of the private rented sector to be brought about by the Housing Act 1988 would lead to a new spate of "Rachmanism". The 1988 Act effectively confined continued Rent Act protection by way of fair rent regulation and security of tenure to pre-1988 Act tenancies. Post-Housing Act tenancies would be at market rents and the new assured shorthold regime offered landlords a form of tenancy which afforded the tenant no security of tenure beyond the contractual term. It was accordingly believed that, without further measures, the potential gains to be had by landlords from unlawfully recovering possession of properties let on Rent Act 1977 protected or statutory tenancies and reletting at significantly higher market rents on assured shorthold tenancies would prove too much of a temptation for a minority of unscrupulous landlords. Some indication of the value of a statutory tenancy can be obtained from the decision in *Murray v. Lloyd* [1989] 1 W.L.R. 1060, where a tenant lost the opportunity of obtaining a statutory tenancy through his solicitor's negligence. The solicitor was liable for damages of £115,000.

As stated above, the new statutory tort seeks to eliminate this risk for tenants by permitting a successful plaintiff who has been excluded and who does not wish to regain possession to recover damages. The damages awarded are to compensate the occupier for loss of possession and are in effect based on the increase in value of the landlord's interest (that is his interest in the building in which the premises are comprised) as a result of the eviction (s.28(1)(2)).

The tort will be committed where a landlord or a person acting on his behalf—

> "(1) unlawfully deprives the residential occupier of any premises of his occupation of the whole or part of the premises (s.27(1)); or
>
> (2) (a) attempts unlawfully to deprive the residential occupier of any premises of his occupation of the whole or part of the premises (s.27(2)(a)); or
>
> (b) knowing or having reasonable cause to believe that the conduct is likely to cause the residential occupier—
>
> (i) to give up occupation of the premises or part; or
>
> (ii) to refrain from exercising any right or pursuing any remedy in respect of the premises;

does acts likely to interfere with the peace or comfort of the residential occupier or members of his household, or persistently withdraws or withholds services reasonably required for the occupation of the premises as a residence and as a result the occupier gives up his occupation of the premises as a residence (s.27(2)(b))".

The formula for measuring damages can produce quite substantial sums which can in an appropriate case appear to have the character of exemplary damages (ss.27(3), 28). Indeed in the first case on section 27 to reach the Court of Appeal—described by Lord Donaldson M.R. as a "cautionary tale for landlords who are minded unlawfully to evict their tenants by harassment or other means"—the Court upheld an award of damages of £31,000 for loss of the tenant's right to occupy a bed-sitting room brought about by the landlord's unlawful conduct (*Tagro v. Cafane* [1991] 2 All E.R. 235). However, the basis on which those damages were assessed is open to question in the light of subsequent case law. (See below.)

The dangers of resorting to premature self help on the part of the landlord were vividly illustrated by *Haniff v. Robinson* (above) where a landlord who had obtained a possession order against a statutory tenant jumped the gun and evicted the tenant without going through the proper channels of obtaining a warrant for possession which could be executed by the bailiff. The tenant was awarded damages of £28,000, but once again the basis on which these damages were assessed must be suspect, in the light of the case law discussed below.

Who is liable? The conduct which is the subject of a claim under section 27 must be that of the landlord (the "landlord in default") or any person acting on behalf of the landlord (s.27(1)).

However, in either case, where liability has arisen, damages are payable only by the landlord in default (s.27(3)). Damages in respect of a section 27 claim cannot be awarded against a person acting on behalf of a landlord on the basis of being a joint tortfeasor, because this would fly in the face of section 27(3) (*Sampson v. Wilson* [1996] Ch. 39, CA, not following dicta to the contrary of Dillon L.J. in *Jones v. Miah* (1992) 24 H.L.R. 578, 586). On the other hand it was held in *Ramdath v. Daley* (1993) 25 H.L.R. 273 that exemplary damages can be awarded in an ordinary tort action against a defendant who is the landlord's agent if that person stood to gain personally from his actions. In that case an award of £1,000 exemplary damages was made against the landlord and one of £6,397 (including £2,500 exemplary damages) against his son who was managing the property and had unlawfully evicted the tenant, following the tenant's refusal to pay a rent increase demanded by the landlord. The Court of Appeal overturned the exemplary damages award against the son because he had not acted in his own right nor obtained any personal profit.

"Landlord" is defined as "the person who but for the occupier's right to occupy, would be entitled to occupation of the premises and any superior landlord under whom that person derives title" (s.27(9)(c)). Thus in *Jones v. Miah* (above) it was held that damages under section 28 could be awarded against the defendants, who had contracted to purchase the landlord's interest in a building which included four bedsitting rooms and had been allowed into occupation as licensees before completion, following which they had unlawfully evicted the residential occupiers.

Basis of assessment As stated above, damages under section 28 are awarded to compensate the occupier for loss of the right to occupy, but they are measured not by reference to the occupier's loss but to the landlord's gain. The court is required to perform this exercise by determining the difference between (a) the value of the landlord's interest (in the building in which the premises are comprised) subject to the plaintiff occupier's right to occupy and (b) the value of that interest if the plaintiff were no longer entitled to occupy. Damages are thus measured by reference to the profit, if any, that the landlord would have made had he been able to determine the plaintiff's rights lawfully at the time of the eviction (s.28(1)(2)).

When performing this calculation the court must value the landlord's interest on the basis of what it could be expected to achieve in a sale on the open market to a willing buyer, on the assumption that neither the occupier nor any of his family is willing to buy and ignoring any development value which would come about from demolition of the building or substantial development of the land (s.28(3)). This will clearly benefit the landlord by reducing the deemed value of the landlord's interest. It is important to emphasise that it is the landlord's interest in the whole building that has to be valued, even though the premises in question may form part only of that building (see section 28(2)).

In *Melville v. Bruton* (1996) 29 H.L.R. 219 a tenant who had been granted a six-month assured shorthold tenancy of part of a freehold property was unlawfully evicted after about five weeks. When she had moved in there were two other occupants of part of the premises, who remained after she had gone. At first instance she was awarded £15,000 damages under section 27 on the basis of the notional difference between the vacant possession value of the building and its value with a sitting tenant. This award was overturned by the Court of Appeal who held that it failed to have regard to the fact (a) that the landlord had not recovered vacant possession of the premises (because there were two other tenants of part who were still in occupation) and therefore the open market value of the building with sitting tenants might be significantly reduced and (b) that the tenant had only lost the five-month residue of a six-month assured shorthold term, a type of tenancy which afforded only negligible security of tenure (see p.238 below). The Court therefore valued the landlord's gain as nil, although the tenant was awarded £500 general damages for the inconvenience, discomfort and distress caused by the eviction. An award of £2,379 for conversion of the plaintiff's possessions was not challenged on appeal.

The same reasoning was employed by the court in *King v. Jackson* [1998] 03 E.G. 138 where, at the time of eviction, the tenant, who had given notice to leave which the landlord had acted upon, thereby had only six days left of his assured shorthold tenancy. The Court of Appeal considered that this was obviously not a particularly valuable asset and overturned the decision of the judge that the landlord was liable for £11,000 damages under section 28. The court substituted an award of £1,500 for breach of the covenant for quiet enjoyment.

It follows therefore that the greater the security which the occupier enjoyed before the eviction, the greater the measure of damages will be. (See *Murray v. Lloyd* (above) where in the case of a negligence claim against a solicitor the loss of the right to acquire a statutory tenancy was valued at £115,000 on the facts of the case). Because most tenants now have assured shorthold tenancies the measure of damages under section 28 will be limited. Only a Rent Act protected tenant who has been evicted is likely to receive substantial damages.

Defences

(1) It is a defence for the landlord to prove that he had believed and had reasonable cause to believe that—

    (a) the residential occupier had ceased to reside in the premises at the relevant time; or

    (b) (in the cases of acts of harassment) he had reasonable grounds for doing the acts or withholding the services in question (s.27(8)).

(2) It is a defence to show that the former residential occupier has been reinstated in the premises, either by court order or otherwise, before the proceedings are finally disposed of (s.27(6)).

In *Tagro v. Cafane* [1991] 2 A11 E.R. 235 the landlord and an accomplice unlawfully evicted the tenant by changing the locks on the door of the flat. The tenant was offered a key to what she discovered to be a 'wrecked' room, in which she refused to stay. The Court held that the landlord's offer did not amount to reinstatement of the tenant. 'Reinstatement does not consist in merely handing the tenant a key to a lock which does not work and inviting her to resume occupation of a room which has been totally wrecked.' P.239 per Lord Donaldson N.R. In any event it was further held that a tenant who is offered reinstatement by the landlord has no obligation to accept that offer. (As noted above, the landlord was held liable for damages of £31,000 in respect of the loss of the tenant's right to occupy and £15,538 for loss and damage to the tenant's belongings. Although observing that these awards were somewhat high, the Court of Appeal did not consider it appropriate tointerfere with them although it was pointed out that the judge had accepted the uncontested evidence of the plaintiff's valuer. The recent decisions in

Melville v. Bruton (above) and *King v. Jackson* (above) suggest that such an award would now be unlikely if proper evidence as to the enhanced value of his interest were introduced by the landlord. (See also *Haniff v. Robinson* (above) where the tenant, who could have been lawfully removed in a matter of days, was awarded damages of £24,751,59 under section 28. This decision seems at odds with the recent case law discussed above.)

It follows that a residential occupier who wishes to claim damages under section 28 should not seek reinstatement or accept an offer of the same. It is possible that even if reinstatement is ordered by the court, the defence will not apply if the tenant chooses not to take up possession (see s.27(6)(b)). If the tenant returns for a short time only, this might not in the circumstances be treated as a reinstatement (see *Murray v. Aslam* (1995) 27 H.L.R. 284).

Failure to mitigate It is provided by section 27(7) that the amount of damages which would otherwise be payable to a successful plaintiff in a section 27 action can be reduced by such amount as the court thinks appropriate if it appears to the court that—

(1) prior to the event which gave rise to the liability, the conduct of the plaintiff or any person living with him in the premises concerned was such that it is reasonable to mitigate the damages for which the landlord in default would otherwise be liable; or

(2) before proceedings were begun the landlord in default had offered to reinstate the plaintiff in the premises in question and either it was unreasonable for him to refuse that offer or, where he has since obtained alternative accommodation, it would have been unreasonable to refuse the landlord's offer had that not been the case.

This provision was considered by the Court of Appeal in *Regalgrand Ltd v. Dickinson* (1996) 29 H.L.R. 620 where it was held that "conduct" has its ordinary meaning and can encompass a wide range of matters. The Court refused to interfere with the decision of the judge who had made deductions from the initial award of £12,000 section 28 damages to reflect (a) withholding rent without prior notice and without justification, (b) the appellants having neglected to inform the landlord that the new boiler which he had installed had failed to cure the heating problems earlier complained of and (c) the firm intention of the appellants to move out three weeks after the date on which they were subsequently evicted. These deductions brought the amount awarded down to £1,500. The Court considered that section 27(7) was not ambiguous and accordingly declined to look at *Hansard* (see *Pepper v. Hart* [1993] A.C. 593) in order to determine whether it was intended that section 27(7) only envisaged a reduced award where there was gross misconduct.

Relationship with other remedies Liability under Housing Act 1988, s.27, which, as stated above, is confined to cases where, as a result of the conduct of the landlord or a person acting on his behalf, the residential occupier gives up occupation, is deemed to be in the nature of liability in tort and is in addition to any other liability in tort or contract that might have been incurred (s.27(4)). Thus, where the necessary elements are present, an additional claim can still be made for breach of the covenant for quiet enjoyment and/or in tort at common law although damages cannot be recovered in respect of both claims on account of the same loss—that is loss of the right to occupy (s.27(5)). The displaced occupier need not elect which damages to seek, but the smaller amount has to be set off against the larger amount. The point is illustrated by the case of *Mason v. Nwokorie* (1993) 26 H.L.R. 60.

The tenant of a bed-sitting room in a building in which the landlord resided was unlawfully evicted following the expiry of an invalid notice to quit. The tenant claimed damages under section 27. The landlord could have lawfully determined the tenancy by four weeks' notice (see p.101 above) following which application could have been made for a possession order. It was agreed that if this course of action had been followed the tenant could have been removed in up to six months' time. Thus the court had to determine the difference between the value of the property with vacant possession and the value of the property with an occupier who could have been lawfully removed in about six months. The plaintiff's expert evidence that this was £4,500 was accepted by the trial judge and the Court of Appeal saw no ground for interfering with that judgment. But the judge had also awarded general damages of £500 and exemplary damages of £1,000. The Court of Appeal considered that the latter amount was really an award of aggravated damages (see above), but in any event both amounts should be offset against the section 27 damages because they were damages in respect of the same loss, the loss of the right to occupy the premises as a residence. (By contrast, in *Kaur v. Gill* (1995) *The Times*, June 15, general damages for breach of the covenant for quiet enjoyment were awarded as well as section 28 damages because the former were not awarded in respect of the loss of the right to occupy). It has been argued that aggravated damages should not in any event be set off against section 27 damages because they are awarded for injury to feelings, rather than for loss of the right to occupy (S.Bridge [1994] Conv. 411). On this point see now *Francis v. Brown* (1998) 30 H.L.R. 143, CA.

Protection from Harassment Act 1997

The Protection from Harassment Act 1997 was passed to deal with the problem of "stalkers" who pressed their unwanted attentions on victims who were thereby put in fear. It was believed by the proponents of the new legislation that the law as it then stood was inadequate to deal with this problem in a satisfactory way. However, the Act is drafted in wide terms and encompasses the actions of a wider group of persons than stalkers. The 1997 Act provides that a person must not pursue a course of conduct which he knows or ought to know amounts to harassment of another (s.1). Breach of section 1 is a criminal offence punishable by up to six months' imprisonment (s.2) and if, on at least two occasions, the conduct caused the victim to fear that violence would be used against him the perpetrator is guilty of a more serious offence which is punishable by up to five years' imprisonment. The court may also impose a "restraining order" on the defendant prohibiting further harassment. Breach of such an order is punishable by up to five years' imprisonment (s.5).

Breach of section 1 also entitles a victim to bring a tort action under the Act. The court may grant an injunction and/or make a damages award which can include damages for anxiety or financial loss (section 3). Breach of an injunction can lead to an application by the victim for a warrant of arrest to be issued. Furthermore it can amount to a criminal offence to do anything, prohibited by the injunction without reasonable cause. It can be seen that the 1997 Act is wide enough to cover harassment of tenants and licensees by landlords or others but in view of the fact that the Protection from Eviction Act 1977 already caters for the crimes of unlawful eviction and harassment, and that there are a number of civil law remedies available at common law or by statute, it is unlikely that landlord and tenant cases will be dealt with under the 1997 Act.

Chapter 6

TERMINATION OF LEASES

Once created, a tenancy can come to an end in a variety of ways. The principal methods are considered in this chapter. When examining this area of law it is important to bear in mind that either the landlord or the tenant might have a very good reason for wanting to terminate a tenancy prematurely. If commercial property rents have risen, and there is no provision for a rent review in the lease, the landlord might be concerned to recover possession in order to relet the property to the tenant or a third party at a higher rent. If, as in the recession of the late 1980s and early 90s, such rents have fallen dramatically, tenants will be eager to determine their tenancies in order to obtain alternative premises at a lower rent. Much of the recent litigation on termination of tenancies has been prompted by such considerations.

When examining the relevant law it is also important to consider any special statutory regime of protection that might affect a particular type of tenancy. It might be the case, for example, that even though the contractual tenancy has come to an end at common law the tenant is permitted to remain beyond that point by statute, as in the case of a protected/statutory tenant under the Rent Act 1977 (See Chapter 10 below). In other cases special statutory rules might provide that certain tenancies can only be ended in ways specified by the particular Act. (See, for example, the rules governing the termination of assured tenancies under the Housing Act 1988 (See Chapter 9 below).

A. TERMINATION BY EFFLUXION OF TIME

The general rule

At common law a tenancy for a fixed term will come to an end on the last day of the term without any need for notice or any other special action by either landlord or tenant (*Cobb v. Stokes* (1807) 8 East 358). Any derivative interest (such as a periodic sub-tenancy) which is still in existence at that time will also end on that date (*Weller v. Spiers* (1872) 20 W.R. 772).

Statutory modifications

As noted above, this rule is modified in its application in the case of any tenancy which is protected by one of a number of special statutory regimes; this means most tenancies.

(1) If the tenancy which has expired is an assured tenancy, or an assured shorthold tenancy, under the Housing Act 1988 the tenant is entitled to remain as a statutory periodic tenant and if the landlord wishes to recover possession he can only do so in accordance with the rules laid down in the Act (See Chapter 9 below).

(2) When a secure fixed-term tenancy under the Housing Act 1985 ends by effluxion of time, a periodic tenancy arises automatically at that point (Housing Act 1985, s.86(1)). This tenancy can only be brought to an end by the landlord by obtaining a court order on one or more of the grounds laid down in the Housing Act 1985 (See Chapter 11 below).

(3) Part I of the Landlord and Tenant Act 1954 provides that certain long residential tenancies at a low rent (as defined) which were created before March 1, 1990 will continue automatically unless or until they are terminated in accordance with the Act (See Chapter 12 below). The Act affords such tenants protection under a scheme corresponding to that applicable to statutory tenants under the Rent Act 1977.

A similar modified assured tenancy scheme (which was introduced by the Local Government and Housing Act 1989 Sched. 10) operates in respect of such tenancies which were granted on or after that date. As in the case of Part I of the Landlord and Tenant Act 1954 the tenant is entitled to remain until the new tenancy afforded by the Acts is terminated in accordance with the relevant provisions.

Furthermore it has been provided that the scheme in Part I of the Landlord and Tenant Act 1954 will cease to apply to any long tenancy created before March 1, 1990 which is still in existence on January 15, 1999. From that date such tenancies will be governed instead by the scheme in the Local Government and Housing Act 1989 (above).

(4) Business tenancies are afforded protection by Part II of the Landlord and Tenant Act 1954 which effects a statutory extension of the contractual tenancy. The landlord can only prevent such an extension arising or recover possession thereafter by observing a procedure laid down in that Act and establishing one of the permitted grounds for possession. Furthermore the tenant has a right to apply to the court for a new tenancy (See Chapter 13 below).

(5) Although a protected tenancy under the Rent Act 1977 may expire by effluxion of time a statutory tenancy can arise in favour of the former protected tenant. If this happens, the landlord can only recover possession by establishing one of the grounds laid down in the that Act. (See Chapter 10 below) The same principle applies in respect of a protected agricultural occupancy under the Rent (Agriculture) Act 1976.

B. TERMINATION BY A BREAK CLAUSE

Introduction

Fixed-term tenancies often contain a provision which gives one or both of the parties the option to determine the tenancy prematurely in accordance with the terms of the option. Such an option, which is commonly referred to as a "break clause", is more frequently included for the benefit of the tenant. Break clauses have become common in recent times. During the recession of the early 1990s, when there was a surplus of commercial property to let, tenants often took advantage of market conditions to negotiate such clauses with their landlords. The advantage of such an option to the tenant is that if rental values fall he has the opportunity of withdrawing from the tenancy and seeking alternative and cheaper premises for his business elsewhere. Conversely, the disadvantage of such a provision for the landlord is that if the option is exercised the tenant will cease to have any liability in respect of the leased premises and the landlord could find it very difficult to relet, save at a much lower rent. For such reasons break clauses will be construed strictly against the person for whose benefit they operate. Landlords are often able to soften the blow by negotiating for a proviso that on exercise of the option by the tenant a "penalty rent" of one or two years' rent will become payable to the landlord. (See S. Tromans, *Commercial Leases* (2nd ed.), p.228.)

A break clause is sometimes found alongside a rent review clause (which permits the rent to be increased from time to time) which is operative by the landlord. In times of rising rental values this would enable the tenant to determine the tenancy if he is faced with a proposal for an increased rent which he does not feel able to afford.

The principal restrictions on the operation of a break clause are as follows.

(a) Who can exercise the option?

If the option is expressed to be exercisable only by a specific named tenant it will not be capable of being exercised by an assignee of the tenancy nor even by the named tenant once the tenancy has been assigned. Thus even if the tenancy is reassigned to the original tenant the break clause will no longer be exercisable by him (*Max Factor Ltd v. Wesleyan Assurance Society* [1996] E.G.C.S. 82. See also *Olympia and York Canary Wharf v. Oil Property Investments* [1994] 2 E.G.L.R. 48). If it were otherwise, an assignee who wanted to get out of a tenancy for whatever reason, such as a decline in rental values, would be able to collude with the original tenant to reassign the tenancy to him to enable the break clause to be exercised, thereby ridding the assignee of any further liability.

In the absence of any restriction as to who can exercise an option to determine the tenancy, the benefit and burden will run with the tenancy and reversion and be exercisable by and against the tenant and landlord for the time being. In *Brown & Root Technology Ltd v. Sun Alliance and London Assurance Co Ltd* [1995] 3 W.L.R. 558, Ch.D it was held that the option is exercisable only by a legal assignee of the term and not by an equitable assignee. Thus in that case, where title to the lease was registered under the Land Registration Act 1925, the original lessee was still able to exercise the option despite a transfer of the lease because the assignee had not been registered as the new lessee in pursuance of the transfer.

If there are joint tenants (or joint landlords in the case of a landlord's option to determine) all will need to participate in the exercise of the option to determine (*Re Viola's Lease* [1909] 1 Ch. 244; *Hounslow London Borough Council v. Pilling* [1993] 2 E.G.L.R. 59). Thus if one or more of the tenants have not signed the notice, they must have authorised that it be signed on their behalf. Otherwise the option will not have been validly exercised. (Contrast a notice to quit (below) and see *Hammersmith LBC v. Monk* [1991] 3 W.L.R. 1144, HL).

(b) Conditions precedent

As in the case of an option to renew a tenancy, any condition precedent to the operation of the option to determine the tenancy must be strictly construed. It is very common for an option to determine to be made conditional on the tenant having performed and observed his obligations under the tenancy. Any failure to comply with such a condition, however trivial the failure, will invalidate the exercise of the break clause. In *Finch v. Underwood* (1876) 2 Ch.D 310, an option to renew was made conditional on the tenants having complied with the terms of the lease. It was held that the landlord was not obliged to grant a new lease in circumstances where the tenant was in breach of a covenant to repair. The rule was applied in *West Country Cleaners (Falmouth) Ltd v. Saly* [1966] 1 W.L.R. 1485 where a tenant had the benefit of an option to renew provided that all the covenants in the tenancy had been duly observed and performed. The tenant was obliged to paint every three years and in the last year of the term. The tenant had not decorated in the last year and one ceiling had never been painted. This was held to invalidate the exercise of the option and accordingly the landlord was not obliged to renew the tenancy. The trivial nature of the breach will be no defence. In *Trane (UK) Ltd v. Provident Mutual Life Assurance* [1995] 1 E.G.L.R. 33 there were trivial breaches of covenant subsisting when the notice exercising the option to determine took effect and this was sufficient to invalidate the exercise of the option. (See also *Bairstow Eves (Securities) Ltd v. Ripley* [1992] 2 E.G.L.R. 47, CA where a failure to decorate, as required, in the last year of the tenancy invalidated an option to renew even though only nominal damages would have been recoverable in respect of that breach of covenant).

On the other hand, a requirement that the tenant must have performed and observed his obligations under the tenancy, to be able to exercise a break clause, will be satisfied where there have been breaches of covenant (whether positive or negative), provided they have been rectified at the relevant time (*Bass Holdings Ltd v. Morton Music Ltd* [1987] 3 W.L.R. 543, CA). It is a matter of construction whether the relevant time is the date of service or expiry of the notice or both. Ideally this would be expressly specified in the break clause, as in *Simons v. Associated Furnishers Ltd* [1931] 1 Ch. 379 where a break clause, conditional on the tenant having performed the covenants in the lease, provided for it to be exercisable where any breaches of covenant had been remedied before expiration of the notice. (See also *Bass Holdings Ltd v. Morton Music Ltd* (above) where the tenants were able to exercise an option to renew, which was conditional on them having duly paid the rent and performed and observed the covenants in the tenancy. Although there had been rent arrears at some time in the past in respect of which the landlord had brought forfeiture proceedings, the tenants had been granted relief against forfeiture on terms with which they had complied).

Rather than being framed in absolute conditional terms, break clauses are sometimes framed so as to be conditional on the tenant having "reasonably" performed and observed the covenants in the tenancy. This means that a tenant who has fairly complied with a covenant, albeit not in strict terms, might still be permitted to exercise the option. An example would be where a covenant to decorate required the use of three coats of paint and only two were used. (See *Reed Personnel Services plc v. American Express Ltd* [1996] N.P.C. 7, where the tenants were held not to have reasonably complied with their repairing obligations). A qualified condition of this kind means that the court is able to judge the tenant's conduct over the whole period of the lease and to take into account also the landlord's conduct or breach of covenant. In *Bassett v. Whitely* (1982) 45 P.& C.R. 87 (a case of an option to renew) a tenant who had withheld rent on two occasions because of the landlord's failure to repair, but had later paid the rent, was held to have reasonably complied with the covenants in the tenancy. However, it should be observed that in *Reed Personnel Services plc v. American Express Ltd* (above) Jacob J. expressed the view that the court should take a more stringent approach to the need for compliance with covenants by the tenant in the case of a break clause than in the case of an option to renew. This is because if, for example, the tenant is under a repairing or decorating obligation, it is more important to the landlord that this is complied with in circumstances when the tenant is leaving (having exercised an option to determine) than when he staying on (having exercised an option to renew). (See further H.W. Wilkinson (1997) N.L.J. 499 and H. Pitchers [1997] 27 E.G. 106).

(c) Construction of notice of exercise

Despite earlier settled authority to the contrary dating back to 1840 (*Cadby v. Martinez* (1840) 11 A.&E. 720, 113 E.R. 87) it has been held by the House of Lords that a notice exercising an option to break the lease will not be invalidated automatically if the wrong date for termination was inserted in the notice. (See *Mannai Investment Co. Ltd v. Eagle Star Life Assurance Co. Ltd* [1997] 3 All E.R. 352, HL followed in *Garston v. Scottish Widows Fund & Life Assurance Society* [1998] 3 All E.R. 596, CA see p.390 below.

In *Mannai* the tenants occupied premises under two leases which had run from January 13, 1992. Each tenancy gave the tenant an option to determine at the end of the third year of the tenancy by giving not less than six months' notice in writing to the landlord or its solicitors, "such notice to expire on the third anniversary of the term commencement date." Following a sharp fall in office rents in the West End of London (where the property was situated) the tenant served a notice on the landlord on June 24, 1994 to determine the lease on January 12, 1995 (that is, one day before the third anniversary of the commencement date). The Court of Appeal held that this was a fatal error; January 12 does not mean January 13. In so doing they followed *Hankey v. Clavering* [1942] 2 K.B. 326, where a notice to quit had stated December 21 instead of December 25. It was held that this was fatal to the validity of the notice even if it was, as the landlord must have realised, a slip on the part of the tenant. This mechanistic approach contrasted with that adopted by Goulding J. in *Carradine Properties Ltd v. Aslam* [1976] 1 W.L.R. 442. In that case a notice exercising a break clause was served on September 6, 1974 purporting to determine the tenancy on September 27, 1973. This was clearly a clerical error because the date specified had already passed. The court accepted that the tenant meant 1975 and the landlord would be expected to have understood it to have that meaning. Of course had the notice stated 1976 that would have been a different matter because there would have been genuine uncertainty as to the intended date and it would not have been obvious that 1975 was intended. Nevertheless, an even more relaxed approach was adopted in *Micrografix Ltd v. Woking 8 Ltd* [1995] 2 E.G.L.R. 32 where the only permitted break date was June 23, 1995. Despite this the tenant's break notice specified March 23, 1994 as the determination date. The court held that in view of the fact that because there was only one possible permitted break date the notice need not have specified the date at all. In the circumstances it was considered that the landlord must have realised that the date specified in the tenant's notice was not the one intended.

It was this second line of authority which commended itself to a majority of the House of Lords in *Mannai* (Lords Goff and Jauncey dissenting). Lord Hoffman (with whom Lords Steyn and Clyde concurred) observed of *Hankey v. Clavering* that "One is bound to be left with a feeling that something has gone wrong here. Common sense cannot produce such a result; it must be the result of some rule of law. If so, what is that rule and is it correct? (p.375)" His Lordship then examined the origins of the rule of construction applied by the Court of Appeal and declared it to be capricious and incoherent. He stated it to be incoherent because it was based on a false assumption as to the function of words. The truth is that words do not inherently refer to people or things. Their application is derived from how people understand a word to have been used in the light of all relevant background information. Thus the wording of a notice exercising a break clause has to be construed in the light of all the relevant circumstances. The consequence of *Hankey v. Clavering* was only to "allow one party to take an unmeritorious advantage of another's verbal error, an adventitious bonus upon which no one can have relied".

The decision in *Mannai* was yet another example of a familiar dilemma in property law. Should the courts opt for a just result whilst injecting a note of uncertainty into the law, or should they make what might be described as a hard decision (such as that of the Court of Appeal in *Mannai*), which is the necessary price to preserve a degree of certainty? The House of Lords chose the former and in future therefore, if an incorrect notice has been served, the person who served that notice will have to ask themselves whether a reasonable landlord would have recognised that the sender intended to determine the tenancy on the permitted date rather than the incorrect date specified in the notice. This element of uncertainty was clearly acknowledged by their Lordships, but the majority felt that their test of the reasonable recipient was the fairest solution to the dilemma. As Lord Clyde stated—

> "Where a notice of termination complies precisely and unambiguously with the provision which empowers the sending of the notice then its validity should be unquestioned. Where the terms of the notice do not altogether accord with the provisions of the contract that may or may not render the notice unenforceable. The problem may then come to be one of finding a fair and reasonable construction of the notice. But there can be cases where the validity of the notice cannot be saved by any construction and will have to be regarded as bad... The standard of reference is that of the reasonable man exercising his commonsense in the context and in the circumstances of the particular case. It is not an absolute clarity or an absolute absence of any possible ambiguity which is desiderated. To demand a perfect precision in matters which are not within the formal requirements of the relevant power would, in my view, impose an unduly high standard in the framing of notices such as those in issue here. While careless drafting is certainly to be discouraged the evident intention of a notice should not in matters of this kind be rejected in preference for a technical precision. (pp.382–3)"

It is finally worth noting that, as Lord Goff pointed out, all the problems in *Mannai* could have been avoided had the tenants served a notice stating that they intended to determine the tenancy "on the third anniversary of the commencement date of this lease", without specifying a particular date. (See further P.Smith [1998] Conv.326].

(d) Effect of premature determination on a sub-tenancy
An interesting issue in connection with break clauses is whether the premature determination of a tenancy under such a clause will automatically bring to an end any subsisting sub-tenancy. According to the Court of Appeal in *Pennell v. Payne* [1995] Q.B. 192, a "tenant's exercise of his right to determine a lease under a break clause is precisely equivalent to his determining a periodic tenancy by notice to quit." This would mean that the sub-tenancy is also determined.

However, it must be appreciated that this will often not be the case because most tenancies are governed by one of several statutory regimes which make express provision with regard to the position of sub-tenants. Where the general rule does apply (*e.g.* to a business tenancy where the parties have contracted out of the Landlord and Tenant Act 1954), it has been suggested that sub-tenants should insist that when the landlord consents to the sub-letting the sub-tenant should be given an option for a lease from the superior landlord should the tenant exercise the break clause. The sub-tenant should also ask to be given notice of any exercise by the tenant of a break clause. (See R. Butler and S. Pemble [1998] 13 E.G. 138.) The decision in *Pennel v. Payne* contrasts with the position (see below) where a tenancy is determined by a surrender or merger of the tenancy with a superior tenancy or the freehold. In both cases the sub-tenancy will survive the ending of the head tenancy.

C. TERMINATION BY SURRENDER

A tenancy will be terminated by surrender where the tenant yields up his tenancy to the immediate reversioner who accepts the surrender. At that point the tenancy determines because it becomes absorbed in the greater interest and the relationship of landlord and tenant between the parties to the tenancy comes to an end. (But the parties can still sue and be sued in respect of a pre-surrender breach of covenant (*Dalton v. Pickard (1911)* [1926] 2 K.B. 545; *Brown v. Blake* (1912) 47 L.J. 495) unless, as is usual in practice, there is a release of liability for past breaches by accord and satisfaction (see *Deanplan v. Mahmoud* (1992) 64 P.& C.R. 409.)

Surrender is either express or is implied by operation of law.

Express surrender

As a general rule, the disposition of a legal estate must be by deed (Law of Property Act 1925, s.52(1)). This requirement applies even to a legal tenancy which need not be *created* by deed (*i.e.* a tenancy taking effect in possession for not more than three years at the best rent reasonably obtainable; s.54(2)). Thus in *Crago v. Julian* [1992] 1 W.L.R. 372 it was held that the assignment of an oral weekly tenancy had to be by deed to pass the legal estate. In principle, therefore, LPA 1925, s.52(1) should apply equally to a surrender of a legal tenancy as it does to an assignment of the legal estate to a third party assignee. This view is subscribed to by Woodfall (*Law of Landlord and Tenant*), but Hill and Redman (*Law of Landlord and Tenant*) p. A909 take the view that an informal legal tenancy (see above) can be expressly surrendered by writing signed by the tenant or his lawfully authorised agent (relying on LPA 1925, s.53(1)). But that provision simply requires that an interest in land can only be disposed of by writing signed either by the person disposing of the interest or his agent lawfully authorised in writing. An instrument which complies with this requirement will at most therefore only effect a surrender of the equitable interest. It does not deal with transmission of the legal estate. The better opinion therefore is that a deed will be required in all cases. Where title to the tenancy is registered under the Land Registration Act 1925 the determination will need to be noted on the register (rule 200, Land Registration Rules 1925). Whether a deed is necessary or not, the point will not matter in most cases because, as will be seen below, failure to comply with the necessary formality may well be cured by the finding of an implied surrender where warranted by the circumstances (see below). An implied surrender does not need to be by deed (s.52(2)(c)).

In the case of a joint tenancy, all the joint tenants must join in the surrender (*Leek & Moorlands Building Society v. Clark* [1952] 2 Q.B. 788; *Greenwich LBC v. McGrady* (1982) 81 L.G.R. 288).

A contract to surrender is valid if it complies with the requirements of section 2 of the Law of Property (Miscellaneous Provisions) Act 1989. But if the premises are held on a business tenancy to which Part II of the Landlord and Tenant Act 1954 applies, the contract will be *unenforceable (LTA 1954, s.38(2); Joseph v. Joseph* [1967] Ch. 78; *Allnatt London Properties v. Newton* [1984] 1 All E.R. 423 (see also p.94 above); *Tarjomani v. Panther Securities Ltd* (1982) 46 P.& C.R. 32).

Implied surrender

A surrender by operation of law comes about not as a result of an express agreement between the parties, but because the law deems it appropriate in all the circumstances to infer that a surrender has come about as a result of the conduct of the parties. An implied surrender is exempt from the normal formalities which govern the passing of the legal estate (LPA 1925, s.52(2)(c)). Thus a deed will not be necessary.

To amount to an implied surrender—

> "the conduct of the tenant must unequivocally amount to an acceptance that the tenancy has ended. There must either be relinquishment of possession and its acceptance by the landlord, or other conduct consistent only with the cesser of the tenancy, and the circumstances must be such as to render it inequitable for the tenant to dispute that the tenancy has ceased. *Tarjomani v. Panther Securities Ltd* (above at p.41 *per* Peter Gibson J. See also *Lyon v. Reed* (1844) 13 M.&W. 285, *per* Parke B.)."

The essence of implied surrender, accordingly, is that the landlord and tenant have been party to a transaction that is inconsistent with the continuance of the tenancy in circumstances which render it inequitable for the tenant to deny that surrender has taken place. It will be necessary therefore to determine what "transactions" are covered by this rule. As indicated in the above passage, the most obvious example is where the tenant gives up possession and the landlord accepts possession unequivocally. The landlord is of course not obliged to act upon a tenant's act of surrender.

What will amount to sufficient conduct on the part of the landlord and tenant to lead to the inference that a surrender has taken place? If the tenant gives up possession it will be a sufficiently unequivocal act of acceptance on the part of the landlord if he relets the premises. On the other hand, if the tenant returns the keys to the property and the landlord accepts them, this will not necessarily amount to a surrender (*Oastler v. Henderson* (1877) 2 Q.B.D. 575). Whether there has been a surrender in such circumstances will depend on the landlord's intention. Thus in *Proudreed Ltd v. Microgen Ltd* [1996] 12 E.G. 127, CA there was no surrender despite the landlord having accepted the keys from the tenant, because the landlord, to the tenant's knowledge, did not intend to accept the offer to surrender unless the property was successfully relet to a surety of the tenant (who had covenanted to take a new tenancy should the tenant become insolvent). (See also *Charville Estates Ltd v. Unipart Group Ltd* [1997] E.G.C.S. 36.) Even an entry into possession of the property by the landlord after possession has been abandoned by the tenant might be an equivocal event. (See *McDougalls Catering Foods Ltd v. BSE Trading Ltd* [1997] 42 E.G. 174, CA where the landlord obtained a possession order against squatters who had gone into possession after the tenants had left. This did not necessarily amount to an implied surrender of the tenancy. The landlord recovered possession from the squatters in order to protect the property. This was not inconsistent with a continuation of the tenancy). By contrast, a surrender was effective where the tenant departed and returned the keys to the landlord who gave them to an agent to enable him to put up a notice to let on the premises and to show people round. In addition the tenant's name on the premises was painted out and the landlord informed him that he had taken possession (*Phene v. Popplewell* (1862) 12 C.B.(N.S.) 334).

Whilst a surrender will not be implied simply by the tenant having abandoned the premises owing substantial rent arrears, it will be possible for a surrender to be brought about when, after a period of absence by the tenant, the landlord resumes possession. In *Preston Borough Council v. Fairclough* (1982) 8 H.L.R. 70, 73, CA, where the tenant had abandoned possession, there was insufficient evidence to enable the court to infer that there had been a surrender. "The bare fact that a tenant leaves premises at a time when he owes rent is certainly insufficient to enable a court to draw the inference that there has been a surrender" (*per* Griffiths L.J.).

Grant of a new tenancy

If the landlord grants a new tenancy to his tenant to take effect before the old tenancy has come to an end, this will operate automatically as a surrender of the old tenancy, irrespective of the intention of the parties (*Jenkin R Lewis & Son Ltd v. Kerman* [1970] 3 All E.R. 414).

In practice, difficulties are more likely to arise over deciding whether a modification of the terms of the existing tenancy amount to a surrender of the tenancy and regrant of a new tenancy. This can be particularly important where the tenant at the time of the variation is an assignee, because, if in law the variation amounts to a surrender of the tenancy and the grant of a new tenancy, all right and obligations in respect of the old tenancy will cease thereafter. It has been held that for this purpose the only variations of a tenancy which will automatically bring about an implied surrender and regrant are where the variation has the effect of either increasing the extent of the premises let to the tenant or the length of the term (*Friends Provident v. British Railways Board* [1996] 1 All E.R. 336. see p.167 below). In all other cases it will be a question of degree in all the circumstances as to whether the variation has the effect of a surrender and regrant.

Change of legal status

An implied surrender will also occur if the tenant agrees to remain on the basis of some other arrangement inconsistent with the continuance of a tenancy. Thus in *Foster v. Robinson* [1951] 1 K.B. 149; CA a tenancy was surrendered where the tenant agreed that he would remain in possession as a rent free licensee. (See Chapter 1 above).

Effect of surrender on sub-tenancies

A surrender of a tenancy does not have the effect of determining a sub-tenancy derived from that tenancy. Thus if L grants a tenancy to T who grants a sub-tenancy to S, a surrender of his tenancy by T will have the effect of terminating the lease and bringing L and S into a direct landlord and tenant relationship (Law of Property Act 1925, s.139). Thus covenants in the former sub-tenancy (which following surrender of the superior tenancy will be the only tenancy) will become enforceable as between L and S.

A mortgagee of a sub-tenancy is similarly unaffected where the head tenant surrenders the tenancy (*ES Schwab & Co. Ltd v. McCarthy* (1975) 31 P.& C.R. 196, CA where the lease and the mortgage were equitable only because the 99-year lease of registered land had not been registered at the Land Registry).

Where there is a surrender of a tenancy and a regrant of a new tenancy to the tenant effecting the surrender, any sub-tenancy will be unaffected and the sub-tenant will continue to hold as a sub-tenant as if the former tenancy had not been surrendered (LPA 1925, s.150(1)).

D. TERMINATION BY MERGER

Requirements

It has been explained above that a surrender comes about when the tenant yields up his tenancy to his immediate reversioner who thereby acquires the tenancy which then becomes absorbed by the superior interest. By contrast, at common law, a tenancy determines by merger when the superior interest, is acquired by the tenant, or both interests are acquired by a third party. The tenancy disappears because the tenant cannot hold a tenancy from himself. Thus the tenancy disappears into the reversion and the covenants in the tenancy are extinguished (*Webb v. Russell* (1789) 3 Term. Rep. 393). Equity placed a gloss on the common law rule by providing that whether merger would occur depended on the intention of the parties. In the absence of direct evidence of intention, it was presumed that despite the two interests becoming united in the tenant, merger was not intended if it was to the interest of the tenant, or only consistent with the tenant's duty, that merger should not take place. An example of a case where a merger would not be consistent with the tenant's duty would be where there is a mortgage of the tenancy because otherwise the mortgagee would lose his security (*Capital Counties Bank Ltd v. Rhodes* [1903] 1 Ch. 631). The primacy of the equitable rule was confirmed by statute which provided that unless merger in equity takes place, there will not be a merger of the legal estate (see now Law of Property Act 1925, s.185).

Effect on derivative interests

As in the case of surrender, merger does not have the effect of determining a sub-tenancy derived from the now merged tenancy. Thus if L grants a tenancy to T, who grants a sub-tenancy to S, and T acquires L's interest, this will have the effect of terminating the lease by merger and bringing L and S into a direct landlord and tenant relationship (Law of Property Act 1925, s.139). Thus covenants in the former sub-tenancy (which following merger of the superior tenancy will be the only tenancy) will become enforceable as between L and S.

E. TERMINATION BY DISCLAIMER

Who can disclaim?

If a tenant becomes bankrupt, or being a company goes into liquidation, the trustee in bankruptcy (personal insolvency) or liquidator (corporate insolvency), as the case may be, is empowered to disclaim the tenancy as onerous property if so desired. (Insolvency Act 1986, ss.315(2)(b); 178(3)(b)). This is most likely to apply to a lease at a full market rent, whether fixed term or periodic. (If as a result of one or more assignments the trustee in bankruptcy or the company being wound up is a tenant of part only of the property let under the original tenancy of the whole, the power to disclaim is exercisable only in relation to that part: Landlord and Tenant (Covenants) Act 1995, s.21(2)). The trustee or liquidator disclaims by serving notice in prescribed form on the landlord. In the case of bankruptcy, where the property is a dwelling-house, a copy of the notice must be served on any person who to the trustee's knowledge is in occupation of the house or claims a right to occupy (s.318)). Any person thereby affected (including a statutory tenant—*Re Vedmay* (1994) 26 H.L.R. 70) can then bring the matter to court and the court can impose conditions or make vesting orders on such terms as it thinks fit in favour of any person prejudiced by the disclaimer, or, where the property is a dwelling-house, any person who occupies or is entitled to occupy the house (ss. 320, 321 and 181,182).

Effect of disclaimer

It is provided by the Insolvency Act 1986 that disclaimer does not affect the rights and liabilities of persons other than the trustee (liquidator) or the bankrupt (company) except so far as necessary for releasing those persons and the property from liability (ss. 315(3) (bankruptcy), 178(4)(b) (liquidation)). The effect of disclaimer where the only persons interested in the property and the obligations in respect of the tenancy are the landlord and tenant is that the tenancy disappears on disclaimer (see *Hindcastle Ltd v. Barbara Attenborough Associates Ltd* [1996] 2 W.L.R. 262, HL). The obligations of the tenant's guarantor also disappear, although in practice the guarantee clause normally requires the guarantor to take up a new tenancy on disclaimer. But if the insolvent tenant was an assignee of the tenancy this can leave untouched the contractual liability of others (*e.g.* former tenants and guarantors) in respect of outstanding breaches of covenant (see further p.171 below).

Any person who sustains loss or damage as result of a disclaimer is deemed to be a creditor of the bankrupt or company to the extent of his loss or damage. This was vividly illustrated recently in *Christopher Moran Holdings Ltd v. Bairstow* [1997] 3 All E.R. 193, CA where a solvent tenant who wanted to get out of an onerous tenancy went into voluntary liquidation and the tenancy was disclaimed. It was held that the landlord was able to recover a sum to compensate him for the rent that he would have recovered had the tenancy continued for the remainder of the term, although this had to be discounted by what the landlord could be expected to obtain by reletting the property on the same terms other than as to rent. (This resulted in the tenant having to pay £2.25 million to represent the lost rent. The rental value of the property had fallen dramatically from £160,000 p.a. when the 20-year tenancy was entered into to £35,000 p.a. at the time of trial). Had the tenant succeeded, many others would have undoubtedly taken the same steps and landlords would have lost billions of pounds. (An appeal to the House of Lords is pending).

F. TERMINATION BY NOTICE TO QUIT

Essential nature

> "A notice to quit is a certain reasonable notice required by law, custom, special agreement or statute, to enable either the landlord or the tenant, or the assignees or representatives of either of them, without the consent of the other, to determine a tenancy from year to year or other periodic tenancy. (Woodfall, para. 17.196.)"

In the absence of express or statutory provision to the contrary, it is of the essence of a periodic tenancy that it can be determined by a valid notice to quit served by either landlord or tenant. Where the tenant has died intestate and a grant of administration has not been made, a notice to quit should be served on the Public Trustee (AEA 1925, s.9 as substituted by Law of Property [Miscellaneous Provisions] Act 1994, s.14 (*Wirrall BC v. Smith* (1982) 43 P.& C.R. 312 where the council landlord was unable to recover possession on the death of the tenant, from other persons who had moved in before the tenant's death, because the tenant had died intestate and the landlord had not served a valid notice to quit terminating that tenancy).

Thus a contractual provision whereby a periodic tenancy can be determined only by one party is void as being repugnant to the nature of a yearly tenancy (*Centaploy v. Matlodge* [1974] Ch. 1). Similarly a provision in the tenancy whereby the landlord will not serve a notice to quit unless the property is required for a particular purpose is also invalid because it renders the tenancy void for uncertainty and leaves it to take effect as an ordinary implied periodic tenancy (*Prudential Assurance Co. v. London Residuary Body* [1992] 2 A.C. 386, HL. But see *Breams Property Investment Co. Ltd v. Stroulger* [1948] 2 K.B. 1 for the possibility of different periods of notice being required of the parties. See p.21 above).

A notice must be clear and certain so that the other party knows what is required of him (*Ahearn v. Bellman* (1879) 4 Ex. D. 201), although a notice to quit a tenancy on or before a specified date will be valid because it simply gives the tenant the option of leaving before that date if he so wishes (*Dagger v. Shepherd* [1946] 1 K.B. 215). The notice required of one party might be different from that required of the other (see above).

A fixed-term tenancy cannot be determined by a notice to quit, although it might be determinable by the exercise of a break clause (see above). There are a number of statutory codes affecting particular types of tenancy which means that the common law position with regard to determination of a tenancy by notice to quit must be read in conjunction with those particular rules. Reference should be made to the appropriate chapters in this book for those special rules.

Effect on a sub-tenancy

It has been explained above that when a tenancy is determined either by the exercise of a break clause, or by a notice to quit, any sub-tenancy derived from that tenancy is also automatically determined, although if the service of the notice by the tenant amounts to a derogation from the grant of the sub-tenancy (see p.122 above), the tenant will be liable in damages to the sub-tenant (see *Pennell v. Payne* [1995] Q.B. 192). Exceptionally, if the notice to quit was served as a consequence of the landlord and tenant colluding to bring about determination of the sub-tenancy, then *Pennell v. Payne* will not apply and the sub-tenancy will not be determined (*Barrett v. Morgan* [1997] 12 E.G. 155, Ch.D).

Length of notice

The period required of a notice to quit is governed by common law, although this will give way to any express or statutory provision to the contrary (see below).

At common law a yearly tenancy is determinable by a half-year's notice given to expire at the end of the first or any subsequent year of the tenancy (*Parker d.Walker v. Constable* (1769) 3 Wils. 25. See also *Sidebotham v. Holland* [1895] 1 Q.B. 378). A half-year notice for this purpose means 182 days, although if the tenancy began on one of the quarter days (Lady Day (March 25), Midsummer Day (June 24), Michaelmas (September 29) or Christmas (December 25)), "half a year" means two quarters. In the case of any other periodic tenancy the common law length of a notice, which must be given to expire at the end of a current or subsequent period of the tenancy, is equivalent to the period of the tenancy in question (*Doe d.Peacock v. Raffan* (1806) 6 Esp.4). Thus a weekly tenancy is determinable by a week's notice, a monthly tenancy by a month's notice and a quarterly tenancy by a quarter's notice.

The notice period can include the date of service of the notice and expiry. However, it is of the essence of a notice to quit at common law that the notice must expire at the end of a current period of the tenancy (see for example *Lemon v. Lardeur* [1946] K.B. 613). Thus a weekly tenancy which began on a Monday can be determined by a notice given on a Monday to expire at midnight on the following (or some subsequent) Sunday, although if the notice states that the tenancy is to determine on the following (or some subsequent) Monday rather than Sunday this will be benevolently construed as referring to the midnight that divides that day from the day before (see *Crate v. Miller* [1947] K.B. 946, CA). A notice to quit at noon on the expiry date is invalid because the tenant is entitled to remain until midnight of that day (see *Bathavon RDC v. Carlile* [1958] 1 Q.B. 461).

Any difficulty caused by not knowing the precise date on which the tenancy commenced can be overcome by serving a notice which requires the tenant to quit on a specified day "or at the expiration of the year (or as the case may be quarter/month/week) of the tenancy which shall expire next after the end of one half year (quarter/month/week/four weeks, from the service of this notice" (see Woodfall, para. 17.257). If the landlord then waits until the end of that period he will necessarily have given the requisite period of notice, whenever the tenancy began.

Statutory rules governing form of notice

Agricultural holdings The above common law rules are modified by statute in the case of a tenancy of an agricultural holding, whatever the period of the tenancy. In such a case, 12 months' notice to quit is required to determine the tenancy (Agricultural Holdings Act 1986, s.25).

Residential lettings Although an oral notice to quit is valid at common law, written notice is sensible as a matter of practice and in any event the Protection from Eviction Act 1977, s.5 provides, subject to the exceptions below, that no notice to quit by a landlord or tenant to quit any premises let as a dwelling is valid unless—

    (1)   it is in writing and contains such information as may be prescribed; and

    (2)   it is given not less than four weeks before the date on which it is to take effect.

Because a notice to quit does not apply to a tenancy at will it has been held that section 5 has no application to such a tenancy (*Crane v. Morris* [1965] 1 W.L.R. 1104).

The need for the notice to be for a period of not less than four weeks is satisfied by a notice which includes the date of service of the notice but excludes the last day (*Schnabel v. Allard* [1967] 1 Q.B. 627 where a notice served on Friday March 4, 1994, which purported to determine a weekly tenancy of a dwelling-house on Friday April 1, was effective).

The prescribed information is contained in the Notices to Quit Prescribed Information Regulations 1988, S.I. 1988 No. 2201 and is designed to make the tenant aware of his legal rights and to advise him to seek legal advice. (It will not be fatal to the validity of a notice to quit that the notice does not use the precise wording of the regulations providing the substance of its contents is conveyed (*Beckerman v. Durling* (1981) 6 H.L.R. 87 where an out-of-date form was used).

The statutory rule in PEA 1997, s.5 was extended to a periodic licence to occupy a dwelling-house by the Housing Act 1988. Thus any notice by the licensor or licensee to determine such a licence, although not technically a notice to quit—a concept which strictly applies only to tenancies—must comply with section 5 of the 1977 Act.

The exceptional cases, referred to above, where section 5 is inapplicable are as follows:

    (1)   Tenancies or licences where a resident landlord/licensor shared accommodation with the tenant/licensee at the end of the tenancy; provided that immediately before the tenancy/licence began the landlord/licensor occupied as his only or principal

home premises of which the whole or part of the shared accommodation formed part (PEA 1977, s.3A(2)). For this purpose "shared accommodation" does not include areas used for storage, nor a staircase, passage, corridor or other means of access (s.3A(4)). Presumably sharing a WC would suffice (*cf.* Rent Act 1977 ss. 21, 22 and Housing Act 1988, s.3). The rationale would seem to be to exclude arrangements where the parties have lived in close proximity to each other. It is the same rationale which motivated the resident landlord exceptions to assured tenancy status under Part I of the Housing Act 1988 and protected tenancy status under the Rent Act 1977 (see pp.219 and 257 below).

The same rule applies where the sharing is with a member of the landlord/licensor's family, who satisfies the same conditions, provided the landlord/licensor also occupied as his only or principal home premises in the same building as the shared accommodation and that building is not a purpose-built block of flats (as defined in Part III Sched. 1 Housing Act 1988) (s.3A(3)).

(2) A tenancy or licence granted as a temporary expedient to a person who had entered the premises in question as a trespasser (s.3A(6)).

(3) A tenancy or licence granted for the purposes only of a holiday. (s.3A(7)).

(4) A gratuitous tenancy or licence (*ibid.*).

(5) A licence to occupy a hostel granted by a local authority or certain other specified public or publicly funded bodies (including a housing association) (s.3A(8)). Occupiers of such accommodation are unlikely to be tenants (*Westminster City Council v. Clarke* [1992] 2 A.C. 288 (see p.309 below)—see also *Mohamed v. Malek and the Royal Borough of Kensington & Chelsea* (1995) 27 H.L.R. 43, CA where it was held that an occupier of hostel accommodation under a temporary licence, granted whilst the local authority made enquiries as to the licensee's statutory entitlement to accommodation as a homeless person, did not occupy a dwelling under a licence for the purposes of this provision).

There is a further requirement that to be an excluded *tenancy*, and therefore outside the ambit of section 5 of the Protection from Eviction Act 1977, the tenancy must have been entered into on or after January 15, 1989, unless in pursuance of a contract entered into before that date. (s.5(1B)(a)). By contrast, an excluded *licence* will not be governed by section 5, whenever the licence was created.

Joint landlords or tenants

In the case of a joint tenancy a notice to quit will be valid provided it is given by at least one of the joint tenants whether or not that person is authorised by the other tenant(s) to serve a notice. The same principle applies to service of a notice to quit by fewer than all the joint landlords where there is more than one landlord (*Parsons v. Parsons* [1983] 1 W.L.R. 1390).

In *Hammersmith & Fulham LBC v. Monk* [1992] 1 All E.R. 1, HL a cohabiting couple, Mr M and Mrs P, were joint tenants of a council house owned and let to them on a weekly tenancy by the plaintiff local authority. When their relationship broke down Mrs P approached the council with a view to being rehoused and the council suggested that she determine her present tenancy. So she served a notice to quit on the council. This put Mr M in a difficult position because if the notice to quit was effective to determine the joint tenancy he would not qualify to remain as a secure tenant under the Housing Act 1985 (see p.318 below). There was long-standing authority that in the case of joint landlords a notice to quit could be served by fewer than all the landlords (*Doe d.Aslin v. Summersett* (1830) 1 B&Ad. 135; and there was Court of Appeal authority that the same principle applied in the case of service of a notice to quit by joint tenants

(Greenwich LBC v. McGrady (1982) 46 P.& C.R. 223). The House of Lords confirmed the *McGrady* decision and held that the notice to quit was effective and therefore Mr M had to leave. The decision thus paves the way for one joint tenant to end the tenancy by serving a notice to quit without the knowledge of the other. It was argued for Mr M that just as the surrender of a joint tenancy or the exercise of a break clause, in the case of a fixed term, required the authorisation of all tenants (see above), the service of a notice to quit should equally require the agreement of all tenants . The House of Lords did not agree and distinguished the case of termination of a tenancy by notice to quit from these other forms of termination. Lord Bridge based this distinction on the principle that as a simple matter of contract law it is implicit that a periodic tenancy continues only so long as that is willed by all parties. Therefore the service of a notice to quit, although positive in form, is negative in substance because "it is by his omission to give notice of termination that each party signifies the necessary positive assent to the extension of the term for a further period" *(per* Lord Bridge at p.9). Thus on this analysis a periodic tenancy is fundamentally different in nature to a fixed term because the latter continues until its fixed date for termination whilst the former continues only so long as this is willed by all parties. Lord Browne-Wilkinson acknowledged that a contract-based solution to the problem was at odds with the rival property law-based analysis, which was grounded in the principle that a tenancy is an estate in land of which an owner should not be divested without his knowledge or consent. Nevertheless he considered that the issue was settled by the rule in *Summersett* (above), which he could see no good reason to alter. The decision in *Monk* has not escaped criticism, not least because of its emphasis on contractual principles when it has long been recognised that tenancies are not like ordinary contracts and are often subject to different rules, both common law and statutory *(e.g.* the Rent Acts) because of their dual nature as property rights. (See, for example, Dewar, (1992) 108 L.Q.R. 375, who also suggested that the two sets of rules could have been reconciled by treating a notice to quit by one joint tenant as operating to release that tenant for the future whilst leaving the tenancy intact as between the landlord and the remaining tenant(s).

Despite the decision in *Monk* it was subsequently contended that a notice to quit served by one of two joint tenants (who were husband and wife) should be invalidated because as co-owners of the legal estate they were trustees for sale for themselves and therefore the tenant who served the notice should have consulted the other beneficiary as required by the Law of Property Act 1925, s.26(3). This argument was rejected by the Court of Appeal in *Crawley B.C. v. Ure* [1996] 1 All E.R. 724, CA. The court held that because the service of a notice to quit by the wife was not a positive act (see *Monk*), there was no duty on her to consult the husband. (For the duty of trustees, see now Trusts of Land and Appointment of Trustees Act 1996, s.11(c).) Nor can it be maintained that serving a notice to quit brings about a renewable disposition under the Matrimonial Causes Act 1973 *(Newlon Housing Trust v. Alsulaimen)* [1998] 4 All E.R. 1 H.L.

Furthermore in *Harrow LBC v. Johnstone* [1997] 1 All E.R. 929, HL where the property held on a joint tenancy by a couple was the matrimonial home the House of Lords held that where the male partner had obtained a court order forbidding the female partner to exclude him from the home, that did not prevent her serving a valid notice to quit.

On the other hand it was decided in *Hounslow LBC v. Pilling* [1994] 1 All E.R. 432 that a notice would be invalid if it is given for less than the period required by the tenancy or by statute where that overrides the agreement (see above). In *Pilling* the tenancy was by its terms determinable by four weeks' written notice or such lesser period as the council might accept when the tenant wished to end the tenancy. The Court of Appeal held that five days' notice by one of two joint tenants was invalid at common law to end the joint tenancy because (a) it was not given to end at the end of a current period of the tenancy (see above) but in any event it would have had to comply with the Protection from Eviction Act 1977, s.5 which (save in exceptional specified cases) requires at least four weeks' notice to quit in the case of any premises let as a dwelling-house (see above). Furthermore although, despite the fact that they cannot contract out of section 5, a landlord and tenant can accept as valid a notice served for a shorter period than that prescribed by law (*Elsden v. Pick* [1980] 1 W.L.R. 898) this would require the assent of all parties, and not just one of the joint tenants. To that extent the provision in the tenancy for a shorter notice was tantamount to a break clause the exercise of which requires the assent of all the joint tenants.

It is of interest to note that in these cases of notice to quit served by one of a couple the party giving notice has often been seeking a council house tenancy and has been encouraged to serve the notice to quit as a prerequisite to being rehoused by the local authority. What seems to get overlooked, or is perhaps considered and rejected as too slow, is the fact that the court has power to transfer a tenancy on divorce or relationship breakdown (see Family Law Act, 1996) and the woman might be better off pursuing this option which will also preserve any accrued right-to-buy entitlement under the Housing Act 1985 (see p.321 below and also C. Williams and P. Luxton (1996) C.F.L.Q. 65).

Repudiation

In principle, a tenancy, like any other contract, can come to an end if by his actions one party repudiates the tenancy and the other party accepts the repudiation thereby bringing the tenancy to an end. In *Hussein v. Mehlmann* [1992] 2 E.G.L.R. 87 it was accepted by Stephen Sedley Q.C. (as he then was), sitting as an assistant recorder of the county court, that a serious breach of his statutory repairing obligations by a landlord of a dwelling-house could, as in that case, amount to a repudiatory breach of contract (p.58 above). The view of Lord Denning M.R. in *Total Oil (Great Britain) Ltd v. Thompson Garages (Biggin Hill) Ltd* [1972] 1 Q.B. 318 that the doctrine of repudiatory breach was inapplicable to leases was considered not to be good law. It was based on an analogy with the doctrine of frustration which at that time was considered not to apply to leases on the basis that a lease is also an estate in land and therefore not determinable in the same way as other contracts. That limitation on the scope of the doctrine of frustration had since been rejected by the House of Lords in *National Carriers Ltd v. Panalpina (Northern) Ltd* [1981] A.C. 675 (see p.133 below). The decision in *Hussein v. Mehlmann* can be seen as part of a wider trend in recent years whereby contractual principles have come to play an increasingly significant role in the law of landlord and tenant at the expense of any special property law rules based on the notion that a tenancy is an estate in land and thereby exempt in many ways from normal principles of contract law.

In this connection it is of interest that the doctrine of repudiatory breach has been applied to leases in other Commonwealth jurisdictions such as Canada (*Highway Properties Ltd v. Kelly, Douglas & Co Ltd* [1972] 2 W.W.R. 28 (where the tenant abandoned the premises)) and Australia (*Progressive Mailing House Pty v. Tabali Pty* (1985) 157 C.L.R. 17 (substantial breach of the covenant to pay the rent)) for the purpose of enabling the landlord to recover damages for prospective losses. This latter aspect of the rule has yet to find its way into English law. (See Biros, Bradgate & Villers, *Termination of Contracts* [1995] at p.165 (P.Luxton)).

If the courts do follow the lead of *Hussein v. Mehlmann*, this will open up interesting avenues. Thus a landlord who alleges that the tenant is in fundamental breach of his tenancy obligations might choose to accept this as a repudiatory breach, thereby sidestepping the elaborate procedures which would be applicable were he to exercise a forfeiture clause and right of re-entry in the tenancy (as to which see below). It was the view of Stephen Sedley Q.C. that the obligation to serve a notice under Law of Property Act 1925, s. 146 and the right of the tenant (or a subtenant or mortgagee) to seek relief against forfeiture (see below) would still need to be complied with. (By contrast it has been held in New Zealand that the doctrine will eliminate the need for compliance with statutory safeguards for tenants in repossession actions where the landlord seeks to forfeit and re-enter for breach of covenant (*Nai Pty Ltd v. Hassoun Nominees Pty Ltd* [1985–1986] Aust. and N.Z. Conv. Rep. 349). (The issues are explored further by Peter Luxton (above). See also [1993] Conv. 71 and [1993] C.L.J. 212.) The Law Commission has formulated a new statutory code on termination of leases for breach of covenant and specifically recommended that the new procedures should displace any action based on repudiatory breach of contract by the tenant. (See p.152 below.)

Frustration

It was axiomatic for centuries that in the absence of express provision by the parties to the contrary, the common law contractual doctrine of frustration did not apply to leases. Thus even though subsequent to the grant of a tenancy the leased property became incapable of being used by the tenant through circumstances beyond the control of either party, the obligations of the tenancy remained unaffected. The rationale for this exception to the general contractual rule was that a lease creates an estate in land which is executed once granted and thus cannot be brought to an end save in one of the ways recognised by English property law. The soundness of this exception was affirmed by the House of Lords in *Cricklewood Property & Investment Trust Ltd v. Leighton's Investment Trust Ltd* [1945] A.C. 221, although the issue of principle as to whether the lease could be frustrated was left open by Viscount Simon L.C. and Lord Wright.

The views expressed by these doubting voices were subsequently endorsed by the House of Lords in *National Carriers Ltd v. Panalpina (Northern) Ltd* (above) when it was held that in exceptional circumstances the doctrine could apply to leases. In that case a 10-year tenancy of a warehouse was granted with a covenant against its use for any other purpose. The road adjoining the premises was closed for an anticipated 20 months. The House of Lords held that this was not a sufficiently serious interruption to a 10-year term as to amount to a frustrating event sufficient to render it inappropriate to enforce the lease. Thus rent remained payable. But their Lordships indicated that a more serious interference might well have led to the doctrine of frustration being applicable. It was also suggested that if the subject matter of the lease physically disappeared (such as through a landslip into the sea, or the destruction of an upper storey flat), a lease might be frustrated. Of course if the land remains and is capable of being built upon, the destruction of any building on the land will not frustrate the lease (*Denman v. Brise* [1949] 1 K.B. 22). Their Lordships thus rejected the notion that like a sale of freehold land, a lease was an executed agreement that once granted was governed by principles of property law and thereafter largely immune from the ordinary principles of contract law—

> "sale of land is a false analogy. A fully executed contract cannot be frustrated; and a sale of land is characteristically such a contract. But a lease is partly executory; rights and obligations remain outstanding on both sides throughout its currency. (*Per* Lord Simon at p.[1981] A.C. 675, 505)."

With regard to the particular case he said that—

> "The reality is that this lessee, for example bargained not for a term of years, but for the use of a warehouse owned by the lessor, just as a demise charterer bargains for the use of this ship. (p.705)"

In practice the parties should wherever possible cater for unexpected events by insurance or by an appropriately worded covenant in the tenancy which allocates responsibility for the consequences of a potentially frustrating event.

G. FORFEITURE

The right to forfeit

A tenancy will contain a number of obligations on the part of the landlord, and considerably more on the part of the tenant. The term "covenant" is strictly confined to an obligation created by deed, but for the sake of convenience it will be used below to mean all express or implied obligations imposed on the parties to a tenancy, whether or not the tenancy has been created by deed. Failure by a landlord or tenant to comply with a covenant will amount to a breach of covenant and this will give rise to an appropriate remedy or remedies, such as an action for damages, specific performance or an injunction. But in the case of a tenant's covenant the landlord for the time being will often have a further weapon in his armoury. Most tenancies will expressly include a provision whereby in the event of a breach of any tenant covenant in the tenancy the landlord will be entitled to forfeit the tenancy by re-entering, thereby putting an end to the tenancy. It is important that such a provision is expressly inserted in the tenancy, because it will not be implied. A provision of this kind is commonly referred to as a forfeiture clause or a right of re-entry. A forfeiture clause will run with the land and hence the benefit will pass to subsequent assignees of the reversion automatically (see Landlord and Tenant (Covenants) Act 1995, s.4 for new tenancies under that Act. see p.196 below). Although forfeiture is clearly a valuable weapon in the hands of a landlord, he may be at the very least reluctant to exercise the right to forfeit the tenancy where property values have fallen (as in the early 1990s) and the rent that would be obtained on a reletting would be significantly lower than that obtainable under the present tenancy.

Covenants and conditions

Covenants need to be distinguished from "conditions". Occasionally a tenancy is made subject to a condition (*e.g.* that the land is not used other than for a particular purpose). If so, breach of a condition gives the landlord the option to forfeit the tenancy even though the tenancy might not contain a forfeiture clause. In practice such conditions are rare and it is more usual to control the use of the property by the tenant by means of a suitably worded covenant coupled with a forfeiture clause. This has the advantage that it gives the landlord a remedy in damages as well as being able to forfeit the tenancy in the event of occurrence of the condition.

A forfeiture clause is therefore a proviso that upon the occurrence of stated events the landlord will have the power to re-enter and forfeit the tenancy. The most usual events will be a breach of any positive or negative tenant covenants in the tenancy.

Other forfeiture events

In a commercial lease it is also usual to provide that a right to forfeit and re-enter will arise on the occurrence of certain insolvency events. Those usually catered for in this way are the tenant becoming bankrupt or having an administration order made, being wound up or having a receiver appointed, making any composition arrangement with creditors, or upon any goods on the premises being taken in execution. For the sake of convenience any event giving rise to a right to forfeit (including such insolvency events) will be referred to below as a breach of covenant. (See also D. Milman and M. Davey [1996] J.B.L. 541.)

Waiver

Because forfeiture can have such critical consequences for the tenant and any other interested party, such as a sub-tenant or a mortgagee of the tenancy, who all stand to lose their interests, both common law and statute have placed obstacles in the way of the landlord. The first of these is the doctrine of waiver, whereby, despite the fact that an occasion giving rise to the right to forfeit has arisen, the landlord will be prevented from exercising that right in certain circumstances.

The doctrine provides that a landlord will not be able to re-enter and forfeit the lease for breach of covenant if he is (a) aware of the acts or omissions which activate this right and (b) (irrespective of his intentions) does some unequivocal act (*e.g.* acceptance of or demand for rent) recognising the continued existence of the lease. (See *Matthews v. Smallwood* [1910] Ch. 777 at 786 *per* Parker J.)

> In *Central Estates (Belgravia) Ltd v. Woolgar (No. 2)* [1972] 3 All E.R. 610, CA the tenant, who was convicted of keeping a brothel, had committed a breach of covenant by permitting the premises to be used for immoral purposes. The landlord's agents therefore commenced the forfeiture process by serving a notice on the tenant under Law of Property Act 1925, s.146 (see below for the need for such a notice) and a partner in the agents' firm then circulated a memorandum in the office to the effect that rent was not to be demanded or accepted from the tenant. The memorandum did not reach a subordinate clerk in the office who demanded and subsequently received the next quarter's rent from the tenant. It was held that irrespective of the landlord's intentions, these actions amounted to a waiver of the right to forfeit the tenancy for breach of covenant. All that was necessary for this purpose was "an unequivocal act done by [or on behalf of] the landlord which recognised the continued existence of the lease after having knowledge of the ground of forfeiture." (The same conclusion was reached in *Van Haarlam v. Kassner Charitable Trust* [1992] 2 E.G.L.R. 59. See further below.)

The doctrine is a harsh one for landlords because of the rule that the intention of the parties, including the tenant's knowledge that the landlord did not intend to waive the breach, was irrelevant. Furthermore it has been held that an unambiguous demand for future rent can by itself be a sufficient act of waiver. This occurred in *David Blackstone Ltd v. Burnett* [1973] 3 All E.R. 782 where Stanwick J. stated that—

> "the knowledge required to put the landlord to his election is knowledge of the basic facts which in law constitute a breach of covenant entitling him to forfeit the lease. Once he or his agents know those facts an appropriate act by himself or any agent will in law effect a waiver of a forfeiture. His knowledge or ignorance of the law is in my judgment, irrelevant." (See also *Cornillie v. Saha* [1996] 28 H.L.R. 561, CA.)

The absolute nature of the doctrine is evident from the decision in *Segal Securities Ltd v. Thoseby* [1963] 1 Q.B. 887 that even if a demand for rent is made "without prejudice", this will not prevent the inference of a waiver. In cases involving an act of waiver other than demand for or acceptance of rent, it will depend on all the circumstances of the case as to whether the landlord has effectively waived the breach. In *Expert Clothing Service and Sales Ltd v. Hillgate House Ltd* [1986] Ch. 340 at 359 Slade L.J. stated that the act of the landlord which is said to constitute the waiver must be "so equivocal that, when considered objectively, it could only be regarded as having been done consistently with the continued existence of a tenancy as at [the relevant date]." (See also *Re National Jazz Centre* [1988] 2 E.G.L.R. 57 where it was held that negotiations between the landlord and the tenant's receiver for a possible new tenancy did not amount to a waiver in the circumstances. This is in accordance with common sense because if it were otherwise, a landlord and tenant would never be able to negotiate to compromise proceedings once a forfeiture claim is made without fear of the landlord having thereby waived the breach).

The same rule does not apply by analogy in the case of a breach of covenant by a statutory tenant under the Rent Act 1977, because such a tenancy cannot be "forfeited" but continues until determined by a court order on one of the grounds laid down in the Act or by notice from the tenant or by the tenant ceasing to occupy the property as his residence (see p.262 below). Thus where a statutory tenant had unlawfully sub-let (a ground for possession), it was held that the demand of rent by the landlord did not amount to an election on his part to treat the sub-tenancy as lawful: (*Trustees of Henry Smith's Charity v. Willson* [1983] 1 All E.R. 73).

It is important to note that for waiver to occur the landlord must have had knowledge of the breach at the time of the alleged act of waiver in question. Knowledge by an agent or employee will be sufficient for this purpose, as in *Metropolitan Properties Co. Ltd v. Cordery* (1979) 251 E.G. 567 where the fact that there had been an unlawful sub-letting of a flat in a block of flats was known to the porter. That knowledge was imputed to the landlord who employed the porter who was under a duty to report to his employer changes of personnel in the flats. In *Official Custodian of Charities v. Parway Estates Ltd* [1984] 3 All E.R. 679 an official notice in the *London Gazette* of a company's winding up (an event which activated the right to forfeit) was not sufficient to fix the landlord with notice of that event.

It is provided by statute that any waiver only operates with regard to the specific breach in question (Law of Property Act 1925, s.148). In the case of a continuing breach, such as disrepair or breach of a covenant to use the premises only for a particular purpose, a waiver is only effective in respect of that breach up to the time of the act which constitutes the waiver. This is because the covenant is continually broken anew as long as the state of affairs which constitutes the breach continues (*New River Co. v. Crumpton* [1917] 1 K.B. 762). It is thus necessary for this purpose to draw a distinction between a once and for all and a continuing breach of covenant.

In *Farimani v. Gates* (1984) 272 E.G. 887, CA the tenancy placed an obligation on the tenant to insure against fire damage and to recover and lay out the insurance money on rebuilding. It was held to be implicit that this was to be done within a reasonable time and that once that time had passed there was a once-and-for-all breach. A breach of the covenant against assigning or sub-letting (see Chapter 4 above) will also be a once-and-for-all breach (*Scala House District Property Co. Ltd v. Forbes* [1974] Q.B. 575).

Procedure

In ancient times a landlord would proceed to forfeit and re-enter by physically retaking possession. In modern times that method has been largely superseded by an action for possession which is commenced by the issue and service of a writ (or the equivalent county court process) claiming possession (*Canas Property Co Ltd v. KL Television Services Ltd*

[1970] 2 All E.R. 795—a case where the writ was issued but not effectively served on the tenant). Once the writ is served this will operate as a (constructive) re-entry by the landlord. From that point the lease is effectively determined and the parties are thereafter released from their obligations under the tenancy. As will be seen below this effect in law can be somewhat misleading for a number of reasons. For example, although the tenant ceases to be liable to pay the rent, he will be liable for "mesne profits" in respect of his use of the land if he remains in possession. These are measured by reference to the current letting value of the property and therefore might be higher or lower than the rent payable under the tenancy. Furthermore the tenant might seek relief against forfeiture and if successful the tenancy will be reinstated automatically and retrospectively (*Hynes v. Twinsectra Ltd* [1995] 35 E.G. 136, CA. See below for relief against forfeiture). In the interim ("twilight") period, such a tenant will remain able to enforce covenants in the tenancy (*Peninsular Maritime Ltd v. Padseal Ltd* [1981] 2 E.G.L.R. 43 where the landlords were required by injunction to use their best endeavours to put a lift in good working order until after trial of the action). Similarly sureties can be liable for rent, notwithstanding a compromise agreement, between the landlord and tenant for the lease to be transferred to the landlord (and hence determine by merger) following forfeiture proceedings by the landlord (*Ivory Gate Ltd v. Spetale and others* [1998] 27 E.G. 139, CA).

As indicated above, in principle re-entry can also effected by what is often referred to as peaceable physical re-entry but this will be rare, and has the potential to be far from peaceful. It has been described as "dubious and dangerous" in *Billson v. Residential Apartments* [1992] 1 All E.R. 141, HL. Furthermore, it is unlawful to enforce a right of re-entry under a residential lease other than by court proceedings where there is somebody lawfully residing in the premises (Protection from Eviction Act 1977, s.2. See Chapter 5 above). Physical re-entry also carries the risk of violence and the possibility of an offence being committed under the Criminal Law Act 1977, s.6 (using or threatening violence to property or to a person in order to secure entry, where the defendant knows that there is a person who is opposed to the entry present on the premises (*ibid*). For all these reasons this remedy is usually only likely to be used where the tenant has vacated the premises. Furthermore if a sub-tenant is in possession it will not be sufficient to determine the head tenancy by peaceable re-entry, for the landlord to come to an agreement with the sub-tenant that the rent is thereafter to be paid to the landlord. Such an arrangement amounts to a recognition of the continued existence of the tenancy. If the landlord is willing for the sub-tenant to remain he should make it clear that this can only be under a new tenancy of the landlord (*Ashton v. Sobelman* [1987] 1 W.L.R. 177).

For purely historical reasons, different procedural rules of forfeiture apply according to whether the covenant broken is a covenant to pay rent, or some other covenant. From early times the Court of Chancery exercised a broad equitable jurisdiction to relieve against forfeiture for non-payment of rent on the basis that the right to forfeit was no more than "security" for the unpaid rent. By contrast that jurisdiction never extended to forfeiture for breach of other covenants, save to a very narrow extent, and it was left to statute law to create such a jurisdiction. Each is examined in turn below. Before doing so it can be noted that it is not uncommon for a host of payments under a tenancy other than rent to be reserved as rent and if this is done the remedies available to the landlord for non-payment of rent by the tenant also apply to the non-payment of those other sums. (See, for example *Escalus Properties Ltd v. Robinson* [1996] Q.B. 231 where a service charge was reserved as additional rent.)

(a) Forfeiture for non-payment of rent
Despite the presence in the tenancy of a covenant to pay rent and a forfeiture clause, the landlord must still make a formal demand for the rent due before forfeiting. This means that he must make a demand at a convenient hour on the premises for the exact sum due on the day that

it is due. In practice this is never necessary because tenancies will be worded so as to waive the need for such a formal demand where the rent is a specified number of days (usually 14 or 21) in arrears.

Even if there is no such waiver in the tenancy itself it is provided by statute (although not without some ambiguity as to its scope: see Law Com. No.142 [1985] para. 2.21) that where the landlord is seeking to forfeit by court proceedings a formal demand will not be necessary where there is at least a half-year's rent in arrears and there are insufficient distrainable goods on the premises to satisfy the arrears which are due (Common Law Procedure Act 1852, s.210) (see County Courts Act 1984, s.139(1) (below) for the equivalent county court rule).

Relief against forfeiture As stated above, because of the drastic consequences of forfeiture, both equity and statute law have intervened so that in an appropriate case a forfeiture can be avoided and the tenant can be permitted to retain his tenancy. This jurisdiction, which is referred to as relief against forfeiture, can also operate in favour of sub-tenants and mortgagees of the tenancy (or sub-tenancy). The rules are frequently both complex and illogical, and are summarised below.

(i) Automatic relief

Even if the landlord has made a formal demand or is exempt from such (see above), if at any time before the trial the tenant pays or tenders to the landlord or his agents, or pays into court, the outstanding rent and arrears and costs the action will be automatically discontinued and relief against forfeiture will be granted (Common Law Procedure Act 1852 s.212. See also *Gill v. Lewis* [1956] 2 Q.B. 1 where it was held that trial means an effective trial and judgment binding on all necessary parties (*e.g.* all joint tenants where there is a joint tenancy)). Unfortunately it has been held that as a matter of construction this provision only applies where there is at least half a year's rent in arrears (*Standard Pattern v. Ivey* [1962] 1 All E.R. 452), although this will not preclude *discretionary* relief being sought and granted under the court's ancient equitable jurisdiction: see below). No such limitation governs the equivalent provision for automatic relief when proceedings are brought in the county court under the County Courts Act 1984 (s.138(2); see below).

(ii) Discretionary relief

If the tenant does not or cannot (see above) take advantage of section 212, he can still apply for relief against forfeiture within six months of the court order (Common Law Procedure Act 1852 s. 210). Such relief will granted by the High Court under section 38 Supreme Court Act 1981.

An analogous and inherent equitable jurisdiction to afford relief also applies at any time after actual peaceable re-entry (see *Lovelock v. Margo* [1963] 2 Q.B. 786 and *Thatcher v. CH Pearce and Sons Ltd* [1968] 1 W.L.R. 748), although the court may apply a six-month bar by analogy with the case of forfeiture by court action (*Howard v. Fanshawe* [1895] 2 Ch. 581).

(iii) Derivative interests

The right to seek relief against forfeiture under section 38 Supreme Court Act 1981 (by virtue of sections 210–212 Common Law Procedure Act 1852) is also available to a sub-tenant or a mortgagee of the tenancy or sub-tenancy (*Doe d.Wyatt v. Byron* (1845) 1 C.B. 623), although it is subject to the same six months' time limit as that which governs an application by the tenant (see above). It may even be exercised in favour of an equitable chargee *(Ladup Ltd v. Williams & Glynn's Bank plc* [1985] 1 W.L.R. 851). If the landlord has actually obtained a court order before relief is sought by the holder of a derivative interest, the tenant (or the last assignee) would need to be a party to the sub-tenant or mortgagee's application because relief involves the revival of the head tenancy and the reimposition of liability on that person *(Hare v. Elms* [1893] 1 Q.B. 604; see also *Escalus Properties v. Robinson* [1996] Q.B. 231, CA as to the retrospective nature of the relief).

Alternatively, a sub-tenant or mortgagee can apply for relief under LPA 1925, s.146(4) but only before the landlord has regained possession. (See below for relief under section 146(4) where the disadvantages, to holders of derivative interests, of relief under this provision are discussed).

(iv) County court proceedings

Where the landlord brings his forfeiture claim in the county court solely on the basis of non-payment of rent, the County Courts Act 1984, ss. 138 and 139 are applicable. (The county court has unlimited jurisdiction in actions for forfeiture and relief against forfeiture (S.I. 1991 No. 724). As in the case of a High Court action there is no need for a formal demand if either the lease so specifies or there are at least six months' arrears and insufficient distrainable goods on the premises (s.139(1).)

If the claim is based solely on non-payment of rent (s.138(6)) and the tenant pays into court or to the landlord at least five clear days before the proceedings all arrears and costs, then the action will cease and the tenant will continue to hold on the terms of the tenancy (s.138(2)). Otherwise if the court is satisfied that the lease should be forfeited it must make a possession order suspended for not less than four weeks which will then take effect unless before that time the tenant pays off all arrears and costs (s.138(3)(5)). This means all the arrears at the time of the order and not the service of the writ *(Maryland Estates Ltd v. Bar-Joseph* [1998] 3 All E.R. 193, CA). The four-week period may be extended on application before possession is recovered by court order (s.138(4)).

If a possession order has been made and the tenant has not taken advantage of the above provisions, he still has six months within which to apply for relief, but after that point he will be "barred from all relief" (s.138(7)(9A)). It has been held that this means that it will not be possible for the High Court to exercise its general equitable jurisdiction to afford relief *(Di Palma v. Victoria Square Property Ltd* [1985] 2 All E.R. 676, CA. In that case the tenant was barred from seeking relief beyond the end of the four-week period after the court order because at that time there was no further leeway; thus a lease worth £30,000 was lost for the sake of £300 unpaid rent. Subsequent to that decision the cut-off point for claiming relief was extended—as stated above—to six months from the date of recovery of possession, by an amendment to s.138 Supreme Court Act 1981, by Administration of Justice Act 1985, s.55).

Relief is available to the tenant, at the court's discretion, on application to the court within six months of re-entry where there is peaceable re-entry (s.139(2)).

A sub-tenant and mortgagee can also seek relief in the county court under section 138 because it has been held that the term "tenant" extends to them *(United Dominions Trust Ltd v. Shellpoint Trustees Ltd* [1993] 4 All E.R. 310). The same six-month time limit also applies in their cases and failure to apply within that period will mean that a sub-tenant or mortgagee will also be barred from all relief whatsoever *(United Dominions Trust Ltd v. Shellpoint Trustees Ltd,* above). Alternatively a sub-tenant or mortgagee can apply for relief under Law of Property

Act 1925, s. 146(4). However, as in the case of a High Court action, there are disadvantages in seeking relief under section 146(4). (See below.)

Is it a bar to relief that the landlord has recovered possession and relet the property to a new tenant? The short answer is no. If L has forfeited T's tenancy and relet to T2, relief can be granted by giving T a lease in reversion to that of T2 so that T becomes T2's landlord. Any premium paid to L by T2 can then be handed over to T (*Fuller v. Judy Properties Ltd* [1992] 14 E.G. 106, CA). But if L and T2 knew that T was seeking relief against forfeiture and yet went ahead with the grant of the new lease, the court might well grant relief by way of ordering that a new lease to be granted to T and that T2 should accordingly lose his lease. This happened in *Bank of Ireland Home Mortgages v. South Lodge Developments* [1996] 14 E.G. 92, where the applicant for relief was a mortgagee of the tenancy which had been forfeited.

A long lease of a flat was granted in 1985 for a premium of £35,000 and an annual rent of £60. Three years later the lease was mortgaged to the plaintiff bank and notice of the mortgage was given to the landlord. Two years later the landlord commenced forfeiture proceedings for non-payment of rent but failed to notify the mortgagee. The landlord re-entered peaceably in March 1992 after obtaining a possession order. Despite the fact that the mortgagee then learned of the possession order and contacted the landlord undertaking to pay the arrears and threatening to apply for relief against forfeiture, the landlord went ahead and granted a new lease to a third party shortly after the mortgagee commenced proceedings for relief under section 138(9) of the County Courts Act 1984. Lightman J. held that the grant of the new lease was not necessarily a bar to relief against forfeiture, but when considering whether relief should be granted he said that—

> "Compliance with the six month limit on applications for relief is a necessary, but not a sufficient precondition for relief. It is incumbent on any applicant for relief, whether a lessee or a person deriving title from a lessee, to make application with all due diligence and keep the lessor informed of his intentions and not leave him in the dark and, if there is any apparent delay, in his evidence fully to explain it. It is not the legislative policy that the premises shall be sterilised producing no return for the lessor during the six month period, let alone that the lessor shall be occasioned loss. So long as the lessor has given those entitled a reasonable opportunity to apply for relief and has reasonably formed the view that no application will be seriously pursued, he may exercise his rights as owner. What is reasonable in this context must depend on the circumstances of the case, *e.g.* the amount of rent due, the seriousness of any breach of covenant, the cost to the lessor of retaining, and preserving the value of the property unlet or unsold and the loss occasioned to the lessor by the delay. (p.93)"

The judge went on to hold that because the lessor knew of the mortgagee's intentions, he should not have gone ahead with the grant of the new lease and the new tenant's solicitor knew this. He was therefore prepared to grant relief against forfeiture by way of a lease to the mortgagee unencumbered by the new lease. In other words the new tenant would lose her lease. Fortunately the plaintiffs were prepared to accept that they should have a lease of the reversion and therefore the new tenant would keep her lease, and the mortgagee would become her landlord, but the premium of £48,000 which she had paid to the landlord had to be handed over to the mortgagee.

(b) Other covenants

Before enforcing a forfeiture in respect of breach of a non-rent covenant by action or otherwise, the landlord must serve a statutory notice on the tenant or the forfeiture will be void (Law of Property Act 1925, s.146(1)). The Landlord and Tenant Act 1927, s.18 also requires that in the case of a breach of a repairing covenant it is for the landlord to establish that the section 146 notice was actually known either to the tenant or sub-tenant (where the tenant had only a nominal reversion), or to the person who last paid the rent and that a reasonably sufficient time for the repairs to be carried out had elapsed since the notice came to the relevant person's attention. Sending the notice by registered post or recorded delivery is prima facie proof that it came to the addressee's attention.

The Law of Property Act 1925, s.146(1) provides that—

"A right of re-entry or forfeiture under any proviso or stipulation in a lease for a breach of any covenant or condition in the lease shall not be enforceable, by action or otherwise, unless and until the lessor serves on the lessee a notice—

(a)   specifying the particular breach complained of; and
(b)   if the breach is capable of remedy, requiring the lessee to remedy the breach; and
(c)   in any case, requiring the lessee to make compensation for the breach;

and the lessee fails, within a reasonable time thereafter, to remedy the breach, if it is capable of remedy and to make reasonable compensation in money, to the satisfaction of the lessor, for the breach."

In the case of an assignment in breach of covenant the assignee will nonetheless become the tenant and therefore any section 146 notice must be served on him because he is the person against whom possession will be sought (*Old Grovebury Manor Farm Ltd v. W Seymour Plant Sales & Hire Ltd* [1979] 1 W.L.R. 1397, see p.83 above).

The aim of section 146 is clearly to enable the claimant to know the allegations against him and to enable him to put the matter right if possible. In a decision which is surprisingly generous to landlords, it has been held that if a section 146 notice has been served in respect of a continuing breach of covenant, and that breach is then waived, the notice will still be effective for the purposes of any subsequent action brought in respect of a continuation of the breach beyond the point of the waiver (*Greenwich LBC v. Discreet Selling Estates Ltd* [1990] 2 E.G.L.R. 65).

Service charges in residential tenancies

Before examining the requirements of the much-litigated section 146 it is necessary to note that since September 24, 1996 a further safeguard has been introduced for the benefit of residential tenants where the landlord seeks to forfeit a tenancy for non-payment of a service charge. The Government was persuaded that some landlords had been aggressively pursuing tenants by way of forfeiture actions or threats of forfeiture for non-payment of service charges. Such charges, which are commonly found in tenancies of flats in a block of flats (see Chapter 12 below), are usually variable from time to time in accordance with the (often complex) terms of the tenancy. For a long time they have been a source of discontent on the part of tenants, who have often considered the charges to be exhorbitantly high. Where, as is often the case, the tenancy is a long tenancy at a low rent which was acquired for a capital sum, often with the benefit of a mortgage loan secured on the lease, the stakes are high and if the tenant is persuaded to give up possession the landlord will often be in a position to make an unmeritorious windfall gain. For this reason it was provided by section 81 of the Housing Act 1996 that a landlord of premises which are let as a dwelling may not forfeit the tenancy for non-payment of a service charge (either by way of court proceedings or by peaceable re-entry) unless the amount of that service charge has been agreed or admitted by the tenant or has been the subject of determination by a court (or an arbitral) tribunal and at least 14 days have elapsed since the decision of the court or tribunal. Court for this purpose means the county court (Housing Act 1996, s.95) although since April 1, 1997, when the power to determine the reasonableness of variable service charge has been exercisable by a leasehold valuation tribunal the court has been able to endorse the decision of an LVT made following an application to the tribunal for determination of the reasonableness of a service charge.

These restrictions do not apply to tenancies within Part II of the Landlord and Tenant Act 1954 (such as business premises with a flat above which are let as a single unit) or agricultural holdings, within the Agricultural Holdings Act 1986, or farm business tenancies under the Agricultural Tenancies Act 1995.

In addition to the safeguards introduced by section 81 of the Housing Act 1996, section 82 of that Act further provides that any section 146 LPA 1925 notice relating to breach of a covenant to pay a service charge must be in a prescribed form. It must state that section 81 of the Housing Act 1996 applies and must set out the effect of section 81(1) in characters which are at least as conspicuous as those used in the notice to indicate that the tenancy may be forfeited or those used to specify the breach complained of (whichever is the more conspicuous). It should be noted that where the service charge has been reserved as rent, a section 146 notice will not be necessary as a preliminary to forfeiture (*Escalus Properties Ltd v. Robinson*, above).

Some critics have suggested that whilst the above recent reforms were necessary to deal with a number of rogue landlords, there is a danger that tenants who have no reasonable case will refer service charges to a leasehold valuation tribunal for a determination as to their reasonableness simply as a ploy to delay paying reasonable and legitimate service charges. (See D. Gilder, [1997] 32 E.G. 79 and A. Myers [1996] 44 E.G. 174.)

No contracting out permitted

Section 146 is mandatory in the cases of those breaches of covenant to which it applies and it is not possible for a landlord and tenant to contract out of its requirements either directly or indirectly. Thus in a case where the tenant was in effect required to surrender his tenancy in the event of a breach of covenant it was held that this was unenforceable and that if the event in question occurred the landlord would be obliged to bring forfeiture proceedings and comply with section 146 (*Plymouth Corporation v. Harvey* [1971] 1 All E.R. 623). In similar vein it was held that a provision in a tenancy which enabled the landlord to give three months' notice to the tenant on breach of covenant was in substance a forfeiture clause (*Richard Clarke & Co. Ltd v. Widnall* [1976] 3 All E.R. 301 (the tenancy otherwise providing that a notice of 12 months on either side was required to terminate the tenancy).

The section 146 notice

The detailed requirements of section 146(1) can now be examined. The reference to "by action or otherwise" makes it clear that the obligation to comply with section 146 applies both to possession actions and cases of peaceable re-entry (*Billson v. Residential Apartments* (above).

The landlord must specify in the notice the breach complained of. As to what this requires it has been said that—

> "I can find nowhere in the section any words which cast upon the landlord the obligation of telling the tenant what it is that he must do. All that the landlord is bound to do is to state particulars of the breaches of covenants of which he complains and call upon the lessee to remedy them. The means by which the breach is to be remedied is a matter for the lessee and not for the lessor. In many cases specification of the breach will of itself suggest the only possible remedy. (*Fox v. Jolly* [1916] A.C. 1 *per* Lord Buckmaster at p.11, see also *Adajio Properties Ltd v. Ausari* [1998] 35 E.G. 86, CA)."

The requirement that the landlord request reasonable compensation does not need to be complied with if such compensation is not wanted by the landlord. Thus its absence will not invalidate the notice (*Lock v. Pearce* [1893] 2 Ch. 271; *Rugby School Governors Ltd v. Tannahill* [1935] 1 K.B. 87, CA).

Remediable and irremediable breaches

It is only necessary for the notice to request that the breach be remedied if "it is capable of remedy".

At first sight this appears to reveal a pitfall because if for whatever reason the notice does not request that the breach of covenant be remedied and the matter goes to trial at which the breach is judged to be remediable, the notice will have been invalid and the landlord will have to start the process all over again. This is precisely what occurred in *Savva and another v. Houssein* [1996] 47 E.G. 138. The tenants had been granted a 12-year tenancy of premises to be used as a cafe, snack bar and a place for operating mini-cabs. The tenant was subsequently in breach of a covenant not to erect certain signs or adverts outside the building and a covenant not to carry out alterations without the landlord's prior written consent. The landlord served a section 146 notice but did not ask for the breaches of covenant to be remedied. Hence the court had to determine whether the breaches were indeed remediable. This turned upon the distinction between remediable and irremediable breaches of covenant.

Staughton L.J. referred to the requirements of section 146 and continued—

> "In my judgment, except in a case of a breach of a covenant not to assign without consent, the question is: whether the remedy referred to is the process of restoring the situation to what it would have been if the covenant had never been broken, or whether it is sufficient that the mischief resulting from a breach of the covenant can be removed. When something has been done without consent, it is not possible to restore the matter wholly to the situation to which it was in before the breach. The moving finger writes and cannot be recalled. That is not to my mind what is meant by a remedy, it is a remedy if the mischief caused by the breach can be removed. In the case of a covenant not to make alterations without consent or not to display signs without consent, if there is a breach of that, the mischief can be removed by removing the signs or restoring the property to the state it was in before the alterations."

The court went on to hold that all the breaches were remediable and therefore the section 146 notice was invalid. The exception in the case of the covenant against assignment was made because of Court of Appeal authority to the effect that the mischief caused by an unlawful assignment or sub-letting was incapable of being remedied (*Scala House and District Property Co. Ltd v. Forbes* [1973] 3 All E.R. 308, CA). The assignment or sub-letting once effected could not be undone (but see below as to relief against forfeiture).

In the past it had been suggested at various times that whilst breaches of positive covenants (*e.g.* covenants to repair) would always be remediable, breach of a negative covenant would not normally be remediable. Another suggestion was that a once and for all breach could never be remedied. With the probable exception of an unlawful assignment or sub-letting (see above), these propositions are clearly no longer tenable in law. Each case will depend on all the circumstances. Thus whilst it has been stated that "breach of a positive covenant to do something can ordinarily for practical purposes, be remedied by the thing actually being done" (*Expert Clothing Service and Sales Ltd v. Hillgate House Ltd* [1986] Ch. 340, 357 *per* Slade L.J.), it has also been said that "I can see no reason why similar reasoning should not apply to negative covenants" (*Savva and another v. Houssein* [1996] 47 E.G. 138 at 140 *per* Aldous L.J.).

In *Expert Clothing Service and Sales Ltd v. Hillgate House Ltd* (above) where the tenant was in long-standing breach of a covenant to reconstruct the leased premises, it was held that the breach was nevertheless remediable. Thus it would seem that a once-and-for-all, or possibly even a continuing, breach of a positive covenant is in most cases likely to be found to be remediable. The test is simply whether the harm done to the landlord is capable of being remedied within a reasonable time. Although the same test would appear to be applicable to breaches of negative covenants, there is more prospect in such a case of it being impossible to remove the offending mischief.

Thus in *Rugby School Governors Ltd v. Tannahill* [1935] 1 K.B. 87 CA; and *British Petroleum Pension Trust Ltd v. Behrendt* [1985] 2 E.G.L.R. 97 breaches of a covenant not to use the premises for immoral purposes were held to be irremediable in the circumstances where the premises had been used for prostitution and where mere cesser of the offending user could not remove the stigma which had become attached to the premises. (See also *Egerton v. Esplanade Hotels London Ltd* [1947] 2 All E.R. 88).

In *Rugby School Governors Ltd v. Tannahill* at p.91 Greer L.J. stated that—

> "I cannot conceive how a breach of this kind can be remedied. The result of committing the breach would be known all over the neighbourhood and seriously affect the value of the premises. Even a money payment together with the cessation of the improper use of the house could not be a remedy."

Despite these decisions it does not follow that immoral user of the premises will never be capable of remedy. Thus in *Glass v. Kencakes* [1966] 1 Q.B. 612 at 629 Paull J. stated that—

> "The fact that the...user involves immorality does not in itself render the breach incapable of remedy, provided that the lessees neither knew of nor had any reason to know of the fact that the flat was being so used, The remedy in such a case, however, must involve not only that immediate steps are taken to stop such a user so soon as the user is known, but that an action for forfeiture of the sub-tenant's lease must be started within a reasonable time."

But even in such a case it was made clear that a breach may still be irremediable in all the circumstances. Examples of such cases would be where the section 146 notice was not the first notice that had had to be served, or if there were "particularly revolting circumstances" attached to the user (*ibid.*). Thus in *Glass v. Kencakes* (above) the breach was held to be remediable by the tenant where the offending use as a brothel had been carried on by a sub-tenant of part without the knowledge of the tenant who, when he discovered the breach took immediate steps to forfeit the sub-tenancy which contained a similar covenant and forfeiture clause. By contrast the breach in *British Petroleum Pension Trust Ltd v. Behrendt* (above) was irremediable because the tenant had turned a blind eye to the immoral user of the premises by a licensee.

The principle in *Rugby School Governors Ltd v. Tannahill* (above) was applied in *Dunraven Securities Ltd v. Holloway* (1982) 264 E.G. 709, CA where a covenant not to use or permit the premises to be used for an illegal purpose was held to have been irremediably broken when the tenant's business manager was guilty of the offence of keeping obscene materials on the premises which were being used, in breach of covenant, as a "sex shop". The same result was reached in *Van Haarlan v. Kasner* (1992) 64 P.& C.R. 214 where the offending use consisted of using the premises for offences (that is acts preparatory to spying) under the Official Secrets Act 1920, although it was made clear that not every illegal user will automatically amount to an irremediable breach of covenant. It will depend on the seriousness and nature of the offence. (See also *Hoffman v. Fineberg* [1949] Ch. 245 where use of the premises for unlawful gaming was held to be an irremediable breach of covenant).

To get over the difficulty faced by a landlord who is uncertain whether the breach is irremediable in law, it is perfectly proper to frame the section 146 notice so as to require the breach to be remedied "if capable of remedy". It would of course even in such a case be necessary to give the tenant a reasonable time in which to remedy the breach (should it prove to be remediable) before proceeding with the forfeiture (see *Glass v. Kencakes*, above).

Time limits

In a case where the breach is capable of remedy the matter of what is a reasonable time will depend on all the circumstances. Three months is usual, at least for a repairing covenant, but "there are no hard and fast rules and all will depend upon what is required to be done" (*Bhojwanui v. Kingsley Investment Trust Ltd* [1992] 2 E.G.L.R. 70 *per* T Morison Q.C. sitting as a deputy High Court judge. See also *Cardigan Properties Ltd v. Consolidated Property Investments Ltd* [1991] 07 E.G. 132 (four weeks was reasonable on the facts where there had been a breach of a covenant to insure by the tenant)). Even in the case of an irremediable breach it is necessary for the landlord to give the tenant an appropriate period of time to consider his position (*Horsey Estates Ltd v. Steiger* [1899] 2 Q.B. 79 at 91). In *Scala House and District Property Co. Ltd v. Forbes* (above), 14 days was considered sufficient for this purpose.

Relief against forfeiture

Even if the tenant cannot (*e.g.* because the breach is irremediable), or does not, forestall further action by complying with the requirements of a section 146 notice, he can still seek relief against forfeiture following service of the notice (LPA 1925, s.146(2)). This is a most important jurisdiction because it gives the court a wide power to prevent forfeiture on appropriate terms if necessary. For this purpose "tenant" includes both a legal assignee and an equitable assignee (*High Street Investment Ltd v. Bellshore Property Investment Ltd* [1996] 2 E.G.L.R. 40). The position is governed by the following propositions:

(a) Statutory power to grant relief

The court has a statutory power to grant relief against forfeiture, following breach of a covenant other than to pay rent. Law of Property Act 1925, section 146(2) provides that—

> "Where a lessor is proceeding, by action or otherwise, to enforce such a right of re-entry or forfeiture, the lessee may in the lessor's action, if any, or in any action brought by himself, apply to the court for relief; and the court may grant or refuse relief, as the court, having regard to the proceedings and conduct of the parties under the foregoing provisions of this section, and to all the other circumstances, thinks fit; and in case of relief may grant it on such terms, if any, as to costs, expenses, damages, compensation, penalty, or otherwise, including the granting of an injunction to restrain any like breach in the future, as the court, in the circumstances of each case, thinks fit."

It now seems to be clear that this statutory power supersedes any inherent equitable jurisdiction to grant relief against forfeiture in respect of a breach of those covenants to which it applies (*Billson v. Residential Apartments* [1991] 3 All E.R. 265, CA (the decision was reversed on appeal by the House of Lords on another point (see below) and so the present issue was left open). In coming to the conclusion that the statutory jurisdiction was the sole source of the court's power to grant relief, the Court of Appeal followed the earlier decisions in *Official Custodian for Charities v. Parway Estates Developments Ltd* [1985] 1 Ch. 151, CA and *Smith v. Metropolitan Properties Ltd* (1986) 1 E.G.L.R. 52, thereby overruling *Abbey National BS v. Maybeech Ltd* [1985] 1 Ch. 190).

(b) Application can be made as soon as section 146 notice served

An application for relief can be made as soon as the section 146 notice is received and at any time until the landlord has obtained judgment and recovered possession (*Pakwood Transport Ltd v. Beauchamp Place Ltd* (1977) 245 E.G. 309, CA and *Billson v. Residential Apartments* [1992] 1 All E.R. 141, HL). (It is of interest to contrast the position where relief is sought in county court proceedings following breach of the covenant to pay rent. In such cases an application for relief may be brought up to six months after the landlord has obtained possession (see p.139 above).)

(c) Peaceable re-entry

If the landlord forfeits by peaceable re-entry the tenant can still seek relief after the service of the section 146 notice and indeed after re-entry. There is no time limit in such a case but in deciding whether or not to grant relief the court will take into account all the circumstances, including any delay by the tenant (*Billson v. Residential Apartments*, above).

In *Billson* the tenants had made alterations to the premises without the landlord's consent. Fourteen days after the service of a section 146 notice the landlords re-entered the premises peaceably, at dawn, and changed the locks. Four hours later, the tenants, through their workmen, then regained possession and the landlord brought court proceedings for possession arguing that the tenants were ineligible to be considered for relief because in the words of section 146(2) the landlords, having re-entered peaceably, were no longer "proceeding by action or otherwise to enforce the re-entry or forfeiture"—they had already enforced it! This argument succeeded at first instance and (not without misgivings) in the Court of Appeal, but not in the House of Lords, where a distaste for peaceable re-entry as a means of recovering possession by a landlord following breach of covenant by the tenant was shown by their Lordships. The House of Lords had to perform some linguistic gymnastics to arrive at the result which they considered to be dictated by justice and the merits of the case. Lord Templeman construed "is proceeding" to mean "proceeds", so that the tenant could still seek relief even though the landlord had already enforced his right. Lord Oliver construed "is proceeding" to mean that where the landlord re-enters by peaceable re-entry the tenant can still seek relief because until his application had been disposed of, the landlord would still be "proceeding", although it could be argued that this renders redundant the words "or otherwise" in section 146(2) (see [1992] E.G. 9202).

Following the decision of the Court of Appeal in *Billson* there had been a sharp increase in the use of peaceable re-entry by landlords. It was swift, cheap and appeared to rule out lengthy and expensive litigation. The decision of the House of Lords reversed that trend. The well-advised landlord has since preferred the certainty of proceeding by court action and obtaining the security of a final possession order and, if relevant, a dismissal of any application for relief by the tenant or others. The decision has also operated to the benefit of mortgagees, who stood to lose their security without their knowledge where the landlord peaceably re-entered.

(d) Relief discretionary

There are no fixed rules governing the exercise of the court's discretion to grant or withhold relief against forfeiture. In practice it will invariably be granted where the breach can be remedied and the tenant undertakes to observe his obligations for the future (*Hyman v. Rose* [1912] A.C. 623). But this will not be possible if for some reason the personal qualifications and suitability of the tenant are at the heart of the lease. This was the case in *Earl Bathhurst v. Fine* [1974] 2 All E.R. 1160, where the tenant of a large country house was an American citizen who had gone abroad and been refused re-entry to the United Kingdom. In the tenancy, which contained an absolute covenant against assignment (save in respect of a cottage on the estate), the tenant had covenanted to reside there and keep the house in a character fitting the estate. While the tenant was abroad execution was levied on the property in respect of unpaid debts and this triggered the operation of a forfeiture clause in the tenancy. Although remaining abroad the tenant sought relief against forfeiture and was refused on the basis that it was essential that he be present and he had proved to be not a fit person to be tenant of the property.

The fact that the breach is irremediable (see above) does not necessarily mean that relief against forfeiture will not be granted (see *Ropemaker Properties Ltd v. Noonhaven Ltd* [1989] 34 E.G. 39 at 49 *per* Millett J.). It will depend upon all the circumstances; although it is clear that the courts have displayed a marked reluctance to grant relief against forfeiture in the case of a breach of covenant by way of immoral or illegal user of the premises. Thus relief was refused in *British Petroleum Pension Trust Ltd v. Behrendt,* above) even though there had been no further breaches, the tenant had offered to enter into a covenant not to sub-let without the landlord's consent, the tenant had paid a premium for the lease on assignment and there was a substantial portion of the term left to run on the lease.

However, the mere fact that the breach in question involves immoral user does not in itself preclude the court from granting relief. "It will, however, be in only the rarest and most exceptional circumstances that the court will grant relief in such a case, particularly where the breach of covenant has been both wilful and serious" (*Ropemaker Properties Ltd v. Noonhaven Ltd* (above) at 46 *per* Millett J.). In the *Ropemaker* case, where a nightclub had been used for prostitution, the judge described the breaches of covenant as of the utmost gravity and a deliberate and continuing disregard by the tenants of their obligations under the lease. Having made such findings it is perhaps surprising that the judge went on to hold that the circumstances were nevertheless sufficiently exceptional to merit granting relief against forfeiture. He listed a number of factors which influenced him in coming to that conclusion: (a) the lease was granted in 1982 for 25 years at a rent of £75,000 p.a. It was now worth considerably in excess of £250,000 p.a.; (b) forfeiture would lead to a substantial financial loss to the defendants out of all proportion to their offence and would result in a windfall gain to the plaintiffs who would acquire the lease for nothing and be able to redevelop the site; (c) the immoral user had ended and was unlikely to be resumed; (d) any stigma was likely to be short-lived; (e) getting rid of the tenants would not remove the stigma which had been created by the club managers and staff, who had left, (f) the defendants had otherwise been excellent tenants; (g) the director of the defendant company was in seriously poor health and had been thinking of retiring and disposing of the lease—he had offered to use his best endeavours to find a purchaser within an appropriate time scale if he were afforded relief. (See also *Central Estates Belgravia v. Woolgar No. 2* [1972] 1 W.L.R. 1048 where relief against forfeiture was granted where the tenant had for a short period and in breach of covenant kept a brothel at the premises).

The court granted relief against forfeiture in *Van Haarlam v. Kasner* (above), even though the breach of covenant was by way of illegal user (spying for a foreign power) and the tenant was serving a lengthy prison sentence. The court considered that it did not necessarily follow that the tenant should be deprived of his 99-year tenancy, for which he had paid a substantial premium. None of the illegal activities performed in the flat were offences *qua* the tenancy. The tenant had paid the ground rent and otherwise observed the covenants in the tenancy. In any event it was necessary to balance the damage sustained by the landlord and whether that is proportionate to the advantages they would obtain if no relief were granted. Harman J. expressed the view that—

> "The advantage to the landlords of obtaining vacant possession of this flat where there is well over 80 years to run at a very low ground rent is so disproportionate to the damage done to it by the acts, illegal as they were and damaging to the state as they were, by Mr Van Haarlem, that had it been my business I would have granted him relief from forfeiture. (On the facts, this did not arise because the landlord was held to have waived the breach by acceptance of rent with full knowledge of the facts amounting to a breach of covenant. See above.)"

Although irremediable, breach of a covenant against alienation (see Chapter 4 above) will not necessarily mean that an application for relief against forfeiture will be denied although it is true to say that the jurisdiction to grant relief will be exercised sparingly (*Creery v. Summersell & Flowerdew & Co.* [1949] Ch. 751). Relief was granted in *Scala House and District Property Co. Ltd v. Forbes* [1973] 3 All E.R. 308, CA because the sub-tenancy had been ended, the transaction which constituted the breach was never intended to take effect as a sub-letting, was the solicitor's fault, did not harm the landlord who could not have reasonably withheld consent had he been asked and if forfeiture had gone ahead the landlord would have benefitted from an increased rent from new tenants. (See also *Lam Kee Ying Sdn Bhd v. Lam Shen Tong* [1975] A.C. 247, PC.)

The court has power in appropriate circumstances to grant relief in respect of part only of the premises leased to the tenant. This will arise where the part which was the subject of the offending user was a physically separate part of the property which could be let and enjoyed as such. In *GMS Syndicate Ltd v. Gary Elliott Ltd* [1981] 1 All E.R. 619 a ground floor and basement of a building were let to the tenant (a men's clothing retailer) who sub-let the basement for use as a sauna bath, gymnasium and health club. The sub-tenant assignees had, in breach of covenant (both to the sub-landlord and the head landlord with whom they had covenanted directly) permitted the use of the basement for immoral purposes. On an application for relief against forfeiture by the tenant the court granted relief in respect of the ground floor but permitted forfeiture of the basement.

A problem can arise where premises are let under a tenancy which contains a forfeiture clause and there is a subsequent assignment of part of the premises. If a breach of covenant occurs which affects only one of the parts it is provided that the forfeiture clause in the tenancy will only be exercisable in relation to that part (Landlord and Tenant (Covenants) Act 1995, s.21(1)).

The court will be reluctant to grant relief where there has been a wilful breach of covenant and no attempt made to remedy the breach. Relief was refused in *Tulapam Properties Ltd v. De Almeida and others* (1981) 260 E.G. 919 (Sir Douglas Frank Q.C. sitting as a deputy High Court judge) where the tenant remained in flagrant breach of a covenant to use the premises for residential purposes for a period of two years, despite service of a section 146 notice. The relevant factors—the conduct of the tenant, the nature and gravity of the breach and its relationship to the value of the property to be forfeited—governing the exercise of the court's discretion in the case of a wilful breach were discussed by the House of Lords in *Shiloh Spinners v. Harding* [1973] AC 691 H.L.

Sub-tenants and mortgagees

At common law a sub-tenancy will be destroyed by forfeiture of the head tenancy. Similarly a mortgagee of either the head tenancy or a sub-tenancy will automatically lose his security. For this reason relief is available at the court's discretion to sub-tenants and mortgagees (whether by sub-demise or by legal charge—*Grand Junction Co. v. Bates* [1954] 2 Q.B. 160) who seek relief against forfeiture under Law of Property Act 1925, s.146(4). This provision applies both to actions for breach of the covenant to pay rent and to actions in respect of breach of other covenants and is applicable in both the High Court and the county court. The principles on which the discretion is to be exercised are the same in each case (*Belgravia Insurance Co. Ltd v. Meah* [1964] 1 Q.B. 436, CA). If successful, the sub-tenant or mortgagee will be granted a new tenancy on the same terms as the forfeited tenancy (and any supplemental tenancy: *Barclays Bank plc v. Prudential Assurance Co. Ltd* [1998] 10 E.G. 159, Hazel Williamson Q.C. sitting as a deputy High Court judge). A sub-tenant or his mortgagee will not be entitled to a lease any longer than the residue of the original sub-tenancy (s.146(4)).

A disadvantage is that the sub-tenant or, more likely, a mortgagee may not learn of the forfeiture proceedings until it is too late, although the landlord is required to endorse the writ or summons claiming possession with the name and address of any sub-tenant or mortgagee who is known to him and to serve a copy on those persons (RSC, Ord. 4 and CCR, Ord. 6, as amended by S.I. 1986 No. 1187).

But relief will not be afforded to a sub-tenant or mortgagee after the landlord has recovered possession by court order against the tenant (*Egerton v. Jones* [1939] 2 K.B. 702) unless the order is set aside (under RSC, Ord. 13, r. 9) to permit an application for relief to proceed, although this will be unlikely where an applicant had been given notice of the forfeiture action. (But note that in the case of breach of a covenant to pay rent an application for relief by the sub-tenant or mortgagee can be made up to six months later under section 138(9) County Courts Act 1984 (see p.139 above).

Relief will normally be afforded to sub-tenants and mortgagees on the usual terms that a successful applicant for relief will pay all outstanding arrears and costs incurred by the landlord. A mortgagee will be given a new tenancy by way of security with the tenant retaining the equity of redemption. This has the side-effect that the tenant will retain his tenancy even though the court would have declined to grant relief to the tenant.

A disadvantage of a sub-tenant or mortgagee obtaining relief under section 146(4) is that relief is by way of a new tenancy and is not retrospective. It follows that a successful applicant will be liable to pay mesne profits on account of the period between the forfeiture (by service of the writ or physical re-entry) and the granting of relief (*Pellicano v. MEPC plc* [1994] 19 E.G. 138). If rental values are higher than the rent payable under the lease, as for example where the tenancy had been granted for a substantial premium and a low rent, this can be very disadvantageous.

However, it has been held by the Court of Appeal that in a case which is not a "rent-only case" this disadvantage can be avoided by the sub-tenant or mortgagee seeking relief under s.146(2) (High Court) which has the advantage that relief is retrospective by way of reinstatement of the tenancy, thus avoiding liability for mesne profits in respect of the period between the date of forfeiture and the granting of relief (*Escalus Properties Ltd v. Dennis* [1996] Q.B. 231). Similarly in a rent-only case in the county court (as compared with the High Court), retrospective relief can be sought by the holder of a derivative interest, under County Courts Act 1984, s.139(9B)(C). (See p.139 above.)

Exceptions to section 146

There are a number of exceptions and modifications to section 146, both in the High Court and the county court (see s. 146(8)(9)) the most important of which are as follows.

First, where the forfeiture occurs on the tenant's bankruptcy (which for this purpose includes liquidation by arrangement and in relation to a corporation, means its winding up: LPA 1925, s.205(1)(i)), or the taking in execution of his interest under the tenancy), section 146 does not apply if the property falls within any one of five categories. They are in effect tenancies of (a) agricultural or pastoral land, (b) mines or minerals, (c) a house used or intended to be used as a public house or beershop, (d) a house let as a dwelling-house with the use of any furniture, books, works of art, or other chattels not being in the nature of fixtures, (e) any property with respect to which the personal qualifications of the tenant are of importance for the preservation of the value or character of the property, or on the ground of neighbourhood to the lessor, or to any person holding under him (s.146(9)).

Secondly, if a forfeiture occurs in the same circumstances as above (*i.e.* bankruptcy, etc.) but the property does not fall into any of the exceptional categories ((a) to (e) above) it is in effect provided that if the lease is sold within one year of the bankruptcy the right to seek relief against forfeiture applies indefinitely for the benefit of the new tenant, thereby enabling that person's title to be confirmed by seeking relief in any forfeiture proceedings. But if the lease is not sold within that year then section 146 only applies during the first 12 months following the bankruptcy. Thereafter the tenant is barred from seeking relief and is therefore vulnerable to a forfeiture action by the landlord. (s.146(10)). As the Law Commission observed, "The effect is to encourage sale within the year (in those cases in which sale is not precluded by the terms of the tenancy) and to enable a sale within that period to be made at a price which is not depressed by the purchaser's fear of having to face an action for possession by the landlord without statutory protection." (Law Com. No. 221 "Termination of Tenancies Bill" (1994), p.123, para. 2.53.) But a mortgagee is not barred and may seek relief under section 146(4) or 146(2). As

Chapter 7

EFFECT OF ALIENATION ON ENFORCEABILITY OF OBLIGATIONS

A. ENFORCEABILITY OF COVENANTS IN THE TENANCY AFTER ASSIGNMENT OF THE TENANCY AND/OR REVERSION

Introduction

It has been axiomatic for centuries that a tenancy of land both creates an estate in the land for a specified period and at the same time constitutes a contract between the original parties (see, *e.g. Walker v. Harris* (1587) Co. Rep. 22a at 23a). The tenancy will contain a number of implied and/or express obligations on the part of the landlord and rather more on the part of the tenant. (For the sake of convenience, whether a legal tenancy is created by deed or not (see Chapter 1 above) these will be referred to in the rest of this chapter as covenants, even though that term is strictly confined to obligations contained in a deed. Indeed the Landlord and Tenant (Covenants) Act 1995 also adopts this wider usage of the term covenant for the purposes of the law of landlord and tenant).

As long as the original parties to the tenancy retain their respective interests in the tenancy and the reversion there is no difficulty with regard to the issue of the enforceability of covenants in the tenancy. They are enforceable between the parties by virtue of the law of contract if either party is in breach. Furthermore, if the landlord has included a provision for forfeiture or re-entry for breach of covenant on the part of the tenant, he may be able to exercise that right in the event of breach of covenant by the tenant (see p.134 above). This contractual liability is commonly referred to as privity of contract liability.

But what is the position where either party disposes of their respective interest(s) under the tenancy during the period of the term and there is non-compliance by an assignee with a covenant in the tenancy or there has been a pre-assignment breach of covenant by landlord or tenant?

We have seen above that a tenancy is more than just a contract. It creates an estate in land that can be dealt with as a property right in a variety of ways notably by way of assignment or the creation of a sub-tenancy of the whole or part of the subject premises. Particularly in the case of a tenancy of some length and of some capital value there could be several such dealings throughout the life of the term originally granted. At the same time the landlord's reversionary interest might also change hands on one or more occasions. In these circumstances it becomes essential to determine the effect of any such disposition(s) by landlord and/or tenant on the enforceability of covenants in the tenancy.

Some legal mechanism was required to enable express or implied obligations under the tenancy to continue to be enforceable after such an event. Despite the fact, as noted above, that the original parties remained contractually liable throughout the term, in the absence of agreement to the contrary, it would especially make sense, and be in accordance with the intention of all parties concerned, if the covenants could be enforced by and against the persons who at the time of any breach are in the relationship of landlord and tenant. Consequently appropriate rules were developed, both common law and statutory, to achieve this outcome.

The Landlord and Tenant (Covenants) Act 1995

Before examining those rules it is necessary to draw attention to the fact that, as will be seen below, the law governing the enforceability of covenants in tenancies where there has been an assignment of the tenancy and/or the reversion was changed significantly by the Landlord and Tenant (Covenants) Act 1995 which applies to qualifying tenancies (known as "new tenancies") granted on or after January 1, 1996. Because that Act is not, save in a number of important respects, retrospective in operation it will still be necessary for many years to come to be familiar with the pre-Act law which still applies to tenancies granted before that date and indeed to certain tenancies granted after that date. It will be convenient to refer to these as "old tenancies". Each set of rules is examined in turn below but before doing so it is necessary to determine whether or not a tenancy is a "new tenancy" for the purposes of the Landlord and Tenant (Covenants) Act 1995.

The meaning of a new tenancy For the purposes of the Landlord and Tenant (Covenants) Act 1995 a "new tenancy" is one granted on after January 1, 1996 (the operative date) unless it was created pursuant to a contract entered into before that date or as a result of a court order (*e.g.* under Part II of the Landlord and Tenant Act 1954 (Chapter 13 below) made before that date (Landlord and Tenant (Covenants) Act 1995, s.1(3)).

A tenancy granted on or after January 1, 1996 in pursuance of an option granted before that date is not a new tenancy whether the option was exercised before or after the operative date (s.1(6)). For this purpose, option includes a right of pre-emption (s.1(7)). The Act makes specific provision to the effect that where after the operative date by virtue of any variation of a tenancy there is a deemed surrender and regrant, this will create a new tenancy for the purposes of the Act (s.1(5)). The circumstances in which a variation will have this effect under the general law were considered in *Friends Provident v. British Railways Board* [1996] 1 All E.R. 336. See p.167 below and p.125 above.

The rules governing "old tenancies"

The enforceability of covenants in such tenancies turns on one or both of two doctrines. The first, which has been referred to above and is examined further below, is the doctrine of privity of contract, which deals with the continuing liability of the original parties throughout the term of the tenancy, irrespective of any dealings with that tenancy and/or the landlord's reversion. The second, which deals with the enforceability of covenants by and/or against assignees following a disposition of the tenancy by way of assignment and/or transfer of the landlord's interest, is the doctrine of privity of estate. (For the sake of convenience, a transaction disposing of the landlord's interest is also referred to below as an "assignment", although strictly speaking this term is not in law appropriate where the landlord's interest is a fee simple).

1. Privity of estate

Privity of estate was said to exist where the parties stood in the relationship of landlord and tenant by virtue of one having the landlord's interest in the property and the other that of the tenant. When a tenancy was granted it followed that the parties had both privity of contract and privity of estate. As noted above, as long as the original parties both held their respective interests, this relationship by way of privity of estate was unimportant from the point of view of their liability under the tenancy for breach of covenant. The covenants would be contractually enforceable in accordance with the terms of the tenancy. However, if either party disposed of their interest in the property the original parties would cease to have privity of estate but would continue to have privity of contract, the significance of which is examined below. By contrast, following an assignment of either the tenancy or the reversion or both, the parties who thereby became for the time being landlord and tenant would then have privity of estate (but not privity of contract) whilst each held their respective interest.

The significance of this is that whilst they remained in the relationship of landlord and tenant those persons would become directly bound by and could enforce certain, but not necessarily all, of the covenants in the tenancy, unless they agreed to the contrary. This was achieved by two rules, one common law and one statutory.

(a) Assignment of the tenancy and/or reversion

On a legal assignment of the tenancy there will pass to the assignee the benefit of all the landlord's covenants and the burden of all the tenant's covenants in the tenancy which "touch and concern the land" (*Spencer's Case* (1583) 5 Co. Rep. 16a). This means that most tenancy covenants entered into by the tenant (*e.g.* to pay the rent, not to assign the tenancy without the landlord's consent, not to use the premises for certain purposes) will be enforceable against the assignee, the new tenant in the same way as they were against the original tenant when that person held the tenancy. Similarly those covenants entered into by the landlord (*e.g.* to repair the property, or to provide services) will be enforceable against the landlord by the new tenant. The rule applies to tenancies made by deed and tenancies in writing (*Boyer v. Warbey* [1953] 1 Q.B. 234) and probably to oral tenancies assuming that the terms can be proved. (But it should be noted that a legal assignment of a tenancy including an oral tenancy must be by deed (*Crago v. Julian* [1992] 1 W.L.R. 372 (see p.30 above)).

By a parallel statutory rule dating back to the Grantees of Reversions Act 1540 and eventually re-enacted in the Law of Property Act 1925, it was provided that on an assignment of the landlord's reversion the benefit and burden of all covenants which "have reference to the subject matter of the lease" would pass to the assignee of the reversion (Law of Property Act 1925, s.141(1) (benefit) and 142(1) (burden)). It has been held that the types of covenant which pass in both cases are the same. In other words, covenants which are deemed to "have reference to the subject matter of the lease" for the purposes of the statutory rule following an assignment of the reversion are exactly the same as those which "touch and concern the land" for the purposes of the rule in *Spencer's Case* (above) following an assignment of the tenancy (*Hua Chiao Commercial Bank Ltd v. Chiaphua Industries* [1987] A.C. 99, PC.

(b) Rationale of the rules

The rationale of the privity of estate rule was explained by Lord Templeman in *City of London Corporation v. Fell* [1994] 1 A.C. 458, 464 when he stated that—

> "The principle that the benefit and burden of covenants in a lease which touch and concern the land run with the term and with the reversion is necessary for the effective operation of the law of landlord and tenant...Common law, and statute following the common law, were faced with the problem of rendering effective the obligations under a lease which might endure for a period of 999 years or more beyond the control of any covenantor. The solution was to annex to the term and the reversion the benefit and burden of covenants which touch and concern the land. The covenants having been annexed, every legal owner of the term granted by the lease and every legal owner of the reversion from time to time holds his estate with the benefit of and subject to the covenants which touch and concern the land."

These obligations, once annexed, endure, whatever happens to the original parties.

> "The effect of common law and statute on a lease is to create rights and obligations which are independent of the parallel rights and obligations of the original human covenantor who and whose heirs may fail or the parallel rights and obligations of a corporate covenantor which may be dissolved. (*per* Lord Templeman p.465)."

It follows that any such annexed obligations will be binding on or enforceable by the landlord and tenant for the time being, but in the absence of any contractual obligation a landlord or tenant will cease to be bound by any such covenant in respect of matters arising after they have parted with the tenancy or the reversion, as the case may be.

> "The liability of an assignee of a lease, begins and ends with his character of assignee...An assignee may, whenever he pleases, assign again; and the moment he divests himself of the character of assignee, he also shakes off his liability...an assignee is only liable by privity of estate, which ceases when he ceases to be assignee, and loses that character. (*Onslow v. Corrie* (1817) 2 Madd. 330; 56 E.R. 357, 360 *per* Plumer, V.-C.)"

(c) Which covenants touch and concern the land?

We saw above that only covenants which touched and concerned the land would pass under the doctrine of privity of estate. In general this means those covenants which affect the landlord in his normal capacity as landlord and the tenant in his normal capacity as tenant, as distinct from those which impose purely personal or collateral obligations (*Hua Chiao Commercial Bank Ltd v. Chiaphua Industries* (above). This is easier to state than explain, but Lord Oliver hazarded an explanation in *P & A Swift Investments (a firm) v. Combined English Stores Group plc* [1988] 2 All E.R. 885, where he cited with approval the test formulated by Bayley J. in *Congleton Corporation v. Pattison* (1808) 10 East 130) and adopted by Farwell J. in *Rogers v. Hosegood* [1900] 2 Ch. 388, 395, that—

> "the covenant must either affect the land as regards mode of occupation, or it must be such as *per se*, and not merely from collateral circumstances, affects the value of the land."

Lord Oliver went on to say that–

"Formulations of definitive tests are always dangerous but it seems to me that without claiming to expound an exhaustive guide, the following provides a satisfactory working test for whether, in any given case, a covenant touches and concerns the land: (1) the covenant benefits only the reversioner for the time being, and if separated from the reversion ceases to be of benefit to the covenantee; (2) the covenant affects the nature, quality, mode of user or value of the land of the reversioner; (3) the covenant is not expressed to be personal (that is to say neither being given only to a specific reversioner nor in respect of the obligations only of a specific tenant); (4) the fact that a covenant is to pay a sum of money will not prevent it from touching and concerning the land so long as the three forgoing conditions are satisfied and the covenant is connected with something to be done on, to or in relation to the land."

Unfortunately Lord Oliver's test, like others, is not devoid of criticism (see Fancourt *Enforceability of Landlord and Tenants Covenants*, 1997, p.32). If the requirements are cumulative it can be argued, for example, that a covenant to pay money in respect of the premises can fall within the second limb (*i.e.* it affects the value of the reversion) but outside the first (because it could still benefit the covenantee even if separated from the reversion) and yet such covenants have been held to touch and concern the land. Furthermore, despite limb (3) of Lord Oliver's test, a covenant expressed to be personal to one party could be enforceable by or against a person other than the covenantee. Thus in *Systems Floors Ltd v. Ruralpride Ltd* [1995] 1 E.G.L.R. 48, by a side letter a landlord gave an undertaking personal to the tenant concerning the modification of certain covenants in the tenancy, including a right to surrender the tenancy in certain circumstances. Following an assignment of the reversion it was held that the obligation ran with the land and was enforceable against the new reversioner. Although personal to the tenant the obligation was not personal to the original landlord. The fact that it was in a side letter did not prevent the burden of the obligation running with the reversion on an assignment of that reversion. (See also LPA 1925, s.142.)

However, despite the criticisms levelled against Lord Oliver's test, it will be satisfied by most, but not all, covenants in the vast majority of tenancies. By way of example, covenants to pay rent (*Parker v. Webb* (1693) 3 Salk. 5) or a service charge, covenants not to dispose of the tenancy by way of assignment (*Goldstein v. Sanders* [1915] 1 Ch. 549) or sub-letting, user covenants (*Wilkinson v. Rogers* (1864) 2 De G.J. & Sm. 62), repairing covenants (*Matures v. Westwood* (1598) Cro. Eliz. 599), are obvious and long-established covenants which touch and concern the land. As Sir Nicholas Browne-Wilkinson V.-C. observed (in *Kumar v. Dunning* [1987] 3 W.L.R. 1167), they either relate to things done on the land itself (*e.g.* repair and user covenants) or affect its value (*e.g.* the covenant to pay rent, which is the major cause of the landlord's reversion having any value during the continuance of the term).

By contrast, purely collateral covenants which do not touch and concern the land do not bind assignees by virtue of the privity of estate doctrine. Examples of such a covenant are (a) a covenant to pay a collateral sum (*i.e.* one not reserved as rent). (In *Re Hunter's Lease, Giles v. Hutchings* [1942] Ch. 124 the tenancy contained an option to renew with a proviso that if the option was not exercised either party might insist on the payment of £500 by the landlord to the tenant. The court held that this obligation did not touch and concern the land and therefore the burden did not pass to the assignee on an assignment of the reversion, and (b) a covenant (in a tenancy of a public house) not to keep a public house within half a mile of the leased public house premises (*Thomas v. Hayward* (1869) 38 L.J.Ex. 175 at 176). The rationale of this last decision seems to be that the covenant does not benefit the land of the covenantee *per se* but a business carried on on that land, although the decision does appear to be somewhat at odds with other decisions in which it has been held that a tie covenant is capable of touching and concerning the land. (See *Clegg v. Hands* (1890) 44 Ch. D. 503 concerning a covenant to buy all beer supplies from a brewer landlord and *Caerns Motor Services Ltd v. Texaco Ltd* [1994] 1 W.L.R. 1249 where the benefit of a covenant by the tenant to buy all petrol supplies from the landlord oil company was held to run with the reversion. But see *Amoco Australia Ltd v. Rocco Bros. Motor Engineering Co. Pty* [1975] A.C. 561, PC for the vulnerability of such covenants to being struck down by the doctrine of restraint of trade. For a discussion of the relevance of the anti-competition provisions of the Treaty of Rome to such covenants, see T. Frazer [1994] Conv. 150). But even though collateral covenants entered into by a tenant would not be binding on an assignee, the landlord might be able to enforce them indirectly by including a right of re-entry, an independent equitable interest, which could be activated by a breach of covenant whoever has caused that breach. (See *Shiloh Spinners Ltd v. Harding* [1973] A.C. 691 at 717, although *Harvey v. Steiger* [1899] 2 Q.B. 79 suggests that this would not be possible in the case of a covenant which does not touch and concern the land). The threat of invoking such a right of re-entry might induce an assignee to comply with the covenant or remedy a breach for fear of losing the tenancy. (See below for a similar issue in connection with the enforceability by the landlord of covenants in the tenancy against a sub-tenant).

It is the more marginal covenants which can cause difficulties when determining whether or not the covenant can be said to touch and concern the land. *Hua Chiao Commercial Bank Ltd. v. Chiaphua Industries* (above) was such a case. The landlord had covenanted to repay to the tenant a deposit paid to secure the performance of covenants under the tenancy by the tenant. The landlord's reversion was assigned to the bank and the original landlord subsequently became insolvent. The tenant sought to recover the deposit from the bank. This required the plaintiffs to establish that the covenant was one which touched and concerned the land (see above). The Privy Council held that it did not. They concluded that the deposit was paid to the landlord as payee and not as landlord. Lord Oliver said that the obligation did not affect the nature, quality or value of the land either during or at the end of the term, nor did it *per se* affect the mode of using or enjoying the subject matter of the tenancy. Whilst it is true that the deposit was paid to secure the performance of covenants under the tenancy by the tenant—

> "The nature of the obligation is simply that of an obligation to repay money which has been received and it is neither necessary nor logical, simply because the conditions of repayment relate to the performance of covenants in a lease, that the transfer of the reversion should create in the transferee an additional and co-extensive obligation to pay money which he has never received and in which he never had any interest or that the assignment of the term should vest in the assignee the right to receive a sum which he has never paid. [1987] AC 99, 113"

The moral of this tale is that the tenancy should make provision for the obligation to pass on an assignment of the reversion thereby enabling this transfer of obligation to be reflected in the price paid for the reversion by the assignee. Similarly the right to sue for return of the deposit should be expressly assigned to the assignee on the assignment of the tenancy. (For further problems see L.Lawrence and S.Petley, "Landlord's Security in a Tenant's Market" [1991] 48 E.G. 54.)

The most important covenant in a tenancy which will not touch and concern the land is one granting the tenant an option to purchase the reversion because this has been held to be a covenant which affects the parties *qua* vendor and purchaser of a different estate in land to that granted by the tenancy (*Woodall v. Clifton* [1905] 2 Ch. 257; *Weg Motors v. Hales* [1962] Ch. 49). It follows that because the benefit of such an option will not pass to an assignee of the tenancy automatically it will be necessary for it to be assigned expressly (*Griffith v. Pelton*

[1958] Ch. 205). By contrast, and anomalously, an option to renew the tenancy does touch and concern the land (*Woodall v. Clifton*, above) although it will also need to be protected by registration under the Land Charges Act 1972 as a class C(iv) land charge (*Beesley v. Hallwood Estates* [1960] 1 W.L.R. 549; *Phillips v. Mobil Oil* [1989] 1 W.L.R. 888; *Taylors Fashions Ltd v. Victoria Trustees Co. Ltd* [1981] 2 W.L.R. 576. For a critical examination of this requirement see M. Thompson (1981) 125 S.J. 816). If title is registered under the Land Registration Act 1925 the option is capable of protection by entry on the register of title of the landlord's estate as a minor interest. If this has not been done it can still be enforceable against an assignee of the reversion as an overriding interest if the tenant is in actual occupation of the land (see LRA 1925, s.70(1)(g); *Webb v. Pollmount Ltd* [1966] Ch. 584. In *Abbey National Building Soc. v. Cann* [1991] 1 A.C. 56 the House of Lords held that the critical moment for determining the status of the occupier for the purposes of section 70(1)(g) is the date of execution of the transfer and not, as in the case of other categories of overriding interest, the date of registration of the transferee).

(d) The rules in action

Passing of the benefit and burden of covenants on assignment of the tenancy This is represented diagrammatically below, where L has granted a tenancy to T who has in turn assigned the tenancy to A. This raises the issues of (a) whether A can sue L on the landlord covenants in the tenancy for breaches which have occurred after the assignment and/or before that date, and (b) whether L can sue A for breaches of covenant which have occurred either before or after the date of the assignment. The liability of A will be examined first.

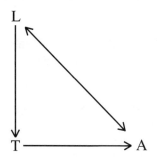

Liability of the assignee of the tenancy to the original landlord As noted above, the effect of a legal assignment of a tenancy is that there will pass to the assignee the benefit of all the landlord's covenants and the burden of all the tenant's covenants in the tenancy which touch and concern the land (*Spencer's Case*, above). An equitable assignment (as under a contract to assign) will not be sufficient to pass the burden of the tenant's covenants to an assignee (*Cox v. Bishop* (1857) 8 De G.M. & G. 815) although an equitable assignee who goes into possession and pays rent may be estopped from denying that he is bound by the covenants in the tenancy (*Rodenhurst Estates Ltd v. WH Barnes Ltd* [1936] 2 All E.R. 3). The assignee becomes liable to the landlord for breach of a covenant that touches and concerns the land which occurs whilst the tenant holds the residue of the term (see below for a possible extension of an assignee's liability beyond that period by contract). In the case of a continuing breach of covenant (such as a covenant to keep in repair) the assignee can become liable for disrepair which began before he became the tenant under the tenancy (*Granada Theatres Ltd v. Freehold Investments (Leytonstone) Ltd* [1959] Ch. 592). Otherwise he is not liable for breaches which have occurred before the assignment (*Churchwardens of St Saviours Southwark v. Smith* (1762) 91 E.R. 179). Nevertheless, despite this absence of liability the assignee may in practice need to rectify any such a breach to obtain relief against forfeiture if the landlord seeks to activate a forfeiture clause in respect of such a breach although this will not be possible if the landlord has waived the breach in question (see p.135 above). (The Law of Property Act 1925, s.141(3) passes the benefit of a right of re-entry to an assignee of the reversion even in respect of pre-assignment breaches. See below.)

An assignee of the tenancy who becomes liable for a continuing breach committed before the assignment to him or who is subject to forfeiture in respect of a pre-assignment breach might be able to sue the assignor on a covenant as to title given on the assignment. (See LPA 1925, s.76; LRA 1925, s.24(1)(a) for assignments before July 1, 1995 and the Law of Property (Miscellaneous Provisions) Act 1994 for (save in specified exceptional cases) assignments on or after that date).

In the case of certain types of letting, such as blocks of flats where flats are let on long tenancies, or tenancies of units on an industrial estate, the tenancy will frequently provide for certain obligations such as covenants to insure, or repair common parts to be performed or observed not by the landlord but by a management company which is made a party to the tenancy and to whom the tenant is required to pay the rent and/or service charge. It has been suggested therefore that it is good practice in such a case either for the tenant's covenants also to be made with the landlord or to require an assignee of the tenancy to enter into a direct covenant with the landlord to make such payments to the management company. This is because it would otherwise be difficult for the management company to sue an assignee of the tenancy for the service charge because there is no privity of estate between them (Fancourt, *op. cit.*, p.85).

Liability of the original landlord to the assignee of the tenancy In the case of the few obligations traditionally undertaken by landlords in tenancies, the effect of an assignment of the tenancy is, as noted above, that the assignee of the tenancy is able to sue the original landlord in respect of breaches of covenant which occur whilst the assignee holds the tenancy. An equitable assignment will be sufficient to pass the benefit of the landlord's covenant to the assignee. An assignee is not able to sue for a breach which occurs before that time unless that right is expressly assigned to him by the assignor tenant who had the right to sue in respect of the breach. The right to sue for a pre-assignment breach otherwise remains with the assignor (see below).

Assignment of the tenancy in part only of the property If there is an assignment of the tenancy in respect of part only of the premises comprised in the tenancy the covenants in the tenancy which touch and concern the part assigned (*e.g.* repairing covenants) are enforceable as between the landlord and the assignee of that part (*Stevenson v. Lambard* (1802) 2 East 575). The statutory indemnity covenants (below) apply with suitable modification. The assignor and assignee tenants can agree an apportionment between themselves as to the rent which will bind their successors in title but this will not bind the landlord unless he is a party to that agreement (LPA 1925, s.190(3)). Where the landlord is not a party to the agreement there is some uncertainty over whether the assignee is liable for the rent attributable to the whole property let or only for a proportionate amount in respect of the part assigned to him. (See Law Com. No. 174, para. 2.29. The point was left open in *Whitham v. Bullock* [1939] 2 K.B. 81, 86.) But in any event the landlord is entitled to levy distress against any part of the property for the rent due in respect of the whole and therefore even if an assignee of part is compelled to pay the rent in respect of the whole that person is entitled to a quasi-contractual indemnity from the tenant of the part retained in respect of the amount fairly attributable to that part (*Whitham v. Bullock*, above).

Passing of the benefit and burden of covenants on an assignment of the reversion This is represented diagrammatically below where L has granted a tenancy to T and has subsequently assigned the reversion to R, raising the issues of (a) whether R can sue T for breach of a covenant in the tenancy, which has occurred either before the reversion was assigned to R or after that time, and (b) whether R becomes liable to T for a breach of covenant which occurs either before or after the assignment.

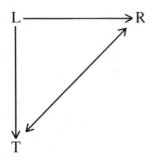

Liability of the original tenant to the assignee of the reversion As noted above, the running of the benefit and burden of covenants in the tenancy following an assignment of the reversion is entirely based on a statutory rule which first appeared in 1540 and is now contained in the Law of Property Act 1925, section 141 of which provides that—

> "(1) Rent reserved by a lease and the benefit of every covenant or provision therein contained, having reference to the subject matter thereof, and on the lessee's part to be observed or performed, and every condition of re-entry or other condition therein contained, shall be annexed and incident to and shall go with the reversionary estate in the land, or in any part thereof, immediately expectant on the term granted by the lease notwithstanding severance of that reversionary estate, and without prejudice to any liability affecting a covenantor or his estate.
>
> (2) Any such rent covenant or provision shall be capable of being recovered, received, enforced, and taken advantage of, by the person from time to time entitled, subject to the term, to the income of the whole or any part, as the case may require, of the land leased."

If the reversion in part only of the land that is let to the tenant is assigned, any right of re-entry or covenant which has reference to the subject matter of the tenancy is annexed to each and every part of the reversion so as to be enforceable by and against the assignee of the severed part (LPA 1925, s.140(1)). Thus an assignee of the reversion in part only of the property would be able to enforce a covenant which touches and concerns that part against the tenant of the whole.

Section 141 makes it clear that the new landlord is able to sue the original tenant for any breach of a tenant's covenant which touches and concerns the land occurring whilst that landlord holds the reversion. But the statute also goes further than this.

It has been established that, as a matter of construction, the effect of LPA 1925, s.141 is that on an assignment of the reversion the assignee alone becomes entitled to sue the tenant in respect of those covenants which have reference to the subject matter of the lease (see above), even in the case of breaches which occurred (or, in the case of a continuing breach of a positive covenant, began) before the assignment (*Re King, Deceased, Robinson v. Gray* [1963] Ch. 459, CA, where there was continuing disrepair under a tenant's repairing covenant; *London and County (A & D Ltd) v. Wilfred Sportsman Ltd* [1971] Ch. 764, where there were rent arrears at the date of the assignment of the reversion). This was held to be the case even if the original tenant in breach had assigned the tenancy before the new landlord acquired the reversion and therefore where there was never privity of contract or estate between the parties (*Arlesford Trading Co. Ltd v. Servansingh* [1971] 1 W.L.R. 1080). The result flows not from the doctrine of privity of estate but from the statute. It follows that after assignment of the reversion the former landlord ceases to be able to enforce the covenants with regard to past or future breaches unless this right has been reserved in the deed of assignment. It should be appreciated that this is a statutory exception to the common law privity of contract rule, applicable to old tenancies, whereby the original tenant remains liable to the original landlord throughout the term of the tenancy for breach of a landlord's covenant whenever that breach occurs (see below).

Despite the above general statutory rule, which permits an assignee of the reversion to sue for breaches of covenants which touch and concern the land, a further obstacle may lie in the way of an assignee landlord who wishes to sue the tenant for breach of covenant. If a landlord makes a written demand to a tenant of premises which consist of or include a dwelling (other than premises comprised in a tenancy which is governed by the business tenancy code in Part II of the Landlord and Tenant Act 1954) for rent or other sums (*e.g.* a service charge) due under the tenancy the demand must include the name and address of the landlord (Landlord and Tenant Act 1987, s.47(1)). If it does not, any service charge is treated as not being due until such time as the information is provided (*ibid.*, s.47(2)). Furthermore the landlord is obliged to give the tenant notice of an address at which notice (including notices in proceedings) may be served on him by the tenant (*ibid.*, s.48(1)). Until such time as this is done any rent or service charge payments under the tenancy are treated as not being due (s.48(2)). Indeed where the reversion assigned is of premises which are or include a dwelling-house, the assignee is obliged to give notice in writing of the assignment, and of his name and address, to the tenant before the next rent day, or if later within two months of the assignment Failure to comply with this requirement is a criminal offence (Landlord and Tenant Act 1985, s.3(1)).

Liability of the assignee of the reversion to the original tenant Law of Property Act 1925, s.142(1) provides that—

> "The obligation under a condition or of a covenant entered into by a lessor with reference to the subject matter of the lease shall, ...be annexed to...that reversionary estate...and may be taken advantage of and enforced by the person in whom the term is from time to time vested...against [the person from time to time entitled to the reversionary estate]."

It follows from this provision that the burden of those landlord covenants in the lease which touch and concern the land will pass to the assignee of the reversion and make that person liable to the original tenant for breaches which occur whilst that landlord has the reversion. Unlike section 141 (which as we have seen effects a transfer of the right to sue for tenant breaches outstanding at the time of assignment), section 142 does not have the effect of transferring to the new landlord the burden of any outstanding breaches of covenant by the original landlord. The lessor at the time the damage was suffered remains liable for such a breach. In *Duncliffe v. Caerfelin Properties Ltd* [1989] 2 E.G.L.R. 38 there was an outstanding breach of the landlord's repairing covenant when the reversion was assigned to the defendants who were clearly liable for the continuing breach. However, they were not liable for past consequential damage to decorations, carpets, furniture and effects which had been caused by disrepair before the date of the assignment. This was the subject of an accrued cause of action separate to the continuing responsibility of the new landlord to remedy all disrepair whether occurring before or after he acquired the reversion.

In those cases where the assignee is obliged, but to give notice fails of the assignment to the tenant (see above) it is provided that until this is rectified the original landlord remains liable for any breach of contract (either by himself or the assignee) as if the assignment had not occurred (Landlord and Tenant Act 1985, s.3(3A)). Where the new landlord is also liable, the assignor and assignee are jointly and severally liable.

Liability as between assignees of the tenancy and the reversion This is represented diagrammatically below where L who has granted a tenancy to T has assigned the reversion to R and T has assigned the tenancy to A. (The same principles apply *mutatis mutandis*, however many assignments there have been of the tenancy or the reversion.)

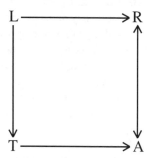

In these circumstances covenants in the tenancy which touch and concern the land are enforceable between the assignees of the tenancy and reversion respectively (*e.g.* R and A above) by virtue of the privity of estate principle and the rules outlined above governing the passing of the benefit and burden of covenants on an assignment of the tenancy (*Spencer's Case*, above), and reversion (LPA 1925, ss. 141 and 142).

Thus any assignees of the tenancy and reversion are liable to each other in respect of any period of time when the reversion and tenancy are vested in them respectively. Hence in the example given above R and A are mutually liable whilst they simultaneously hold their respective interests. If A were to reassign to A2 he would cease to be liable to R for any breach of covenant thereafter by an assignee and A2 and R would become mutually liable whilst they hold their respective interests. If R then assigned to R2, privity of estate would arise between R2 and A2 for as long as they mutually held their respective interests.

Of course the same modifications to the privity of estate principle which were discussed above in relation to the assignment of the reversion apply in the case where there has been an assignment of both interests under the tenancy. (See *Re King, Deceased, Robinson v. Gray*, above; *London and County (A & D Ltd) v. Wilfred Sportsman Ltd*, above; and *Arlesford Trading Co. Ltd v. Servansingh*, above).

The principles governing the enforceability of covenants following an assignment of the tenancy and/or reversion only give a partial picture of who is able to sue whom in respect of a breach of covenant occurring after such an event. The full picture is obtained only by examining also the rules governing the continuing *contractual* liability of original parties or in some cases assignees of the tenancy and/or the reversion. These rules are examined next.

2. Privity of contract liability

(a) Introduction

We saw above that because a tenancy is a contract the original parties remain bound by the covenants in the tenancy throughout the term, in the absence of agreement to the contrary (*Stuart v. Joy* [1904] 1 K.B. 362).

Thus if a tenancy has been assigned and there has subsequently been a breach by the tenant for the time being of a covenant in the tenancy which touches and concerns the land, the landlord will have a choice of defendants. This contractual liability can be enforced by the original landlord (if he still has the reversion) or an assignee of the reversion (by virtue of LPA 1925, s.141 (above)). If, for example, a subsequent assignee of the tenancy fails to pay the rent the landlord would ordinarily expect to look to that person for redress (see *Allied London Investments Ltd v. Hambro Life Assurance Ltd* [1984] 1 E.G.L.R. 62 at 63, *per* Walton J.) However, if for whatever reason (*e.g.* insolvency of the assignee) he chooses not to do so he can turn instead to the original tenant who will remain liable by virtue of privity of contract. It will not be open to the original tenant to argue, in a case where there is a qualified covenant against assignment (see p.85 above) that there was an implied term in the tenancy that in its dealings with assignees the landlord would take reasonable care to ensure that such an assignee was financially viable to meet its obligations under the tenancy (*Norwich Union Life Insurance Society v. Low Profile Fashions Ltd and Others* [1992] 1 E.G.L.R. 86).

(b) For how long does contractual liability last?

The meaning of "the term" for determining the extent of the original tenant's contractual liability has been explored in a number of cases. Thus in *Baker v. Merckel* [1960] 1 Q.B. 657 the court made it clear that a former tenant's liability continued during any extension of the original term which had come about by virtue of the exercise by an assignee of an option to extend the tenancy contained (or incorporated) in the original tenancy before assignment. This was because the effect of the option in that case was to extend the original term. It would follow that by contrast the original tenant's liability would not continue during any new tenancy granted to an assignee in pursuance of an option in the original tenancy because this would be a quite separate term (see M. Pawlowski [1990] 50 E.G. 38). Furthermore the House of Lords refused to extend the privity rule so as to impose liability on an original tenant during any statutory continuation of a tenancy under Part II of the Landlord and Tenant Act 1954.

In *City of London Corporation v. Fell* [1994] 1 A.C. 458 the defendant tenant (the City firm of solicitors, Wilde Sapte) had taken a 10- year tenancy which they later assigned to a company who remained in occupation after the end of the contractual term by virtue of the continuation provisions of Part II of the Landlord and Tenant Act 1954 (see Chapter 13 below). The assignees then went into liquidation and the landlord sued the defendant, for arrears of rent which had accrued during the statutory continuation period, on the basis of the original contract. The House of Lords held that the defendants were not liable. Their contract was to pay the rent during the term. That term was extended by the 1954 Act which did not expressly impose any liability on anyone apart from the landlord and tenant at that time. To hold otherwise would make the tenant liable for rent which they never covenanted to pay for a term which they had never enjoyed. Of course if the tenant had contracted to pay the rent during any statutory extension as well, then this would bind him and he could be sued for unpaid rent accruing whilst that extended term was vested in an assignee. But the tenant will not be liable for an interim rent determined by the court under section 24A of the Landlord and Tenant Act 1954 (see p.390 below) unless the tenancy so provides. In *Herbert Duncan Ltd v. Cluttons* [1993] Q.B. 589 where the tenant had contracted to pay the rent reserved under the tenancy during the term, which was defined in the tenancy as including any statutory extension, the tenant's liability was limited to that amount (£70,000 p.a.) and did not extend to the interim rent of £200,000 p.a. which had been agreed between the landlord and assignee by a consent order. Following these decisions it became common practice to extend privity of contract liability to cover any statutory period of continuation under the Landlord and Tenant Act 1954 and any interim rent under s.24A of that Act (see, *e.g. Collins Estates Ltd v. Buckley* [1992] 2 E.G.L.R. 78).

(c) Effect of variations of the tenancy

The potentially extensive nature of privity of contract liability for the defaults of assignees of the tenancy is revealed by a series of reported cases concerning rent review clauses. They establish that if the original tenancy contains a rent review clause which, following assignment of the tenancy, is operated by the landlord and assignee to increase the rent, the original tenant will be liable for that increased rent if sued in the event of non-payment by the assignee (*Centrovincial Estates plc v. Bulk Storage Ltd* (1983) 46 P.& C.R. 393 where the rent had increased from £17,000 p.a. to £40,000 p.a.). This is because the increase was obviously contemplated by the terms of the original tenancy. The decision was followed in *Selous Street Properties Ltd v. Oronel Fabrics Ltd* (1984) 270 E.G. 643 where the reviewed rent reflected improvements. Although these improvements were originally carried out in breach of covenant the landlord had later waived the breach by granting retrospective approval; and *Gus Management Ltd v. Texas Homecare Ltd* [1993] 2 E.G.L.R. 6 where the landlord and the assignee of the tenancy had agreed a rent review. These decisions must be read in the light of the later decision of the Court of Appeal to the effect that an original tenant will not be responsible for increases which occur as a result of variations in the terms of the tenancy by the landlord and an assignee of the tenancy, to which that tenant was not a party and which were not contemplated by the terms of the tenancy at the date of the assignment (*Friends Provident v. British Railways Board* [1996] 1 All E.R. 336). The earlier decisions discussed above can now only be justified if the variations in question were as a matter of construction permitted by the terms of the original tenancy in each case. In so far as they are based on the proposition that a post-assignment variation always binds an original tenant they cannot be supported because that proposition was rejected by the Court of Appeal in the *Friends Provident* case.

(d) Positive and negative covenants

It will be noted that the reported cases discussed above involve actions against original tenants for breach of a positive covenant by a successor where breach by the successor necessarily entails breach by the original covenantor because the latter has covenanted that he will do something and that it does not matter that it has not been done by somebody else, *i.e.* an assignee. But does the same reasoning apply to negative covenants? Is a covenant not to do something broken by the actions of somebody else? It is commonly believed that this makes no difference because the original covenantor must be taken as having warranted that the covenant will not be broken either by himself or a successor in title. This argument relies on LPA 1925, s.79 which says that—

> "A covenant relating to any land of a covenantor... shall, unless a contrary intention is expressed, be deemed to be made by the covenantor on behalf of himself his successors in

title and the persons deriving title under him or them, and, subject as aforesaid shall have effect as if such successors and other persons were expressed."

The conventional view that this provision, which also applies to freehold covenants, makes the covenantor liable for the acts of all successors in title, however remote, is not universally subscribed to and at least one commentator has suggested that section 79 is merely a word-saving provision which does no more than provide that such a covenant is one which is intended to run with the land of the covenantor (T.M. Fancourt, p.25 *Enforceability of Landlord and Tenant Covenants* (1997)). The point is clearly an open one and it may well be that contrary to the conventional wisdom (see *e.g.* Megarry and Wade, *The Law of Real Property* (5th ed. 1984)) a court would hold that an original tenant is not liable for breach of a negative covenant by an assignee of the tenancy.

(e) Release of a contracting party

The contractual liability of the original tenant will come to an end only with the termination of the tenancy by whatever method or by a release of the tenant (or an assignee in whom the tenancy is vested) by the landlord or assignee of the reversion (*Deanplan v. Mahmoud* [1993] Ch. 151). Release of the guarantor will not by itself be enough to release the primary debtor from his contractual liability (*Allied London Investments v. Hambro* (1983) 269 E.G. 41).

A surrender by operation of law and deemed regrant will come about if the landlord and assignee vary the original tenancy by altering the subject premises or the term, *i.e.* the length of the tenancy (*Friends Provident v. British Railways Board*, above). Whether other purported variations will amount to a surrender and regrant will be a matter of construction in each case.

(f) Statutory exceptions to privity of contract liability

A statutory exception to the privity of contract rule is provided by the Family Law Act 1996, Sched. 1, para.2(2) whereby a tenant who transfers the tenancy to his or her former spouse in pursuance of a court order following divorce does not have continuing liability under any covenant "having reference to the dwelling house".

We saw in Chapter 1 above that a perpetually renewable lease takes effect by statute as a lease for 2,000 years (LPA 1922, s.145, Sched. 15, para. 5). It is further provided that in such a case the lessee is contractually liable only for the period when the lease is vested in the lessee or his personal representatives, notwithstanding any stipulation to the contrary (para. 11(1)).

(g) Continuing contractual liability of an assignee

By virtue of the rules governing privity of estate an assignee's liability lasts only as long as he holds the tenancy or the reversion respectively.

> "The assignee is not liable for a breach of covenant committed after the assignee has in turn assigned the lease because once he has assigned over he has ceased to be the owner of the term to which the covenants are annexed. (*City of London Corporation v. Fell above, per* Lord Templeman.)"

However, it had long been common practice, on an assignment of a tenancy, for the landlord to require the assignee to covenant directly with the landlord to observe the covenants in the tenancy for the remainder of the term. By this means the assignee could be made liable for breaches which occurred even after any further disposal of the tenancy by assignment when privity of estate between himself and the landlord would have ceased (*Estates Gazette Ltd v. Benjamin Restaurants Ltd* [1994] 26 E.G. 140, CA). Furthermore because he had made himself contractually liable, the assignee's liability even extended to covenants in the tenancy which did not touch and concern the land. Such a direct covenant will pass to an assignee of the reversion at common law (see *P & A Swift Investments (a firm) v. Combined English Stores Group plc* [1998] 2 All E.R. 885, HL, dealing with a surety covenant by a guarantor of the original tenant).

Qualified covenants against disposition (see Chapter 4 above) have usually made provision of such covenants by the assignee a reasonable condition of granting a licence to assign.

(h) Assignee of the reversion not usually contractually liable

By contrast to the position where the tenancy is assigned, it was not usual practice in the cases of old tenancies for an assignee of the reversion to covenant directly with the original tenant.

(i) Contractual liability of a surety

In the case of many commercial tenancies it had long been standard practice for landlords to require a tenant or, in cases where a direct covenant was required (see above), an assignee, to provide a surety for performance of the tenant covenants in the tenancy. The contractual liability of such a surety is normally, unless restricted or extended, co-extensive with that of the principal debtor (*Thames Manufacturing Co Ltd v. Perrotts (Nichol & Peyton) Ltd* (1984) 271 E.G. 284, 287 and *Johnsey Estates Ltd v. Webb* [1990] 19 E.G. 94). Thus if that liability is discharged by the creditor the obligation of the surety will correspondingly be discharged. (*Coastplace Ltd v. Hartley* [1987] 2 W.L.R. 1287). But there is an important qualification under the general law. If the obligation of the principal debtor (the tenant) is changed by agreement between the landlord and tenant or if the landlord allows the tenant any time or indulgence such that it cannot be said without enquiry that the surety would not be prejudiced thereby, the surety will be released unless, as is frequently the case in practice, the guarantee provides otherwise (*Holmes v. Brunskill* (1877) 3 Q.B.D. 495). Such a release will also operate in respect of any obligation to take a new tenancy in the event of disclaimer on insolvency of the tenant (as to which, see below) (*Howard de Walden Estates v. Pasta Place Ltd* [1995] 1 E.G.L.R. 77). It has, however, been held that a surety for a former tenant will not be affected by a variation between the landlord and a subsequent assignee of the tenancy because the obligation guaranteed by the surety is the contractual obligation of the former tenant (*Metropolitan Properties Co. (Regis) Ltd v. Bartholomew* [1996] 1 E.G.L.R. 82: but *cf.* section 18 below for post-1995 variations).

Furthermore if the person whose obligations are guaranteed by the guarantor becomes insolvent and the tenancy is disclaimed (see below) this will not discharge the guarantor from liability (see *Hindcastle Ltd v. Barbara Attenborough Associates Ltd* [1996] 1 All E.R. 737, HL).

It has also been common in practice to include a covenant by the surety that if the tenancy is disclaimed on insolvency (see below) they will take up a new tenancy on the same terms as the former tenancy.

A surety covenant is of course not a covenant in the tenancy by either landlord or tenant. It is therefore not governed by the statutory rule in the LPA 1925, s.141 (above) dealing with the passing of the benefit of a tenant's covenant which has reference to the subject matter of the tenancy to an assignee of the reversion . But in *P & A Swift Investments (a firm) v. Combined English Stores Group plc* (above) the House of Lords held that the benefit of such a surety covenant would, even in the absence of an express assignment, pass to any subsequent assignee of the landlord's estate by virtue of the common law rules governing covenants affecting land. The landlord's reversion is clearly "land" for this purpose. At common law the benefit of a covenant which touches and concerns that land will pass to a successor in title to the reversion.

The test to be applied is the same as that applicable to a tenant's covenant in the tenancy and because the surety covenant guarantees the performance of primary obligations which are themselves covenants which touch and concern the land then that surety covenant can also be said to touch and concern the land. The same principle was applied in *Coronation Street Industrial Properties Ltd v. Ingall Industries plc* [1989] 1 W.L.R. 304 in respect of a covenant by a surety to take up a new tenancy in the event of termination of the tenancy by disclaimer on insolvency.

The landlord is not permitted to recover twice over from the surety and the principal debtor. Thus where a landlord recovered a sum in respect of rent arrears from a tenant's surety he had to set off that sum in a subsequent action in respect of the arrears against the tenant (*Milverton Group Ltd v. Warner World Ltd* [1995] 2 E.G.L.R. 28).

Where the tenancy and the guarantee are under seal the limitation period is six years (Limitation Act 1980, s. 19; *Romain v. Scuba TV Ltd* [1996] 2 All E.R. 377).

(j) The use of indemnities as a protection against continuing contractual liability (and their limitations)

Original tenants under "old tenancies" have very few means of protecting themselves against future contractual claims save by verifying the creditworthiness of their immediate assignees as well as insisting on the presence of a clause in the original tenancy which compels the landlord to take a direct covenant from assignees.

A first assignor of the tenancy frequently takes an express indemnity from his assignee in respect of the assignor's contractual liability in respect of post-assignment breaches of covenant. That assignee would then on a further assignment take an indemnity from his assignee and so on, enabling liability to be ultimately revisited on the assignee in default. An express indemnity will extend the liability of the assignee to breaches of any of the tenancy covenants committed at any time during the remainder of the term. Even in the absence of an express indemnity a statutory indemnity to the same effect applies in the case of assignments for valuable consideration of tenancies to which title is unregistered; Law of Property Act 1925, s.77(1)(c), Sched. 2, Pt. IX. (In *Johnsey Estates Ltd v. Lewis & Manley (Engineering) Ltd* [1987] 2 E.G.L.R. 69 the Court of Appeal held that the primary obligations undertaken by the assignee towards the landlord amounted to valuable consideration passing to the assignor for the purpose of the statutory indemnity covenant). In the case of registered titles the indemnity applies to all transfers by way of assignment; Land Registration Act 1925, s.24(1).

Quite apart from any express or statutory indemnity, the original tenant also has a quasi-contractual claim against the defaulting assignee based on the principle that as between the tenant and the assignee the liability of the latter is primary and that of the former secondary and that there is a restitutionary obligation to indemnify another who has been compelled by law to discharge the primary debtor's liability (*Moule v. Garrett* (1872) L.R. 7 Exch. 101 at 104). This obligation is quite separate from any obligation arising under the statutory indemnity covenant and therefore an express exclusion of the latter will not exclude the former (*Re Healing Research Trustee Co. Ltd* [1992] 2 All E.R. 481). The weakness of these remedies is obvious. As far as the express (or statutory) indemnity is concerned, it is always possible that there will turn out to have been an assignment at some stage where an indemnity had not been taken, thereby breaking the chain. But even more serious, in the case of both the express (or statutory) indemnity and the quasi-contractual claim, is the fact that the assignee who has given the indemnity or the assignee in default in default will prove to be not worth suing. This will usually be the case if the landlord has felt it necessary to resort to the original tenant. (In *RPH Ltd v. Mirror Group Holdings Ltd* (1992) 65 P.& C.R. 252 the original tenant who had a claim by way of indemnity against an insolvent assignee was unable to compel that assignee to sue his solvent assignee or to assign to the original tenant the indemnity obtained from that assignee).

(k) Insolvency of an assignee of the tenancy

If the defaulting assignee tenant becomes insolvent and the tenancy is disclaimed by the trustee in bankruptcy, the assignee will be free from liability (Insolvency Act 1986, s.315. A similar rule applies in relation to a disclaimer by the liquidator of an insolvent company; *ibid.*, s.178). This is because the effect of a disclaimer is to determine as from the date of the disclaimer the rights interests and liabilities of the company or the bankrupt and the trustee in the tenancy (ss.315(3)(a) and 178(4)(a)). But this affords no relief to the former tenant, because his liability (and that of his surety; *Warnford Investments v. Duckworth* [1979] Ch. 127) remains unaffected as does that of a guarantor of the bankrupt or insolvent assignee (*Hindcastle Ltd v. Barbara Attenborough Associates Ltd* [1996] 1 All E.R. 737, HL).

Similar problems have arisen in connection with individual and company voluntary arrangements. These are schemes which can operate in cases of personal or corporate insolvency respectively whereby a meeting of creditors is able to agree an arrangement with the debtor which avoids bankruptcy or (in the case of corporate insolvency) liquidation. One problem which has arisen is whether, if the debtor is an assignee tenant and the landlord is left short by the arrangement, the landlord can sue the original tenant. It has been held that unless the IVA provided for forfeiture, disclaimer or variation of the tenancy, or made express provision in relation to former tenants, their privity of contract liability is preserved (*Mytre Investments Ltd v. Reynolds* [1995] 3 All E.R. 588; *RA Securities Ltd v. Mercantile Credit Co Ltd* [1995] 3 All E.R. 588. (*Cf. Burford Midland Properties Ltd v. Marley Extrusions Ltd* [1995] 2 E.G.L.R. 15 where the terms of the arrangement were that the creditors would not pursue the original tenant). This principle was applied in *Johnson v. Davies* [1997] 1 All E.R. 921. The plaintiffs were sureties of a company's liability under a tenancy. They owned virtually all the shares in the company. The shares were then sold to three individuals and the plaintiffs ceased to have any interest in the business. The buyers agreed to indemnify the plaintiffs against any claims in respect of the tenancy. A claim was subsequently made against the plaintiffs which they satisfied. They then sued two of the three buyers under the indemnity. It was held that those persons had not been released by an IVA (of which the plaintiffs had had notice) which had been entered into by the third co-debtor. Any such release would need to have been provided for in the IVA. (See also *March Estates plc v. Gunmark Ltd* [1996] 2 E.G.L.R. 38.)

Even if the former tenant is in a position to have recourse by way of indemnity to an insolvent tenant, he will only be an ordinary creditor of the insolvent estate (ss. 315(5), 178(6)). However, a small measure of relief is provided by the decision in *Becton Dickinson U.K. Ltd v. Zwebner* [1989] Q.B. 208 at 217 that if there is a solvent guarantor of a later assignee, an original tenant who is sued is entitled to be indemnified by that guarantor. (For a criticism of that decision on the basis that the liability of the surety is secondary only, see Fancourt, *op. cit.*, p.59 who suggests that to avoid doubt the assignor should where possible seek an indemnity from the guarantor of the assignee.)

(l) Continuing contractual liability of the original landlord

As we have seen above, by virtue of the doctrine of privity of contract an original landlord remains liable to his original tenant throughout the term, despite an assignment of the reversion. Thus in *Eagon v. Dent* [1965] 3 All E.R. 334 the tenant was unable to exercise an option in the tenancy against an assignee of the reversion because it had not been protected by registration under the Land Charges Act 1925. The tenant then sued the original landlord who was held liable in damages. It is therefore necessary, and indeed standard practice, to take the precaution of obtaining an indemnity from any purchaser of the landlord's interest in respect of any obligations in the tenancy on the part of the landlord (*e.g.* an option to renew the tenancy or to purchase the landlord's interest). In similar fashion a tenant who has assigned the tenancy can sue the original landlord in respect of breaches which occur either before or after the assignment (although in the case of the latter loss would be difficult to prove in practice): *City & Metropolitan Properties Ltd v. Greycroft Ltd* [1987] 3 All E.R. 839 where the landlord was liable for loss caused to the tenant by a breach of repairing covenant before the tenant assigned the tenancy. The court considered that by analogy with the rule that a tenant's contractual liability survived an assignment, the landlord's liability should similarly survive.

Indeed it was even suggested by the Court of Appeal that the effect of the Law of Property Act 1925, s.142(1) (above) was to make an original landlord directly liable to an assignee of the tenancy who only became tenant after the landlord had assigned the reversion; *Celsteel Ltd v. Alton House Holdings Ltd (No. 2)* [1987] 1 W.L.R. 291, 296.

(m) Equitable tenancies (see also *Smith* [1978] C.C.J. 98)

An equitable tenancy is created either by a specifically enforceable contract for a tenancy or in circumstances where the need for a deed to create a legal tenancy has not been complied with (see pp.22 and 30 above). Where such a tenancy has been created there is authority (albeit much criticised) that an assignee of the tenancy is not, in the absence of a direct covenant with the landlord, bound by the burdens of tenant covenants in the tenancy (other than restrictive covenants) because there is no legal estate in the land to which the landlord and the assignee are both privy (*Purchase v. Lichfield Brewery Co. Ltd* [1915] 1 K.B. 184). By contrast it was Lord Denning's view in *Boyer v. Warbey* [1953] 1 Q.B. 234 that an equitable assignee who has taken possession should be liable on the covenants in the tenancy. There are no such problems with the benefit of covenants in equitable tenancies because the benefit can pass automatically to an assignee of the equitable term (*Manchester Brewery v. Coombs* [1901] 2 Ch. 608).

The legal position following an assignment of the reversion is as outlined above in the case of legal tenancies (*i.e.* it is governed by the Law of Property Act 1925, ss. 141 and 142) (*Weg Motors Ltd v. Hales* [1962] Ch. 49). Thus the benefit and burden of covenants in the equitable tenancy will pass to an assignee of the reversion.

The above difficulties disappear in the case of new tenancies under the Landlord and Tenant (Covenants) Act 1995, which applies to legal and equitable tenancies.

Law reform: the terms of debate

We saw above that the law governing old tenancies was radically altered by the Landlord and Tenant (Covenants) Act 1995 for "new tenancies" granted on or after January 1, 1996. The principal achievement of the Act is, subject to important qualifications, to abolish the privity of contract principle which as we have seen provides that a landlord or tenant who covenants to be bound by obligations in a tenancy throughout the term is thereby liable even for breaches of covenant which occur after he has disposed of his interest in the property. The Act also contains a new statutory code governing the enforceability of (non-personal) landlord and tenant covenants in tenancies following assignment of the tenancy and/or the reversion. This code provides that the benefits and burdens of such covenants will be annexed to the tenancy and the reversion respectively.

The above outline of the pre-1995 Act law which still governs "old tenancies" reveals many of the defects of that law the existence of which fuelled a campaign in the 1980s and early 1990s to reform the law.

Although the principle of privity of contract applied to all (pre-1995 Act) tenancies, whatever the nature of the property, and applied equally to landlord and tenant, it attracted greatest criticism with regard to its application to former tenants under a tenancy of commercial property. Although, as noted above, the doctrine of privity of contract had been around for centuries it did not seem to have caused problems on a sufficiently large scale to have provoked any significant outcry until comparatively recent times. The reasons for this would appear to lie in changes to the traditional landlord and tenant relationship which occurred because of developments in the property world. The most notable change was that in the attitude to commercial property as an investment vehicle by a class of landlords typically constituted by institutional investors such as banks, life insurance companies and pension funds. This led to the growth of sophisticated upwards-only rent review clauses (see, *e.g.* Law Com. No. 162 "Landlord and Tenant: Reform of the Law", (1987) para. 3.17) and an increasing insistence on the provision of an elaborate chain of sureties (see above) as landlords sought to shift as much of the risk of the venture as possible away from themselves and onto other parties. In this changed climate it was only a matter of time before businesses failed and former tenants, who had long since disposed of their property, would face unexpected ruin as they were made responsible for breaches of covenant occurring long after they had disposed of the leasehold interest and therefore over which they had no control. The dangers were most obvious in relation to non-payment of rent by an assignee and breach of repairing obligations over which the former tenant would have no control. (See *Thames Manufacturing Co. Ltd v. Perrotts (Nichol & Peyton) Ltd* (1984) 271 E.G. 284, 287.)

The limitations of the means by which tenants might seek to protect themselves by way of indemnities from assignees are discussed above.

The precarious position of former tenants was in marked contrast to that of the landlord who would invariably have reserved to himself the power to approve the identity of a proposed assignee. In addition the landlord had the powerful remedy of forfeiture in the event of non-compliance with a covenant by the present tenant. Even worse were cases where the landlord preferred to have recourse to the original tenant for unpaid rent because market rental levels had fallen since the tenancy was granted and therefore he would not benefit by repossessing and reletting the property which might be occupied by the tenant in default or have been abandoned. In those circumstances the original tenant would undoubtedly prefer to be able to have recourse to the leasehold property but was unable to do so in the absence of a provision for re-entry in the assignment itself.

The widespread media publicity surrounding the cases arising in the early 1980s provoked demands for reform of the law and in 1986 a Law Commission Working Party examined the matter and initiated a wide-ranging consultation. In 1988 the Commission published a comprehensive report (Law Com. No. 1974, "*Landlord and Tenant Law: Privity of Contract and Estate Law* [1988]"; for a summary see H.Wilkinson [1989] Conv.). The report concluded that there was an overwhelming case for reform covering both existing and future tenancies, albeit stopping short of the complete abrogation of the privity of contract principle which had been provisionally recommended by the earlier Working Party (Law Com. WP No. 95, "*Landlord and Tenant: Privity of Contract and Estate: Duration of Liability of Parties to Leases*" (1986)).

The Law Commission found that whilst there was considerable support for the complete abrogation solution, there were a significant number of respondents to the consultation (almost exclusively landlords or those interested on their behalf) who were opposed to it and indeed to any statutory reform.

The principal objection was that privity of contract liability arose as a result of a voluntary assumption of contractual liability by the tenant when he entered into the tenancy and that he could equally have bargained for his liability not to survive an assignment of the tenancy, or otherwise to limit his potential liability. The Law Commission had little difficulty in disposing of this objection, pointing out that such bargains were rare, which was not surprising in view of a considerable body of evidence that any such market freedom was largely illusory because of the inequality of bargaining power between landlords and tenants. The somewhat unreal nature of this objection becomes even more apparent in the light of the Law Commission finding of widespread ignorance among tenants as to the nature of the doctrine and its applicability to them. Furthermore, few tenants were in a position to protect themselves against a potentially disastrous contingent liability by setting funds aside even if they had appreciated the true legal position.

The remaining objections were less easily disposed of. They were all rooted in an argument that it would be detrimental not only to the commercial rented sector but to the economy as a whole by altering such a fundamental principle on which institutional leases had long been based. As we have seen above, in recent times the commercial property market has come to be dominated by institutional investors such as pension funds, banks and insurance companies and, increasingly, foreign investors for whom property is an investment medium with the need for a secure income stream. Privity of contract provides the guarantee that this need will be met. It was thus argued that abolition of the doctrine would increase the risk for the landlord and would very likely lead to a number of effects which would have harmful consequences for tenants as a whole and indeed the economy itself as property lost its competitive edge over gilts and equities. The consequences predicted included damage to the investment value of existing tenancies; a diminution in the development of properties to let, thereby stifling new development; a compensatory rise in rent levels and a slowing down of assignment negotiations as landlords took more care over the selection of assignees.

In response to these arguments the Law Commission took the view that whilst the predicted consequences were necessarily a matter for speculation, they were satisfied that it was reasonable to conclude that abolition would bear hard on some landlords in some cases and that although there was a case for reform, some flexibility was required. It was for this reason that, instead of endorsing the provisional conclusion of the Working Party that the principle of privity should be completely abrogated, a compromise solution was proposed. This recommended a new rule that although a tenant (whether original or otherwise) should normally have no continuing liability after parting with the tenancy it would be possible for a landlord who reasonably needed the security of a guarantee from the assigning tenant covering the performance of some or all of the tenant covenants by his successor assignee, to insist upon this as a condition of consent to a proposed assignment. The Law Commission reasoned that this would offer landlords adequate protection because they would be able to judge the financial strength of the assignee and where reasonable to do so insist upon a guarantee from the assignor as a condition of the consent to assign. In proposing that the reform should cover both existing and future tenancies the Law Commission clearly rejected the landlords' objection that this would be unjustified retrospective legislation. (The *Financial Times* of October 6, 1992 carried a report that the Prudential was threatening an appeal to the European Court of Human Rights, on the basis that changes to institutional leases including the abrogation of privity of contract would amount to confiscation).

Paradoxically, by 1993, when the Lord Chancellor announced that the Government had decided to implement the Law Commission Report, new tenants, unlike those who had signed their tenancies in more prosperous times, found themselves bargaining in a very different climate. Market conditions had changed dramatically since the Law Commission Report was published in 1988. The recession had significantly altered the balance of bargaining power between landlords, and tenants and prospective tenants were now in a much better position to drive harder bargains with landlords including, in some cases, a contractual modification or exclusion of the privity principle and for the grant of tenancies either for shorter fixed terms than the traditional 25-year term or for the tenancy to include more frequent break clauses in the tenant's favour. The value of privity of contract to landlords under such tenancies was clearly less significant than it had been in times past. All this had made landlords less resistant to a reform provided that privity of contract was retained for existing tenancies. The British Property Federation now seemed to accept the inevitability of reform and sought instead to water down further the Law Commission proposals. In these circumstances it is perhaps not surprising that the landlord lobby, although unable to persuade the Government that legislative reform was no longer necessary, by the time-honoured device of suggesting a Code of Practice instead, was nevertheless able to dictate further significant Government concessions when legislation could no longer be avoided. In fact the Government's hand was eventually forced by the Mr Peter Thurnham M.P., who, with all-Party support, introduced a Private Members Bill (under the Ten Minute Rule) to implement the reforms proposed in the Lord Chancellor's announcement of March 1993.

The details of the debate surrounding the Bill are recorded elsewhere (see *Davey*, [1996] 59 M.C.R. 79), but suffice to say that the precise details of what ultimately became the Landlord and Tenant (Covenants) Act 1995, were the result of a deal struck by the British Property Federation (representing institutional landlords) and the British Retail Consortium (representing major retailers). The first element of the deal was that privity of contract liability would be abolished for new post-Act tenancies (save that in certain circumstances the landlord would be able to require an outgoing tenant to guarantee the obligations of his immediate assignee, but no further). The second major element was that changes would be made to section 19 of the Landlord and Tenant Act 1927 whereby landlords would be given more control over the conditions on which a commercial tenancy could be assigned (see p.94 above). The quid pro quo was that tenants would be offered a package of measures designed to ameliorate any continuing contractual liability of former tenants under both old and new tenancies. How successful this hastily enacted measure will prove to be remains to be seen.

New tenancies: the Landlord and Tenant (Covenants) Act 1995

(a) Introduction: a new statutory code

The Act replaces the common law rules governing the effect of assignment of a tenancy or the reversion on the enforceability of covenants in the tenancy which touch and concern the land by virtue of privity of estate with a new rule that the benefit and burden of all landlord and tenant covenants (as defined in section 28(1)) of the tenancy are to be annexed to the whole and each and every part of the premises and the reversion and are to pass on any assignment of the tenancy or the reversion (s.3(1)).

"Covenant" is widely defined as including any term, condition and obligation in the tenancy whether , express, implied or imposed by law. The new rules thus apply to terms of all types of tenancy whether created by deed or other writing or orally (s.28(1)). Indeed the term "tenancy" extends to all types of tenancy including a specifically enforceable agreement for a tenancy (see p.22 above) (s.28(1)). Also covered by the new scheme are covenants (as defined above) in collateral agreements (see, *e.g. Systems Floors Ltd v. Ruralpride* [1995] 1 E.G.L.R. 48) or agreements which supplement or qualify the tenancy agreement (s.28(1)).

"Landlord covenant" means a covenant falling to be complied with by the landlord of premises demised by the tenancy and "tenant covenant" means a covenant falling to be complied with by the tenant of premises demised by the tenancy (s.28(1)).

It follows that whether a covenant can be said to "touch and concern" the land or "have reference to the subject matter of the tenancy" becomes irrelevant in the case of "new" tenancies. Thus *Spencer's Case* becomes redundant for new tenancies and the Law of Property Act 1925, ss.141 and 142 are repealed in relation to such tenancies. There are a few limited exceptions which govern certain covenants given by a tenant either on a sale by assignment to him by a local authority or housing association under the statutory "right to buy" or of a house within a National Park. The covenants in question oblige the covenantor to repay the discount if he disposes of the tenancy within a limited period of time or in one case to prevent the further disposal of a house in certain National Park, etc., areas. In each of these cases therefore the tenant's obligation will not be destroyed by an assignment of the tenancy.

But the new rule does not enable a covenant which is expressed to be personal to any person to be enforceable by or (as the case may be) against any other person (s.3(6)(a)). Thus a covenant which is for example expressed to operate only whilst X is the tenant or Y is the landlord will not be enforceable once the named party disposes of his interest.

Furthermore the new rule does not remove the need for protection under the Land Charges Act 1972 or the Land Registration Act 1925 where the covenant creates a registrable interest under that Act (s.3(6)(b)). Examples of a landlord's covenant would be an option to renew the tenancy (see *Phillips v. Mobil Oil* [1989] 1 W.L.R. 888) or to purchase the reversion (see *Beesley v. Hallwoood Estates* [1960] 1 W.L.R. 549), whilst an example of a tenant's covenant would be an obligation on the tenant to offer to surrender the tenancy before seeking consent to an assignment (see *Greene v. Church Commissioners* [1974] Ch. 467. and p.93 above). Although it will be recalled that where title to the land is registered under the Land Registration Act 1925, non-registration will not be an obstacle where the tenant has the benefit of the interest and is in actual occupation (see LRA 1925 and *Webb v. Pollmount* [1966] Ch. 584).

The benefit of a landlord's right of entry (which is a legal or equitable interest depending on whether the tenancy is legal or equitable (see LPA 1925, s.1(2)(e)(3)) is also annexed to the whole and each and every part of the reversion in the demised premises and will therefore pass on an assignment of the whole or any part of the landlord's reversion in the premises (s.4(2)).

The passing of the benefit of surety covenants remains subject to the general law (see above).

(b) Assignment of the tenancy

Following the assignment of a tenancy by the tenant the assignee is bound thereafter by all (non-personal) landlord and tenant covenants except to the extent that (a) immediately before the assignment they did not bind the assignor or (b) they fall to be complied with in relation to any demised premises not comprised in the assignment (*e.g.* where there is an assignment of part (s.3(2)). Thus the assignee is not bound by any covenants to the extent that they have been waived or released by a party with the benefit of the covenant before the assignment, unless the waiver or release was expressed to be personal to the assignor tenant (s.3(4)).

The assignee becomes correspondingly entitled to the benefit of the landlord covenants, save in so far as they relate to any demised premises not comprised in the assignment (s.3(2)(b)).

Assignment is widely defined as extending to an equitable as well as a legal assignment, an express assignment and an assignment by operation of law and an assignment in breach of covenant (s.28(1)).

The assignee does not have any liability for pre-assignment breaches of covenant (s.23(1). That liability remains with the assignor (s.24(1)(3)). Nor does the assignee become entitled to sue the landlord for a breach of covenant committed before the assignment unless that right has been expressly assigned to him at some stage. Otherwise that right remains with the assignor (s.24(4)).

(c) Assignment of the reversion

The same rule as in section 3(2) above applies *mutatis mutandis* on an assignment of the reversion. Thus following the assignment of the landlord's whole interest in the reversion whether by the landlord or a third party, (*e.g.* a trustee in bankruptcy or personal representative) in the whole or part of the premises the assignee is bound thereafter by all (non-personal) landlord and tenant covenants except to the extent that (a) immediately before the assignment they did not bind the assignor, or (b) they fall to be complied with in relation to any demised premises not comprised in the assignment (s.3(3)). As in the case of old tenancies (see above) the assignee is not liable for pre-assignment breaches of covenant by a predecessor landlord. The latter remains liable for such breaches (s.24(1)).

The assignee becomes correspondingly entitled to the benefit of the tenant covenants save in so far as they relate to any demised premises not comprised in the assignment (s.3(2)(b)). But the assignee of the reversion does not thereby become entitled to sue in respect of a pre-assignment breach of a tenant's covenant (s.23(1)) unless that right has been expressly assigned to him (s.23(2)). A comparison can be made with the law governing old tenancies where the effect of the now repealed LPA 1925, s.141 is that (save where provision is made to the contrary) the assignee of the reversion acquires the right to sue in respect of a pre-assignment breach and the assignor loses that right (*Re King, Deceased, Robinson v. Gray* [1963] 2 W.C.R. 629, CA; *London and County (A & D Ltd) v. Wilfred Sportsman Ltd* [1970] 2 All E.R. 600, CA). Curiously, although the landlord cannot sue in respect of a tenant's breach of covenant occurring before the assignment of the reversion, he can exercise any right of re-entry in the tenancy in respect of that breach (section 23(3) above), in which case the tenant might seek relief against forfeiture. But this would only normally be given on condition that the breach is remedied!

(d) Effect of the assignment of the tenancy

When a tenant assigns (either legally or equitably) the residue of his term in the whole of the premises comprised in the tenancy he is thereafter released from the tenant covenants of the tenancy and ceases to be entitled to the benefit of the landlord covenants of the tenancy (s.5(1), (2)). This is the abolition of privity of contract for tenants.

If a tenant assigns his interest to the extent of only part of the premises let to him he will be released from the tenant covenants in the tenancy as from that date and will thereafter no longer be entitled to the benefit of the landlord covenants in the tenancy in so far as they fall to be complied with in relation to that part of the premises let (s.5(3). See further s.28(2)).

Thus if, for example, a tenancy of a building comprising a shop with a flat above is let and the tenant assigns the tenancy in so far as it relates to the shop but retains the flat, the assignor tenant will be released from any user covenants which relate to the business premises. He will remain bound by covenants which are attributable solely to the residential part which has been retained.

With the abrogation of privity of contract liability the need for indemnity covenants is obviated and therefore the implied statutory indemnity covenants in the Law of Property Act 1925 and the Land Registration Act 1925 (see above) are accordingly abolished for new tenancy assignments (s.14). Of course this does not prevent an assignor taking an express indemnity from the assignee, nor does it exclude quasi-contractual liability on the part of the assignee arising under the rule in *Moule v. Garret* (above).

The assignor remains liable to the landlord for pre-assignment breaches of a tenant covenant whether or not he is released from the tenant covenants thereafter (s.24(1), (3)). (As we have seen above, the assignor remains able to sue the landlord for a pre-assignment landlord breach of a landlord covenant (s.24(4)).)

Where a tenant is released from the tenant covenants in the tenancy in accordance with the above provisions a guarantor of the assignor tenant's obligations is also released to the same extent (s.24(2)).

(e) Effect of the assignment of the reversion

Unlike the abolition of privity of contract liability for a tenant on assignment of the tenancy, a different rule applies on the assignment of the whole or part of the reversion in the premises comprised in the tenancy. The rationale for the difference is that the tenant has no control over the identity of the assignee of the reversion. In such a case therefore it is provided that any assignor landlord will, unless released, remain bound by the landlord covenants in the tenancy for the remainder of the term even if that term is assigned. This is a result of the combined effect of section 3, which is to annex the benefit of the covenants to the term and of section 6, which says that the assignor landlord remains bound unless released in accordance with the Act. (By contrast, an original landlord under an "old tenancy" who has assigned would not be liable thereafter to an assignee of the term—as opposed to the original tenant—because he had neither privity of contract nor estate with that assignee tenant).

The effect is that the assignor and assignee of the reversion will become jointly and severally liable to the assignee for breaches of covenant occurring after the date of the assignment (s.13).

To seek release, the landlord must serve a notice on the tenant informing him of the proposed assignment and requesting a release, as from the date of the assignment, from the landlord covenants (s.6(6)). (See also the Landlord and Tenant (Covenants) Act 1995 Notices Regulations 1995, S.I. 1995 No. 2964.)

If a landlord assigns the reversion of only part of the premises let he can apply for release from the landlord covenants in so far as they fall to be complied with in relation to that part of the premises let (s.6(3)).

In so far as the Act renders a landlord who is an assignee liable for the remainder of the term, in the absence of release under the above procedure, this also marks a change from the law applicable to "old tenancies". Under that law, as explained above, an assignee landlord is liable for breaches occurring only whilst he holds the reversion because his liability stems from the principle of privity of estate.

In order to activate the release procedure the relevant notice must be served before or within four weeks of the assignment (s.8(1)). (For forms of service see section 27(5) and Landlord and Tenant Act 1927, s.23.) If the tenant (or tenants, where the tenancy has already been assigned in part to one or more tenants) objects (by serving a notice in prescribed form on the landlord) within four weeks of service of the landlord's notice, the landlord can apply to the county court for a declaration that it would be reasonable for him to be released (s.8(2)). The court may reject the request or grant the declaration and if they take the latter course the landlord will be released.

The landlord will also be released from the date of the assignment in the event of (a) the tenant not objecting within four weeks of service of the landlord's notice, or (b) the tenant serving a notice in writing on the landlord consenting to the release, or if he has objected, stating that the objection is withdrawn (s.8(2), (3)).

It should be noted that nothing in the 1995 Act is to be read as preventing a party to a tenancy from releasing a landlord from a landlord covenant of the tenancy. Thus even if the landlord is not released in one of the above ways, it would seem that the tenant can at any time release the landlord from a landlord covenant. However, what cannot seemingly be done is for the parties to agree in the tenancy or elsewhere that the landlord will be released from the landlord covenants following an assignment other than in accordance with the statutory procedure outlined above. Any such agreement would appear to fall foul of the anti-avoidance mechanism in section 25 of the Act (see below).

An assignor landlord who for whatever reason does not get released in any of the above ways (as above) may seek release again in the same way (see above) on the occasion of a subsequent assignment of the reversion (s.7(2), (3)). He should therefore make provision to be notified of any such assignments.

If a landlord is released the assignee landlord will not acquire the right to sue for pre-assignment breaches of covenant by the tenant. This will remain with the assignor unless expressly assigned to the assignee (s.24(4)).

(f) Apportionments

We have seen above that on an assignment of the tenancy in part only of the premises let the assignor remains liable only for those covenants which are attributable to the part retained and is released as to those relating solely to the part assigned. But in some cases covenants are so expressed that they are attributable to the whole of the premises as let and not just to any particular part. The most obvious and important example would be a covenant to pay rent or a service charge. Such covenants are referred to as "non-attributable" covenants. To cater for such obligations it is provided that on an assignment of part the assignor and assignee are thereafter jointly and severally liable for performance of the relevant covenant in respect of the part assigned (s.13). In the case of a covenant to pay rent this could render the assignee liable for the whole rent under the tenancy. To enable the parties to avoid this consequence the Act provides a procedure for securing that an agreement for apportionment of the liability as between the parties is binding on a third party (sections 9 and 10). A similar procedure is available, to cater for "non-attributable" landlord covenants where there is an assignment of the reversion in part only of the premises (s.9(2)).

(g) Excluded assignments

An assignment in breach of covenant or an assignment by operation of law is an excluded assignment and therefore there cannot be any cessation of liability between an assignor and the other party to the tenancy (or as the case may be the reversion) until and from (if any) a subsequent non-excluded assignment (s.11). Thus on an excluded assignment of the tenancy the assignor tenant will remain bound by any tenant covenants in the tenancy and entitled to the benefit of any landlord covenants therein. This is by way of contrast to the position in the case of old tenancies where the liability of the assignee ceases on assignment of the tenancy. The tenant and assignee will have joint and several liability in the case of the former and be jointly entitled to enforce the latter (s.13). The same rules will apply *mutatis mutandis* on an excluded assignment of the reversion.

In the case of an excluded assignment of the reversion it follows that the landlord will not be able to seek release from the landlord covenants in the tenancy until the occasion of a non-excluded assignment. Any release will then only be as from the date of that later assignment.

An assignment by operation of law means one which vests the legal or equitable interest in the tenancy or reversion in the assignee without any voluntary disposition by the assignor. An example would be where a tenancy vests in the executors of a deceased tenant or where on insolvency of the tenant a tenancy vests in the trustee in bankruptcy.

(h) Third-party covenants and rights

It was explained above that it is not uncommon in the case of a long residential tenancy, or even a commercial tenancy, for services to be provided by a third party, such as a management company. This is particularly useful for example where a building is let off in parts (*e.g.* a block of flats or offices) and the management company provides services to the flats including possibly repair and maintenance of the common parts of the building. In such a case the tenancy may provide for the rent and/or service charge to be payable to the management company which agrees to provide the services and or carry out the repairs in question. Such arrangements may be in the tenancy itself or some other supplemental or collateral agreement. The 1995 Act contains provisions whereby the benefit of such obligations can pass in the same way as landlord or tenant covenants under the tenancy. Thus in the example above the management company's obligation to provide services for the benefit of the tenant would be treated as a "landlord covenant" for the purposes of the Act enabling an assignee of the tenancy to enforce it against the management company. Similarly the burden of the tenant's obligations under the arrangement (*e.g.* to pay the service charge) will pass to the assignee of the tenancy.

(i) Authorised guarantee agreements

We saw above that the Law Commission had proposed that, despite an assignor tenant being released from the covenants in the tenancy following the assignment (see above), the landlord when consenting to an assignment (*i.e.* where there was an absolute or qualified covenant against assignment) should be able to impose a condition that the assignor tenant guarantees the performance of the tenant covenants by his successor. But this should normally last only until the following non-excluded assignment. The Commission's proposal was implemented by section 16 of the Act.

Section 16 effectively provides that following a release of the tenant from any or all of the tenant covenants in the tenancy an authorised guarantee agreement (AGA) can be imposed on that tenant if certain conditions are satisfied—

(1) that there is an absolute or qualified covenant against assignment in the tenancy;
(2) that any consent thereby required is given subject to a condition (lawfully imposed) that the tenant is to enter into an agreement guaranteeing the performance of the relevant covenant(s)by the assignee; and
(3) that the agreement is entered into by the tenant in pursuance of that condition (s.16(3)).

In this way the landlord can ensure that the strength of the tenant covenants in the tenancy is undiluted at least until the next assignment when he can call for a guarantee covenant from the first assignee which will last whilst the second assignee holds the residue of the tenancy and so on. Thus each assigning tenant who enters into an AGA will have a strong incentive to choose his assignee with care. The most usual circumstances in which such an obligation will be "lawfully imposed" is where, by virtue of section 19(1A) the alienation covenant in the tenancy permits the same (see p.94 above). In other cases it will turn on the court's view of whether it is reasonable for the landlord to impose such a requirement, which will no doubt depend on all the circumstances such as the comparative covenant strength of the assignee (see p.89 above).

In so far as an AGA purports to impose liability on an assignor for events occurring after a further assignment of the tenancy it will be ineffective. Otherwise it will be effective during the time that the assignee, the performance of whose obligations is guaranteed, holds the term (ss.16(4) and 25(1)).

It is clear from the wording of the Act that any liability imposed under an AGA can be primary rather than secondary, as is the case in normal guarantee agreements (s.16(5)(a)). Thus to this extent an obligation identical to the old privity of contract liability can apply for the duration of an AGA. Alternatively the AGA can impose secondary liability as a guarantor in respect of the assignee's performance of the relevant covenant(s)(s.16(5)(b)) whereby the guarantee can be activated in the event of default by the assignee.

The terms of an AGA may also provide that if the assignee becomes insolvent and the trustee in bankruptcy or liquidator disclaims the tenancy, the landlord can required the guarantor to take a new tenancy (but not so as to expire later than the term of the assigned tenancy and on terms no more onerous than those of that tenancy) (s.16(5)). (*Cf. Hindcastle Ltd. v. Barbara Attenborough Associates Ltd.* [1997] AC 70 H.L.) It follows that on a subsequent assignment of that term he may be required to enter into a new AGA (s.16(7)).

Where an assignor tenant under an excluded assignment is only released on the occasion of a later assignment (see above) it is provided that he can be obliged to enter into an AGA on that occasion guaranteeing the performance of the tenant covenants in the tenancy by that later assignee (s.16(6)).

An AGA, like any other guarantee agreement, can be discharged by any variation of the main contract which is not on the face of it non-detrimental to the guarantor unless the agreement (as is common in the case of normal surety agreements) provides that any such variation will have no effect on the guarantee.

Further relief for tenants under "old" and "new" tenancies

(a) Fixed charges

As explained above, the package deal which permitted the Bill to proceed offered tenants, under both old and new tenancies, some concessions to alleviate difficulties produced by continuing contractual liability following an assignment. The Lord Chancellor's announcement in March 1993 had already indicated that any reform of the law of privity would include a new requirement that a landlord would be unable to pursue a former tenant or guarantor for arrears created by a subsequent assignee's failure to pay rent or a service charge unless formal notice of the arrears had been given to the former tenant or guarantor within nine months of those arrears arising. This would enable the persons affected to make provision for any possible future claim. The package deal in late 1994 included an agreement that the relevant period should be reduced to six months.

The change is effected by section 17, which is expressed to apply to a covenant under which any fixed charge is payable by the former tenant. It applies where a tenant under an old or new tenancy has a continuing contractual liability after an assignment. In the case of a new tenancy this will come about either as a result of the tenant entering into an AGA or where there has been an excluded assignment thereby precluding a release from the tenant covenants in the tenancy.

Fixed charge means—

(1) rent;
(2) any service charge (as defined in the Landlord and Tenant Act 1985, s.18, *viz.* an amount payable for services, repairs, maintenance or insurance or the landlord's costs of management, the whole or part of which varies or may vary according to the costs incurred in connection with the matters for which the service charge is payable); and

(3)   any other liquidated sum in the case of breach of any other tenant covenants of the tenancy (s.17(6)). This will cover such cases as where there is a specified penalty for each fixed period that the tenant is in breach of certain covenants.

Rent is undefined, although when the 1995 Act was passing through Parliament the Lord Chancellor tentatively suggested that it amounted to any payment of a recurring nature given in consideration of the occupation of the premises let to the tenant. (*Hansard*, H.L. Vol. 565, col. 277, June 24, 1995). It should be noted that tenancies sometimes reserve a variety of payments including VAT as rent for the purposes of the tenancy (see *Escalus Properties Ltd v. Robinson* [1996] Q.B. 231) and in such a case such payments would fall within the definition of a fixed charge for the purposes of section 17.

When section 17 applies the landlord cannot recover from a former tenant (or his guarantor) any amount in respect of the fixed charge which has become due and is unpaid without first having served notice on that person within six months beginning with the date when the charge becomes due. The number of potential defendants will potentially be much wider in the case of old tenancies than new because under the latter an assignor tenant's liability will only continue either by virtue of an AGA or because the assignment under which he divested himself of the tenancy was an excluded assignment. In the first case under the 1995 Act to be reported it was held that where a landlord has served a section 17 notice on a guarantor of a former tenant he is not prevented from recovering from the guarantor by the fact that he did not also serve a section 17 notice on the former tenant whose performance was being guaranteed (*Cheverell Estates Ltd v. Harris* [1998] 02 E.G. 127).

The statutory notice to the former tenant or guarantor (including, in the case of a new tenancy, a guarantor under an authorised guarantee agreement) of a former tenant under section 17 must specify the amount due and inform him that the landlord intends to recover from the recipient the amount specified in the notice and (where payable) interest and the terms on which it is accruing (s.17 (S.I. 1995 No. 2964)). Once it is served there is no bar on the landlord subsequently suing (within the normal six-year limitation period for rent) for an amount no more than that specified in the notice.

It has been pointed out that there is a gap in the section 17 procedure. Suppose L grants a tenancy to T and T then assigns the tenancy to T1 in breach of covenant. This is an excluded assignment. T1 then assigns the tenancy to T2. The landlord might lawfully require, on that later occasion, that not only must T1 enter into an authorised guarantee agreement with regard to the observance of the tenant covenants in the tenancy by T2, but that T also enter into an identical authorised guarantee agreement (s.16(6) above). In these circumstances T is not a guarantor for the purposes of section 17 because he is guaranteeing the performance of the covenants not by *his* assignee but by the present tenant. Thus T can be pursued in respect of breach by T2 even if the landlord has not served him with a section 17 notice (see Fancourt, *op. cit.*, p.203).

A six-month period beginning on January 1, 1996 operated in respect of outstanding breaches at that date, unless proceedings had been instituted before then; Landlord and Tenant (Covenants) Act 1995, s.17(5).

(b) Post-assignment variations

The second of the concessions referred to above was designed to meet the objection that under the pre-1995 Bill case law a former tenant (or guarantor) could be contractually liable following non-observance by an assignee of a covenant which had been varied since that former tenant or guarantor held the tenancy. The obvious example was where the assignee had negotiated a rent review or altered other terms of the tenancy which had opened up avenues of potential liability for the former tenant not envisaged when the tenancy was assigned. Examples are provided by the decisions in *Centrovincial Estates Plc v. Bulk Storage Ltd* (1983) 127 S.J. 443 and *Selous Street Properties Ltd v. Oronel Fabrics Ltd* (1984) 270 E.G. 643, 743.

By coincidence, the statutory solution to this dilemma was rendered virtually redundant before it came into force, by virtue of the decision of the Court of Appeal in *Friends Provident v. British Railways Board* (above) which, as we have seen, provides that the contractual liability of an assignor tenant (or his guarantor) would not extend to obligations not contemplated by the terms of the tenancy when held by that tenant. (This is by no means the only example of a statutory reform being anticipated by the courts. See, for example, the Court of Appeal decision in *Woodward v. Docherty* [1974] 1 W.L.R. 966, which to all intents and purposes anticipated the extension of full Rent Act security to furnished tenancies by the Rent Act 1974. see p.193 below).

The statutory solution was implemented by section 18, which provides that the contractual liability of a former tenant or guarantor, under an "old" or "new" tenancy, will not extend to any increase in rent which is solely attributable to a "relevant variation" (on or after January 1, 1996) of the terms of the tenancy by the landlord and a subsequent assignee (s.18(1), (2)).

A "relevant variation" is one where at the time of the variation the landlord either has an absolute right to refuse to allow it or would have had such a right if the former tenant had sought such a variation immediately before he assigned the tenancy but, between then and the variation, the terms of the tenancy had been varied to deprive the landlord of that right (s.18(4)). For the purpose of determining whether a landlord had such a right to prohibit the variation, regard must be had to all the circumstances, including the effect of any statutory provision (s.18(5)).

As an example of the above, suppose that a tenancy, as originally worded, restricts user of the premises to a specific use and contains an absolute covenant against change of user by the tenant. If the tenant assigns the tenancy and the landlord then waives the absolute covenant against change of use, with the result that a rent increase becomes payable, the original tenant will not be liable for that increase if an assignee fails to pay. (But he will be liable up to the amount of the original rent.) This is because at the time the tenancy was assigned, the landlord had an absolute right to prohibit the change of use.

If in the same circumstances a post-assignment variation had deleted the covenant against change of user following which a change of user had occurred bringing about a rent increase, the tenant will again not be liable for the increase because the absolute covenant against change of use was deleted after the assignment.

If the original covenant against change of user was a qualified covenant and the landlord had after assignment permitted a change of user by an assignee which had resulted in a rent increase, the original tenant's liability in respect of that increase would depend on whether it was reasonable or not for the landlord to have given his consent (s.18(6)).

It follows of course that a rent increase by virtue of a rent review clause in the tenancy which bound the former tenant would not be a relevant variation. (The rule that, in the absence of provision to the contrary, a guarantor's liability might in any event be wholly discharged by a variation of the tenant covenants, is preserved by s.18(3). For that rule, see p.169 above.)

It should be remembered of course that a variation amounting to a surrender and regrant will put an end to the original tenancy and with it any continuing liability of a former tenant or guarantor under that tenancy (see above p.125 for the circumstances amounting to a surrender and regrant).

(c) Overriding leases

The final concession to tenants and their guarantors, which is embodied in section 19, was designed to meet the "responsibility without power" jibe; that is, that an original tenant or guarantor who has been sued following breach of covenant by an assignee will normally have no recourse to the leased premises. Its purpose accordingly, is to allow any such person who has made full payment to the landlord of a fixed charge following a section 17 notice (see above) to call for the landlord to grant him, at the tenant's cost, an "overriding lease" which will slot in as a headlease in reversion on the tenancy held by the defaulting tenant who will thereby become a sub-tenant of the former tenant (s.19(1)). (The request will create an estate contract which can be protected by notice or caution as a minor interest under the Land Registration Act 1925 or, where title to the land is unregistered as a class C(iv) land charge under the Land Charges Act 1972 (1995 Act s.20(6)). It can be seen that this provision will not assist a former tenant who has been forced to indemnify another former tenant who has been forced to pay by virtue of privity of contract liability. For example a tenant, T, under an old tenancy granted to him by L, assigns his tenancy to T1 (with the benefit of an express or statutory indemnity covenant from T1, who then assigns to T2). T2 then fails to pay the rent and L sues and recovers the arrears from T. But If T then successfully recovers from T1 under the indemnity covenant this will not enable T1 to claim an overriding lease. (See S.Elvidge and P. Williams, "Overriding Importance" [1996] 47 E.G. 132.)

A section 19 claim must be made within 12 months of making payment and the landlord must grant the lease within a reasonable time thereafter unless the relevant tenancy has been determined (s.19(5), (6)). The overriding lease is for three days longer than the unexpired residue of the existing tenancy. If more than one person who has paid a fixed charge applies, the lease is to be granted to the first applicant (s.19(7)). When granted, the overriding lease will enable the former tenant who has paid, to regain control of the property by forfeiture and thereby recover or limit his loss. An overriding lease will automatically bind a mortgagee of the landlord's interest without the need for any consent by the mortgagee (s.20(4)).

A disadvantage of the procedure is that, in the absence of agreement to the contrary, the terms of the overriding lease will be on the same terms as the defaulting tenant's tenancy, save for any personal or spent covenants. This will include any post-assignment variations whether or not they were contemplated by the terms of the tenancy at the time it was assigned by the claimant. Thus this might extend that person's liability beyond what it would have otherwise been (see section 18 (above)). If the tenancy of the defaulting tenant was an old tenancy the overriding lease will also be an old tenancy when granted even though of necessity that will be after January 1, 1996. The overriding lease must state whether it is an old or new tenancy (s.20(1)).

Anti-avoidance

The Landlord and Tenant (Covenants) Act 1995 contains a very wide-ranging anti-avoidance provision which was obviously designed to deal with cases where a landlord persuades a tenant to agree to curtail or eliminate the benefits which are afforded to the tenant by the Act. (The provision is actually drafted in terms which also protects a landlord from adverse agreements, although in practice it is more likely to be of benefit to tenants).

Thus section 25(1) provides that any agreement relating to a tenancy is void to the extent that—

(1)   it would otherwise have effect to exclude, modify or otherwise frustrate the operation of any provisions of the Act;

(2)   it provides for—

   (a)   the termination or surrender of the tenancy or
   (b)   the imposition on the tenancy of any penalty, disability or liability
         in the event of the operation of any provision of the Act; or
(3)   it provides indirectly for any of the results specified in (2)(a) or (b) above.

No other limits are placed on the benefits of this provision which covers any such agreement whether in the tenancy itself or made before the creation of the tenancy (s.25(4)). The better opinion is that an agreement made after the tenancy would similarly be covered by section 25.

It follows that if a new tenancy provides for the tenant to remain contractually liable under the tenancy following a (non-excluded) assignment, that provision will be void. However, the Act specifically provides that two types of agreement are not caught by section 25. The first is an absolute or qualified covenant against assignment in so far as it can be said that the presence or operation of the covenant has the effect of excluding or frustrating the operation of the 1995 Act to release the tenant from his covenants. The second is an authorised guarantee agreement in so far as it conforms to the requirements of the Act relating to such agreements (see section 16 and above for AGAs).

It is an open, and at the time of writing an undecided, point, as to whether section 25 will operate to strike down any requirement (whether arising from the surety agreement or the landlord's conditional consent to an assignment, as to which see section 19(1A), above) that the guarantor of a former tenant, who is lawfully required to enter into an AGA, must also act as a guarantor of the obligations of that former tenant under the AGA. Although the better opinion is that such a requirement would be struck down, there is an argument that the obligation of the former tenant to enter into an AGA as a condition of the licence to assign is a tenant covenant from which the tenant is not released on an assignment and therefore it is legitimate to require the guarantor of that tenant to guarantee the obligations of the former tenant under the AGA, an AGA not being covered by section 25 (see [1996] 19 E.G. 118, 32 E.G. 68 and 32 E.G. 64). It has also been argued that a landlord who by the terms of the tenancy bans an assignment but permits the tenant to sub-let for a duration one day less than the residue of the tenancy, possibly with other restrictions governing the rent payable under the sub-tenancy and the need for a direct covenant with the landlord by the sub-tenant, will very likely fall foul of section 25 (P. Walter, "The Landlord and Tenant (Covenants) Act 1995: A Legislative Folly" [1996] Conv. 432,433). This was the stated opinion of the Lord Chancellor's Department. Whether a court will take the same view remains to be seen, although in practice it may prove nigh on impossible to obtain a tenant on such terms.

Conclusion

Finally, it is worthy of note that despite the best efforts of the law reformers whose labours produced the Landlord and Tenant (Covenants) Act 1995, its potential for assisting former tenants has been considerably reduced by the recession-induced move towards shorter tenancies of commercial property during the 1990s. Thus research has shown that since 1989 there has been a dramatic shortening in the length of tenancy terms. The survey in question revealed that 55 per cent of all new tenancies granted in 1996 were for less than five years, whilst the average length of a new tenancy had fallen to eight years, as against 20 years in 1989 (see *Property Week*, January 13, 1998). In these circumstances the abolition of privity of contract liability is hardly likely to be of great concern to landlords. The near universal imposition of an AGA following an assignment will mean that in the case of a large number of tenancies the original tenant will remain liable for the remainder of the term. (Research shows that most tenants do not seek to assign for five to seven years). In such circumstances the abolition of privity of contract liability would appear to have been bought at a high price, given that in return landlords have gained a powerful measure of control over assignments by virtue of the changes to section 19 of the Landlord and Tenant Act 1927 (see p.94 above) (For a critical assessment, see G. Acheson, "Too little too late" [1997] 03 E.G. 132.)

B. ENFORCEABILITY OF COVENANTS IN THE TENANCY BY AND AGAINST A SUB-TENANT

When a tenant creates a sub-tenancy there is no privity of estate between the landlord under the head tenancy and the sub-tenant under the sub-tenancy because, unlike the case of an assignment (above), the tenant retains his estate in the land. At the same time he creates a new estate between himself and the sub-tenant. Thus if L creates a five-year term in favour of T who one year later sub-lets to ST for three years, there is neither privity of contract nor privity of estate between L and ST. (Had the purported sub-tenancy been for a period equal to or greater than that comprised in the residue of the tenancy at that time, the "sub-tenancy" would have operated not as a sub-tenancy but as an assignment by operation of law instead (*Milmo v. Carreras* [1946] K.B. 306).

It follows that as a general rule, where a valid sub-tenancy has been created, the head landlord (or any assignee) and the sub-tenant cannot sue each other on covenants in the head tenancy. This general rule is qualified in a number of cases by special statutory rules which provide for the sub-tenant to become the tenant of the head landlord where the intermediate tenancy comes to an end (see Landlord and Tenant Act 1954, s.65(2)) (business tenancies; Rent Act 1977, s.137 and Housing Act 1988, s.18 (residential tenancies)).

It is also qualified in the case of covenants in the head tenancy which are restrictive covenants. Where title to the land is not registered under the Land Registration Act 1925 a sub-tenant will be bound by any such covenant under the ordinary principles of land law, because as an equitable interest it will bind everybody except the bona fide purchaser for value without notice of a legal estate in the land burdened by the covenant (*Hall v. Ewin* (1887) 37 Ch D 74; *Teape v. Dowse* (1905) 92 L.T. 319). The sub-tenant will not be able to claim that he is without notice of the covenant because he has a statutory right to call for and inspect the head tenancy (LRA 1925, s.44(2), (4), (5))and will therefore have constructive notice of the covenant. (Covenants between landlord and tenant are not governed by the registration requirements of the Land Charges Act 1972 s.2(5)(ii) even if they relate to land other than that comprised in the tenancy. Thus in *Cleveland v. Dartstone Petroleum Ltd* [1969] 1 W.L.R. 1807 a covenant in a tenancy that the landlord would not build on adjoining land which he owned could not be enforced against a purchaser of that land who was a bona fide purchaser for value of the legal estate without notice of the covenant. A purchaser in such circumstances is only likely to have notice where he also happens to purchase the reversion of the tenancy). Where title to the head tenancy is registered under the Land Registration Act 1925 the sub-tenant will be bound by any covenants which affects the sub-landlord's title (LRA 1925, s.23). The position in equity with regard to the enforceability of restrictive covenants in tenancies is preserved by the Landlord and Tenant Act 1995, s.3(5).

It follows that in the case of a restrictive covenant in a head tenancy the head landlord will be able to enforce the covenant against the sub-tenant by seeking an injunction. (See also *Hemingway Securities Ltd v. Dunraven Ltd* [1995] 09 E.G. 322 where the judge at first instance granted a mandatory injunction ordering the subtenant, to whom a sub-tenancy had been granted by the tenant in breach of a covenant against subletting, to surrender the sub-tenancy).

Quite apart from the case of restrictive covenants, a head landlord might be able to enforce covenants in the tenancy against a sub-tenant indirectly by bringing forfeiture proceedings against the tenant where the tenancy contains a forfeiture clause. If the tenancy is forfeited the sub-tenancy will also end. Thus if the sub-tenant wishes to remain he will need to seek relief against forfeiture which if granted is likely to be on condition that the sub-tenant remedies the breach of condition committed by the tenant (for forfeiture see p.134 *et seq* above). Furthermore, where rent under a head tenancy is in arrears the landlord is permitted to serve notice directing the sub-tenant to pay his rent to the superior landlord until the arrears are discharged (Law of Distress Amendment Act 1908, s.6). Thus the sub-tenant's obligation to pay rent to the tenant is made enforceable by the head landlord, with whom the sub-tenant has neither privity of contract nor privity of estate. Finally, it has now been made clear that a landlord cannot rely on LPA 1925 s.56(1) to enforce a covenant in the tenancy against a sub-tenant (*Amsprop Trading Ltd v. Harris Distribution Ltd* [1997] 2 All E.R. 990), although this will not prevent a landlord from requiring that the sub-tenant directly covenant with the landlord to observe the covenants in the tenancy.

Chapter 8

REGULATION OF RESIDENTIAL RENTS AND SECURITY OF TENURE

The residential property market

At the present day the rented sector of the housing market is comprised principally of three sub-sectors. The first is the social rented sector where the landlord is a local authority. The second is a hybrid category, where the landlord is a housing association funded from both public and private sources. The third is the independent private rented sector where the landlord is either a private individual or a property company.

At the beginning of the twentieth century the private rented sector housed virtually the whole population. The modern origins of this sub-sector lay in the economic boom of the mid-nineteenth century. The private landlord flourished during this period of unprecedented population growth and urbanisation. (The population increased from 9 million in 1801 to 32 million in 1901). By 1914 the private rented sector accounted for 90 per cent of the total housing stock in Great Britain. Local authorities were not to have any significant role to play as landlords until after 1945, when the Government embarked upon an ambitious programme of public sector building for rent. In 1914 local authority lettings accounted for an insignificant 0.2 per cent of the housing stock, whilst the fledgling owner-occupied sub-sector comprised only 10 per cent of the housing stock.

By 1995 the position had changed dramatically. The private rented sector now accounted for only 9.9 per cent of the total housing stock whilst the level of owner occupation had risen to 66.8 per cent. Local authority lettings accounted for 18.9 per cent and the remaining 4.3 per cent consisted of lettings by housing associations (Housing and Construction Statistics, DOE, 1997).

Clearly a seismic shift in the composition of the housing market had occurred over the previous 80 years, characterised not least by the dramatic decline in the role played by the once dominant private rented sector. Many explanations have been offered to account for this development. A frequently indicted culprit has been the regulatory regime governing rent control and security of tenure, popularly known as "the Rent Acts", which first appeared as a temporary feature of the English law of landlord and tenant in 1915. However, like that other well-known "temporary" measure, the income tax of 1799, the Rent Act regime proved to be rather more enduring than originally envisaged.

Regulation versus freedom of contract

Ever since the first "Rent Act" of 1915 there have been acute political differences over the need for, or the form of, a regulatory code, and therefore it should come as no surprise that the relevant law has been modified on many occasions. (The code first enacted in 1915 is traditionally referred to as "the Rent Acts", although in fact the first statute to bear this title was the Rent Act 1957.) As we will see below, the current Rent Act 1977 applies only to tenancies which began before January 15, 1989. Most tenancies granted on or after that date are governed instead by the minimalist code of protection to be found in the Housing Act 1988.

Because of this background the present chapter explores the historical evolution of the current schemes with the aim of throwing light on what might otherwise be unintelligible provisions. It also highlights the important economic, social and political dimensions of legislation which until very recent times has rarely failed to expose bitter divisions between the main political parties. (For a discussion of the policy background see J. Doling and M.Davies, *Public Control of Privately Rented Housing* (1985); A.Nevitt, "The Nature of Rent Controlling, Legislation in the UK", Environment & Planning (1970) Vol.2 pp. 127–136.)

The origin of controls: an emergency measure

Before 1914 rents were regulated by the open market. It was a market characterised by overcrowding, unfit and insanitary accommodation and insecurity of tenure. Land was expensive and so were rents, which had to cover acquisition costs, current maintenance and profit. However, by 1914 the number of houses built for rent each year was already falling as capital found more attractive alternative forms of investment. Building controls imposed on the outbreak of war in 1914 exacerbated the growing scarcity of rented accommodation. Rents began to rise and the scene was set for the emergence of a resistance movement. In 1915 there was a wave of rent strikes coupled with widespread industrial unrest throughout the United Kingdom, particularly on Clydeside where there was a large concentration of munitions workers in desperate need of affordable accommodation. The grudging political response, made under pressure, was swift. The Increase of Rent and Mortgage Interest (War Restrictions) Bill was introduced by the President of the Board of Trade on November 25, 1915 and was law by December 23 of the same year. (For an excellent account of the background to this measure, see David Englander, *Landlord and Tenant in Urban Britain 1838–1918* (1983). See also M.J.Daunton, *A Property Owning Democracy? Housing in Britain* (1985).)

The 1915 Act adopted a simple measure of control by freezing rents of unfurnished dwelling-houses at the level payable on August 14, 1914. Increases beyond this "standard rent" were permitted only in limited circumstances (*e.g.* structural improvements or alterations by the landlord). The Act also reflected recognition of the obvious fact that rent control would be useless by itself without security of tenure, otherwise landlords would be able to avoid controls by evicting tenants and selling or letting elsewhere at a higher rent.

Widespread political misgivings over state intervention in the private rented sector were typified by Sir Walter Essex, who said of the Bill, with a considerable degree of astute prescience, that—

> "It illustrates very strikingly the disruptive and disintegrating effects of the War, and I think those who harbour the comforting thought that this is a temporary measure, temporary in its entirety, temporary in its acceptance of a principle, are hugging a delusion which they are certain to find is a delusion before they are many years older. (British Parliamentary Papers *Hansard*, H.C. 787 1915.)"

Sir Walter Essex clearly foresaw that the solution of what was perceived to be an immediate short term problem had considerable potential to create a very different set of problems. Once the principle of intervention had been accepted, albeit as a solution to what was thought to be a temporary hiccup in the ordinary operation of market forces as a result of peculiar wartime conditions, withdrawal was always going to be a difficult business. Indeed when the war ended, the shortage of housing for rent was worse than ever. The 1915 Act had been extended by other measures throughout the war and in 1920 the legislation was consolidated in the Increase of Rent and Mortgage Interest (Restrictions) Act 1920. A tenant protected by the Act could not be removed at the end of the contractual tenancy and was entitled to remain in possession on the same terms as before as a "statutory tenant". Furthermore, limited succession rights to a statutory tenancy were introduced for certain close relatives on the death of the protected or statutory tenant. (These features, albeit subsequently modified, remain part of the current Rent Act scheme).

Decontrol and a return to controls

The slow post-war economic recovery ensured that the controls first introduced during the First World War remained a feature of the inter-war years, although as the housing shortage gradually became less severe a number of decontrolling measures were enacted in the 1930s. They provided that controls would cease to apply to a property once the landlord was able lawfully to recover possession of that property. This method was colloquially referred to as "creeping decontrol". Another method employed at the time was known as block decontrol, whereby controls were removed *en bloc* from properties with a rateable value above a specified limit. However, in 1933 houses with very low rateable value were given immunity from creeping decontrol and this method was virtually abandoned in 1938.

Despite decontrol, four million houses remained in control when war broke out in 1939 (Cullingworth, *Essays in Housing Policy*, p.62). Following that event identical arguments to those employed in 1915 saw controls reimposed, save that the standard rent for properties newly controlled was measured by reference to that payable on September 1, 1939. In similar fashion controls were retained after the war. However, by now an important change of housing policy had occurred. The new Labour Government of 1945 looked not to the private rented sector for a solution to the housing shortage, but to a massive public building programme of houses to rent from local authority landlords. By 1951 that sub-sector had grown to 17 per cent of the total housing stock, whilst the private rented sub-sector now accounted for 52 per cent. The third element of the equation was the owner-occupied sector which had in the meantime grown to 31 per cent of the housing stock (Housing and Construction Statistics, DOE). Home ownership had now become a much more viable option for many encouraged by the rapid growth of building societies from the 1930s onwards, coupled with generous tax relief for mortgage-payers.

The return of decontrol

The return of a Conservative Government in 1951 saw a shift of policy away from council house provision and towards the expansion of owner occupation. The Government argued that the post-war shortage of housing had all but disappeared, and with it the *raison d'être* of controls. (Over three million dwellings were let at a net weekly rent of 10 Shillings (50 pence) or less and of these, nearly one million were let at less than 5 Shillings (25 pence) per week: White Paper, *Rent Control: Statistical Information*, Cmnd. 17 (1956), (quoted in Cullingworth, *op. cit.*, p.62). Hence the controversial Rent Act 1957 heralded a process of extensive "creeping" and "block" decontrol whilst at the same time providing that the principal legislation would no longer apply to tenancies newly created on or after July 6, 1957. In the meantime the rents of tenancies remaining in control were pegged by reference to 1956 gross values with increases permitted beyond the new limits only to reflect subsequent repairs and/or improvements to the property by the landlord.

Despite this ambitious attempt at a restoration of economic orthodoxy to the private rented sector, a number of studies established that the market did not behave in a text book fashion (see Cullingworth, *op. cit.*, p.64). Not all landlords increased rents, although many did. The higher rents did not result in widespread and extensive repair by landlords. Indeed, many of them took the opportunity of regaining possession to withdraw from the private rented sector by selling the houses. Furthermore, the increased rents brought about by decontrol narrowed the price gap between poor and good housing to such an extent that many tenants decided to buy and improve previously rented houses. Although the Act did not therefore lead to a revival of the private rented sector or widespread disaster for tenants, it did have one unfortunate by-product which was to haunt the Government and contribute to its downfall in 1964. Decontrol, coupled with an absence of satisfactory regulation of houses in multiple occupation and inadequate protection for tenants against unlawful eviction and harassment, led to a housing crisis in Greater London, where shortages of accommodation were acute. The activities of a small number of unscrupulous landlords, including the notorious Perec Rachman, who exploited these circumstances (see Shirley Green, *Rachman* (1970), led to the appointment in August 1963 of a Committee of Inquiry (the Milner Holland Committee) into the whole housing situation in Greater London, with particular reference to privately rented accommodation. Before the Committee reported, the Government suffered defeat at the general election of 1964 and a Labour Government was returned to office for the first time since 1951. The Report of the Milner Holland Committee was eventually published in March 1965 (*Report of the Committee on Housing in Greater London*, Cmnd. 2605, (1965)). It castigated successive governments, which for 50 years had sought to deal with complex problems by a piecemeal series of crude measures of control and decontrol. The Report called for a common dogma-free approach to the problem which would encourage all classes of landlord, public, private and housing associations to make their contribution to a lasting solution to the housing problem.

Regulated tenancies

The failure of decontrol to reverse the decline in the fortunes of the private rented sector, coupled with the Rachman scandal and the findings of the Milner Holland Committee, sounded the death knell for the 1957 Act which was repealed (without an adverse vote by the Conservative Opposition) by the temporary Protection From Eviction Act 1964. That Act retained the old controls, both in respect of rent and security of tenure, for tenancies of properties which had not yet been decontrolled by the Rent Act 1957. The 1964 Act was soon replaced by the Rent Act 1965 which brought back into protection all remaining unfurnished tenancies of dwelling-houses of which the rateable value on March 23, 1965 did not exceed £400 in Greater London of £200 elsewhere, provided the principal legislation would have applied to the tenancy but for the (now repealed) decontrolling provisions of the 1957 Act. The rateable value limits operated to exclude only a small number of luxurious properties. However, whilst the existing provisions governing security of tenure were for the most part extended to tenancies brought into protection by this measure, a novel system of rent regulation was introduced for these tenancies. The Government accepted that in such cases landlords and tenants should be permitted to agree a rent between themselves unfettered by a statutory formula which had arguably kept rents at an artificially low level. Consequently, a new system of rent regulation was devised for what were designated "regulated tenancies".

The aim of the new system of rent regulation was to permit the landlord and tenant of a regulated tenancy to negotiate a rent, but subject to the proviso that either of them or both jointly could at any time during the tenancy seek determination of a "fair rent" by a newly created official called a "rent officer". Provision was made for what was in effect an appeal to an independent tribunal (a Rent Assessment Committee), which was empowered to consider the matter afresh. The rent registered, following a determination by the rent officer or rent assessment committee, became the maximum recoverable rent for that, and any subsequent, regulated tenancy of the premises. Save in exceptional circumstances, it was not possible to seek alteration of a registered rent, which was to be by way of a subsequent re-registration, other than at three-yearly intervals. It is probably true to say that the Labour Government was not so much concerned to increase the supply of privately rented accommodation (it preferred to expand the social rented sector), but rather to stabilise the existing level of supply at fair rents.

Thus, after the 1965 Act, rents of tenancies governed by the Rent Acts were subject to one of two systems of rent restriction. The first was that contained in the principal legislation and applied to those tenancies which had not been decontrolled by the 1957 Act before its repeal. These were to be known as "controlled tenancies" and their rent limits were calculated by reference to 1956 rateable values with rent increases permitted beyond that limit only to reflect subsequent repairs and/or improvements to the property by the landlord. The second regime was the "fair rent system" contained in the 1965 Act and applicable to those tenancies newly designated as "regulated tenancies" (see above). In general, the system of security of tenure for both types of tenancy was the same although certain additional grounds for possession were made available to landlords of regulated tenants.

Furnished tenancies

From their beginning, the Rent Acts had excluded furnished tenancies from the ambit of the principal controls, although from the 1920 Act onwards they had attempted, with limited success to eliminate "excess profits" from such tenancies. However, the Furnished Houses (Rent Control) Act 1946 set up a different system of controls for contracts (thus applying to tenancies and licences with exclusive possession) to occupy furnished premises as a residence, whereby the contract could be referred, by either party or the local authority, to an independent rent tribunal which had power to confirm the contractual rent or reduce it to whatever was considered "reasonable" in all the circumstances. (The Rent Act 1974 subsequently gave the tribunal the additional power to increase the rent). The Act also made provision for a limited degree of security of tenure by providing for a delay in the operation of a notice to quit if served after the contract had been referred to the tribunal, whether before the tribunal's decision or within three months thereafter. The 1946 Act had been due to expire on December 31, 1947 but was subsequently extended and continued in force until made permanent by the Rent Act 1965.

Consolidation

In 1968 almost all the Rent Acts then in force, including the furnished tenancy code, were repealed and consolidated in the Rent Act 1968. All tenancies which had remained controlled by the principal legislation, as well as those brought into protection by the Rent Act 1965, were henceforth to be known as "protected tenancies" whilst the tenancy remained contractual and "statutory tenancies" if the contractual tenancy had ended (or the protected tenant had died leaving a qualifying successor). The controlled/regulated dichotomy continued to apply for rent restriction purposes. Contracts for the occupation of furnished accommodation became known as "Part VI contracts".

Controlled tenancies abolished

Following a change of government in 1970 a Report was commissioned on the working of the new system outlined above. Both the Committee appointed and a subsequent government White Paper accepted, whilst acknowledging the need for minor reforms, that the fair rent system was working well (*Report of the Committee on the Rent Acts* (The Francis Committee), Cmnd. 4609 (1971); *Fair Deal for Housing*, Cmnd. 4728 (1971)). However, the Government was concerned that controlled rents had become frozen at unacceptably low levels. The Rent Act 1965 already provided that on a second statutory succession a controlled tenancy should become a regulated tenancy and the Housing Act 1969 had provided for conversion to regulated tenancies of controlled tenancies of dwellings in good repair which had been equipped by landlords with standard amenities (as defined). The new Conservative Government introduced the Housing Finance Act 1972 which replaced the conversion provisions in the 1969 Act with a staged process of conversion whereby all controlled tenancies would eventually become regulated tenancies subject to the fair rent system. Although halted, following the election of a Labour Government in 1974, by the Housing Rent and Subsidies Act 1975, this process was finally completed, following the return of a Conservative Government in 1979, by the Housing Act 1980 which converted any remaining controlled tenancies into regulated tenancies on November 28, 1980, thereby bringing them within the scope of the fair rent system.

Consolidation and further reform

Consolidation occurred again with the Rent Act 1977. Part VI contracts were renamed "restricted contracts", but regrettably no attempt was made to rationalise the Byzantine web of substantive law. The complex and unintelligible nature of much of that law was further bedeviled by the Housing Act 1980 which made a number of radical amendments to the operation of the Rent Act scheme not just by amending the 1977 Act but also by substantive provisions in the 1980 Act itself.

Protection extended

In the meantime, the Labour Government, which had been returned to office in 1974, retrospectively extended full Rent Act protection to furnished tenancies (following the recommendation in the Minority Report of the Francis Committee). As a political compromise new exceptions to protection were introduced. They were tenancies created by resident landlords (which were specifically accorded Part VI contract status, whether the premises were furnished or not); tenancies granted to students by specified educational institutions and holiday lettings. Thus the focus of the Part VI code shifted from furnished lettings, which were now mostly fully protected, to post-1974 Act resident landlord lettings.

Housing association tenancies protected

Housing associations, which are voluntary bodies formed to provide accommodation for rent at affordable rent levels, have been around since the nineteenth century but were given a much more expanded role to play in housing provision following the changed funding arrangements contained in the (Conservative) Housing Act 1974. Whilst unenthusiastic about expanding the public rented sector, Conservative governments were willing to provide public funding for housing associations which were seen as less bureaucratic, monolithic and more ideologically acceptable as providers of housing to groups in greatest need than local authority landlords. Indeed a political consensus was to emerge on the desirability of supporting this small but growing sub-sector of the rented property market, which by 1995–96 accounted for 5 per cent of all households, albeit that the rate of growth has been slowed down in recent years by reduced levels of government funding.

The Housing Finance Act 1972 extended the fair rent scheme (but not the security of tenure code) in the Rent Act 1968 to tenancies where the landlord's interest was held by a registered housing association. These tenancies became known for this purpose as "housing association tenancies" and will be referred to hereafter as such. (As will be seen below, most housing association tenants were also subsequently afforded the status of "secure tenants", thereby giving them broadly the same security of tenure as that afforded to tenants of local authorities under the separate code first introduced by the Housing Act 1980 and now contained in the Housing Act 1985).

The Housing Act 1980—the road to deregulation

The Housing Act 1980 was a watershed. Since 1965 there had been a broad political consensus on the need for the retention of security of tenure and rent regulation under the Rent Act, albeit with disagreements as to where precisely the balance between the interests of landlords and tenants should lie. There was also a considerable degree of consensus on the need for a significant role to be played as housing providers by both local authorities and housing associations, with a more marked degree of enthusiasm for the latter than for the former by Conservative administrations. All this was to change in the 1980s. A neo-liberal economic policy was espoused by the Conservative Government elected in 1979 under the leadership of Margaret Thatcher. Classical free market economic theory had little time for regulatory mechanisms such as rent control, and the stage was set for a return to decontrol. In a replay of 1957 it was once again argued that state intervention through rent regulation had interfered with the free play of market forces by encouraging some landlords to withdraw from the market once possession has been obtained, and others to decide not to make properties available for rent when they would otherwise have done so. (See, for example, D.C. Stafford, *The Economics of Housing Policy*, (Croom Helm, London 1978). Curiously, this argument seemed to fly in the face of evidence documenting the continued decline in the size of the private rented sector following the decontrolling 1957 Act.

Nevertheless, the 1980 Act cautiously sought to implement the new policy, not by returning to wholesale deregulation but by shifting the balance of power in favour of landlords. Thus it introduced additional Rent Act grounds for possession and extended some of the existing grounds. The minimum period between rent registrations was reduced from three to two years. The limited degree of rent tribunal security of tenure enjoyed by holders of restricted contracts was abolished for those contracts entered into on or after November 28, 1980, although their rents remained vulnerable to review by the rent tribunal. Rent tribunals as such were abolished and their functions transferred to rent assessment committees—which when exercising those functions were to be known as rent tribunals! (In practice, rent assessment committees and rent tribunals had been drawn from the same body of persons since 1965).

Protected shorthold tenancies

One of the reforms in which the Government placed great faith was the new "protected shorthold tenancy" which was made available by the 1980 Act. This permitted a landlord to let for a fixed term, being not less than one nor more than five years, free from the normal Rent Act security of tenure but subject to the fair rent scheme, provided that before the grant the landlord gave the tenant a valid notice stating that the tenancy was to be a protected shorthold tenancy. The court could waive the need to comply with this notice requirement if it subsequently considered it just and equitable to order possession. There were complex provisions which required a formal notice to be served by the landlord to cause the tenancy to be terminated at the expiration of the fixed term which, if not adhered to, could result in the tenant becoming entitled to remain for at least a further year. If all these procedural requirements were satisfied by the landlord, he was guaranteed recovery of possession at the end of the fixed term.

Assured tenancies

Another novel form of tenancy created by the 1980 Act, and intended to stimulate new building for rent, was the "assured tenancy". This was a tenancy which in all respects would be an ordinary protected tenancy but which, by virtue of the Act, was freed from Rent Act security and rent regulation. Before this freedom could be obtained certain conditions had to be satisfied. Thus the landlord had to be an "approved body". Approval was by statutory instrument and in practice extended to certain building companies, insurance companies, pension funds, etc. Furthermore the dwelling-house had to be, or form part of, a building which was erected (and on which construction work began) on or after August 8, 1980. This was subsequently extended by the Housing and Planning Act 1986 to cover dwellings built before that date but which had been substantially improved or repaired or converted at a cost greater than a prescribed amount.

Finally, it should be noted that although such a letting was to be free of Rent Act security of tenure and rent regulation, it was to be subject to the statutory scheme of protection for business tenancies contained in the Landlord and Tenant Act 1954, as appropriately modified for this purpose. The right to renewal of the lease under that scheme included provision for the county court to settle both the terms and the rent of the renewed term in the event of failure to agree on these matters by the parties. The assured tenancy scheme got off to a slow start and was never a great success. By the end of 1987 just under 3,000 assured tenancies had been created, mainly involving sheltered accommodation for the elderly constructed by housing associations.

The end of consensus

The now increasingly fragile political consensus on the principle of Rent Act regulation finally broke down following the re-election of a third successive Conservative Government in May 1987, despite the fact that as late as December 1986 it was reported that: "Mr Patten [the Minister of Housing] re-affirmed his commitment, to maintain the Rent Acts and emphasised the importance of political consensus if any changes in them were proposed." (*Financial Times,* December 9, 1986 quoted in R. Albon and D. C. Stafford, *Rent Control* (1987), p. 83.)

The White Paper, *Housing: The Government's Proposals*, Cm. 214 (1987) went further than at any time since the 1957 Act down the road of deregulation. It heralded a radical shake-up of the existing system with the express objective of putting "new life into the independent rented sector" and ensuring that "The letting of private property will again become an economic proposition" (*ibid.*, para. 1.15). The case against controls, as summarised in the White Paper, was based on four propositions. First, that rent controls had prevented landlords from getting an adequate return on their investment. Second, that people who might have been prepared to grant a temporary letting had been deterred by the laws on security of tenure which made it impossible to regain possession of their property when necessary. Third, that low rents meant that many private landlords had difficulty in finding sufficient resources to keep their property in good repair. Fourth that tenants themselves had not benefited as a whole from rent restrictions, since the supply of privately rented housing had shrunk below what was needed. (For academic arguments which emphasised the link between controls and decline of the private rented sector in the United Kingdom, see further P.Minford, M. Peel and P. Ashton, *The Housing Morass* (The Institute of Economic Affairs, London 1987) and J. Gyourko, "*Controlling and assisting privately rented housing*" (1990) *Urban Studies*, Vol. 27 No. 6, pp. 785–793. See also A.Ogus *Regulation: Legal Forces and Economic Theory* (1994) p.297; N.Duxbury, "Law, Markets and Valuation" (1995) *Brooklyn Law Review* Vol. 61 p.657. Cf. R.G.Lee, "*Rent Control—The Economic Impact of Social Legislation*" (1992) 12 O.J.L.S. 543–557.)

The new way—partial deregulation

The Government response to the problems of the private rented sector was to propose a new statutory regime for rents end security of tenure in the private rented sector. With very limited exceptions, mainly for the benefit of existing tenants, the Rent Act 1977, with some amendments, described in the White Paper as "minor", would be retained only for those tenancies created before the operative date of the new legislation. Once the landlord was able to regain possession of those properties the Rent Act regime would cease to apply and if the premises were relet it would be on the basis of the new regime. Under that regime, applicable to tenancies created after the coming into operation of the foreshadowed legislation, rents would be at the market level, with the aim of stimulating an increased supply of rented accommodation.

At the same time, the White Paper also stated that the Government did not favour total decontrol of the market, leaving rents and security of tenure to be settled contractually between landlord and tenant with no statutory restraint, on the basis that this would not give sufficient protection to tenants' interests—

> "It is reasonable that, when entering a tenancy, the tenant should expect to have to pay the market rent for the property, with suitable adjustments over time. But once a tenant has a market rent tenancy and is occupying a property as his or her home it is right that he or she should have a reasonable degree of security of tenure."

Consequently it was proposed that the normal type of tenancy under the new regime would be a revamped "assured tenancy" under which the tenant would pay a market rent but obtain security of tenure. Despite the Government's decision not to go down the road of total decontrol, it soon became clear that the Government's proposals did not form the basis of a political consensus. Indeed they were to provoke a long and bitter parliamentary battle over the Housing Bill 1987, which took a full year to emerge relatively unscathed as the Housing Act 1988.

The Housing Act 1988

The Act adopted a process of "creeping deregulation" in the sense that, save for a small number of exceptional cases, it became impossible on or after January 15, 1989 to create a protected tenancy, a housing association tenancy or a restricted contract. However, at the same time, the Rent Act 1977, as amended by the 1988 Act, continues to apply to any of these categories of tenancies or contracts created before January 15, 1989 (and in the few exceptional cases referred to above, to tenancies—or as the case may be, contracts—created on or after that date). Thus the use of the term "deregulation" here refers to the replacement of one regulatory mechanism by another much weaker form of regulation much more favourable to landlords.

New-style assured tenancies

Part I of the Housing Act 1988 provided that, subject to a number of exceptional cases which were closely modelled on the 1977 Rent Act exceptions, most residential tenancies granted on or after January 15, 1989 to an individual or individuals would take effect as "assured tenancies". It is important to note that the new regime applies also to tenancies created on or after January 15, 1989 where the landlord's interest is held by a housing association, reflecting their new location within a quasi-private rented sub-sector of the housing market.

The nomenclature of the 1988 Act was most unfortunate and apt to mislead. Unlike the 1980 Act assured tenancies, there is no need for a landlord of a 1988 Act assured tenancy to be an approved landlord, nor need the dwelling in question be new or newly converted. Furthermore, assured tenants have a security of tenure based not on Part II of the Landlord and Tenant Act 1954, but on provisions which prevent a landlord gaining possession save on certain mandatory or discretionary grounds which are modelled on the Rent Act scheme.

It became impossible to create 1980 Act assured tenancies on or after January 15, 1989. Any 1980 Act assured tenancy in existence at that date was converted automatically into the new type of assured tenancies provided for by the Housing Act 1988.

Rent fixing for assured tenancies is governed by market forces and is therefore left to agreement between landlord and tenant. However, there is limited scope, mainly on the occasion of proposed rent increases, for a rent assessment committee, on application, to determine a market rent for the tenancy where the landlord and tenant are unable to agree on a new rent.

Assured shorthold tenancies

Although the White Paper proposed that the assured tenancy was expected to be the normal letting regime, in practice this proved not to be the case. This was because the Act offered landlords an attractive alternative form of tenancy. That alternative was the "assured shorthold tenancy" which was modelled on, but not to be confused with, the protected shorthold tenancy introduced by the Housing Act 1980. As originally enacted, the Housing Act 1988 provided that an assured shorthold tenancy was an assured tenancy—

(1)   created for a term of not less than six months;

(2)   in respect of which there was no power (other than by way of a forfeiture clause) for the landlord to determine the tenancy at any time earlier than six months from the beginning of the tenancy; and

(3) in respect of which the landlord had served a notice in the prescribed form on the tenant at the start of the tenancy stating that it was to be an assured shorthold tenancy.

All the grounds of possession applicable to assured tenancies were also made applicable to shorthold tenancies. However, there was also the important additional ground that, once the shorthold tenancy has ended, provided the landlord has given at least two months' notice stating that he requires possession, the court must order possession.

It was further provided that a tenant of an assured shorthold tenancy (which was not a renewed shorthold tenancy) could at any stage during that tenancy refer his rent to a rent assessment committee for assessment. If the committee considered that there were a sufficient number of similar dwelling-houses in the locality let on assured or assured shorthold tenancies and that, by reference to the levels of those rents, the rent under the tenancy referred to them was significantly higher than that which the landlord might reasonably have expected to have obtained, the committee could then determine in effect a reasonable market rent. The rent determined would become the maximum recoverable rent under that tenancy.

Partial or total deregulation?

Although the assured tenancy afforded the tenant security of tenure as a quid pro quo for a market rent, it was always doubtful from the outset as to how many landlords would create such tenancies, given the more attractive alternative of the assured shorthold tenancy, in respect of which possession was guaranteed once the tenancy had expired. The deterrent of a possible early reference of the rent to a rent assessment committee was arguably more theoretical than real. This was because, as explained above, the committee could only register a rent if satisfied that the rent payable under the tenancy was substantially higher than prevailing rents of other assured tenancies (whether shorthold or not) in the locality. Even if the committee were so convinced, they were limited to determining a market rent, albeit one which reflected the lack of security. Furthermore, even if the tenant was convinced that he or she had made an unwise bargain, the fear of eviction at the end of the tenancy was likely to prove a sufficient disincentive to apply to the rent assessment committee. Indeed by 1995 there were fewer than 1,500 applications a year out of 826,000 assured tenancies. (Government Consultation Paper (linked to the White Paper, *Our Future Homes*) *The Legislative Framework for Private Renting*, DOE, June 1995, para. 2.12.)

Nevertheless, although some landlords would freely choose to let on assured tenancies, others had no choice. Landlords who availed themselves of the Business Expansion Scheme tax advantages provided for by the Finance Act 1988 were compelled to let on assured tenancies. The scheme offered tax relief at the top marginal rate to taxpayers who invested from £500 to £40,000 in new ordinary shares of unquoted British companies which specialised in providing and maintaining properties for the purpose of letting under the new assured tenancy scheme. To obtain the full tax relief the shares must have been issued after July 29, 1988 and before the end of 1993 and be held for at least five years. If sold after five years the profit is exempt from capital gains tax. If the company sells the property or the shares after five years it will be exempt from corporation tax. The scheme proved to be very popular. Indeed so popular that the scheme came to an end on 31 December 1993.

The other main group of landlords who primarily let only on assured tenancies are housing associations. Whilst there is no legal constraint on the use of assured shorthold tenancies by registered housing associations, guidance has been issued by the Housing Corporation to the effect that—

"Associations are expected to give their tenants long term security where possible. Therefore assured shorthold tenancies should be used only in exceptional circumstances, which an association may be required to justify to the Housing Corporation, where shorthold is the only practicable way of meeting the association's housing objectives. (*The Tenant's Guarantee*: issued by the Housing Corporation (HC/43/88))."

Thus most housing association tenancies are assured tenancies. In this connection it can be noted that under Part IV of the Housing Act 1988 (until its repeal by the Housing Act 1996) an approved landlord body, which might be a housing association or private company or tenants' co-operative, could apply to take over ownership of the whole or specific parts of a local authority's housing stock, subject to a right of veto by affected tenants. Most such transfers were to housing associations and therefore the tenants have become assured tenants. (Tenants can also become assured tenants as a result of a voluntary transfer of its housing stock by a local housing authority).

Although an assured tenant whose landlord is a registered housing association is subject to the statutory regime in Part I of the Housing Act 1988 in exactly the same way as any other assured tenant, the "Tenants' Guarantee" issued by the Housing Corporation states that associations are expected to give their assured tenants additional contractual rights within the terms of the tenancy agreement similar to those afforded to secure tenants under the Housing Act 1985. (See Chapter 11 below).

Finally, in connection with assured tenancies under which the landlord is a housing association, it should be noted that the Government considered it unlikely that any proposed rent increase would be challenged before a rent assessment committee. Indeed they were of the opinion that where accommodation has been provided with the assistance of public subsidy, or has been transferred—from a public body such as a local authority, ... it is intended to be accessible to people on low incomes. Associations were therefore expected to set and maintain their rents at levels within the reach of those in low paid employment which would usually entail setting rents below market rental levels.

Despite the government's expectation, many tenants have failed to appreciate this and have ill-advisedly challenged proposed increases before a rent assessment committee who are then required to determine a market rent, which is likely to be considerably higher than the affordable rent sought by the association. This development raises a serious question as to whether such tenancies should remain within the ambit of the rent assessment committee's jurisdiction.

Assured shortholds the norm: the Housing Act 1996

The overwhelming superiority, from the landlord's viewpoint, of the assured shorthold tenancy, meant that, save in those cases outlined above, where the landlord was required to let on a fully assured tenancy, the former type of tenancy inevitably became the norm (see below). It therefore came as no surprise that in 1995 the Government concluded that there was little point in providing for the assured tenancy as the default type of tenancy when most tenancies created were assured shortholds. (By 1995–96, there were 1,319,000 assured tenancies of which 877,000 were shortholds.) Thus the Housing Act 1988 was amended by the Housing Act 1996, thereby providing that, save in specified exceptional cases, any new assured tenancy created on or after February 28, 1997 will take effect automatically as an assured shorthold tenancy. It is now inevitable that save for lettings by housing associations, virtually all new tenancies will take effect as assured shorthold tenancies. To that extent the protections for fully assured tenants in Part I of the Housing Act 1988 are to all intents and purposes a dead letter.

Market rents

How successful the 1988 Act reforms would prove to be in achieving the aim of reviving the private rented sector was always heavily dependent upon how far tenants would be able to afford the higher market rents. The role of housing benefit was critical in this respect because under the new market rent regime subsidy is concentrated on the tenant rather than the property. Even where a market rent is registered by a rent assessment committee that registration only affects the tenancy in question. This is in marked contrast to the fair rent scheme in the Rent Act 1977 whereby a registered rent also bound any subsequent regulated tenancy of the same premises.

The changing role of the rent officer

Rent officers have continued to have a role to play, since January 15, 1989, in determining fair rents under the Rent Act 1977 for regulated tenancies, and housing association tenancies. However, as explained above, save in a limited number of instances, it has not been possible since that date to create new regulated tenancies or housing association tenancies. Consequently the role of the rent officer has changed. The Rent Act workload has gradually diminished as landlords have recovered vacant possession of properties which had been let on regulated tenancies. However, the Housing Act 1988 conferred new functions upon them. Since April 1, 1989 they have been required to scrutinise the levels of rents which are being met by housing benefit, not for the purpose of being able to alter the recoverable rent, but for the purpose of limiting the amount of housing benefit payable by the local authority. The purpose of this procedure is to prevent market rents being "benefit led", which would otherwise enable landlords to recover excessive rents at the expense of the taxpayer.

The dual regulatory regimes

It can be seen that most tenants in the private rented sector now inhabit one or other of two legal worlds, each of which reflects markedly differing political solutions to a highly charged and complex issue. The first world, governed by the Rent Act 1977, is that of "fair rents" and extensive security of tenure. The second world, governed by the Housing Act 1988, is one of "market rents" and insecurity of tenure. The two worlds are different not only in respect of the regulatory regimes which govern them, but also in the nature of the housing stock of which they are comprised and the tenants who occupy those properties.

Most of the stock in the private rented sector is elderly. The General Household Survey of 1995–96 (*Housing in England 1995–96* (HMSO, 1997)) revealed that 45 per cent of private rented dwellings were built before 1919. These are mainly properties in poor condition, held on Rent Act protected unfurnished tenancies and likely to be occupied by older people, although some properties will have been improved by landlords, often with the aid of an improvement grant.

Improvements have been rendered less frequent since the Housing Act 1988 made most improvement grants discretionary rather than mandatory, whilst at the same time lowering the standard of improvement to be attained. By contrast, properties let on assured shorthold (or fully assured) tenancies under the Housing Act 1988 are likely to be in better condition and let furnished. Tenants are also likely to be younger people, often sharing, and the tenancies will invariably be relatively short-term (a year is typical). Other tenants might be single parents, many of whom will be dependent upon housing benefit.

In the course of time, as regulated tenants move or die, landlords will either sell with vacant possession or relet under the Housing Act 1988 and, in the absence of further regulatory measures, the Rent Act sector will eventually wither away. In 1989 there were 1,071,000 regulated tenancies. However, by 1995–96 the number had dropped to 272,000 (*Housing in England, op. cit.*).

The future of the private rented sector

It can be seen from the above survey that in recent years, government policy has been heavily influenced by a laissez-faire free market ideology with regard to regulation of the private rented sector. Legislators have been convinced that the removal of most regulatory controls will not only halt, but put into reverse the hitherto inexorable decline of that sector. This policy relies heavily on a belief that controls have almost single-handedly been responsible for that decline. But is this true?

Most commentators accept that the explanation for the small size of the private rented sector in the United Kingdom does not lie solely in the long-term existence of rent controls, although this has undoubtedly been a factor in discouraging supply. Favourable tax treatment (through mortgage interest and capital gains tax relief), along with cheap credit coupled with traditionally high levels of inflation, have given home ownership an artificial comparative advantage in the United Kingdom during a period of rising income levels. A further boost was provided by the "right to buy" introduced by the Housing Act 1980 which gave council tenants the mandatory right to swell the ranks of the owner-occupied sector by buying the property which they rented, often with substantial discounts and readily available finance. Thus the trend towards owner occupation has been far stronger in the United Kingdom than elsewhere in Europe. (At the time of writing, home ownership is at an all-time high, comprising 68 per cent of all households: *Housing in England, op. cit.*).

Another important factor was the post-1945 shift in government policy towards large-scale state provision of council housing for rent. The public rented sector accounted for 10 per cent of the total housing stock in 1938. This figure had risen to 17 per cent by 1951 and by 1981 had reached its all-time high figure of 30 per cent, before falling back to 18 per cent in 1995–96 largely through a switch to owner occupation following the introduction of the "right to buy" in 1980 and to a lesser degree as a result of increased provision by housing associations, from 2 per cent in 1981 to 5 per cent in 1995–96. (*Housing in England, op. cit.*). Indeed the shift from local authority to housing association provision has been encouraged since the 1980s by a number of government-led initiatives. (On the changing face of the social rented sector, see A. Murie, "The Social Rented Sector, Housing and the Welfare State in the UK" (1997) 12 *Housing Studies* 437).

At the same time, United Kingdom governments have not consistently afforded private landlords sufficiently attractive tax breaks to persuade them to enter or remain in the market in sufficient numbers. As indicated above, one of the features of United Kingdom law over a long period of time has been a remarkably high degree of political conflict over housing policy, discouraging risk-taking by prospective landlords. Indeed, this almost permanent climate of uncertainty, along with its damaging effects, had been highlighted as long ago as 1965 in the Report of the Milner Holland Committee.

Before examining whether, in the nine years since the deregulating Housing Act 1988 came into force, there has been a restoration of the fortunes of the private rented sector we might consider who can be expected to be seeking accommodation in that (deregulated) sector. All the indications are that this sector caters for increasing numbers of younger persons and single or single-parent households. Some of these tenants will be using the private rented sector as a staging post *en route* to owner occupation. Others will have no alternative in the face of declining public sector provision and for them it will be a tenure of last resort. Flexible labour markets, with decreased job security, will preclude owner occupation as a viable option for many householders. Thus the private rented sector will need to expand to cater for increasing numbers of persons in each of the above groups, but is never likely to grow to the proportions to be found in neighbouring European states which exhibit markedly divergent patterns of tenure from those in the United Kingdom as a result of very different political and cultural histories.

Judging by the experience of the last 10 years, there is some evidence which suggests that, following the implementation of the Housing Act 1988 in January 1989, there has been an increase in the size of the private rented sector. Thus between 1989 and 1995–96 the number of households renting privately rose from an all-time low of 8.6 per cent to 10.1 per cent. Part of this increase has undoubtedly come about as a result of the deregulation provisions in the Housing Act 1988, and a small boost in supply was provided by the BES scheme. However, this scheme has been described as a short-term, if expensive success. (See R. Best, P. Kemp, D. Coleman, S. Merrett and T. Crook *The Future of Private Renting, Consensus and Action* (Joseph Rowntree Foundation, York, 1992). See further J. Hughes, "The impact of the Business Expansion Scheme on the supply of privately-rented housing" (1995) *Journal of Property Finance* Vol. 6 No. 2, pp. 1–32.) By contrast, a significant part of the increase since 1989 appears to be attributable to the slump in the housing market, which left many owner occupiers who had been forced to move, usually as a result of changing jobs, with no alternative other than to let out their property on a temporary basis. Furthermore the huge increase in mortgage repossession cases during the recession of the early 1990s meant that many former owner-occupiers were forced to turn to the private rented sector.

Although, as noted above, a largely deregulated market has emerged since 1989, this has resulted in sharp levels of rent increase which in turn have fuelled levels of housing benefit payments to tenants in the private rented sector. Thus public subsidy has shifted from dwellings (through rent regulation) to tenants (and indirectly to landlords). Housing benefit paid to private sector (and housing association) tenants rose from £1.03 billion in 1986–87 to (an estimated) £5.8 billion in 1996–97. (DSS, *Social Security Statistics* (HMSO, 1997). Approximately 50 per cent of this amount was paid to tenants in the private rented sector. Housing benefit now underpins not only the majority of revenue (65–70 per cent) to local authority and housing association landlords but also around one-third for private landlords, and has spiralled to such a degree that a number of changes were made to the relevant regulations in an attempt to reduce the overall level of government expenditure on housing benefit. (See further S. Wilcox, *Housing Review 1996/97*, (Joseph Rowntree Foundation, York, 1996); G. Bramley, "Housing policy: a case of terminal decline?" (1997) 25 *Policy & Politics* 387. These developments may indicate that any upturn in the fortunes of the private rented sector could prove to be a temporary phenomenon. (See further T. Crook, J. Hughes and P. Kemp, *The Supply of Privately Rented Homes: Today and Tomorrow* (Joseph Rowntree Foundation, York, 1995).

Thus there are good grounds for believing that by itself deregulation will not be enough to effect a significant increase in the size of the private rented sector. As we have seen above there are many other factors apart from regulation, such as the existence of more attractive alternative investment opportunities elsewhere, which have affected the willingness of landlords to enter or remain in the private rented sector. (See D. Maclennan, "Private rental housing: Britain viewed from abroad" in *The Private Provision of Rented Housing* (ed. P.Kemp), Avebury, Aldershot, (1998) pp. 147–174; M. Harloe, *Private Rented Housing in the United States and Europe* (Croom Helm, London, 1985).

The simple fact is, as is revealed by an examination of the private rented sector in other states within the European Union, that the text book free market where supply and demand interact in an unregulated fashion does not exist. (See M. Oxley and J. Smith, *Housing Policy and Rented Housing in Europe* (E&F Spon, 1997)). For numerous reasons the size of the sector has been declining for decades throughout most of Western Europe, albeit at a faster rate in the United Kingdom than elsewhere. (Germany provides an exception, although significantly that country provides state incentives for investors to remain in and enter the market. The cost of housing in Germany is also relatively far higher than in the United Kingdom and there is only a very small public rented sector). Nevertheless the private rented sector remains significantly higher in most European states other than in the United Kingdom and in all of those countries the level of both demand and supply are actively supported by the state. Until government is prepared to adopt a more extensive political framework, which revitalises and supports both demand for and supply of privately rented accommodation, it can confidently be predicted that by itself the removal of rent controls and security of tenure will not prove any more successful than previous attempts to restore the fortunes of the private rented sector. The provisions of the Finance Act 1995 which are designed to encourage institutional investment in the private rented sector by allowing investment trusts to be formed with the benefit of capital gains tax exemption and a reduced rate of corporation tax have yet to induce a positive response from the market. As one commentator has observed, "had it been the long-term objective to kill off the private landlord, British housing policy has achieved a remarkable degree of success" (Cullingworth, *Essays in Housing Policy*, p.73.) (See further P. Kemp, "Deregulation, markets and the 1988 Housing Act" (1990) 24 *Social Policy & Administration* 145; A. Bovaird, M. Harloe and C.M.E. Whitehead, "Private rented housing: Its current role" (1985) 14 *Journal of Social Policy*. For criticism of the return of the rent fixing process to market forces see J. Ivatts, "Rented housing and market rents: a social policy critique" (1988) 22 *Soc. Policy and Admin.* 197).

It remains to be seen what difference will be made by the return of a Labour Government in May 1997. The Labour Party's earlier commitment to repeal Part I of the Housing Act 1988 has been dropped and to that extent a new political consensus on the need to revive the private rental sector appears to have emerged. In those circumstances it seems unlikely that there will be an extension of Rent Act controls. In the meantime, although in steady decline, the Rent Act protected sub-sector still comprises a significant number of tenants and therefore a knowledge of the regulatory regimes contained in the Rent Act 1977 and the Housing Act 1988 will remain necessary for some time. The next chapter examines each of these schemes.

Chapter 9

SECURITY OF TENURE AND RENT REGULATION IN THE PRIVATE SECTOR: (1) THE HOUSING ACT 1988

A. INTRODUCTION

As explained in Chapter 8 above, most residential tenancies created by private landlords or housing associations on or after January 15, 1989 take effect as either assured or assured shorthold tenancies under the Housing Act 1988. An assured tenancy for the purposes of the Housing Act 1988 is a type of tenancy which affords the tenant security of tenure, under a statutory regime of protection which, to a large degree, is broadly modelled on the scheme in the Rent Act 1977 which governs protected and statutory tenancies. By contrast an assured shorthold tenancy, which is more specifically a sub-species of assured tenancy, is a type of tenancy which affords the tenant very little protection. This is because once the shorthold tenancy has ended, and provided the landlord has given the tenant at least two months' notice stating that he requires possession, the court must order possession when the landlord brings the appropriate proceedings. In reality, therefore, an assured shorthold tenancy offers very little by way of assurance to the tenant, who has negligible security of tenure beyond that provided for by the terms of the tenancy.

We also saw in Chapter 8 that, although the Housing Act 1988 originally provided that most tenancies created on or after January 15, 1989 would take effect as fully assured tenancies, unless the landlord specifically created an assured shorthold tenancy, the position has been reversed since February 28, 1997, when the Housing Act 1988 was amended by the Housing Act 1996. Assured tenancies created on or after that date will take effect as assured shorthold tenancies unless the parties choose to create a fully assured tenancy. We have thus now arrived at the position where the vast majority of tenancies will be of the assured shorthold variety. Indeed even before the changes brought about by the Housing Act 1996 the proportion of shortholds had been growing rapidly. Nevertheless, it is still necessary, when considering the law governing assured shorthold tenancies, to begin by examining the statutory definition of an assured tenancy. This is because all assured tenancies, whether fully assured or shorthold, must comply with this definition. Furthermore, there are still a significant number of fully assured tenancies in existence, most of which will have been created before February 28, 1997. The majority of those created on or after that date will have been granted by housing associations which are for the most part required to let on fully assured tenancies (see p.200 above).

B. DEFINING ASSURED TENANCIES

Introduction

The statutory definition of an assured tenancy in the Housing Act 1988 draws heavily upon terminology familiar from the regimes contained in the Rent Act 1977 (definition of a protected tenancy) and the Housing Act 1985 (definition of a secure tenancy) (see Chapters 9–11 below). It would therefore seem natural, when exploring the ambit of the 1988 Act, to consider how the courts have construed equivalent terminology in the earlier legislation. At the same time it should be appreciated that the primary purpose of statutory construction is to determine what is the ordinary natural meaning of the word within the context of the section in which it appears. Thus, although the case law on the earlier schemes may undoubtedly be of assistance when construing the Housing Act 1988, it will at the same time be necessary to have regard to the purpose of the provision in question and the mischief at which it is aimed (see *Quillotex Co. Ltd v. Minister of Housing and Local Government* [1966] 1 Q.B. 704, per Salmon L.J. and *Annicola Investments v. Minister of Housing and Local Government* [1968] 1 Q.B. 631).

Assured tenancies defined

Section 1 of the Housing Act 1988 provides that, save for specified exceptional cases—

> "A tenancy under which a dwelling-house is let as a separate dwelling is for the purposes of this Act an assured tenancy if and so long as
>
> > (a)   the tenant, or as the case may be, each of the joint tenants, is an individual; and
> > (b)   the tenant, or as the case may be, at least one of the joint tenants occupies the dwelling-house as his only or principal home."

No contracting out of the Act

Despite the absence of any statutory prohibition on contracting out of the protection of the Act, in principle it should not be possible for the parties to a tenancy which takes effect as an assured tenancy to agree that the Act will not apply to that tenancy. This has long been accepted in the case of the Rent Acts and it is believed that the courts would apply a similar rule to the Housing Act 1988. (For the judicial prohibition on contracting out of the Rent Act, see *Barton v. Fincham* [1921] 2 K.B. 291; *A.G. Securities v. Vaughan; Antoniades v. Villiers* [1988] 3 W.L.R. 1205, *per* Lord Templeman).

Elements of the definition

Element One

> "A tenancy under which a dwelling-house is let as a separate dwelling…"

In so far as the definition requires there to be a tenancy of a "dwelling-house let as a separate dwelling", it mirrors the same requirement for a protected tenancy contained in section 1 of the Rent Act 1977 (see Chapter 10 below).

Tenancy/let The only clue in the Act itself as to the meaning of tenancy for this purpose is that it extends to a sub-tenancy and an agreement for a tenancy or a sub-tenancy (s.45). Nevertheless, it is clear, from earlier case law on the Rent Acts, that the definition applies to all types of tenancy. Thus it covers fixed-term and periodic (*e.g.* weekly or monthly) tenancies, whether they arise expressly or by implication. Also covered is a tenancy taking effect in equity, provided it is specifically enforceable as such under the principle in *Walsh v. Lonsdale* (1882) 21 Ch. 9 (For the statutory formalities governing contracts, see Chapter 1 above).

As we saw in Chapter 1, the fact that mainstream protection under the Rent Acts was confined to tenants led many landlords to seek to avoid the Rent Act by purporting to create an occupational arrangement other than a tenancy. Indeed, as Evershed M.R. observed in *Foster v. Robinson* ([1951] 1 K.B. 149 at 158), there was—

> "nothing to prevent the parties from so arranging matters that there is nothing to which the Acts can apply, providing the transaction in question is a genuine transaction and not a mere sham."

The most popular, but by no means only, device employed by owners to avoid (or evade?) the Rent Acts was the occupational licence, and reference should be made to Chapter 1 above for an account of the law governing the outcome of that campaign.

During the passage of the Housing Act 1988 through Parliament, the Government resisted an Opposition attempt to extend the scope of the 1988 Act to embrace contractual licences; it was considered that this matter could be left safely to the courts. As we have already seen, the courts have not always found it easy to determine how particular occupational arrangements should be classified. Nevertheless, as far as the Housing Act 1988 is concerned, that is now of very little consequence. The introduction of the assured shorthold tenancy by the 1988 Act removed any incentive for most private landlords to attempt to create a licence rather than a tenancy. Landlords can now let at a market rent on an assured shorthold tenancy which guarantees them possession at least six months after commencement of the tenancy. Furthermore, even where a tenancy rather than a licence is inadvertently created, the consequences are much less severe for landlords in the case of arrangements entered into on or after February 28, 1997. This is because, as we have seen above, such a tenancy will take effect automatically as an assured shorthold tenancy, whereas before that date it would have been a fully assured tenancy.

A dwelling-house Section 1 of the Housing Act 1988 provides that to be an assured tenancy, there must be a letting of a dwelling-house (which may be a house or part of a house (s.45)). The Act does not provide any further definition of the term "dwelling-house". However, the Rent Act 1977 affords protected tenancy status to a tenancy of a dwelling-house, and in that context the term has been extensively considered by the courts since it first appeared in the Increase of Rent and Mortgage Interest (Restrictions) Act 1920.

In *Horford Investments v. Lambert* [1976] Ch. 39, 51 Scarman L. J. stated that—

> "It must be a question of fact whether premises are a house or not...if the agreement is to let a barn, the tenant even though he lives there cannot be heard to say that it is let as a dwelling-house."

The term clearly includes a flat, whether purpose-built or not, (*Langford Property Co v.*

Goldrich [1949] 1 K.B. 511, 516, CA and can even extend to a single room (*Curl v. Angelo* [1948] 2 All E.R. 189, 190, CA *per* Lord Greene M.R.) provided it has all the essential facilities for normal residential living. This was found not to be the case in *Central YMCA Housing Association v. Goodman* (1991) 24 H.L.R. 98, CA (a decision which concerned the definition of a secure tenancy contained in the Housing Act 1985, s.79) where the defendant was granted the right to occupy a room, with no cooking facilities, in a hostel. The court held that the room could not be described as a dwelling-house any more than a hotel room.

The term also extends to two or more properties, whether contiguous or not, let together on a single tenancy as one home (*Langford Property Co. v. Goldrich* (above) and *Whitty v. Scott-Russell* [1950] 2 K.B. 32, CA. (Such an arrangement can be contrasted with that in *Grosvenor (Mayfair) Estates v. Amberton* (1983) 265 E.G. 693, where two flats were let under one tenancy with a covenant by the tenant to use as *a* private residence only. This was impossible because one flat was occupied at the time by licensees. It was held that because the property was let as two flats with no imminent prospect of use as one dwelling they could not be treated as having been let as a single dwelling). The same result occurred in *Metropolitan Properties Co. (F.G.C.) v. Barder* [1968] 1 W.L.R. 286, CA where a tenant of a flat later obtained another tenancy of a single room in the building for occupation by an au pair girl. The fact that the two units were let at separate times and on different terms meant that they could not be said to amount to a single dwelling.

Doubts have occasionally arisen over the status of less permanent structures. In *Elitestone v Morris* [1997] 2 All E.R. 513, HL a wooden bungalow which rested on its own weight upon concrete pillars was held by the House of Lords to have become part of the realty, and therefore to be a dwelling-house for the purposes of section 1 of the Rent Act.

Whether a caravan qualifies as a dwelling-house depends upon the circumstances of the letting. In principle, caravans would be excluded but in appropriate circumstances they might qualify as a dwelling-house, as in *Makins v. Ekon* [1977] 1 W.L.R. 221, where the caravan wheels had been raised and permanent services connected. By contrast, in the later case of *R. v. Rent Officer of the Nottinghamshire Registration Area, ex parte Allen* (1985) 52 P.& C.R. 41 the Court referred to a number of relevant factors to which regard should be had, including whether or not the caravan retained its mobility and whether it was occupied as a permanent home. On the facts of that case, it was held that the caravans in question did not qualify, because although connected to the mains supplies of electricity and sewage, they were fully mobile and were occasionally moved by the owner for the purpose of carrying out repairs and renovations. The services were easily connected and disconnected.

Let as a separate dwelling

(a) The tenancy must provide for residential user The dwelling-house in question must be "let as a separate dwelling". The first two words indicate that residential user must be provided for, expressly or impliedly, by the terms of the tenancy (*Horford Investments v. Lambert*, above). In deciding what is the purpose of the letting, it is necessary to consider the terms of the tenancy in the light of the surrounding circumstances and in particular the nature of the premises. Once again it will be instructive to examine the interpretation afforded by case law to the identical expression used in section 1 of the Rent Act 1977 (definition of a protected tenancy) and section 79 of the Housing Act 1985 (definition of a secure tenancy).

In *Wolfe v. Hogan* [1949] 2 K.B. 194, CA premises in Chelsea, London were let for business purposes (use as an antiques shop). Although this purpose was not expressly stated in the tenancy, this did not matter. In such circumstances actual user will generally supply the relevant purpose of the letting and in this case that purpose was clear because when let the premises were used as a shop. The landlord subsequently agreed to a request by the tenant that she be permitted to sleep at the premises in view of the difficulty in returning home during bombing raids on London. In fact (as she had always intended), she began to live there permanently and the issue arose as to whether she was protected by the 1920 Act. The Court of Appeal held that because the (implied) terms of the tenancy provided for business user the premises could not be said to be let as a dwelling-house, in the absence of a consensual variation in the terms of the tenancy. Such a variation will not be implied simply because the landlord accepts rent knowing of the actual changed user (p.203 per Denning L.J. See also *Ponder v. Hillman* [1969] 1 W.L.R. 1261).

Similar problems can arise where a tenancy is granted of property, part of which is used for residential purposes and part for business purposes, such as a shop with a flat above. It will be seen below that an assured tenancy will be precluded where the tenancy falls within Part II of the Landlord and Tenant Act 1954 (*i.e.* where the whole or any part of the premises subject to the tenancy is occupied by the tenant for the purposes of a business carried on by him or for those and other purposes (s.23(1)). Nonetheless, a subsequent cessation of the business use will not mean that the tenancy will automatically become an assured (or assured shorthold) tenancy.

In *Trustees of Henry Smith's Charity Kensington Estate v. Wagle* [1990] 1 Q.B. 42, CA premises were let for the purposes of an artist's or sculptor's residential studio on what was acknowledged to be a business tenancy within Part II of the Landlord and Tenant Act 1954 even though the premises included living accommodation. At some subsequent stage the premises were used by the then tenants for residential purposes only. The court held that even though the effect of this was that the 1954 Act no longer applied it did not follow that the premises were 'let as a dwelling-house' in the absence of an agreement by the landlord to a variation in the terms of the tenancy. (See also *Pulleng v. Curran* (1980) 44 P.& C.R. 58, CA, *Russell v. Booker* (1982) 5 H.L.R. 10, CA and *Webb v. Barnett LBC* (1988) 21 H.L.R. 228, CA. See further J. Martin [1983] Conv. 390.)

(b) The premises must be let for use as a single dwelling The reference to "a" separate dwelling indicates that if premises which consist of several units of accommodation (such as bed sitting rooms or flats) which are let to a non-occupying tenant for the purpose of sub-letting to separate occupiers, the head tenancy would not be within section 1. This is because the premises are not let as a dwelling, but as several dwellings (*Horford Investments v. Lambert*, above). This is to be contrasted with the circumstances in *Regalian Securities v. Ramsden* [1981] 1 W.L.R. 611, where a flat and maisonette were held to be let as a separate dwelling even though the maisonette was subsequently sub-let.

The principle in *Horford Investments v. Lambert* (above) was applied in *St Catherine's College v. Dorling* [1980] 1 W.L.R. 66, CA where the purpose of a tenancy, whereby a house was let to the College, was for individual study/bedrooms in the house to be sub-let by the College to students who would share the kitchen and bathroom. The Court held that the house was not let to the College as a separate dwelling. Thus the College was subsequently unable to apply for a fair rent to be registered by the rent officer because the tenancy was not a regulated tenancy within the Rent Act 1977. Occasionally such an arrangement might give rise to a business tenancy within Part II of the Landlord and Tenant Act 1954. This occurred in *Groveside*

Properties Ltd v. Westminster Medical School (1983) 47 P.& C.R. 507, CA where a tenancy of a flat, consisting of four individual study rooms to be occupied by medical students with shared use of a kitchen, bathroom, lavatories and sitting room, was granted to the Medical School. It was held that, because of the substantial degree of control which it exercised over the use of the premises by the students, the Medical School occupied the flat for the purposes of its business as an educational institution providing student accommodation, and therefore the tenancy was governed by Part II of the Landlord and Tenant Act 1954.

Such "direct leasing" schemes were, and continue to be, commonly used by universities and colleges as a means of providing student accommodation, which guarantees payment of the rent to the head landlord, by the use of tenancies outside the ambit of special statutory codes such as those contained in the Rent Act 1977 and the Housing Act 1988. This is because of the exemptions from those regimes for lettings *to* a qualifying educational institution: (see pages 218 and 256 below). Of course the attraction of such schemes to prospective landlords, as a means of avoiding the fair rent and security of tenure codes in the Rent Act 1977, disappeared from January 15 1989 when the Housing Act 1988 prohibited the creation of new Rent Act protected tenancies. Nevertheless, many landlords still prefer such an arrangement with an educational institution rather than dealing direct with the student occupiers.

(c) Shared use of part may exclude an assured tenancy   The requirement for the letting to be of a "separate" dwelling directs attention to the issue of sharing. We have already seen that if an occupier does not have exclusive occupation of any living accommodation, there cannot be a tenancy (see p.1 above). Of course it may be the case that several occupiers are joint tenants of the whole of the premises and accordingly they will have an assured tenancy of the whole. As long as at least one of the joint tenants occupies the premises as his only or principal home, the tenancy will be assured (Housing Act 1988, ss.1 and 45).

However, other cases of sharing can present difficulties. A particular problem could arise if, under the terms of his tenancy, an occupier has exclusive use of separate accommodation (not capable of use on its own as a dwelling) and shares, more or less equally, other "living accommodation" with one or more other persons. (For this purpose, "living accommodation" includes sitting rooms and kitchens, but not bathrooms (*Cole v. Harris* [1945] K.B. 474, CA)).

The state of affairs described above is the common house- or flat-sharing scenario where a group of people live under the same roof, each having an agreement which grants each occupier the right to exclusive possession of a separate bedroom along with shared use with the other occupiers of the kitchen, bathroom and living room(s). At first sight this would seem to deprive the occupier of assured tenancy status, because he cannot be said to be occupying a dwelling-house as a "separate" dwelling. (See *Neale v. Del Soto* [1945] K.B. 144, CA; *Goodrich v. Paisner* [1957] A.C. 65, HL and *Marsh v. Cooper* [1969] 1 W.L.R. 803, CA on the equivalent provision in what is now Rent Act 1977, s.1). This is also the case under the secure tenancy code in the Housing Act 1985. (See *Parkins v. Westminster City Council* [1997] E.G.C.S. 163, where a sharing of living accommodation in a local authority-owned flat by an occupier with exclusive possession of a bedroom precluded a secure tenancy, on the basis that there was not a separate dwelling for the purposes of section 79 of the Housing Act 1985 (definition of a secure tenancy). See also *Central YMCA Housing Association Ltd v. Saunders* (1990) 23 H.L.R. 212, CA).

The Housing Act 1988 deals with this problem by providing that, notwithstanding the requirements of section 1, a sharing of living accommodation with a person or persons other than the landlord will not by itself preclude there being a (deemed) assured tenancy of the accommodation exclusively occupied by the tenant (Housing Act 1988, s.3(1) which is modelled on Rent Act 1977, s.22). There is no similar saving for an assured tenancy of the separate accommodation where the sharing is with the landlord (*cf.* Rent Act 1977, s.21). However, in most such cases an assured tenancy will be precluded in any event by the separate resident landlord provisions in the Housing Act 1988 Sched. 1, para. 10 (see below).

(d) Effect of sub-letting of part By contrast with the cases examined above, it is provided that if an assured tenancy of a house or flat is granted to a person who then sub-lets part, as a result of which the sub-tenant has shared use of living accommodation with the tenant, this will not prevent the head tenant from having an assured tenancy (Housing Act 1988, s.4 which is modelled on Rent Act 1977, s.23). This is an enactment of the decision of the House of Lords in *Baker v. Turner* [1950] A.C. 401. Of course, in these circumstances the sub-tenant will probably not have an assured tenancy, because *he* is sharing with *his* landlord. In any event he is likely to be excluded by the resident landlord exception (see below).

(e) Premises must be used for residential purposes The requirement that the dwelling-house be let as a dwelling points to a need for the premises to be capable of being used for normal residential purposes such as sleeping, cooking and eating (*Curl v. Angelo* [1948] 2 All E.R. 189, 192, CA). Use for the purposes of sleeping, although a necessary requirement (*Wimbush v. Cibulia* [1949] 2 K.B. 564, CA), is not by itself sufficient. Thus in *Metropolitan Properties v. Barder* (above), the "annexe" let for the use as a bedroom by the au pair girl did not qualify.

The remaining parts of the definition of an assured tenancy part company with the Rent Act model.

Element two

> "the tenant, or as the case may be, each of the joint tenants, is an individual..."

The tenant must be an individual As will be seen (see Chapter 10 below), a Rent Act protected tenancy can exist even where the tenant is not an individual (for example, where the tenant is a company or an institution). This would enable the tenant to claim the protection of the fair rent regime contained in the Rent Act 1977. But the tenant would not be able to claim that a statutory tenancy has arisen at the end of the contractual tenancy. A statutory tenancy will only arise at that time if the person who immediately beforehand was the protected tenant occupies the dwelling-house as his residence (p.262 below). Because, necessarily, this requirement cannot be satisfied other than by an individual or individuals, a company or some other institutional tenant cannot be a Rent Act statutory tenant (*Hiller v. United Dairies (London) Ltd* [1934] 1 K.B. 57). Even if the tenancy were granted to the company on the terms that someone else was to reside in the house, a statutory tenancy cannot arise in favour of that person (*S.L. Dando Ltd v. Hitchcock* [1954] 2 Q.B. 317; *Firstcross Ltd v. East West (Export/Import) Ltd* (1980) 255 E.G. 355).

By contrast, the requirement in the Housing Act 1988, that an assured tenant be an individual, means that a letting to a company tenant will clearly be completely outside the Act from the outset. It is not surprising that because of the extensive security of tenure afforded to statutory tenants by the Rent Act 1977, the temptation to avoid that security by creating a company let proved to be irresistible to some landlords, who chose to take that route rather than the risky alternative of attempting to create an occupational licence (see Chapter 1 above). Of course, since January 15, 1989, most landlords have been able to create an assured shorthold tenancy at a market rent which affords the tenant only a very limited right to remain once the tenancy has ended, and to that extent the temptation to create a company let for avoidance purposes has been significantly diminished. Where a company let has been employed the relevant case law on the Rent Acts, discussed in Chapter 10, will prove instructive if there is any doubt over the genuineness of the transaction.

Element three

"...occupies the dwelling house as his only or principal home."

This expression is not defined in the Act. It is identical to that employed in the definition of a secure tenancy contained in section 81 of the Housing Act 1985 (see Chapter 11 below). Its terms clearly prevent the possibility of a tenant having an assured tenancy in more than one property. In the case of a joint tenancy, the tenancy will be assured as long as at least one of the joint tenants satisfies the requirement. It would seem to follow that another joint tenant would not be prevented from enjoying an assured tenancy of another property.

It has been decided, in *Crawley Borough Council v. Sawyer* (1988) 20 H.L.R. 98, a case involving the construction of section 81 of the Housing Act 1985, that occupation as a home is the same as occupation as a residence. Hence if a single tenant occupies more than one property as a residence, it will be a question of fact as to which is his principal home. It was held in that case that when the tenant went to live elsewhere with his girlfriend but continued to pay the rent and rates for his flat, which he visited once a month, he was still occupying that dwelling-house as his principal home. The evidence showed that he only occupied his girlfriend's home on a temporary basis. (This was not the case in *Ujima Housing Association v. Ansah* (1997) *The Times*, November 20, CA where the tenant had sub-let his flat, and then departed not leaving any furniture behind. The court said that looked at objectively, it could not be said that the departed tenant had the necessary intention to maintain occupation of the dwelling-house as his principal home).

Effect of tenant ceasing to be an individual or to occupy the dwelling-house as his only or principal home If either of these second and third elements of the definition ceases to be satisfied at any time, the tenancy will cease to be an assured tenancy because the Housing Act 1988 states that the tenancy will only be assured if and so long as the tenant (or one of them if there is a joint tenancy) is an individual and occupies the dwelling-house as his or her only or principal home (see section 1(1) above). This would suggest that if the tenant returns before the landlord recovers possession, the tenancy will presumably become assured again.

Consequently if the tenant ceases to occupy the dwelling-house as his only or principal home, the tenancy will no longer be assured. Thus on the ending of the tenancy the landlord will be able to recover possession free of the Housing Act restrictions (but see Chapter 5 above). By contrast, section 2 of the Rent Act 1977 provides that a statutory tenancy which has arisen under that Act will continue "if and so long as [the tenant] occupies the dwelling-house as his residence." There is a body of case law on the meaning of this expression which has been interpreted generously to permit a tenant to maintain a statutory tenancy in one home which he occupies as a residence whilst maintaining another residence elsewhere (see p.263 below). Whilst these cases might be of some guidance to the meaning of cessation of occupation, for the purposes of the Housing Act 1988, s.1, it must be remembered that a physically absent tenant who wishes to keep his assured tenancy alive will need to establish constructive occupation of the premises as his principal home, which will be more difficult than establishing constructive occupation of premises merely as a residence.

Spouses and cohabitants Since the Matrimonial Homes Act 1967, where the matrimonial home is held on a tenancy in the name of one spouse, the other has had a statutory right to occupy the home. The 1967 Act was subsequently extended and then consolidated in the Matrimonial Homes Act 1983. On October 1, 1997 that Act was itself replaced by Part IV of the Family Law Act 1996.

One consequence of this statutory code is that if a married sole assured tenant leaves the matrimonial home, but that person's spouse has a statutory right to occupy (now referred to as "matrimonial homes rights"), any payment or tender of rent by that spouse will be as good as if made by the absent/tenant spouse (Family Law Act 1996, s.30(2), replacing Matrimonial Homes Act 1983, s.1(5)). Furthermore, as long as the tenancy continues it will remain assured if, and so long as, the remaining spouse occupies the property as his or her only or principal home. This is because the occupying spouse's occupation will be treated as that of the absent tenant/spouse (Family Law Act 1996, s.30(3), replacing Matrimonial Homes Act 1983, s.1(6)). However, once the marriage comes to an end by a decree of divorce the matrimonial homes rights of the occupying spouse also come to an end (unless they have been extended beyond the marriage, following an application made during the marriage under s.33(5)). Therefore the tenancy will cease to be assured.

The occupying spouse can seek to avoid this difficulty by asking the divorce court to exercise the power which it has to vest the tenancy in the non-tenant spouse under Schedule 7 to the Family Law Act 1996 (replacing Schedule 1 to the Matrimonial Homes Act 1983).

The court's powers to transfer a tenancy subsist until remarriage of an applicant. Nevertheless, in practice that spouse must make the application for a transfer before the decree absolute is pronounced (or, when Part II of the Family Law Act 1996 is brought into force, when a divorce order is made). This is because on divorce the claimant will cease to be a spouse and therefore her/his occupation will cease to be treated as that of the absent spouse, and the tenancy will no longer be assured. For the same reason the extension, by the Family Law Act 1996, of the court's power to order a transfer of the tenancy on application by a former spouse who has not remarried will not assist the non-tenant former spouse because, as explained above, the tenancy will normally have ceased to be assured on divorce.

The power of the court to transfer a tenancy also applies with regard to protected and statutory tenancies under the Rent Act 1977 and secure tenancies under the Housing Act 1985 where it is likely to be of more value. This is because, as one commentator has observed, most assured tenancies will be assured shorthold tenancies which, as we have seen above, afford the tenant negligible security of tenure (S.Bridge, *"Transferring tenancies of the family home"* [1998] Fam. law 26).

By contrast to spouses, non-married cohabitants of assured tenants were in a vulnerable position before October 1, 1997 where the tenant departed leaving a non-married cohabitant in sole occupation. The provisions of the Matrimonial Homes Act 1983 did not provide for her/his occupation to be treated as that of the tenant in such circumstances, nor for a transfer of tenancy order. Since that date it has been provided by the Family Law Act 1996 that a cohabitant who has the benefit of an occupation order under section 36 of the 1996 Act will have equivalent matrimonial homes rights to those of a spouse and thus be able to seek transfer of a tenancy. Nonetheless, because there is no statutory provision whereby occupation by a non-tenant cohabitant is deemed to be that of the departed (assured) tenant, the tenancy will cease to be assured if the tenant ceases to occupy the premises as his only or principal home.

The definition expanded—dwelling-house let with other land

If a dwelling-house is let together with other land then, provided that the main purpose of the letting is the provision of a home for the tenant, or in the case of joint tenants at least one of them, the other land is treated as part of the dwelling-house for the purposes of Part I of the Housing Act 1988 (s.2). There is an exception where the land is agricultural land within the meaning of the General Rate Act 1967, s.26(3)(a) exceeding two acres in extent : s.2(2) and Sched. 1, para. 6. See below. In *Bradshaw v. Smith* (1980) 255 E.G. 699, CA a field in excess of two acres was held not to be agricultural land as defined (for the purposes of the parallel provision in Rent Act 1977—see below) because it was used mainly or exclusively for recreational purposes. Save for the "main purpose" modification, this provision mirrors similar provisions in the Rent Act 1977 and the Housing Act 1985 (see page 255 below).

C. EXCLUSIONS

The Housing Act 1988 provides that certain tenancies cannot be assured tenancies even if the requirements of the definition of an assured tenancy are otherwise satisfied (ss.1(1)(c) and 1(2)). The exclusions are mostly modelled on those to be found in the Rent Act 1977 scheme for protected tenancies. In this connection, it is interesting to note that the Rent Act exclusion of tenancies where the rent includes payments in respect of board or substantial payments in respect of attendance (Rent Act 1977, s.7) is not replicated in the Housing Act list of exclusions. The Government took the view that its presence in the Rent Act had led to abuse by landlords, although in cases of board and/or attendance, it may be that the occupier's status is that of a lodger and therefore his agreement would not be that of an assured tenancy in any event.

Tenancies and contracts created before January 15, 1989

A tenancy entered into before, or pursuant to a contract made before, January 15, 1989, cannot be an assured tenancy save in the following cases.

(a) Conversion of Housing Act 1980 assured tenancies or contracts

Any old-style Housing Act 1980 assured tenancies in existence immediately before January 15, 1989 were converted into assured tenancies under the 1988 Act as from that date (Housing Act 1988, s.37(1)). A contract for such a tenancy was treated as a contract for a 1988 Act assured tenancy unless it would be excluded by paras 11 or 12 of Sched. 1) (Housing Act 1988, s.1(2), Sched. 1, para. 1).

(b) Transfer of tenancies from public to private sector

Most local authority tenancies are governed not by the Rent Act 1977 or the Housing Act 1988 regimes for protected and assured tenants respectively, but by the secure tenancy code contained in Part IV of the Housing Act 1985 (see Chapter 11 below). However, it has been government policy for some years to diminish the role of the public rented sector by encouraging local authorities to transfer their rented housing stock in whole or in part to housing associations or the private sector. Without further provision this would mean that if any such transfer related to property let on a tenancy created before January 15, 1989, such a tenancy could not become an assured tenancy because it was created before the operative date. The Housing Act 1988 accordingly provides that—

(1) where a public sector landlord disposes of its interest in a property on or after January 15, 1989 the tenancy will be assured if all the other requirements of an assured tenancy are satisfied notwithstanding the fact that it was created before the operative date (s.38(1)(3));

(2) similarly, where because of a change of landlord a "housing association tenancy" (*i.e.* one governed by the Part VI of the Rent Act 1977) ceases to qualify as such on or after January 15, 1989, the tenancy can become an assured tenancy, notwithstanding that it might have been created before January 15, 1989 (s.38(2)(3)).

Dwelling-houses with high rents

A tenancy which is entered into on or after April 1, 1990 under which the rent payable for the time being exceeds £25,000 a year cannot be an assured tenancy (Housing Act 1988, Sched. 1 para. 2(1) as substituted by the References to Rating (Housing) Regulations 1990 (S.I. 1990 No. 434). This figure applies to tenancies of all dwelling-houses affected, no distinction being drawn between London and elsewhere.

For the purpose of this exception rent does not include any sum payable by the tenant which is expressed to be payable in respect of rates, services, management, repairs, maintenance or insurance. Thus "rent" only covers sums which are properly to be regarded as reserved by the landlord in respect of occupation of the dwelling. For example, if a property is let at a gross rent of £26,000 p.a. including a service charge of £2,000 p.a. the tenancy will not be excluded by the high-rent exception.

The crucial time for determining the application of this exemption is whenever the issue falls to be determined, and therefore if the rent fluctuates from time to time a tenancy will correspondingly move in and out of being assured. Thus if the rent of an assured tenancy is legitimately increased beyond this limit the tenancy will cease to be assured. (See *R. v. London Rent Assessment Panel, ex parte Cadogan Estates Ltd* [1997] 33 E.G. 88, below, where it was held that if a rent assessment committee determined a market rent of above £25,000 p.a. the tenancy would cease to be assured).

The high-rent exclusion was introduced as a result of the replacement of domestic rates by the community charge (subsequently replaced itself by the council tax). Other tenancies are governed by the following exclusion.

Dwelling-houses with high rateable values

A tenancy (a) which was entered into before April 1, 1990, or on or after that date in pursuance of a contract made before that date, and (b) under which the dwelling-house had a rateable value on March 31, 1990 which, if it is in Greater London, exceeded £1,500, and if it is elsewhere exceeded £750, cannot be an assured tenancy (Housing Act 1988, Sched. 1, para. 2A as added by S.I. 1990 No. 434). The rateable value limits are considerably simpler than those contained in the equivalent exclusion from Rent Act protection (see Rent Act 1977, ss.4 and 5).

Tenancies at a low rent

A tenancy under which for the time being no rent is payable cannot be an assured tenancy (Housing Act 1988, Sched. 1, para. 3 as substituted by S.I. 1990 No. 434 reg. 2. Sched., para. 30). It will be appreciated that as in the case of the high rent exemption, a tenancy may fall within or outside this exclusion from time to time if the rent payable fluctuates above or below the limit (*J.F. Stone Lighting & Radio v. Levitt* [1947] A.C. 209, HL).

A tenancy is also prevented from being an assured tenancy if it is entered into on or after April 1, 1990 and the rent payable for the time being is payable at a rate of, if the dwelling-house is in Greater London, £1,000 or less a year, or, if it is elsewhere, £250 or less a year (Housing Act 1988, Sched. 1, para. 3A as substituted by S.I. 1990 No. 434).

Also excluded are low-rent tenancies entered into before April 1, 1990. For this purpose, a low-rent tenancy is one under which the rent for the time being is less than two- thirds of the rateable value of the dwelling-house on March 31, 1990 (Housing Act 1988, Sched. 1, para. 3B as substituted by S.I. 1990 No. 434).

For the above purposes, as in the case of the high-rent exemption, "rent" does not include any sum payable by the tenant which is expressed to be payable in respect of rates, services, management, repairs, maintenance, or insurance (Housing Act 1988, Sched. 1, para. 3 as substituted by S.I. 1990 No. 434). This is principally designed to prevent a long tenancy, under which the rent includes a service charge, from being an assured tenancy solely by virtue of the service charge bringing the rent above the level at which the exception would otherwise cease to apply (see Chapter 12 below for "long tenancies").

Apart from the above qualification rent is not otherwise defined. However, case law on the parallel provision in the Rent Act 1977 established that rent must be payable in, or quantifiable in terms of money. Thus services rendered to the landlord by the tenant, for example as a caretaker, can only count as rent if they are treated as being representative of an agreed monetary quantification (*Montague v. Browning* [1954] 1 W.L.R. 1039, CA where the tenant's services as a caretaker of a synagogue had been quantified as equivalent to the rent payable for the property let to him by his employers. This can be compared with *Barnes v. Barratt* [1970] 2 Q.B. 657, CA where a tenant purportedly sub-let part of his accommodation to a couple who did not pay rent but rendered unquantified domestic services for the tenant. The court held that the absence of quantification was fatal to a claim that a sub-tenancy had been granted at a rent. (The court also held that in any event a licence rather than a tenancy had been created. See further *Bostock v. Bryant* (1990) 22 H.L.R. 449.)

Business tenancies

A tenancy to which Part II of the Landlord and Tenant Act 1954 applies (business tenancies) cannot be an assured tenancy (Housing Act 1988, Sched. 1, para. 4).

We have already seen that a tenancy cannot be within section 1 of the Housing Act 1988 unless the premises in question comprise a dwelling-house *let as* a separate dwelling (above). Therefore a tenancy granted for business purposes cannot become an assured tenancy simply by reason of subsequent residential user. Similarly a tenancy granted for mixed residential and business purposes (*e.g.* a shop with a flat above) cannot become assured simply by subsequent cessation of the business user.

On the other hand, where a dwelling-house is initially let as a dwelling, within section 1 of the Housing Act 1988, but the premises are subsequently used partly for business purposes, the question whether the Housing Act is excluded depends upon whether the business tenancy code in Part II of the Landlord and Tenant Act 1954 applies to the tenancy. If it does the Housing Act 1988 is excluded. If not, the Housing Act will continue to apply.

The business tenancy code applies to a tenancy where the whole or any part of the premises subject to the tenancy is occupied by the tenant for the purposes of a business carried on by him or for those and other purposes (Landlord and Tenant Act 1954, s.23(1)). "Business" means the carrying on of a trade, profession, or employment (s.23(2)). It should be noted that Part II of the 1954 Act does not apply to a tenancy for a fixed term of not more than six months unless there is an option to renew beyond that time or the tenant or his predecessor in the business has been in occupation for more than six months (LTA 1954, s.43).

It will be noted that for the 1954 Act to apply there is no requirement that the initial letting be for business purposes. In practice most difficulty is likely to be encountered in deciding whether a particular activity can be said to be a "business use" or, if it is, whether that use is of minimal significance. This is a question of fact. If the activity is not a business use or amounts to a business use of minimal significance then, as stated above, Part II of the 1954 Act is inapplicable and the tenancy will remain assured.

> In the Rent Act case of *Lewis v. Weldcrest* [1978] 1 W.L.R. 1107 it was held that where a tenant sub-let rooms to lodgers on a bed and breakfast basis for little or no profit, she was not reaping any commercial advantage and therefore was not occupying the premises partly for business purposes. Hence the tenancy was not excluded from Rent Act protection. (See also *Gurton v. Parrott et al.* (1990) 23 H.L.R. 418, CA where as a hobby the tenant, for a number of years, ran a business, of kennelling, grooming and breeding of dogs, from her home. It was held that this was incidental to the main residential purpose of the tenancy and insufficient to attract the application of Part II of the Landlord and Tenant Act 1954).
>
> The Court of Appeal reached the same conclusion in *Royal Life Saving Society v. Page* [1978] 1 W.L.R. 1329 where it was held that the 1954 Act did not apply to a maisonette occupied as his home by a doctor who (with the landlord's permission) saw the occasional patient there. The doctor, who had consulting rooms in Harley Street, was principally employed as medical adviser to the Selfridges store where he worked five days a week. (By contrast, it was held in *Cheryl Investments v. Saldanha* [1978] 1 W.L.R. 1329 that a tenant's business use of his rented flat was a significant purpose of his occupation and hence attracted the application of Part II of the 1954 Act.)

Tenancies of licensed premises

A tenancy under which the dwelling-house consists of or comprises premises licensed for the sale of alcohol for consumption on the premises cannot be an assured tenancy (Housing Act 1988, Sched. 1, para. 5).

Tenancies of agricultural land

A tenancy under which agricultural land (within the meaning of the General Rate Act 1967, s.26(3)(a)) exceeding two acres is let with the dwelling-house cannot be an assured tenancy (Housing Act 1988, Sched. 1, para. 6).

Tenancies of agricultural holdings

A tenancy under which the dwelling-house is comprised in an agricultural holding and is occupied by the person responsible for the control of the farming of the holding (*i.e.* a farm manager) cannot be an assured tenancy (Housing Act 1988, Sched. 1, para. 7). Such a tenancy is governed by the code contained in the Agricultural Holdings Act 1986.

Student lettings

Most lettings to students by a "specified institution or body of persons" will not be assured tenancies (Housing Act 1988, Sched. 1, para. 8). For this purpose "student" is widely defined as a person who is pursuing, or intends to pursue, a course of study. They can be studying either at the landlord institution or another. The specified institutions are listed in S.I. 1998 No. 1967 (as amended), which covers a wide range of bodies including universities and other publicly funded institutions of higher and further education. Thus students who live in university-owned accommodation will not be assured tenants. Indeed in practice they are unlikely to be tenants at all and will more probably occupy under the terms of a licence agreement. It follows that students who occupy privately owned accommodation which has been let to the university for the purpose of sub-letting to students will not have an assured tenancy. (see p.210 above).

Holiday lettings

A tenancy the purpose of which is to confer on the tenant the right to occupy the dwelling-house for a holiday cannot be an assured tenancy (Housing Act 1988, Sched. 1, para. 9). The equivalent provision in section 9 of the Rent Act 1977 was originally introduced by the Rent Act 1974 to affirm that a tenant under a genuine holiday let should not have Rent Act protection. At the same time it was intended that landlords should not abuse this privilege by creating sham "holiday lets" for the purpose of evading the Rent Act. The Rent Act exemption has thus been replicated in Schedule 1 to the Housing Act 1988, although in neither case is "holiday" defined.

It will come as no surprise to learn that the main problem with the Rent Act exception was discovering whether or not a purported holiday letting was in fact a sham transaction set up to evade the protection of the Act. The courts made it clear that, despite a general rule that where a tenancy was described as a holiday letting the onus would be on the tenant to establish that this is not so, they would be astute to detect sham transactions. (See *Buchmann v. May* [1978] 2 All E.R. 993, CA and *R. v. Rent Officer for the London Borough of Camden, ex parte. Plant* (1980) 7 H.L.R. 15. See further T. J. Lyons [1984] Conv. 286). Such problems are much less likely to arise since the Housing Act 1988 came into force. Few, if any, landlords will go to the lengths of creating a holiday let for the sole purpose of avoiding the Housing Act 1988. The certainty of an assured shorthold tenancy offers far less risk at little cost.

Crown tenancies

A tenancy under which the landlord's interest is held by the Crown or is held by or on trust for a government department cannot be an assured tenancy. (Certain tenants whose landlord is either the Secretary of State or an NHS Trust are also excluded by the National Health Service and Community Care Act 1990, Sched. 1, para. 11.) The exception does not extend to where that interest is under the management of the Crown Estates Commissioners (Housing Act 1988, Sched. 1, para. 11.)

Local authority lettings

A tenancy under which the landlord's interest is held by a local authority or any of certain other specified public bodies (including a Housing Action Trust established under Part III of the Housing Act 1988) cannot be an assured tenancy (Housing Act 1988, Sched. 1, para. 12). Most of these tenancies will take effect instead as secure tenancies under the Housing Act 1985 (see Chapter 11 below).

Tenancies under which the landlord's interest is held by a housing association are not generally excluded, but they will be if the interest belongs to a fully mutual housing association (para. 12).

Transitional cases

A protected tenancy, within the meaning of the Rent Act 1977, a "housing association tenancy" (also within the meaning of the Rent Act 1977) and a secure tenancy, within the meaning of the Housing Act 1985, cannot be assured tenancies (Housing Act 1988, Sched. 1, para. 13).

These are not strictly transitional cases. Protected tenancies and "housing association tenancies" (both of which are governed by Rent Act 1977 regulatory regimes—see Chapter 10) are specifically excluded because, as will be seen, it is still possible, in exceptional cases, for such tenancies to be created on or after January 15, 1989 (for example, where a new tenancy is granted to an existing protected or housing association tenant of the same landlord, or where the tenancy was granted in pursuance of a contract entered into before January 15, 1989). Of course, the vast majority of protected and housing association tenancies will have been created before January 15, 1989 and will therefore be excluded for that reason.

Resident landlord lettings

A tenancy is excluded from being an assured tenancy where there is a "resident landlord" (Housing Act 1988, Sched. 1, para. 10).

The resident landlord exclusion is closely modelled on that contained in section 12 and Schedule 2 to the Rent Act 1977, save that under the 1988 Act the resident landlord is required to occupy the relevant premises as his only or principal home, rather than as his residence. Subject to that distinction the relevant case law on the Rent Act provisions will be equally applicable to the 1988 Act exception.

(a) Elements of the resident landlord exception

The necessary conditions for the application of the resident landlord exception are as follows.

That the dwelling-house forms part only of a building and, except in the case where the dwelling-house also forms part of a flat, the building is not a purpose-built block of flats It will usually be obvious whether a dwelling-house forms part of a building. An example would be a flat in a house converted to flats. The rationale for excluding purpose-built blocks of flats from the scope of the exemption is that if the landlord and tenant are occupying such flats they can hardly be said to be living in close proximity to each other and therefore the landlord is not in need of the power to recover possession swiftly if the arrangement should prove to be unsatisfactory. It is otherwise where the dwelling-house is part of such a purpose-built flat, although it is probable that where this is the case there will be such a degree of sharing of common living accommodation that section 1 will be excluded by virtue of the absence of a letting as a separate dwelling. (see p.210 above)

As in the case of the analogous provision in the Rent Act 1977, a purpose-built block of flats is defined as a building which as constructed (as distinct from converted: *Barnes v. Gorsuch* (1982) 43 P.& C.R. 294, CA) contained, and contains, two or more flats; and for this purpose "flat" means a dwelling-house which forms part only of a building and is separated horizontally from another dwelling-house which forms part of the same building.

That the tenancy was granted by an individual who, at the time when the tenancy was granted, occupied as his only or principal home another dwelling-house which also forms part of the building (or the flat where the tenant's dwelling-house forms part of a flat in a purpose-built block) In practice the difficulties most likely to be encountered here are in deciding whether the landlord can be said to have been "occupying a dwelling-house as his only or principal home" and whether the landlord and tenant were occupying dwelling-houses in the same building.

(i) Occupation of a dwelling-house as his only or principal home by the landlord A landlord may fail to qualify as a resident landlord because the premises in the building of which he has use may not qualify as a dwelling-house.

> In *Lyons v. Caffery* (1982) 5 H.L.R. 63, CA the landlord of a basement consisting of a bed-sitting room, kitchen, bathroom, lavatory and sun-room created a tenancy of the bed-sit and shared the use of the kitchen and lavatory with the tenant. It was held that the sun-room, which was unsuitable for use as a bedroom, could not be said to be a separate dwelling-house occupied by the landlord. This would indicate that sleeping accommodation is an essential component of a dwelling-house for this purpose.

The landlord may also fail to qualify because he cannot be said to be occupying a dwelling-house "as his only or principal home". Case law on the Rent Act resident landlord exception indicates that a landlord will not be prevented from qualifying as a resident landlord merely because he does not permanently reside on the premises or indeed has other accommodation where he lives. This would permit an absent landlord to qualify, provided he has the intention to return which is manifested in some way, usually by the presence of furniture or a representative occupier in his absence. (Page 259 below).

This case law must be treated with extreme caution in the context of the Housing Act 1988 because the parallel Rent Act provision only requires the landlord to occupy a dwelling-house in the same building "as a residence" rather than as his only or principal home. Thus an absentee landlord would be more readily able to argue that he was a resident landlord for the purposes of the Rent Act 1977, notwithstanding that he had two or more homes (*ibid*). In the case of the Housing Act 1988 the landlord faces the much harder task of proving that the dwelling-house which he occupies in the same building as the tenant is his only or principal home.

(ii) The same building The Act does not define what is meant by building and it will be a question of fact as to whether the dwelling-house occupied by the landlord is in the same building as that occupied by the tenant.

In *Bardrick v. Haycock* (1976) 31 P.& C.R. 420, CA the landlord of a large house, which had been converted into six self-contained flats, had constructed an adjoining two-storey extension in which he lived. The extension was tied into the main house but the two had separate entrances and there was no internal connection between them. The court held that on these facts the landlord did *not* occupy a dwelling-house in the same building as the tenants. The Court had regard to the purpose of the resident landlord exception being to prevent the tenant having long-term security of tenure in view of the potential social embarrassment which could arise from his living in close proximity to the landlord where the arrangements were such that their paths were likely to cross. This was not likely to arise in that case (unlike the later county court case of *Guppy v. O'Donnell* [1979] C.L.Y. 1627, CC where there was an internal connection between the two parts of the building). Nonetheless, the issue of what amounts to the same building for the purposes of this exception is still a question of fact in every case as illustrated by the decision of the Court of Appeal in *Griffiths v. English* (1981) 2 H.L.R. 126, CA where the exception was held to apply even though the tenant occupied an extension to one side of a building and the landlord an extension to the other side of that building, there being no internal connection between either extension and the main building. See also *Wolff v. Waddington* (1989) 22 H.L.R. 72.

At all times since the tenancy was granted, the interest of the landlord under the tenancy has belonged to an individual who, at the time he owned that interest, occupied as his only or principal home another dwelling house in that building (or that flat where the leased dwelling forms part of a flat in a purpose-built block) The clear aim of this requirement is that there should have been a resident landlord at all times since the beginning of the tenancy although such residence need not always have been in the same "dwelling-house" within the building. Special provision has been made to provide for cases where a resident landlord dies or transfers his interest to another person who does not take up residence immediately (see below). If the landlord's interest is held on trust and a beneficiary under the trust occupies another dwelling-house in the same building as the tenant, as his only or principal home, the continuous residence requirement is deemed to be satisfied (Housing Act 1988, Sched. 1, para. 18).

Joint landlords In the case of joint landlords it is sufficient if any one of the landlords satisfy either or both of the second and third elements above (Housing Act 1988, Sched. 1, para. 10(2)). The same rule was held to apply to the analogous Rent Act exclusion which did not cater for the case of joint landlords (*Cooper v. Tait* (1984) 271 E.G. 105, CA).

(b) Existing assured tenants

It will be seen (p.260 below) that the parallel exclusion in the Rent Act 1977 does not apply in the case of a letting by a resident landlord to a person who immediately before the grant of the tenancy was a protected or statutory tenant of the same dwelling-house or of another dwelling-house in the same building. This was included to prevent a landlord moving into a building and offering an existing protected tenant a new tenancy of his dwelling-house, or another dwelling-house in the same building in an attempt to deprive him of the protection which he enjoyed under his former tenancy.

Similarly the Housing Act 1988 resident landlord exclusion does not apply if:

(1) the tenancy is granted to a person who immediately before it was granted was a tenant under an assured tenancy of the same dwelling-house or another dwelling-house in the same building; and

(2) the landlord under the new and former tenancies was the same person (Housing Act 1988, Sched. 1, para. 10(2)).

If either of the tenancies was granted by joint landlords it will suffice if the same person under the two lettings is the landlord or one of the landlords under each tenancy.

(c) Continuous residence by landlord

Complex provisions apply for the purpose of determining the application of the present exception, where there are periods during which there is no occupation by the landlord or a successor. This may occur either because of the death of the landlord or because the landlord has otherwise disposed of his interest (Housing Act 1988, Sched. 1 Part III, paras 17–21). The relevant provisions are, with some modifications (*e.g.* to provide for the case of joint landlords), very similar to those in the Rent Act 1977.

D. ASSURED TENANCIES—SECURITY OF TENURE

Fixed-term tenancies—expiry of the fixed term

(a) The statutory periodic tenancy

The Housing Act (HA) 1988 provides that if a fixed-term assured tenancy comes to an end either by effluxion of time or by the landlord exercising a break clause (see below), the tenant is nevertheless entitled to remain in possession under a "statutory periodic tenancy" of the dwelling-house (HA 1988, s.5(2), (3) and (7)). However, a statutory periodic tenancy will not arise if at the end of a fixed-term assured tenancy the tenant is granted a new tenancy of the same or substantially the same dwelling-house (HA 1988, s.5(4)).

The periods of a statutory periodic tenancy are the same as those for which rent was last payable under the fixed-term tenancy. Thus if rent was payable on a monthly basis it will become a monthly tenancy. The other terms of the tenancy are the same as those of the immediately preceding fixed term, except that if there is a provision for determination by the landlord or the tenant (other than for forfeiture or re-entry), that provision shall not have effect while the tenancy remains an assured tenancy (HA 1988, s.5(3)). If the tenancy subsequently ceases to be assured then that provision will revive. The "provision" referred to would seem to be a break clause which would otherwise permit a party to determine the fixed term prematurely (see p.119 above for break clauses).

The Act contains an anti-avoidance provision to nullify any agreement or document purporting to be a surrender, notice to quit, etc., made or given in advance by a prospective assured tenant which would otherwise have the effect of bringing the tenancy to an end (HA 1988, s.5(5)). Such an agreement is also ineffective in relation to the statutory periodic tenancy if made at any time before that tenancy begins.

(b) Varying the terms

The Act contains a procedure whereby either landlord or tenant may serve notice in the prescribed form (S.I. 1988 No. 2203, Form 1) on the other party proposing a variation in the terms of the statutory periodic tenancy other than as to rent. If the landlord or the tenant considers it appropriate, the notice may also propose an adjustment of the amount of the rent to take account of the proposed terms (HA 1988, s.6(1), (2)).

The notice must be served not later than the first anniversary of the day on which the preceding fixed-term tenancy came to an end (HA 1988, s.6(2)).

Once the notice has been served on him, the recipient has three months during which he may, by an application in the prescribed form (S.I. 1988 No. 2203, Form 2), refer the notice to a rent assessment committee (HA 1988, s.6(3)(a)). If the recipient does not refer the notice to the rent assessment committee, then the terms proposed in the notice will, from such date specified in the notice, automatically become terms of the tenancy in substitution for any of the existing terms dealing with the same subject matter. Furthermore if a consequential adjustment in the rent payable has been proposed in the notice, the rent will also be varied automatically to the proposed amount (s.6(3)(b)). The date specified for the changes must not be earlier than three months after service of the notice.

Where a section 6 notice has been referred to the committee they are directed to consider the terms proposed in the notice. They must then determine whether those terms or some other terms (dealing with the same subject-matter as the proposed terms) are such as, in the committee's opinion, might reasonably be expected to be found in an assured periodic tenancy of the dwelling-house concerned. Thus the committee has a choice of either endorsing the proposed variation, or specifying some alternative variation dealing with the same subject-matter (*e.g.* as to repairs or services), or leaving the original terms unaltered. It seems clear that the Act envisages the possibility of only one determination under section 6 in respect of the same tenancy.

Where the committee adopt either of the first two courses open to them, they may also, if they consider it appropriate, specify an adjustment of the rent under the statutory periodic tenancy to take account of the varied terms. They may do so whether or not a new rent was requested by the person who served the section 6 notice (s.6(5)). The variation of terms as specified by the Committee, along with any rental adjustment, will take effect from the date specified by the committee (which cannot be earlier than the date specified in the section 6 notice) unless the parties agree otherwise.

(c) Ending the statutory periodic tenancy

Once a statutory periodic tenancy has arisen it may be brought to an end by the landlord only by obtaining a court order on one or more of the grounds specified in the Act (see below).

Restrictions on recovery of possession during fixed term

Although the relevant statutory provision, Housing Act 1988, s. 5(1), is cryptically worded, its effect is that the landlord of a fixed-term assured tenancy is unable to bring that tenancy to a premature end save by one of two means.

The first is by obtaining a court order on one of the grounds provided for by the Act (see below), although it will suffice if the tenant is prepared to admit that the ground has been made out (*R. v. Bloomsbury and Marylebone County Court, ex parte. Blackburne* [1985] 2 E.G.L.R. 157).

The second is applicable only where there is a provision in the tenancy which gives the landlord power to determine it by the exercise of that power (HA 1988 s.5(1)). If this is the case the landlord can exercise the power and thereby determine the tenancy. Although it is not made explicit by the Act, it seems clear that the power referred to is confined to a "break clause" which provides for premature determination of the term by the landlord at a specified point in time by notice. This is because it is specifically provided that any reference to a power to determine by the landlord does *not* include a power of re-entry or forfeiture for breach of any term or condition of the tenancy (HA 1988, s.45(4)). Thus the landlord is not able to determine the tenancy by forfeiture or re-entry for breach of a term or condition of the tenancy. (But see below as to the relevance of such a clause).

Although the Act preserves the right of a landlord who has inserted a break clause in the tenancy to operate that clause and thereby determine the term prematurely, the tenant is nevertheless still entitled to remain. This is because on the ending of the fixed term a statutory periodic tenancy will normally arise under section 5(2) (see above), and as we have seen, such a tenancy cannot be determined by the landlord save by obtaining a court order on one or more of the grounds specified in the Act.

By contrast a tenant is able to determine a fixed-term assured tenancy prematurely by any means available to him, such as surrender or by operating a break clause, but it should be remembered that in the case of a joint tenancy, surrender requires the consent of all joint tenants (*Leek & Moorlands Building Society v. Clark* [1952] 2 Q.B. 788, CA).

Assured periodic tenancies

The rule here is straightforward. Whether the periodic tenancy is contractual or statutory (see above), a court order on one more of the permitted grounds is needed before possession can be recovered by the landlord. The Act specifically provides that the service of a notice to quit is of no effect (s.5(1)).

It should be noted that the above restriction applies only to determination of the tenancy by the landlord and therefore a tenant can determine an assured periodic tenancy by any permitted common law method such as serving a notice to quit or surrender of the tenancy (*Hammersmith and Fulham BC v. Monk* [1992] 1 A.C. 478 where in the case of a (secure) joint tenancy one of two joint tenants was able to give an effective notice to quit, thereby ending the tenancy without the agreement of the other tenant–see p.130 above).

Proceedings for possession

(a) Mandatory and discretionary grounds for possession

It was explained above that if the landlord seeks possession of a dwelling-house let on an assured tenancy he can only do so by obtaining a possession order from the court. In turn the court can only make a possession order on one of the grounds set out in the Act (HA 1988, s.7(1) and Sched. 2). These restrictions are confined to proceedings by the landlord and do not relate to proceedings for possession of a dwelling-house which are brought by a mortgagee who has lent money on the security of the assured tenancy (HA 1988, s.7(1)).

This form of security of tenure is very familiar and is similar to that adopted in respect of protected and statutory tenancies under the Rent Act 1977 and secure tenancies under the Housing Act 1985. The grounds on which a possession order can be made by the court are classified as either mandatory or discretionary. Thus if one or more of the mandatory grounds (grounds 1 to 8, below) is established by the landlord, the court *must* make a possession order, whilst in the case of the discretionary grounds (grounds 9 to 17, below) the court *may* make a possession order if it considers it reasonable to do so (s.7(3), (4) and Sched. 2, Parts I and II).

(b) Restricted grounds where fixed term not yet expired

Where the tenancy in respect of which possession is sought is a fixed-term tenancy which has not expired, the grounds upon which the court can grant a possession order are limited. In such a case the court is not empowered to grant a possession order unless the ground relied upon is ground 2 or ground 8 (mandatory grounds) or any of the discretionary grounds (save for grounds 9 and 16). Furthermore, in such cases the landlord must overcome an additional hurdle by establishing that the terms of the tenancy provide for it to be brought to an end on the ground in question. This can be by way of provision for forfeiture, right of re-entry, notice or otherwise (HA 1988, s.7(6)). It is unclear whether the provision in the tenancy must specifically refer to the ground(s) in the Act or whether it will suffice for it to cover the same circumstances as catered for by the ground in question.

For example, a tenancy agreement might contain a forfeiture clause permitting the landlord to forfeit the tenancy in the event of the tenant having been convicted of using or permitting the premises to be used for illegal or immoral purposes. Although no reference is made to any particular ground for possession it is arguable that although the landlord will not be permitted to exercise the forfeiture clause, its presence will permit him to seek an order on the basis of ground 14 (nuisance or illegal or immoral user—see below), because its wording covers the circumstances catered for by that ground.

Once a possession order is made it will operate to terminate any statutory periodic tenancy which might have arisen under section 5 on the end of the fixed term if this has occurred in the meantime (*e.g.* by expiry) before the court order is made. If on the other hand the effect of the court order is to determine the fixed term (*i.e.* where it would otherwise have continued) it will also prevent a statutory periodic tenancy arising at that time thereby entitling the landlord to possession (s.7(7)).

(c) Notice of intended possession proceedings

Before a landlord begins possession proceedings it is first necessary for him to serve a notice of proceedings for possession (in the prescribed form: S.I. 1997 No. 194, Form 3 on or after February 28, 1997), in accordance with section 8 of the Housing Act 1988, which specifies the ground(s), and particulars of it, relied upon. The grounds specified in the notice may subsequently be added to or altered with the leave of the court provided the notice as served is a valid notice.

In the case of joint landlords it will suffice that at least one of them has served the section 8 notice. Despite a failure by the landlord to serve such a notice the court may still entertain the possession proceedings if it considers it just and equitable to dispense with the notice requirement. In *Kelsey Housing Association Ltd v. King* (1995) 28 H.L.R. the possession claim was based on a history of bad behaviour by the tenants amounting to a nuisance and annoyance to neighbours. The court was prepared to dispense with the need for service of a section 8 notice where the tenants had ample warning and could not but have realised in view of their serious misconduct that immediate proceedings would be inevitable. A similar dispensation power appears in a number of places in the Housing Act 1988 (Sched. 2, grounds 1–3, 12 and 20) and the Rent Act 1977 (Sched. 15, cases 11, 12 and 20) in connection with the need for a landlord to serve notice and reference should be made to the relevant sections.

The Court of Appeal considered the validity of a section 8 notice in *Marath v. MacGillivray* (1996) 28 H.L.R. 484, CA where ground 8 (three months' rent arrears) was relied upon. The notice did not set out the full amount of the arrears but alleged that a specified amount was owing at a particular date and that no rent had subsequently been paid. The Court held that this was a valid notice. It was sufficient that (a) the notice made it clear that the landlord was alleging that more than three months' rent arrears was due at the date of the notice and (b) that there was some method whereby the tenant could determine the amount alleged to be due. (By contrast, in *Torridge DC v. Jones* (1985) 18 H.L.R. 107, CA, a decision on the analogous requirement in the Housing Act 1985, s.82 the Court of Appeal held that a notice which simply alleged "non-payment" of rent was defective. (See p.319 below).

It will be noticed that section 8 requires not only the ground relied upon but also the particulars of the ground to be set out in the notice. It was held in *Mountain v. Hastings* (1993) 25 H.L.R. 427 that a notice which failed to give the tenant the information necessary to take steps to protect himself was defective and invalid. In that case the ground relied upon was ground 8 in respect of which it was necessary to alert the tenant to the fact that under that ground, rent arrears need to be outstanding both at the date of service of the notice and at the hearing.

The section 8 notice must specify that the proceedings will begin—

(a)   not earlier than a date specified in the notice; and
(b)   not later than 12 months from the date of service of the notice.

The date specified for the purposes of (a) above must not be earlier than—

(1)   the date of service of the notice in the case of ground 14 (nuisance or illegal or immoral user);
(2)   two months from the date of service of the notice in the case of grounds 1 (landlord requires possession); 2 (mortgagee requires possession); 5 (property required for a minister of religion); 6 (landlord's intention to demolish or reconstruct); 7 (death of periodic tenant); 9 (suitable alternative accommodation to be made available) and 16 (service tenant whose employment has ended);
(3)   two weeks from the date of service of the notice in the case of all other grounds (s.8(3), (4), (4A), (4B)).

If the tenancy is periodic and could be determined by a notice to quit given by the landlord which is longer than the minimum period as calculated above then this will become the minimum period instead for the purposes of the section 8 notice (s.8(6)). Thus in the case of a yearly tenancy, which would require a notice to quit of six months in the absence of any provision to the contrary, the relevant period for the purposes of (a) above would be six months.

Where possession is being sought on the ground of domestic violence against a partner (ground 14A), the section 8 notice must be served on a non-tenant partner who has left as a result of domestic violence (s.8A added by the Housing Act 1996, s.150) (see further below).

In any case where the proceedings are based on one of the discretionary grounds for possession, the county court has—

(1)   power to adjourn the proceedings for such period or periods as it thinks fit; and
(2)   a discretion to stay or suspend execution of the order or postpone the date of possession for such period or periods as it thinks fit. In doing so the court may impose such conditions as it deems appropriate and indeed must impose conditions with regard to payment of any rent arrears unless it considers that to do so would cause undue hardship to the tenant or would otherwise be unreasonable (Housing Act 1988, s.9).

These powers can also be exercised in favour of a spouse who has matrimonial homes rights (under Family Law Act 1996 Part IV) and is in occupation of the dwelling-house (s.9(5)).

The court has no discretion with regard to possession proceedings brought on any of the mandatory grounds for possession. In such cases possession can only be postponed for a maximum of 14 days or, where it appears to the court that exceptional hardship would be caused to the tenant, six weeks (Housing Act 1980, s.89).

The accelerated possession procedure

Grounds 1, 3, 4 and 5 are subject to a "fast track" possession procedure in the county court provided that (a) the section 8 notice has been served, (b) the only purpose of the proceedings is to recover possession, (c) no other claim is being made and (d) the requisite notice for that ground was served not later than the beginning of the tenancy (CCR, Ord. 49, r. 6A as amended by S.I. 1997 No. 1837). This procedure enables the issue to be decided on the basis of affidavit evidence, provided there is no contest and without the need for attendance. It is important to get the application right because otherwise the application might be rejected and the landlord will have to go through the normal procedure, thus causing further delay (see N. Madge (1998) N.L.J. 546). This procedure is also available in respect of claims to possession under section 21 (assured shorthold tenancies—see below).

The mandatory grounds (1–8)

Before examining these grounds it is necessary to note that the first five grounds all require that the landlord must have given written notice to the tenant not later than the beginning of the tenancy stating that possession might be recovered under the ground in question.

Despite this requirement for written notice it is provided that in the case of grounds 1, 2 and 8 the court, if of the opinion that it is just and equitable to do so, is empowered to dispense with the notice requirement.

> The principles on which this discretion will be exercised were examined in the context of ground 1 in *Boyle v. Verrall* (1996) 29 H.L.R. 436, CA. Mrs Boyle purchased the freehold of a flat. Because she and her husband lived elsewhere she decided to let the flat on a furnished tenancy until they needed to live there. Mrs Boyle had intended to create an assured shorthold tenancy but she failed to complete the appropriate notice required at that time by section 20 of the Housing Act 1988 (see below) and which she had previously given to the tenant. Thus the tenancy took effect as a fully assured tenancy. The tenant realised the landlord's mistake and failed to draw it to her attention. The Court of Appeal held that despite not having served a notice for the purposes of ground 1, Mrs Boyle should be permitted to rely on that ground. In a conversation with the tenant she had made it clear that she and her husband would need the flat at some time in the future. It was found that this did not amount to oral notice.
>
> Nevertheless, the Court made it clear that oral notice was not an essential prerequisite to the exercise of the discretion to dispense with the notice requirement, although it might in all the circumstances be a relevant factor. (See also *Mustafa v. Ruddock* (1988) 30 H.L.R. 495, CA where an owner-occupier instructed agents to let the property on an assured shorthold tenancy but the agents omitted to serve a section 20 notice, with the result that a fully assured tenancy was created. The court permitted the landlord to recover possession under Ground 1 and dispensed with the need for the appropriate notice to have been served).

Ground 1

This ground applies in two cases—

(1) Where the landlord who is seeking possession or, in the case of joint landlords who are seeking possession, at least one of them, occupied the dwelling-house as his only or principal home at some time before the beginning of the tenancy.

(2) Where the landlord who is seeking possession or, in the case of joint landlords who are seeking possession at least one of them, requires the dwelling-house as his or his spouse's only or principal home. It is not necessary for the landlord to establish that his requirement for the home is reasonable. He simply needs to establish that he bona fide wants and genuinely has the intention of using the property for that purpose (*Boyle v. Verrall*, above).

In this second case the landlord (or in the case of joint landlords seeking possession, any of them) must not have acquired the reversion by purchase for money or money's worth but need not himself have occupied it at any stage as his sole or principal home.

The obvious aim of this ground is to encourage owners to let out property during a temporary absence (*e.g.* whilst working abroad) with a guarantee that they will recover possession on their return.

Ground 2

This enables the landlord to recover possession where a mortgage over the property was granted before the tenancy began and the mortgagee requires vacant possession in order to sell in pursuance of the exercise of his power of sale under the Law of Property Act 1925, s.101. The notice requirement (see above) will be satisfied for the purposes of this case by a notice served in relation to ground 1 or 2.

Ground 3

Although not strictly so limited, in practice this ground permits the landlord to recover possession in the case of an out of season holiday let which has ended. It applies to a tenancy for a term certain of not more than eight months of a dwelling-house which, at some time in the 12 months before the tenancy was granted, had been occupied under a right to occupy it for a holiday.

Ground 4

This ground applies to a tenancy for a term certain of not more than 12 months of a dwelling-house which, at some time in the 12 months before the tenancy was granted, had been occupied on a student let within paragraph 8 of Schedule 1 (lettings to students by specified educational institutions). It thus facilitates recovery of vacation lets of student accommodation.

Ground 5

This ground permits recovery of possession where the dwelling-house is held for the purpose of being available for occupation by a minister of religion as a residence from which to perform the duties of his/her office and the court is satisfied that the dwelling-house is available for occupation by a minister of religion for such a residence.

Ground 6

This complex ground applies where the landlord (or, if the landlord is a registered housing association or charitable housing trust, a superior landlord) intends either (a) to demolish or reconstruct the whole or a substantial part of the dwelling-house or (b) to carry out substantial works on the dwelling-house or any part of it or any building of which it forms part.

In addition it must be established that the work cannot reasonably be carried out without the tenant giving up possession of the dwelling-house because—

(1) the tenant is not willing to permit a variation of the terms of the tenancy which permit access or otherwise facilitate the carrying out of the proposed works; or

(2) the nature of the intended work is such that no such variation is practicable; or

(3) the tenant is not willing to accept an assured tenancy of part so as to permit the landlord to carry out the works in question; or

(4) the nature of the intended work is such that a tenancy is not practicable.

To rely on this ground the landlord must have acquired his interest in the property before the current tenancy but in the case where the tenant was the tenant under a previous assured tenancy, this means before that earlier tenancy. Thus a landlord who acquires the reversion subject to the tenancy and then grants the tenant a new tenancy cannot rely on ground 6. Ground 6 is also inapplicable where the assured tenancy is one which has arisen by succession on the death of a Rent Act tenant (see p.267 below).

This ground is based upon the ground of opposition to a new business tenancy in section 30(1)(f) of the Landlord and Tenant Act 1954 (see p.392 below). A landlord who successfully relies on ground 6 is required to pay compensation to the tenant (under section 11).

Ground 7

This ground gives the landlord a right to recover possession where the tenancy is a periodic tenancy (including a statutory periodic tenancy) which has devolved under the will or intestacy of the former tenant (*i.e.* it has not passed to a surviving spouse under the terms of HA 1988 section 17, see below). It thus gives the landlord who decides that he does not want a non-spouse successor in title as a tenant the opportunity to recover possession.

Possession proceedings must be begun not later than 12 months after the death of the former tenant, although the court may direct that this period should run from the date on which in the court's opinion the landlord, or in the case of joint landlords, one of them became aware of the former tenant's death. For the purposes of this ground a landlord who accepts rent from a new tenant, such as a person living as a member of the deceased's household, after the death of the former tenant, is not thereby to be treated as having created a new periodic tenancy unless there is a written agreement by the landlord to a change in the rent payable, the period of the tenancy, the premises which are let or any other terms of the tenancy.

Ground 8

The landlord is entitled to recover possession if at the date of service of the section 8 notice of intended possession proceedings (see above) *and* at the date of the hearing—

(1) where rent is payable weekly or fortnightly at least eight weeks' rent is unpaid (the specified period of arrears was reduced from 13 weeks to eight by the Housing Act 1996);

(2) where rent is payable monthly at least two months' rent is unpaid (the period of arrears was reduced from three months to two by the Housing Act 1996);

(3) where rent is payable quarterly, at least one quarter's rent is more than three months in arrears; and

(4) where rent is payable yearly, at least three months' rent is more than three months in arrears.

It has been argued by advice agencies that the tightening up of this ground by the Housing Act 1996, coupled with widespread delays in the payment of housing benefit, will make even more tenants than before vulnerable to possession proceedings on this ground.

Discretionary grounds

Ground 9
This ground, which mirrors the similar ground for possession provided for by section 98 and Schedule 15 Part IV of the Rent Act 1977, is applicable where suitable alternative accommodation is available for the tenant or will be available for him when the possession order will take effect (see p.285 below). Suitable alternative accommodation is defined for this purpose in Part III of Schedule 2, which specifies—

(1) that a certificate of the local housing authority that it will provide suitable alternative accommodation at the appropriate date is conclusive evidence that such accommodation will be available; and

(2) that the landlord will otherwise need to establish that the alternative accommodation will (a) offer reasonably similar security of tenure to that enjoyed at present and (b) be reasonably suitable to the means and needs of the tenant and his family with regard to extent and character and proximity to place of work.

These criteria have been considered at length by the courts in relation to the Rent Act 1977.

The issue of the tenant's needs was addressed in *Hill v. Rochard* [1983] 1 W.L.R. 478, CA where the tenants had a statutory tenancy of a period country house which had the benefit of a staff flat, a stable and one and a half acres of land including a paddock and outbuildings. The tenants rejected the offer of a tenancy of a more modest modern detached house on the outskirts of a village. The Court held that the accommodation offered was reasonable, and that whilst 'extent and character' denoted some degree of subjectivity, the loss of friends, paddocks and outbuildings for animals were not material because they related to the tenant's desires and wishes, rather than housing needs.

On the other hand, in *Yewbright Properties Ltd v. Stone & Others* (1980) 40 P.& C.R. 402 it was held that the accommodation offered in Dulwich in south east London was not reasonably suitable to the tenant's needs, when she lived and worked mainly in south west London.

It has also been held that when considering the issue of extent and character of the alternative accommodation, the court can take into account not only the physical characteristics of the accommodation, but also environmental matters.

In *Redspring Ltd v. Francis* [1973] 1 W.L.R. 134 it was considered relevant that the alternative accommodation offered to the tenant, who lived in a quiet residential road, was unsuitable. It was in close proximity to a fish and chip shop, a hospital, a cinema and pub, and there were proposals for a tram shed opposite (*cf. Warren v. Austen* [1948] 2 K.B. 82).

The *Francis* decision was distinguished in *Siddiqui v. Rashid* [1980] 1 W.L.R. 1018 where the tenant, who lived in London, was offered alternative accommodation in Luton which was suitable with regard to his means, rental and extent and was closer to his place of work. The landlords wanted to sell the property currently occupied by the tenant in order to buy a larger property for the Muslim community. The tenant's submission that it was nevertheless unsuitable because it would take him away from his local mosque and cultural centre and circle of friends was rejected. The court held that these were not relevant environmental considerations because they did not relate to the character of the property.

The offer, as alternative accommodation, of part only of that currently let to the tenant can be suitable in appropriate circumstances. In *Mykolyshin v. Noah* [1970] 1 W.L.R. 1271 the tenant did not occupy all of her present accommodation and the landlord required possession of a third room for a member of his family, whereas in *McDonnell v. Daly* [1969] 1 W.L.R. 1482 an offer of two of the three rooms currently occupied by the tenant was not deemed to be suitable. The under user by the tenant in the former case would appear to be a critical distinguishing feature between the two decisions.

It must be remembered that even if the ground is made out the court still has to consider whether it is reasonable to order possession in all the circumstances. Thus in *Battlespring Ltd v. Gates* (1983) 268 E.G. 355, CA it was held that despite the fact that the landlord had offered the tenant suitable alternative accommodation in the same road as the property in question, it was still not reasonable in all the circumstances to order possession. The tenant had lived in her flat for 35 years and was attached to it by her memories. The Court of Appeal held that it was not wrong for the judge to have considered the motive of the landlord who had recently acquired the property to make a 'quick profit'.

By contrast, the Court of Appeal held that it was not unreasonable for the court to have ordered possession in *Gladyric Ltd v. Collinson* (1983) 11 H.L.R. 14 where the tenant of a cottage was offered as alternative accommodation either a flat in a converted house or a flat in a house in multiple occupation. It seems to have been an important feature of the decision that the tenant, a lecturer at Oxford University, had been told that the tenancy of the cottage was only to be for a short time.

Ground 10

This provides that it is a ground for possession if some rent lawfully due is unpaid when the possession proceedings are begun and there were arrears at the date of service of the section 8 notice (save where the court considers it just and equitable to waive the requirement for a section 8 notice).

Ground 11

Whether or not there are any rent arrears when possession proceedings are begun, the tenant has persistently delayed paying rent which has become lawfully due. This ground is clearly of use to a landlord who is unable, for whatever reason, to avail himself of either the mandatory ground 8 or the discretionary ground 10.

Ground 12

Any obligation of the tenancy (other than one related to the payment of rent) has been broken or not performed. Thus if, for example, the tenant uses the premises for business purposes in breach of covenant, the landlord might seek possession on this ground.

Ground 13

This ground applies where the tenant, or any person residing in the dwelling-house, has caused the condition of the dwelling house or any common parts to deteriorate as a result of acts of waste or neglect or default. If the deterioration was caused by a lodger or sub-tenant, this ground will apply if the tenant has not taken such steps as he ought to have taken to remove the offending occupier. In *Holloway v. Povey* (1984) 15 H.L.R. 104, CA it was made clear that failure to control the garden (treated as part of the dwelling-house) during the growing season so that it becomes overgrown can be deterioration by neglect for the purposes of this ground.

Ground 14

This ground, which was amended by the Housing Act 1996, applies where the tenant, or any person residing in or visiting the dwelling-house has (a) been guilty of conduct causing or likely to cause a nuisance or annoyance to a person residing, visiting or otherwise engaging in a lawful activity in the locality or (b) has been convicted of (i) using the dwelling-house, or allowing it to be used for illegal or immoral purposes or (ii) an arrestable offence committed in the house or the locality see, *e.g. West Kent Housing Association v. Davies* [1998] E.G.C.S. 103 (late night car repairs a nuisance).

The widening of this ground by the Housing Act 1996 was clearly designed to permit the removal of anti-social tenants whose activities have spread wider than the dwelling-house itself. Indeed it would permit the removal of convicted criminals such as local drug dealers.

Ground 14A

This ground was added by the Housing Act 1996, s.149 and applies where the dwelling-house was occupied by a married couple, or a couple living together as man or wife, and one or both of them is a tenant. It is only available where the landlord seeking possession is a registered social landlord *i.e.* a housing association or a charitable housing trust.

To be applicable (a) one of the partners must have left the dwelling-house because of threats of violence by the other partner towards the one who has left or a member of that person's family who was residing with him/her immediately before the partner left, and (b) the court must be satisfied that the partner is unlikely to return.

The purpose of this ground is to enable the landlord to recover possession of family-sized accommodation occupied by somebody who has driven their partner out by violence or threats of violence in circumstances where the victim is likely to be seeking alternative accommodation from the local authority or a housing association.

Ground 15

This is similar to ground 13, save that it relates to deterioration of the condition of furniture provided for use under the tenancy.

Ground 16

The dwelling-house was let to the tenant in consequence of his employment by the landlord seeking possession or a previous landlord under the tenancy and the tenant has ceased to be in that employment. It should be noted that unlike the equivalent Rent Act ground (see p.276 below), use for a new employee is not required although clearly this will be relevant to how the court should exercise its discretion.

Ground 17

The tenant is the person, or one of the persons, to whom the tenancy was granted and the landlord was induced to grant the tenancy by a false statement made knowingly or recklessly by the tenant or a person acting at the tenant's instigation.

E. Rents of Assured Tenancies

We have seen above that a primary objective of the Housing Act 1988 was to provide that, save in exceptional cases, most tenancies created on or after January 15, 1989, where the landlord's interest is held by a private landlord or housing association, would be free of the regulatory fair rent regime of the Rent Act 1977. In the case of assured tenancies the Government considered it "reasonable that, when entering a tenancy, the tenant should expect to have to pay the market rent for the property, with suitable adjustments over time" (White Paper, *Housing: The Government's Proposals*, Cm.214 (1987), para. 3.9).

This policy is embodied in the rent-fixing provisions of the Housing Act 1988. The basic principle is that the rent recoverable under an assured tenancy is the amount which the parties have provided for in the tenancy agreement subject to any variation that the parties might have subsequently negotiated.

However, this central principle of freedom of contract is modified by those provisions of the Act which permit or provide for a non-negotiated variation in the agreed rent in limited circumstances. The two exceptional procedures provided for are contained in sections 6 and 13 of the Act.

Section 6—statutory periodic tenancies

We have already seen above that under section 6 of the Housing Act 1988 either landlord or tenant may obtain a variation in the terms, other than as to rent, of a statutory periodic tenancy and that this may result in a consequential variation in the rent payable (p.222 above). The section 6 procedure is available only in respect of a statutory periodic tenancy. In other words, there must have been a preceding fixed-term tenancy. Furthermore, the procedure must be brought into operation before the first anniversary of the day on which the former fixed term came to an end.

Section 13—periodic tenancies (contractual or statutory)

Section 13 of the Housing Act 1988 contains a quite different procedure to that in section 6. This procedure enables the landlord to seek a rent increase in respect of—

(1) a statutory periodic tenancy (which for this purpose includes an assured periodic tenancy arising by succession on the death of a Rent Act protected or statutory tenant: HA 1988, s.39(6)(f)). see p.270 below); and

(2) any other (*i.e.* contractual) periodic tenancy (other than one which contains its own binding rent review mechanism).

Thus in the case of (a) there must have been a contractual fixed term which has ended, whereas in the case of (b) the tenancy will have been periodic from the outset. However, it must be noted that, in this second instance, the procedure will not apply if the tenancy contains its own review machinery under which, if operated, the rent will or may be increased. Many housing associations now include such a mechanism in their tenancy agreements (see Davey [1992] 11 Lit. 144).

Initiating the procedure

For the purpose of obtaining a rent increase under the section 13 procedure , the landlord must serve on the tenant a notice in the prescribed form proposing a new rent to take effect at the beginning of a new period of the tenancy specified in the notice (s.13(2)). The specified period must begin not earlier than—

(1) the minimum period after the date of service of the notice; and
(2) except in the case of a statutory periodic tenancy, the first anniversary of the date on which the first period of the tenancy began.

The "minimum period" referred to above depends upon the type of tenancy. In the case of a yearly tenancy it is six months and in the case of a tenancy where the period is less than a month it is one month. In all other cases it is a period equal to the period of the tenancy (s.13(3)).

Thus, it can be seen that in the case of a tenancy which was periodic from the outset, the notice may not specify a date of operation for a proposed increase earlier than 12 months after the tenancy began. On the other hand, in the case of a statutory periodic tenancy, the only constraint on the specified date is that provided by the "minimum period". It seems clear that the notice may be served before the 12 months have expired in the first case, and probably before the statutory periodic tenancy has arisen in the second case, although to be safe a landlord should wait until that point in time because the statute is unclear as to whether an earlier notice would be valid.

Effect of landlord's notice

Once a section 13 notice has been served, the rent increase will take effect from the specified date unless before that time—

(1) the tenant by application in the prescribed form refers the landlord's notice to a rent assessment committee; or
(2) the landlord and tenant agree on a variation of the rent which is different from that proposed in the notice, or agree that the rent should not be varied (s.13(4)).

The application form to the rent assessment committee must be signed by the tenant or his or her agent as the case may be, and if there are joint tenants each tenant or agent must sign, unless one signs on behalf of the rest with their agreement.

Procedure

The procedure to be followed by the rent assessment committee following a reference under section 13 is exactly the same as that applicable to a reference under section 6.

In both cases it will be important to decide as a preliminary matter whether the reference is a valid one and that the rent assessment committee has jurisdiction to consider it. This will mean verifying that there is a tenancy within the Act and that all the statutory requirements as to notices and time limits, etc., have been satisfied.

Function of the rent assessment committee

If a section 13 notice has been referred to the rent assessment committee they must determine the rent at which they consider that the dwelling-house concerned might reasonably be expected to be let in the open market by a willing landlord under an assured tenancy—

(1) which is a periodic tenancy having the same periods as those of the tenancy to which the notice relates;

(2) which begins at the beginning of the new period specified in the notice;

(3) the terms of which (other than those relating to the amount of rent) are the same as those of the tenancy to which the notice relates;

(4) in respect of which the same notices, if any, have been given under any of grounds 1 to 5 of Schedule 2 to the 1988 Act as have been given (or have effect as if given) in relation to the tenancy to which the notice relates (s.14(1)).

The grounds referred to in (4) above are those mandatory grounds for possession which are dependent for their operation on the service of a notice by the landlord at or before the beginning of the tenancy, stating that possession might be recovered under the ground in question if the appropriate conditions are satisfied (see above). It is clearly envisaged that if any such notice has been served, this will have an effect upon the rent payable, although this is questionable. In the case of the first two grounds, it should be recalled that the court may dispense with the notice requirement if of the opinion that it is just and equitable to do so (p.227 above).

Market rents

It will be seen that, by way of marked contrast to their function under the fair rents scheme contained in the Rent Act 1977, the rent assessment committee's function under section 14 of the Housing Act 1988 is to determine a market rent. Beyond the basic assumptions set out above, no further guidance is offered to committees as to how they ought to carry out this task.

The matter therefore turns around the question of the basis on which the committee will form its reasonable expectation as to the appropriate rent. The answer must be on the basis of recent freely negotiated rents for similar properties in the same or a comparable locality, with adjustments for any differences which will affect the rental level and allowing for the statutory "disregards". Consequently the evidential emphasis will be on establishing those comparable market rents to which the necessary adjustments will need to be made. This will be a matter not just for the parties, but also for the rent assessment panels who will have built up a bank of evidence which, because of the fluctuating nature of the property rental market, will need to be constantly monitored to ensure that it reflects the current state of the market.

Disregards

When making a determination under section 14, the committee are directed to disregard a number of matters. These include any increase in the value of the dwelling-house attributable to a relevant improvement carried out by a person who at the time it was carried out was the tenant (unless the tenant had contracted to carry out the improvement concerned) (s.14(2)(b)). Otherwise, the landlord would be obtaining the benefit of a tenant's voluntary improvements by way of increased rent. Similarly any reduction in the value of the dwelling-house attributable to a failure by the tenant to comply with his obligations under the tenancy is to be disregarded. (It has been held that, in the case of an assured tenancy arising by way of succession (see p.270 below), failure to comply with a repairing obligation by the tenant's predecessor is not to be taken into account when assessing the rent: *N & D London Ltd v. Gadson* (1991) 24 H.L.R. 64).

The Rent Act 1977 also requires certain improvements to be disregarded when assessing a fair rent (see p.294 below) but unlike the Rent Act, the Housing Act 1988 does not define the term "improvement". This may present a rent assessment committee with some difficulty. This is because the Rent Act 1977 provides that when disregarding certain tenant's improvements for the purpose of assessing a fair rent, "improvement" includes the replacement of any fixture or fitting (Rent Act 1977, s.70(4)). The absence of a corresponding statutory definition of improvement for the purposes of Part 1 of the Housing Act 1988 would seem to preclude a rent assessment committee, when determining a market rent under section 14 or 22 (see below), from disregarding a tenant's replacement of fixtures or fittings as a relevant improvement, although many committees will no doubt feel able to give the term "improvement" a similar meaning to that which it carries in the Rent Act 1977.

The meaning of rent

For the purposes of section 14, "rent" does not include a "variable" service charge within the meaning of section 18 of the Landlord and Tenant Act 1985 (HA 1988, s.14(4)). In other words, it does not include any sum payable by a tenant of a dwelling as part of or in addition to the rent which is attributable to services, repairs, maintenance or insurance or the landlord's costs of management, the whole or part of which varies or may vary according to the relevant costs (Landlord and Tenant Act 1985, s.18 as amended by the Landlord and Tenant Act 1987). It is not uncommon for housing associations to provide for a variable service charge where the amount payable by the tenant for services can fluctuate from year to year according to the costs of providing the services in question.

The reason that variable service charges are excluded, is that the tenant is given protection in respect of unreasonable charges by the Landlord and Tenant Act 1985 which since September 1997 (following the Housing Act 1996) enables these to be challenged before a leasehold valuation tribunal.

Coincidence of references under section 6 and 13

Circumstances may occur where a committee receives around the same time both:

(1) a reference under section 6(2) by either landlord or tenant, as the case may be, seeking an adjudication on a proposed variation of terms of a statutory periodic tenancy; and

(2) a reference under section 13(2) by the tenant under the same tenancy seeking determination of a market rent.

If the date specified in the section 6 notice is not later than the first day of the new period specified in the section 13 notice, the committee may propose to hear the two references together. If they do so, they are required to determine the section 6 reference before making a determination in relation to the section 13 reference. Accordingly the terms of the tenancy to be taken into account on the section 13 determination will be the terms as varied by virtue of the section 6 determination (s.14(6)).

Effective date of rent determined by the committee

Unless the landlord and tenant otherwise agree, the rent determined by the committee following a section 13 reference is to be the rent payable under the tenancy with effect from the beginning of the new period specified in the notice. Consequently it is important for committees to deal expeditiously with references. Any rates in respect of the dwelling-house (such as those for water and sewage disposal) which are borne by the landlord or a superior landlord are added to the rent determined by the committee (s.14(7)).

If the rent assessment committee consider that the operative date for the increase would cause undue hardship to the tenant, then the committee may direct a later date, but not one later than the date of the committee's determination (s.14). No indication is given as to what is meant by "undue hardship" and it is a matter for the discretion of the committee in each case. It is important to realise that the rent determined by the committee becomes the maximum rent payable *unless the landlord and tenant otherwise agree*. Thus unlike registration of a fair rent under the Rent Act 1977, the market rent determined by the rent assessment committee does not become a statutory limit.

Furthermore, if, at any time before the committee's determination of a rent for the dwelling-house, the landlord and tenant give notice in writing that they no longer require such a determination, or if the tenancy has come to an end, the committee are not required to continue with their determination (s.14(8)). This would seem to give the committee a discretion as to whether to continue or not, but little would seem to be achieved by continuing in such circumstances because either the landlord and tenant will ignore the rent determined by the committee, or, if the tenancy has come to an end, the landlord will re-let and the rent determined by the committee will not affect that new tenancy.

If a rent has been increased by virtue of a section 13 notice or a determination by a rent assessment committee under section 14, then the landlord may seek further increases by notice under section 13. However, the date specified for the purposes of when the increase is to take effect must not be earlier than the "minimum period" after the date of service of the notice *and* the first anniversary of the date on which the previous increase took effect by virtue of section 13 or a determination by the rent assessment committee under section 14. Thus it will be possible for the rent to be reviewed annually.

F. ASSIGNMENT, ETC., OF ASSURED TENANCIES

The ordinary rules governing alienation of tenancies and their interaction with the statutory rules in section 15 Housing Act 1988 are dealt with in Chapter 4, to which reference should be made.

Sub-tenancies

If an assured tenant has lawfully created a sub-tenancy and the tenancy subsequently comes to an end, the sub-tenant will thereafter hold directly of the landlord on an assured tenancy, provided his new landlord is not disqualified from being a landlord under an assured tenancy (s.18).

Succession to assured tenancies

On the death of a tenant who held under a fixed-term assured tenancy, the tenancy will devolve in accordance with the laws of testate or intestate succession depending on whether or not the tenant effectively disposed of the property by will. By contrast, the Housing Act 1988 provides for a very limited statutory right of succession on the death of the tenant under an assured periodic tenancy. It applies where the tenant was the sole tenant and immediately before the death the tenant's spouse was occupying the dwelling-house as his or her only or principal home. In those circumstances the tenancy will vest by statute in the spouse. This will be so irrespective of the terms of the tenant's will or the law of intestacy (Housing Act 1988, s.17(1)).

This right of succession will not apply if the tenant was himself a successor, as defined. The tenant will himself be a successor if—

(1) the tenancy became vested in him by virtue of section 17 or under the will or intestacy of the previous tenant; or
(2) at some time before his death the tenancy was a joint tenancy and he had become the sole surviving tenant; or
(3) he had become an assured tenant by succession following the death of a Rent Act protected or statutory tenant (s. 17(2); see p.270 below).

An additional succession will not occur where a successor tenant as defined above takes a new tenancy of the same or substantially the same dwelling-house and then dies (s.17(3)).

For the purposes of section 17 a person who was living with the tenant as his or her wife or husband is to be treated as the tenant's spouse (s.17(4)). In *Harrogate BC v. Simpson* [1986] 2 F.L.R. 91, CA it was held that the same expression did not enable a same-sex partner to succeed to a secure tenancy under the Housing Act 1985. This decision was followed in the Rent Act case of *Fitzpatrick v. Sterling Housing Association* [1997] 4 All E.R. 991 to deny a statutory tenancy by succession to the surviving partner of a homosexual couple who had lived together for many years (see p.272 below).

If more than one person qualifies as a successor such one of them as may be decided by agreement, or, in the absence of agreement, by the county court is to be treated as the tenant's spouse for the purposes of succession to the tenancy (s.17(5)).

G. ASSURED SHORTHOLD TENANCIES

Defining assured shorthold tenancies

The first point to notice is that an assured shorthold tenancy is a sub-species of the assured tenancy. Consequently all the provisions in the Housing Act 1988 which are expressed to apply to assured tenancies also apply to assured shorthold tenancies unless for this purpose they are specifically modified or excluded by the Act. It follows that if a tenancy is at any time excluded by the Act from being an assured tenancy, it cannot at the same time be an assured shorthold tenancy.

We have already seen that between January 15, 1989 and February 28, 1997 the (fully) assured tenancy was the default tenancy if all the requirements of an assured tenancy (discussed above) were satisfied. A landlord could, in the first instance, only create an assured shorthold tenancy if he complied with a number of stringent requirements including the service of a special form of notice on the tenant before the commencement of the tenancy. Failure to do so usually resulted in the creation of a fully assured tenancy. The position is now reversed in the case of lettings on or after February 28, 1997. Such a tenancy which satisfies all the requirements of an assured tenancy will now, save in specified exceptional circumstances, take effect not as a (fully) assured tenancy but as an assured shorthold tenancy instead (Housing Act 1988, s.19A—added by Housing Act 1996, s.96(1) and S.I. 1997 No. 225).

It is thus necessary to distinguish between those tenancies created before and those created after the operative date.

1. Tenancies created on or after February 28, 1997

As noted above, all "new" assured tenancies are assured shorthold tenancies save in the following exceptional cases. Thus there is no need for any warning to the tenant that the tenancy is to be a shorthold tenancy nor any need to notify the tenant of his/her rights.

For this purpose a "new" tenancy is—

(1)   a tenancy which is expressly created on or after February 28, 1997; or
(2)   a tenancy which comes into being as a statutory periodic tenancy by virtue of section 5 (see p.222 above), on the coming to an end of a fixed-term assured tenancy which was itself created on or after February 28, 1997 (HA 1988, s.19A).

The exceptional cases where a tenancy will still take effect as an assured shorthold tenancy are—

(1)   Tenancies entered into on or after February 28, 1997 in pursuance of a contract made before that date (s.19A(a)).
(2)   Tenancies where at any time before or after the tenancy began the landlord has given the tenant notice (for which no special form is required) that the tenancy is not to be an assured shorthold tenancy (Housing Act 1988, Sched. 2A, paras 1 and 2). Note that the notice can be served even during the term.

This exception is most likely to be used by housing associations because as we have seen (see p.200 above) guidance has been issued by the Housing Corporation to the effect that—

"Associations are expected to give their tenants long term security wherever possible. Therefore assured shorthold tenancies should be used only in exceptional circumstances, which an association may be required to justify to the Housing Corporation, where shorthold is the only reasonable way of meeting the association's housing objectives. (*The Tenants' Guarantee:* issued by the Housing Corporation under the Housing Associations Act 1985, s.36A as inserted by the Housing Act 1988, s.49 (HC/43/88).)"

An exceptional circumstance where an assured shorthold tenancy must be granted is provided for by the Housing Act 1996. That Act provides that when a local authority discharges its statutory obligation to house homeless persons it does so by securing that suitable accommodation is made available. That accommodation can be from the authority's own stock or might be owned by a housing association or a private landlord. In the case of a housing association it is provided that the tenancy can only be an assured shorthold tenancy and this cannot be turned into an assured tenancy by notice unless the property is being made available in accordance with the authority's normal allocation criteria (*i.e.* not under the special homelessness provisions) (HA 1996, s.209).

(3)   Tenancies which expressly provide that the tenancy is not to be an assured shorthold tenancy (Housing Act 1988, Sched. 2A, para. 3).

(4)   Assured tenancies by succession (Housing Act 1988, Sched. 2A, para. 4).
Since January 15, 1989 all Rent Act successions, on the death of the protected or statutory tenant, by family members (other than spouses) and all second successions result in the successor obtaining an assured tenancy under the Housing Act 1988 rather than a statutory tenancy under the Rent Act 1977 (Housing Act 1988, s.39, see p.270 below).
The present exception to the Housing Act 1988, s.19A means that such tenancies arising by way of succession on or after February 28, 1997 will still take effect as fully assured tenancies.

(5)   An assured tenancy which becomes an assured tenancy on ceasing to be a secure tenancy (Housing Act 1988, Sched. 2A, para. 5).
Since January 15, 1989, where a local authority transfers its rented housing stock to a private sector or housing association landlord its formerly secure tenants will cease to be secure because the landlord's interest is no longer held by a qualifying public sector landlord (see p.310 below). Thus those tenants will normally become (fully) assured tenants. The purpose of the present exception is to preserve this position where such an event occurs on or after February 28, 1997.

(6)   Tenants under certain long tenancies at a low rent which have expired (Housing Act 1988, Sched. 2A, para. 6).
On the expiry of certain long tenancies at a low rent on or after January 15, 1989 the tenant acquires an assured tenancy (see Local Government and Housing Act 1989, Sched. 10, para. 6; see p.352 below). The present exception provides that where such a tenancy arises on or after February 28, 1997 the tenancy will not be an assured shorthold tenancy.

(7)   Tenancies replacing assured tenancies (Housing Act 1988, Sched. 2A, paras. 7 and 8).
The exception in paragraph 7 is designed to prevent a landlord (alone or jointly with others) granting a new tenancy on or February 28, 1997 to a tenant (alone or jointly with others) who immediately before that tenancy was granted was an assured tenant (or in the case of a joint tenancy, one of the joint tenants) under a fully assured tenancy of that landlord (or one of the joint landlords).
However, the exception will not apply where the prospective tenant (*i.e.* all the tenants, in the case of a joint tenancy) has served a notice in the prescribed form on the prospective landlord (or in the case of joint landlords, one of them) stating that the tenancy is to be an assured shorthold tenancy. This option, which was not foreshadowed in either the White Paper or the Consultation Documents which preceded the 1996 Act, is not open to the landlord. It is difficult to imagine the circumstances in which a tenant might want to take such steps and the scope for abuse by unscrupulous landlords who would seek to procure the conversion of a fully assured to a shorthold tenancy seems plain. (See Driscoll (1996) N.L.J. 1699).
If a fixed-term (fully) assured tenancy ends, the statutory periodic tenancy which arises under section 5 will not be an assured shorthold tenancy (Housing Act 1988, Sched. 2A, para. 8).

(8)   Assured agricultural occupancies (Housing Act 1988, Sched. 2A, para. 9).

Occupiers of tied agricultural and forestry properties, whether by way of a tenancy or a licence, are afforded protection by Part I of the Housing Act 1988 under a parallel scheme (with necessary modifications) to that afforded to assured tenants by the 1988 Act. They are known as assured agricultural occupancies.

The present exception ensures that the regime in Section 19A which provides for "new" assured tenancies to take effect automatically as shorthold tenancies does not extend to assured agricultural occupancies unless the landlord by serving a notice in the prescribed form, chooses to opt into that scheme. However, this option is not available to a landlord who is seeking to grant a new (shorthold) tenancy to a tenant who (or in the case of joint tenants, one of whom) immediately beforehand was a tenant or licensee of that landlord (or one of them, in the case of joint landlords) under an assured agricultural occupancy.

Furthermore when a fixed-term fully assured tenancy ends the statutory periodic tenancy which arises under section 5 will be an assured shorthold tenancy if the fixed term tenancy was one in respect of which the landlord had served the notice referred to in the above (Housing Act 1988, Sched. 2A, para. 9(1)). But this will apparently not be the case if he chooses to grant a new tenancy instead. (See M. Johnstone [1997] E.G. 150).

2. Tenancies created before February 28, 1997

An assured tenancy entered into before February 28, 1997 will be an assured shorthold tenancy provided it satisfies the following conditions—

(1)   It is a fixed-term tenancy granted for a term certain of not less than six months. (In *Bedding v. McCarthy* (1994) 27 H.L.R. 103, CA a tenancy which was signed at midday on December 18 and was to expire on the following June 17 was deemed to have commenced at the beginning of December 18 and hence to be for the requisite six-month minimum period.)

(2)   In respect of which there is no power for the landlord to determine the tenancy at any time earlier than six months from the beginning of the tenancy (other than by way of forfeiture or right of re-entry—s.45(4)).

(3)   In respect of which a notice was served as mentioned below (Housing Act 1988, s.20(1)).

The notice referred to in (3) above must be in the prescribed form, or one substantially to the like effect (S.I. 1988 No. 2203, Sched. Form 7). It must have been served on the prospective tenant(s) by the prospective landlord (or at least one of the landlords in the case of joint landlords) (Housing Act 1988, s.20(6)(a)) before the assured tenancy was entered into, and it must state that the assured tenancy to which it relates is to be a shorthold tenancy (s.20(2)). If there are joint tenants it must have been served on all of the tenants (s.45(3)). In practice, many landlords treated the need for a section 20 notice as a necessary inconvenience and obtained the tenant's signature at the same time as the tenancy agreement was entered into. It was a question of fact as to which had actually occurred first (*Bedding v. McCarthy* (above)).

The courts have taken a strict view of the need for compliance with section 20. Thus in *Panayi & Pyrkos v. Roberts* (1993) 25 H.L.R. 408, a notice which stated that the tenancy would end in six months, when in fact it was to last for a year, was held to be invalid. The error would not have been apparent to anyone reading the notice, unlike an obvious clerical error. However, in *Andrews v. Brewer* (1998) 30 H.L.R. 203 the Court of Appeal held that a notice which stated the date of termination of the tenancy to be four days after the contractual date did not invalidate the notice; nor did the omission of one of the prescribed notes (relating to the payment of council tax) on the basis that the tenant was not thereby adversely affected.

Reference should also be made to the decisions in *Mustafa v. Ruddock* [1998] 30 H.L.R. 495, CA and *Boyle v. Verrall* (1996) 29 H.L.R. 436, CA, (p.227 above) where, in both cases, the court allowed a landlord who had not served a section 20 notice to recover possession of the assured tenancy thereby created by relying on ground 1, despite no notice having been served on that ground.

Existing fully assured tenants

If a landlord has granted a tenancy to a person or persons who (or at least one of whom, as the case may be) immediately before the tenancy began was a tenant of the same landlord under an assured tenancy which was not a shorthold tenancy, the new tenancy cannot be a shorthold tenancy even if all the requirements referred to above have been satisfied. The tenancy will take effect instead as an ordinary (fully) assured tenancy (s.20(3)). This provision was designed to prevent a landlord reducing a tenant's protection by granting him an assured shorthold tenancy (of the same or a different dwelling-house) when his assured tenancy (under which he had security of tenure) came to an end.

In the circumstances discussed below an assured shorthold tenancy will arise despite the fact that the requirements in items (1)–(3) above were not fulfilled in relation to that tenancy.

Renewal of an assured shorthold tenancy

If an assured shorthold tenancy came to an end and the landlord at that time granted the former tenant a new tenancy of the same or substantially the same premises, then if and so long as the new tenancy of the same or substantially the same premises is an assured tenancy, it will be an assured shorthold tenancy (Housing Act 1988, s.20(4)). (For the meaning of "landlord" and "tenant", see s.45(3)).

Similarly any statutory periodic tenancy which arises on the coming to an end of the shorthold tenancy will also be an assured shorthold tenancy so long as it remains an assured tenancy (see *Lower Street Properties Ltd v. Jones* [1996] E.G.C.S. 37). The only situation where the above rules is where, before the new tenancy was entered into, or as the case may be, the statutory periodic tenancy took effect in possession, the landlord served notice (for which there is no prescribed form) on the tenant that the new tenancy (or statutory periodic tenancy) was not to be a shorthold tenancy. If there were joint landlords it is sufficient for one of them to have notified the tenant (Housing Act 1988, ss.20(5), (6)(b)).

The rationale of this rule is that if the landlord and tenant have negotiated a new tenancy they are presumed to have been satisfied with the shorthold arrangement and therefore it can be assumed that both would wish to continue on that basis. This explains why the tenant under a shorthold tenancy created before February 28, 1997 cannot refer the rent to a rent assessment committee under section 22 below following expiry of the initial fixed term.

The other cases of deemed shorthold are as follows.

Assured tenancy by succession

If, following the death of a tenant who was a protected or statutory tenant of a dwelling-house under the Rent Act 1977, a person was entitled to succeed to a Housing Act 1988 assured tenancy by succession of the dwelling-house, that tenancy will be an assured shorthold tenancy whether or not it fulfils the conditions mentioned above, if under the earlier tenancy the landlord might have recovered possession of the dwelling-house under Case 19 of Schedule 15 to the Rent Act 1977 (Housing Act 1988, s.39(7)). Case 19 relates to recovery of possession in the case of protected shorthold tenancies (see p.293 below). The purpose of this exception is to ensure that if in respect of the former tenancy the landlord had the benefit of a mandatory ground for possession under Case 19, the successor tenant should not be in any better position than the former tenant. He is therefore entitled only to an assured shorthold tenancy.

Renewals in favour of certain tenants

A similar rule applies in two cases where there has been a renewal on or after January 15, 1989 in favour of a person who immediately beforehand was a protected or statutory tenant of the landlord.

(1) The first case is where the renewal on or after January 15, 1989 is in favour of a tenant who immediately beforehand held under a protected shorthold tenancy (which will necessarily have been created before January 15, 1989)

(2) The second case arises where, before January 15, 1989, a former protected shorthold tenant (or a statutory successor on death) remained in occupation under a new contractual tenancy or a statutory tenancy and there is a grant of a new tenancy on or after January 15, 1989 to that person.

In each of these cases the landlord would have had the benefit of the mandatory ground for possession in Case 19 of Schedule 15 to the Rent Act 1977 against the tenant under the former tenancy and therefore it would not be right to permit that tenant to acquire a fully assured tenancy by taking a new tenancy on or after January 15, 1989. (The normal rule is that where there is a renewal in favour of a protected or statutory tenant the tenant would not lose Rent Act protection—Housing Act 1988, s.34(1)(b).)

The solution adopted by the Housing Act 1988 is to provide that on such a renewal the tenant will acquire instead an assured shorthold tenancy under the Housing Act 1988 unless, before the tenancy is entered into, the landlord serves notice that it is not to be a shorthold tenancy (Housing Act 1988, s.34(3)).If the landlord does serve such a notice the tenancy will be an assured tenancy.

Assured shorthold tenancies—recovery of possession

The two main attractions for landlords of the assured shorthold tenancy as a form of letting are (a) as in the case of a fully assured tenancy, the ability to let at a market rent with minimal regulation (see above), and (b) the ability to recover possession by a simple procedure following termination of the tenancy. This second feature is examined below.

The first point to notice is that an assured shorthold tenancy is a sub-species of assured tenancy and therefore all the grounds for possession in Schedule 2 are equally applicable to an assured shorthold tenancy. Furthermore in the case of the assured shorthold tenancy an additional ground for possession is in effect provided by section 21 of the Housing Act 1988.

(a) Fixed-term shorthold tenancies

Section 21 provides that once a fixed-term assured shorthold tenancy comes to an end, the court must order possession, provided the following conditions are satisfied—

(1) no further assured tenancy (whether shorthold or not) has been created other than an assured shorthold periodic tenancy (whether statutory or not); and

(2) the landlord (or in the case of joint landlords, at least one of them) has given the tenant not less than two months' notice in writing stating that he requires possession of the dwelling-house. The notice may be given before or on the day on which the tenancy ends and is effective also in respect of any statutory periodic tenancy which arises at the end of the fixed term. Indeed when the court orders possession, any such statutory periodic tenancy will determine automatically when the order takes effect. There is nothing which prevents the notice being given at the beginning of the fixed term, although this is not usual in practice.

For example, if L has granted T a six months fixed term and at the end of that period T remains in possession paying rent on a periodic basis, an assured shorthold statutory periodic tenancy will have arisen automatically unless the landlord has expressly created (a) a new fully assured tenancy or (b) a new assured shorthold fixed term or (c) a new assured shorthold periodic tenancy.

Nevertheless, save in cases (a) and (b), the landlord can then at any time seek a possession order provided a notice as in (2) above has been served.

(b)   Periodic assured shorthold tenancies

In the cases where on the ending of a fixed-term shorthold tenancy either (a) a (shorthold) statutory periodic tenancy has arisen or (b) the tenant has been granted a new contractual (shorthold) periodic tenancy and the landlord has not served a notice at or before the ending of the fixed term (see above), he can still initiate a procedure to recover possession.

Thus it is provided that the court must grant a possession order if in such a case the landlord (or in the case of joint landlords at least one of them) has given the tenant not less than two months' notice in writing stating that after the end of the notice period (which must end on the last day of a period of the tenancy) possession will be required for the purposes of section 21. The date specified for this purpose must not be earlier than the date on which the tenancy could have been ended by a notice to quit given by the landlord on the same day as the notice.

We saw above that until February 28, 1997 it was not possible to create an initial assured shorthold tenancy other than for a minimum fixed term of six months (s.20). However, since that date all new assured tenancies (save in the exceptional cases discussed above—such as where the landlord opts for a fully assured tenancy) take effect as assured shorthold tenancies. Thus it is now open to the landlord to create from the beginning an assured shorthold fixed term of less than six months or alternatively a periodic assured shorthold tenancy.

To cater for this the Housing Act 1988 was amended (by the Housing Act 1996) to provide that although the landlord is permitted to initiate the notice procedures described above in respect of such tenancies, any court order for possession cannot take effect earlier than six months after the beginning of the tenancy. To cater for the possibility of more than one tenancy between the parties within that period, whether contractual or statutory, it is provided that in the case of a "replacement tenancy" any possession order cannot take effect earlier than six months after the commencement of the original tenancy.

Accelerated possession procedure

A landlord seeking possession of property let on an assured shorthold tenancy may be able to use the special fast track procedure in the county court (see p.227 above).

Rents of assured shorthold tenancies

As in the case of an ordinary assured tenancy, the rent recoverable for a shorthold tenancy, at least initially, will be that provided for by the tenancy agreement. However, unlike the case of fully assured tenancies, there is a mechanism enabling the tenant only to seek a rent determination by the rent assessment committee. It is designed to protect a tenant who considers that his or her contractual rent is significantly higher than local market rental levels for that type of property.

Thus it is provided that a tenant under an assured shorthold tenancy may apply in the prescribed form (S.I. 1997 No. 194 Form 6) to a rent assessment committee for a determination of the rent which, in the committee's opinion, the landlord might reasonably be expected to obtain under the assured shorthold tenancy (s.22(1)).

The procedure described above is not available in the following cases—

(1) Where the tenancy is one granted (or, in the case of a statutory periodic assured shorthold tenancy, one arising) on or after February 28, 1997 and more than six months have elapsed since the beginning of the tenancy, or, in the case of a replacement tenancy, since the beginning of the original tenancy. (If the tenancy began before February 28, 1997 the tenant has a right to refer the rent to a rent assessment committee at any time during the initial fixed term, however long that might be).

(2) Where the original tenancy has ended and a new tenancy of the same or substantially the same premises has come into being (*i.e.* either by renewal or by virtue of section 5—assured periodic tenancy) between the landlord and tenant, whether or not a section 20 notice has been served in respect of the later tenancy.

Once a rent assessment committee have determined a rent under section 22, no further application is permitted in relation to that tenancy (s.22(2)(a)). The procedure to be followed by the rent assessment committee following an application under section 22 is the same as that following a reference under section 6 or section 13.

Function of the rent assessment committee

As noted above, the rent assessment committee to whom an application is made under section 22 are required to determine the rent which, in the committee's opinion, the landlord might reasonably expect to obtain under the assured shorthold tenancy (s.22(1)). However, before they can do so, an obstacle must be overcome. It is provided that the committee are not to make such a determination unless they consider—

(1) that there is a sufficient number of similar dwelling-houses in the locality let on assured tenancies (whether shorthold or not); and

(2) that the rent payable under the assured shorthold tenancy in question is significantly higher than the rent which the landlord might reasonably expect to obtain under the

tenancy having regard to the level of rents payable under those other tenancies (s.22(3)).

Although the test to be applied by the committee is similar to that applicable to a determination under section 14, it should be observed that the function of the committee under section 22 is more stringently qualified. First, only if open-market rents reveal the rent in question to be "significantly higher" than the appropriate level can the committee determine a rent.

Secondly, the committee is required to draw its comparables from the "locality" in which the subject property is located. The Act gives no indication as to what is meant for this purpose by "significantly higher", nor by "locality", and therefore these terms are arguably matters of fact for the committee to determine (see also p.291 below).

It is interesting that the Government's expectation was that rents under assured shorthold tenancies would be set at lower levels than those for comparable properties let on ordinary assured tenancies, to reflect the absence of security of tenure for the former (Hansard, H.C. Vol. 134, col. 623, November 30, 1987). However, in practice it has been found that shorthold rents tend to be higher than assured rents.

If the landlord and tenant give notice in writing to the committee that they no longer require a determination, or if the tenancy has come to an end, the committee is not required to continue with its determination (ss.22(5), 14(8)). As already explained, it is unlikely that any committee would proceed to a determination in these circumstances unless perhaps in the latter case a backdated determination would benefit one party.

Effect of rent assessment committee's decision

If the rent assessment committee do determine a rent, the new rent will have effect from such date as the committee may direct. They may not direct a date earlier than the date of the application. If at any time the rent payable under the tenancy is in excess of the rent so determined, the excess is irrecoverable from the tenant (s.22(4)). Although not explicitly stated in the Act, it is presumed that this will permit a tenant to recover any overpayment made before the determination if the committee direct an effective date earlier than that of their decision. The landlord will not be permitted to serve a notice under section 13(2) (see p.234 above) until after the first anniversary of the date on which the section 22 determination takes effect (s.22(4)).

For the purposes of a determination under section 22, "rent" is given the same meaning as in section 14(4) (s.22(5), see p.236 above). Similarly where the rates are borne by the landlord or a superior landlord, any rent determined will be rate-exclusive and therefore, if by the terms of the tenancy the rent is inclusive of rates, the rates will be recoverable in addition to the rent determined by the rent assessment committee.

Since April 1, 1990 this only affects water rates because domestic rates ceased to exist from that date.

The Secretary of State has a reserve power exercisable by statutory instrument to provide that section 22 shall not apply in such cases or to tenancies of dwelling-houses in such areas or in such other circumstances as may be specified in the orders (s.23).

Increase of rent under an assured shorthold tenancy

A landlord who wishes to increase the rent under a periodic assured shorthold tenancy, or a statutory periodic assured shorthold tenancy, may avail himself of the section 13 procedure where applicable. However, it is far more likely that he will simply bring, or threaten to bring, possession proceedings if the tenant is unwilling to pay a higher rent.

Information on rents

It is provided that the President of every rent assessment panel is required to keep certain specified information with respect to rents under assured tenancies which have been the subject of references or applications to, or determinations by, rent assessment committees. In other words, registers of rents are kept and the register entry for a particular tenancy will be sent to both parties. This information is to be made available to the public, without charge, at the panel office (Housing Act 1988, s.42(1) and S.I. 1988 No. 2199, art. 4).

The information relates to cases where the rent assessment committee for an area have made a determination following a reference to them under section 13 or section 22 of the Housing Act 1988, or where they are precluded from making a determination under section 22 because the conditions set out in section 22(3) have not been satisfied.

Jurisdictional disputes

Apart from those matters which fall within the jurisdiction of a rent assessment committee, the county court has jurisdiction to hear and determine any question arising under, *inter alia*, Part I of the Housing Act 1988. Because an application for a determination under the procedure laid down in section 6 or section 13 or section 22 of the Housing Act 1988 is made to a rent assessment committee, the committee will have to make a preliminary decision as to whether or not it has jurisdiction.

Challenging the decision of the rent assessment committee

Although the Housing Act 1988 does not provide for an appeal from a rent assessment committee's decision on the substantive issue of the rent there is a right of appeal on a point of law from a decision of the rent assessment committee under the Tribunals and Inquiries Act 1992, s.11(1). A committee's decision may also be open to challenge by way of judicial review (see p.288 below).

Chapter 10

SECURITY OF TENURE AND RENT REGULATION IN THE PRIVATE SECTOR: (2) THE RENT ACT 1977

Introduction

The Rent Act (RA) 1977 contains a number of special regulatory regimes which afford tenants differing levels of protection by way of rent regulation and /or security of tenure depending on the type of tenancy in question. Save in exceptional cases the protection of the Act is confined to tenancies which were created before January 15, 1989. The principal regime, which provides a dual form of protection by way of fair rent regulation and security of tenure, applies to what are known as protected or statutory tenancies. In practice this means most tenancies created before the above date, where the landlord's interest is held by a landlord other than a public sector authority or a housing association.

The main exception to this regime comprises resident landlord lettings created since the Rent Act 1974 came into operation on August 14, 1974 and before January 15, 1989. They are afforded a lesser form of protection under the separate Restricted Contract code also contained in the Rent Act 1977. Tenancies created before January 15, 1989 where the landlord's interest is held by a housing association are brought within the fair rent regime by virtue of Part VI of the Act.

A. PROTECTED TENANCIES

Date of creation of protected tenancy

Before examining the concept of the protected tenancy it is very important to remember that the Housing Act 1988 provides that, save in a number of exceptional circumstances, it has not been possible to create a new protected tenancy under the Rent Act 1977 on or after January 15, 1989 (the operative date of Part I of the Housing Act 1988). Thus the Rent Act 1977 is now mainly confined to tenancies created before that date.

The exceptional cases where a Rent Act protected tenancy may still be created on or after January 15, 1989 are as follows:—

1. Where the tenancy was entered into in pursuance of a contract made before the operative date (Housing Act 1988, s.34(1)(a)).

2. Where a landlord grants a tenancy to a person (whether solely or jointly with others) who immediately beforehand was a protected or statutory tenant of that landlord (whether he was a sole or joint landlord under that earlier tenancy) (Housing Act, s.34(1)(b)).

    This is clearly designed to prevent a landlord removing Rent Act protection from a protected or statutory tenant by offering the tenant a new tenancy of the same or different premises after the Housing Act 1988 came into force.

    This exception will not apply where the earlier tenancy was a protected shorthold tenancy or where the tenant under such a tenancy was holding over under a new tenancy or a statutory tenancy following the expiry of the initial fixed term. In such a case the new tenancy will be an assured shorthold tenancy unless the landlord gives notice to the contrary, in which case it would become a fully assured tenancy (Housing Act 1988, s.34(2), (3)).

    It will be noted that this exception is only of benefit to a person who immediately before the grant of the new tenancy was a protected or statutory tenant. Thus in *Bolnore Properties v. Cobb* (1996) 29 H.L.R. 202 a gap of 24 hours between the earlier tenancy ending and the grant of the new tenancy was sufficient to mean that the tenant was not a protected or statutory tenant immediately beforehand.

    Furthermore, in the case of a new tenancy to joint tenants it will suffice for that tenancy to be protected even though only one of the tenants was protected under the earlier tenancy. (See further Davey (1991) 11 Lit. 22).

3. Where the tenancy is granted to a person (alone or jointly with others) following a possession order under the Rent Act 1977 made on the ground of suitable alternative accommodation (see p.285 below) and where—

    (a) the tenancy is of the premises which constitute the suitable alternative accommodation as to which the court was satisfied; and

    (b) the court considered, in the possession proceedings, that the grant of an assured tenancy under the Housing Act 1988 would not afford the required security and accordingly directed that the tenancy should be a protected or, as the case may be, statutory tenancy (Housing Act 1988, s.34(1)(c)).

An assured tenancy clearly affords the tenant a more closely circumscribed form of security than that afforded by a Rent Act protected tenancy. Whether such a tenancy will offer the particular tenant "the required security" may be a different matter.

The issue was considered by the Court of Appeal in *Llaimond Properties Ltd v. Al-Shakarchi* [1998] E.G.C.S. 21. The tenant was a monthly protected tenant of a London flat. The landlord served a notice to quit and sought possession on the basis of the availability of suitable alternative accommodation offering either (a) a Rent Act protected tenancy or (b) a Housing Act 1988 assured tenancy of a flat elsewhere which the landlord company held on a 20-year lease. The Court held that Housing Act 1988, s.34(1)(b) (which, as we have seen above, preserves Rent Act protection where the landlord grants a new tenancy to a person who was his protected or statutory tenant immediately before the grant of the new tenancy) does not apply in the context of an action for possession on the basis of suitable alternative accommodation. In such a case that provision is displaced by s.34(1)(c) whereby Rent Act protection is preserved only if the court is satisfied that the grant of an assured tenancy will not provide the required security. In the present case the Court refused to upset the judge's finding that an assured tenancy, provided it was not an assured shorthold tenancy, would provide the required security.

Statutory definition

Having dealt with the circumstances in which a protected tenancy may still be created even after January 14, 1989, we can now turn to the statutory definition of a protected tenancy—

"Subject to this Part of this Act a tenancy under which a dwelling-house (which may be a house or part of a house) is let as a separate dwelling is a protected tenancy for the purposes of this Act. (RA 1977, s.1)."

"Tenancy" includes a sub-tenancy (s.152(1)).

Thus if a tenancy comes within the terms of this provision then, subject to the exceptions examined below, it will be a protected tenancy and the tenant will enjoy the security of tenure afforded to him by the Act. Furthermore it will be a regulated tenancy for the purposes of rent regulation (see below).

Although the Rent Acts have never expressly prohibited a landlord and tenant from contracting out of the Act, the courts have long since held that this is not permitted (*Barton v. Fincham* [1921] 2 K.B. 291; *cf. A.G.Securities v. Vaughan* [1988] 3 W.L.R. 1205, HL).

In the past some landlords have sought to evade the Rent Act controls by dressing up a tenancy as a sale agreement whereby the "purchaser" agrees to buy the property over a period of time paying the "purchase price" in instalments by way of periodical payments. In cases where the agreement is clearly not genuine the courts have ignored the label placed upon the arrangement and given effect to the true substance of the agreement, which will often be a tenancy (see *Martin v. Davies* (1952) 159 E.G. 191). But quite apart from this it has been provided that a court order for possession is needed in the case of property held on the terms of a "rental purchase agreement" and the court is given power in possession proceedings to adjourn those proceedings, stay execution or postpone the date of possession and impose such conditions as it thinks fit (Housing Act 1980, s.88 extending the Protection From Eviction Act 1977 to such cases).

It should be noted that the inclusion of the opening seven words of section 1 makes it clear that even if a tenancy satisfies the necessary conditions, it will not be a protected tenancy if it falls within any of the exceptions set out elsewhere in Part I.

We have already seen in Chapter 9, above that the salient features of section 1, namely—

- a tenancy
- of a dwelling-house
- let as a separate dwelling

have been much litigated, and reference should be made to that chapter for a discussion of each of these terms. In addition the following features of the definition should be noted.

Effect of sharing

As in the case of assured tenancies under the Housing Act 1988 (see p.210 above), special rules apply where the occupier has exclusive use of some accommodation but the terms of his agreement provide for a sharing of other accommodation with another or others. Case law on the early Rent Acts established that if the right to share by the other (a) approached equal occupation rather than some limited user; and (b) related to "living accommodation", which included sitting rooms and kitchens but not bathrooms (*Cole v. Harris* [1945] K.B. 474, CA) the occupier would not have a protected tenancy (see *Neale v. Del Soto* [1945] K.B. 144, CA; *Goodrich v. Paisner* [1957] A.C. 65, HL and *Marsh v. Cooper* [1969] 1 W.L.R. 803, CA).

Any sharing arrangements which did not satisfy requirements (a) and (b) above did not prevent the tenant being fully protected. To deal with those cases where the degree of sharing was sufficient to prevent a protected tenancy arising, statute law subsequently provided that where the sharing was with a person or persons other than the landlord, the tenant would nevertheless be deemed to have a protected tenancy of the accommodation of which he has exclusive possession. The relevant provision is now Rent Act 1977, s.22 which also gives the tenant rights with regard to his use of the "shared accommodation". The time to test the issue of sharing under these provisions is the time of any relevant proceedings (*Tovey v. Tyack* [1955] 1 Q.B. 57, CA).

Where the shared user, which prevented the tenancy from being a protected tenancy, was with the landlord, statute provided that the tenant would instead have what is now known as a restricted contract (a less secure form of protection). The relevant provision, Rent Act 1977, s.21 was later repealed by the Housing Act 1988 save for tenancies created before January 15, 1989. In any event it had already been rendered redundant in most cases by the "resident landlord exception" (see below) introduced by the Rent Act 1974. That exception, which is now contained in the Rent Act 1977, s. 12 provides that where the landlord occupies another dwelling-house in the same building as the tenant then, even in the absence of sharing, the tenancy will not be a protected tenancy. Section 20 provided that the tenancy (which will necessarily have been created before January 15, 1989) would take effect instead as a restricted contract.

It has been held, for the purposes of section 21, that it does not matter that the "person" with whom the occupier shares is a corporate body.

> *In Mortgage Corporation v. Ubah* (1996) 73 P.& C.R. 500 a tenancy was precluded from being a protected tenancy, and took effect instead as a restricted contract, because the kitchen had been shared with the landlord. The court rejected the occupier's argument that when the landlord's mortgagee acquired the (formerly resident) landlord's interest a protected tenancy arose, on the basis that the mortgage company was incapable of using a kitchen.

Exclusions

Despite the fact that a tenancy might fall within section 1 of the Rent Act 1977 and therefore prima facie take effect as a protected tenancy, the tenancy can nevertheless still fall within one of the following exceptions to protection provided for by the Act.

1. Dwelling-house above certain rateable values

The purpose of this exclusion is to ensure that higher value properties are outside the protection of the Rent Act 1977, on the assumption that tenants who can afford such accommodation are not in need of statutory protection. The provisions are complex because of the domestic rating system which was abolished in April 1990. Before that date every domestic property had a "rateable value" attributed to it by the district valuer for the purpose of assessing liability for local taxes (rates). That rateable value was assessed by reference to the letting value of the property. Thus a relatively more expensive property would have a higher rateable value than a less expensive property. The Rent Act 1977 accordingly excludes very expensive property from protection by the present exception to protection. As noted above, the domestic rating system was abolished from April 1990, although the current system still attributes a value to all properties, each of which is placed in one of a number of value "bands" for the purpose of local taxation.

(a) Tenancies entered into before April 1, 1990 (or in pursuance of a contract made before that date)

For these tenancies the test is the rateable value on "the appropriate day" (*i.e.* the day when the rateable value of the property was first entered in the valuation list—unless that date was before March 23, 1965 in which case March 23, 1965 is the appropriate date).

The tenancy will be excluded if the rateable value on the appropriate day exceeds the limits set out below. The higher value applies to properties in Greater London and the lower value to properties elsewhere. The limits are:

(1) where the appropriate day is on or after April 1, 1973, £1,500 or £750;
(2) where the appropriate day is on or after March 22, 1973 but before April 1, 1973, £600 (£300) on the appropriate day *and* £1,500 (£750) on April 1, 1973;
(3) where the appropriate day is before March 22, 1973 £400 (£200) on the appropriate day **and** £600 (£300) on March 22, 1973 **and** £1,500 (£750) on April 1, 1973.

The complexity arises because of the nationwide general revaluation of properties on the valuation list which occurred on April 1, 1973.

(b) Tenancies entered into on or after April 1, 1990

In the case of such tenancies the high rateable value test has been replaced by a test based on the rent payable for the time being. If it is payable at a rate exceeding £25,000 per year the tenancy will not be protected. (In practice this exception will rarely be needed because only in rare cases will a tenancy created on or after January 15, 1989 be capable of being a protected tenancy: see Housing Act 1988, s.34 and p.249 above).

2. Tenancies at a low rent

(a) Tenancies entered into before April 1, 1990 (or in pursuance of a contract made before that date)

Such a tenancy is not a protected tenancy if either (a) there is no rent payable under the tenancy or (b) the annual rent payable under the tenancy is less than two-thirds of the rateable value on the appropriate day (Rent Act 1977, s.5: see ss.152(1) and 25(3) for the appropriate day).

(b) Tenancies entered into on or after April 1, 1990

A tenancy is prevented from being a protected tenancy if—

(1) it is entered into on or after April 1, 1990 (unless in pursuance of a contract made before that date); and

(2) under the tenancy for the time being either no rent is payable or the rent is payable at a rate of, if the dwelling- house is in Greater London, £1,000 or less a year, and if the dwelling-house is elsewhere, £250 or less a year (Rent Act 1977, s.5(2A) added by S.I. 1990 No. 434, reg. 2, Sched., para. 18).

This method of determining whether a tenancy is governed by the low rent exception was introduced in order to deal with the abolition of domestic rates from April 1, 1990, although once again it should be remembered that, save in a few exceptional instances, most tenancies created on or after January 15, 1989 will be governed by the Housing Act 1988 rather than the Rent Act 1977.

The following points should be noted about the low rent exception—

(1) The rent payable is to be determined at the time the matter arises. Consequently a tenancy may move in or out of protection if the rent goes up or down (see *Stone (J&F.) Lighting and Radio v. Levitt* [1947] A.C. 209, HL). However, because section 5 does not in terms apply to a statutory tenancy, it has been suggested that if a rent officer or rent assessment committee fixes a rent which reduces the rent payable under a statutory tenancy below the limit specified in section 5 (*e.g.* because the premises are unfit for habitation) the tenancy will remain protected ([1980] Conv. 389). (See also [1981] Conv. 325–6 where it is further suggested that even if the recoverable rent of a protected tenancy is reduced by registration, section 5 will not render the tenancy unprotected because the reference to rent payable is arguably confined to the contractual rent).

(2) "Rent" is not defined in the Act (*cf.* ss.71 and 85) but has been held to mean the total monetary payment to be paid by the tenant to the landlord as rent (*Sidney Trading Co. v. Finsbury Corporation* [1952] 1 All E.R. 460, 461, DC *per* Lord Goddard C.J.). Services rendered to the landlord by the tenant, for example as caretaker, can only count as rent for the purposes of the Rent Act if they are treated as being representative of an agreed monetary quantification (*Montague v. Browning* [1954] 1 W.L.R. 1039, CA; *Barnes v. Barratt* [1970] 2 Q.B. 657, CA). A genuine premium is not rent, but the courts will be astute to find a sham where what is in reality rent is described as a premium (*Samrose Properties v. Gibbard* [1958] 1 W.L.R. 235, CA). Premiums are not usually payable except for long leases.

(3) If a tenancy has been granted for a term in excess of 21 years which cannot be determined before the end of that period by the tenant giving notice then for the purposes of determining whether the tenancy is excluded by section 5, "rent" does not include such parts of any sums payable by the tenant expressed to be payable in respect of rates, services, repairs, maintenance or insurance (Rent Act 1977, s.5(4), (5). This is to prevent a long tenancy at a ground rent being brought into protection by a service charge of an amount which would otherwise be above the limits of the low rent exception.

(4) The fact that a tenancy at a low rent is excluded from protection does not prevent a sub-tenancy of the same dwelling-house from being a protected tenancy.

3. Shared ownership leases

(For details of the different ways in which such leases may arise see Alder and Handy, *Housing Association Law* (3rd ed., 1997).

This term refers to schemes whereby a tenant takes a long lease (usually for 125 years) under which he pays an initial premium representing a proportion of the market value of the dwelling-house. The premium will usually be raised by a mortgage loan which will be paid back with interest in the usual way. The tenant also pays a rent for the dwelling-house but with a deduction to take account of the premium. If the premises are a flat, the tenant will usually be required to pay a service charge, which may be variable. The essence of the scheme is that at any time the tenant will be able to purchase further "slices" of the equity at the prevailing valuation. As the tenant buys successive slices of the equity there will be a corresponding reduction in the amount of rent payable under the lease. When the tenant has acquired a 100 per cent share in the equity he will, in the case of a house, be able to buy the freehold for a nominal amount.

It is unlikely that it was ever envisaged that shared ownership leases would be within the ambit of the rent regulation provisions of the Rent Act 1977. Nonetheless, it became clear that at least in the early stages, such a lease could prima facie take effect as a protected tenancy because the rent was high enough not to be caught by the low-rent exception in section 5 of the Rent Act 1977. The position is now governed by an amendment to the Rent Act. The Housing and Planning Act 1986 amended the Rent Act so as to provide that a tenancy is not a protected tenancy if it is a qualifying shared ownership lease (Housing and Planning Act 1986, Sched. 4, para. 1). This exclusion only applies to qualifying leases granted after December 10, 1987 (*ibid.*, para. 11(1)). Such a lease granted before that date may still be a protected tenancy.

In practice the new exclusion is, on the face of it, of little significance as far as protected tenancies are concerned because virtually all shared ownership leases are granted by housing associations or a public authority and therefore could not take effect as protected tenancies for that reason (Rent Act 1977, s.15.) They can, however, take effect as a "housing association tenancy" under Part VI of the Rent Act 1977 for the purpose of rent regulation (see Rent Act 1977, s.89 below and p. 299), although this will no longer be possible in the case of a "qualifying shared ownership lease" granted after December 10, 1987 (Rent Act 1977, s.86). It must be remembered that in any event, save in a few exceptional instances, it is not possible to grant a new "housing association tenancy" on or after January 15, 1989 (Housing Act 1988, s.35).

4. Dwelling-house let with other land

A tenancy is not a protected tenancy if the dwelling-house which is the subject of the tenancy is let together with land other than the site of the dwelling-house (Rent Act 1977, s.6). This exclusion has to be read along with section 26 which provides that any land or premises let together with a dwelling-house shall, unless it consists of agricultural land exceeding two acres in extent, be treated as part of the dwelling-house. The courts have reconciled these apparently inconsistent provisions by applying a "dominant purpose" test. That is, if the dwelling-house is let as an adjunct to something else (*e.g.* a campsite), then section 6 applies and there is no protected tenancy. On the other hand, if the other "land" (including buildings, such as a garden or a garage), is let as an adjunct to the dwelling-house, then section 26 applies and the tenancy can be protected (*Feyereisel v. Turnidge* [1952] 2 Q.B. 29, CA and *Bradshaw v. Smith* [1980] E.G.D. 394, CA *Cf. Pender v. Reid* (1948) S.C. 381).

5. Payments for board and attendance

It is provided that a tenancy is not a protected tenancy if under the tenancy (*i.e.* when granted) the dwelling-house is bona fide let at a rent which includes payments in respect of board or attendance (Rent Act 1977, s.7(1)). There is a statutory requirement that in the case of attendance, the amount of rent which is fairly attributable to the attendance, having regard to the value of that attendance to the tenant, must form a substantial part of the whole rent if the tenancy is to be excluded from protection by this provision (*ibid*. s.7(2).) This need for the payments to be substantial does not apply to payments in respect of board. "Board" means a daily meal or meals prepared and served by or on behalf of the landlord. The need for the meal to be served by or on behalf of the landlord prevents tenancies falling outside protection where the landlord simply provides the tenants with the ingredients or a meal voucher (*Gavin v. Lindsay* 1987 S.L.T. 12, Sh Ct). Subject to a *de minimis* test, partial board will suffice. Thus a "continental breakfast" of bread rolls, butter, jam and marmalade and tea or coffee is sufficient (*Otter v. Norman* [1989] A.C. 129, HL; *Holiday Flat Co. v. Kuczera* 1978 S.L.T. 47, Sh Ct). The dividing line seems to be between an "early morning cup of tea" on the one hand and "bed and breakfast" on the other (*Otter v. Norman*, above, at 326, *per* Lord Bridge).

"Attendance" means the provision of services which are personal to the tenant, and performed by an attendant provided by the landlord (*Palser v. Grinling* [1948] A.C. 291, 310, HL). Examples are cleaning of the dwelling-house, the removal of dirty linen and the supply of fresh linen (*Marchant v. Charters* [1977] 1 W.L.R. 1181, CA and *Nelson Developments Ltd v. Taboada* (1992) 24 H.L.R. 462). Services in relation to the common parts of a building (*e.g.* cleaning of common hall and stairs) are not sufficient (*Palser v. Grinling* [1948] A.C. 291, 318, HL; *cf. King v. Millen* [1922] 2 K.B. 647, DC). The meaning of "substantial" is dealt with below. (See p.258)

The effect of the tenancy being excluded from protection because of board or substantial attendance might be that it will take effect instead as a restricted contract (p.303 below). However, substantial payments for board would also rule out even this weaker form of protection (*ibid*). Furthermore it may well be that the nature and degree of any attendance would mean that the occupier does not have exclusive possession and would therefore be a licensee only (see p.11 above).

6. Lettings to students

A tenancy is not a protected tenancy if it is granted to a person who is pursuing, or intends to pursue, a course of study provided by a specified educational institution and is so granted by that institution or by another specified institution or body of persons (Rent Act 1977, s.8(1)). This exception was first introduced by the Rent Act 1974. The specified bodies are as designated by statutory instrument and include universities and other publicly funded institutions of further and higher education (s.8(2)) and the Assured and Protected Tenancies (Lettings to Students) Regulations 1998 (S.I. 1998 No.1967). These regulations are consolidating regulations and specify the relevant bodies for the purposes of section 8 of the Rent Act 1977 and the equivalent exclusion in the Housing Act 1988, Sched. 1, para. 8 (p.218 above)). Thus lettings to students by the specified bodies are outside rent controls and do not attract the security of tenure afforded to protected and statutory tenants.

In practice because virtually all existing student tenancies will have been granted on or after January 15, 1989 they cannot be protected tenancies in any event and will be governed by the parallel provisions in the Housing Act 1988 which exclude such lettings from being assured tenancies (see p.218 above).

7. Holiday lettings

A tenancy is not a protected tenancy if the purpose of the tenancy is to confer on the tenant the right to occupy the dwelling-house for a holiday (Rent Act 1977, s.9). This exception was also first introduced by the Rent Act 1974. It is identical to the assured tenancy exclusion in Housing Act 1988, Sched. 1, para. 8 (see p.218 above). Once again in practice it is now virtually a dead letter for it is difficult to imagine that there are at present any holiday lettings which were created before January 15, 1989!

8. Agricultural holdings

A tenancy is not a protected tenancy if the dwelling-house is comprised in an agricultural holding (within the meaning of the Agricultural Holdings Act 1986 (formerly 1948)) or farm business tenancy (within section 1 Agricultural Tenancies Act 1995) and is occupied by the person responsible for the control of the farming of the holding (Rent Act 1977, s. 10). It is identical to the assured tenancy exclusion in Housing Act 1988, Sched. 1, para. 7 (p.218 above).

9. Licensed premises

A tenancy of a dwelling-house which consists of or comprises premises licensed for the sale of intoxicating liquors for consumption on the premises is not a protected tenancy (Rent Act 1977, s.11). Thus tenancies of public houses are excluded. There is a parallel assured tenancy exclusion in Housing Act 1988 Sched. 1, para. 5 (p.217 above). Such tenancies are likely to be business tenancies within Part II of the Landlord and Tenant Act 1954 (see the Landlord and Tenant (Licensed Premises) Act 1990).

10. Resident landlords

This exception was introduced by the Rent Act 1974 and, as subsequently amended, is now contained in section 12 of the Rent Act 1977. It prevents a tenancy from being a protected tenancy (a) where the landlord lives in the same building, not being a purpose block of flats, as the tenant and (b) in the case of a purpose-built block of flats, where the dwelling-house is part of a flat in that block and the landlord occupies as his residence another dwelling-house in that flat. Its purpose is clearly to exclude from protection lettings where the landlord and tenant live in close proximity in the same building (*e.g.* a converted house). If created before January 15, 1989 such tenancies will take effect instead as restricted contracts (Rent Act 1977, s.20 : see p.303 below). The relevant provisions are very similar to but not identical with the assured tenancy exclusion in Housing Act 1988, Sched. 1, para. 10 (see p.219 above) which was modelled on the Rent Act exclusion.

The relevant differences are as follows.

(a) The tenancy must have been granted on or after August 14, 1974
The Rent Act 1974 extended full protection to furnished lettings whether created before August 14, 1974 or on or after that date. At the same time, the present resident landlord exception was introduced, but only in respect of tenancies created on or after August 14, 1974.

It was not extended to unfurnished tenancies granted before the operative date because this would have deprived existing protected tenants of full protection. No such objection could be made to excluding from full protection resident landlord furnished lettings granted before that date because they were already without full protection by virtue of being furnished. Consequently such tenancies remained excluded from full protection. (Rent Act 1977, Sched. 24, para. 6.) For this purpose a tenancy is a furnished letting if:

(1)   the premises are bona fide let at a rent which includes any payments in respect of furniture; and

(2)   the amount of rent fairly attributable to the use of furniture, having regard to the use value of that furniture to the tenant, forms a substantial part of the whole rent (Rent Act 1977, s.7 as originally enacted). The pre-1974 Act case law established that "substantial" is here used in the sense of "considerable, solid, or big." (*Palser v. Grinling* [1948] A.C. 291, 316, HL). The test is to be applied to the circumstances as at the time of the grant of the tenancy (*Bowness v. O'Dwyer* [1948] 2 K.B. 219, CA; *Jozwiak v. Hierowski* [1948] 2 All E.R. 9, CA).

The case law indicates that a broad common sense approach should be taken, rather than any set formula. In practice the normal approach is to take the capital cost of providing the actual furniture at the time of creation of the tenancy, and then take a percentage of that value as representing the amount of rent fairly attributable to the use of the furniture to the tenant allowing for such matters as depreciation and interest on capital. This figure can then be compared with the whole rent to see whether it represents a substantial part of that rent (*Woodward v. Docherty* [1974] 1 W.L.R. 966, CA; *Christophides v. Cuming* (1976) 239 E.G. 275, CA). It will be appreciated that since by definition we are here dealing with pre-August 14, 1974 tenancies, there may be evidential difficulties in coming to a decision. It is difficult to say what will be regarded as "substantial" for the present purposes. Whilst 20 per cent or more is likely to be regarded as substantial, it is not obvious where the line should be drawn. Indications are that it is around 15 per cent, but much will depend on the facts of the particular case.

(b) The landlord (and any successor(s)) must have occupied a dwelling-house in the same building (or flat) as his residence

(In the case of the assured tenancy exception the requirement is that the landlord occupy the relevant dwelling-house as his only or principal home). In the case of joint landlords, residence by at least one will be sufficient (*Cooper v. Tait* (1984) 48 P.& C.R. 460, CA).

This raises the issue of whether in a particular case the landlord can be said to have been "occupying a dwelling-house as a residence".

1. Dwelling-house The question of what is a dwelling-house was dealt with in *Palmer v. McNamara* (1991) 23 H.L.R. 168. Part of a house was let to a tenant and the landlord lived in a room elsewhere in the house. The landlord lived in the room, but by choice did not cook there. A question arose as to whether this prevented him arguing that he occupied a dwelling-house in the same building as the tenant. It had been urged upon the court that the cases on the meaning of "dwelling-house" for the purposes of section 1 (above) suggested that the room would need to have facilities for cooking, sleeping and eating to be a dwelling house for the purposes of section 12. The court held that this was not necessarily so. Dillon L.J. said: "It seems to me quite clear that in considering whether a room or series of rooms is a dwelling-house one has to look not only at the physical surroundings, but at the purpose. (p.171)"

In the present case the landlord chose to eat cold meals or bring in take-away meals. It could not be said that this meant that his room was not a dwelling-house for the purposes of section 12. The cases on section 1 were not necessarily conclusive on the issue in the present context.

2. Occupied as a residence By contrast it is expressly provided that for the purposes of section 12 a person shall be treated as occupying a dwelling-house as his residence if, so far as the nature of the case allows, he fulfils the same conditions as by virtue of section 2(3) are required to be fulfilled by a statutory tenant of a dwelling-house. The effect of this provision is to incorporate all the Rent Act case law on the meaning of "occupying . . . as a residence for the purposes of section 2" (see p.263 below). The significance of these cases in the context of section 12 is that a landlord can qualify as a resident landlord even though the dwelling-house which he occupies is not his only home.

Similarly an absent landlord would arguably still qualify provided he has the intention to return which is manifested in some way, *e.g.* by the presence of furniture or a representative occupier in his absence. Such a claim failed in *Jackson v. Pekic* (1990) 22 H.L.R. 9. The landlord granted the tenant a tenancy of a bed-sitting room in a house other parts of which were let to other tenants. The landlord was not in actual occupation at that time and only moved in to one of those other rooms in 1997, following the departure of the tenant of that room. The argument that during that four-year absence the presence of furniture or the occupier in the room amounted to proxy residence by the landlord was rejected by the Court of Appeal. The landlord had not left any personal effects of furniture of her own indicating that during her absence she was treating the room as her home. "There is no principle of law which says that the mere presence of furniture, consistent with an ordinary furnished letting at market rent, could serve for that purpose" (*per* Gibson L.J. p.19).

Thus it becomes a question of fact and degree, in the circumstances, as to whether the landlord is occupying the dwelling-house in question as a residence.

It should be noted that the decisions in some of the reported cases on the nature and degree of residence required of a statutory tenant are rather generous towards the tenant, presumably because of the underlying Rent Act policy of protecting tenants. By way of contrast it can be argued that the application of the section 2(3) test should be modified in the context of the resident landlord, in view of the different "mischief" which that exception is aimed at; that is preventing security arising where the landlord, or his representative, is living in close proximity to the tenant. In other words the courts should be reluctant to find a landlord to be a resident landlord in the more marginal cases of residence. Thus whilst a landlord should not be prevented from qualifying as a resident landlord merely because he does not permanently reside on the premises (such as where he works away and only comes home from time to time), the courts should be suspicious where the landlord does not reside in the same building as the tenant in any real sense of the term. The difficulties of applying the section 2(3) test in the context of section 12 are illustrated by *Palmer v. McNamara* (above) where the landlord, who suffered from a physical disability and needed help in dressing and undressing, slept every night at the house of a friend who lived a mile or so away. He spent the daytime hours at the room in his house where all his possessions were. The Court held that on the facts he still occupied the room as his residence.

This decision in *Palmer v. McNamara* can be contrasted with that in *Cliffe v. Standard* (1982) 132 N.L.J. 186, where a landlord retained a furnished room in a house which contained a number of flats, but slept in another house where his wife and children also lived. It was held that he was not a resident landlord of the former property.

This does not mean, however, as noted above, that a landlord cannot be a two-home landlord. Thus in *Wolff v. Waddington* (1989) 22 H.L.R. 72, the Court of Appeal refused to upset the trial judge's decision that a landlord was resident. The original landlord became ill and died. Shortly before her death her daughter went to live with her. The daughter inherited the property on her mother's death and remained there for 13 months before attempting to sell up. Despite her principal home being in the USA where she intended to return, she was held to be a resident landlord.

(c) Tenancies granted by a resident landlord to existing tenants

The resident landlord exception will not apply where immediately before the tenancy was granted the person to whom it is granted was a protected or statutory tenant of the same, or another, dwelling-house in the same building (RA 1977, s.12(2)). This will safeguard the position of a protected or statutory tenant who has entered into a new tenancy with a landlord who moved into the building after the original tenancy was granted and then created a new tenancy in favour of the tenant.

(d) Continuous residence by landlord

The landlord (or his successor(s)) must at all times have occupied as his (their) residence another dwelling-house in the same building (or flat where the dwelling house is a flat in a purpose-built block).

Complex provisions, which are replicated with some modification (*e.g.* to provide for the case of joint landlords) by the parallel assured tenancy exception in the Housing Act 1988 (see Sched. 1, Part III, paras 17–21 of the 1988 Act), apply for the purpose of determining the application of the present exception, where there are periods during which there is no occupation by the landlord or a successor (RA 1977 Sched. 2, para. 1). This may occur either because of the death of the landlord or because the landlord has otherwise disposed of his interest.

(i) Death of the resident landlord

Periods of deemed residence. If on the death of a resident landlord on or after November 28, 1980, his interest becomes vested in personal representatives acting as such, then for any period not exceeding two years for which they so hold the landlord's interest, the "continuous residence requirement" of section 12(1)(c) is deemed to be satisfied.

Thus the personal representatives will have all the rights of a resident landlord during that period. It follows that if the tenancy is periodic, the personal representatives may determine the tenancy within the period of deemed residence by service of a notice to quit. They may then recover possession whether before or after that period has ended. The position otherwise is that if the new landlord does not take up residence by the end of the period the tenancy will become a protected tenancy.

Periods of disregard. In contrast to the cases of deemed residence examined above, it is provided that where a deceased resident landlord's interest becomes vested in the Public Trustee (*i.e.* pending the appointment of administrators where the deceased died intestate) or "trustees as such" (*e.g.* where the personal representatives have vested the landlord's interest in trustees of a trust created by the landlord's will), any period not exceeding two years during which that interest remains so vested shall be "disregarded" for the purposes of the requirement of continuous residence. If by the end of a period of disregard a new resident landlord has not moved in, the tenant becomes fully protected. The significance of a period of disregard is that if the tenancy comes to an end during such a period (*e.g.* by expiry or notice to quit), then, in the absence of any Rent Act ground(s) for possession, the (non-resident) holder of the landlord's interest will be able to obtain possession but not until the end of the period of disregard (RA 1977, Sched. 2, para. 3; and *Landau v. Sloane* [1982] A.C. 490).

We saw above that if the landlord's interest is at any time held on trust and a beneficiary occupies another dwelling-house in the same building as the tenant, the continuous residence requirement is deemed to be satisfied (RA 1977, Sched. 2, para. 2). Thus if a trust of the landlord's interest arises under the landlord's will or intestacy and there is an occupying beneficiary under that trust, he will have all the rights of a resident landlord, including the right to terminate the tenancy and thereafter to recover possession. In these circumstances therefore there is no period of disregard, despite the landlord's interest being vested in trustees as such.

(ii) Inter vivos transfer by a resident landlord Where the landlord transfers his interest under the tenancy during his lifetime there is a 28-day "period of disregard" which, by written notice to the tenant within that period, can be extended to not more than six months. Thus if the contractual tenancy has not ended by the end of that period, the tenant is fully protected if the new landlord has not moved in (RA 1977, Sched. 2, para. 1).

11. Landlord's interest held by the Crown

A tenancy cannot be a protected or statutory tenancy at any time when the landlord's interest is held by the Crown or is held by or on trust for a government department. This exclusion does not extend to tenants of the Duchies of Lancaster or Cornwall or the Crown Estates Commissioners (RA 1977, s.13).

12. Landlord's interest belonging to a local authority or certain other public bodies

A tenancy cannot be a protected or statutory tenancy at any time when the landlord's interest is held by a local authority or any of certain other public bodies including the Commission for the New Towns, a New Town Development Corporation and the Development Board for Rural Wales (RA 1977, s.14).

It will be noted that in the case of each of the last two exclusions, a protected or statutory tenancy will cease to be protected by the Rent Act 1977 if the landlord's interest is subsequently acquired by the Crown or a local authority or one of the other specified public bodies.

13. Landlord's interest belonging to a housing association

It is provided that a tenancy shall not be a protected or statutory tenancy at any time when the interest of the landlord under that tenancy belongs to a registered housing association, or a co-operative housing association. Nor can there be a protected or statutory tenancy at any time when the landlord's interest is held by the Housing Corporation or a charitable housing trust. (RA 1977, s.15). If the landlord's interest is held by any of the above bodies and is transferred to a private landlord on or after January 15, 1989 the tenancy cannot become a protected tenancy, despite having been created before that date (Housing Act 1988, s.38(2)(3)). It is important to remember that a special housing association fair rent scheme, contained in Part VI of the Rent

Act 1977, applies to all tenancies (other than co-ownership tenancies) that are outside full Rent Act protection solely because of the operation of sections 15 and 16 of the Rent Act 1977. This is dealt with below (p.299). A co-ownership tenancy is a tenancy granted by a co-operative housing association and under which the tenant is entitled to a capital sum on giving up the tenancy.

Tenancies granted on or after January 15, 1989 where the landlord is a housing association will usually be assured tenancies (p.200 above).

14. Landlord's interest belonging to a housing co-operative

A tenancy cannot be a protected tenancy at any time when the landlord's interest belongs to a housing co-operative within the meaning of section 27B of the Housing Act 1985 (RA 1977, s.16).

15. Premises with a business use

As in the case of assured tenancies, a tenancy to which Part II of the Landlord and Tenant Act 1954 applies (business tenancies) cannot be a regulated tenancy (Rent Act 1977, s. 24) (for business tenancies see Chapter 13 below).

B. THE STATUTORY TENANCY

When will a statutory tenancy arise and what are its terms?

When a protected tenancy ends, for example where a fixed term expires or a periodic tenancy is ended by a notice to quit, the tenant, if and so long as he occupies the dwelling-house as a residence, is entitled to remain as a "statutory tenant". This requirement can be satisfied in the case of a joint tenancy even though all the joint tenants are not in residence at the end of the tenancy. The tenant(s) in residence at that time will become the statutory tenant(s) (*Lloyd v. Sadler* [1978] Q.B. 774, CA). The dwelling-house is then said to be subject to a statutory tenancy, and the tenant will hold on the same terms as the original contract of tenancy in so far as they do not conflict with the requirements of the Act (Rent Act 1977, s.3(1)). If the landlord simply continues to accept rent from a statutory tenant this will not give rise to a new contractual tenancy.

It is an implied term of a statutory tenancy that the tenant shall afford to the landlord access to the dwelling-house and all reasonable facilities for executing therein any repairs which the landlord is entitled to execute (Rent Act 1977, s.3(2)). If notice to quit was required under the contractual tenancy then the tenant must give the same notice in respect of the statutory tenancy if terminating it by notice to the landlord. If no period of notice was required under the protected tenancy (*e.g.* because it was for a fixed term) then a notice of not less than three months is required (s.3(3)). A notice to quit by the tenant must be in writing and comply with section 5 of the Protection From Eviction Act 1977 (see p.129 above). The statutory tenancy cannot be ended by the landlord other than by obtaining a court order on one of the grounds set out in Schedule 15 to the Rent Act 1977.

Nature of the statutory tenancy

The requirements of the statutory tenancy will now be examined in more detail. Before doing so we can note that the statutory tenancy is not a tenancy in the sense of being a legal or equitable interest but is a statutory right which affords the tenant a "status of irremovability" (*Jessamine Investment Co Ltd v. Schwarz* [1978] Q.B. 264, 267, *per* Stephenson L.J.). Furthermore it cannot be assigned by the tenant (*Keeves v. Dean* [1924] 1 K.B. 685) because it is not an estate or interest in the land. If the tenant ceases to occupy the dwelling-house as a residence the statutory tenancy will cease (see above). Just as a statutory tenancy cannot be assigned nor in principle can there be a sub-letting. Indeed as in the case of an assignment any purported sub-letting of the whole dwelling-house will also be a nullity and mean that the tenancy will cease to be a statutory tenancy because the tenant will no longer be in residence, thereby enabling the landlord to recover possession. However, it has been held that despite the fact that a statutory tenant has no estate or interest in land, a sub-letting of part will be permitted if this is not prohibited by the terms of the immediately proceeding (contractual) protected tenancy (*Roe v. Russell* [1928] 2 K.B. 117). Presumably any such sub-letting on or after January 15, 1989 will be an assured tenancy (or if on or after February 28, 1997, an assured shorthold tenancy). (See S. Bridge, *Residential Leases* (1994), p.130).

Transmission of a statutory tenancy

Despite the restrictions on assignment discussed above, the Rent Act makes provision for "transmission" of the statutory tenancy in two instances. The second is on death and is dealt with below. The first is a transmission *inter vivos* (s.3(5) and Sched. 1, Part II). In order to be effective the landlord must be made a party to the transfer which must be in writing. The effect of any such transmission is that the incoming tenant is treated as stepping into the shoes of the outgoing tenant (Sched. 1, para. 13). It is an offence for the outgoing tenant to ask for or receive any sum or any other consideration by a person other than the landlord as a condition of giving up possession of the dwelling-house (Sched. 1, para. 12).

There is also a statutory power for the court to transfer a statutory tenancy to a former partner of the tenant under the Family Law Act 1996, Part IV.

Occupation as a residence

We saw above that a statutory tenancy will only exist if and so long as the statutory tenant occupies the dwelling-house as a residence. This is to be determined by reference to the case law which has built up over the years since the Act of 1920.

(a) Company lets

The requirement of residence means that whilst a company or other institution can be a protected tenant (and hence seek registration of a fair rent), it cannot become a statutory tenant when the contractual tenancy comes to an end. This gave rise to schemes whereby the landlord granted a lease of a dwelling-house to a company nominated by the intended occupier in order to forestall any statutory tenancy arising on determination of the protected tenancy. Of course this would not prevent the company from seeking a registered rent whilst the protected tenancy exists. Company tenancy schemes usually operate by the landlord requiring the occupier to purchase an "off the shelf company" with which the landlord enters into an agreement to occupy. The agreement gives the company, of which the intended occupier is appointed managing director, the right to nominate the occupier of the property. That person then nominates himself. The Court of Appeal has held in a number of cases that if there were no common intention by the landlord and tenant to dress up a private tenancy as a company let to avoid the relevant Rent Act provisions, then if the facts are consistent with the purported transaction, the arrangement should not be overridden on grounds of public policy. Thus the occupier will not be entitled to a statutory tenancy when the protected tenancy comes to an ends. (See *Hilton v. Plustitle Ltd* (1988) 21 H.L.R. 72; *Firstcross Ltd v. East West Ltd* (1980) 7 H.L.R. 298; *Estavest Investments Ltd v. Commercial Investments Ltd* (1987) 21 H.L.R 106, CA; *Kaye v. Massbetter Ltd & Kanter* (1990) 24 H.L.R. 28). This strict application of the traditional sham doctrine in *Snook v. London and West Riding Investments Ltd* [1967] 2 Q.B. 786 contrasts sharply with the more critical approach adopted by the House of Lords towards "licences" designed to avoid Rent Act protection. (See *Street v. Mountford* [1985] A.C. 809 and *A-G Securities Ltd v. Vaughan*; *Autoniades v. Villiers* [1990] 1 A.C. 417 H.L. See p.6 above).

(b) Constructive residence

A tenant is clearly not expected physically to occupy the property at all times in order to preserve his status as the statutory tenant. Thus ordinary periods of absence (such as for holidays or as a hospital in-patient) will not terminate that status. But what of longer periods, whether voluntary or involuntary (such as during a prison sentence)? The courts have taken a liberal view of what amounts to residence for the purposes of a statutory tenancy. Thus it has been held that if absence is sufficiently prolonged or non-intermittent to give rise to the prima facie inference of a cessation of possession or occupation this will merely shift the onus on to the tenant to rebut the presumption that his possession has ceased. Whether the tenant's absence is sufficient to raise the initial presumption is one of fact and degree. In order to rebut the presumption the tenant will need to establish (a) a *de facto* intention on his part to return, coupled with (b) some manifestation of that intention on the premises; *i.e.* some visible and genuine symbol such as a representative occupier or furniture.

> In *Brown v. Brash* [1948] 2 K.B. 247 the tenant was sent to prison for two years. Whilst he was there his partner left the house and took their two children and much of the furniture with her. The Court of Appeal applying the above test held that, notwithstanding the tenant's intention to return, there ceased to be any manifestation of that intention once his partner and children left with most of the furniture. Thus at that point he forfeited his status as a statutory tenant. (See also *Skinner v. Geary* [1931] 2 K.B. 546 where the tenant who went to live elsewhere with no intention of returning but permitted his sister to occupy the premises was held not to be occupying the property as his residence.)

There must be a practical or real possibility of the intention to return being fulfilled within a reasonable time. What is a reasonable time is again a question of fact and degree, as illustrated by the following group of cases, some of which are notable for the generosity afforded to tenants by the courts who are anxious not to deprive tenants of Rent Act protection save where this is clearly warranted.

> In *Gofor Investments v. Roberts* (1975) 29 P.& C.R. 366 the tenant and her family lived in the flat in question until 1970, when she and her husband along with four of their six children went to live in Malta. She left her furniture in the flat. The tenant stated that when she left she intended to return to the flat in about eight to 10 years, although when the landlord sought possession, following expiry of the seven-year fixed term, in 1975, she stated that she intended to return in the following year. During the tenant's absence the flat

was occupied by the two children who had remained and it was used from time to time by the husband. The Court of Appeal refused to upset the decision of the county court judge that the tenant had maintained her status as a statutory tenant. (See also *Bevington v. Crawford* (1974) 232 E.G. 191, where it was held to be sufficient for the landlord to have left furniture in the property and a caretaker despite having visited the property for only 10 days a year over a seven-year period).

The same conclusion was reached in the later case of *Brickfield Properties Ltd v. Hughes* (1987) 20 H.L.R. 108, CA. The tenant had a statutory tenancy of a London flat but from 1978 he and his wife lived in a cottage in Lancashire which his wife had inherited. They left their four children living in the property and three of them still lived there at the time of the possession proceedings by the landlord in 1987. During that nine-year interval the tenant had never been back to London and his wife had made only three visits to the property. Nevertheless, the tenant maintained that they would probably return to live there in a few years time once it became more difficult to cope in the more primitive and uncomfortable conditions in the cottage. The Court of Appeal agreed that the tenant had established the necessary *animus revertendi* and *corpus possessionis* to maintain his tenancy.

By contrast, in *Duke v. Porter* (1986) 19 H.L.R. 1 the tenant was held to have abandoned his statutory tenancy of a cottage by going to live in a flat in a property which he owned. Four years later he sublet part of the cottage and thereafter he returned from time to time only to collect the rent. The rest of the cottage was used simply as a store for his furniture. It was held that the tenant had effectively abandoned his intention to return and thereby lost his status as a statutory tenant.

Occupation by a spouse

At common law it was held that a statutory tenant's tenancy could be maintained by his wife's occupation which would be treated as that of the tenant himself even if he did not intend to return. Thus in *Brown v. Draper* [1944] K.B. 309 the protected tenant left, leaving his wife and child in occupation. It was held that when the landlord served a notice to quit a statutory tenancy arose in favour of the former protected tenant and therefore his wife was not a trespasser. This rule applied only as long as the marriage subsisted (*Robson v. Headland* (1948) 64 T.L.R. 596, CA). The common law rule was subsequently enshrined in a statutory rule, in the Matrimonial Homes Act 1967, which also applied to the case of a wife tenant who leaves her spouse in occupation. The 1967 Act was subsequently extended and then consolidated in the Matrimonial Homes Act 1983. On October 1, 1997 that Act was itself replaced by Part IV of the Family Law Act 1996.

One consequence of this statutory code is that if a married protected or statutory tenant leaves the matrimonial home, but that person's spouse has a statutory right to occupy (now referred to as "matrimonial homes rights"), any payment or tender of rent by that spouse will be as good as if made by the absent/tenant spouse (Family Law Act 1996, s.30(2) replacing Matrimonial Homes Act 1983, s.1(5)).

Furthermore, as long as the tenancy continues it will remain protected if, and so long as, the spouse remaining occupies the property as his or her residence. This is because the occupying spouse's occupation will be treated as that of the absent tenant/spouse (Family Law Act 1996, s.30(3) replacing Matrimonial Homes Act 1983, s.1(6)).

However, once the marriage comes to an end by a decree of divorce the matrimonial homes rights of the occupying spouse also come to an end (unless they have been extended beyond the marriage following an application made during the marriage under s.33(5)). Therefore the statutory tenancy will cease automatically (*Metropolitan Properties Ltd v. Cronan* (1982) 44 P.& C.R. 1).

The occupying spouse can seek to avoid this difficulty by asking the divorce court to exercise the power which it has to vest the tenancy in the non-tenant spouse under Schedule 7 to the Family Law Act 1996 (replacing Schedule 1 to the Matrimonial Homes Act 1983). But there is a potential trap here. Despite the fact that a court's powers to transfer a tenancy subsist until remarriage of an applicant, in practice that spouse must make the application for a transfer before the decree absolute is pronounced (or, when Part II of the Family Law Act 1996 is brought into force, a divorce order is made) because, as noted above, on divorce the claimant will cease to be a spouse and therefore her/his occupation will cease to be treated as that of the absent spouse, and the statutory tenancy will therefore be forfeited.

For the same reason the extension, by the Family Law Act 1996, of the court's power to order a transfer of the tenancy on application by a former spouse who has not remarried will not assist the non-tenant former spouse of the statutory tenant because, as explained above, the tenancy will normally have ceased on divorce.

By contrast to spouses, non-married cohabitants of protected or statutory tenants were in a vulnerable position before October 1, 1997 where the tenant departed leaving a non-married cohabitant in sole occupation. This was because the provisions of the Matrimonial Homes Act 1983 did not provide for her/his occupation to be treated as that of the tenant in such circumstances, nor did the court have power to make a transfer of tenancy order. (In *Colin Smith Music v. Ridge* [1975] 1 W.L.R. 463 a statutory tenant left and surrendered his tenancy to the landlord, who was held to be entitled to possession as against the tenant's mistress and children who had remained in occupation). The position has since been altered by the Family Law Act 1996. Since October 1, 1997 a cohabitant who has the benefit of an occupation order under section 36 of the 1996 Act will have equivalent matrimonial homes rights to those of a spouse and thus be able to seek transfer of a tenancy. But because there is no statutory provision whereby occupation by a non-tenant cohabitant is deemed to be that of the departed (assured) tenant, then the tenancy will cease automatically on the departure of the tenant.

Two-homes cases

It will have been observed from the discussion above that in many of the cases involving an absent tenant who claims that he is a statutory tenant despite his absence, the tenant has another home elsewhere. Similar issues arise where there is only partial user of the property in question because the tenant has another home elsewhere. This raises the issue of the "two-home tenant".

The leading case is the decision of the House of Lords in *Hampstead Way Investments Ltd v. Lewis-Weare* [1985] 1 W.L.R. 164.

> The tenant of a flat who, following his marriage, lived there with his wife and step-children, bought a house nearby for his family. The tenant continued to sleep at the flat for five nights a week, when he worked late at a night club, but he took all his meals at the house. The tenant's step-son lived at the flat full-time. The tenant kept his clothes at the flat and had his mail addressed there. The Court held that in principle it was possible for a tenant to occupy a rented property as his residence, whilst at the same time having a home elsewhere. Whether he did so occupy his rented accommodation was a question of fact and degree. On the facts of the case the tenant's limited use of the flat was insufficient to amount to occupation of it as his residence. The court acknowledged that it was possible to use more than one property as a home, but in the present case—

"The flat was in truth, the home, not of the tenant, who slept there on five nights a week and kept his clothes there, but that of the adult step-son, who carried out all an ordinary person's living activities there (*per* Lord Brandon p.171)."

(For other cases of limited occasional user, see *Walker v. Ogilvy* (1974) 28 P.& C.R. 288 and *Regalian Properties Ltd v. Scheuer* (1982) 263 E.G. 973. See also *DJ Crocker Securities (Portsmouth) Ltd v. Johal* [1989] 42 E.G. 103, CA. In that case an overseas student came to the United Kingdom to study law and took a flat. He later married but subsequently returned to Malaysia in 1977 where he stayed thereafter, although he made occasional short visits to the United Kingdom and stayed in the flat which, since 1985, had been used by his niece or other persons living there with her permission. The court held that the flat could not in any sense of the term be described as the tenant's home in all the circumstances, having regard to the fact that his place of work and home were clearly in Malaysia. (*Cf. Langford Property Co. Ltd v. Tureman* [1949] 1 K.B. 29 where a man with a cottage in the country took a weekend flat in London where he slept on average for two nights a week. He rarely ate at the flat, which was occupied by a friend and his wife. The court held that it was nevertheless occupied as his home and in principle because one could have two homes, each was occupied as a residence.)

Once again, it can be seen that the courts have exhibited a marked tendency to lean in favour of protection for the tenant, save in cases where it cannot be said that the tenant is occupying the property in question as his residence in any real sense of the term.

A statutory tenancy by succession

The Rent Acts have from their earliest days afforded rights of succession to certain family members of a deceased protected or statutory tenant. As will be seen below those provisions were generous and could lead to the landlord being unable to recover possession of a property initially let on a protected tenancy for a very long time indeed, spanning more than one generation. Although as a general rule it has not been possible, following the Housing Act 1988, to create new Rent Act protected tenancies since January 15, 1989, any protected or statutory tenancies in existence at that date are still governed by the Rent Act regime, although it is important to appreciate that significant amendments were made to the succession provisions of the Rent Act 1977 in respect of such tenancies in the case of deaths on or after January 15, 1989.

When will a statutory tenancy by succession arise?

A "statutory tenancy by succession" may arise in favour of another (to be determined according to the rules in Rent Act Act 1977, Sched. 1) on the death of a protected or statutory tenant. If immediately before his death the tenant was a protected tenant, the contractual tenancy continues in favour of whoever is entitled to it under the tenant's will or intestacy but the rights and obligations of that person (if he or she is not the statutory successor) are suspended during the subsistence of the statutory tenancy (*Moodie v. Hosegood* [1952] A.C. 61). In *Whitmore v. Lambert* [1955] 1 W.L.R. 495, where the protected tenant's widow took under his will, it was held that this overrode her statutory right to succeed, thereby permitting a first statutory succession to occur on her subsequent death.

The statutory tenancy will last as long as the successor occupies the dwelling-house as his or her residence.

There may even be a second succession on the death of the first successor. As noted above, who is entitled to a statutory tenancy by way of succession depends upon the date of death of the original and/or, as the case may be, the successor tenant. The rules, which are contained in Schedule 1, are complicated and are summarised as follows.

1. First succession

(a) Death of original tenant before January 15, 1989

Surviving spouse: If the deceased tenant was survived by his or her spouse, the spouse, if residing in the dwelling-house immediately before the tenant's death, would qualify as statutory tenant by succession if and so long as he or she occupied the dwelling-house as his or her residence (para. 1).

In the case of deaths before November 28, 1980 this rule only applied to widows and not widowers. A widower could only qualify as a family member (see below). The position of husband and wife was equated by the Housing Act 1980 in the case of deaths on or after the above date enabling a surviving widower to qualify in exactly the same way as a surviving widow. There was also a rule applicable in the case of deaths before November 28, 1980, that the survivor had to be residing (in the dwelling-house) with the tenant at the time of his or her death, thus excluding a separated spouse whose husband was no longer living in the house at the time of his death. This requirement was also removed by the Housing Act 1980, for the benefit of widows or widowers, where the tenant died on or after November 28, 1980.

Other family members: In the absence of a qualifying surviving spouse, any member of the original tenant's family who was residing with the tenant at the time of, and for at least six months immediately before, his or her death could qualify as the statutory tenant if and so long as he or she occupied the dwelling-house as his or her residence (para. 2). By way of contrast to the rule set out above, it should be noted that the successor need not have resided in the dwelling-house for the qualifying period (*Waltham Forest LBC v. Thomas* [1992] 2 A.C. 198 (a decision on section 87 of the Housing Act 1985 that in the absence of clear words to that effect, this requirement would not be implied). If there was more than one qualifying person the statutory tenant by succession was to be determined by agreement or in default of agreement by the county court (see para. 3 and *Williams v. Williams* [1970] 1 W.L.R. 1530, CA where the judge favoured the claim of the widower who was in greater need, to that of the adult son of the deceased, whose claim was considered more meritorious from the point of view of conduct). There was no provision for a joint succession (*Dealex Properties Ltd v. Brooks* [1966] 1 Q.B. 542).

The meaning of the term "residing with" has been the subject of considerable judicial examination, as a result of which it would appear that some degree of family living together by the deceased tenant and the claimant is required.

In *Swanbrae Ltd v. Elliott* (1987) 19 H.L.R. 86, CA Swinfen Thomas J. stated that "residing with" means that a claimant "must show that he or she has made a home at the premises which they are claiming and has become in a true sense a part of the household." The claimant in that case, who had a permanent home elsewhere, was unable to fulfil this requirement simply by having stayed at her sick mother's house, which was two miles away, on a part-time basis (*i.e.* three or four nights a week) for over six months. Whilst it was not impossible for a "two-home" claimant to succeed, it was necessary to show more than mere residence at the property in question. It is a question of fact and degree as to whether the necessary degree of communal living has been established.

In *Hildebrand v. Moon* [1989] 37 E.G. 123 it was held that the necessary degree of communality had been shown by the claimant daughter who moved back to nurse her ill mother whilst retaining her own flat elsewhere, although it seems to have been of significance that she had contemplated selling the flat a few months before her mother's death.

The fact that the tenant might not have been in the property for the whole of the requisite period will not necessarily be sufficient to prevent a successful claim. Thus in *Hedgedale Ltd v. Hards* [1991] 15 E.G. 107, CA a man moved into his grandmother's flat, shortly after she had broken her arm in an accident, intending to form a family unit with her. Despite the tenant's absence for four months whilst she visited her daughter, the claimant grandson was held entitled to succeed as a statutory tenant on his grandmother's death. By contrast in *Foreman v. Beagley* [1969] 1 W.L.R. 1387, CA the tenant was confined to hospital for the last three years of her life. During the last year her son lived at the premises in question. The Court held that he had not established the necessary degree of communal living so as to be "residing with" his mother. The necessary intention to establish a joint household was missing.

(b) Death of original tenant on or after January 15, 1989

Surviving spouse: A surviving spouse, who was residing in the dwelling-house immediately before the death of the original tenant, may still qualify as statutory tenant by succession if and so long as he or she occupies the dwelling-house as his or her residence.

For this purpose a person who was living with the original tenant as his or her wife or husband is to be treated as a spouse of the original tenant (para. 2(2)). In the rare case where this creates a conflict between more than one "surviving spouse" (*e.g.* a genuine spouse and one treated as such in accordance with this provision), they must agree who is to be entitled and in default of agreement the successor can be determined by the county court (para. 2(3)).

The meaning of the expression "living with the original tenant as his or her wife or husband" has been explored in the context of the secure tenancy regime contained in the Housing Act 1985 which uses the same expression (Housing Act 1985, s.113) as well as the present context.

In *Westminster City Council v. Peart* (1991) 24 H.L.R. 389 (a Housing Act 1985 case) the Court of Appeal held that to establish that a man and woman were living together as husband and wife it was not sufficient simply to show that they lived together in the same household. Thus in that case the defendant failed to establish that she was living with her divorced husband in his flat, during a period of reconciliation, at a time when she had retained her own flat elsewhere.

What is clear is that these provisions contemplate that the parties are respectively male and female. In *Harrogate Borough Council v. Simpson* (1984) 17 H.L.R. 205 a woman was not permitted to succeed, under the Housing Act 1985, to a secure tenancy on the death of her lesbian lover with whom she had been living in the property in question for two and a half years.

This decision was followed, with great reluctance, by the Court of Appeal in the Rent Act case of *Fitzpatrick v. Sterling Housing Association Ltd* [1997] 4 All E.R. 991. The claimant had lived in a close stable and loving homosexual relationship with the deceased statutory tenant from 1976 until the tenant's death in 1994. The Court of Appeal by a majority (Ward L.J. dissenting) held that it was bound by the *Simpson* case (above) to hold that the claimant and the deceased were not living together as husband and wife.

The Court in *Fitzpatrick* further held that the claimant also failed on the alternative basis that he was a member of the deceased tenant's family) (see below).

Member of the family: In the absence of a surviving spouse, a member of the original tenant's family who was residing with him in the dwelling-house at the time of his death may succeed, but only if that person has also been residing with the deceased in the

dwelling-house for at least two years immediately before his or her death (para. 3). Thus the period of qualifying residence has been increased from six months to two years and it is specified that residence must have been in the dwelling-house in question. Furthermore the successor obtains an assured tenancy by succession, governed by the Housing Act 1988, and not a statutory tenancy by succession under the Rent Act 1977 HA 1988, s.39. There can be no succession to such an assured tenancy. If the former tenancy was a protected shorthold tenancy the successor acquires an assured shorthold tenancy (HA 1988, s.39(7)). Transitional provisions safeguard the position of the successor where the tenant died within 18 months of January 15, 1989. In such a case a relative will be deemed to have satisfied the residence requirement provided he or she was residing with the tenant at the time of his or her death and for the six-month period immediately before that death (para. 3(2)). The reference to the claimant "residing with" the deceased tenant indicates that the claimant must have established a settled home with the applicant (see above).

2. Second succession

(a) Death of first successor before January 15, 1989

On the death of the statutory tenant by succession (the first successor) before January 15,1989, save in a small number of exceptional cases, there could be a second succession in favour of the first successor's spouse or a member of the first successor's family as the case may be (paras 6 and 7). It should be noted that the relevant family for this purpose is that of the first successor (*Sefton Holdings Ltd v. Cairns* (1987) 20 H.L.R. 124). Similar rules to those applicable on the death of the original tenant applied to determine the second successor. No further succession was permitted on the death of the second successor (paras 5–7). A statutory tenant by succession could not obtain further rights of transmission by taking a new contractual tenancy of the dwelling-house. Thus if a first successor took a new tenancy and died, any successor would be a second successor. Where such a succession took place before August 27, 1972 this rule applied only if the first of any further tenancies was granted on or after that date (para. 10(4)).

(b) Death of first successor on or after January 15, 1989

On the death of the statutory tenant by succession (the first successor) on or after January 15, 1989, the original tenant having died before that date, there can be a second succession, but only in favour of a person who:

(1) was a member of the original tenant's family immediately before that tenant's death; and

(2) was a member of the first successor's family immediately before the first successor's death (paras 5 and 6).

Thus there is no longer an automatic right to succeed in favour of a surviving spouse who was residing in the dwelling-house immediately before the death of the first successor. Furthermore it is now necessary for a second successor to establish membership of both the family of the original tenant and that of the first successor at the relevant times.

Finally it should again be appreciated that succession is to an assured tenancy by succession, to which there can be no further succession, and not to a statutory tenancy by succession under the Rent Act 1977. In order to qualify, the successor must be residing in the dwelling-house with the first successor at the time of, and for the period of two years immediately before, the first successor's death. If more than one person qualifies they must decide amongst themselves who is to succeed and in default of agreement the county court may decide. Similar transitional provisions to those operating on the death of an original tenant applied on the death of a first successor within 18 months of January 15, 1989 (para. 6(2)).

Where the original tenant also died on or after January 15, 1989 there cannot be a second succession (to an assured tenancy by succession—see above) unless the first successor was a surviving spouse.

The meaning of "family"

(a) Heterosexual cohabitants

Neither the Rent Act 1977 nor the Housing Act 1988 defines the term "family". Consequently it has been left to the courts to deal with, and a considerable body of case law developed before the 1988 Act changes. Much of the case law has considered whether a person cohabiting with, but not married to, the deceased tenant could be treated as a member of the tenant's family for the purpose of acquiring a statutory tenancy by succession. As we have seen above, where the original tenant has died on or after January 15, 1989 a person who was living with that deceased tenant at the time of death as his/her wife/husband will qualify as a surviving spouse. In cases where the tenant died before that date, a cohabitant could only succeed by establishing that he or she was a member of the deceased tenant's family.

Earlier case law was prepared to find the necessary family relationship where the couple had had children and thus created a family unit (*Hawes v. Evenden* [1953] 1 W.L.R. 1169 where the couple had lived together for 12 years and had two children) but not where a childless couple lived together for 20 years (*Gammans v. Ekins* [1950] 2 K.B. 328). However, in the light of changing social mores this distinction was later abandoned by the Court of Appeal in *Dyson Holdings Ltd v. Fox* [1976] 1 Q.B. 503, where a man was permitted to succeed to a statutory tenancy on the death of his female partner of 21 years with whom he had lived as man and wife, although they were not legally married to each other. A number of factors were deemed to be relevant to the issue of whether the necessary family nexus existed. These included the presence or absence of children, the length of the cohabitation and whether or not the partners held themselves out as husband and wife. Although this change of approach was not at first universally accepted by the judiciary, it was endorsed by the Court of Appeal in *Watson v. Lucas* [1980] 1 W.L.R. 1493. In that case the claimant had lived with the statutory tenant, who was a widow, for 19 years during which time the claimant was legally married to somebody else. The Court held that he could nevertheless be treated as a member of his deceased partner's family despite the fact that they had not used the same surname or held themselves out as being a married couple.

Thus it emerged from the case law that there could be said to be a family relationship if, at the time of the tenant's death, the parties were and had been living together in a sufficiently stable and permanent relationship, whether or not they had children and whether or not one of the parties was married to somebody else.

Although the chance of establishing a right to succeed was improved the longer the relationship had lasted, no particular time limit was imposed by the courts. Thus whilst in *Dyson Holdings Ltd v. Fox* [1996] Q.B. 503, CA and *Watson v. Lucas* [1980] 1 W.L.R. 1493, CA the relevant periods were 21 years and 19 years respectively, a claim succeeded in *Chios Property Investment Ltd v. Lopez* [1987] 05 E.G. 57 where the length of cohabitation between two persons who intended to marry was only two years. On the other hand, in *Helby v. Rafferty* [1979] 1 W.L.R. 13 a claim by a cohabitant to succeed on the death of his partner failed where the evidence established that despite five years' cohabitation the relationship between the couple lacked permanence and stability.

The extended meaning of surviving spouse in the case of deaths on or after January 15, 1989 (see above) now makes it much easier for a cohabitant to qualify as a statutory successor. To satisfy the extended definition, no particular period of cohabitation should be required, nor will the presence or absence of children be relevant. Nor should it matter that one of both of the parties is married to somebody else (as in *Watson v. Lucas,* above).

(b) Other relationships

The courts have had little difficulty with those cases of claims to succeed where there is a legal or quasi-legal nexus (*e.g.* step-children). Indeed this has been held to include a niece by marriage (*Jones v. Whitehill* [1950] 2 K.B. 204) and a case where the tenant had, at a time when legal adoption was not possible, *de facto* adopted the claimant, who was now 41, when she was six years old (*Brock v. Wollams* [1949] 2 K.B. 388). However, it is equally well established that a "family" relationship cannot be established by two unrelated adults living together in a platonic relationship, *e.g.* as "aunt and nephew" or "sisters".

In *Carega Properties SA (formerly Joram Developments Ltd) v. Sharratt* [1979] 1 W.L.R. 928 the claimant was a man of 43 who had lived in the tenant's house for 21 years until her death at the age of 94. The tenant was the widow of the late Mr Justice Salter who had died in 1929. She and the claimant had enjoyed a close platonic relationship and he had referred to her as "aunt". The House of Lords held that he was not entitled to succeed as a statutory tenant by succession on her death. Similarly in *Sefton Holdings Ltd v. Cairns* [1988] 14 E.G. 58, CA a woman who had lived with a family as a daughter of the original tenants since she was 23 was held not to be entitled to succeed as statutory tenant on the death of their daughter (the first successor) because she was living as a member of the household, as distinct from being a member of the family. (She was too old when she went to live with the family to be treated as having been *de facto* adopted. *Cf. Brock v. Wollams*, above.)

By contrast to the more enlightened attitudes of recent times towards heterosexual cohabitants the Court of Appeal has considered itself unable to extend the analogy to same-sex couples. Thus in *Fitzpatrick v. Sterling Housing Association Ltd* [1997] 4 All E.R. 991, CA a claim to succeed to a statutory tenancy made by a homosexual partner of the deceased statutory tenant on the basis that the claimant was a member of the deceased tenant's family failed. The judgments reveal a deeply felt awareness by all three judges of the social changes which had taken place since the succession provisions were first introduced into the Rent Acts in an earlier and very different social climate. At first sight the signs looked good for Mr Fitzpatrick's claim to succeed on the death of his partner. All three members of the Court of Appeal were critical of the discriminatory nature of the relevant statutory provision.

Waite L.J. stated that—

> "If endurance, stability, interdependence and devotion were the sole hallmarks of family membership, there could be no doubt about this case at all. Mr Fitzpatrick and Mr Thompson lived together for a longer period than many marriages endure these days. They were devoted and faithful, giving each other mutual help and support in a life which shared many of the highest qualities to be found in heterosexual attachments, married or unmarried. To adopt an interpretation of the statute that allowed all sexual partners, whether of the same or the opposite sex, to enjoy the privilege of succession to tenancies protected by the Rent Acts would, moreover, be consistent not only with social justice but also with the respect accorded by modern society to those of the same sex who undertake a permanent commitment to a shared life (at p.103)."

Nevertheless, his Lordship felt unable to depart from binding authority to the effect that—

"the law in England regarding succession to statutory tenancies is firmly rooted in the concept of the family as an entity bound together by ties of kinship (including adoptive status) or marriage. The only relaxation, first by court decision and then by statute, has been a willingness to treat heterosexual cohabitants as if they were husband and wife (p.1004)."

His Lordship (along with Roch L.J.) considered that any change to what he described as an "arbitrary and discriminatory" law be made by Parliament who would have to grapple with intricate policy questions such as whether, and if so in what circumstances, friends should be included within the definition of family. They would also have to balance the conflicting social goals, inherent in the Rent Act, of protecting occupiers and respecting the rights of owners to possession of their property. Statutory succession rights, like the Rent Act itself, necessarily invades the rights of home owners to recover possession of their property. What is more difficult is to determine the proper limits of such an invasion. In a bold, wide-ranging and powerful judgment, Ward L.J., not without considerable hesitation, dissented from the majority and considered that it was open to the Court to hold that not only should Mr Fitzpatrick have been held to have been a member of his deceased partner's family but that he should have succeeded also on the basis that he had lived with the deceased "as his husband or wife" because in his view there was "no essential difference between a homosexual and heterosexual couple." He concluded by quoting from Bingham M.R.'s judgment in *R. v. Ministry of Defence, ex parte. Smith* [1996] Q.B. 517 at 554 that "A belief which represented unquestioned orthodoxy in year X may have become questionable by year Y and unsustainable by year Z (see further *N.Wikeley* (1998) 10 C.F.L.Q.)" His Lordship considered that *Harrogate Borough Council v. Simpson* (above) was decided in year Y and that 1997 was year Z (see further *N. Wikeley* (1998) 10 C.F.L.Q. 191).

C. SECURITY OF TENURE

The scheme of security of tenure adopted by the Rent Act 1977 provides that, notwithstanding the position at common law, a court is not able to make a possession order in respect of a dwelling-house let on a protected or secure tenancy save on one of the grounds permitted by the Act. Thus if, for example, the contractual tenancy is ended by effluxion of time or by a landlord's notice to quit, the tenant can remain as a statutory tenant until the landlord is able to establish a ground for possession. Similarly if a landlord were to forfeit a protected tenancy for breach of covenant this would only have the effect of ending the contractual tenancy and not any statutory tenancy that might arise at that point. He would therefore also need to establish a ground for possession at the same time to enable that statutory tenancy to be terminated by court order. Even then he might not recover possession because it is not always sufficient simply to establish a ground for possession (see below).

It can be noted in passing here that a mortgagee whose mortgage was subject to a protected tenancy of the mortgaged property is in no better position with regard to recovery of possession than the landlord where that tenancy has ended and a statutory tenancy has arisen because the protected tenancy will be binding on the mortgagee either as a legal estate where title to the land is unregistered or as an overriding interest under section 70(1) paragraph (g) or (k) where title to the land is registered (see, for example, *Woolwich Building Society v. Dickman* [1996] 3 All E.R. 204 where a protected tenancy was binding on the mortgagee, despite the tenants having

signed a consent form postponing their rights to the rights of the Society). Thus despite the fact
that the mortgagor has defaulted and the mortgagee is seeking to exercise his power of sale, he
will not be able to obtain possession against the statutory tenant without first establishing one of
the relevant grounds in the Rent Act (see below), some of which are in any event discretionary.
(But see Case 11 below).

If on the other hand the mortgage has priority because the protected tenancy was granted
after the mortgage and in breach of the mortgage deed (that is, where the deed excludes the
mortgagor's power of leasing without the mortgagee's prior consent), then neither that tenancy
nor a subsequent statutory tenancy arising on the end of that tenancy will bind the mortgagee,
who can assert a paramount title (*Dudley & District Benefit Building Society v. Emerson* [1949]
2 All E.R. 452; *Britannia Building Society v. Earl* [1990] 1 W.L.R. 422, CA).

But note the result in *Barclays Bank plc v. Zaroovabli and others* [1997] 2 All E.R. 19. This
was an unusual case where a protected tenancy was granted two months after the property was
mortgaged to the plaintiffs, the mortgage excluding the mortgagor's power of leasing. Had title
to the land been unregistered the mortgagee would have acquired a legal estate on the granting
of the mortgage and, as we have seen above, the tenancy would not have been binding on the
mortgagee. But title to the land in the present case was registered and the mortgagee did not
register the mortgage, and thereby acquire a legal mortgage until after the contractual tenancy
had ended and a statutory tenancy had arisen. This was fatal to the mortgagee's claim that they
were not bound by the tenancy. Until registration of the mortgage the contractual tenancy and
later the statutory tenancy had priority to the mortgage, which at that point was only a minor
interest. When the mortgagee was registered it would undoubtedly have been bound by the
contractual tenancy as an overriding interest under section 70(1)(k), had it still subsisted.
(Paragraph (k) covers legal leases granted for a term not exceeding 21 years.) But this was not
the case. The contractual tenancy had ended and been superseded by the statutory tenancy.
Nevertheless the judge (Sir Richard Scott V.-C.) held that the subsequent statutory tenancy was
equally binding because any other result would be inconsistent with the protection intended to
be afforded to a statutory tenant by the Rent Act 1977.

The tenant could not rely on the Land Registration Act 1925 s.70(1)(g) which protects as an
overriding interest the "rights of every person in actual occupation", because, even on the
assumption that a statutory tenancy can be such a "right", the crucial time for determining
whether the mortgagee was bound by an overriding interest under paragraph (g) was the
granting of the mortgage rather than its subsequent registration. (See *Abbey National Building
Society v. Cann* [1991] A.C. 56 H.L.)

Grounds for possession

The statutory grounds fall into one of three categories each of which has different
consequences.

(a) Discretionary grounds

The first set of grounds (called "Cases") are contained in Rent Act 1977, Sched. 15, Part 1
(Cases 1 to 10). If one or more of these grounds is established the court may make a possession
order if it considers it reasonable to make such an order. Thus it is not sufficient merely to
establish such a ground; the court must also exercise its discretion in favour of the landlord if he
is to be able to recover possession (RA 1977, s.98(1)(b)). Furthermore in cases based on one or
more of the discretionary grounds the court has additional powers to adjourn the proceedings or
to stay or suspend the possession order or to postpone the date for possession for such period(s)
as the court thinks fit (Rent Act 1977, s.100).

(b) Mandatory grounds

By contrast the second set of grounds which are contained in Part II of Schedule 15 (Cases 11 to 20) are the mandatory grounds for possession . If one or more of these Cases is established in possession proceedings by the landlord the court must make a possession order (RA 1977, s.98(2)).

(c) Suitable alternative accommodation

The third way in which the landlord might recover possession is by relying on the present or imminent availability of suitable alternative accommodation for the tenant (Rent Act 1977, s.98). Although this is not encompassed by any of the Cases in Schedule 15 it is in effect a ground for possession and is dealt with as such below. Possession can only be ordered on this ground if the court considers it reasonable in all the circumstances to make the possession order.

The discretionary grounds

Case 1—rent unpaid or other breach of obligation

The first limb of this ground provides that a possession order may be made if any rent is unpaid. This means that at the time proceedings were commenced, rent was lawfully due (in the sense that the obligation had arisen and not been discharged) and that such rent remained unpaid and untendered (*Bird v. Hildage* [1948] 1 K.B. 91, CA). In practice, possession will only be ordered where there is a history of serious non-payment and in most cases the court will exercise its powers under section 100 to grant a stay etc. on condition that arrangements are made for discharge of arrears and undertakings as to future compliance are given.

The second limb covers breach of any express or implied obligation of the tenancy, such as by using the premises for non-residential purposes (*Florent v. Horez* (1983) 12 H.L.R. 1), whether remediable or not (see p.143 above for when a tenancy covenant is irremediable). The doctrine of waiver (see p.135 above) has no application in this context (*Trustees of Henry Smith's Charity v. Willson* [1983] Q.B. 316).

Case 2—conduct which is a nuisance or annoyance or conviction

This ground is virtually identical to ground 14 of the assured tenancy code in the Housing Act 1988 which was modelled on this Case. It was amended by the Housing Act 1996 and is discussed in Chapter 9 above (see p.232).

Case 3—deterioration in condition of the dwelling house by culpable acts or neglect

This ground is framed in very similar terms to ground 13 of the assured tenancy code in the Housing Act 1988, save that that ground extends to deterioration of the common parts (see p.232 above).

Case 4—deterioration of furniture

This ground is virtually identical to ground 15 of the assured tenancy code in the Housing Act 1988 which was modelled on this Case (see p.232 above).

Case 5—tenant's notice to quit

This ground applies where the tenant has served a notice to quit and as a consequence the landlord has contracted to sell or let the dwelling-house or has taken other steps as the result of which he would in the court's opinion be seriously prejudiced if he could not recover possession.

Case 6—assignment or sub-letting

This ground is applicable where the tenant has assigned or sub-let the whole of the dwelling-house or sub-let part of the dwelling-house, the remainder already being sub-let (see p.286 below).

Case 7

This case was repealed by the Housing Act 1980.

Case 8—dwelling-house reasonably required as a residence for the landlord's employee

This ground applies if a number of conditions have all been satisfied—

(1)   The dwelling-house is reasonably required by the landlord for occupation as a residence for a person who is a full-time employee either of the landlord or a tenant of the landlord or with whom a contract of employment has been made conditional on housing being provided. The crucial time at which the satisfaction of this condition is to be determined is the date of the hearing. Furthermore it must also be established that it is reasonable to make a possession order in all the circumstances (*R.F.Fuggle v. Gadsen* [1948] 2 K.B. 236).

(2)   The tenant was an employee of the landlord or a former landlord (*i.e.* when the premises were let to him).

(3)   The dwelling-house was let to him in consequence of that employment. It does not matter that the tenant was ignorant of this fact (*Royal Crown Derby Porcelain Co v. Russell* [1949] 2 K.B. 417, CA).

(4)   That employment has ceased.

This ground is also available against a successor to the tenant from whom the premises were let even though that person was never in the landlord's employment (*Bolsover Colliery Co. Ltd v. Abbott* [1946] 1 K.B. 8, CA).

Case 9—dwelling-house reasonably required for occupation by the landlord or a member of his family

This ground (which can be compared with Case 11) applies where the dwelling-house is reasonably required by the landlord for occupation as a residence by:

(1)   himself; or
(2)   any son or daughter of his over the age of 18; or
(3)   his father or mother; or
(4)   his or her mother-or father-in-law.

It does *not* apply if the landlord became landlord by purchase (subject to the tenancy) after:

(1)   November 7, 1956, in the case of a tenancy which was then a controlled tenancy;
(2)   March 8, 1973, in the case of a tenancy which became a regulated tenancy by virtue of the Counter Inflation Act 1973;
(3)   May 24, 1974, in the case of a regulated furnished tenancy;
(4)   March 23, 1965, in the case of any other tenancy.

The onus of establishing the reasonableness of the landlord's requirement must be discharged at the date of the hearing (*Smith v. McGoldrick* (1976) 242 E.G. 1047; *Alexander v. Mohamadzadeh* (1985) 18 H.L.R. 90, CA).

The premises must be required for use as a residence by the appropriate person. This requirement will not be satisfied where the landlord is seeking possession in order to sell after a short period of residence (*Rowe v. Truelove* (1976) 241 E.G. 533; contrast the case 11 case of *Lipton v. Whitworth* (p.280 below).

In the unusual circumstances of *Smith v. Penny* [1947] 1 K.B. 230 it was held that where the landlord required the dwelling-house for occupation by his minor children who would be looked after there by other carers this would count as occupation by the landlord. In *Richter v. Wilson* [1963] 2 Q.B. 426 at 430 it had been said that the word "himself" must include all natural emanations of the landlord (*per* Willmer L.J.).

The reference to "landlord" in Case 9 includes joint landlords beneficially entitled. It has been held that if possession is sought for the purpose of residence by "the landlord" the wording means that they must both require the dwelling-house as a residence for themselves (*McIntyre v. Hardcastle* [1948] 2 K.B. 82, CA. This limitation was treated as an open point by the House of Lords in *Tilling v. Whiteman* [1980] A.C. 1 at 19 (p.281below)) but

By contrast where, in a joint landlords case, the property is required for residence not by the landlord but by a specified relative, it will suffice that that person is related to at least one of the joint landlords. In *Potsos v. Theodotou* (1991) 23 H.L.R. 356, CA therefore, it was sufficient that the property was required by married joint landlords for the wife's natural son (aged 22) from a previous marriage who had been brought up by the husband landlord since he was 18 months old, even though he had never been adopted by the husband. This refusal to extend the joint landlord concept further than necessary is to be welcomed.

"Landlord by purchase" means that the landlord acquired the property for money or money's worth. This is designed to exclude landlords who have bought the property with a sitting tenant, rather than acquired it through deed of gift, or family arrangement or as a result of succession on death. In *Thomas v. Fryer* [1970] 1 W.L.R. 845, CA it was held that where the landlord, who acquired the property by a family arrangement on her mother's death, had made adjusting payments to her siblings this did not make her a landlord by purchase. (See also *Mansukhani v. Sharkey* (1992) 24 H.L.R. 600, CA where a transfer of a mortgaged flat made in consideration of natural love and affection, and a covenant by the recipient to pay the mortgage was held to be a gift.) It must also be appreciated that the court will still need to be satisfied that it is reasonable to order possession.

Furthermore, there is an additional hurdle applicable to this Case only which the landlord will need to surmount if he is to succeed in recovering possession. This is that even if the requirements of Case 9 have been satisfied, "a court shall not make an order for possession . . . . if the court is satisfied that having regard to all the circumstances of the case, including the question whether other accommodation is available for the landlord or the tenant, greater hardship would be caused by granting the order than by refusing to grant it" (RA 1977 Sched. 15, Part III, para. 1). The onus of establishing that this will be the case is on the tenant (*Piper v. Harvey* [1958] 1 Q.B. 439).

It has been held that when determining this matter—

> "The court should take into account hardship to all who may be affected by the grant or refusal of an order for possession—relatives, dependents, lodgers, guests and the stranger within the gates—but should weigh such hardship with due regard to the status of the persons affected and their proximity to the landlord or tenant, and the extent to which consequently hardship to them would be hardship to him. (*Harte v. Frampton* [1948] 1 K.B. 73, 79, CA.)"

Hardship to the tenant if the order is made will often be made out if the tenant will have great difficulty in finding alternative unfurnished accommodation. Indeed, since January 15, 1989 any such accommodation may now be at a much higher rent because it will more than likely be on an assured shorthold tenancy, with no security of tenure. In a number of cases it has been held that a failure by the tenant to show that he had searched for such accommodation without success was fatal to a claim of greater hardship (see, *e.g. Piper v. Harvey* (above) and *Alexander v. Mohamadzadeh* (above), although in *Bassett v. Fraser* (1981) 9 H.L.R. 105, CA and *Baker v. MacIver* (1990) 22 H.L.R. 328, CA it was said that it is open to the court to recognise that any such search would be in vain. This is less likely to be the case since the early 1990s if the claim frequently voiced by landlords that there is much more property available since deregulation of the market by the Housing Act 1988 is true (see p.203 above). (See also *Manaton v. Edwards* (1985) 18 H.L.R. 116.)

Case 10—sub-letting at excessive rents

This ground for possession applies where the tenant has sub-let part of the dwelling-house on a protected or statutory tenancy or restricted contract at a rent in excess of the permitted rent. It is of little significance today because most tenancies created since January 15, 1989 will be outside the ambit of the Rent Act and in any event if there is a sub-letting of part the landlord is likely to be a resident landlord and therefore the tenancy will not even be an assured tenancy shorthold or otherwise. Hence no rent restrictions will apply.

Mandatory grounds

Once a landlord has established one or more of grounds 11 to 20, the court must order possession (RA 1977, s.98(3) above). Possession can be postponed for a maximum of only 14 days unless this would cause exceptional hardship in which case possession may be postponed for a maximum of six weeks (Housing Act 1980, s.89(1)).

The mandatory grounds for possession all have a common feature. This is that no later than the "relevant date" the landlord must have given notice to the tenant that at some time in the future possession might be required on the ground in question. There is no prescribed form of notice but the notice must make it clear that possession might be recovered under the case in question (*Fowler v. Minchin* (1987) 19 H.L.R. 224). The relevant date is in general the date of commencement of the tenancy although later dates are specified in the case of some tenancies which came into protection as a result of particular measures which extended full Rent Act protection to tenancies hitherto outside the code.

It follows that in each of these cases if the relevant notice has been served and the landlord is able to establish that the conditions of the ground in question are satisfied the tenant will be vulnerable to successful possession proceedings once the contractual term has come to an end such as by expiry of a fixed term. Thus to this limited extent it is possible for the parties to contract out of the security of tenure provisions of the Act which would otherwise apply. In these circumstances it is not surprising that the need for service of the appropriate notice at the relevant time is vital. However, in four cases (*viz.* Cases 11, 12, 19 and 20) the court has a discretion to waive the need for service of that notice if it considers that it would be otherwise just and equitable to make a possession order.

In *Fernandes v. Parvardin* (1982) 5 H.L.R. 33 the Court of Appeal refused to interfere with a waiver of the need to have served written notice under Case 11 (below) where satisfied that oral notice had been given to the tenant by the relevant date. By contrast it was not considered just and equitable to dispense with the notice requirement, for the purposes of Case 11, in *Bradshaw v. Baldwin-Wiseman* (1985) 49 P.& C.R. 382 where there had been no intention to create a Case

11 tenancy at the relevant time and where the person seeking possession was the successor in title to the original landlord (his mother) who had not had any intention of recovering possession at the end of the tenancy. The court held that when considering whether it is just and equitable to dispense with the need for notice, courts should consider the circumstances affecting the landlord and his successors in title, and the circumstances of the tenant along with the circumstances in which the failure to give written notice arose. In *White v. Jones* (1994) 26 H.L.R. 477 the landlords, who had moved abroad in 1964 before letting the house, had indicated orally at that time that they might return to England and require possession at some time. This was held to be insufficient ground for waiving the need for a written notice. This was a case where the tenancy was a furnished letting which had become protected as a result of the Rent Act 1974 which extended full security to furnished tenancies. Thus the relevant date for service of the appropriate notice was not later than February 13, 1975. In these circumstances the oral notice was not particularly significant because nobody believed that there was security at that time. It was outweighed by the hardship that would be caused to the tenant by granting possession.

Special rules apply to enable the landlord to recover possession by a speedy process based on affidavit evidence when relying on the mandatory grounds for possession if certain conditions are satisfied (Rent (County Court Proceedings for Possession) Rules 1981, S.I. 1981 No.139).

Case 11—owner occupier

This ground which was introduced by the Rent Act 1965 was considerably extended by the Housing Act 1980. Case 11 applies where a person (the owner occupier) who let the dwelling-house on a regulated tenancy had at any time before the letting occupied it as his residence and—

(1) not later than the relevant date (see above) the landlord gave notice in writing to the tenant that possession might be recovered under this case; and
(2) the dwelling house has not since that date been let on a protected tenancy by the owner occupier with respect to which the notice requirement had not been satisfied; and
(3) the court is of the opinion that one of the conditions set out below is satisfied.

Furthermore if the court is of the opinion that it is just and equitable to order possession it may do so notwithstanding that one or both of the conditions in (1) and (2) have not been satisfied. (See above for the exercise of this discretion by the court.)

The conditions referred to in (3) above are that—

(1) The dwelling-house is required as a residence for the owner or any member of his family who resided with the owner when he last occupied the dwelling-house as a residence.
(2) The owner has died and the dwelling-house is required as a residence for a member of his family who was residing with him at the time of his death.
(3) The owner has died and the dwelling-house is required by a successor in title as his residence or for the purpose of disposing of the property with vacant possession.
(4) The dwelling-house is subject to a mortgage made by deed before the tenancy was created and the mortgagee requires possession in or to sell with vacant possession in exercise of the mortgagee's express or statutory power of sale.
(5) The dwelling-house is not reasonably suitable to the needs of the owner having regard to his place of work and he needs to be able to sell with vacant possession in

order to acquire as his residence a dwelling-house which is more suitable to those
needs.

The primary aim of Case 11 as originally enacted was to permit a person who owns a
property to let it on a protected tenancy but to preserve his right to recover possession after the
tenancy has ended by serving notice on the tenant no later than the relevant date (see above). An
example would be where somebody goes to work abroad for a year intending to return (see the
observations of Lord Wilberforce in *Tilling v. Whiteman* [1980] A.C. 1 with regard to this
purpose behind Case 11).

At one time there was a trap for a landlord who let on a Case 11 tenancy, went away and
whilst away relet on another Case 11 tenancy, the first having come to an end in the meantime.
It was held in *Pocock v. Steel* [1984] 1 W.L.R. 229 on the wording of the statute at that time that
the landlord could not rely on Case 11 because he had not been the owner-occupier
immediately before the tenancy in respect of which he was now seeking possession. This trap
was removed by the Rent Act (Amendment) Act 1985 which provided that intervening
occupation was not required by the landlord where there had been two or more consecutive
Case 11 lettings. Further amendments were made by the Housing Act 1980.

It will be noted that prior residence by the landlord (but not necessarily as an
owner-occupier) is necessary as well as the fact that the property is required as a residence.
Prior residence by somebody else with the landlord's permission is not sufficient.

The Court of Appeal considered what is meant by "required as a residence" in *Naish v.
Curzon* (1984) 51 P.& C.R. 229. The landlord who sought possession on the basis of Case 11
lived and worked mainly in South Africa. Before letting the property in 1980 he had occupied it
intermittently since he had bought it in 1971. His intention was that after recovering possession
he would visit the United Kingdom once or twice a year for between two to six weeks at a time
and use the flat as a residence during his visits. The tenant's argument that the landlord would
not occupy the property permanently and therefore should not be granted possession failed.
The Court of Appeal held that Case 11 does not require permanence with regard to occupation
by the landlord as a residence. It is simply a question of fact in each case.

The Court reached a similar conclusion in *Davies v. Peterson* (1989) 21 H.L.R. 63 where the
landlord, who was a lawyer in Sierre Leone, regularly visited England once a year and stayed
for at least three months. The fact that the residence for which the landlord desired possession
would be intermittent was not fatal to his claim. As Slade L.J. observed in *Mistry v. Isidore*
(1990) 22 H.L.R. 281, 289, "temporary, or intermittent residence, which may suffice for the
purpose of Case 11, by no means necessarily involves occupation as a home." His Lordship
noted that for the purposes of the resident landlord exception in section 12 (above), Parliament
had expressly imported the case law on the meaning of occupation as a residence for the
purposes of section 2(3) whereas any such cross-reference was conspicuously absent from
Case 11.

The same result was reached in *Lipton v. Whitworth* (1994) 26 H.L.R. 293 where it was
claimed that the premises were required for use as a residence by the landlord's wife and
daughter. Possession was granted but the wife stayed only for a few weeks before going to live
elsewhere, following which the property was sold. The tenant's appeal was dismissed on the
basis that an intention to live in the property for a short while pending sale was not inconsistent
with occupying the house as a residence for the purposes of Case 11. (Contrast the Case 9 case
of *Rowe v. Truelove* (1977) 241 E.G. 553.)

There is also no requirement that the dwelling-house is reasonably required by the landlord.
The Court of Appeal has held that the present condition—

"means no more than bona fide wanted and genuinely intended to be occupied as a residence at once, or at any rate within a reasonable time but so wanted and intended whether reasonably or unreasonably, even from the landlord's point of view (*Kennealy v. Dunne* [1977] 1 Q.B. 837 at 849 *per* Stephenson LJ. *Cf* Case 9 above.)"

For the purposes of Case 11 it is sufficient in the case of a tenancy granted by joint landlords that possession is required for occupation as a residence by one or more of them. (See *Tilling v. Whiteman* [1980] A.C. 1 where possession was required to enable one of the two joint landlords to occupy the property as a residence.) (*Cf.* Case 9 above as applied in *McIntyre v. Hardcastle* [1948] 2 K.B. 82).

Although this was not a strict conveyancing interpretation of the relevant wording of Case 11 it was considered by the House of Lords to be in accordance with common sense and the policy behind this provision which supported a construction facilitating recovery of possession for occupation by fewer than both (or where more) all the joint landlords in the case where the tenancy was created by joint owner-occupiers. That policy was articulated by Lord Salmon—

"At the time when the [Act] was passed, there existed and had for many years existed a serious shortage of residential accommodation. There were many cases of persons in occupation of homes which they owned jointly who, for one reason or another, had to leave them temporarily, sometimes for considerable periods; they would have liked to let them during their absence, but refrained from doing so for fear of losing them forever to their tenants. Accordingly, many homes remained unoccupied, which would otherwise have been let to persons urgently in need of them. Case [11] was in my view designed to safeguard persons who occupied their home against the danger of losing them should they let them during their absence; and accordingly enabled more living accommodation to become available to the public than would otherwise have been the case, p.22."

The expedited possession procedure referred to above (p.279) is available in the case of a claim based on Case 11 where the dwelling-house is required for occupation by the owner or any member of his family who resided with him when he last occupied it as his residence. However, it will not be available where the landlord is relying on the court exercising its power to dispense with the need to have served a Case 11 notice on the tenant (see p.278 above).

Case 12—landlord's retirement home

This ground was introduced by the Rent Act 1974, and extended considerably by the Housing Act 1980 amendments to Rent Act 1977, Sched. 15. It applies where the landlord intends to occupy the dwelling-house as his residence at such time as he might retire from regular employment and has let it on a regulated tenancy before he has retired. Its purpose therefore is to enable a landlord who intends to retire to a property to let it in the meantime secure in the knowledge that when he comes to retire he will be able to recover possession. There is no requirement that there be occupation as a residence by the landlord before the grant of the tenancy.

In order for the landlord to recover possession under Case 12 it must be established that—

(1)   not later than the relevant date (see above) the landlord gave notice in writing to the tenant that possession might be recovered under this case; and

(2)   the dwelling house has not since August 14, 1974 been let on a protected tenancy by the owner occupier with respect to which the notice requirement had not been satisfied; and

(3)   the court is of the opinion that one of a number of specified conditions is satisfied.

The specified conditions referred to in (3) above are:

(1)   the owner has retired from regular employment and requires the dwelling-house as a residence;
(2)   the owner has died and the dwelling-house is required as a residence for a member of his family who was residing with him at the time of his death;
(3)   the owner has died and the dwelling-house is required by a successor in title as his residence or for the purpose of disposing of the property with vacant possession;
(4)   The dwelling-house is subject to a mortgage made by deed before the tenancy was created and the mortgagee requires possession in or to sell with vacant possession in exercise of the mortgagee's express or statutory power of sale.

It can be seen that the last three conditions are the same as in Case 11 (see above). As is the case of the ground in Case 11, if the court is of the opinion that it is just and equitable to order possession, it may do so notwithstanding that one or both of the conditions in (1) and (2) have not been satisfied. (See above for the exercise of this discretion by the court.)

The expedited possession procedure referred to above is available in the case of a claim based on Case 12 where the dwelling-house is required for occupation by the owner or (where he has died) for any member of his family who resided with him when he last occupied it as his residence. However, it will not be available where the landlord is relying on the court exercising its power to dispense with the need to have served a Case 11 notice on the tenant (see p.278 above).

Case 13—holiday lets

The purpose of this ground, which was also introduced by the Rent Act 1974, was to enable a landlord to let a dwelling-house normally used as a holiday home at other times of the year (either by the landlord or somebody else) without the tenancy attracting Rent Act protection. It applied to a tenancy for a term certain not exceeding eight months where at some time within the 12 months before the relevant date (see above) the dwelling-house was occupied under a right to occupy it for the purposes of a holiday and where not later than the "relevant date" the landlord gave notice in writing to the tenant that possession might be recovered under this Case. It is effectively historic now because new Rent Act protected tenancies cannot in any event, save in exceptional cases, be created since January 15, 1989. (See above for the equivalent ground under the Housing Act 1988).

Case 14—vacation lettings of student accommodation

This ground was also introduced by the Rent Act 1974. Its purpose was to enable a landlord to create vacation lettings of a dwelling-house normally used for occupation by students during the academic year, without that vacation tenancy attracting Rent Act protection. It applies to a tenancy, for a term certain not exceeding 12 months, of a dwelling-house which at some time within the 12 months before the relevant date (which is usually the date of creation of the tenancy) was occupied under a tenancy to which section 8 applied. (It will be recalled that section 8 exempts from Rent Act protection lettings to students by specified educational institutions). For Case 14 to apply the landlord must have given to the tenant, not later than the "relevant date", notice in writing that possession might be recovered under this case. This ground was thus not confined to vacation lettings by educational institutions (who would normally employ a licence for such purposes). It was also of advantage to landlords participating in "direct leasing schemes" whereby during term time the landlord would let to a university which would sub-let to students whilst during vacations the landlord could let the property out with a Case 14 notice. As in the case of Case 13 this ground is effectively historic now because new Rent Act protected tenancies cannot in any event, save in exceptional cases, be created since January 15, 1989. (See p.228 above for the corresponding ground for possession under the Housing Act 1988).

Case 15—minister of religion

This ground permits recovery of possession where the dwelling-house is held for the purpose of being available for occupation by a minister of religion as a residence from which to perform the duties of his/her office and where not later than the "relevant date" the landlord gave notice in writing to the tenant that possession might be recovered under this Case. The court must be satisfied that the dwelling-house is required for occupation by a minister of religion for such a residence.

Case 16—agricultural employees

This case applies where the dwelling-house was at any time occupied by a person under the terms of his employment as a person employed in agriculture and where the current tenant neither is nor was such a person nor the widow of any person so employed. It permits the landlord to recover possession provided that not later than the "relevant date" the landlord gave notice in writing to the tenant that possession might be recovered under this case. In order for possession to be granted the court must be satisfied that the dwelling-house is required for occupation by a person employed or to be employed by the landlord in agriculture.

Cases 17 and 18—former farmhouses

These grounds both deal with circumstances where following an amalgamation scheme (Case 17) or in other circumstances (Case 18) a dwelling-house formerly occupied by a farmer or his widow has become redundant and been let to a tenant on whom not later than the relevant date a notice in writing was served stating that possession might be recovered under the relevant case.

In order for possession to be granted, the court must be satisfied that the dwelling-house is required for occupation by—

(1) a person employed or to be employed by the landlord in agriculture (Case 17); or
(2) either a person to be responsible for control of the farming of the land or a person employed or to be employed by the landlord in agriculture (Case 18).

Case 19—protected shorthold tenancies

Protected shorthold tenancies were introduced by the Housing Act 1980, s.52, as a means of permitting a landlord to let, on or after November 28, 1980, on a fixed-term regulated tenancy of one to five years with the certainty of being able to recover possession at the end of the term. A protected shorthold tenancy could not be created in favour of a person who was immediately beforehand a protected or statutory tenant of the dwelling-house. Furthermore it was necessary for the landlord to have given the tenant notice in the prescribed form stating that the tenancy was to be a protected shorthold tenancy. Despite the landlord having a mandatory ground for possession the tenant did have the benefit of rent regulation. To be a protected shorthold tenancy the landlord must not have been able to terminate the fixed term other than by forfeiture or re-entry for breach of covenant by the tenant (s.52(1)(a)). By contrast, the tenant could terminate the tenancy during the fixed term by giving one month's notice if the term was for two years or less; otherwise three months' notice was required (HA 1988, s.53).

The court was empowered to dispense with the need to have served the initial protected shorthold notice (referred to above) if it considered it nevertheless just and equitable to grant possession (HA 1980, s.55(2)). In *R.J.Dunnell Property Investments Ltd v. Thorpe* (1989) 21 H.L.R. 559, CA the Court held that it was just and equitable to dispense with this requirement where the tenant knew about the nature of the tenancy from the outset.

It has not been possible to create new protected shorthold tenancies since January 15, 1989, save in pursuance of a contract entered into before that date. Even a renewal of a tenancy in favour of a former protected shorthold tenant (or statutory successor) will create only an assured shorthold tenancy under the Housing Act 1988 (s.34(2)(3)) contrary to the general rule that a renewal on or after January 15, 1989 in favour of an existing protected or statutory tenant will create a protected tenancy (HA 1988, s.34(1)(b)): see p.250 above).

It follows that possession of most properties which were let on protected shorthold tenancies will by now have been recovered by the landlord. Nevertheless there will still be some cases where the fixed term has expired but the former protected tenant (or his statutory successor on death) is still holding over. Case 19 remains available in respect of such a tenant. It also applies where such a tenant has (before January 15, 1989) taken a new tenancy of the dwelling-house, notwithstanding that in neither case will the tenant be a protected shorthold tenant following expiry of the initial fixed term. (See section 55(2) and *Gent v. de la Mere* (1988) 20 H.L.R. 199).

Case 19 provides that possession proceedings have to be begun within three months of expiry of a written notice served on the tenant by the landlord stating that proceedings for possession under Case 19 may be brought after its expiry. This is of course quite distinct from the pre-tenancy shorthold notice. The notice of intended possession proceedings must expire not earlier than three months after it is served, but if the tenancy is a periodic tenancy, it must also expire not earlier than the date on which that periodic tenancy could be brought to an end by a notice to quit served by the landlord on the same day if that is later than three months. (For the requirements of a valid notice to quit, see p.127 above).

A Case 19 notice must be served within the three-month period before the date on which the protected shorthold tenancy comes to an end. Otherwise it must be served in the period of three months immediately before any anniversary of that date. Thus if the initial fixed term has ended without notice having been served by the landlord there will be a three-month period in each successive year when the landlord will have the opportunity to serve a Case 19 notice on the tenant and then bring possession proceedings. If the landlord serves a valid Case 19 notice and does not act upon it, any subsequent notice will not be valid if it is served earlier than three months after expiry of the earlier notice. (See *Ridehalgh v. Horsefield and Isherwood* (1992) 24 H.L.R. 453, CA) If the tenancy has become periodic the landlord will also need to end that tenancy by a notice to quit.

Case 20—servicemen

The purpose of this ground, which was added by Housing Act 1980, s.67, was to permit a member of the armed forces to let a dwelling-house to a tenant and to be able to recover possession at some time in the future if certain conditions are satisfied. The conditions are that—

(1)   the dwelling-house is required as a residence for the owner; or

(2)   the owner has died and the dwelling-house is required as a residence for a member of his family who was residing with him at the time of his death; or

(3)   the owner has died and the dwelling-house is required by a successor in title as his residence or for the purpose of disposing of the property with vacant possession; or

(4) the dwelling-house is subject to a mortgage made by deed before the tenancy was created and the mortgagee requires possession in or to sell with vacant possession in exercise of the mortgagee's express or statutory power of sale; or

(5) the dwelling-house is not reasonably suitable to the needs of the owner, having regard to his place of work, and he needs to be able to sell with vacant possession in order to acquire as his residence a dwelling-house which is more suitable to those needs.

The ground, although wider in terms, is clearly designed for the benefit of a member of the armed forces who has bought a property with a view to retirement from the forces but has let the property in the meantime.

In order to rely on this ground the landlord must have given notice in writing to the tenant not later than the tenancy began that possession might be recovered under this case. As noted above the court has a discretion to waive the need for service of that notice if it considers that it would be otherwise just and equitable to make a possession order.(See p.278 above for the exercise of this discretion by the court.)

The expedited possession procedure referred to above is available in the case of a claim based on Case 20 where the dwelling-house is required for occupation by the owner or (where he has died) for any member of his family who resided with him when he last occupied it as his residence. However, it will not be available where the landlord is relying on the court exercising its power to dispense with the need to have served a Case 11 notice on the tenant (see p.279 above).

Suitable alternative accommodation

We saw above that even if the landlord is unable to recover possession on the basis of one or more of the above grounds for possession a possession order will nevertheless still be made if the court is satisfied both that it is reasonable to make a possession order and that suitable alternative accommodation is available for the tenant or will be available for him when the possession order takes effect (RA 1977, s.98(1)(a) and Sched. 15, Part IV). The relevant provisions are very similar to those in the Housing Act 1988, Sched. 2, Part III and reference should be made to the discussion in Chapter 9 above). It should also be recalled that since January 15, 1989 any new tenancy will normally be an assured or assured shorthold tenancy under that Act and not a Rent Act protected tenancy (p.205 above). Nevertheless, if the court is satisfied that it is appropriate to order possession on the basis of the availability of suitable alternative accommodation, it may direct that the tenancy be a protected tenancy if further satisfied that in the circumstances an assured tenancy (or presumably since February 28, 1997 an assured shorthold tenancy) will not afford the tenant the required security (Housing Act 1988, s.34(1)(c)). (See also *Laimond Properties Ltd v. Al-Shakarchi* [1998] E.G.C.S. 21 (p.250 above).

D. ASSIGNMENT AND SUB-LETTING

Protected tenancy

A protected tenant can at common law lawfully assign or sub-let the whole or part of the premises in the same way as any other contractual tenancy unless of course the relevant transaction is prohibited by the terms of the lease. (see p.79 above). An unlawful assignment will be a breach of covenant and may give rise to possession proceedings on the basis of the discretionary ground for possession in Case 1 of Rent Act 1977, Sched. 15 (see p.275 above). Furthermore, even if the assignment is not in breach of covenant, Case 6 provides a discretionary ground for possession where the tenant has since December 8, 1965 (or certain other dates for tenancies which became regulated by legislation subsequent to the Rent Act 1965) assigned the whole of the dwelling-house, or sub-let part the remainder having already been sub-let, without the consent of the landlord. Of course where the assignment or sub-letting is not in breach of covenant the landlord will otherwise need to be able to determine the contractual tenancy before seeking possession of the dwelling-house.

Statutory tenancy

We have seen above that if a statutory tenant purports to assign or sub-let the whole dwelling-house and goes out of occupation the tenancy will cease to be a statutory tenancy because the tenant will no longer be occupying the dwelling-house as a residence for the purposes of Rent Act 1977, s.2. But it should also be remembered that a lawful sub-letting of part may be possible.

Protection of sub-tenants

Where the tenancy of a protected or statutory tenant who has sub-let the dwelling-house comes to an end (for whatever reason), the sub-tenant will then be deemed to hold as a tenant directly of the head landlord as if the tenant's statutorily protected tenancy (whether it be contractual or statutory) had continued (Rent Act 1977, s.137(2), (4)). Thus the sub-tenant will replace the tenant on the same terms under which the latter formerly held. A possession order against the tenant will not give the landlord an automatic right to recover possession as against the sub-tenant (s.137(1)). Nonetheless, if the sub-letting, albeit not in breach of covenant, did not have the landlord's consent then Case 6 (above) can be used not only against the tenant but also the sub-tenant. Otherwise it would in practice be useless to landlords (*Leith Properties Ltd v. Byrne* [1983] Q.B. 433).

Head-lease not protected

Section 137(3) of the Rent Act 1977, provides somewhat cryptically that—

"Where a dwelling-house—

(a)   forms part of premises which have been let as a whole on a superior tenancy but do not constitute a dwelling-house let on a statutorily protected tenancy; and

(b)   is itself subject to a protected or statutory tenancy

then, from the coming to an end of the superior tenancy, this Act shall apply in relation to the dwelling-house as if, in lieu of the superior tenancy, there had been separate tenancies of the dwelling-house and of the remainder of the premises, for the like purposes as under the superior tenancy, and at rents equal to the just proportion of the rent under the superior tenancy."

In recent years there has been considerable controversy over the issue of whether this provision gives a sub-tenant Rent Act protection on determination of his landlord's lease where that lease was not a protected or statutory tenancy.

A common scenario is where the head tenancy is a business tenancy (within Part II of the Landlord and Tenant Act 1954) of premises which include a dwelling-house which has been sub-let to a sub-tenant. The question to be determined is whether on the coming to an end of the head tenancy the sub-tenant is entitled to remain as a protected or statutory tenant.

In *Pittalis v. Grant* [1989] Q.B. 605 there was a tenancy of a shop with a flat above. The flat was sub-let for a term on a protected tenancy which became statutory on expiry of the contractual term. When the head lease was surrendered the head landlord sought possession as against the sub-tenant. The Court of Appeal held, controversially, that the sub-tenant did not become protected as against the head landlord because the subject matter of the head lease (the shop and flat), "the premises", was not a dwelling-house for the purposes of the Rent Act 1977. (It was a tenancy within Part II of the Landlord and Tenant Act 1954). The Court of Appeal considered itself bound by the decision of the House of Lords in *Maunsell v. Ollins* [1975] A.C. 373 where it had been held that the sub-tenancy of a cottage on a farm did not become protected on the determination of the head tenancy, the subject matter of which comprised the whole farm which was not premises which could be described as a dwelling-house. The actual decision in *Maunsell v. Ollins* was subsequently reversed by the addition of section 137(4) which ensures that where the head tenancy is of an agricultural holding the sub-tenant can nevertheless become protected on the ending of the superior tenancy. However, the decision in *Pittalis v. Grant* was not statutorily reversed, in so far as it precluded protection for residential sub-tenants of business tenants on the coming to an end of the head tenancy. Indeed the decision was followed by the Court of Appeal in *Bromley Park Garden Estates Ltd v. George* [1991] 2 E.G.L.R. 95 (where leave to appeal to the House of Lords was refused) and *London Regional Transport v. Brandt* (1996) 29 H.L.R. 441. Nevertheless, despite this strong line of authority, the Court of Appeal has now held these decisions to be *per incuriam* and thus not to be followed.

In three appeals, *Wellcome Trust Ltd v. Hammad, Ebied and another v. Hopkins and another* and *Church Commissioners for England v. Baines* [1998] 1 All E.R. 657 the Court of Appeal held in each case that, on the true construction of Rent Act 1977, s.137(3), a sub-tenant of a dwelling-house which comprised part of larger premises held on a business tenancy became protected as against the freeholder when the head tenancy came to an end. The Court also held that the earlier Court of Appeal authority to the contrary had failed to have regard to the wording of Rent Act 1977, s.24(3). This provides that "A tenancy shall not be a regulated tenancy if it is a tenancy to which Part II of the Landlord and Tenant Act 1954 applies (*but this provision is without prejudice to the application of any other provision of this Act to a sub-tenancy of any part of the premises comprised in such a tenancy*)" (italics supplied). This necessarily assumes that the 1954 Act can apply to premises which can be a dwelling-house for the purposes of the Rent Act. Indeed it was the Court's view that this was recognised as such in *Maunsell v. Ollins*.

E. RENT REGULATION

Introduction

The history of rent control in the private rented sector of the housing market is long and chequered (see Chapter 8 above). As we have seen it has to all intents and purposes been abandoned for virtually all tenancies created on or after January 15, 1989, although rent regulation remains in force for tenancies still governed by the Rent Act 1977. For the purposes of rent regulation under the Rent Act 1977 a "regulated tenancy" is defined as a protected or statutory tenancy (s.18(1)). Furthermore where a regulated tenancy is followed by a statutory tenancy of the same dwelling-house the two are treated together as constituting one regulated tenancy (s.18(2)).

The concept of the fair rent is at the heart of the scheme of rent regulation for regulated tenancies which was first introduced by the Rent Act 1965 and is now contained in Part IV of the Rent Act 1977. The Act enables either the landlord or tenant (or both jointly) under a regulated tenancy to apply to a local rent officer for determination and registration of a "fair rent" which, when registered, will provide a rent limit for any regulated tenancy of the dwelling-house which is the subject of the tenancy (see Rent Act 1977, Part IV and Schedules 10 and 11 for the relevant machinery). A party who is dissatisfied with the rent officer's determination may ask for the matter to be referred to an independent tribunal, a rent assessment committee. The committee, who will consider the matter of the fair rent afresh, may confirm the rent determined by the rent officer or determine a different rent which will then be registered. The rent confirmed or determined by the committee will be effective from the date of the committee's decision (RA 1977, s.72). After first registration of a rent under Part IV of the 1977 Act, application for a fresh registration by landlord or tenant (unless made by them jointly) can only be made at two-yearly intervals save in exceptional circumstances provided for by the Act (e.g. where there has been a material change in the condition of the house, such as a modernisation of the property by the landlord) (RA 1977, s.67(3)). Rent assessment committees are required, if requested, to state the reasons for their determination in writing (Tribunal and Inquiries Act 1992, s.10 and Sched. 1 and S.I. 1971 No.1065 reg. 10A). Although any party who is dissatisfied with a Committee's decision may appeal to the High Court on a point of law, in practice many appeals are on the alternative ground of judicial review. Indeed it has been held that this is the most appropriate route where what is being challenged are the reasons given by the Committee for their decision (*Ellis & Sons Fourth Amalgamated Properties v. Southern Rent Assessment Panel* (1984) 270 E.G. 39; *R. v. London Rent Assessment Panel, ex parte. Chelmsford Building Co.* (1986) 278 E.G. 979). This is because it enables the Committee to be represented (they are not party to a statutory appeal) and permits a further appeal to the Court of Appeal and or House of Lords.In this context it is likely that inadequate reasons will of themselves be ground for quashing an assessment on the basis that they lead to an inference that the decision making process was irrational or otherwise unlawful (*Crake v. Supplementary Benefits Commission* [1982] 1 All E.R. 498, 507 *per* Woolf L.J. and *Curtis v. London Rent Assessment Committee* [1997] 4 All E.R. 842, 868 *per* Auld L.J.).

The rent before registration

(a) During the contractual tenancy

The general rule, where a rent has not been registered for a regulated tenancy under Part IV of the Rent Act 1977 is that there is no statutory rent limit during the contractual period of any regulated tenancy, save where the tenant under the regulated tenancy is a "tenant having security of tenure". A person is a "tenant having security of tenure" if immediately before the grant of his tenancy, he was either—

(1) a regulated tenant of the dwelling-house; or

(2) a person who might have succeeded as a statutory tenant the person who was the regulated tenant of the dwelling-house at that time (s.51(1)).

In such cases the rent recoverable cannot exceed the rent under the earlier tenancy unless the new tenancy agreement satisfies certain statutory requirements. These require the agreement to be in writing and signed by both parties. It must also inform the tenant that the agreement will not prevent the landlord or tenant from applying at any time to the rent officer for registration of a fair rent (subss.51(3) and (4)).

In similar vein, if a tenant under a protected tenancy which is a regulated tenancy agrees to a rent increase this will be a "rent agreement with a tenant having security of tenure" and will need to comply with the above statutory requirements. These requirements do not apply where the increase comes about as a result of the operation of a rent review clause in the tenancy agreement, although the tenant can of course seek registration of a fair rent at a subsequent stage (see *Sopwith v. Stuchbury* (1983) 17 H.L.R. 50, CA).

(b) Statutory periods

The general rule, where there is no registered rent, is that the recoverable rent for any statutory period cannot exceed the rent recoverable for the last contractual period of the regulated tenancy (s.45(1)).

The fair rent scheme

(a) Effect of registration of a fair rent

Where a rent for a dwelling-house has been registered under Part IV of the Rent Act 1977 the rent recoverable under any regulated tenancy of the dwelling-house (both for the contractual and statutory periods of such a tenancy) is limited to the registered amount (ss. 44(1), 45(1)). Thus once a rent has been registered that will become the rent limit until altered by a subsequent registration. It forms the limit not only for the regulated tenancy in respect of which the rent is registered but also for any subsequent regulated tenancy or tenancies of the dwelling-house (see, *e.g. Rakhit v. Carty* [1990] 2 Q.B. 315).

It will be recalled that because, save in exceptional cases, it has not been possible to create new regulated tenancies since January 15, 1989, the number of regulated tenancies is gradually diminishing. Of those that still exist many will already have a fair rent registered. However, others will not and it is therefore still possible for an application for first registration to be made in such cases. The effect of such a registration is as follows—

(1) If the contractual rent or, as the case may be, the rent payable for any statutory period is higher than the registered rent, the excess is irrecoverable from the tenant (ss.44(2)

and 45(2)(a)). Any overpayment can be recovered by proceedings against the landlord and/or by withholding rent up to the amount in question (s.57(2)).

(2) If the rent payable immediately before registration is lower than the registered rent the landlord will (in the absence of a contractual provision for variation of the rent) have to wait until the contractual tenancy has determined before he is able to obtain an increase in the recoverable rent up to the registered amount. He will be able to do this by serving a notice of increase (in the prescribed form) which can be served before or after the contractual tenancy has ended (s.49(3)). If the contractual tenancy is a periodic tenancy terminable by notice to quit the landlord may instead serve a notice of increase which has the dual effect of acting as a notice to quit to terminate the contractual tenancy as well as increasing the rent. This is provided that the date from which the tenancy could have been determined by a notice to quit is earlier than that specified in the notice of increase as the effective date of the increase (s.49(4)). If the tenancy was already a statutory tenancy immediately before registration of the fair rent then following registration the rent may be increased up to the registered amount by a notice of increase specifying the date from which the increase is to take effect (s.45(2)(b)).

(b) What is a fair rent?

It should not come as a surprise to learn that the term "fair rent", laden as it is with unarticulated values, receives little statutory elaboration. The architects of the Rent Act 1965 studiously avoided any attempt to provide a statutory definition. Instead of a definition the Rent Act 1977 provides a number of criteria either to be taken into account or to be ignored by rent officers and rent assessment committees when performing the task of determining a fair rent.

Factors to be taken into account The Rent Act 1977, s.70(1) provides that when assessing a fair rent—

"regard shall be had to all the circumstances (other than personal circumstances) and in particular to:

(a) the age, character, locality and state of repair of the dwelling-house;
(b) if any furniture is provided for use under the tenancy; the quantity, quality and condition of the furniture; and
(c) any premium, or sum in the nature of a premium, which has been or may be lawfully required or received on the grant, renewal, continuance or assignment of the tenancy."

Each of these factors will be examined in turn.

"All the circumstances (other than personal circumstances)" This is clearly a reference to those circumstances which affect the rental value of the property. (*Palmer v. Peabody Trust* [1975] Q.B. 604 at 608, DC, *per* Lord Widgery C.J.; see also *Metropolitan Property Holdings v. Finegold* [1975] 1 W.L.R. 349, DC where the presence of a school - in the St John's Wood area of London - whose intake was restricted to the children of American families in London, was held to be a factor to be taken into account). In the leading case of *Mason v. Skilling* [1974] 1 W.L.R. 1437,1443 Lord Kilbrandon considered that the decision about which circumstances are relevant and which are not was a matter calling for the application of a valuer's professional skill and experience. Despite the undoubted truth of this observation the issue is not entirely devoid of legal principle and it is possible to identify the sort of circumstances which are in law relevant or irrelevant. In order to define "all the circumstances" some guidance can be obtained from other sections of the Rent Act which clearly assume the relevance of certain factors to the rent fixing process.

(a) The terms of the existing tenancy These are clearly relevant. The Rent Register entry will state the contractual allocation between the parties of responsibility for internal and external repairs and decorations and will usually state whether the statutory repairing obligations in sections 11–17 of the Landlord and Tenant Act 1985 as amended are applicable (see p.50 above).

(b) Services The Rent Act provides that the registered rent shall include any sums payable by the tenant to the landlord for the use of furniture or for services, whether or not those sums are included in the rent or payable under a separate agreement (RA 1977, s.71(1)). This clearly entails consideration of any relevant services when determining the fair rent.

When it comes to the valuation of services the actual costs are only a guide and it may prove to be necessary to make appropriate adjustments to those figures to reflect the value of the services to the tenant. In *Metropolitan Properties Co. v. Noble* [1968] 1 W.L.R. 838 a rent assessment committee was held to have acted properly when it reduced the sum attributable to the cost of central heating to a dwelling-house on the basis that the system was inefficient. (See also *R. v. London Rent Assessment Panel, ex parte. Cliftvylle Properties Ltd* (1983) 266 E.G. 44.)

"The age, character, locality and state of repair of the dwelling-house" It is clear that the registered rent should reflect these matters from the effective date (*Nicoll v. First National Developments* (1972) 226 E.G. 301). That date is the date of registration in the case of a determination by the rent officer. In the case of a determination by a rent assessment committee it is the date of the committee's determination (RA 1977, s.72).

(a) Locality The reference to locality clearly directs rent officers and committees to have regard to the proximity or absence of amenities such as shops, transport, etc., and locational disadvantages such as nearby industry or other detrimental features. Features which are of benefit because of the personal preferences of a particular tenant should in principle be disregarded. The selection of the bounds of the "locality" for the purpose of this provision is a matter for the discretion of the rent officer or committee (*Palmer v. Peabody Trust*, above, at p.610 *per* Lord Widgery C.J.). Although there is no authority on the limits (if any) to this discretion, it has been said that the reference to locality in section 70(1) "will normally, though not always, mean the immediate locality, because as a rule only the character of the immediate neighbourhood is likely to affect the value of the house" (Report of the Committee on the Rent Acts, Cmnd. 4609 (1971), p.61).

(b) State of repair Rent officers and committees are required to assess a rent on the basis of the actual state of repair of the property at the relevant time. Therefore they must take into account any disrepair brought about by the landlord's failure to comply with his repairing obligations. However, it has also been held that the landlord's covenant to repair is of some value to the tenant (*Sturolson v. Mauroux* (1988) 20 H.L.R. 332, CA). Thus even if there has been a closing

order in respect of the premises, it does not follow that the fair rent should be nil (*Williams v. Khan* (1982) 43 P.& C.R. 1, CA. On the other hand it has also been held that a rent officer was justified in determining a nominal rent for uninhabitable premises where the disrepair was attributable to neither the landlord nor the tenant (*McGee v. London Borough of Hackney* (1969) 210 E.G. 1431 (where it was alleged that the disrepair was attributable to the work of a poltergeist!). It should be noted that the tenancy may then cease to be protected because of the low-rent exception to protection (Rent Act 1977, s.5. see p.253 above). The repairing obligations of the parties will depend upon the terms of the lease in conjunction with any obligations implied by common law and/or by statute. (see Chapter 13 above). In connection with the issue of repair, it should be noted that if a property is in good repair because of the tenant carrying out repairs which in law are the responsibility of the landlord, the fair rent will be on the basis of the property as repaired. In other words the tenant does not get a discount by way of reduced rent (*Stewart's Judicial Factor v. Gallacher* (1967) S.C. 59).

"The quantity, quality and condition of any furniture provided" When assessing the amount in the rent attributable to the use of furniture, the use value of the furniture to the tenant should be considered. A tenant may legitimately claim that to him a Chippendale chair is something to sit on and has the same utility as an ordinary mass-produced chair. In *Palser v. Grinling* [1948] A.C. 291, Viscount Simon stated that it is the value of the landlord's covenant to provide furniture which controls the figure to be arrived at, and that whilst the burden of wear and tear falls on the landlord he is not, in the absence of an express covenant, under any obligation to repair or renew the furniture from time to time. He went on to make it clear that if a landlord provides more furniture than the tenant reasonably needs having regard to the nature of the accommodation, then the rent will be limited to the use of the articles for which there is such a need. However, it has subsequently been held that if the landlord has a contractual obligation to provide furniture if requested to do so by the tenant, then the tenancy may be a furnished tenancy for the purposes of rent assessment, even if at the tenant's request none of the landlord's furniture is physically on the premises and all the furniture which is there was provided by the tenant (*R. v. London Rent Assessment Panel, ex.parte. Mota* (1988) 20 H.L.R. 159).

"Any premium, or sum in the nature of a premium, which has been or may be lawfully required or received on the grant, renewal, continuance or assignment of the tenancy" In the case of some tenancies covered by the fair rent scheme the general ban on premiums in connection with the granting and assigning of protected tenancies is inapplicable. In such cases, therefore, premiums are taken into account.

Scarcity

It was explained above that rent officers and committees are given little guidance as to what is meant by a "fair rent". Nevertheless, the Act does direct them to assume that—

> "the number of persons seeking to become tenants of similar dwelling-houses in the locality on the terms (other than those relating to rent) of the regulated tenancy is not substantially greater than the number of such dwelling-houses in the locality which are available for letting on such terms (s.70(2))."

The purpose of this provision is clear. If there is an excess of demand over the supply of rented accommodation of the kind in question, then it can be expected that the market rent will be higher than would be the case were supply and demand to be approximately in balance. Therefore a rent officer or committee is to fix a fair rent on the assumption that there is such a balance, despite the true factual state of affairs. Hence the calculation of a "fair rent" will require some discount to be made on the market rent to eliminate that element of the rent which reflects the scarcity in question (*Western Heritable Investment Co. v. Husband* [1983] 2 A.C. 849, HL). Of course this process is only part of the overall task of assessing a fair rent and therefore it does not mean that if supply exceeds demand or that supply and demand are broadly in balance, the agreed contractual rent will automatically be a fair rent. The rent officer or committee still has to assess a fair rent in the light of all the criteria discussed above. The concept of scarcity, which lay dormant for many years has recently been revived as a contentious issue and is discussed further below.

Locality

It has been held that the sort of scarcity envisaged by section 70(2)—

"is a broad, overall general scarcity affecting a really substantial area (*Metropolitan Property Holdings v. Finegold*, above at p 354 *per* Lord Widgery C.J.)."

The Court held that the fixing of the locality for this purpose is a matter for the rent officer or committee who, bearing in mind that different parts of the country require different considerations, were advised "to draw their inspiration from the area with which they are familiar in their work." (See also *Northumberland and Durham Property Trust Ltd v. London RAC* [1998] E.G.C.S. 56).

Statutory disregards

It was mentioned above that the Rent Act not only requires rent officers and rent assessment committees to take into account specific matters when assessing a fair rent, but also requires them to disregard certain other factors, which are examined below.

(a) Personal circumstances

The personal circumstances of either the landlord or the tenant play no part in the assessment of a fair rent. Thus the personal means and characteristics of the landlord and tenant are obviously not relevant.

Problems can sometimes arise in connection with housing association lettings. Because of their funding arrangements and social purposes such landlords have often sought registration of an "affordable rent" at a level below that which the rent officer or rent assessment committee would normally consider appropriate for the property in question. In law the social nature of the landlord is clearly a personal circumstance and to be disregarded. In practice a lower level of rents has in the past tended to emerge for housing association tenancies, although in recent years the gap between housing association and private sector fair rents has significantly narrowed. This is because the funding arrangements have changed since 1989 making associations more reliant on non-government sources of finance which have to be obtained on the open market on commercial terms. Hence associations have been under increasing pressure to maximise their rental income thereby weakening the incentive to seek relatively lower fair rents.

(b) Any disrepair or other defect attributable to a failure by the tenant under the regulated tenancy or any predecessor in title of his to comply with any terms thereof (RA 1977. s.70(3)(a))

In this connection it should be recalled that in the case of tenancies granted on or after October 24, 1961 the major structural and external repairing obligations are placed by statute on the landlord and the parties cannot contract out of this position (see p.50 above). In so far as a repairing obligation is otherwise legitimately placed upon the tenant any disrepair which is a breach of that obligation is to be disregarded when assessing a fair rent. In other words the fair rent is to be assessed as if the obligation had been complied with.

(c) Any improvement carried out otherwise than in pursuance of the terms of the tenancy by the tenant under the regulated tenancy or any predecessor in title of his (RA 1977, s.70(3)(b))

This "disregard" is included to prevent any injustice arising from an assessment which would otherwise have been based upon the present physical state of the property even where that state had been improved by the tenant or a predecessor in title.

"Improvement" for this purpose (contrary to the general rule) includes the replacement of any fixture or fitting, *e.g.* replacing old fixtures with their modern equivalent (RA 1977 s.70(4)). This is an extension to the general definition for the purposes of Part IV whereby (save where the context requires otherwise) "improvement" includes structural alteration, extension or addition and the provision of additional fixtures or fittings, but does not include anything done by way of decoration or repair (s.75(1)). Thus, as noted above, if a tenant carries out repairs which are the landlord's obligation, then the rent will be fixed for the property in its improved state with no allowance to the tenant. Predecessor in title refers to a previous tenant under that tenancy (*Henry Smith's Charity Trustees v. Hemmings* (1982) 45 P.& C.R. 377, CA). In practice this is taken to extend, in the case of a statutory tenancy, to improvements carried out by the former protected tenant. The reference to the need for the improvements to have been carried out "under the regulated tenancy" means that if they were carried out by the tenant before he took the tenancy they are probably not to be disregarded unless he had the benefit of a contract for a tenancy at that time. (The point was left open in *Hemmings*).

(d) Tenant's improvement of or damage to furniture provided by the landlord

If any furniture is provided for the tenant's use under the regulated tenancy, any improvement to the furniture by the tenant or any predecessor in title of his is to be disregarded. Also to be disregarded is any deterioration in the condition of the furniture due to any ill-treatment by the tenant, any person residing or lodging with him or any sub-tenant of the tenant (RA 1977, s.70(3)(e)).

Methods of determining a fair rent

Although, as explained above, the Rent Act 1977 specifies particular matters which must be taken into account or, as the case may be, disregarded when assessing a fair rent, it perhaps understandably gives no further guidance on how the fair rent is actually to be assessed. When the system of rent registration was first introduced, rent officers and rent assessment committees had to feel their way slowly, being guided by the limited statutory criteria and such assistance as could be gleaned from the court decisions which gradually emerged. Needless to say a number of different methods of assessment were proposed, particularly by or on behalf of landlords, and in practice the decisions of rent officers and committees across the country reflected these different approaches to the crucial issue of how one arrived at a fair rent.

Eventually the validity of these differing approaches was tested in court. The principal methods which emerged are discussed below.

(a) Market rent less scarcity—phase 1

This method, which was described as "a well recognised and thoroughly reputable route" (*Metropolitan Property Holdings Ltd v. Laufer* (1974) 29 P.& C.R. 172, 174, *per* Lord Widgery C.J.) first entails the assessment of a market rent for the type of dwelling-house in question, noting the matters which under the Act are to be taken into account or disregarded as the case may be. There must then be deducted from that rent such percentage as appears to represent any scarcity element in the rent, if that element is substantial. When the system of fair rent regulation was introduced in 1965 this method of assessment was frequently adopted and reference was made, by rent officers and rent assessment committees, to market rents recently negotiated for properties which did not have a registered rent. This comparable evidence could then be adjusted to take account of all relevant difference including the "scarcity factor" in order to arrive at the fair rent for the property whose rent was being determined. However, in the course of time such evidence was hard to come by as more and more rents were registered and the rents of those tenancies which had not been registered came to be negotiated in the "shadow of the Rent Act". Thus the market rent less scarcity method fell out of favour and resort was increasingly had to an alternative method assessment. This was the use of registered "comparables".

(b) Registered comparables

In the leading case of *Mason v. Skilling* [1974] 1 W.L.R. 1437,1439, Lord Reid said that section 70 leaves it open to the rent officer or rent assessment committee to adopt any method or methods of ascertaining a fair rent provided that they do not use any method which is unlawful or unreasonable and then went on to state that—

> "The most obvious and direct method is to have regard to registered rents of comparable houses in the area. In the initial stages this method may not be available but as the number of comparable registered rents increases the more likely it will be that it will lead to a correct result."

The validity of this approach was endorsed in *Western Heritable Investment Co. Ltd v. Husband* [1983] 2 A.C. 849, 859, where Lord Brightman declared that—

> "If comparables are available which do not reflect, or are discounted to reflect, scarcity value, such comparables are the best guide to a fair rent."

The rationale of the comparables method was explained in *Tormes Property Co. v. Landau* [1971] 1 Q.B. 261 by Lord Parker C.J., when he said that—

> "It must surely be of the essence to this whole scheme that there should be uniformity, and no doubt as the volume of registered fair rents increases in the future no one will go to market rent less scarcity, they will go straight to the enormous volume of fair rents that have been registered."

He went on to approve a passage in the 27th edition of Woodfall, *The Law of Landlord and Tenant*, to the effect that if there were no suitable comparables, the best test was that of market rent less a percentage reduction to reflect scarcity, if substantial, and that a fair return on the landlord's capital investment may be a guide or check on rental values, but it is by no means conclusive.

This last observation is a reference to another method of assessment which is based on a "fair" return on capital value.

(c) Return on capital value

A dictum of Lord Reid is often cited in support of this method of assessment. His Lordship stated that a committee is—

> "entitled to have regard to the capital value. A fair rent should be fair to the landlord as well as fair to the tenant and it can be regarded as fair to the landlord that he should receive a fair return on his capital. (*Mason v. Skilling* [1974] 1 W.L.R. 1437,1440.)"

Too much should not be read into this observation, which simply says that the capital value method of assessment is not an unfair method. It does not say that it must be used. Indeed Lord Reid went on to approve the registered comparables method as the most appropriate method in most cases at that time.

The return on capital value method has always been considered a less than reliable instrument in its application to the fair rent scheme. The method involves attributing a capital value to the premises to which a notional rate of return is applied with deductions where relevant for factors such as onerous obligations in the lease or scarcity where this is reflected in the capital value. It suffers from a number of drawbacks not least the difficult task of determining the basis for the appropriate capital value and the appropriate rate of return. Landlords often suggest a sum representing their estimate of the vacant possession value of the property with which tenants would not necessarily agree. For reasons such as these this method of assessment was also eclipsed by the registered comparables method. Indeed the courts went so far as to hold that where registered comparables were available, the committee was impelled to reject any alternative basis of assessment that might have been urged upon them (*Ellis & Sons Fourth Amalgamated Properties v. Southern Rent Assessment Panel* (1984) 270 E.G. 39). Thus the argument frequently advanced by landlords, that, as the difference between market rents and registered rents under the Rent Acts widened, it became more and more necessary, if fairness was to be done by the landlord, to fix rents by reference to capital values and not merely by reference to existing registered rents, found little favour with the judiciary (see *e.g. Guppy's Properties Ltd v. Knott (No. 1)* (1978) 245 E.G. 1023, DC). Indeed a doctrine of precedent of sorts emerged as a result of the decision of the Court of Appeal in *London Rent Assessment Committee v. St George's Court* (1984) 48 P.& C.R. 230, CA where the court quashed the decision of a rent assessment committee which when determining a fair rent for a purpose-built flat disregarded a fair rent which had been assessed by another committee only three months earlier for the same type of flat in the same block. Griffiths L.J. observed (at p.234) that—

> "Unless it can be demonstrated to a rent assessment committee that the rent assessed for a comparable property has been arrived at upon such a fundamental misapprehension, then it is the duty of that rent assessment committee to regard such a previous assessment as a proper assessment of the fair rent and as the best evidence of the rent which would be fair for the property that it has under consideration. Of course all the circumstances have to be taken into account but when one is dealing with flats of the same layout, one on top of another, very weighty reasons would have to be shown before it would be permissible to depart, certainly to depart substantially, from the fair rent which had very recently been assessed for one of those similar flats."

(d) Market rent less scarcity—phase 2

We saw above that as more and more rents were registered, the market rent less scarcity method of assessment was largely supplanted by the registered comparables method. This was based on the assumption that the registered comparables were ultimately derived from rents determined under the market rent less scarcity method. In other words that they had a built in allowance for scarcity where present. Doubts were thrown on the validity of this assumption following the introduction of an unregulated market in the private rented sector for post-Housing Act 1988 tenancies. Landlords increasingly argued that market rental evidence for comparable properties had now become available. This evidence could therefore be used for the purposes of fair rent assessment for those tenancies which remained regulated, thereby facilitating the revival of the market rent less scarcity method of assessment. This was said to be consistent with the comparables method of assessment save that the comparables relied upon are not registered comparables decided without reference to market rental evidence but are current assured (or assured shorthold) tenancies let at market rents. Indeed it was strongly argued that traditional registered fair rents were markedly out of line with current market rental levels even when adjusted for scarcity and therefore were an unreliable guide for the purposes of fair rent assessment when registered rents came up for review. This argument succeeded at first instance in *BTE Ltd v. Merseyside & Cheshire Rent Assessment Committee* (1991) 24 H.L.R. 514 and was endorsed by the Court of Appeal in *Spath Holme Ltd v. Chairman of the Greater Manchester and Lancashire Rent Assessment Committee* (1996) 28 H.L.R. 107 and *Curtis v. London Rent Assessment Committee* [1997] 4 All E.R. 842. In the former case it was held that—

> "the fair rent to be determined is a market rent less the disregards and discounted for scarcity. Thus...if there is no scarcity and no disregards then the rents should be the same whether the tenancy is a regulated tenancy or an assured tenancy (*per* Morritt L.J. at 122–123.)"

In both cases the court held that following the Housing Act 1988, the best evidence of fair rent was close market rent comparables, and where such comparables were available enabling the identification of a market rent as a starting point, there was normally no need to refer to registered comparables at all. Indeed if there was a significant difference between registered fair rent comparables and close market rent comparables the committee could not prefer the former to the latter without some cogent explanation and analysis. Because of the significant gap which had emerged between levels of registered rents and market rents the above decisions have led to steep increases in fair rents in recent years. This, largely unforseen, result has been produced by a side-wind from the introduction of unregulated tenancies by the Housing Act 1988 and many of the tenants affected have felt betrayed in the light of assurances given at that time that the Act would not have any impact on existing Rent Act protected tenants. (See Hansard, H.C. cols 121–128, January 26, 1998 and the DETR Consultation Paper (*Limiting Fair Rent Increases* (May 1998) which proposed that increases be limited to RPI plus 10 per cent and thereafter RPI plus 5 per cent).

Arguments before rent officers and rent assessment committees now focus principally on two issues. The first relates to the differences between alleged market rent comparables and the subject property and the consequential adjustments that might need to be made to enable a fair rent to be determined. It is invariably the case that assured tenancy comparables are not close comparables in the sense that they will often be furnished lettings of improved and modernised properties. By contrast, many regulated tenancies are of properties which are unmodernised and let unfurnished. Because there may be little or no direct market rental evidence as to the latter it is necessary to arrive at a fair rent by making appropriate adjustments to the market rental evidence which is available for the better furnished properties.

The other main area of debate is focused on the issue of scarcity which has now been revived as a source of contention between landlord and tenant. In the past it was said that the decision as to whether relevant scarcity existed and to what degree if any was a matter of professional judgment. The Francis Committee stated that they had received a good deal of evidence "to the effect that the assessment of the scarcity element in the rent is an extremely difficult task and, indeed, that scarcity is incapable of measurement except by way of an intelligent guess." It was held that whilst landlords or tenants may suggest with or without supporting evidence an appropriate percentage deduction, if any, there was no obligation on a committee to quantify any element which it had allowed for scarcity (*Metropolitan Property Holdings v. Laufer* (1974) 29 P.& C.R. 172). However, a new approach to the issue in the context of reasons for decisions is required by *Curtis v. London Rent Assessment Committee* (above). Committees that have made a deduction from market rental evidence in respect of scarcity will be required to explain how any scarcity which they have found to exist has affected the rent in a particular case and to justify the particular discount applied (*Northumberland & Durham Property Trust Ltd v. London Rent Assessment Committee and others* [1998] E.G.C.S. 42. See also cases repealed at [1988] 24 E.G. and [1988] E.G.C.S. 56).

It is clear that much higher standards are now expected of rent assessment committees than in the early days of the fair rent scheme. In particular it has been held that where there is a marked difference between the rent indicated by the relevant market rental comparables and the rent determined by the committee an explanation for the difference with the use of some figures is now required. Failure to do so could lead to the decision being quashed on the basis that an error of law is thereby disclosed (see above).

F. PREMIUMS

The draughtsmen of the original rent controlling legislation were fully aware that rent controls would prove to be useless in themselves unless provision was also made to combat attempts to circumvent those controls by the taking of a premium in addition to or instead of rent. Consequently the legislation included appropriate anti-avoidance provisions. The relevant provisions are now contained in Part IX of the Rent Act 1977. Broadly speaking, they are designed to outlaw the taking of premiums on the grant, renewal, continuance or assignment of a protected tenancy.

In this connection it should be recalled that they only affect protected tenancies or restricted contracts under the Rent Act 1977. Assured tenancies and assured shorthold tenancies under the Housing Act 1988 are not subject to any prohibitions on premiums. Thus the relevant provisions are now likely to be applicable only in very limited circumstances such as where a premium is taken in consideration of the grant of a protected tenancy in one of those rare cases where such a tenancy can be created since January 15, 1989 (the most likely being a renewal in favour of an existing protected tenant).

Part IX of the Rent Act 1977 also contains complex provisions which govern permissible premiums on assignment where a premium was paid in respect of a tenancy at a time when it was lawful to require payment of a premium, but where the tenancy subsequently became protected and thus within the statutory prohibition on unlawful premiums.

G. Housing Association Tenancies

Introduction

We saw above that tenancies created before January 15, 1989 cannot take effect as protected (or statutory) tenancies under the Rent Act 1977 at any time where the landlord's interest is held by a housing association (Rent Act 1977, s.15). On the other hand, most of these tenancies will take effect as "housing association tenancies" and will be governed by the fair rent regime contained in Part VI of the Rent Act (s.86). That system of rent regulation was first applied to such tenancies by Part VIII of the Housing Finance Act 1972. "Housing association tenancies" will for the most part also be secure tenancies under the Housing Act 1985, and thus attract the security of tenure afforded to such tenancies by Part IV of that Act. (See Chapter 11 below).

It is important to remember that, save in specified exceptional cases, a tenancy created on or after January 15, 1989, under which the landlord's interest is held by a housing association will not take effect as a "housing association tenancy" or as a secure tenancy but will be governed by the new scheme for assured tenancies contained in Part I of the Housing Act 1988.

Thus tenants of the same association in the same development may be governed by different statutory codes. However, in practice, as far as security of tenure is concerned, their position will usually be equalised to some degree by additional contractual rights afforded to them under their tenancies, whilst their rents are likely to be lower than market rents because of government subsidy to associations and the "affordable rents" policy which they follow.

Definitions

A "housing association tenancy", for the purposes of the Rent Act 1977, is defined as a tenancy (other than a co-ownership tenancy) where:

(1) the interest of the landlord belongs to a housing association or housing trust, or to the Housing Corporation (or Housing for Wales); and

(2) the tenancy would be a protected tenancy but for section 15 or 16 of the Rent Act 1977; and

(3) it is not a tenancy to which Part II of the Landlord and Tenant Act 1954 applies (RA 1977, s.86).

It follows that if any of the exceptions to a protected tenancy in Part I of the Rent Act 1977, other than those contained in sections 15 and 16 are applicable, the tenancy cannot be a housing association tenancy. Thus "qualifying shared ownership leases" will be excluded from Part VI of the Rent Act 1977 because they are prevented from being a protected tenancy by section 5A of the Rent Act 1977 and not by either of sections 15 or 16. Consequently they cannot take effect as housing association tenancies. "Housing Association" has the same meaning as in the Housing Associations Act 1985 (RA 1977, s.86(3)).

A "co-ownership tenancy" is a tenancy granted by a cooperative housing association within the meaning of the Housing Associations Act 1985, where under the terms of the tenancy the tenant is entitled on giving up the tenancy to a sum representing a proportion of the capital value of the property (RA 1977, s.86(3A)).

"Housing trust" has the same meaning as in section 15 of the Rent Act 1987 (RA 1977, s.86(4)).

Date of creation

As already explained above, save in exceptional cases, a tenancy created on or after January 15, 1989 cannot be a protected tenancy.

It is similarly provided that, save for the exceptional cases set out below, a tenancy created on or after January 15, 1989 cannot be a "housing association tenancy" (Housing Act 1988, s.35). Consequently the rules relating to housing association tenancies which are examined below will, for the most part, apply only to tenancies created before January 15, 1989. Tenancies created by housing associations on or after that date will usually take effect in the same way as tenancies created by private landlords, *i.e.* as assured tenancies under the 1988 Act. However, it should be noted that where, on or after January 15, 1989, the landlord's interest under a protected or statutory tenancy becomes held by a housing association, a housing trust, the Housing Corporation or Housing for Wales the tenancy is not thereby prevented from being a housing association tenancy (HA 1988, s.35(5), (6)).

The principal exceptional circumstances in which a tenancy granted on or after January 15, 1989 ("the operative date") can be a housing association tenancy governed by Part VI of the Rent Act 1977 are—

(1)   where the tenancy was entered into in pursuance of a contract made before the operative date (Housing Act 1988, s.35(2)(a));

(2)   where it is granted to a person (alone or jointly with others) who, immediately before the tenancy was granted, was a tenant under a housing association tenancy and is so granted by the person who at that time was the landlord under that previous tenancy (HA 1988, s.35(2)(b)). The new tenancy may be of the same or different premises. This is designed to ensure that a tenant who was holding under a housing association tenancy when the Housing Act 1988 came into force will not be prejudiced by taking a new tenancy of the same or different premises after that date;

(3)   where it is granted to a person (alone or jointly with others) following a possession order under the Housing Act 1985 (s.84(2)(b), (c)) made on the basis of the availability of suitable alternative accommodation and where:

   (a)   the tenancy is of the premises which constitute the suitable alternative accommodation as to which the court was so satisfied; and

   (b)   the court considered in the possession proceedings that the tenancy would be a housing association tenancy (Housing Act 1988, s.35(2)(c)).

The primary significance of a tenancy being a housing association tenancy as defined in section 86 of the Rent Act 1977 is that the fair rents regime contained in Part VI of the 1977 Act will apply.

Registration of rents

The provisions of Part IV of the 1977 Act relating to application to the rent officer for determination of a fair rent and the criteria to be applied when making that determination (*i.e.* sections 67, 70, 71 (save for subsection (3)) and 72) are applied to housing association tenancies (RA 1977, s.87(1), (2)). The provisions dealing with the procedure to be followed on an application and any "appeal" to the rent assessment committee, along with those governing the effects of registrations are also applied to housing association tenancies (RA 1977, s.87(1), (6)).

Rents are to be registered in a separate part of the register kept under Part IV, and if the landlord's interest under the tenancy ceases to be held by a housing association, etc. any rent registration remains as effective as if it had been registered in the part of the register relating to regulated tenancies (RA 1977, s.87(1), (2)). Where a rent for a dwelling-house is registered, the rent limit is the amount so registered (RA 1977, s.86(1), (2)).

Rent limit before registration

There is still a rent limit for housing association tenancies even where a rent has not been registered. If the tenancy was created before January 1, 1973, the rent limit is the rent recoverable under the tenancy, as varied by any agreement before that date but not as varied by any agreement after that date (RA 1977, s.88(4)(a)).

If the tenancy was created on or after January 1, 1973 and not more than two years before the tenancy began the dwelling-house was subject to another tenancy (whether before 1973 or later), the rent limit is the rent recoverable under that other tenancy (or if more than one, the last of them) for the last rental period of that tenancy (RA 1977, s.88(4)(b)(5)).

In any other case the rent limit is the rent payable under the terms of the lease (and not that rent as varied by any subsequent agreement) (RA 1977, s.88(4)(c)).

The rent under a fixed term housing association tenancy can only be increased if there is a rent review clause in the lease. However, if a housing association tenancy is a weekly or other periodic tenancy, the rent may be increased with effect from the beginning of any rental period by the landlord serving a written notice of increase which specifies the date on which the increase is to take effect and is given to the tenant not later than four weeks before that date (RA 1977, s.93(1)). In reality any increase will be sought by means of an application to the rent officer. Indeed most housing association tenancies will have a registered rent.

Overpayment

There are provisions for the recovery of excess rent paid by the tenant similar to those applicable to regulated tenancies (RA 1977, s.94).

H. RESTRICTED CONTRACTS

Introduction

Until the Rent Act 1974, mainstream Rent Act protection by way of rent control and security of tenure was confined to unfurnished tenancies. Furnished tenancies and licences were governed by a separate code of protection which dated from the Furnished Houses (Rent Control) Act 1946. That Act was extended and amended from time to time, before being made permanent by the Rent Act 1965. The furnished lettings code was consolidated, along with the Rent Acts in Part VI of the Rent Act 1968 and the tenancies and licences in question were renamed "Part VI Contracts".

The scheme introduced by the 1946 Act established district rent tribunals to whom either party to the contract or the relevant local authority could refer the contract. The tribunal could then register a reasonable rent. If they did so it became unlawful to require or receive a rent exceeding the registered rent or payment of any premium in addition to the rent. The tribunal was also empowered to defer the operation of a notice to quit, thereby affording some degree of security of tenure.

The Rent Act 1974 dramatically altered the ambit of the two codes of protection by retrospectively extending full Rent Act protection to furnished tenancies which were reclassified as regulated tenancies rather than Part VI contracts. At the same time the 1974 Act provided that a "resident landlord" letting created on or after August 14, 1974 would no longer be capable of being a protected or statutory tenancy. Such a tenancy would take effect instead as a Part VI contract, even if the rent did not include payments in respect of furniture or services. Resident landlord *furnished* tenancies created before August 14, 1974 remained Part VI contracts and did not become protected or statutory tenancies. When the Rent Act legislation was consolidated in the Rent Act 1977, Part VI contracts were renamed "Restricted Contracts" (Rent Act 1977, s.19).

Further important changes were made by the Housing Act 1980. The power of the rent tribunal to defer the operation of a notice to quit was removed in relation to restricted contracts created on or after November 28, 1980. The only security afforded to occupiers in such cases is that where the contract has come to an end, *e.g.* by expiry of a fixed period or operation of a notice to quit, and the landlord obtains a possession order, the court has power to stay or suspend execution of the order or postpone the date of possession but not beyond a date later than three months after the making of the order (Rent Act 1977, s.106A as added by s.69(2) of the Housing Act 1980).

Restricted contracts were finally dealt a death blow by the Housing Act 1988 which provides that no new restricted contracts can be created on or after January 15, 1989, unless entered into in pursuance of a contract made before that date (Housing Act 1988, s.36(1)). It is further provided that if, on or after January 15, 1989 there is a variation in the terms of a restricted contract which affects the amount of the rent payable under the contract for the dwelling in question, the contract will be treated as a new contract entered into at the time of the variation (s.36(2)(a)).

The effect of this provision is that the "new" contract will not be a restricted contract. Any variation in the rent which comes about either as a result of a rent tribunal determination, or as a result of an agreement by the parties to make the rent payable the same as the registered rent is not treated as a variation for this purpose (s.36(3)). A variation on or after January 15, 1989 of any other terms will not automatically give rise to a new contract (s.36(2)(b)). It will thus be a matter of construction to determine whether the variation is sufficient to amount to the creation of a new contract.

Because restricted contracts traditionally tended to be relatively short term arrangements, the rate of decline of such contracts since January 15, 1989 has been rapid and far greater than that of protected tenancies which are usually longer term arrangements. The number of restricted contracts created before November 28, 1980 is now negligible. For these reasons the following discussion of the relevant provisions is limited to a relatively brief summary.

Restricted contracts defined

Restricted contracts arise in each of the following cases.

(1)   The first is a contract whereby one person (the "lessor") grants to another person (the "lessee"), in consideration of a rent which includes payment for the use of furniture

or for services, the right to occupy a dwelling (*i.e.* a house or part of a house) as a residence (Rent Act 1977, s.19). The definition thus extends to contractual licences. However this definition is subject to a number of exceptions. The most important of these exceptions applies where the contract creates a regulated tenancy, although it must be remembered that save in a few exceptional cases it has not been possible to create either a regulated tenancy or a restricted contract since January 15, 1989.

As noted above, since the Rent Act 1974 a tenancy where the rent payable includes a significant amount in respect of furniture was no longer precluded from being a regulated tenancy unless it was a pre-August 14, 1974 resident landlord letting, in which case it remained a restricted contract. After August 14, 1974 therefore, the most likely reason for a tenancy not being regulated, and thus capable of qualifying as a restricted contract under section 19, is where the rent includes payment for furniture or services (which brings it within section 19) but also includes payments in respect of board or substantial payments in respect of attendance (which prevents it being a regulated tenancy by virtue of Rent Act 1977, s.7). (But if a substantial element of the rent is in respect of board the contract cannot even be a restricted contract).

(2) The Rent Act 1977, s.20 provides that a resident landlord tenancy which is excluded by section 12 from being a protected or statutory tenancy (see p.257 above) will automatically take effect as a restricted contract whether or not the rent includes payment for the use of furniture or for services.

(3) A tenancy will also take effect automatically as a restricted contract, whether or not the rent includes payment for the use of furniture or for services, where the tenant has exclusive occupation of accommodation and the terms of the tenancy include the use of other "living" accommodation in common with the landlord (or the landlord and others) such that there is not a letting of a separate dwelling-house within section 1 of the 1977 Act (see p.252 above) (Rent Act 1977, s.21).

In practice, the introduction of the much wider resident landlord exception by the Rent Act 1974 (see above) will preclude the need to determine whether a tenancy is a restricted contract by virtue of section 21, because in the sharing cases where that provision applies, the landlord will usually be a resident landlord within section 12 and the tenancy will be treated as a restricted contract by virtue of section 20.

In all the above cases the rent must not have been varied since January 15, 1989 other than as a consequence of a rent tribunal determination.Otherwise the contract will be deemed to be a post-Housing Act 1988 contract and therefore cease to qualify as a restricted contract.

Excluded dwellings and contracts

The Rent Act 1977, s.19 provides for a number of other exclusions from the restricted contract regime including (a) premises with high rateable values, (b) contracts where the landlord is a local authority or one of certain specified public bodies or the Crown and (c) contracts which create a housing association tenancy within Part VI of the Rent Act 1977.

Rent control

The Housing Act 1980 abolished rent tribunals and transferred their functions to rent assessment committees who, when performing those functions, were to be known as rent tribunals. The scheme of rent control governing restricted contracts is as follows.

Either party under a restricted contract of a dwelling-house in respect of which there is no rent registered under Part V. of the Rent Act may make an application to a rent tribunal for determination of a reasonable rent. Of course if the rent is varied by agreement after January 15, 1989 a new contract is created and this will not be governed by the Rent Act 1977.

Rent tribunals are directed to do one of three things:

(1) to approve the rent payable under the contract; or
(2) to reduce or increase the rent to such sum as they may, in all the circumstances, think reasonable; or
(3) if they think fit in all the circumstances, dismiss the reference (RA 1977, s.78(2)).

Effect of registration of rent

Where the rent payable for any dwelling is entered in the register under Part V, it is not lawful to require or receive on account of rent for that dwelling under a restricted contract payment of any amount in excess of the rent so registered (RA 1977, s.81). Further applications may be made at intervals of not less than two years, save where the application is made jointly by the parties or where there has been a relevant change of circumstances so as to make the registered rent no longer a reasonable rent (RA 1977, s.80(1)).

Security of tenure

The position as to security of tenure for holders of restricted contracts was radically altered by the Housing Act 1980. Thus it is necessary to consider whether a restricted contract was entered into before November 28, 1980 or on or after that date.

(a) Contracts entered into before November 28, 1980

It should be noted that, because this limited form of security is linked to service of a notice to quit, it is not available to fixed term lessees where (as will usually be the case) the contract does not provide for its premature determination by notice.

Fixed-term contracts created before November 28, 1980 will now be encountered infrequently in practice, if at all. As noted above, the Act also applies to contractual licences determinable by notice despite the fact that technically such a notice is not a "notice to quit", which is a term properly reserved for a notice determining a tenancy. At common law whether a contractual licence has been validly determined by notice will depend upon the terms of the contract.

The position of lessees under periodic restricted contracts entered into before November 28, 1980 is set out below. References to referral of a contract to the tribunal mean a reference for the purpose of determining a reasonable rent which initially at least is a necessary condition of obtaining security even if there is no dispute about the rent.

Automatic security If a restricted contract is referred to the tribunal by the lessee any notice to quit served by the lessor on the lessee at any time before the tribunal's decision is given or within the six months thereafter shall not take effect before the expiry of that (six-month) period, unless the tribunal substitutes a shorter period (RA 1977, s.103(1)).

Application for security Where a notice to quit has been served, the lessee can apply to the rent tribunal for deferral of the operation of the notice provided that the period at the end of which the notice to quit takes effect, whether that be under the general law or by virtue of section 103, has not expired (RA 1977, s.104(1)).

If the lessee does make such an application the notice to quit cannot take effect before the application is determined by the tribunal who may direct that the notice to quit shall not have effect until the end of such period as they specify being not later than six months after the date on which the notice to quit would otherwise have taken effect (s.104(3)).

If the notice was served after the restricted contract was referred to the rent tribunal, but before the tribunal's decision is given or within six months after that decision then, as explained above, the operation of the notice is automatically deferred by section 103. In these circumstances section 104 enables the tribunal, on application by the lessee, to extend deferral of the operation of the notice to quit for a further period of up to six months after the date on which it was automatically deferred by the operation of section 103.

Furthermore, it is provided that as long as any period specified by the tribunal under section 104 has not expired, further applications may be made under section 104 for the period of security to be extended again. Such applications may be made indefinitely but in practice a tribunal is unlikely to continue granting security in this way.

If the rent tribunal refuse to give a direction under section 104 it is provided that the notice to quit is not to have effect before the expiry of seven days from the determination of the application. No subsequent application may be made under section 104 in relation to that notice to quit (s.104(4)).

In certain cases of misconduct by the lessee the tribunal has power to reduce the period of postponement of the notice to quit (s.106). Special rules apply in relation to recovery of possession by certain owner occupiers (s.105). However, few such contracts will exist today.

There are clearly very few remaining restricted contracts created before November 28, 1980 and the rent tribunal's jurisdiction is thus becoming obsolete. There were only 25 applications to rent tribunals throughout England and Wales in 1997.

(b) Contracts entered into on or after November 28, 1980

If the contract was entered into on or after November 28, 1980 the provisions of the Rent Act 1977 relating to security of tenure which are outlined above are inapplicable. Consequently once the contract has come to an end (*e.g.* by expiry of a notice to quit) the lessor may seek a possession order if the lessee refuses to leave.

On the making of an order for possession or at any time before execution of the order, the court may either stay or suspend execution of the order, or postpone the date of possession for such period or periods as the court thinks fit (s.106A(1)(2)). The power to delay possession is subject to an important qualification in that the court may not by any such order postpone the giving up of possession to a date later than three months after the making of the order (s.106A(3)).

Upon granting any such stay, suspension or postponement the court must, unless it considers that it would cause unreasonable hardship to the lessee or would otherwise be unreasonable, impose conditions with regard to the payment by the lessee of any arrears of rent (if any) and rent or mesne profits and impose such other conditions as it thinks fit (s.106A(4)).

Chapter 11

SECURE TENANCIES

Introduction

"Until 1980 public sector landlord and tenant law was something of a non-subject, mostly (if at all) treated as a legal clothes peg for public housing law to hang housing relationships upon, and featuring little in books or courses on landlord and tenant law. (*Hill and Redman's Law of Landlord and Tenant*, Vol. 2, para. D1.)"

The reason for the late development of a public sector law of landlord and tenant is that until the Housing Act 1980, public sector tenants had no security of tenure comparable to that afforded to tenants in the private sector by the Rent Acts. They were governed by the ordinary law of landlord and tenant. The assumption was that local authorities and other public bodies, who are of course politically accountable for their actions, could be relied upon to treat their tenants fairly. Any decisions which were in breach of the rules of natural justice or in excess of their statutory powers could be challenged by way of judicial review. (See *Bristol District Council v. Clark* [1975] 3 All E.R. 976). As Hill and Redman state (*op. cit.*): "General principles of public law and 'collectivist' housing policy ruled the roost." All this changed in 1980. In its manifesto for the 1979 general election, the Labour Party proposed that council tenants should be granted the benefit of a statutory code of protection which would cover security of tenure, limited succession rights, a right to exchange and other benefits, dealt with below. The election was lost but the new Conservative Government adopted much of the former Labour Government's proposals and the Tenant's Charter was eventually enacted in the Housing Act 1980. That Act introduced a new concept, "the secure tenancy", to describe the normal form of tenancy granted to public sector tenants which would attract the new statutory rights. The Act was retrospective in the sense that, along with new tenants, all existing tenants who satisfied the definition also became secure tenants. The Housing Act 1980 also introduced a right which the previous Government had certainly not been in favour of—the statutory right to buy. This enabled a qualifying local authority tenant to compel the landlord to sell him/her the freehold or grant him/her a long lease of their rented house at a favourable discount. The 1980 Act code, which became consolidated in the Housing Act 1985, was subsequently modified and extended in important ways by a number of Housing Acts (most notably the Housing and Building Control Act 1984, the Housing Act 1985, the Housing and Planning Act 1986, the Housing Act 1988, the Local Government and Housing Act 1989, the Leasehold Reform, Housing and Urban Development Act 1993 and the Housing Act 1996).

The present chapter comprises an examination of the concept of the secure tenancy and the rights afforded to secure tenants by the statutory code contained in the Housing Act 1985. Save where otherwise indicated, all references below are to that Act.

Secure tenancies

Save in specified exceptional cases, a tenancy under which a dwelling-house is let as a separate dwelling is a secure tenancy at any time when the conditions described in sections 80 and 81 as the landlord condition and the tenant condition are satisfied (s.79(1)(2)(a)). The exceptions are set out in Schedule 1.

"a dwelling-house is let as a separate dwelling" This is a hallowed expression which has been borrowed from the definition of a protected tenancy in section 1 of the Rent Act 1977 and has been used also by the Housing Act 1988, s.1 (definition of an assured tenancy). Reference should be made to Chapters 9 and 10 above for a discussion of its meaning where it will be seen that if premises are let for mixed residential and business purposes (and therefore within Part II of the Landlord and Tenant Act 1954) subsequent cessation of the business user element will not automatically render the tenancy secure because "let as" refers to the purpose of the letting (*Webb v. London Borough of Barnet* (1989) 21 H.L.R. 228, CA). At this point, however, it is worth noting that an occupant with exclusive possession of a hostel room or flat who (under the terms of the tenancy) is also required to share other living facilities with another occupier or occupiers of a separate part of the building will not have a secure tenancy because he will not have a "separate dwelling" for the purposes of section 79 (see *Parkins v. Westminster City Council* [1997] E.G.C.S. 163 and *Central YMCA Housing Association Ltd v. Saunders* (1990) 23 H.L.R. 212, CA). By contrast it is specifically provided that a person can still have a Rent Act protected tenancy of any exclusively occupied accommodation such as a bed-sitting room even though he also shares living accommodation with an occupier of another dwelling (Rent Act 1977, s.22 and p.252 above. See also Housing Act 1988, ss. 3 and 10).

It can be important to determine the extent of the accommodation comprised in the secure tenancy for a variety of reasons, including the applicability of the "right to buy" provisions of the Housing Act 1985 (see below). In *Tyler v. Royal Borough of Kensington and Chelsea* (1990) 23 H.L.R. 380 a secure tenant of a ground-floor flat was given a licence to occupy a first-floor flat whilst works were carried out on the ground-floor flat. The works were never done and the tenant continued to occupy both flats. He then exercised his right to buy the ground-floor flat, following which he moved upstairs and claimed to be able to buy that flat "as his principal home". It was held that the intention was that the top-floor flat was only licensed to be used in conjunction with the tenancy of the ground floor flat, and once that ended the licence also ended.

"...at any time when..." This indicates that the tenancy may move in and out of protection as a secure tenancy, according to who holds the landlord's interest at any one time. (See *Crawley Borough Council v. Sawyer* (1988) 20 H.L.R. 98 below. See also Rent Act 1977, ss.13–16 for a similar rule in relation to protected tenancies). *Basingstoke & Deane BC v. Paice* (1995) 27 H.L.R. 433 was an unusual example of the meaning of this element of the definition of a secure tenancy. The tenant of a local authority owned garage converted part of it to a flat which he (unlawfully) sub-let. When the head tenancy was surrendered the sub-tenant became a secure tenant because his landlord was now the local authority following the surrender. (See p.125 above for the effect of surrender of tenancy in a sub-tenancy).

Licences

To avoid the lease/licence problem, which had caused so much difficulty in connection with the application of the Rent Acts (Chapter1 above), it is provided that the provisions in Part I of the Housing Act 1985 governing the rights of secure tenants (but not the right to buy) apply in relation to a licence to occupy a dwelling-house (whether or not granted for a consideration) as they apply in relation to a tenancy (s.79(3)).But this does not extend to a licence granted as a temporary expedient to a person who entered the dwelling-house or any other land as a trespasser (*i.e.* a "squatter"), whether or not another licence of the same or a different dwelling-house had been granted to that person (s.79(4)).

Despite the extension of secure tenancy status to licensees, problems have still arisen in connection with licences. In *Westminster City Council v. Clarke* [1992] 2 A.C. 288 H.L. it was settled by the House of Lords that to be a qualifying licence under section 79(3), the licensee must have exclusive possession. (Page 9 above). However, since *Street v. Mountford,* [1985] A.C. 809 H.L. save in exceptional cases, an occupier with exclusive possession will be found to be a tenant in any event. Thus there will be few licences which fall within s.79(3). On the other hand the *Clarke* decision raises once again the complex issue of what amounts to exclusive possession). In that case the local authority ran a hostel which was intended to provide a temporary refuge for homeless single men including those with personality disorders and physical disabilities. The intention was that they could then move on to more permanent accommodation. To this end Mr Clarke was given a licence to occupy a single room with cooking facilities in the hostel for a weekly charge by virtue of an agreement which was described as a licence to occupy. The agreement stated that it was not intended to create a tenancy and that Mr Clarke was not to have exclusive accommodation of any particular room that might be allotted to him. This was emphasised by provisions to the effect that the council were permitted to move him to other accommodation without notice, that he could be required to share his room with another occupant and that he was only entitled to occupy in common with the council whose representative could enter at any time. Had this been a private sector arrangement the courts would have viewed these provisions with great suspicion as an attempt to avoid protective legislation applicable to tenants but not licensees (see *Street v. Mountford* (above)). But the circumstances here were special. The nature of the accommodation and its purpose were such that it was in the interests of everybody that the council retained as much control as possible over the arrangements. To have given occupiers security of tenure would have thwarted the purpose of the scheme. Thus Mr Clarke was held not to have exclusive possession, and could be evicted by notice on account of his behaviour, although Lord Templeman emphasised that—

> "This is a very special case which depends on the peculiar nature of the hostel maintained by the council, the use of the hostel by the council, the totality, immediacy and objectives of the powers exercisable by the council and the restrictions imposed on Mr Clarke. The decision in this case will not allow a landlord private or public to free himself from the Rent Acts or from the restrictions of a secure tenancy merely by adopting or adapting the language of the licence to occupy. (p.302)"

Occupiers of "shortlife" accommodation who have been granted the right to occupy pending redevelopment are also unlikely to have the necessary degree of exclusive possession for a secure tenancy where the local authority retains rights of control over the property (*Camden LBC v. Shortlife Community Housing* (1992) 25 H.L.R. 330, p.16 above). (See also *Bruton v.*

London and Quadrant Housing Trust [1997] 4 All E.R. 970, CA) where the authority interposed a voluntary housing trust licensee between the council and the sub-licensee occupier who was not a tenant by estoppel.)

Let

Difficult issues also arise where it is alleged that there was no intention to create a tenancy. Because of the social character of publicly funded bodies there might be more scope for this contention in the public sector context than in the private sector where, because the courts are wary of bogus intentions, an "intention" not to create a tenancy has been largely confined to acts of generosity and the like. (See *Street v. Mountford* above; and p.13).

In *Westminster City Council v. Basson* (1991) 23 H.L.R. 225 the defendant had been living in a council flat with the secure tenants. She remained in occupation after the secure tenants had left and the tenancy had been determined. The council wrote to her stating that she must leave, but inviting her to pay "damages by way of use and occupation charges" pending her departure. The council did not seek to recover possession for over a year during which time another department had awarded the defendant housing benefit and given her a rent book. Nevertheless, it was held that it had been made clear that there had never been any intention to grant her a tenancy and therefore she had not acquired the status of a secure tenant. (*Cf. Tower Hamlets LBC v. Ayinde* (1994) 26 H.L.R. 631 where the council made it clear that a non tenant occupier who had remained following the departure of the secure tenants was being treated as the new tenant).

The same rule applies where the local authority has obtained a possession order against an occupier but as an act of indulgence permits that person to remain in occupation subject to payment of a weekly charge and gradual discharge of rent arrears. This will not create a new tenancy and therefore the possession order can subsequently be enforced. Such an occupier has been described as a "tolerated trespasser" pending either the revival of the old tenancy or the breach of the agreed conditions (*Burrows v. Brent LBC* [1997] 11 E.G. 150, HL. See also *Southwark LBC v. Logan* (1995) 29 H.L.R. 40). This is a sensible rule because local authorities would otherwise be reluctant to afford such an indulgence to an occupier for fear that should he further default the whole process of possession proceedings would have to be gone through again notwithstanding the earlier possession order.

The landlord condition

The purpose of the landlord condition is to confine secure tenancy status to tenants of public sector landlords. For the most part this means a local authority, but also comprises a number of other bodies. Thus "the landlord condition" will be satisfied if the interest of the landlord belongs to one of a number of authorities or bodies including—

(1) a local authority;
(2) a new town corporation;
(3) a housing action trust;
(4) an urban development corporation, the Development Board for Rural Wales;
(5) certain housing co-operatives.

It will be noted that registered housing associations (renamed "registered social landlords" by the Housing Act 1996) are not included in this list. They were originally included but were removed as from January 15, 1989 by the Housing Act 1988. A tenancy entered into on or after that date by a housing association will normally be an assured tenancy under the Housing Act 1988 (see Chapter 9 above) and cannot be a secure tenancy save in the following exceptional cases—

(1) Where the tenancy or licence was entered into in pursuance of a contract made before the operative date (Housing Act 1988, s.35(4)(c)),

(2) Where it is granted to a person (alone or jointly with others) who, immediately before the tenancy was granted, was a secure tenant and is so granted by the body who at that time was the landlord under that previous tenancy (HA 1988, s.35(4)(d)).
The new tenancy may be of the same or different premises. This is designed to ensure that a tenant who was holding under a secure tenancy from a housing association landlord when the Housing Act 1988 came into force will not be prejudiced by taking a new tenancy of the same or different premises after that date.

(3) Where it is granted to a person (alone or jointly with others) following a possession order under the Housing Act 1985 made on a ground which requires the court to be satisfied that suitable (alternative) accommodation is to be made available to the tenant (see below) and where—

 (i) the tenancy is of the premises which constitute the suitable accommodation as to which the court was so satisfied; and

 (i) the court considered in the possession proceedings that the tenancy should be a secure tenancy because an assured tenancy would not provide appropriate security (HA 1988, s.35(4)(e)).

(4) Where it was granted pursuant to an obligation (under s.554(2A) of the Housing Act 1985) to repurchase a defective dwelling from a person who had bought that dwelling under the right to buy (see below) (HA 1988, s.35(4)(f)).

A tenancy granted before January 15, 1989 by a housing association can still be a secure tenancy because at that time the above list included such a body. (Such a tenancy will also remain governed by the fair rent scheme of the Rent Act 1977. See p.299 above). The same rule applies where on or after January 15, 1989 a housing association landlord acquires the landlord's interest under a protected or statutory tenancy created before that date (HA 1988, s.35(5)).

It should be noted that if, on or after January 15, 1989, a public landlord who satisfies the landlord condition disposes of its interest in a property which is subject to a secure tenancy to a private landlord (including for this purpose a housing association), the teancy will cease to be secure (Housing Act 1988 s.38).

Introductory tenancies

The Housing Act 1996 (ss. 124–143) has given local authorities and housing action trusts the opportunity to create a tenancy outside the secure tenancy regime of the Housing Act 1995. Such a tenancy is known as an "introductory tenancy" and offers the tenant only a very limited security of tenure along the lines of that afforded to assured shorthold tenants under the Housing Act 1988 (see Chapter 9 above), although the tenant will have the benefit of other statutory rights (e.g. as to succession, assignment and the right to have repairs carried out expeditiously) afforded to secure tenants. An introductory tenancy will come into being where the authority has, in the exercise of its discretion, decided to introduce an "introductory tenancy regime" as a means of combating anti-social behaviour on certain estates. Save in exceptional cases, once such a regime has been adopted any tenancy granted which would otherwise have been a secure tenancy will instead be an introductory tenancy under which the tenant will in effect be "on probation" and will not become a secure tenant until the end of a 12-month trial period. During, or at the end of, that period the landlord will be able to recover possession if the tenant should misbehave by invoking a notice procedure and seeking a court order. It remains to be seen how popular the new powers, which are fraught with potential difficulties, will prove to be. (See further, J. Driscoll, *Hill and Redman's Guide to the Housing Act 1996*). Authorities may prefer to deal with the problem of anti-social tenants by relying on the grounds for possession (expanded by the Housing Act 1996) provided for by the Housing Act 1985 (see below).

The tenant condition

The tenant condition is that the tenant is an individual and occupies the dwelling-house as his only or principal home; or, where the tenancy is a joint tenancy, that each of the joint tenants is an individual and at least one of them occupies the dwelling-house as his only or principal home (s.81).

The principal issue in relation to joint tenants is that even though only one of them might occupy the dwelling-house as his or her principal home, that right can be brought to an end if the other serves a notice to quit on the landlord. This will have the effect of terminating the tenancy which will leave the occupier vulnerable to a claim for possession by the landlord. (See *Hammersmith & Fulham LBC v. Monk* [1992] 1 All E.R. 1, HL; see p.130 above). Indeed the landlord will frequently have instigated the absent tenant to take this course of action as a prelude to being offered a sole tenancy of the same or other premises.

"...occupies the dwelling-house as his only or principal home" The requirement that the tenant must occupy the dwelling-house as his only or principal home differs from the Rent Act 1977 scheme, in that occupation is not a requirement of a protected tenancy under that Act. (Although it becomes vital when determining whether a statutory tenancy arises or continues following the ending of the protected tenancy or death of the protected tenant (p.262 above).) On the other hand this element is identical to that required for an assured tenancy under the Housing Act 1988 which to that extent was modelled on the definition of a secure tenancy.

The meaning of "only or principal home" was examined in *Crawley Borough Council v. Sawyer* (1988) 20 H.L.R. 98. (See further S.Bridge [1988] Conv. 300) The Court of Appeal held that occupation as a home is the same as occupation as a residence. Hence if a single tenant does occupy more than one property as a residence, it will be a question of fact as to which is his principal home. (The Court, perhaps questionably, reasoned by analogy with the case law on the Rent Act 1977 as to whether a person was occupying a dwelling-house as a residence for the purpose of acquiring or maintaining a statutory tenancy of that dwelling-house. See p.263 above). It was held in *Sawyer* that when the tenant went to live elsewhere with his girlfriend but continued to pay the rent and rates for his flat which he visited once a month, he was still occupying that dwelling-house as his principal home. The evidence showed that he only occupied his girlfriend's home on a temporary basis. (This was not the case in *Ujima Housing Association v. Ansah* (1997) *The Times,* November 20, 1997, CA where the tenant had sub-let his flat, and then departed not leaving any furniture behind. The court said that looked at objectively it could not be said that the departed tenant had the necessary intention to maintain occupation of the dwelling-house as his principal home).

The issue of whether a secure tenant who is physically absent from the dwelling-house can maintain his status as a secure tenant through representative occupation by others has, not surprisingly, proved to be difficult and contentious.

The normal rule where a secure tenant ceases to occupy the property as his sole or principal home, is that occupation by others will not be treated as constructive occupation by the departed tenant. (See, for example, *Jennings v. Epping DC* (1993) 25 H.L.R. 241 where the tenant moved into a nursing home and his wife (who was a joint tenant) took a flat nearby to be near to him. Their council house was then sub-let. It was held that the tenants had forfeited their status as secure tenants. See also p.338 below).

Significant problems can occur if a sole secure tenant ceases to occupy the home as his residence leaving a spouse or partner in occupation. Statute has sought to deal with this issue generally. The issues, and relevant rules, are examined in Chapter 9 above in relation to assured tenancies under the Housing Act 1988 to which reference should be made because the same principles apply to secure tenancies.

Secure tenancies—exclusions

Even though a tenancy or licence satisfies the requirements of section 79 it will nevertheless not be a secure tenancy if it falls within one of the specified exceptions contained in Schedule 1 to the Housing Act 1985. Nor will it remain secure in certain circumstances if the tenant dies or assigns or sub-lets the whole of the dwelling-house (see below for the effect of death or assignment on the status of a secure tenancy). It follows that if, for whatever reason, a tenancy is not, or ceases to be, secure, the occupant will become vulnerable to a possession claim by the landlord following termination of the tenancy by a minimum of four weeks' notice to quit (Protection From Eviction Act 1977, s.5. See *Cannock Chase District Council v. Kelly* [1978] 1 W.L.R. 1.)

The specified exceptions referred to above are examined below and are numbered so as to correspond with the relevant paragraph of Schedule 1.

1. Long tenancies
A tenancy is not a secure tenancy if it is a "long tenancy". This in essence means a tenancy granted for a term certain exceeding 21 years, whether it is (or may become) terminable before the end of that term by notice given by the tenant or by re-entry or forfeiture. It also includes a perpetually renewable lease (see p.19 above) and a tenancy granted in pursuance of the right to buy under Part V of the Act (see below) (HA 1985, s. 115).

1A. Introductory tenancies
A tenancy is not a secure tenancy if it is an introductory tenancy or a tenancy which has ceased to be an introductory tenancy either because (a) it has been disposed of on death to a non-qualifying person (see HA 1996, s.133(3)) or (b) by virtue of the tenant or, in the case of a joint tenancy, every tenant ceasing to occupy the dwelling-house as his only or principal home (HA 1996, s.125(5)).

2. Premises occupied in connection with employment
A tenancy is not a secure tenancy if the tenant is an employee of the landlord, or of certain other listed public bodies, and his contract of employment requires him to occupy the dwelling-house for the better performance of his duties. ("Contract of employment" means a contract of service or apprenticeship, whether express or implied and (if express) whether oral or in writing). The listed bodies are a local authority, a new town corporation, a housing action trust, an urban

development corporation, the Development Board for Rural Wales, and the governors of an aided school. A similar exclusion applies in respect of service tenancies granted to police officers and fire authority employees.

It is also possible for a landlord to withhold secure tenancy status from a non-service tenancy of a dwelling-house which has been let on a service tenancy within the three years before the grant of the tenancy. To obtain this immunity the landlord must, before the grant, give notice in writing to the tenant to this effect. If such notice is given, and the landlord is not a local authority, the tenancy will not be secure until three years have passed without a service tenant in occupation. If on the other hand the landlord is a local authority it will not be secure unless and until the local authority notify the tenant in writing to that effect.

Despite the reference to a service tenancy in paragraph 2, the expression "for the better performance of his duties" is a long-established feature of a service occupancy (*i.e.* a licence) as opposed to a service tenancy. However, as noted above, the lease/licence distinction is of minimal significance for the purposes of determining whether a secure tenancy exists under the Housing Act 1985 (see s.79(3) above)).

The most troublesome aspect of this particular exclusion has proved to be the issue of whether the requirement that the premises be occupied for the better performance of his duties is a term of the employee's contract of employment.

The matter came before the House of Lords in *Hughes v. Greenwich LBC* [1994] 1 A.C. 170. The contentious issue was whether a person was able to establish a secure tenancy in order to exercise the statutory right to buy. The case involved a retired head teacher of a local authority special boarding school who whilst employed had occupied a house in the school grounds which was owned by the landlord. He remained living there after he retired and claimed the right to buy. His contract of employment had made no reference to the need to live in any particular accommodation and the House of Lords rejected the council's claim that it was an implied term of the plaintiff's contract that he be required to live in the property provided let alone for the better performance of his duties. To succeed in this claim the council would have needed to establish that the tenant could not have performed his duties unless he lived in that particular accommodation. They were unable to do so and hence the tenant was able to exercise the right to buy.

It is possible for a secure tenant's status to change where subsequent to the grant of the tenancy he enters into an employment contract with the landlord which requires him to live in the dwelling-house in question for the better performance of his duties. At that point his tenancy would cease to be secure (*Elvidge v. Coventry CC* [1994] Q.B. 241, where the tenant changed jobs on promotion and his contract was altered to require him to live in his cottage for the better performance of his new job as an assistant ranger).

Furthermore, if a service tenant retires and his contract of employment ends he will not thereby become a secure tenant. If it were otherwise the landlord would not be able to recover possession from a tenant whom the exception was designed to exclude from secure tenant status (*South Glamorgan CC v. Griffiths* (1992) 24 H.L.R. 334).

3. Land acquired for development

A tenancy is not a secure tenancy if the dwelling-house is on land which has been acquired for development (as defined by section 55 of the Town and Country Planning Act 1990) and the dwelling-house is used by the landlord, pending development of the land, as temporary housing accommodation.

The purpose of this exclusion is to enable "short life property" to be let pending development without the tenant being able to claim a secure tenancy and thereby thwart the development. It will be sufficient that there is a continuous thread of intended development throughout, albeit that the particular development intended might not be the same at all times (*Attley v. Cherwell DC* (1989) 21 H.L.R. 613). Furthermore it need not be the immediate landlord who requires the land for development, as in *Hyde Housing Association v. Harrison* (1990) 23 H.L.R. 57, where land was acquired for road-widening purposes by the Department of Transport who then granted the plantiff housing association the right to use it for housing purposes. It was held that a tenancy granted by the association was not secure. (*cf. Lillieshall Road Housing Co-operative Ltd v. Brennan* (1992) 24 H.L.R. 193 where the intention to develop appeared to have been abandoned and therefore the tenancy became secure).

4. Accommodation for homeless persons

A local authority has a range of duties and powers with regard to housing homeless persons under Part VII of the Housing Act 1996. Whilst performing those functions it can accommodate an applicant and such an arrangement can be by way of a secure tenancy even though only provided in pursuance of the authority's statutory duties (*Family Housing Association v. Jones* (1989) 22 H.L.R. 45, CA); but since the Housing Act 1996 a tenancy will not be secure unless and until the authority notifies the tenant to that effect.

This paragraph will also apply where the accommodation is by arrangement (under HA 1996, s.209) provided by a landlord other than the local authority. This will usually, but not necessarily, be a housing association, as in *Family Housing Association v. Miah* (1982) 5 H.L.R. 94. In such a case the issue will be whether or not the tenancy is an assured tenancy (see Chapter 9 above). In this connection it is provided that a tenancy cannot be an assured tenancy before 12 months from the applicant being notified of the authority's decision unless the landlord notifies the tenant that the tenancy is to be an assured shorthold or fully assured tenancy. Where the landlord is a housing association the landlord cannot serve such a notice making the tenancy an assured tenancy other than an assured shorthold tenancy (s.209)).

5. Temporary accommodation for persons taking up employment

A tenancy is not a secure tenancy if—

(1) the person to whom the tenancy was granted was not, immediately before the grant, resident in the district in which the dwelling-house is situated;

(2) before the grant of the tenancy, he obtained employment, or an offer of employment, in the district or its surrounding area;

(3) the tenancy was granted to him for the purpose of meeting his need for temporary accommodation in the district or its surrounding area in order to work there, and of enabling him to find permanent accommodation there; and

(4) the landlord notified him in writing of the circumstances in which this exception applies and that in its opinion the proposed tenancy would fall within this exception,

Except where the landlord is a local authority the tenancy will become secure after one year, or on the landlord notifying the tenant to that effect before that date. Where the landlord is a local authority the tenancy will become secure only if the landlord notifies the tenant that it is to be secure. The aim of this exception would appear to be to encourage persons from outside the area to take up employment in the area by providing them with local authority (or other public) accommodation as a temporary measure until they become established and are able to make their own arrangements.

6. Short-term arrangements

This exception is designed to ensure that where a private landlord makes short life accommodation available to the local authority, expressly for use as temporary housing accommodation (such as for homeless persons), any sub-tenancy or licence granted by the authority will not become a secure tenancy. It applies even where the private landlord has granted a licence, rather than a tenancy, to the local authority (*London Borough of Tower Hamlets v. Miah* (1991) 24 H.L.R. 199; *Tower Hamlets London Borough Council v. Abdi* (1993) 25 H.L.R. 80).

7. Temporary accommodation during works

A tenancy is not a secure tenancy if—

(1) the dwelling-house has been made available for occupation by the tenant (or a predecessor in title of his) while works are carried out on the dwelling-house which he previously occupied as his home; and

(2) the tenant or predecessor was not a secure tenant of that other dwelling-house at the time when he ceased to occupy it as his home.

This is most commonly used where a local authority has served a repairs notice on a private landlord under the Housing Act 1985 (see p.72 above) and is temporarily accommodating the tenant whilst the repairs are carried out.

8. Agricultural holdings, etc.

This exception (which is derived from Rent Act 1977, s.10) is designed to prevent a farm manager from obtaining secure tenancy status whether he works for the landlord or the tenant of the farm.

9. Licensed premises

A tenancy is not a secure tenancy if the dwelling-house consists of or includes premises licensed for the sale of intoxicating liquor for consumption on the premises. (See also Rent Act 1977, s.11.)

10. Student lettings

This exception is designed to prevent student lets, which by their nature are not intended as long term arrangements, attracting secure tenancy status. (See also Rent Act 1977, s. 8 and Housing Act 1988, Sched. 1, para. (8).)

A tenancy of a dwelling-house is not a secure tenancy if—

(1) it is granted for the purpose of enabling the tenant to attend a designated course at an educational establishment; and

(2) before the grant of the tenancy the landlord notified him in writing of the circumstances in which this exception applies and that in its opinion the proposed tenancy would fall within this exception. (See also the Secure Tenancies (Designated Courses) Regulations S.I. 1980 No. 1407, as amended by S.I. 1993 No. 931).

Except where the landlord is a local authority, then (a) in the case where the tenant attends a designated course at the educational establishment specified in the landlord's notice the tenancy will become secure six months after the tenant ceases to attend that (or any other) designated course at that establishment and (b) where the tenant does not take up the course it will become secure six months after the grant of the tenancy. In both cases the tenancy can become secure at an earlier stage if the landlord notifies the tenant to that effect.

On the other hand, where the landlord is a local authority it will become secure at any time only if the landlord notifies the tenant that the tenancy is to be treated as secure.

11. Business tenancies

This exclusion, which is modelled on Rent Act 1977 s.24, provides that a tenancy is not a secure tenancy if it is one to which Part II of the Landlord and Tenant Act 1954 applies (tenancies of premises occupied for business purposes. See Chapter 13 below).

12. Almshouses

Some charities do not have power to grant tenancies and therefore cannot create a secure tenancy in any event. But because a licence can be a secure tenancy it was felt prudent to provide that a licence of an almshouse granted by or on behalf of a charity cannot be a secure tenancy.

Security of Tenure

The basic scheme of that part of the Housing Act 1985 which governs security of tenure for secure tenants is that the secure tenancy, whether fixed-term or periodic, cannot be ended by the landlord other than by obtaining a court order on one or more of the grounds laid down in Schedule 2 to the Act (s.82(1)).

"Consent orders" for possession without establishing a ground are not possible. In *Wandsworth London BC v. Fadayomi* [1987] 1 W.L.R. 1473 Parker L.J. stated that in order to justify an order being made without an investigation of the facts, what was required was not a mere consent to the making of the order but an express admission of facts, which, if they had been proved, would have given the court jurisdiction to make the order. Reference should also be made to *R. v. Worthing BC, ex parte Bruce* (1994) 26 H.L.R. 223, CA where the tenant conceded that he was not a secure tenant and therefore a consent order that he give up possession was not disturbed by the court.

Where the landlord does obtain an order for possession of the dwelling-house, the tenancy ends on the date on which the tenant is to give up possession in pursuance of the order (s.82(2)). Unlike the Rent Act 1977 scheme, which governs protected tenancies, there is no concept similar to the statutory tenancy and therefore no need for the contractual tenancy to be ended by one of the usual methods of termination, such as by exercise of a break clause or by service of a notice to quit, or by forfeiture etc. (See Chapter 6 above). But there is a similarity with the Rent Act 1977 scheme in another sense, because the grounds on which the court is able to order possession are closely modelled on those set out in Schedule 15 to the Rent Act 1977 which governs the circumstances in which a landlord can recover possession of a dwelling-house which is let on a protected or statutory tenancy (see p.273 above).

Fixed term followed by periodic tenancy

Once a fixed-term secure tenancy comes to an end by effluxion of time (or by order of the court under section 82(3)—proceedings for possession by way of forfeiture—see below) a periodic tenancy arises under the Act unless the landlord has granted the tenant another tenancy to commence on the ending of the fixed term. The period of this new tenancy will depend on the periods for payment of rent under the former fixed term (*e.g.* weekly, monthly, etc.). The parties and terms of the tenancy are the same as those of the first tenancy at the end of it, except that the terms are confined to those which are compatible with a periodic tenancy and do not include any provision for re-entry or forfeiture (s.86).

Termination by the tenant

Nothing in the Housing Act 1985 prevents the tenant terminating the tenancy by any method permitted in law. These include surrender, as in *R. v. Croydon LBC, ex parte Toth* (1986) 20 H.L.R. 576, where the tenant abandoned the property and the landlord re-entered and changed the locks. (But a joint tenancy can only be terminated by surrender by or with the authority of all joint tenants: *Leek & Moorlands Building Society v. Clark* [1952] 2 Q.B. 788.) Other methods include, in the case of a periodic tenancy, service of a valid notice to quit, or, in the case of a fixed-term tenancy, the exercise of a break clause in the tenancy. Since the Housing Act 1988, s.117 came into force, a secure periodic tenancy can also be ended by disclaimer by the tenant's trustee in bankruptcy.

By contrast with the case of surrender, there is nothing to prevent one of two or more joint tenants, with or without the consent of the other tenant(s), ending the tenancy by notice to quit (*Hammersmith & Fulham LBC v. Monk* [1992] 1 All E.R. 1, HL. see p.130 above). But notice by fewer than all joint tenants will not suffice where the landlord accepts a notice for less than the statutory minimum period of four weeks which is required by the Protection from Eviction Act 1977, s.5 (*Hounslow LBC v. Pilling* [1994] 1 All E.R. 432. see p.131 above).

Termination by the landlord

As noted above, a secure tenancy cannot be ended by the landlord save by virtue of a court order on one of the grounds specified in the Act and therefore the normal methods of termination of tenancies such as by notice to quit or by forfeiture are inapplicable (s.82(1)). It is further provided by the Housing Act 1985 that the process of recovery of possession must be initiated by the landlord serving a statutory notice on the tenant (s.84). This requirement closely resembles the procedure which was subsequently adopted in respect of assured tenancies by the Housing Act 1988 (see p.225 above). It was amended by the Housing Act 1996, s.147.

Special provision is made for fixed-term tenancies with a proviso for re-entry or forfeiture. Section 82(3) provides that the court shall not order possession of the dwelling-house in pursuance of such a proviso, but in a case where the court would have made such an order (had it not been prevented by s.82(1) above) it shall instead make an order terminating the tenancy on a date specified in the order. (Section 146, Law of Property Act 1925 (save for subsection (4)) and all the other rules governing forfeiture will also apply. See p.134 above).

Once the court has made such an order, section 86 (which, as noted above, provides that on the ending of a fixed-term secure tenancy a periodic tenancy arises) will then apply (s.82(3)). Thus the effect of the forfeiture clause is preserved but the prematurely determined fixed term is then replaced by a periodic tenancy! At first sight this would appear to require the landlord to go through the process of ending that periodic tenancy by further proceedings for possession, but the better opinion is that this could be done in the earlier proceedings. Thus the court could end both the fixed-term and the periodic tenancy which then springs up (under section 86, below) in one fell swoop, if of course it is minded to do so in the circumstances. It might be content simply to terminate the fixed term and give the tenant another chance.

Notice of intended possession proceedings

As noted above, Housing Act 1985, s. 83(1) (as amended) provides that the court shall not entertain proceedings for the possession of a dwelling-house let under a secure tenancy, or proceedings for the termination of a secure tenancy, unless (a) the landlord has served on the tenant a notice complying with the provisions of that section or (b) the court considers it just and equitable to dispense with the requirements of such a notice. The dispensation power in (b) was added by the 1996 Act amendments and is identical to that which applies in the case of the notice procedure in section 8 of the Housing Act 1988 governing termination of assured tenancies. (See *Kelsey Housing Association v. King* (1995) 28 H.L.R. 270 and p.225 above).

The section 83 notice must be in the prescribed form (see S.I. 1987 No. 755 (the Secure Tenancies (Notices) Regulations 1987)) or a form substantially to the same effect (*Dudley Metropolitan Council v. Bailey* (1990) 22 H.L.R. 424, CA) and must specify the ground on which the court will be asked to make an order for possession of the dwelling-house or for the termination of the tenancy and give particulars of that ground (s.83(2)). The ground(s) so specified may be altered or added to with the leave of the court (s.84(3)). In *Torridge District Council v. Jones* (1986) 18 H.L.R. 107 where ground 1 was relied on, the notice simply stated that "The reasons for taking this action are non-payment of rent." This was held to be insufficient because the notice should at least have specified the amount claimed. The court stated that the purpose of the section 8 notice is to make the tenant aware of what he needs to do to put matters right. In *Dudley Metropolitan Council v. Bailey* (above) it was held that an error in the particulars will not necessarily invalidate the notice, although it may well affect the decision of the court on the merits. In *Bailey* the specified arrears of rent were alleged to be £145.96, but in fact that figure included rates and water rates, the actual rent arrears amounting to £72.88. The notice was held to be valid.

Where the tenancy is a periodic tenancy and ground 2 in Schedule 2 (nuisance or other anti-social behaviour) is specified, the notice must also (a) state that possession proceedings may be begun immediately and (b) specify the date on which the landlord requires the tenant to give up possession (s.83(3)(a)). The notice will be inoperative 12 months after that date (s.83(3)(b)); thus any proceedings must be brought within that period (s.83A(1)).

If ground 2 is not specified the notice must specify a date after which proceedings for the possession of the dwelling-house may be begun (s.83(4)(a)). The notice will cease to be operative 12 months after the specified date (s.83(4)(b)). Consequently any proceedings must be begun within that time and after the date specified in the landlord's notice (s.83A(2)).

In both the above cases the date specified must not be earlier than the date on which the tenancy could, but for section 82(1)(above), be brought to an end by notice to quit given by the landlord on the same date as the section 83 notice (s.83(5)). (See the Protection from Eviction Act 1977, s. 5 requirements as to the need for a minimum of four weeks' notice (p.129 above).

Where a section 83 notice is served with respect to a fixed-term secure tenancy it has effect also with respect to any periodic tenancy arising on the termination of that tenancy by virtue of section 86 (above) and the above provisions governing notices in respect of periodic tenancies are inapplicable in such a case (s.83(6)).

Additional requirements in cases of domestic violence

Where possession is being sought on the ground of domestic violence by the tenant against a partner (ground 2A; see further below) a copy of the section 83 notice must also be served on the partner who has left as a result of the violence if that person is not a tenant, or it must be established that all reasonable steps were taken to effect service on that person (s.83A(3), (6) added by the Housing Act 1996, s.150) (see further below). Equally if the landlord seeks to amend a section 83 notice, once served, by adding ground 2A (see above for the addition of grounds) the court must be satisfied that the landlord has served, or taken all reasonable steps to serve, a copy on the partner who has left (s.83A(4), (6)). But in either case if ground 2 (nuisance or anti-social behaviour) is also specified in the notice the court may dispense with the requirements as to service in relation to the partner who has left the dwelling-house if it considers it just and equitable to do so (s.83A(5)).

Grounds for possession

As noted above, the court has no power to make an order for the possession of a dwelling-house let under a secure tenancy except on one or more of the grounds set out in Schedule 2 (s.84(1)).

The grounds fall into three categories. The court cannot make an order for possession—

(1) on any of the grounds in Part I of Schedule 2 to the Act (grounds 1 to 8), unless it considers it reasonable to make the order (this means reasonable with regard to the interests of the parties and the public: *London Borough of Enfield v. McKeown* [1986] 1 W.L.R. 1007, CA, where it was held to be relevant that the tenant had served a notice claiming the right to buy although this fact would not prevent the authority from seeking possession);

(2) on any of the grounds in Part II of Schedule 2 (grounds 9 to 11), unless the court is satisfied that suitable accommodation will be available for the tenant when the order takes effect;

(3) on any of the grounds in Part III of Schedule 2 (grounds 12 to 16), unless it both considers it reasonable to make the order *and* is satisfied that suitable accommodation will be available for the tenant when the order takes effect,

Part IV of Schedule 2 sets out the criteria for determining whether suitable accommodation will be available for a tenant.

In the case of proceedings which rely on any of the grounds in Parts I and III above (being cases in which the court must be satisfied that it is reasonable to make a possession order) the court has a wide discretion to adjourn the proceedings for such period or periods as it thinks fit (s.85(1)). The court also has a discretionary power to stay or suspend the execution of a possession order, or postpone the date of possession, for such period or periods as it thinks fit (s.85(2)). If a suspended order is made the tenancy will end when the terms of the order are breached (see s.82(2) and *Thompson v. Elmbridge BC* (1986) 19 H.L.R. 526). These powers mirror those available to the court in the case of possession proceedings both under the Rent Act 1977 (see s.100) and under the Housing Act 1988, s.9 where any of the discretionary grounds for possession are relied upon.

On any such adjournment, stay, suspension or postponement the court is required to impose conditions with respect to the payment by the tenant of arrears of rent (if any) and rent or payments in respect of occupation after the termination of the tenancy (mesne profits), unless it considers that to do so would cause exceptional hardship to the tenant or would otherwise be unreasonable. It may also impose such other conditions as it thinks fit (s.85(3)). If the conditions are complied with, the court may, if it thinks fit, discharge or rescind the order for possession (s.85(4)).

Provision is also made for a departed tenant's spouse (or former spouse) who has matrimonial home rights under the Family Law Act 1996. (The matrimonial home rights normally cease on termination of the marriage but may be extended to a former spouse under s.33(3).) Such a spouse (or former spouse) is entitled to pay the rent and her occupation will be treated as that of the departed spouse thereby maintaining the secure tenancy despite the absence of the tenant (Family Law Act 1996 s.30(4)(b)). Furthermore a spouse (or former spouse) with matrimonial home rights who is in occupation can enjoy the benefit of the court's powers as to adjournment, etc. in the event of possession proceedings (Housing Act 1985, s.85(5)). The same benefits as to adjournment etc. are also extended to a cohabitant or former cohabitant who has the benefit of a court order under section 36 of the Family Law Act 1996 (s.85(5A)). But it has been argued that this will be of no avail to such a tenant where the tenant has departed because, unlike the case of spouses (see above), there is no provision in the Family Law Act 1996 for payment of rent by a cohabitant or former cohabitant to be treated as payment by the secure tenant for the purposes of keeping the secure tenancy alive. Thus the tenancy would cease to be secure on the tenant's departure, assuming that the dwelling-house has ceased to be his or her principal home (see above). (For the same reason it would appear that the court's power under FLA 1996 Sched. 7 to transfer a secure tenancy to a cohabitant or former cohabitant with the benefit of a matrimonial home rights order under section 36 of that Act would be similarly ineffective in those circumstances.) (See Encyclopedia of Housing etc. vol. 1, para. 1–1667.)

A. GROUNDS ON WHICH THE COURT MAY ORDER POSSESSION IF IT CONSIDERS IT REASONABLE

Ground 1

Rent lawfully due from the tenant has not been paid or an obligation of the tenancy has been broken or not performed.

This ground is derived from the similar ground in Case 1 of Schedule 15 to the Rent Act 1977. Accordingly, similar principles should apply and reference should therefore be made to the discussion in Chapter 10 p.274. It should also be appreciated that a tenant who has withheld rent might nevertheless not be in breach of covenant if he pleads and establishes a breach of covenant by the landlord (*e.g.*to repair) by way of counterclaim thereby affording him a right of set-off (see *Brent LBC v. Carmel* (1995) 28 H.L.R. 203 and p.71 above). Ground 1 is commonly relied on and the court often exercises its discretion not to order possession or its powers to adjourn or suspend etc. the order on terms. In *Woodspring District Council v. Taylor* (1982) 4 H.L.R. 95, CA the court considered it unreasonable to order possession on this ground against a tenant who had been a good tenant for 24 years but who had recently fallen into serious arrears as a result of a bout of ill-health and unemployment. For a case where possession was granted on the ground of persistent rent arrears, see *Haringey LBC v. Stewart* (1991) 23 H.L.R. 557.

With regard to the second limb of this ground, the court will consider such matters as the nature of the breach, its seriousness and remediability and the likelihood of its continuance. (See *Sheffield City Council v. Green* (1994) 26 H.L.R. 349 and *Sheffield City Council v. Jepson*

(1993) 25 H.L.R. 299, CA, both of which involved the keeping of a dog, contrary to the terms of the tenancy agreement).

Ground 2

The tenant or a person residing in or visiting the dwelling-house (a) has been guilty of conduct causing or likely to cause a nuisance or annoyance to a person residing, visiting, or otherwise engaging in a lawful activity in the locality, or (b) has been convicted of (i) using the dwelling-house or allowing it to be used for immoral or illegal purposes or (ii) an arrestable offence committed in, or in the locality of, the dwelling-house.

Ground 2, as currently worded, was introduced by the Housing Act 1996, s.144, and replaced the original more narrowly worded ground in order to permit the removal of anti-social tenants whose activities have spread wider than the dwelling-house itself, perhaps to another part of an estate. (But for a liberal interpretation of the earlier ground, the first limb of which was confined to conduct which was a "nuisance or annoyance to neighbours", see *Northampton Borough Council v. Lovatt and another* [1998] 07 E.G. 142, CA where the term "neighbours" was interpreted to mean "all persons sufficiently close to the sources of the conduct complained of to be adversely affected by that conduct", thereby enabling the authority to remove socially undesirable tenants on an estate).

Nuisance (which is used here in the colloquial rather than technical legal sense) and annoyance have been held to extend to racial and sexual harassment (*Woking BC v. Bistram* (1993) 27 H.L.R. 1, CA; *Kensington & Chelsea RBC v. Simmonds* (1996) 29 H.L.R. 507). The conduct complained of need not be that of the tenant himself (see *Kensington & Chelsea RLBC v. Simmonds*, above, where the conduct complained of was that of the tenant's son). It can be conduct which affects a wide range of people, not just neighbours, and would extend for example to conduct affecting council employees working in the area. The second limb of this ground is sufficiently wide to encompass a conviction for an offence, which need not have been committed in the dwelling-house itself. Indeed it would permit the removal of convicted criminals such as local drug dealers.

Ground 2A

This ground was added by the Housing Act 1996, s.145 and applies where the dwelling-house was occupied by a married couple, or a couple living together as man or wife, and one or both of them is a tenant.

To be applicable, (a) one of the partners must have left the dwelling-house because of threats of violence by the other partner towards the one who has left or a member of that person's family who was residing with him/her immediately before the partner left, and (b) the court must be satisfied that the partner is unlikely to return.

The purpose of this ground is to enable the landlord to recover possession of family-sized accommodation occupied by somebody who has driven their partner out by violence or threats of violence in circumstances where the victim is likely to be seeking alternative accommodation from the local authority. To permit the perpetrator to remain could be to endorse the inefficient use of scarce local authority housing stock by allowing the tenant to occupy a property which is larger than that which is suitable having regard to his or her needs. An alternative course of action to solve the problem, which would require a positive act on the part of the victim partner, but would circumvent the need for a court order, would be for the victim to serve a notice to quit on the local authority which would end the tenancy. (See *Hammersmith & Fulham LBC v. Monk* [1992] 1 All E.R. 1 H.L.).

Ground 3

The condition of the dwelling-house or of any of the common parts has deteriorated owing to acts of waste by, or the neglect or default of, the tenant or a person residing in the dwelling-house and, in the case of an act of waste by, or the neglect or default of, a person lodging with the tenant or a sub-tenant of his, the tenant has not taken such steps as he ought reasonably to have taken for the removal of the lodger or sub-tenant.

This is modelled on case 3 in Schedule 15 to the Rent Act 1977 and is identical to ground 13 in Schedule 2 to the Housing Act 1988 (see pp.275 and 232 above).

Ground 4

The condition of furniture provided by the landlord for use under the tenancy, or for use in the common parts, has deteriorated owing to ill-treatment by the tenant or a person residing in the dwelling-house and, in the case of ill-treatment by a person lodging with the tenant or a sub-tenant of his, the tenant has not taken such steps as he ought reasonably to have taken for the removal of the lodger or sub-tenant. (See also RA 1977, Sched. 15, case 4 and HA 1988, Sched. 2 ground 15.)

This is similar to ground 3 save that it relates to deterioration of the condition of furniture provided for use under the tenancy. This is of limited significance to secure tenancies, which are rarely furnished tenancies.

Ground 5

The tenant is the person, or one of the persons, to whom the tenancy was granted and the landlord was induced to grant the tenancy by a false statement made knowingly or recklessly by the tenant or a person acting at the tenant's instigation. This ground, which was modified by the Housing Act 1996, s.146, does not have a Rent Act parallel but an identical ground for possession (ground 17) was added to Schedule 2 to the Housing Act 1988. It is designed to combat people who obtain accommodation by false pretences, often at the expense of legitimate applicants and thereby jumping the queue. (See *Shrewsbury & Atcham BC v. Evans* (1997) 30 H.L.R.)

Ground 6

The tenancy was assigned to the tenant, or to a predecessor in title of his who is a member of his family and is residing in the dwelling-house, by an assignment made by virtue of section 92 (assignments by way of exchange) and a premium was paid either in connection with that assignment or the assignment which the tenant or predecessor himself made by virtue of that section. In this paragraph "premium" means any fine or other like sum and any other pecuniary consideration in addition to rent.

This ground is designed to prevent tenants who have been permitted to exchange (see below for the right to exchange) from taking a premium as consideration for any assignment in pursuance of that right.

Ground 7

The dwelling-house forms part of, or is within the curtilage of, a building which, or so much of it as is held by the landlord, is held mainly for purposes other than housing purposes and consists mainly of accommodation other than housing accommodation, and—

    (a)   the dwelling-house was let to the tenant or a predecessor in title of his in consequence of the tenant or predecessor being in the employment of the landlord, or of a local authority, a new town corporation, a housing action trust, an urban development corporation, the Development Board for Rural Wales, or the governors of an aided school, and

(b)   the tenant or a person residing in the dwelling-house has been guilty of conduct such that, having regard to the purpose for which the building is used, it would not be right for him to continue in occupation of the dwelling-house.

This ground permits the landlord to remove, for misconduct, an employee (*e.g.* a boarding school teacher or a caretaker) of that landlord or some other public body, who is a tenant of accommodation in what are primarily non-residential premises.

Ground 8

The dwelling-house was made available for occupation by the tenant (or a predecessor in title of his) while works were carried out on the dwelling-house which he previously occupied as his only or principal home and—

(a)   the tenant (or predecessor) was a secure tenant of the other dwelling-house at the time when he ceased to occupy it as his home,

(b)   the tenant (or predecessor) accepted the tenancy of the dwelling-house of which possession is sought on the understanding that he would give up occupation when, on completion of the works, the other dwelling-house was again available for occupation by him under a secure tenancy, and

(c)   the works have been completed and the other dwelling-house is so available.

The purpose of this ground is to provide that, if a tenant has been required to move elsewhere to another local authority property whilst works are carried out on his home, the landlord will have a discretionary ground for possession if the tenant refuses to go back home when the works have been completed.

B. GROUNDS ON WHICH THE COURT MAY ORDER POSSESSION IF SUITABLE ALTERNATIVE ACCOMMODATION IS AVAILABLE

Ground 9

The dwelling-house is overcrowded, within the meaning of Housing Act 1985 Part X, in such circumstances as to render the occupier guilty of an offence. (See Part X for offences in connection with overcrowding where it is provided (by s.324) that a house is overcrowded if the number of persons sleeping in the house is in excess of the "space standard" (as to which see s.326) or if two or more persons being 10 years old or over, of opposite sexes, and not being persons living together as husband and wife, must sleep in the same room (the "room standard" as defined in s.325).)

Ground 10

The landlord intends, within a reasonable time of obtaining possession of the dwelling-house—

(a)   to demolish or reconstruct the building or part of the building comprising the dwelling-house, or

    (b) to carry out work on that building or on land let together with, and thus treated as part
        of, the dwelling-house, and cannot reasonably do so without obtaining possession of
        the dwelling-house.

This ground is based upon the ground of opposition to a new business tenancy in section
30(1)(f) of the Landlord and Tenant Act 1954 (see p.392 below). A tenant who loses his home
on this ground is entitled to home loss payments under the Land Compensation Act 1973, s.29.
In order to establish this ground the landlord must show a settled and clearly defined intention
to carry out works, similar to that required of a business tenancy landlord who relies on LTA
1954, s.30(1)(f). (See *Cunliffe v. Goodman* [1950] 2 K.B. 237; *Betty's Cafe's v. Phillips
Furnishing Stores* [1959] A.C. 20). In *Wansbeck DC v. Marley* (1988) 20 H.L.R. 247, CA a
clearly defined and settled intention to carry out work on an employee's cottage was not
established by the landlord and in any event the court considered that it had not been
established that the proposed, relatively minor, works could not reasonably have been carried
out without the need for possession by the landlord.

Ground 10A

The dwelling-house is in an area which is the subject of a redevelopment scheme approved
by the Secretary of State or the Housing Corporation in accordance with Part V of Schedule 2
and the landlord intends within a reasonable time of obtaining possession to dispose of the
dwelling-house in accordance with the scheme.

This ground was added by the Housing and Planning Act 1986 and facilitates recovery of
possession where the landlord intends to dispose of the property, within a reasonable time to a
private landlord for renovation or modernisation. The dwelling-house must be in an approved
redevelopment scheme (as defined in Part V of Schedule 2) which can only be entered into after
consultation with the tenants. A tenant who loses his home on this ground is entitled to home
loss payments under the Land Compensation Act 1973, s.29.

Ground 11

The landlord is a charity and the tenant's continued occupation of the dwelling-house would
conflict with the objects of the charity.

C. GROUNDS ON WHICH THE COURT MAY ORDER POSSESSION IF IT
CONSIDERS IT REASONABLE, AND SUITABLE ALTERNATIVE
ACCOMMODATION IS AVAILABLE

Ground 12

This ground (which resembles Case 8 of Schedule 15 to the Rent Act 1977) permits recovery
of possession of a dwelling-house which forms part of, or is within the curtilage of, a building
which is held mainly for purposes other than housing purposes and consists mainly of
accommodation other than housing accommodation, or is situated in a cemetery.
    For this ground to apply—

    (a) the dwelling-house must have been let to the tenant or a predecessor in title of his in
        consequence of the tenant or predecessor being in the employment of the landlord or
        of another specified public body and that employment has ceased, and
    (b) the landlord must reasonably require the dwelling-house for occupation as a
        residence for some person either engaged in the employment of the landlord, or of

such a body, or with whom a contract for such employment has been entered into conditional on housing being provided.

The aim of this provision is to permit the landlord to recover tied accommodation from an ex-employee in order to make it available for another employee. (*c.f.* ground 7 above which is superficially similar but dealing with a different problem (namely the conduct of the employee).)

Ground 13

The dwelling-house has features which are substantially different from those of ordinary dwelling-houses and which are designed to make it suitable for occupation by a physically disabled person who requires accommodation of a kind provided by the dwelling-house and—

(a) there is no longer such a person residing in the dwelling-house, and
(b) the landlord requires it for occupation (whether alone or with members of his family) by such a person.

This ground enables a landlord to recover possession of specially adapted property from a statutory successor to a disabled tenant (see below for succession) or in circumstances where a disabled occupier, for whose benefit the property was provided, has departed. It clearly makes sense to enable the property to be offered for occupation by another disabled person and for the displaced occupier to be offered appropriate (non-specially adapted) alternative accommodation.

Ground 14

The landlord is a housing association or housing trust which lets dwelling-houses only for occupation (whether alone or with others) by persons whose circumstances (other than merely financial circumstances) make it especially difficult for them to satisfy their need for housing, and—

(a) either there is no longer such a person residing in the dwelling-house or the tenant has received from a local housing authority an offer of accommodation in premises which are to be let as a separate dwelling under a secure tenancy, and
(b) the landlord requires the dwelling-house for occupation (whether alone or with members of his family) by such a person.

This ground is similar to and complementary to ground 11. It is confined to a secure tenancy under which the landlord is a housing association. For the most part this will mean a tenancy granted before January 15, 1989 because most tenancies granted on or after that date will be Housing Act 1988 assured tenancies (see p.205 above).

Once again it is designed to permit optimal use of property provided for persons with particular needs.

Ground 15

The dwelling-house is one of a group of dwelling-houses which it is the practice of the landlord to let for occupation by persons with special needs and—

(a) a social service or special facility is provided in close proximity to the group of dwelling-houses in order to assist persons with those special needs,

   (b)   there is no longer a person with those special needs residing in the dwelling-house, and

   (c)   the landlord requires the dwelling-house for occupation (whether alone or with members of his family) by a person who has those special needs.

Like the previous two grounds this is also concerned with seeking to ensure that property provided for persons with special needs is kept available for use by such persons. It applies where there is a group of such houses.

Ground 16

The accommodation afforded by the dwelling-house is more extensive than is reasonably required by the tenant and—

   (a)   the tenancy is vested in the tenant by virtue of section 89 (succession to periodic tenancy), the tenant being qualified to succeed by virtue of section 87(b) (members of family other than spouse), and

   (b)   notice of the proceedings for possession was served under section 83 (see above) more than six months but less than 12 months after the date of the previous tenant's death.

The matters to be taken into account by the court in determining whether it is reasonable to make an order on this ground include—

   (a)   the age of the tenant,

   (b)   the period during which the tenant has occupied the dwelling-house as his only or principal home, and

   (c)   any financial or other support given by the tenant to the previous tenant.

Ground 16 is aimed at preventing "under occupation" where the periodic tenant has died and a non-spouse family member who has succeeded to a periodic tenancy is occupying the property which is too big for his or her reasonable needs. Notice must be served not earlier than six months but not later than 12 months after the death of the tenant.

Suitability of accommodation

For the purposes of section 84(2)(b) and (c) above (that is cases in which the court is not to make an order for possession unless satisfied that suitable accommodation will be available) accommodation is suitable if it consists of premises—

   (1)   which are to be let as a separate dwelling under a secure tenancy; or

   (2)   which are to be let as a separate dwelling under a protected tenancy, not being a tenancy under which the landlord might recover possession under one of the cases in Part II of Schedule 15 to the Rent Act 1977 (the "mandatory grounds" where the court must order possession); or

   (3)   which are to be let as a separate dwelling under an assured tenancy which is neither an assured shorthold tenancy, within the meaning of Part I of the Housing Act 1988, nor a tenancy under which the landlord might recover possession under any of grounds 1 to 5 (the "mandatory grounds") in Schedule 2 to that Act,

and, in the opinion of the court, the accommodation is reasonably suitable to the needs of the tenant and his family.

It is provided that in determining whether the accommodation is reasonably suitable to the needs of the tenant and his family, regard shall be had to the following factors—

   (1)   the nature of the accommodation which it is the practice of the landlord to allocate to persons with similar needs;

   (2)   the distance of the accommodation available from the place of work or education of the tenant and of any members of his family;

   (3)   its distance from the home of any member of the tenant's family if proximity to it is essential to that member's or the tenant's well-being;

   (4)   the needs (as regards extent of accommodation) and means of the tenant and his family;

   (5)   the terms on which the accommodation is available and the terms of the secure tenancy;

   (6)   if furniture was provided by the landlord for use under the secure tenancy, whether furniture is to be provided for use in the other accommodation, and if so the nature of the furniture to be provided.

It has been held that this list of factors is not exhaustive (*Enfield LBC v. French* (1985) 17 H.L.R. 211, CA,).

Alternatively, where the landlord is not a local housing authority, a certificate from the local housing authority that they will provide suitable accommodation for the tenant by a specified date is conclusive evidence that accommodation will be available for him by that date (para. 4).

It can be seen that, according to Schedule 2 Part IV, every member of a tenant's family living with him is a person with a potential interest in any possession proceedings. Thus if the tenant does not wish to raise a matter affecting such a family member, that person can seek to be joined as a party to the proceedings (*Wandsworth London BC v. Fadayomi* [1987] 1 W.L.R. 1473).

The suitable accommodation requirement is conceptually similar to the ground for possession based on the availability of suitable alternative accommodation and contained in Rent Act 1977, s.98(1)(a) and Schedule 15 Part IV although the relevant factors to which the court is to have regard are specified in more detail in the Housing Act 1985. Reference should therefore be made to Chapter 10 p.285 for a discussion of the relevant case law on the Rent Act ground. One material difference between the two Acts is that any reference to the suitability as to character of the alternative accommodation is omitted from the secure tenancy code. In *Enfield London Borough Council v. French* (above) this was stated to be deliberate (at p. 216 *per* Stephenson L.J.). (*cf.* the different wording of Rent Act 1977, Sched. 15, Part IV, para. 5(b) and *Redspring Ltd v. Francis* [1973] 1 W.L.R. 134 where the decision of a judge who had deliberately rule out of consideration the environmental facilities of the alternative accommodation was overturned).

In *Enfield London Borough Council v. French* (above) the defendant was a single man who had been left alone in a two-bedroom flat following the death of his mother. The flat had the benefit of a garden in which the defendant, whose hobby was gardening, had done a lot of work. In that particular case it was council policy to allocate a two bedroomed flat with a living room to a couple with a child and not to a single person. The council accordingly sought possession relying on ground 13 (above) and offered the tenant a one-bedroom flat without a garden. Quite apart from the different wording of the Rent Act and the Housing Act provisions on alternative accommodation, the judge did in fact take into account the tenant's desire for a garden but considered it to be outweighed by other considerations. (Indeed, para. 2(a), which is unique to the public sector code, brings into play, as a relevant consideration, the needs of tenants other than the tenant who is the subject of the possession proceedings.) In those circumstances the Court of Appeal would not interfere with the judge's exercise of his discretion to order possession.)

Ground 9: additional factors

Where possession of a dwelling-house is sought on ground 9 (overcrowding such as to render the occupier guilty of an offence), it is provided, somewhat surprisingly, that other accommodation may still be reasonably suitable to the needs of the tenant and his family, notwithstanding that the permitted number of persons for that accommodation, as defined in section 326(3) (overcrowding: the space standard), is less than the number of persons living in the dwelling-house of which possession is sought.

Thus it is a ground for possession that the dwelling-house is overcrowded even though the alternative accommodation to be provided would also be overcrowded according to one limb of the definition of that term.

Succession on death of secure tenant

(a) Devolution of periodic tenancies

(i) The right to succeed Before the Housing Act 1980 there was no right to succeed to a council tenancy on the death of the tenant, although in exercise of their discretion local authorities often permitted a close family member to remain as a tenant. The position with regard to succession on death is now regularised by the Housing Act 1985 which provides that on the death of a secure periodic tenant the tenancy will vest by statute in a qualifying successor (s.89(1), (2)). In the absence of a qualifying successor the tenancy will cease to be secure and therefore be determinable by the landlord who can serve an ordinary notice to quit thereby ending the tenancy.

A person is qualified to succeed under section 89 if he occupies the dwelling-house as his only or principal home at the time of the tenant's death and is either—

(1) the tenant's spouse, or
(2) another member of the tenant's family who has resided with the tenant (as a family member: *Westminster City Council v. Peart* (1991) 24 H.L.R. 389) throughout the period of 12 months ending with the tenant's death (s.87),

provided (in either case) that the tenant himself was not a successor (as defined in section 88 (see below)).

(ii) Some key elements

(1) Only or principal home This term has already been encountered when examining the essential elements of a secure tenancy (above).

(2) Member of the tenant's family It is provided (by section 113) that for (the purposes of Part V) a person is a member of another's family if—

(1) he is the spouse of that person, or he and that person live together as husband or wife (s.113(1)(a)); or

(2) he is that person's parent, grandparent, child, grandchild, brother, sister, uncle, aunt, nephew or niece (s.113(1)(b)). For this purpose, relationships by marriage and half-blood are treated as whole-blood relationships; a person's stepchild is treated as his child, and an illegitimate child is treated as the legitimate child of his mother and reputed father (s.113(2)).

(iii) Cohabitants It will be noted that cohabitants are not to be equated with spouses for the purposes of Part V. (*cf.* the case of statutory succession under the Rent Act 1977. See p.271 above). A cohabitant can be a family member but not a spouse of his or her partner. For a cohabitant to qualify it is necessary to establish that he or she and the tenant were living together as husband and wife. This expression is used in other legislation such as the Family Law Act 1996 and the Social Security (Miscellaneous Provisions) Act 1977. In the Family Law Act 1996 cohabitants are defined, for the purposes of Part IV of the Act (family homes and domestic violence), as " a man and woman who, although not married to each other, are living together as husband or wife" (s.62(1)(a)). This replicates the definition in the (now repealed) Domestic Violence and Matrimonial Proceedings Act 1976.

In *Adeoso v. Adeoso* [1980] 1 W.L.R. 1535 it was held that that definition still applied to a couple whose relationship had broken down, who had ceased to talk to each other and lived in separate rooms in the same flat. Despite this they shared household expenses and utility bills. It was held that they were still living together as husband and wife. Despite the fact that in that context (remedies in respect of domestic violence), the courts might be expected to afford the term a liberal meaning it is quite likely that a similar approach would be adopted towards the definition in section 113 of the Housing Act 1985.

Rent Act case law on the question of whether a cohabitant is a member of the tenant's family for the purposes of the succession provisions in that Act is also clearly of some relevance to the issue of whether people are living together as husband and wife for the purposes of Part V of the Housing Act 1985. Reference should be made to Chapter 10 p.271 for an account of that case law.

In the context of the Housing Act 1985 it was held by the Court of Appeal in *Westminster City Council v. Peart* (1991) 24 H.L.R. 389 that to establish that a man and woman were living together as husband and wife it was not sufficient simply to show that they lived together in the same household. Thus in that case the defendant failed to establish that she was living with her divorced husband in his flat, during a period of reconciliation, at a time when she had retained her own flat elsewhere.

The vexed issue of same-sex cohabitants was raised in *Harrogate Borough Council v. Simpson* (1984) 17 H.L.R. 205, where it was held that the wording of the Act meant that a woman was not permitted to succeed, under the Housing Act 1985, to a secure tenancy on the death of her lesbian lover with whom she had been living in the property in question for two and a half years. The Court of Appeal held that the expression 'living together as husband and wife' connotes a heterosexual relationship and not a same-sex relationship. This decision was followed, with great reluctance, by a majority of the Court of Appeal in the Rent Act case of *Fitzpatrick v. Sterling Housing Association Ltd* [1997] 4 All E.R. 991, where it was decided that a homosexual partner of the deceased tenant could not qualify as a statutory successor under the Rent Act 1977 as a 'member of the tenant's family' (see p.272 above). In a powerful dissenting judgment, Ward L.J., not without considerable hesitation, dissented from the majority and considered that it was open to the Court to have held that not only was Mr Fitzpatrick a member of his deceased partner's family, but that he should have succeeded also on the basis that he had lived with the deceased 'as his husband or wife', because, in his view, there was 'no essential difference between a homosexual and heterosexual couple.' He concluded by quoting from Bingham M.R.'s judgment in *R. v. Ministry of Defence, ex parte. Smith* [1996] Q.B. 517 at 554 that 'A belief which represented unquestioned orthodoxy in year X may have become questionable by year Y and unsustainable by year Z'. His Lordship considered that *Harrogate Borough Council v. Simpson* (above) was decided in year Y (1984) and that 1997 was year Z. (See the comment at (1998) 10 C.F.L.Q. 191 by N. Wikeley.)

(3) Resided with the tenant for 12 months before the tenant's death It was originally held by the Court of Appeal that this meant that the successor and the deceased tenant had to have resided together for the requisite period in the dwelling-house to which a tenancy by way of succession was being claimed (*South Northamptonshire DC v. Power* [1987] 1 W.L.R. 1433), but this was overruled by the House of Lords in *London Borough of Waltham Forest v. Thomas* (1992) 24 H.L.R. 622, HL). Thus, provided that the tenant and successor resided together in a council house at the time of the tenant's death it does not matter where they resided together before then. This interpretation was justified on the basis that any other result would be calculated to produce "unwelcome and unjustifiable distress and hardship in the event of an untimely death" (*per* Lord Templeman).

The meaning of "resided with" was considered in *Peabody Donation Fund Governors v. Grant* (1986) 6 H.L.R. 41 where the court emphasised that the requirement involved the claimant having spent a significant amount of time with the person with whom s/he was allegedly residing. In that case the tenant's daughter lived at her father's flat for most of the week to look after him. Her books were there and she had come to regard it as home.The Court of Appeal refused to interfere with the judge's decision that the daughter had established that the statutory requirements for her to succeed to a secure tenancy of her father's flat on his death had been satisfied. A more marginal case perhaps was *Camden LBC v. Goldenberg and another* (1992) 24 H.L.R. 36. The claimant lived with his grandmother in her council flat. But when he married he and his wife went to look after the house of friends who were abroad for 10 weeks. He intended not to return to the flat if he and his wife could find suitable accommodation at the end of that period. When they could not they separated and he returned to his grandmother's flat where he remained until her death. By a majority the Court of Appeal held that the continuity of residence had not been broken by the claimant's departure because he had left his possessions there and the prospects of finding somewhere else to live were too distant to displace that intention.

(iv) The tenant must not have been a successor As noted above a person cannot qualify as a successor if the tenant himself was a successor as defined in section 88. That section provides that the tenant will be a successor in the following cases.

(1) Where the tenancy vested in him by virtue of section 89 (see above). A second succession on death is therefore precluded.

(2) Where he was a joint tenant and has become the sole tenant. Thus there cannot be a statutory succession on the death of a person who had been a joint tenant but before his or her death had become the sole tenant under that tenancy. But where a tenant was a joint tenant but became a sole tenant of the house under a *new* tenancy he will not be a successor for the purpose of section 88. In *Bassetlaw DC v. Renshaw* [1992] 1 All E.R. 925 a husband and wife were joint tenants. The husband gave notice to quit thereby ending the tenancy (see *Hammersmith & Fulham LBC v. Monk* A.C. 478, HL) and the council granted the wife a new tenancy. On her death her son was entitled to succeed to that tenancy because she had not become a sole tenant under the previous joint tenancy.

(3) Where the tenancy arose by virtue of section 86 and the former tenancy was granted to another person or jointly to him and another person. (As noted above, section 86 provides that a periodic tenancy arises by statute where a fixed term secure tenancy has ended, for example by effluxion of time or (in effect) by forfeiture (see above).)

(4) Where he became the tenant on the tenancy being assigned to him although (i) where that assignment came about as a result of a court order under sections 23A or 24 of the Matrimonial Causes Act 1973 (*i.e.* where the divorce court has ordered a transfer from one spouse to the other) or section 17(1) of the Matrimonial and Family Proceedings Act 1984 (property adjustment order after overseas divorce, etc.) the tenant will only be treated as a successor if the assignor was a successor (s.88(2)), and (ii) where the assignment to him was by way of exchange (under section 92 below) he will be a successor only if he had been a successor to the tenancy which he assigned as his part of the exchange (s.82(3)). Hence if tenant A (who is a successor tenant) exchanges with tenant B (a non-successor tenant), A will remain a successor under his new tenancy and B will still be a non-successor under his tenancy.

(5) Where he became the tenant on the tenancy being vested in him on the death of the previous tenant. This is also designed to prevent more than one succession on death. But there can be cases where there is doubt as to whether the tenant who has died had himself succeeded on the death of the previous tenant. Before the Housing Act 1980 there was no statutory right to succeed. At that time if a council tenant died the tenancy would pass under the law of testate or intestate succession. This is what happened in *Epping Forest District Council v. Pomphrett and Another* (1990) 22 H.L.R. 475. On the death of the tenant intestate in 1978 no letters of administration were ever taken out. The tenancy therefore vested in the President of the Family Division under the Administration of Estates Act 1925, (Since the Law of Property (Miscellaneous Provisions) Act 1994, s.19, it would vest in the Public Trustee). The widow and her children remained living in the property and the council promised that they would "formally transfer the tenancy to her". But they neither determined nor transferred that tenancy. The inference to be drawn therefore was that by permitting her to remain and accepting rent they had granted the widow a new tenancy. This meant that on her subsequent death in 1985 one of the children was able to succeed under the Housing Act 1985 because the tenant had not succeeded on the death of her husband. She had a new tenancy, of which one of her children could be a statutory successor.

(6) Where the tenancy was previously an introductory tenancy (see above) and he was a successor to the introductory tenancy.

It is further provided that if the tenant was a successor under periodic tenancy A which has come to an end and within six months becomes a tenant, of the same house or of the same landlord, under tenancy B he will be a successor in relation to tenancy B unless that tenancy provided otherwise (s.88(4)).

(v) More than one qualifying successor Where there is more than one qualifying successor, the tenant's spouse (if any) will become the successor. Otherwise the qualifying successors will choose one of themselves by agreement and in the absence of agreement the landlord is empowered to make the choice. (By contrast the Rent Act 1977 provides for the choice to be made by the county court. See, *e.g. Williams v. Williams* [1970] 1 W.L.R. 1530.)

(vi) Position where there is no successor Where there is no person qualified to succeed the tenant, the tenancy will devolve in accordance with the laws of testate and intestate succession, depending on whether the tenant has effectively disposed of it or not by will.

The tenancy will accordingly cease to be secure—

(1) where it is vested or otherwise disposed of in the course of the administration of the tenant's estate, unless the vesting or other disposal is in pursuance of a property adjustment order made under section 24 of the Matrimonial Causes Act 1973 in matrimonial proceedings (*e.g.* where the parties are or are to be divorced) or under s.17(1) of the Matrimonial and Family Proceedings Act 1984 (property adjustment order after overseas divorce, etc.) or under paragraph 1 of Schedule 1 to the Children Act 1989 (under which the court can order transfer of the tenancy to a child in an application for financial relief against a parent or parents); or

(2) when it is known that when the tenancy is so vested or disposed of it will not be in pursuance of such a court order (s.89(3)).

A tenancy which thereby ceases to be a secure tenancy cannot subsequently become a secure tenancy (s.89(4)).

(b) Devolution of a fixed-term secure tenancy
There is no statutory right of succession in respect of a fixed-term secure tenancy on the death of the secure tenant. The tenancy will devolve in the normal way according to the laws of testate or intestate succcession. It will remain a secure tenancy until—

(1) it is vested or otherwise disposed of in the course of the administration of the tenant's estate unless that vesting or disposal is (i) in pursuance of a court order under section 24 of the Matrimonial Causes Act 1973 (see above) or (ii) to a qualified successor (s.90(1),(2)(a),(3)); or

(2) it is known that when it is so vested or disposed of it will not be a secure tenancy (s.90(1),(2)(b)).

If on the tenant's death the tenancy ceases to be a secure tenancy, it cannot subsequently become a secure tenancy (s.90(4)).

D. ASSIGNMENT, SUB-LETTING AND LODGERS

The general law governing a tenant's freedom or lack of freedom to alienate his interest by way of an assignment of the tenancy or by granting a sub-tenancy is examined in Chapter 4 above. Because of the special nature of council tenancies, which are tenancies of publicly owned housing stock available for tenants with identified needs, and for which there will often be a waiting list, there are special rules which govern a secure tenant's freedom to deal with his tenancy. Indeed as we have already seen, if the secure tenant ceases to occupy the dwelling-house as his only or principal home the tenancy will cease to be secure and therefore terminable in accordance with the ordinary law of landlord and tenant.

Assignment

The general rule is that a secure tenancy which is either a periodic tenancy or a fixed-term tenancy created on or after November 5, 1982 is not capable of being assigned (Housing Act 1985, s.91(1)) except in one of the three exceptional cases set out below.

(1)   an assignment by exchange under section 92;

(2)   an assignment in pursuance of a court order under sections 23A or 24 of the Matrimonial Causes Act 1973; or under section 17(1) of the Matrimonial and Family Proceedings Act 1984 (property adjustment order after overseas divorce, etc.) or under paragraph 1 of Schedule 1 to the Children Act 1989 (under which the court can order transfer of the tenancy to a child in an application for financial relief against a parent or parents);

(3)   an assignment to a potential statutory successor on death (s.91(3)). This is a potentially useful provision which could avoid post-mortem disputes by rival claimants.

In each exceptional case therefore the assignment is perfectly effective and the assignee can become a secure tenant even if there is an absolute prohibition on assignment in the tenancy (*Governors of the Peabody Donation Fund v. Higgins* [1983] 1 W.L.R. 1091. But see section 84 and ground 1 of Schedule 2 above for possible recovery of possession by the landlord).

Whether a family court will exercise its statutory powers (see (2) above) to order transfer of a tenancy between family members powers will probably depend on the attitude of the local authority, especially if there is a prohibition on assignment in the tenancy agreement (*Thompson v. Thompson* [1976] Fam. 25 and *Jones v. Jones* (1996) 29 H.L.R. 561). The court also has a quite separate power to transfer a secure tenancy as between spouses and cohabitants under the Family Law Act 1996, Sched. 7.

A fixed-term tenancy created before November 5, 1982 can be assigned but this will result in permanent loss of secure status, save in one of those three exceptional cases (s.91(2)).

Assignments by way of exchange   The right to exchange in section 92 provides that a secure tenant may exchange his or her tenancy with another secure tenant with the written consent of their landlord(s), such consent not to be unreasonably withheld except on one of the grounds set out in Schedule 3 (s.92(1),(2)). The landlord can only rely on such a ground where he has notified the tenant of the ground and the relevant particulars within 42 days of the tenant's application for consent (s.92(4)).

The principal grounds are—

(1)   that by reason of a court order the tenant is obliged or will be obliged to give up possession at a date specified in the order;

(2)   that possession proceedings have begun under any of the first six grounds in Part 1 of Schedule 2 (above) or a section 8 notice has been served on one of those grounds;

(3) that the accommodation afforded by the dwelling-house is substantially more extensive than is reasonably required by the proposed assignee;

(4) the extent of the accommodation afforded by the dwelling-house is not reasonably suitable to the needs of the proposed assignee and his family.

Other grounds relate to the nature of the property (*e.g.* where it is designed for a disabled person and the proposed assignee or a member of his family is not disabled) or the circumstances of the letting (*e.g.* certain tenancies in connection with employment of the assignor tenant).

If consent is withheld on any ground other than one set out in Schedule 3, it is deemed to have been granted (s.92(3)).

The landlord can give consent conditionally where there are rent arrears or there is some other outstanding breach of covenant or obligation of the tenancy. The condition is that the tenant pay the outstanding arrears or rectify the breach as the case may be (s.92(5)). Any other condition is to be disregarded (s.92(6)).

Thus secure tenants can exchange even if they have different landlords. Exchange may also take place with an assured tenant whose landlord is a registered housing association (or the Housing Corporation, Housing For Wales or a charitable housing trust)(s.92(2A)).

Sub-letting and lodgers

Section 93(1) provides that it is a term of every secure tenancy that the tenant (a) may take in lodgers (see, *e.g. Monmouth BC v. Marlog* (1994) 27 H.L.R. 30, CA (see p.10 above) and *Huwyler v. Roddy* (1996) 28 H.L.R. 551) but (b) will not, without the written consent of the landlord sublet or part with possession of part of the dwelling-house. (The Landlord and Tenant Act 1988 (see p.87 above) does not apply to a secure tenancy.)

Consent to a sub-letting (which may be given retrospectively: s.94(4)) must not be unreasonably withheld (and if unreasonably withheld, is to be treated as given: s.94(2)). The onus is on the landlord to show that consent was withheld reasonably (s.94(2)). Conditional consent is not permitted and if conditions are imposed consent is to be treated as given and the conditions can be ignored (s.94(5)).

A failure to respond to a request for consent within a reasonable time is to be taken as a refusal of consent (s.94(6)(b)).

If consent is requested in writing the landlord must give written reasons to the tenant where consent is refused (s.94(6)(a)).

However, if the secure tenant parts with possession, or sub-lets the whole (including sub-letting part and then the remainder), the tenancy ceases to be a secure tenancy and cannot become a secure tenancy again (s.93(2)). This would permit the landlord to end the tenancy by a notice to quit.

A tenancy which ceases to be secure because the tenant condition in section 81 (occupation by the tenant) ceases to be satisfied remains subject to the restrictions in sections 91 and 93 above (s.95).

E. THE RIGHT TO BUY

Introduction

Since 1952 local authorities have had power by general consent to dispose of council houses to their tenants with a 20per cent discount, although between 1968 and 1970 limits were imposed on sales in the main conurbations. What was novel about the Housing Act 1980 was that it introduced, for the first time, a statutory *right* to buy, exercisable by most secure tenants. That scheme, which was subject to important amendments, was subsequently consolidated in the Housing Act 1985, Part V and has since been further amended. It affords a qualifying tenant the opportunity to acquire from their landlord either the freehold of the house, or (as the case may be) a 125-year lease of the flat in which they live.

To forestall councils who, for political reasons, were minded to procrastinate over an application by a tenant to exercise the right to buy, the Secretary of State was empowered to intervene and complete the sale by the exercise of a power to "do all such things, as appear to him necessary or expedient" to enable tenants to exercise the right to buy. This power was described, in *R. v. Secretary of State for the Environment, ex. parte. Norwich City Council* [1982] Q.B. 808 as "a most unusual and draconian default power framed so as to maximise the power of the Secretary of State and to minimise any power of review by the court"). Discounts from the market value of the property were available according to how many years a qualifying tenant had been a council tenant. Under the 1980 Act the discounts began at 32per cent for tenants of three years' standing (the minimum qualifying period of residence) rising to 50per cent for those who had accumulated 20 years or more of qualifying residence. Prospective purchasers could claim a council mortgage of 100per cent although given that most purchasers obtained mortgages from banks or building societies, this right proved to be loss popular than anticipated and was eventually abolished as from October 11, 1993 by the Leasehold Reform, Housing and Urban Development Act 1993. To prevent profiteering by tenants who had exercised the right to buy it was provided that if the property was re-sold within five years a repayment would be due to the local authority former landlord.

The right to buy policy was a flagship measure of the first Thatcher Government and was bitterly opposed by the Labour Party, which promised to repeal it if returned to power. This opportunity never arose because the scheme proved to be astoundingly successful, netting £23 billion in sales receipts by 1992, by far the most successful measure of privatisation. The Labour Party eventually accepted that continued opposition to the scheme was unlikely to win much support and dropped its pledge to repeal the right to buy. From 580 right-to-buy sales in 1980, the number rose to 196,430 in 1982 (the highest figure in any one year). Sales then slackened off to 82,251 in 1986. The Government's response to declining sales was to boost the scheme by reducing the minimum residence period to two years and by increasing the maximum discount to 60per cent. (Housing and Building Control Act 1984). As from January 7, 1987 further incentives were provided. The minimum discount for flats was raised to 44per cent and the maximum to 70per cent after 15 years' residence, whilst the repayment period following resale was reduced from five to three years (Housing and Planning Act 1986). This raised sales to 181,370 in 1989 before the recession set in leading to a dramatic decline in sales to a low point of 46,350 in 1995. By that time a total of 1,569,321 council dwelling-houses had been sold since 1980, amounting to 25per cent of the total stock of that year. The unforseen recession also led to many former tenants, who had exercised the right to buy and could no longer afford the mortgage repayments, being forced to sell at depressed prices or have their homes repossessed by their mortgagee. This was one drawback of the right-to-buy policy. Another unhappy feature of the scheme was that it had operated very unevenly—

> "It is very important to note that the pattern of these sales was very uneven geographically and socially. A high proportion of the sales were in the south of England where owner occupation was already high. The vast majority of RTB tenants were middle aged, skilled manual workers with adolescent or grown up children. Very few high rise flats were sold compared to the rapid purchase of houses on the more suburban estates, and so these sales created a much less diverse housing stock causing considerable housing management problems... The major effect of the RTB policy has been, therefore to create a residual housing sector increasingly occupied by the poorest sections of society and disproportionately representing the long-term unemployed, elderly people and single parent households living in less desirable housing types such as high rise flats, and less favoured housing locations in inner city areas or on socially stigmatised 'hard-to-let' estates. (Hughes and Lowe, Social Housing Law and Policy (1995) p.60.)"

Right to buy on rent-to-mortgage terms

In an attempt to cater for those tenants who were unable to afford to buy, even with the discounts available, a statutory shared ownership scheme was introduced by the Housing and Building Control Act 1984. (Would-be purchasers could already defer completion for up to two years in the hope that their circumstances would improve.) This scheme enabled a tenant, who had claimed to exercise the right to buy and the right to a council mortgage, to be granted a "shared ownership lease" where he was not entitled to a full mortgage (because of his income). Under this scheme the tenant purchaser could acquire a proportion of the beneficial interest in the property, usually 50per cent, on a long lease and then buy further tranches in multiples of 12.5per cent. The tenant would at the same time remain a periodic tenant and pay a proportionately reduced rent on the remainder at any time. Once the whole beneficial interest had been acquired in this way the tenant could call for the freehold to be conveyed to him. The scheme was little used and abolished for new purchasers from November 1, 1993, when it was replaced by the rent to mortgage scheme introduced by the Leasehold Reform Housing and Urban Development Act 1993. The complex details of this scheme are in new sections 143–151B and Schedule 6A to the Housing Act 1985 as inserted by sections 108–120 of the 1993 Act, and only a summary is provided here.

The scheme operates by permitting a tenant, who is qualified to exercise the right to buy (at a discount) and has made a valid claim to exercise that right, to initiate a notice procedure by serving notice on the landlord exercising the right to acquire on rent-to-mortgage terms. At the end of this procedure, and if entitled, the tenant will then be able to pay the landlord part of the purchase price outright with a loan obtained from a private source (*e.g.* through a building society or bank mortgage loan). This payment is referrred to as the "minimum initial payment". The balance is left outstanding as a liability secured by a charge (ranking in priority after that granted to finance the initial payment) which would be paid when the property is disposed of *inter vivos* or on death although it can be reduced or cleared at any time by voluntary payments. From the beginning the tenant purchaser becomes the owner of the freehold (in the case of a house) or a 125-year lease (in the case of a flat), in both cases burdened by a covenant to repay the balance as outlined above. The rent formerly payable is converted to mortgage repayments on the loan raised to cover the initial payment.

The scheme was thus designed to attract tenants who could not otherwise afford to pay a private mortgage for the full (discounted price) but could afford mortgage repayments at the same level as the rent formerly payable. For this reason a tenant whose income is above a specified limit is not eligible because he can exercise the right to buy in the normal way. On the other hand the tenant must have a certain income level to enable him to meet his commitments. Thus the right to buy on rent-to-mortgage is also not exercisable by a tenant who either (a) is or was entitled to housing benefit (a means tested benefit to help with rental payments) or (b) has claimed housing benefit in the period beginning twelve months before the tenant claims to exercise the right and ending with the day on which the conveyance or grant is executed (s.143A).

Right to buy—main features

The following account is concerned primarily with the circumstances in which the right to buy is exercisable. The actual process of exercise of the right is dealt with only briefly.

(a) Who is eligible?
The right to buy, in the case of a freehold house, or to acquire a long lease in the case of a flat (as defined in section 183) or a leasehold house, is exercisable by a secure tenant of the dwelling-house in question (ss. 118(1)).

If there are joint tenants the right is exercisable jointly as long as at least one of them occupies the dwelling-house as his only or principal home (s.118(2)). Alternatively it can, by agreement between the joint tenants, be exercisable by one or more of them provided that at least one of the persons to whom the right belongs occupies the dwelling as his or her only or principal home.

In addition to being a secure tenant, a person will only be entitled to claim to exercise the right to buy if that person satisfies the residence requirement. That is they must have been a public sector tenant (as widely defined in Schedule 4 paras 6–9) for a period of (or periods amounting to) at least two years. This need not necessarily have been in the same premises or indeed with the same landlord (s.119(1) and Sched. 4). In the case of joint tenants the residence requirement need only be satisfied by at least one of them (s.119(2)), which need not necessarily be the purchaser.

A secure tenant is permitted, in his notice claiming the right to buy, to require that not more than three members of his family who are not joint tenants but who occupy the dwelling-house as their only or principal home, to share the right to buy with him (s.123). This could boost the discount available.

The family member must either be the tenant's spouse or someone who has been residing with the tenant throughout the period of 12 months ending with the service of his notice. Where this right is exercised the purchasers will be treated as joint tenants. A person is a member of another's family if (a) he is that person's spouse or he and that person live together as husband or wife or (b) he is that person's parent, grandparent, child, grandchild, brother, sister, uncle, aunt, nephew or niece. Half-blood relationships are treated as whole blood, a step-child as a child of the step-parent and an illegitimate child as the legitimate child of his mother and reputed father (s.118).

(b) How is the required period of residence satisfied? (s.119 and sched.4)
It is possible to count towards the period of qualifying residence any time during which (a) the secure tenant or (b) his or her spouse or (c) his or her deceased spouse was a public sector tenant provided that during that time the individual concerned was occupying the property as his or her only or principal home (as to which, see section 81 above). (Sched.14 para. 2). A joint tenant is deemed to have fulfilled this requirement as long as he or she occupied the dwelling as his or her only or principal home (para. 3).

A period of residence by a spouse only counts if the secure tenant and the spouse were at that time living together (para. 2). Similarly residence by a deceased spouse only counts if the secure tenant and the spouse were living together at the time of the spouse's death (para. 3). The child of a public sector tenant who becomes a secure tenant is also permitted to count a period before s/he became the secure tenant, when s/he was over 16 and during which he or she resided in a dwelling-house (of which a parent was a sole or public sector tenant), as his or her only or principal home. Such period must be immediately before he took over the tenancy or be a period ending not more than two years before that date (para. 4).

In addition a period or periods (before service of the notice claiming the right to buy) during which the tenant or his or her spouse or deceased spouse occupied armed forces accommodation can be counted. Once again the spouse and the secure tenant must have been living together at the time and in the case of a deceased spouse the secure tenant and the deceased spouse must have been living together at the time of the spouse's death (para. 5).

Similar provisions apply in respect of a period during which the tenant (or his or her spouse or deceased spouse) was a qualifying person for the purposes of the preserved right to buy (as to which, see below) (para. 5A).

(c) Exceptions to the right to buy (s.120 and Sched.5)

The first group of exceptions deals with landlords against whom the right to buy is not permitted. They are (a) a charitable housing association or housing trust, (sch.5 para. 1) (b) a co-operative housing association (para. 2), (c) a housing association which has never had public funding (para. 3), (d) a landlord who does not own the freehold or has an insufficient leasehold estate to be able to grant a lease of at least 21 years if a house and of at least 50 years if a flat (para. 4), and (e) the Crown (save for certain exceptions) (para. 12).

The second group of exceptions all relate to the type of property or the purpose for which it has been let. It comprises the following.

(1) Where the dwelling-house is (a) within the curtilage of a building held by the landlord for non-housing purposes and consisting mainly of accommodation other than housing or is in a cemetery and (b) was let to the tenant (or a predecessor in title) in consequence of the tenant (or predecessor) being in the employment of the landlord or of certain other public bodies (para. 5).

The clear aim here is to exclude tied property from the right to buy. The meaning of "curtilage" was considered in *Dyer v. Dorset CC* [1989] Q.B. 346 where the tenant was a college lecturer who was secure tenant of a house in the college grounds, the landlord being the authority/employer. His application to exercise the right to buy was upheld and the court, as a matter of interpretation, rejected the landlord's argument that his house was within the curtilage of a particular building or collection of buildings rather than the college grounds as a whole. (The lecturer was not excluded from being a secure tenant by Sched.1, para. 2 because his contract did not require him to live there).

(2) Where the dwelling-house has features which are different from those of ordinary dwelling-houses and are designed to make it suitable for occupation by physically disabled persons and both (a) it is one of a group of dwellings which it is the landlord's practice to let for occupation by such persons and (b) a social service or special facilities are provided in close proximity for the purpose of assisting those persons (para. 7).

In this context "designed" means that the property was designed and built or converted with the particular features in question, and not merely "intended" by reason of the addition of special features for occupation by a disabled person. Furthermore the Act contemplates features such as ramps, lifts and special doors, etc. and not ones which might be found in an ordinary dwelling. The fact that an ordinary property had been modified so as to have a downstairs lavatory intended for use by the tenant's disabled daughter did not mean that the property was "designed" to make it suitable, etc. (*Freeman v. Wansbeck DC* (1983) 10 H.L.R. 54).

(3) Where the dwelling-house is one of a group which it is the landlord's practice to let to mentally disordered persons and where a social service or special facilities are provided (not necessarily in close proximity) for the purpose of assisting those persons (para. 9).

(4) Effectively excludes a dwelling-house where it is one of a *group* of dwelling-houses with certain special features (location, size, design etc.) which are part of a sheltered housing scheme for the elderly (*i.e.* persons aged 60 or above) or elderly and disabled persons and which have the benefit of a residential or non-residential warden facility along with a common room (para. 10). For this exception to apply the dwelling must have been first let before January 1, 1990.

(5) Excludes a similar *single* dwelling with such features which was let to the tenant or a predecessor in title for occupation by a person aged 60 or more (para. 11).

Circumstances where the tenant cannot claim (or continue with) the right to buy

(1) Where the tenant is, or will be, obliged to give up possession by a court order (s.121(1)). Thus in *London Borough of Enfield v. McKeon* [1986] 1 W.L.R. 1007 a possession order was made after the tenant had served notice claiming to exercise the right to buy. It was held that the process was continuing and hence the tenant could be prevented from continuing to completion. (See also *Tanolridge DC v. Bickers* [1998] 41 E.G. 220, CA). But if all stages have been gone through save completion by execution of the transfer, possession proceedings after that point probably will not preclude completion if the tenant has sought an injunction (under s.138(3) below). (*Dance v. Welwyn Hatfield DC* [1990] 1 W.L.R. 1097, as explained in *Bristol City Council v. Lovell* [1998] 1 W.L.R. 446).

(2) Certain cases where the tenant is bankrupt or there are pending bankruptcy proceedings against the tenant or the tenant has made a composition with creditors (s.121(2)).

(3) Where the tenant ceases to be a secure tenant before the whole process is completed, as in *Sutton LBC v. Swann* (1985) 18 H.L.R. 140, where the tenant left his council flat and bought a house elsewhere having earlier claimed the right to buy the flat. He thereby forfeited his status as a secure tenant and the right to buy a long lease of his flat, (See also *Bradford Metropolitan City Council v. McMahon* [1994] 1 W.L.R. 52 where the tenant died before completion and it was held that the personal representatives could not compel completion. But contrast *Harrow LBC v. Tonge* (1993) 25 H.L.R. 99 where the deceased tenant (herself a statutory successor) had (under s.123) joined her daughter in the right to buy thereby enabling the daughter, as a deemed joint secure tenant (see above), to complete the purchase). *Sutton LBC v. Swann* (above) was applied in *Muir Group Housing Association Ltd v. Thornley* (1993) 25 H.L.R. 89 where after having exercised the right to buy but before completion, the tenant departed and sub-let the whole house. It was held that he had forfeited his secure tenancy status by the sub-letting and also lost the right to complete the right-to-buy process. This result was consistent with the policy of the Act. As Glidewell L.J. observed—

"the statutory regime gives the secure tenant considerable benefits—not merely to require his landlord to sell him the freehold but also to sell it to him at a discount—which result in corresponding disadvantages for the landlord. It would follow therefore that the provisions of the statute should be strictly construed so as to preclude a person who has, for whatever reason, ceased to be a secure tenant from being able to claim the advantages. (p.98)"

The procedure

The Act provides for an elaborate procedure of notices and counter notices which, once the right to buy has been established, enables the tenant to discover a number of matters including the price, information as to any service charge, the value of the dwelling and how that was arrived at, the appropriate discount applied and the discount period taken into account and the provisions to be included in the transfer or lease. The tenant must also be informed of the rent to mortgage scheme (see above) (ss.122–125E). Once all stages of the process have been concluded save completion, the landlord must convey the freehold or, as the case may be, grant the lease. This obligation is enforceable by injunction (s.138). (See *Taylor v. Newham LBC* [1993] 2 All E.R. 649 where the court refused to treat the grant of an injunction as discretionary in these circumstances and granted it as of right). The tenant can withdraw at any time before completion by serving written notice to that effect on the landlord (s.122). If the tenant fails to complete on time the landlord can serve a preliminary notice to complete within not less than 56 days followed by a second notice if the tenant fails to comply with the first. When the second notice period expires the tenant is deemed to have withdrawn his application to exercise the right to buy (ss.141 and 142). On completion the transfer will be an occasion for compulsory registration of title if title, is not already registered (s.154).

The price

The price payable is that which the dwelling-house would realise, at the time when the tenant serves his initial notice, if sold on the open market by a willing vendor and subject to the following assumptions:

(1) that the vendor was selling the fee simple with vacant possession or as the case may be was granting a lease for the appropriate term (as defined in Para. 12 of Sched. 6), which is usually 125 years at a ground rent of no more than £10 per annum;

(2) that neither the tenant nor a member of his family (see below) residing with him wanted to buy or take the lease (thus excluding any enhanced hypothetical bid that might have been expected from such a sitting tenant or family member);

(3) that there be disregarded any improvements made by certain specified persons or any disrepair attributable to any of those persons. (The persons listed are the secure tenant or any predecessor in title under that tenancy or an introductory tenancy; and any member of his family (see below) who immediately before the secure tenancy (or an immediately preceding introductory tenancy) was a secure tenant or introductory tenant of the dwelling-house.) (Ss.126 and 127.)

Any dispute as to value is determinable by the district valuer following reference of the matter to him (s.128).

The price is then discounted according to any qualifying period of residence. (See above for calculation of the qualifying period of residence). The minimum qualifying period is two years. The minimum discount is 32 per cent in the case of a house, where the qualifying period is less than three years, rising by 1 per cent for each complete year, to a maximum of 60 per cent. In the case of a flat the minimum discount is 44 per cent rising by 2 per cent for each complete year to a maximum of 70 per cent. (s.129).

Where the right to buy died is being exercised by joint tenants the qualifying period used is that of the one who has the greatest entitlement. The discount is also reduced by any discount given on a previous right to buy sale to either the purchaser or one of the purchasers or the spouse or deceased spouse of one of them (provided that such spouse and the secure tenant were living together at the time and in the case of a deceased spouse that the secure tenant and the deceased spouse were living together at the time of the spouse's death) (s.130).

There is a maximum discount prescribed by the Secretary of State (currently £50,000) and a maximum by reference to the amount that has been spent on the dwelling by the landlord in the previous eight years. If the price before discount is below that amount there is no discount allowed (s.131).

Where the tenant who had claimed the right to buy died before completion and her daughter had succeeded as periodic tenant by succession (see below) the daughter was able to obtain a discount based on her mother's (longer) period of occupation as a public sector tenant (*McIntyre v. Merthyr Tydfil DC* (1989) 21 H.L.R. 320).

Other terms

The terms on which sales take place are contained in section 139(1) and Schedule 6. The schedule sets out in particular the detailed provisions which govern the terms of any long lease including length (normally 125 years), service charge, repairing obligations, and provides for an absolute right to assign and sub-let (see also *Sheffield CC v. Jackson* [1998] 3 All E.R. 260, CA).

The obligation to repay a discount

The purchaser must covenant that if the dwelling-house is disposed of within three years of the purchase, a proportion of the discount must be repaid if demanded. The amount is one-third for each year less than three years and the liability to repay is a charge on the premises which will bind successors in title to the purchaser (ss.155 and 156).

The relevant disposals which will trigger off the obligation are a conveyance of the freehold or an assignment of the lease or the grant of a (non-mortgage lease) for a term of more than 21 years otherwise than at a rack rent (s.159). A number of disposals are not relevant disposals for this purpose. They are—

(1) A disposal as a result of a court order following marital breakdown (*i.e.* under Matrimonial Causes Act 1973, ss. 23–24A; or s.17(1) of the Matrimonial and Family Proceedings Act 1984 (property adjustment order after overseas divorce, etc.) or under paragraph 1 of Schedule 1 to the Children Act 1989 (under which the court can order transfer of the tenancy to a child in an application for financial relief against a parent or parents)) is excluded from this definition. (S.160(1)(c) and (3)(a) as amended, reversing *R. v. Rushmore BC, ex parte. Barrett* (1988) 20 H.L.R. 366, CA where it was held that an order for sale under the Matrimonial Cause Act, s.24A 1973 was not exempt because at the time this provision was not one of those listed in s.160.)

(2) A disposal which is a vesting of the dwelling-house in a person taking under a will or on an intestacy (s.160(1)(b)) or a disposal made following an order under section 2 of the Inheritance (Provision for Family and Dependants) Act 1975 (s.160(1)(c) and (3)(b)).

(3) Certain disposals between qualifying family members (s.160(1)(a) and (2)(a)–(c)).

(4) A disposal by way of compulsory purchase (ss.160(1)(d) and 161).

(5) A disposal of land included (under s.184) in the original purchase.

Restrictions on resale

We saw above that on certain disposals by the purchaser within three years of the exercise of the right to buy, a proportion of the discount could be demanded by the original vendor. But even more restrictive provisions govern the actual disposal of certain types of property.

Thus in the case of sale of a dwelling-house in (a) a National Park or (b) an area designated as of outstanding natural beauty under the National Parks and Access to the Countryside Act 1949, s.87 or (c) an area designated by the Secretary of State as a rural area, the landlord is permitted to insert one of two types of restrictive covenants in the transfer which will restrict the freedom of disposition of the purchaser, save in the case of exempt disposals. Accordingly a covenant may be required that any relevant disposal will require the landlord's written consent, such consent not to be withheld in the case of a person who has had his only or principal home in, or worked in, a designated region (which will include in whole or in part such a National Park or area) for the last three years (s.157). (See sections 159 and 160 above for the meaning of "relevant" and "exempt" disposals.)

The clear aim of this provision is to preserve homes in designated areas for residents or workers in or around that or a similar area.

Alternatively the landlord (with the consent of the Secretary of State or in the case of a housing association, the Housing Corporation) might choose to include a right of pre-emption whereby save for an exempt disposal, no relevant disposal may be made within the next 10 years unless the tenant/purchaser or his successor in title offers to reconvey the dwelling-house or (as the case may be) surrender the lease, at a price to be determined in accordance with section 158, to the landlord and the landlord has refused or failed to accept the offer within one month after it was made (s.157(4)).

Preserved right to buy

Special provisions preserve the right to buy for a secure tenant who has continued to occupy the property as his or her only or principal home and whose landlord's interest has been transferred to the private sector or (since January 15, 1989) to a housing association with the consequence that the tenancy ceases to be secure because the landlord condition is no longer satisfied (ss. 171A–171H Housing Act 1985, added by the Housing and Planning Act 1986). The right is registrable under the Land Charges Act 1972 or the Land Registration Act 1925 and thereafter enforceable against a successor landlord. The right can also be exercised by a qualifying successor which means a family member who has acquired the tenancy on the death of the tenant or by assignment or by court order under the Matrimonial Causes Act 1973 or the Family Law Act 1996.

Right to buy for housing association tenants

Although in general housing association secure tenants could qualify for the statutory right to buy in Part V of the Housing Act 1985, most housing associations are registered charities and as such were until recently exempt from the statutory right-to-buy scheme. This was altered by Part I of the Housing Act 1996 which extended the statutory right to buy to assured or secure tenants of registered housing associations, but only where the dwelling has been built or acquired with public money on or after April 1, 1997.

There is also a voluntary purchase scheme in respect of certain dwellings which has been in operation since April 1996. (See Hill and Redman, *Special Bulletin on the Housing Act 1996*, paras 321–327.)

Other rights of secure tenants

The Housing Act 1985 affords secure tenants a number of other rights including the right to receive a written statement from the landlord explaining in simple terms the nature of a secure tenancy and the statutory and contractual rights afforded to the tenant (s.104). Any variation of those terms by the landlord other than by agreement with the tenant must be by way of at least four weeks' notice (or if longer, the rental period) after a preliminary consultation process with the tenant (ss.102 and 103. See *Palmer v. Sandwell MBC* (1988) 20 H.L.R. 74). Other rights include a right to have qualifying repairs carried out and compensation if they are not (s. 96) and in effect a right to make improvements subject to the landlord's consent, which is not to be unreasonably withheld or given subject to unreasonable conditions (ss.97–101). There is also a scheme whereby at the end of their tenancy tenants can receive compensation from the landlord for qualifying improvements carried out since February 1, 1994 (ss. 99A and 99B (added by the Leasehold Reform Housing and Urban Development Act 1993, s.122) and S.I. 1994 No.613). There is a discretionary power for the landlord to give compensation in the case of improvements carried out since October 3, 1980 when the secure tenancy code first came into operation under the Housing Act 1980 (s.100).

Chapter 12

LONG LEASES

Introduction

We saw in Chapter 1 above that tenancies can last for as long or as short a period as the parties choose to agree. Thus it is almost as common to encounter a weekly tenancy as a 999-year tenancy. The reasons for the former are obvious. The parties either envisage a short-term arrangement or the landlord wishes to give himself the option of allowing the tenancy to last for as long or as short as he might choose. A periodic tenancy will continue until either the landlord or the tenant chooses to terminate it by notice to quit or some other permitted method of termination (see Chapter 6 above).

In practice this simple objective has been bedeviled, as far as landlords are concerned, by statutory intervention which, since 1915, has afforded protection to tenants in the private rented sector on a scale hitherto unenvisaged. The story of the subsequent long war of attrition between the protagonists is told elsewhere, but suffice to say at this point that landlords have won the war and virtually all private sector tenancies granted since February 28, 1997 will have no statutory security of tenure to speak of beyond a minimum of six months from commencement of the tenancy (see Housing Act 1988 as amended by the Housing Act 1996. Chapter 8 above).

The public rented sector is a different story. As we have seen in Chapter 11, local authorities regularly grant weekly tenancies to tenants who in fact remain tenants for decades, if not for their lifetimes. Furthermore, since the Housing Act 1980 most local authority and other public sector tenants are "secure tenants", and as such have been afforded the benefit of a special statutory code of protection. This code prevents the landlord from recovering possession other than by obtaining a court order, which can only be granted if one or more specified grounds are satisfied, and even then the court will often have a discretion as to whether or not to order possession. (See now Housing Act 1985 and Chapter 11 above.)

When regulation applies it will not usually matter what particular form the contractual term takes for the purposes of determining whether the tenant is afforded statutory security. Thus it might be a periodic tenancy (*e.g.* weekly or monthly), or for a fixed term. However, traditionally, "long tenancies at a low rent" have been exempt from the principal codes of protection governing tenancies in the private and public residential sectors of the housing market. This is because such tenancies will have been granted for a premium and the relationship of the parties has been perceived by lawmakers as more akin to that of vendor and purchaser rather than landlord and tenant. Nevertheless, whilst it is true to say that the "tenant" has "bought" the lease, the parties remain landlord and tenant and their relationship is governed by the law of landlord and tenant. Furthermore the lease is a limited estate which will expire one day, thereby ending the tenant's interest in the property. The question arises therefore whether such tenants are deserving of any special treatment.

The function of long leases

Before dealing with how the law has answered this question it is important to understand why longer leases are, or have in the past been, granted by landlords. For this purpose it is necessary to distinguish between a house and a flat. A landlord who lets a house for a long fixed term will usually receive a premium at the outset, as he would if he were selling the freehold and receiving the purchase price outright. He will also in addition receive a small ground rent throughout the term. Whether a tenant is willing to pay a premium, and if so how much, will depend on market forces and the length of the proposed term. In general the longer the lease the greater will be its capital value making it more likely that the tenant will be willing to pay a premium rather than a market rent for the property.

Once granted, a lease has the disadvantage that it is a wasting asset and has a progressively diminishing value as it draws towards its expiry date. This makes it increasingly difficult not only to use the lease as security for a mortgage loan but also to sell it by way of assignment. Of course the corresponding benefit to the landlord of this arrangement is that he is making a long-term investment because at the end of the term, however remote, possession will revert to the holder of the interest which is immediately in reversion on the tenancy, although clearly the longer the residue of the lease, the less value this reversionary interest will have.

So why do landlords want to let on very long terms such as 99 years or even 999 years? To most people the latter if not the former looks very similar in principle to a disposal of the fee simple. A purchaser will pay exactly the same for a 999 year lease as for the fee simple. The answer to this question is that the reasons are partly historical, partly technical and partly economic.

The long-term residential lease, as a feature of English property law, first appeared as a means of financing speculative building in the late eighteenth century. For this purpose "long term" is for the purpose of most statutes taken to mean a lease originally granted for more than 21 years, although in practice most building leases were for periods of 99 years or longer. In many cases the original leaseholder will have been a developer who would have constructed the house on the plot leased from the freeholder who might have been the trustees under a family trust who have let the land as a long-term investment. The developer will then have either sold the lease or granted a sub-lease for a premium, having retained a nominal leasehold reversionary interest. For example, a developer with a 99-year lease might have granted a sub-lease of 99 years less 10 days. From the tenant's point of the main problem with such leases, as we have noted above, is that one day they will come to an end and without any statutory intervention the landlord will be able to recover possession of the property.

The other, not unconnected, main reason for the emergence of long residential leases stems from the fact that English law has never developed a satisfactory mechanism for enabling positive covenants to run with freehold land. If a developer builds on plots of land on an estate and sells each house off to a purchaser in fee simple he can take covenants from that purchaser. Such covenants might be restrictive in nature (*e.g.* not to use the property for non-residential purposes, not to build more properties on the land and so on) or positive (*e.g.* to keep boundary fences in repair).

Restrictive covenants are equitable interests in the land and capable of binding subsequent purchasers of the land quite irrespective of whether that purchaser has agreed to be bound or not. Positive covenants, by contrast, are purely contractual in nature and therefore do not as such bind persons other than the original covenantor or his or her estate. Hence a purchaser of land subject to such a covenant will not be bound to observe that covenant. This clearly diminishes the utility of positive covenants as far as the person or persons with the benefit of the covenant is concerned. But if, instead of selling the fee simple, the developer were to grant purchasers a 999 year lease with identical covenants, both the positive and negative covenants would be capable of binding subsequent purchasers because of the special rules governing the enforceability of most covenants in leases, be they positive or negative covenants (see Chapter 7 above). Hence for this purpose the long lease is a conveyancing device used for the ulterior motive of ensuring the durability of covenants affecting the land irrespective of a change of lessee.

As indicated above, another purpose of the long lease has been to provide the original developer not only with a premium but also with a regular ground rent. This will be a worthwhile enterprise where the developer, or the freeholder where he has carried out the development himself, has several hundred or even thousands of houses to sell. A disadvantage of such an arrangement is that ground rents are relatively low and will decline in value over the years as inflation takes its toll, although in recent decades some long leases have provided for periodic increases in the ground rent. In practice the right to receive such rents has tended not to remain with the original developer or his successors in title. They are frequently acquired in significant numbers by large-scale speculators who buy and sell them at auction.

Quite apart from the use of long leases in connection with housing developments the device has had a vital role to play in connection with flats intended for ownership rather than for periodic or short-term letting. A flat forms part only of a building and unlike the whole building is not susceptible to freehold ownership. Each flat will depend for its utility upon matters outside the control of the individual flat owner. Thus there might be common parts or facilities such as gardens, car parking, stairs, landings and corridors, boilers, lifts, etc., the maintenance and/or furnishing of which will need to be the responsibility of somebody. Furthermore, provision will also need to be made for the maintenance and repair of the structure of the whole building, which can have a bearing on the enjoyment and value of the individual flats. The traditional solution to such problems has been for individual flats to be sold on long leases and for the landlord to be made responsible for the matters outlined above for which the tenants will pay through their rent and/or a service charge. Long leasehold flat developments are to be found all over England and Wales, although there are concentrations in particular areas such as London. This use of the long lease has created its own set of problems. Examples include (i) whether the lease has made adequate provision for responsibility for the maintenance and repair of common parts; (ii) disputes over the performance or non-performance of maintenance obligations and/or the provision of services by the landlord; (iii) disputes over service charges and (iv) whether the lease will attract purchasers and whether it will be acceptable security for a mortgage loan.

As in the case of long leasehold houses, reversions on long leasehold flats have been acquired by companies. Many of these companies are household names, who have acquired the freeholds as part of large commercial property portfolios. There are profits to be made not only when the reversions fall into possession but also in the interim by the management of services for which management fees can be charged.

It can be seen that long leases can create problems for tenants. The principal problem for long leaseholders of houses is that one day the lease will expire and at common law possession will revert to the immediate reversioner (*i.e.* another leaseholder or the freeholder as the case may be). This problem has been addressed at different times and in different ways by a number of statutory provisions which are examined below. As in the case of long leases of houses there have been several statutory attempts to deal with the dilemmas faced by long leaseholders of flats and these are also examined below.

A. LONG LEASES OF HOUSES

The basic problem in relation to long leases is stated above. The contractual term of such a lease will expire one day and the right to unencumbered ownership and possession will then revert to whoever holds the reversion on that lease (whether that be a superior leaseholder or the freeholder). Not only that, the tenant might be faced with a large bill for dilapidations in order to put the property into a proper state of repair (see Chapter 3 above). The apparent injustice of this result is that, as well as paying a ground rent, the occupying leaseholder or a predecessor will have paid a premium for the lease and in many cases the premium will be as near as makes no difference to what would have been paid for the unencumbered freehold of that property. In many cases, as noted above, the original leaseholder will have been a developer who would have constructed the house on the plot leased whilst the leaseholder and/or his predecessors in title will have maintained and improved the property since it was constructed. Nevertheless, as a matter of contract law, the land and any buildings on that land will revert to the superior title holder at the end of the lease and the leaseholder in possession will be deprived of his/her home.

Of course, many supporters of the long leasehold system would argue that such arrangements should not be upset precisely because they are based on contracts freely entered into by the original leaseholder and accepted by those who subsequently acquire the lease. This freedom of contract rationale did not commend itself to nineteenth century reformers who perceived a fundamental injustice at play and in 1880 the principle of compulsory enfranchisement made its first appearance as a serious political demand. Compulsory enfranchisement means that the landlord would by statute be compelled to sell the reversion under a residential long lease to a qualifying tenant at a price determined in accordance with rules prescribed by statute. Although nothing came of the demand it did not go away and pressure groups such as Town Tenant's League (1906) kept the issue alive. The principle of compulsory enfranchisement was first examined in the Report of the Royal Commission on the Housing of the Working Classes, 1884–5 which revealed a division of opinion on the issue, although in a special supplementary report 10 of the 15 members concluded that—

> "The prevailing system of building leases is conducive to bad building, to deterioration of property towards the close of the lease, and to a want of interest on the part of the occupier in the house he inhabits; and that legislation favourable to the acquisition on equitable terms of the freehold interest on the part of the leaseholder would conduce greatly to the improvement of the dwellings of the people of this country. (Reports from Commissioners, 1884–5, Vol.30.)"

Despite these arguments the issue was not considered after 1889 (when it was rejected by the Select Committee on Town Holdings) until the Leasehold Committee, which was appointed in 1948, reported in 1950 (The Leasehold Committee Final Report, Cmd.7982). This Report contains an account of the historical background to the issue of leasehold enfranchisement up to 1950. Like the Report of 1889, the 1950 Report once again rejected the notion of compulsory leasehold enfranchisement, although following a recommendation made in the Majority Report, Part I of the Landlord and Tenant Act 1954 was enacted.

Long leases at a low rent—Part I of the Landlord and Tenant Act 1954

The Landlord and Tenant Act 1954 was designed to provide a measure of security of tenure for a tenant on the expiry of a qualifying long tenancy at a low rent, which but for the low rent exclusion in the Rent Act 1977 would have been a regulated tenancy. In such a case the tenancy is continued until it is brought to an end in accordance with the Act when the tenant will usually become a statutory (regulated) tenant. The landlord is then only able to recover possession by establishing one or more of certain specified grounds. These grounds are similar to those applicable in the case of an ordinary regulated tenancy under the Rent Act 1977 with one additional ground; *viz.* that for the purposes of redevelopment the landlord proposes to demolish or reconstruct the whole or a substantial part of the premises for which he reasonably requires possession. The rent under the statutory tenancy is determined in accordance with the fair rent regime of the Rent Act 1977 (see Chapter 10 above).

Following the coming into force of the Housing Act 1988 on January 15, 1989 it was decided that just as there could be no new Rent Act protected tenancies created on or after that date, save in exceptional cases, nor should new long tenancies be capable of taking effect as statutory tenancies under Part I of the Landlord and Tenant Act 1954. Thus it was provided (by the Local Government and Housing Act 1989, s.186 and Sched. 10) that such tenancies entered into on or after April 1, 1990 would instead be subject, on termination, to a regime of security of tenure and rent fixing broadly parallel to that applicable to assured tenancies under the Housing Act 1988. It was further provided that any tenancy which remained within the scope of the 1954 Act would also become subject to this new regime as from 15, January 1999 if it had not been terminated at that date. The only exception is where the landlord has served a notice under section 4 of the 1954 Act specifying a termination date earlier than January 15, 1999 (see below). Unfortunately, there is a problem with regard to long tenancies granted on or after January 15, 1989 and before April 1 1990. Such tenancies might be governed by neither regime. This is because, as will be seen below, the application of Part I of the 1954 Act turns upon whether the tenancy would have been Rent Act protected but for the low-rent exception. But, as noted above, save in specified exceptional cases, it has not been possible to create a Rent Act protected tenancy since 15, January 1989. It would seem to follow therefore that a long tenancy granted on or after that date cannot fall within Part I of the 1954 Act. Furthermore if it is entered into before April 1, 1990 it will not be governed by the modified scheme in the Local Government and Housing Act 1989. Despite this apparent lacuna, some commentators believe that when the time comes (which cannot be before 2010) the courts will engage in some purposive statutory interpretation of the 1989 Act to bring such tenancies within the code contained in that Act (as to which see below).

Part I of the Landlord and Tenant Act 1954

As noted above, the Act applies to a qualifying tenancy at a low rent which was entered into before January 15, 1989 and which has terminated before January 15, 1999. The relevant requirements are as follows (all references are to the 1954 Act). It is not possible for the parties to contract out of the Act (s.17).

(a) A long tenancy
The Act only applies to a long tenancy as defined in the Act (s.2(1)). This means a tenancy which was granted for a term exceeding 21 years, whether or not that term was subsequently extended by the parties or by any enactment (s.2(4)). By way of anti-avoidance it is provided that if a long tenancy comes to an end and the tenant is granted a new tenancy at a low rent (or

by implication of law becomes a tenant under a new tenancy) that new tenancy will be deemed to be a long tenancy irrespective of its terms (s.19(1). See also Schedule 4 for the position where the new tenancy is a periodic tenancy).

(b) At a low rent

The tenancy must be a tenancy at a low rent, which for this purpose means a tenancy whose annual rent does not exceed a certain limit. For tenancies entered into before April 1, 1990 that limit is two-thirds of the rateable value (as determined in accordance with section 5 of the Rent Act 1977 which excludes from mainstream Rent Act protection a tenancy at a "low rent" thereby excluding most long tenancies. (see p.253 above) (s.2(5)(a)). For tenancies entered into on or after April 1, 1990 the rental limit is £1,000 a year in Greater London and £250 a year elsewhere (s.2(5)(b)). (Note that such tenancies will in fact be governed by Schedule 10 to the Local Government and Housing Act 1989.)

In determining whether a long tenancy is, or at any time was, a tenancy at a low rent, there must be disregarded such part (if any) of the sums payable by the tenant which are expressed to be payable in respect of rates (*e.g.* water rates), council tax, services, repairs, maintenance or insurance unless it could not have been regarded by the parties as a part so payable (s.2(7)). This is to prevent a long tenancy at a ground rent being excluded from Part I of the Landlord and Tenant Act 1954 by a service charge of an amount which would otherwise take the tenancy outside the limits of the low-rent requirement.

(c) The tenant must satisfy "the qualifying condition"

This means that "the circumstances (as respects the property comprised in the tenancy, the use of that property and all other relevant matters) are such that on the coming to an end of the tenancy at that time the tenant would, if the tenancy had not been one at a low rent, be entitled, by virtue of the Rent Act 1977, to retain possession of the whole or part of the property comprised in the tenancy" (s.2(1)).

In other words, all the elements of a Rent Act protected tenancy must be satisfied and the tenancy must not have been excluded from protection under that Act for any reason other than the "low rent exception" in section 5. Those requirements are examined in detail in Chapter 10 above to which reference should be made.

The qualifying condition must be satisfied both at the beginning of the tenancy and the date when the issue of the applicability of the 1954 Act falls to be determined (*i.e.* when possession is sought by the landlord). But to avoid difficulties of proof, given that many long tenancies will have begun in the nineteenth century, it is provided that for the purpose of determining (a) whether the property was let as a separate dwelling and (b) the nature of the property or relevant part at that time, it is to be assumed that the position was the same at the beginning of the tenancy as it is when the issue falls to be determined (s.22(3)).

This has sometimes resulted in protection being afforded to tenants who have bought up the "fag end" (*i.e.* the remaining short residue) of a 99-year tenancy at a low rent of a property which has been sub-divided into two or more units. If the tenant has gone into occupation, and can establish that s/he intends to convert the property to a single dwelling for occupation as a residence, the protection of Part I of the Landlord and Tenant Act can be claimed (see *Haines v. Herbert* [1963] 1 W.L.R. 1401 and *Herbert v. Byrne* [1964] 1 W.L.R. 519. In *Herbert v. Byrne* the tenant claimant only occupied one of the units, the remainder being let to protected sub-tenants).

Thus in *Regalian Securities Ltd v. Ramsden* [1981] 1 W.L.R. 611 a penthouse maisonette and a flat were let together on a 42-year lease from 1936. The tenant of the whole property lived in the flat whilst his sub-tenant lived in the maisonette under a sub-tenancy due to expire on the day before the expiry of the head tenancy. When the head tenancy expired the sub-tenant refused to leave. Nevertheless the tenant was able to claim the protection of the 1954 Act because he had the intention of occupying the whole as a separate dwelling-house following the departure of the sub-tenant.

There is a mechanism whereby this outcome can be avoided by the landlord. If the qualifying condition is not satisfied the landlord can apply to the county court at any time within the 12 months before the expiry date of the tenancy for a declaration that Part I of the 1954 Act does not apply. The court can make such a declaration if satisfied that it is unlikely that the qualifying condition will be satisfied at the expiry date of the tenancy and for this purpose it is to be presumed that circumstances will not change by that date (s.2(2)).

However, the above provision will be of no value after January 15, 1999 because any long tenancy which has not been terminated by that date will be governed, if at all, by the 1989 Act and not the 1954 Act (unless the landlord has served a termination notice (see below) which specifies a termination date earlier than January 15 1999. Indeed this phasing out of the 1954 Act scheme must be borne in mind when considering the rules below.

The scheme of Part I of the 1954 Act is that if a tenancy falls within Part I immediately before its term date and has not by that date been ended in accordance with the Act, it will continue automatically on the same terms as before including the rent until so determined (s.3(1)). If the tenant has sub-let part, the rent for the part retained will be determined by apportionment between the two or more parts (s.3(2)(b)). The contractual tenancy will be continued in accordance with section 3 even if the circumstances thereafter change so that the qualifying condition is no longer satisfied (s.3(1)).

(d) Termination by the tenant

The LTA 1954, Part I provides that the tenant can end the tenancy on the term date by giving one month's notice in writing to the landlord (s.5(1)). If the tenancy has been continued by virtue of section 3 the tenant can end it at any time by giving such notice either before or after the term date (s.5(2)).

(e) Termination by the landlord

The landlord can terminate the tenancy on the term date or a later date by giving notice in writing to the tenant not more than 12 nor less than six months before the specified date (s.4(1),(2)).

The notice must specify the premises which the landlord believes to be, or to be likely to be, the premises qualifying for protection (s.4(3).

The landlord's notice must take one of two forms—

(1) A notice which contains a proposal for a statutory tenancy (s.4(3)(a)). Such a notice must set out the proposed terms as to rent and repairs (as to which see sections 7 and 8). Any disagreement as to these matters can be determined by the county court (s.7. See *Etablissement Commercial Kamira v. Schiazzano* [1985] Q.B. 93). On termination of the tenancy by such a notice the provisions of the Rent Act 1977 governing statutory tenancies (including the right to seek registration of a fair rent by the rent officer) will apply thereafter (s.6(1)). But this will not be the case if at the end of two months after service of the landlord's notice the qualifying condition was not fulfilled, unless the tenant has elected (under s.4(4) below) to remain in possession (s.6(2)).

(2) A notice which states that if the tenant is not willing to give up possession on the termination of the tenancy, the landlord intends to apply for a possession order on

one or more of the grounds contained in section 12. (These grounds correspond with suitable modifications to the discretionary grounds in Part 1 of Schedule 15 of the Rent Act 1977 (see p.275 above)). A local authority or other public body (as specified in the Leasehold Reform Act 1967, s.28) can also rely on the additional ground that for the purposes of redevelopment the landlord proposes to demolish or reconstruct the whole or substantially the whole of the relevant premises (LTA 1954, s.12(1)(a) and LRA 1967, s.38(1)). The notice must specify the particular ground(s) relied on (s.4(3)(a),(b)). (See section 13 for the procedure to be followed by the landlord.) If the landlord fails to obtain an order he can within one month serve a notice proposing a statutory tenancy (see (1) above) specifying a termination date not earlier than three months after the giving of that notice (s.14(3)).

The section 4 notice must invite the tenant to notify the landlord in writing, within two months, whether he is willing to give up possession at the date of termination of the tenancy (s.4(4)).

Schedule 10, Local Government and Housing Act 1989

As noted above, for tenancies created on or after April 1, 1990, a qualifying tenancy at a low rent will be governed not by the Landlord and Tenant Act 1954 but by the modified assured tenancy scheme in Schedule 10, Local Government and Housing Act 1989. It should be remembered also that this scheme applies to a tenancy granted before that date which has not been terminated by January 15, 1999, unless the landlord has served a termination notice specifying a termination date before that date (LGHA 1989, s.186(3)).

The basic principles of the LGHA 1989 scheme are, with suitable modifications, broadly parallel to those which govern Part I of the Landlord and Tenant Act 1954. (All references below are to Schedule 10 to the 1989 Act unless otherwise stated). "Long tenancy" and "low rent" are defined as in the 1954 Act scheme. Thus for a tenancy which was entered into on or after April 1, 1990, the low rent test is that the rent does not exceed £1,000 per annum if the property is in Greater London and £250 if it is elsewhere (paras. 2(3)–(4)).

The "qualifying condition" (see above) is that the circumstances must be such that had the tenancy not been excluded from the protection of the assured tenancy code in the Housing Act 1988 by the low rent exception (see section 1 and Sched. 1, para. 3 of that Act) the tenant would have been entitled, to remain in possession of the whole or part of the property comprised in the tenancy by virtue of that Act (para. 1(1)).

In other words, all the elements of a Housing Act 1988 assured tenancy must be satisfied and the tenancy must not have been excluded from protection under that Act for any reason other than the "low rent exception" (in Housing Act 1988, Sched. 1, para. 3). Those requirements are examined in detail in Chapter 9 above, to which reference should be made. It should be noted that for this purpose the tenancy is specifically excepted from the general rule that assured tenancies granted on or after February 28, 1997 are assured shorthold tenancies (see Housing Act 1996, Sched. 2A, para. 6; page 240 above).

As in the case of the 1954 Act, it is provided that for the purpose of determining (a) whether the property was let as a separate dwelling and (b) the nature of the property or relevant part at that time, it is to be assumed that the position was the same at the beginning of the tenancy as it is when the issue falls to be determined (para. 1(7)).

Continuation of the term

Unless and until a long tenancy within Schedule 10 is terminated in accordance with the Act it will continue as a long tenancy, at the same rent and on the same terms as before, beyond the term date, even if the circumstances thereafter change so that the qualifying condition is no longer satisfied (para. 3).

Termination by the tenant

The Act provides that the tenant can end the tenancy on the term date by giving one month's notice in writing (para. 8(1). Alternatively the tenant can end the tenancy at any time after that date by giving such notice either before or after the term date (para. 8(2)).

Termination by the landlord

The landlord can terminate the tenancy on the term date or a later date by giving notice in writing to the tenant not more than 12 nor less than six months before the specified date (para. 4(1)).

The landlord's notice must take one of two forms—

(1) A notice which proposes an assured monthly periodic tenancy and a rent for that tenancy. The notice must also contain a statement that the other terms are to be the same as the long tenancy immediately before it was terminated unless (under para. 6) the landlord proposes other terms instead (para. 4(5)(a)). In such a case the tenant may make a counter proposal and any disagreement is to be determined by a rent assessment committee (para. 10). On termination of the tenancy by the landlord's notice the provisions of the Housing Act 1988 governing assured periodic tenancies will apply thereafter (para. 9(1),(2)). But this will not be the case if at the end of two months after service of the landlord's notice the qualifying condition was not fulfilled, unless the tenant has elected (under para. 7) to remain in possession (para. 9(3)).

When the landlord serves his notice, or at any time after that date and before the termination date, the landlord may propose an interim rent. If the tenant disagrees with that proposed rent he can refer the matter to a rent assessment committee for determination of a market rent on (see paras 6 and 7).

(2) A notice which states that if the tenant is not willing to give up possession on the termination of the tenancy the landlord intends to apply for a possession order on one or more of the grounds contained in para. 5(1).The notice must specify the particular ground(s) relied on (para. 4(5)(b)).

The para. 4 notice must invite the tenant, to notify the landlord in writing, within two months, whether (a) in the case of a notice proposing an assured tenancy, the tenant wishes to remain in possession and (b) in the case of a notice to resume possession, that he is willing to give up possession at the date of termination of the tenancy (para. 7).

If in the case of (b) the tenant is not willing to give up possession the landlord can seek a possession order from the county court.

The specified grounds are—

    (a)   Ground 6 in Housing Act 1988, Sched. 2 (landlord's intention to demolish reconstruct or carry out substantial works, etc. see p.229 above). This ground is not available in the case of a former 1954 Act tenancy which has become governed by the LGHA 1989 Act (as to which see above) (para. 5(2)).

    (b)   The discretionary grounds for possession in Housing Act 1988, Sched. 2, Part II (*viz*, grounds 9–16. see p.230 above) save for ground 16 (tenancy granted in consequence of employment).

    (c)   That for the purposes of redevelopment the landlord proposes to demolish or reconstruct the whole or substantially the whole of the relevant premises. This ground is only available where the landlord is a local authority or specified public body (para. 5(4)).

    (d)   That the premises or part of them are reasonably required by the landlord for occupation as a residence for himself or any son or daughter of his over 18 years of age or his or her spouse's father or mother. This ground is not available where the interest of the landlord was acquired or created after February 18, 1966.

If the landlord fails to obtain an order he can, within one month, serve a notice (see (1) above) proposing an assured periodic tenancy specifying a termination date not earlier than three months after the giving of that notice (para. 15(3),(4)).

B. LEASEHOLD ENFRANCHISEMENT—REFORM AT LAST: THE LEASEHOLD REFORM ACT 1967

Introduction

In strong contrast to the conclusion of the Majority Report (see p.348 above), two members of the Jenkins Committee signed a Minority Report in which they recommended that as a general rule an occupying tenant (or sub-tenant) of a house let on a long tenancy at a low rent should have a right to acquire compulsorily the freehold interest (along with any intermediate leasehold reversions) of that property. No qualifying period of residence was proposed, although it was recommended that tenants who bought their tenancies in the last 10 years of the term should be excluded. This proposal clearly went far beyond the limited reforms, which as we have seen above, were subsequently introduced by Part I of the Landlord and Tenant Act 1954.

Perhaps predictably, nothing came of the Jenkins Committee's Minority Report and there the matter rested until 1966 and the publication of the White Paper, *Leasehold Reform in England and Wales* Cmnd. 2916 1966) by a new (but not New) Labour Government. The problem had become acute at that time because many building leases were granted in the latter half of the nineteenth century, at a time when landlords had used their monopoly power to prevent development taking place other than on long leasehold terms. These tenancies, typically granted for 99 years, would soon expire, producing hardship for the tenants who not only stood to lose their houses but also faced the prospect of being presented with large bill for "dilapidations" (see above).

Furthermore, even in cases where a long tenancy was not about to expire, tenants who wished to sell and move also suffered hardship because the residue of the term might have diminished to a point (usually 50 years or thereabouts) beyond which institutional lenders were not prepared to grant mortgage loans. Moreover, the capital value of the tenancy would thereafter diminish at an ever-accelerating pace placing the landlord in an unparalleled and very unequal bargaining position and leaving the tenant with no incentive to repair or improve the property.

Having rehearsed these difficulties the White Paper stated that enfranchisement legislation would be introduced to redress the problem. Although the White Paper and the 1967 Act were confined to houses, very similar arguments applied to tenancies of maisonettes and flats. Additionally, these tenants often had other difficulties to contend with in connection with unfair service charges and poor management (see above). Nonetheless, nothing was done about them and it was left to later legislation to fill this lacuna in the statutory scheme. The basic scheme of the 1967 Act (as amended by subsequent legislation) is set out below.

A statutory right to enfranchise or obtain an extended tenancy

(a) The statutory rights

The Leasehold Reform Act 1967 (s. 1) gives a tenant of a house under a tenancy granted for a term of more than 21 years, the right to acquire on fair terms the freehold in fee simple (s.8) or to be granted an extended tenancy for a further 50 years following the expiry of the current tenancy (s.14).

(b) Qualifying conditions

Before examining each of the qualifying conditions it must be noted that, because of subsequent statutory amendments which govern the application of those conditions, it is necessary to distinguish between three types of cases—

(1) The statutory right to enfranchise or obtain an extended tenancy are conferred on a tenant who at the relevant time (that is the time when he gives notice of his desire to enfranchise or have an extended lease), occupies the house as his residence and is a tenant under a long tenancy at a low rent subject to financial limits related to the rateable value or letting value of the property (s.1(1)(2)).

Furthermore the tenant must, at the relevant time (see above), have been occupying the house under for the last three years or for periods amounting to three years in the last 10 years, as his only or main residence (LRA 967, s.1(1) and 1(2)).

The requirement that the tenant must occupy the house as a residence means that he must in right of his tenancy occupy it in whole or in part as his only or main residence (whether or not he also uses it for other purposes) (s.1(2)).

(2) The statutory right to enfranchise (but not to obtain an extended lease) is also conferred on—

    (a) a tenant who satisfies the qualifying conditions save that his house is outside the financial limits referred to above (s.1A added by the Leasehold Reform Housing and Urban Development Act 1993, s.64) and

    (b) a tenant (who satisfies the qualifying conditions) whose tenancy (which is not an excluded tenancy as defined) fails to satisfy the low rent but is a tenancy which was granted for a term of years certain exceeding 35 years (s.1AA inserted by Housing Act 1996, Sched. 9, para. 1).

Each of the main elements of the statutory right to enfranchise or obtain an extended tenancy
will be examined in turn.

1. A house

The 1967 Act deals with enfranchisement of "houses". For this purpose the term "house" is
defined as including—

> "any building designed or adapted for living in and reasonably so called, notwithstanding
> that the building is not structurally detached, or was or is not solely designed or adapted
> for living in, or is divided horizontally into flats or maisonettes; and—
>
> (a) where a building is divided horizontally, the flats or other units into which it
>   is so divided are not separate 'houses', though the building as a whole may
>   be; and
> (b) where a building is divided vertically the building as a whole is not a house
>   though any of the units into which it is divided may be."

Considerable thought clearly went into this definition, but what does it mean? First, that
"flats" are not "houses" although a building, let to one tenant, which contains two or more flats
or other units can be a house. (See *Malpas v. St Ermin's Property Ltd* [1992] 1 E.G.L.R. 109,
where it was held that two maisonettes, one on the ground floor and one an upper floor, which
were used as a single residence, could together constitute a house). (*Cf. Peck v. Anicar
Properties* [1971] 1 All E.R. 517). Second, that a terraced house is a "house" notwithstanding
that it is part of a larger building (the terrace), which is clearly not a house. The same applies to
a semi-detached house. Beyond this, marginal cases have presented, and no doubt will continue
to present, difficulties. However, it is established that whether premises are a house or not is a
question of law and not fact.

In *Tandon v. Trustees of Spurgeon's Houses* [1982] A.C. 755 premises which comprised a
shop with a flat above, and which were let on a single tenancy, were held to be a house within
the meaning of the Leasehold Reform Act 1967. As long as a building of mixed use can
reasonably be called a house it is within the statutory definition, even though it might also
reasonably be called something else—

> "Small corner shops and terraced shops combined with living accommodation are to be
> found in almost every town and village in England and Wales. Parliament plainly intended
> that a tenant who occupied such premises as his residence should have the benefit of the
> Act if the building could reasonably be called a 'house' (*per* Lord Roskill)"

In reaching this conclusion the House of Lords were clearly conscious of the conflict of
interests inherent in the Act and for the need to hold a balance between those interests.

Where a house is not structurally detached and a material part of it lies above or below a part
of the structure which is not comprised in the house it cannot be a "house" for the purposes of
the 1967 Act (LRA 1967, s.2(2)). In *Duke of Westminster v. Birrane* [1995] 2 W.L.R. 270 it was
held that "material" means—

> "of sufficient substance or significance to make it likely that enfranchisement will
> prejudice the enjoyment of the house or another part of the structure , whether by reason of

the ability of one freehold owner to enforce positive obligations against successors in title of the other or otherwise. (At p.277 *per* Nourse L.J.)"

Thus if the enjoyment of part of the house is dependent on rights over the part of the adjoining property which is below or above the house, it is likely to be material for this purpose. (See also *Parsons v. Viscount Gage (Trustees of Henry Smith's Charity)* [1974] 1 W.L.R. 435; *Wolf v. Crutchley* [1971] 1 W.L.R. 99 and *Gaidwoski v. Gonville & Caius College Cambridge* [1975] 1 W.L.R. 1066).

The Act also specifically provides that the tenant can include in the claim premises let with the house, which for this purpose is to be taken as referring to "any garage, outhouse, garden, yard and appurtenances which at the relevant time are let to him with the house and are occupied with and used for the purposes of the house or any part of it by him or another occupant" (s.2(3)). See also *Methuen-Campbell v. Walters* [1979] 1 W.L.R. 223 where a "paddock" not within the curtilage of the house was held to be excluded. *Cf. Cadogan v. McGirk* [1996] 4 All E.R. 643. (See below).

2. Occupied by the tenant as his only or main residence

It is provided that the reference in section 1 to the tenant occupying the house as his only or main residence is satisfied where the tenant occupies part only (s.1(2)). Thus it is clear that the tenant might live in one part of the house and sublet another part and yet still enfranchise in respect of the whole. (See, for example, *Harris v. Swick Securities Ltd* [1969] 1 W.L.R. 1604).

A company or other artificial person cannot be an occupying tenant for the purposes of the Act (s.37(5)).

Whether a tenant occupies the house as his residence is a question of fact and degree. For this purpose a tenant who is absent can still be occupying the house as his residence provided that he is keeping it ready for himself to go into occupation as and when he pleases, although the likelihood is that in such circumstances he cannot be said to be occupying the house as his main residence which is probably elsewhere (*Poland v. Earl Cadogan* [1980] 3 All E.R. 544). It also follows that a tenant cannot be said to be occupying the house as his residence if it is occupied by a sub-tenant or a mortgagee who has taken possession (*Poland v. Earl Cadogan*, above).

A qualified sub-tenant is also entitled to exercise the statutory rights (s.5(4) and Sched. 1). If he enfranchises he will need to acquire the freehold and any intermediate leasehold interests. For this purpose an intermediate leaseholder or the freeholder is nominated as "the reversioner" who will conduct the sale on behalf of all concerned.

3. For the last three years or periods amounting to three years in the last 10 years

Originally the Act only applied where the tenant had occupied the house as his residence under a long tenancy at a low rent for five years before he gave notice to enfranchise or extend, or for periods amounting to five years within the previous 10 years (s.1(1)(b)). This was reduced to three years by the Housing Act 1980 Sched. 21, para. 1(1) to bring it into line with the public rented sector "right to buy" provisions of Part I of that Act (now Part V. of the Housing Act 1985 (see Chapter 11 above)). But there was no further reduction of the qualifying period under the LRA 1967 when the residence requirement under the "right to buy" was reduced to two years by the Housing and Building Control Act 1984, s.3.

It should also be noted that if the occupying tenant dies while occupying the house as his residence a member of his family who becomes entitled to the tenancy (*e.g.* on succession), and who wishes to claim the benefit of the LRA 1967, can count towards the qualifying period of occupation not only any relevant periods of occupation by himself but also those of the deceased tenant (section 7, which applies to deaths before and after the Act).

It is provided (by section 7(7)) that a person is a member of another's family if that person is (a) the other's wife or husband or (b) a son or daughter (or son- or daughter-in-law) of the other or of the other's wife or husband, or (c) the father or mother of the other or the other's wife or husband. Step-children are included in (b), as are illegitimate children and adopted children.

4. Under a long tenancy (at a low rent, where relevant: see above)

The tenant must occupy the property under a long tenancy both at the relevant date (*i.e.* when he serves his notice of claim) and throughout the necessary three-year period of residence.

Thus this requirement was not satisfied where the tenant had occupied under a Rent Act protected sub-tenancy but then acquired the head lease thereby becoming a tenant under a long tenancy (*Harris v. Plentex Ltd* (1980) 40 P.&C.R. 483. The earlier period as a sub-tenant did not count towards the qualifying period).

A long tenancy is a tenancy granted for a term of years certain for a term exceeding 21 years (s.3(1)). (This means that the term from the date of the grant (and not from any earlier commencement date that might be expressed in the grant) must be in excess of 21 years (*Roberts v. Church Commissioners for England* [1972] 1 Q.B. 278).

For this purpose any right of the landlord to determine the tenancy prematurely by exercising a right of re-entry or forfeiture is to be ignored (s.3(1)). A perpetually renewable lease is deemed to be a long tenancy unless it is a sub-tenancy and the superior tenancy is not a long tenancy (s.3(1)). Where the tenant under a long tenancy which comes to an end is granted another long tenancy of the whole or part of the premises, the two are treated as one long tenancy (s.3(3)). A term for less than 21 years with an option to renew (without payment of a premium) which is exercised and thereby brings the aggregate of the two terms to more than 21 years will make the original tenancy a long tenancy for the purposes of the Act (s.3(4)).

If a long tenancy comes to an end and the tenant is granted a new tenancy (or by implication of law becomes a tenant under a new tenancy) that tenancy will be deemed to be a long tenancy irrespective of its terms (LRA 1967 s.3(2)). Thus if, for example, a 25-year lease ends and the tenant is granted a new 10-year lease that new tenancy will be a long tenancy. Indeed this will still be the case even if the tenant assigns the new tenancy. Thus the assignee will be able to enfranchise as and when he satisfies all the other necessary conditions of the 1967 Act (*Austin v. Dick Rickards Properties Ltd* [1975] 1 W.L.R. 1033).

Some long tenancies created before April 18, 1980 had been drafted deliberately so as to avoid the 1967 Act by providing that the tenancy would be terminable on notice after a death or marriage (often that of a member of the Royal Family, not infrequently the Prince of Wales). The effect of this was that the lease was not a "long tenancy" within the Act (because of the uncertainty point). The Housing Act 1980 dealt with this device by providing that such leases, if granted on or after April 18, 1980, would be qualifying leases. The Housing Act 1980 left outside the LRA 1967, leases granted before that date. The LRHUDA 1993 removed this anomaly and brought those leases within the scope of the 1967 Act right to enfranchise (but not the right to obtain an extended lease) (LRA 1967, ss.3(1) and 1B inserted by the Leasehold Reform Housing and Urban Development Act 1993, s.64(1)).

A long tenancy includes any statutory extension under Part I of the Landlord and Tenant Act 1954 or Sched. 10 to the Local Government and Housing Act 1989 (above) (LRA 1967, s. 3(5)).

The requirement of a low rent As noted above, the rights under section 1 of the 1967 Act only apply in the case of a tenancy at a "low rent" (see below). Following the Housing Act 1996 this requirement has, save in exceptional cases, been retrospectively and prospectively removed for leases granted for 35 years or more (LRA s.1AA inserted by Housing Act 1996, para. 1, Sched. 9. Thus the low rent requirement will now only apply to tenancies for between 21 years and 35 years.

The low rent test, which was designed to exclude from the LRA 1967 a tenancy at a market rent is contained in LRA 1967 s.4 as amended.

Where the tenancy was entered into before April 1 1990 (or in pursuance of a contract entered into before that date) the annual rent must be less than two-thirds of the rateable value of the house on the appropriate date (which will be March 23, 1965 or the date of the letting if later) (s.4(1)). Where the tenancy did not have a rateable value when let the relevant date will be the first date thereafter before April 1, 1990 when it did have such a value. (See Housing Act 1996, s.105).

For the purpose of the low-rent requirement, it is further provided that a tenancy granted after August 1939 and before April 1963 will not be a tenancy at a low rent (provided it was not a building lease) if its rent exceeded two-thirds of the letting value of the property at its commencement. The onus of establishing that this is the case is on the landlord (s.4(5)). See also *Hembry v. The Trustees of Henry Smith's Charity* (1987) 19 H.L.R. 533, CA). (Letting value means the best annual rent obtainable in the open market for the grant of a long lease on the same terms whether this is achieved by letting at a rack rent or letting at a lower rent plus the payment of a premium (*Johnson v. Duke of Westminster* [1981] 1 Q.B. 323).

In determining "rent" for the purposes of the low rent requirement there is to be disregarded any part of the rent expressed to be payable by way of service charges, or for repairs, maintenance or insurance (s.4(1)).

In the case of tenancies entered into on or after April 1, 1990 (other than in pursuance of a contract entered into before that date), when domestic rates were abolished, the right to enfranchise or extend is excluded if the rent is over £1,000 p.a. in Greater London or £500 elsewhere.

An alternative test By an amendment introduced by the LRHUDA 1993 it was provided that where a tenancy fails the low rent test in the 1967 Act an alternative test becomes applicable (Leasehold Reform Act 1967, s.4A added by LRHUDA 1993, s.65). This test is based on the ground rent in the first year of the tenancy and will enable some tenants who are excluded by the normal test (based on the rent at the time of enfranchisement) to acquire their freehold.

The alternative low rent test is as follows—

(1) In the case of tenancies entered into before April 1, 1963 the rent must not have been more than two-thirds of the letting value on the first day of the term.

(2) If the lease was granted on or after April 1, 1963 and before April 1, 1990 the rent must not have been more than two-thirds of the rateable value of the house on the date the lease started or (if later) the date on which it first appeared in the valuation list.

(3) If the lease was granted on or after April 1, 1990, or if the house did not have a rateable value before that date, the rent must not have been higher than £1,000 in Greater London or £250 elsewhere.

The alternative test is designed to catch cases where the rent has been reviewed and set at a level which means that it would fail the original low rent test. It does not apply for the purposes of lease extension.

5. Rateable value limits

In a concession to prominent landlords of some of the large London estates, the 1967 Act provide that the statutory rights do not apply to houses with rateable values, on March 23, 1965 (or on the date on which the house first appeared in the valuation list), of more than £200 or, if in Greater London, £400. By a series of complex amendments these limits were subsequently adjusted on a number of occasions (as explained below) before the exclusion of higher value properties from the right to enfranchise (but not the right to an extended tenancy) was finally abolished as from November 1, 1993 by the Leasehold Reform Housing and Urban Development Act 1993 (but not for "excluded tenancies"—see below).

However, as we will see below, tenancies brought within the right to enfranchise by the abolition of the rateable value limits are subject to a different, and much less generous, valuation test when it comes to determination of the price to be paid (see below).

Where the value limits continue to apply (see above) it is necessary to distinguish between tenancies entered into before April 1, 1990 (or in pursuance of a contract entered into before that date) and those entered into on or after that date (other than in pursuance of an earlier contract). This is because of the replacement of domestic rates (and hence rateable values) as from April 1, 1990, first by the Community Charge and then by the Council Tax.

(1) For tenancies entered into on or after April 1 1990 (other than in pursuance of a contract entered into before that date), the value of the premises is calculated by a formula based on the premium paid as a condition of the grant of the tenancy and its length when granted (S.I. 1990 No. 434, reg. 5).
(2) For tenancies entered into before that date the house and premises must not have had a rateable value at the appropriate date above the specified limits (see s.4(1),(5),(6) for those limits).

When determining rateable values it is possible for the tenant to establish that a lower notional value should be adopted because of structural improvements carried out by the tenant. This can result in the tenant paying a lower price on enfranchisement (see *Pearlman v. Keepers and Governors of Harrow School* [1978] 3 W.L.R. 736 (installation of central heating)).

Exclusions

The Act excludes a house at any time when—

(1) it is let to the tenant and occupied by him with other land or premises to which the house is ancillary (s.1(3)(a));
(2) it is comprised in either an agricultural holding for the purposes of the Agricultural Holdings Act 1986 or a holding held under a farm business tenancy under the

Agricultural Tenancies Act 1995 (s.1(3)(b)). This exclusion applied in *Lester v. Ridd* [1989] 2 Q.B. 430 even though the agricultural land with which the house had been let had been partitioned and separately assigned by the tenant.

Other exclusions include a shared ownership lease granted by a specified public body or housing association (LRA 1967, s.33A and Sched. 4, added by the Housing and Planning Act 1986, s.18 and Sched. 4). Although the Act does not apply to tenancies held of the Crown the Crown will often volunteer to be bound.

Also excluded from the right to enfranchise (but not from the right to an extended tenancy) are properties vested inalienably in the National Trust (LRA 1967, s.32) as well as certain property owned by a listed public body which is earmarked for development in the next 10 years as certified by a Minister of the Crown (LRA 1967, s.28).

The LRHUDA 1993 introduced two new exclusions. The first is a tenancy where the immediate landlord is a charitable housing trust and where the house is part of the housing accommodation provided by the trust as part of its charitable purposes (LRA 1967, s.1(3)(b) as amended by 1993 Act, s.67(2)). The second concerns any house which has been designated by the Treasury as property of outstanding scenic, historic, architectural or scientific interest (*i.e.* under the Inheritance Act 1984, s.31(1)) and in respect of which an undertaking has been given on transfer that it will be preserved and maintained by the transferee and that the public will be given reasonable access (s.32(A1) added by LRHUDA 1993, s.68). (The purpose of such arrangements is to prevent a charge to inheritance tax will arising on the transfer). Without the LRA 1967 exclusion, enfranchisement would give rise to a charge to tax on the landlord. Both of these new exclusions apply only to tenancies granted on or after November 1, 1993 save that, in the case of tenancies brought within the LRA 1967 by the LRHUDA 1993 (see above) they will apply whenever the tenancy was created (LRHUDA 1993, ss.67(3) and 32A(1)).

Procedure

The 1967 Act provides for a systematic procedure of notices and counter notices which has to be initiated by the tenant claimant before compulsory enfranchisement or statutory lease extension can take place (LRA 1967, Sched. 3). Service of the initial notice of claim operates as a contract for sale or a lease as the case may be (s.5(1)). The benefit of the contract can be assigned (s.5(2)).Once the tenant's application has been made, provided it was made in good faith, the landlord cannot start forfeiture proceedings in respect of the tenancy without leave of the court. But the fact that the landlord has commenced forfeiture proceedings before the tenant applies to enfranchise or for an extended tenancy is no bar to such an application provided the forfeiture claim is dismissed or there is a subsisting counterclaim for relief against forfeiture (*Hynes v. Twinsectra Ltd* (1995) 28 H.L.R. 183).

Landlord's overriding rights

Where a tenancy has been extended in accordance with section 14 it is provided that at any time during that extension or within the last 12 months of the original term, the landlord may seek a possession order on the basis that for the purposes of redevelopment he proposes to demolish or reconstruct the whole or substantially the whole of the relevant premises (s.17(1)). This right can also be exercised where the tenant makes an application for an extension.

Section 18 allows the landlord to oppose a claim for enfranchisement or an extended lease on the ground that the premises or part of them will be reasonably required by the landlord for occupation as the only or main residence of the landlord or any person who is at that time an adult member of the landlord's family (as defined in section 18(3)). This ground of opposition is not available where the interest of the landlord was acquired or created after February 18, 1966. However, the court can refuse an order on the ground that it is satisfied that greater hardship would be caused by making the order than by refusing it (s.18(4)).

A landlord who successfully relies upon sections 17 or 18 will be required to pay compensation to the tenant.

The price to be paid on enfranchisement

The price to be paid on enfranchisement has always been a contentious issue. The Minority Report of the Jenkins Committee of 1950 had recommended that the price payable on compulsory enfranchisement should be a fair market value of the reversion with a sitting tenant protected by the Rent Acts and excluding the value of any improvements effected by the tenant or a predecessor in title for which the landlord had not given consideration. As we have seen above the recommendations in that Report were not adopted.

When the principle of enfranchisement was finally accepted in 1966, the Government and Opposition were sharply divided on the central question of the price to be paid on enfranchisement. According to the 1966 White Paper the legislation proposed at that time was to be based on the principle that "the land belongs in equity to the landowner and the house belongs in equity to the occupying leaseholder". The word "equity" is of course used in the sense of meaning "morally". In accordance with this principle, that "in equity" the bricks and mortar already belonged to the tenant, the Bill provided that the price payable for the freehold should be calculated by reference to what the freehold would fetch if sold on the open market by a willing seller subject to the lease on the assumption that the tenant had no right to enfranchise but that (if he has not already done so) he would exercise his right under the Act to obtain a 50 year extension to his present term. It was on this issue of the price to be paid that the all party consensus crumbled. The Opposition considered this provision to be nothing less than robbery. Their view was that the leaseholder should pay a fair market price for both land and house on the basis that it is a fundamental legal axiom that what is attached to the soil becomes part of it and that everybody who had dealt with the lease or the reversion since the granting of the lease must be taken to have acted on that basis.

Fears, voiced by the Opposition, that the proposed basis of compensation would give tenants a windfall gain at the expense of landlords who would be deprived of the true value of their reversions were subsequently echoed by one legal commentator who observed that—

> "Although the 1967 Act was passed primarily to meet the anxieties of ordinary householders in South Wales and other areas where the long leasehold system was widespread, it is notorious that the persons who in fact derived most benefit from the 1967 Act were relatively wealthy purchasers of short residues of long tenancies of houses in Belgravia, Chelsea, Kensington, Westminster and similar expensive areas of London, just under the £400 Greater London rateable value limit. (Hague, *Leasehold Enfranchisement* (Sweet & Maxwell, 2nd ed., 1987))."

Nevertheless, despite the objections of the Opposition and of many powerful landlords, the LRA 1967 provided for compensation along the lines foreshadowed in the White Paper.

Section 9 accordingly provides that (where the rateable value is below £1,000 in Greater London or £500 elsewhere) the price payable for the house and premises is to be the amount which at the relevant time the house and premises, if sold in the open market by a willing seller *(with the tenant and members of his family who reside in the house not buying or seeking to buy)* might be expected to realise on the assumption that the vendor was selling the fee simple subject to the tenancy but on the assumption that the tenant had no right to enfranchise under the LRA 1967 and on the assumption that the tenancy was to be extended for 50 years. (Such an extended tenancy is at site value only). The words in italics were added by the Housing Act 1969, s.82 to make it clear that the tenant etc. was not to be considered a hypothetical bidder.)

The formula provided by section 9 effectively means that where a tenant enfranchises the landlord will receive no compensation for the house and his only loss in most cases, where the site value would be nominal, will be the capitalised value of the ground rent (see *Farr v. Millerson Investments Ltd* (1971) 218 E.G. 1177). Indeed where the reversion is very distant it may be virtually incapable of valuation, in which case an investment approach is taken (see *e.g. Janering v. English Property Co Ltd* (1977) 242 E.G. 388 where there were 900 years unexpired and the Lands Tribunal simply applied a formula of ground rent times 9.1 years purchase). Indeed in such cases the reversion might be considered to be of negligible value and a nominal amount determined. (But see *Windsor Life Assurance Co Ltd v. Austin and another* [1996] 34 E.G. 93 where the Lands Tribunal held that it would be wrong to say that a reversion subject to an unexpired term of some 77 years was not of some value. A price of £796 was determined).

Similarly in the case where a tenant claims an extended lease it is provided that the rent payable would be a revised modern ground rent which ignores the value of the building (s.15).

The effects of this formula on the position of landlords, particularly those with large numbers of properties in prime locations, was severe. An attempt, by the trustees of the estate of the Duke of Westminster, to obtain a declaration by the European Court of Human Rights that the Leasehold Reform Act 1967 was in breach of the European Convention failed in *James v. United Kingdom* (1988) 8 E.H.R.R. 123. (See Andrews (1986) 11 E.L.Rev. 366 and Merrills, British Yearbook of International Law Vol.LVII p.450). The trustees gave evidence that since the inception of the Act they had had to sell 80 house at a total loss of £2,529,903.

Compensation in higher value cases

As noted above, a different basis for evaluation of the purchase price to be payable on enfranchisement was provided for both (a) those tenancies with higher rateable values which were brought within the ambit of the 1967 Act by the Housing Act 1974 (LRA 1967, s.9(1A) added by Housing Act 1974, s.118(4)) and (b) those tenancies which come within LRA 1967, s.1A, or 1B following the Leasehold Reform, Housing and Urban Development Act 1993 (LRA 1967, s.9(1C) as inserted by 1993 Act, s.66(1)) as well as (c) those (non-excluded) tenancies granted for a term exceeding 35 years and which are therefore within the right to enfranchise even though they fail the low rent test (LRA s.1AA added by Sched. 9, para. 1 Housing Act 1996).

This alternative test is designed to ensure that the price to be paid is closer to the market value of the reversion to the site including the building. The test is the same as in section 9 save that (a) it is not to be assumed that the tenant is entitled to remain with his present tenancy extended by 50 years and if the tenancy has been extended it is to be assumed that it will end on the original term date, (b) the higher bid that might be expected from the sitting tenant is not to be excluded from the calculation, (c) it is to be assumed that at the end of the tenancy the tenant would be entitled to remain under the terms of Part I of the Landlord and Tenant Act 1954 or Schedule 10 to the Local Government and Housing Act 1989 as the case may be (as to which see above; but see also *Vignaud v. Keepers and Governors of the Possessions Revenues and Goods of the Free Grammar School of John Lyon* [1996] 37 E.G. 144) and (d) that the price is to be diminished by the value of any improvements carried out by the tenant or his predecessors in title at their own expense (s.9(1A)). For the purposes of determining whether the tenancy is of a property with a higher rateable value that value can be adjusted to take account of tenant's improvements in accordance with Schedule 8 to the Housing Act 1974 (s.9(1B)).

The test is qualified in cases of enfranchisement under the new rights introduced by the LRHUDA 1993 Act or the Housing Act 1996. In such cases it is not to be assumed that the tenant will have any statutory right to remain at the end of his tenancy (Leasehold Reform Act 1967, s. 9(1C)(a),(b) as added by LRHUDA 1993 (and amended by Housing Act 1996, Sched. 9, para. 2(4)). Furthermore the landlord will always be entitled to receive at least half of any "marriage value", along with compensation for "severance" (*i.e.* any diminution in value of other land affected by the loss of the land enfranchised) and any other consequential loss caused to other property including loss of development value (LRA 1967, s.9A added by LRHUDA 1993, s.66 and amended by Housing Act 1996, Sched 9, para. 2(5)).

"Marriage value" refers to the value which the tenant would place on the freehold subject to his own occupancy under the long tenancy. This is clearly more than the value which would be placed on it by a third party purchaser who, unlike the tenant purchaser, would not acquire the right to the unencumbered freehold. When the tenant enfranchises, the tenancy merges into the reversion and the tenant now has vacant possession of an unencumbered freehold at his disposal. The value which he will place upon this right is clearly more than the combined value of (a) the freehold reversion subject to the tenancy and (b) the tenancy itself. But this additional value is only unlocked by the merger. As we have seen it is expressly excluded from the formula in section 9 for calculating the price to be paid for the relatively lower value properties which remain governed by that formula. But it *is* included for the purposes of calculating the purchase price in those cases brought within the 1967 Act by the 1993 and 1996 reforms.

Estate management schemes

The qualms voiced by estate owners, that enfranchisement could destroy the character of an estate which had been created and preserved by comprehensive enlightened management, were met by provisions in the LRA 1967 for the approval by the appropriate Minister of schemes of estate management on application by a landlord. This would thereby have enabled the character of an estate to be preserved, after enfranchisement of some of the properties on the estate had taken place, by the continued enforcement of covenants affecting the enfranchised property in exercise of the landlord's powers of management (LRA 1967, s.19). Under the LRA 1967 any scheme had to be certified as appropriate by a Ministerial certificate and be approved by the High Court. An application for a scheme also had to be made within two years of the coming into force of the 1967 Act (*i.e.* by January 1 1970). Such powers could also be retained by tenant applicants which would be of value where a whole estate was sold off to tenants under the LRA 1967. Where there is a section 19 scheme and more of that landlord's property on the estate is acquired under the new right to enfranchise which came about as a result of the abolition of the low rent test for certain tenancies by the Housing Act 1996 (see LRA 1967, s.1AA above) an application may be made to a Leasehold Valuation Tribunal for termination or variation of the existing scheme to take account of the new purchases (LRHUDA 1993, s.75). The LVT also has power to approve new schemes for estates where the new right to enfranchise is exercised (LRHUDA 1993, s.70). An application must be made before April 1, 1999.

C. LONG LEASES OF FLATS

Introduction

We saw above, that when the LRA 1967 was passed, flats and maisonettes were excluded from its ambit. The reasons given in the 1966 White Paper were first, that flats had only been let on long leases on any widespread scale since the Second World War and therefore the problem was not as acute, and second, that there were technical conveyancing difficulties arising in the case of freehold flats. The second reason is a reference to the common law rule that the burden of positive covenants does not run with freehold land (*Austerberry v. Oldham Corporation* (1885) 29 Ch D 750; followed in *Rhone v. Stephens* [1994] 2 All E.R. 65). So far nothing has been done to implement the recommendation of the Report of the Wilberforce Committee on Positive Covenants Affecting Land (Cmnd. 2719,1965) that this rule be reversed nor the later Law Commission Report on the Law of Positive and Negative Covenants Law Com. No.127, 1984. Indeed in March 1998 the Lord Chancellor announced that the Government has decided not to implement Law Com. No. 127).

Neither of the above reasons for excluding flats from the Act was particularly compelling. The principles on which the legislation was based apply with equal force to flats as to houses. Furthermore the right to an extended lease does not create technical difficulties as to the enforcement of positive covenants. Of course even if these difficulties were to be eradicated to enable flats to be sold freehold there would still be problems with regard to other difficulties which are specific to flats such as the maintenance of common parts, the provision of services and responsibility for the repair and general management of the block.

Disputes between landlords and tenants over service charges, and poor management particularly in relation to blocks of flats, is a chronic problem and an enduring feature of the long leasehold system of flat tenure in England and Wales. Indeed, despite the absence of any root and branch reform of the leasehold tenurial system the pressure for action by government has been so great that from time to time governments have at least made some attempt to solve these difficulties, although often with very limited success. Most recently a press release from the then Department of the Environment was issued on January 18, 1996 by the Secretary of State who referred to a written answer which he had given to a Parliamentary Question from an M.P. On that occasion he had said—

> "I have received a large number of representations [from M.P.s and leaseholders, particularly in London] about allegations that some landlords have been behaving unreasonably. The allegations are that a number of landlords have been buying up freeholds of blocks of flats and then presenting the leaseholders with very large maintenance and service charge bills. The amounts demanded appeared to be excessive in relation to the work required, and the landlords can make a substantial profit by employing associated surveyors, contractors and managing agents, and earning commission. Any leaseholders who challenge the service charges are met with aggression and intimidation from the landlord and threatened with forfeiture of the lease."

A number of related problems are highlighted here. First the thorny issue of service charges and their reasonableness, including the related matter of the landlord's remedy of fofeiture of the lease in respect of unpaid service charges. Second the controversial issue of sales of freeholds to unscrupulous purchasers without the tenants' knowledge.

Service charges

The first attempt to deal with unfairness to tenants in relation to service charges by way of statutory regulation was by the Housing Finance Act 1972 (s. 90). The relevant provisions were extended by the Housing Act 1974 and then replaced by the Housing Act 1980, s.136 and Sched. 19. They are now consolidated in the Landlord and Tenant Act 1985, ss. 18–30) and have since been amended and extended by the Landlord and Tenant Act 1987 and the Housing Act 1996. The relevant provisions operate primarily by providing tenants with rights of challenge in respect of unfair service charges by way of an application for a determination from a local leasehold valuation tribunal. (Until September 1 1997 the jurisdiction was vested in the county court). Other related provisions are designed to enable a tenant to obtain information about service costs (ss.21–25).

For the purposes of this code of protection "service charge" is defined as—

"an amount payable by a tenant of a dwelling as part of or in addition to the rent—

    (a)   which is payable directly or indirectly, for services, repairs, maintenance or insurance, or the landlord's costs of management, and

    (b)   the whole or part of which varies or may vary according to relevant costs. (LTA 1985, s.18(1).)"

"Relevant costs" are defined as being "costs or estimated costs incurred or to be incurred by or on behalf of a landlord or a superior landlord, in connection with the matters for which the service charge is payable" (LTA 1985, s.18(2)). What services are to be provided, and by whom and at what cost, will of course depend upon the terms of the tenancy in question.

LTA 1985, s. 19(1) provides that "relevant costs" should be taken into account in determining the amount of a service charge of a dwelling—

    (1)   only to the extent that they are reasonably incurred, and

    (2)   where they are incurred on the provision of services or the carrying out of works, only if the services or works are of a reasonable standard.

Where, as is common, the service charge is payable in advance, any amount charged must be reasonable and adjusted subsequently in the light of the actual costs incurred (s.19(2)). There is an incentive for the landlord to notify the tenant within 18 months of having incurred any relevant costs, that those costs have been incurred and that the tenant will be required to contribute to them by way of a service charge payment. If the landlord fails to so notify the tenant then those costs will be irrecoverable (LTA 1985, s.20B).

Further protection is provided in respect of the costs incurred in connection with "qualifying works" which in relation to service charges means "works (whether on a building or on any other premises) in respect of which the tenant is required by the terms of his lease to contribute by way of a service charge." If the amount incurred is in excess of the permitted limit the excess cannot be taken into account in determining the amount of the service charge unless what are called the "relevant requirements" have been complied with or dispensed with by the court (s.20). The limit is whichever is the greater of the prescribed amount (at present £50) times the number of dwellings let to the tenants concerned or £1,000 (or such other sum as may be prescribed). The relevant requirements are to be found in a detailed statutory information and consultation process to be engaged in by the landlord with the tenants and their representative body if any. The requirements include the need for the landlord to obtain at least two estimates as to the costs of the proposed works. The court has power to dispense with these requirements if it is considered that the landlord has acted reasonably (*e.g.* in an emergency) (LTA 1985, s.20(9)).

As indicated above, until September 1, 1997 it was possible for a landlord or tenant(s) to seek a declaration from the county court as to the reasonableness of costs or as to whether the relevant services or works were of a reasonable standard. Following the Housing Act 1996, it is now provided that since that date the jurisdiction to rule on the reasonableness of service charges etc. is exercisable by a local leasehold valuation tribunal (LVT) with an appeal to the Lands Tribunal with leave of the LVT or (if refused) the Lands Tribunal itself. A fee is payable by the applicant and the tribunal does not have power to award costs (although it can order a party to pay the applicant's fee as it thinks fit). The tribunal can now, at the request of either party, make a determination as to the reasonableness of costs incurred or the standard of works or services for which costs have been incurred or whether an advance sum is reasonable (LTA 1985, s.19(1A). The tribunal can also rule prospectively on the reasonableness of proposed costs, services or works and what advance payments before costs are incurred would be reasonable (LTA 1985, s.19(1B)). No such application can be made in respect of matters which have been agreed by the tenant or determined by a court or arbitral tribunal or in respect of which the tenant has agreed that it be referred to arbitration (LTA 1985, s.19(2C). The tribunal can also at the tenant's request rule that the landlord's costs before the LVT are not to be recoverable by way of the service charge if it considers this to be just and equitable (LTA 1985, s.20C).

The rights afforded to tenants by sections 18–25 of the Landlord and Tenant Act 1985 do not apply to service charges paid by a tenant of a local authority or certain other public bodies unless the tenancy is a long tenancy (as defined). They only apply to a regulated tenancy with a registered fair rent under the Rent Act 1977 if that rent is registered as variable (*i.e.* under Rent Act 1977, s.71(4)).

The LVT also has jurisdiction to determine disputes with regard to the reasonableness of insurance provision and the premiums charged where the tenant challenges the landlord's choice of insurer. If the tribunal is satisfied that the cover is unsatisfactory or that the premiums are excessive the landlord can be ordered to nominate another insurer (LTA 1985, sched.).

Further protection is given to tenants who belong to a recognised tenant's association (in accordance with LTA 1985, s.29). The association is empowered to appoint a surveyor to advise on matters relating to, or which may give rise to, service charges payable to a landlord by one or more members of the association. The surveyor will be entitled to access to relevant documents (Housing Act 1996, s.84 and Sched. 4).

Finally it should be noted that the Housing Act 1996, s.81 introduced important restrictions on the right of a landlord to forfeit a residential lease for non-payment of service charges. These are dealt with in Chapter 6 above. As noted above, this reform was considered necessary because of the increased incidence of landlords buying up reversions and then threatening tenants with forfeiture unless the tenant met what were often unreasonable demands by the landlord for service charge payments. Tenants were thus being intimidated into compliance for fear of legal costs and or losing their home.

Management problems

Following the Report of the Nugee Committee (Report of the Committee of Enquiry on the Management of Privately Owned Blocks of Flats, 1985), problems caused by bad management were addressed by the Landlord and Tenant Act 1987.

The Landlord and Tenant Act 1987

The primary objectives of the Landlord and Tenant Act 1987 were—

(1) to introduce new powers for the appointment of a manager by the courts where a landlord was not fulfilling his obligations (LTA 1987 s.21). The power to appoint a new manager of the building in which a flat is situated is now exercisable by the LVT where satisfied that the landlord's management is unsatisfactory (LTA 1987, s.24A as added by Housing Act 1996, s.85. This right is not available in the case of a public sector or housing association landlord or where the premises are not purpose built and the landlord is a resident landlord as defined in s.58(2) (s.21(3)(a)).

(2) In extreme cases, where the appointment of a manager has not worked, or is deemed by the court to be an insufficient remedy, to give tenants a right of compulsory acquisition of the landlord's interest (LTA 1987, Part III as subsequently amended by the Housing Act 1996). Once again (as in (1) above), exempt landlords are excluded.

(3) To give a right of pre-emption to qualifying tenants (see below) where a landlord wishes to dispose of his interest in premises to which the Act applies.

The right of first refusal

Part I of the Landlord and Tenant Act 1987 applies to a building (whether purpose-built or not) which contains two or more flats held by qualifying tenants, provided that at least 50 per cent. of the flats in the building are held by qualifying tenants (s.1(2)). It does not apply where more than 50 per cent of the surface area of the building is occupied or intended for occupation by tenants other than residential tenants (s.1(3)).

A disposal which triggers off the right can be by way of sale of the freehold or grant of a long lease (s.4(1)) or a contract for the same (s.4A inserted by the Housing Act 1996 thereby reversing the decision of the Court of Appeal in *Mainwaring v. Henry Smith's Charity Trustees* [1996] 2 All E.R. 220 that a contract to sell by the landlord was not a relevant disposal). Disposals by a mortgagee are also included.

Certain disposals are exempt. They include disposals within a family or a trust, or on bankruptcy or by way of a compulsory purchase order (s.4(2)). (See also below with regard to company transfers within a group).

The essence of the scheme in Part I of the LTA 1987 is that before making a relevant disposal of property containing flats the landlord is compelled to offer the property to (90 per cent of) the qualifying tenants at the price requested by the landlord (s.5. See *Mainwaring v. Henry Smith's Charity Trustees* [1996] 2 All E.R. 220). More than 50 per cent of the tenants can accept or reject this offer within two months, following which the tenants have a further two months to nominate a purchaser on their behalf. If he wishes to sell the landlord then has a month to send a contract (s.8A). From receipt of the contract the tenants will have two months in which to sign and pay a deposit of not more than 10 per cent. If the tenants reject the initial offer, the landlord can then, within the next 12 months, sell the property to somebody else. But if he does so he must offer it at a price no lower than that which he asked of the tenants (s.7). If the landlord does go ahead and sell for a higher price, or without having offered the property to the tenants in the first place, the tenants must be notified by the purchaser of the change of ownership (LTA 1985, s.3). They then have the right to obtain information about the sale from the purchaser (s.11) and, if they wish, to buy the property from the purchaser at the same price as was paid by him for the property.

There is also a procedure (in section 18) whereby a prospective purchaser can serve a notice on 80 per cent of the tenants (whether qualifying or not) informing the tenants of the proposed sale and enquiring as to whether the landlord has served a section 5 notice and whether the tenants would want to exercise that right. If not more than 50 per cent reply within two months (extended from 28 days by the Housing Act 1996) or if more than 50 per cent reply but they do not regard themselves as qualified or wish to exercise the right, the prospective purchaser may treat the premises as ones to which Part I of the LTA 1987 does not apply. But this does not absolve the landlord from serving a section 5 notice (*Mainwaring v. Henry Smith's Charity Trustees*, above).

Landlords who are bound by the right of first refusal provisions of the LTA 1987 are freeholders, or a superior landlord where the immediate landlord has a lease of less than seven years (ss. 2 and 58). Tenants who qualify for the benefits of the Act are in practice mainly long leaseholders and regulated tenants under the Rent Act 1977 (but not assured tenants under the Housing Act 1988) (s.3(1)). Other excluded tenants include service tenants (*i.e.* where the tenancy is linked to employment), agricultural tenants, sub-tenants of qualifying tenants, business tenants and tenants of three or more of the flats in the building being sold.

Certain landlords are also exempt (s.1(4)). They include public sector bodies and registered housing associations and resident landlords where the building is not a purpose built block (s.58). A resident landlord is one who has occupied a flat in the block as his only or main residence for the previous 12 months.

The drawback of this scheme when introduced was that it was badly drafted and was passed with very little debate.

In one case the Master of the Rolls observed that—

> "I readily appreciate the complexities of the task that confronted the draughtsman in seeking to give legislative effect to this ambitious scheme. But the history of these proceedings is a dismal commentary on a measure intended to help tenants in mansion blocks, many of them of limited means. As it is the legal profession would appear to be the main beneficiaries of this obscure statute. (*Belvedere Court Management Ltd v. Frogmore Development Ltd* [1996] 1 E.G.L.R. 59, CA *per* Bingham M.R.)."

The main problem with the 1987 Act as originally drafted was that it was too restrictive and contained insufficient anti-avoidance provisions. Furthermore the sanctions for non-observance were so weak that the Act was largely ignored by landlords.

The Housing Act 1996 sought to meet many of these criticisms of the right of first refusal in the LTA 1987. Thus since October 1, 1996—

(1)   It is a criminal offence for the landlord (a) to fail to serve a section 5 notice or (b) to sell at a higher price after the tenants have rejected his offer. (The maximum punishment at present is a £5,000 fine (s.10A).)

(2)   Failure of a third party purchaser to notify the tenants of the sale and of their rights by serving a section 3A notice is also a criminal offence (maximum fine £2,500).

(3)   The time limits for tenants to exercise their rights do not begin to run until they have been notified.

(4)   Transfer of the landlord's interest to an associated company is not an exempt disposal where the associated company has been an associated company for less than two years (s.4(2)). Before this amendment any disposition to an associated company

was exempt and this had led to widespread avoidance of the Act by selling to an associated company (an exempt transfer) followed by a sale of the shares in that company to a purchaser.

(5) The Housing Act 1996 also introduced an alternative procedure whereby the landlord can auction the property at a public auction following which the tenants can take the place of the successful bidder (LTA 1987, s.5B). Before this the landlord faced a dilemma. If he pitched the offer to the tenants too low they would obtain a bargain. If he pitched it too high he would have great difficulty in selling to anybody.

Enfranchisement of flats

Despite the legal protections outlined above, there was widespread belief that they were inadequate by themselves in so far as they only dealt with some of the problems faced by long leaseholders of flats and even then the legal solution was complex and bristling with difficulties which made that solution more theoretical than real.

Before the 1992 general election all political parties were agreed on the need for leasehold reform. A Consumers' Association survey had revealed that nearly 50 per cent of leaseholders of flats encountered serious problems with their freeholders. Strong tenants' campaigning groups emerged, such as the Leasehold Enfranchisement Association and the Enfranchisement League, and the Prime Minister promised action. The result of this pressure was the Leasehold Reform Housing and Urban Development Act 1993.

The Leasehold Reform Housing and Urban Development Act 1993

Part I of LRHUDA 1993 (which has since been amended by the Housing Act 1996) seeks to solve the problems outlined above by granting to certain flat owners a right to collective enfranchisement in relation to the freehold of the block in which they live. (The 1993 Act leaves in place the right of compulsory purchase in the 1987 Act although the right is now enhanced by removal of the prerequisite need for the Court to consider whether the appointment of a manager is an adequate remedy; LRHUDA 1993, s.85). The Act also gives an individual tenant the alternative right to an extended tenancy. Estimates as to the number of leaseholders likely to be affected varied somewhat. At the Bill's Second Reading in the Commons, the Secretary of State for the Environment, Michael Howard, suggested a figure of 550,000 (*Hansard*, H.C. col. 164, November 3, 1992) whilst when the Bill was read for a second time in the Lords a figure of 750,000 was given by Lord Strathclyde; *Hansard*, H.L. Deb vol col 86, February 23, 1993).

The scheme of the 1993 Act is for the freehold to be acquired by a nominee or nominees of those tenants exercising the right who can then procure the grant to themselves of new long leases and run their own management (s.15). This may be an individual or individuals or one or more companies or a combination of the two. In many cases it is likely that it will be a trust or a company formed for that purpose.

The ideological pedigree of the new rights granted by the LRHUDA 1993 was the long-term programme to extend home ownership which had begun in 1980 with the introduction of the right to buy for qualifying council tenants (see Chapter 11 above). This programme was of course itself part of a wider political strategy to create a popular capitalism and thereby change social attitudes. It was also the first plank in the process of abolition of long leasehold residential tenure. Despite this ideological justification it is difficult to avoid the conclusion that the impetus for further reform came from a strong tenant lobby whose views were forcibly represented in Parliament by a number of M.P.s who represented constituencies, mainly in London and the South East, with the greatest concentration of tenants affected.

The Act was opposed by a number of estate owners including the "Great Estates" (*e.g.* the Grosvenor and Cadogan Estates and the Church Commissioners). In many ways this echoed the battles fought over the Leasehold Reform Act 1967 which, as we have seen, was also opposed as "confiscatory" legislation. Although the opponents of the 1993 Act were unable to prevent its arrival on the statute book, they did deal the Bill as originally introduced some very severe blows and hence diluted its eventual impact. Of course, it could be argued that landlords have less room to complain about the 1993 measure which, as we will see below, compensates the landlord on a market price basis for his lost interest. Indeed as we have seen above, more generous compensation provisions also apply to enfranchisement claims in respect of higher value properties under the LRA 1967.

The right to enfranchise

The right to enfranchise applies in respect of premises if they—

(1) consist of a self-contained building or part of a building (as defined in s.3(2));
(2) contain two or more flats held by qualifying tenants; and
(3) the total number of flats held by such tenants is not less than two-thirds of the total number of flats contained in the premises (s.3(1)).

The tenants may also seek to purchase appurtenant property let under the tenancy(s), such as gardens or garages (s.1(2),(3),(4)). Indeed in some circumstances the landlord might be able to compel this.

Excluded premises

Certain premises are excluded from the statutory right.

The first is where a building contains a non-residential part (excluding common areas) which is more than 10 per cent of the internal floor area of the building (s.4(1)). Attempts to increase the 10 per cent limit were defeated at the Commons Committee stage. Although there is power for this percentage to be increased, the previous Government stated that it had no intention of using this power.

The second is where, in the case of a building (not being a purpose-built block of flats) which comprises four or fewer flats there is a resident landlord (s.4(4)). (See section 10 for the meaning of resident landlord which is in parallel terms to section 12 of the Rent Act 1977; see p.257 above. Essentially this is where the freeholder or an adult member of his family (as defined in section 10(5)) occupies one of the flats as his only or principal home and has done so for a period of at least the previous 12 months. A purchaser of the landlord's interest who goes into occupation within 28 days can satisfy this condition (s.10(6)).

Also excluded are National Trust properties which are held inalienably (s.95) and properties which have been designated for conditional exemption from inheritance tax (s.31) (see p.361 above) or are within the precincts of a cathedral close (s.96). The legislation does not bind the Crown (s.94), but an undertaking has been given that the Crown will comply with the Act in most cases.

Qualifying tenants

A person is a qualifying tenant of the flat if he is a tenant under a long lease which is at a low rent or for a "particularly long term" (LRHUDA 1993, s.5 as amended by Housing Act 1996, Sched. 9, para. 3).

Certain leases are excluded: *viz.* (a) a business tenancy, (b) where the immediate landlord is a charitable housing trust and the flat forms part of the housing accommodation provided by it in pursuit of its charitable housing purposes and (c) where the lease was a sub-lease out of a superior lease other than a long lease at a low rent or for a "particularly long term" and there has been no waiver of that breach by the superior landlord (s.5(2)).

Long lease is defined in section 7 in very similar terms to those in LRA 1967 s.3 (see above). Thus it will usually mean the holder of a lease originally granted for more than 21 years. (But see above for the extended meaning of the term). The definition of a low rent is identical to the new section 4A of the 1967 Act (see above) (LRHUDA 1993, s.8). Where the tenancy fails the low-rent test it can still qualify if it is a "particularly long lease", which essentially means a tenancy granted for more than 35 years (LRHUDA 1993, s.8A added by Housing Act 1996, Sched. 9, para. 3).

If there is more than one long lease of a flat at a low rent the tenant who can qualify is the one with the inferior interest (s.5(3),(4)(a)). Where any person would otherwise be a qualifying tenant of more than two flats in any building that person cannot be regarded as a qualifying tenant of any flat (s.5(5)). (As originally drafted a tenant with more than one flat could have qualified in respect of each). It is further provided that all companies in a group are considered as one person for this purpose (s.5(6)).

Residence requirement

It is provided that, although a tenant does not need to be a resident to qualify, not less than one half of the qualifying tenants by whom the initial notice is given must satisfy the residence requirement (s.13(2)).

The residence requirement is that the tenant has occupied the flat wholly or partly as his only or principal home (but not necessarily under a qualifying lease) for the previous 12 months or for three years in the last 10 years, whether or not he has used it for other purposes (s.6). This residence condition did not appear in the original Bill. The concept of only or principal home is taken from the requirements of a secure tenancy in section 81 Housing Act 1985 (see p.312 above Compare LRA 1967, s.1 "occupying as his residence"). Where a flat is let to joint tenants, only one need satisfy the residence condition. The residence requirement can be satisfied by a beneficiary under a trust (s.6(4)).

Landlord's right to resist a claim

A landlord can defeat an application for enfranchisement if at least two-thirds of all the long leases in the block are due to terminate within five years of the date of the original notice of intention to enfranchise and he or she can demonstrate (to the county court) an intention to redevelop the whole or a substantial part of the premises, after that time, which could not reasonably be carried out without obtaining possession (s.23). This is more generous than the three years permitted under Part II of the Landlord and Tenant Act 1954. It is further provided (s. 36 and Sched. 9) that where a property to be enfranchised includes non-residential parts or flats not let to qualifying tenants (*e.g.* those on shorter leases) the landlord may by notice require the nominee purchaser to grant a leaseback for 999 years at a peppercorn rent to the freeholder of a particular flat or other unit. This will ensure that the freeholder remains the landlord of certain excluded tenants (*e.g.* a business tenant or one of premises where the freeholder is resident). In the case of flats let on secure tenancies under the Housing Act 1985 by local authorities or other public landlords, a leaseback is compulsory, as also in the case of flats let by a housing associations to non-qualifying tenants (Sched. 9, paras 2 and 3).

Procedure

In order to make a successful application to enfranchise the applicants must initiate a complex system of notices and counter notices, all subject to strict time limits, some very short, by serving a notice to purchase (under section 13) after having obtained information regarding the ownership of the freehold and intermediate leasehold interests. Although it would be prudent it is no longer obligatory (since Housing Act 1996) to have obtained a valuation, by a qualified surveyor, of the interest(s) to be acquired.

The notice is registrable as a land charge under the Land Charges Act 1972 or as a minor interest (by way of caution or notice) under the Land Registration Act 1925 (LRHUDA 1993, s.97(1)). For the procedure to be followed, unless otherwise agreed, in giving effect to a claim to exercise the right to collective enfranchisement or a claim to exercise the right to lease renewal under Part I, see the Leasehold Reform (Collective Enfranchisement and Lease Renewal) Regulations 1993, S.I. 1993 No. 2407.

Interestingly, there is no obligation on the qualifying tenants who choose to serve a notice to inform any other tenants of their actions; an omission which might create dissent between tenants within a block. Side agreements to allow other tenants to participate after completion of the process (with the aim of reducing the marriage value—see below) must be disclosed (s.18). Disputes as to the terms of acquisition (*viz*, the interests to be acquired, the extent of the property concerned, the purchase price, apportionment, etc. and the provisions of the conveyance (s.24(8)) are to be settled by a leasehold valuation tribunal on application (within six months of service of the counter notice or further counter notice) if the parties are still in dispute two months after service of the reversioner's counter notice (s. 24). The procedure to be followed by tribunals is contained in the Rent Assessment Committee (England and Wales) (Leasehold Valuation Tribunal) Regulations 1993, S.I. 1993 No. 2408. Disputes as to eligibility to enfranchise are dealt with by the County Court (ss. 22 and 23).

Recalcitrant reversioners who fail to enter into a contract can be sidestepped on application to the court by the nominee purchaser who can pay into court and take a conveyance from the person designated by the court (ss. 24, 25 and Sched. 5). There is also a complex court-based procedure for a nominee purchaser to obtain a vesting order following payment into court where there is a missing or untraceable landlord (ss. 26 and 27). It is an understatement to say that this part of the Act is bristling with complexities and constitutes a potential minefield for any group of tenants which is not professionally advised.

The price to be paid

Of course a crucial feature of the new scheme, as well as the original scheme applicable to houses, is the price which must be paid on enfranchisement (s.32(1) and Sched. 6). If there are also intermediate leasehold interests to be acquired, the freeholder must share the purchase price proportionately with the holders of those interests (Sched. 6, para. 12).

The Act requires (see Sched. 6, para. 2) the nominee purchaser to pay (a) the value of the freeholder's interest, (b) at least 50 per cent of any "marriage value" (see Sched. 6, para. 4(1)) and (c) an amount to reflect any loss caused to the value of other property retained by the freeholder through severance brought about by enfranchisement (injurious affection) (Sched. 6, para. 5).

In *Blackstone Investments Ltd v. Middleton-Dell Management* [1997] 14 E.G. 135 it was held by the Lands Tribunal that the purchase price should include an amount to compensate the landlord for loss of commission which he had received on insurance premiums recoverable under a service charge in the lease and to which he would no longer be entitled following enfranchisement.

The value of the freeholder's interest is its anticipated open market value on the assumption that it is sold by a willing seller subject to the existing leases of the purchasers and any intermediate leases (with neither the nominee purchaser nor any participating tenant buying or seeking to buy). Certain statutory assumptions are to be made, including the disregard of any improvements carried out at his own expense by a participating tenant or any predecessor in title (Sched. 6, para. 3).

As we have seen above, the concept of marriage value is not new and is normally understood as referring to the fact that the value of two interests when brought together is often more than the sum of the values of the individual interests before merger. In the context of collective enfranchisement under the 1993 Act it means the increase in the aggregate value of the freehold and leasehold interests in the hands of the nominee purchaser (and thus under the control of the participating tenants) as compared with their value before enfranchisement; thereby reflecting the potential ability of the participating tenants to compel the nominee purchaser to grant them new leases without restriction as to length of term and without payment of any premium (para. 4(2)).

Although it seems clear what is intended by this definition, the concept is of course somewhat artificial in this context because there is no true "marriage" of the different sets of interests, unlike cases of house enfranchisement. The apportionment of the marriage value is controversial. The Act provides that the nominee purchaser can have no more than 50 per cent. It does not say that the landlord is similarly restricted. Hence landlords will argue for anything up to and including 100 per cent in order to compensate them for the enforced sale of their interests. Indeed some Members of Parliament argued that it should always be 100 per cent, whilst Opposition Members contended that it should be nil on the basis that in most cases the value of the house or flat is attributable entirely to payments made by the leaseholder and/or his or her predecessors. It is worth observing that in practice, as in the case where marriage value has been apportioned under the separate basis of valuation for higher value properties under the Leasehold Reform Act 1967 (see above), leasehold valuation tribunal often adopt a fifty-fifty apportionment as the most equitable.

The nominee purchaser is in general liable for the reasonable costs incurred by the respondent or other relevant landlords but not any costs in connection with leasehold valuation tribunal proceedings (s.33(5)) nor where the initial section 13 notice ceases to have effect because the landlord has established an intention to redevelop (s.33(4)). Costs under court proceedings are dealt with under the usual litigation costs rules.

The individual right to a new lease

As an alternative to enfranchisement for those tenants who are unable to qualify for collective enfranchisement, or do not wish to participate in such a venture, the LRHUDA 1993 has also introduced the individual right to a new lease. This addresses the wasting asset problem (but not the issue of bad management). The right is to the grant of a new lease for a period equivalent to the unexpired portion of the old lease plus 90 years, at a peppercorn rent but on payment of a market value premium, in substitution for the existing lease (s.56(1) and Sched. 13). The right can be exercised on an unlimited number of occasions.

In order to qualify, a tenant must satisfy two conditions on the day that notice of exercise of the right is given. He or she must first be a qualifying tenant of the flat and second, satisfy a residence qualification of at least three years in the last 10 (s.39(2)). However, occupation need only have been of at least part of the flat and not necessarily by virtue of any lease (s.39(5)). Occupation must be as the tenant's only or principal home, whether or not he has also used it for other purposes. It follows that company leases are excluded, thereby opening an avoidance route for freeholders.

The question of whether a tenant is a qualifying tenant is determined in accordance with sections 5, 6, 7, 8 and 8A (discussed above), save that a tenant may qualify in respect of more than one flat at a time (s.39(4)).

The procedure is activated by a tenant's notice which creates a (registrable) contract with the competent landlord who may serve a counter-notice admitting the tenant's claim or denying it and using the redevelopment ground of opposition, which will only apply if the tenant's current lease is due to expire within five years. (see ss. 42–45 and Scheds 11 and 12). As in the case of the procedure for collective enfranchisement, there are strict time limits to be complied with.

Disputes as to terms are again dealt with by a leasehold valuation tribunal (s.48). The new lease may contain provision for payments for services, repairs, maintenance and insurance (s.57). The premium is calculated in accordance with Schedule 13. The landlord is entitled to the diminution in value of the reversionary interest on the lease and not less than 50 per cent of the marriage value (Sched. 13, paras. 2 and 4(1)) along with any compensation for any other injurious affection suffered by the landlord (see p.364 above). In this context, marriage value means the difference between (a) the aggregate value of the interests of all parties (including any intermediate landlords) before the grant of the new lease and (b) the aggregate values of such interests after the grant (para. 4(2)).

Landlord's right to resist the claim

A landlord can defeat an application for enfranchisement if the tenant's lease of his flat is due to terminate within five years of the date of the original notice of intention to claim a new lease and that he or she can demonstrate (to the county court) an intention to redevelop the whole or a substantial part of the premises, after that time, which could not reasonably be carried out without obtaining possession (s.47). Tenants will need to be careful to watch out for this trap.

Landlord's right to terminate new lease

The right to a new lease contains a serious drawback. Where a new lease has been granted (under s.56) following a section 14 claim, it is provided that at any time within the last 12 months of the original term, or within five years ending with the term date of the new term, the landlord may seek a possession order on the basis that for the purposes of redevelopment he proposes to demolish or reconstruct the whole or substantially the whole of the relevant premises in which the flat is contained and that he could not reasonably do so without obtaining possession (s.61). If successful the landlord may have to pay compensation to the tenant (under Schedule 14).

Landlord's right to compensation

When a tenant makes a claim for a new tenancy under the 1993 Act and the outcome is not established until after the current term has expired, he does not have to pay a market rent for the period after the date of expiry and before the grant of the new tenancy. However, it is now provided that (as from January 16, 1989) where the claim for a new lease is made in the last two years of the current term and the claim ultimately proves to be ineffective (save by virtue of section 47 above or as a result of a compulsory purchase order: see section 55) the tenant will have to pay the landlord compensation for the difference between the ground rent and the market rent that he would have otherwise been able to obtain under Schedule 10 to the Local Government and Housing Act 1989 (see above) (LRHUDA 1993, ss.61A and 61B added by Housing Act 1996, Sched. 11, para. 3).

Estate management schemes

The Act also contains provisions similar to those in the Leasehold Reform Act 1967 which will enable landlords of estates to apply within two years (*i.e.* by April 1 1999) to retain unified management control over those estates and raise service charges by way of approved management schemes without depriving leaseholders of the right to enfranchise (ss. 69–75). This is to enable landlords to preserve the character and amenities of an area and protect it from piecemeal development or alteration. Unlike the original section 19 of the LRA 1967, whereby as we have seen above, the landlord had to obtain approval from the Secretary of State and then the High Court, the new system enables a leasehold valuation tribunal to give approval. Tenants can also apply and in default a local authority or English Heritage may apply.

Conclusion

The 1993 Act removes the arbitrary value limits in the Leasehold Reform Act 1967 and logically extends to flats the principle of leasehold enfranchisement. However, the provisions of the original Bill relating to collective enfranchisement, although in many ways deficient and badly drafted, were so extensively emasculated by the successful sabotage actions of the large landlords and their lobbyists that the right is likely to prove more illusory than real. It is quite likely that given the formidable obstacles in the way of collective enfranchisement, the right to an individual new lease will prove to be the much more frequently used of the reforms introduced by the 1993 Act. Indeed the extended availability of this right which had a much more limited range when the Bill was originally drafted is likely to prove much more attractive either as an end in itself or as a staging post on the way to collective enfranchisement. Collective enfranchisement, in areas of high property values, can be expensive, and institutional lenders are likely to prove hesitant when asked to lend to nominee purchasers. The nominee purchaser represents tenants who could move on, creating difficulties if they do not assign at the same time as their lease their interest in the management company, if any. Of course it should not be assumed that collective enfranchisement, even where achieved, will necessarily prove to be the panacea hoped for by many victims of the present long leasehold system. The management of a block of flats can be a complex, time-consuming and expensive affair and has the potential to create different battlegrounds of conflict, both between participating tenants as well as between enfranchising tenants and other tenants in a block. On the other hand the legislation is in place and it is possible for a willing government to amend it in ways which will enhance the attractiveness of the right of collective enfranchisement. The rights afforded by the 1993 Act must also give some peace of mind to tenants whose interests had become virtually unmarketable. Furthermore the difficulties identified above are much less likely to apply in the many cases of small blocks of flats where enfranchisement can be relatively inexpensive and problem free. The Act seeks to anticipate many avoidance devices by way of anti-avoidance provisions but others remain, many of them deliberately placed there by amendments accepted by the government as the price to be paid for ensuring passage of the Act onto the statute book. Finally, the legislation can be seen as a staging post on the road to the replacement of long leasehold tenure with the much-heralded commonhold whereby flat owners will effectively become freeholders of their flats with the building controlled by a commonhold association under the control of the flat owners. The implementation of this proposed reform was repeatedly deferred by the last Conservative Government until it was too late. Whether the present Government will grasp the nettle remains to be seen. (See further the Report of an Inter-Departmental working group under the chairmanship of Trevor Aldridge, *Commonhold—Freehold flats and freehold ownership of other interdependent buildings* Cm. 179 (1987); *Commonhold*—Consultation Paper issued by the Lord Chancellor's Department, Cm. 1345 (1990); *Commonhold—A Consultation Paper*, Lord Chancellors Department, July 1996 and L.Crabb, *The Commonhold Association—As You Like It?* [1998] Conv. 283.

Chapter 13

BUSINESS TENANCIES AND SECURITY OF TENURE

A. TENANCIES PROTECTED

---

1. Introduction

The principal code governing the protection of business tenants is contained in Part II of the Landlord and Tenant Act 1954 whose origins lay in the Final Report of the Leasehold Committee Cmn. 7982 (1950). That Committee had been faced with the task of deciding how best to achieve a balance between the interests of landlords and tenants of property used for professional or business purposes. Such tenancies are of course governed by the general principles and rules of the ordinary law of landlord and tenant. Nevertheless, as in the case of other types of tenancy, such as residential or agricultural tenancies, a question arises as to whether there should be some statutory regulation of the contractual bargain, either by way of rent control or security of tenure. As we have seen (Chapter 8 above) there had been regulation in the private residential sector since 1915, although support for regulation was by no means universal. But whatever the merits of such controls, it was generally acknowledged that when compared to the residential market the arguments for rent regulation were far less compelling in the case of the business sector. The parties were much more likely to have been legally advised and there was frequently a less marked imbalance in the bargaining power of the parties. There was also a widespread perception that excessive regulation could reduce the quantity of properties available to rent as investors look elsewhere. After careful consideration of the matter the Leasehold Committee concluded that there should not be any form of rent regulation and that this was a matter which should be left to the parties.

Security of tenure was a different matter. The landlord's interest in the property is invariably viewed by him as a long term investment producing a regular income and potentially a capital gain. The tenant sees matters rather differently. The property is the source of the tenant's livelihood. A business built up over a number of years will acquire a "goodwill" which will be lost if the business is forced to relocate. Thus there is a strong case for permitting a tenant to remain beyond the end of the contractual term provided that the terms are fair and that the landlord is not financially prejudiced by such a right. Indeed, quite irrespective of any statutory entitlement on the part of the tenant, landlords and tenants frequently agree to a new tenancy and this will be foreshadowed in some tenancies by the inclusion of an option to renew the tenancy.

The first steps towards a code of protection for business tenants were taken by the enactment of the Landlord and Tenant Act (LTA) 1927. Part I of that Act is designed to compensate the tenant at the end of the tenancy (a) for any authorised improvements which he has carried out and which have added to the letting value of the property at that time and (b) for any goodwill which he will lose by having to give up possession. The Act provided for a limited right to a new tenancy where the compensation for loss of goodwill would be inadequate. The rights in (b) were available only to tenants who had carried on a trade or business and therefore tenants who had used the premises for professional purposes or for a non-profit making activity were thus excluded. The limited scope of the LTA 1927 was criticised by the Jenkins Committee which recommended a more extensive framework of protection for business tenants in general, whereby, following termination of the existing tenancy, the tenant would have a statutory right to a new tenancy, at a market rent, (but ignoring the tenant's improvements) subject to the landlord being able to defeat that right by establishing the existence of one or more specified grounds of opposition. In the case of some of these grounds it was recommended that a landlord who recovered possession might have to pay compensation to the tenant.

Most, but not all, of the recommendations of the Jenkins Committee were accepted. The compensation for improvements scheme of the Landlord and Tenant Act 1927 was retained and remains in force today, although it is little used in practice. It does not cover improvements which the tenant is contractually obliged to carry out. The landlord can therefore avoid the compensation provisions by ensuring that when he agrees to a tenant's request for permission to make an improvement the tenant is for consideration obliged to carry out the proposed improvement. The Law Commission has recommended that the statutory scheme be abolished (Law Com. No. 178 *Landlord and Tenant Law: Compensation for Tenants' Improvements* (1989) but the recommendation has not been implemented.

At the same time the provisions in the Landlord and Tenant Act 1927 dealing with compensation for goodwill were repealed and a new comprehensive code of protection for business tenants was enacted in Part II of the Landlord and Tenant Act 1954, which came into force on October 1, 1954. Although that measure has been subject to some amendments since it first appeared, notably by the Law of Property Act 1969, (following the Law Commission's Report on the Landlord and Tenant Act 1954, Part II (1969) Law Com. No. 17) it has stood the test of time and has remained for the most part unchanged. As Hill and Redman observe:

> "The provisions of the Landlord and Tenant Act 1954, Part II have proved generally successful in achieving a reasonable degree of security of tenure for tenants without imposing unnecessarily great burdens on landlords."

The Law Commission examined the scope and operation of Part II in a report published in 1992 in which it was recommended that the code be retained although some recommendations for amendment were also made. (*Business Tenancies: A Periodic Review of the Landlord and Tenant Act 1954, Part II* (Law Com. No. 208. See also the preceding Working Paper No. 111 (1988)). The Act is complex at times and provides a detailed procedure whereby at, or following, the end of a business tenancy either the tenant is able to obtain a new tenancy or the landlord can recover possession of the premises.

2. Tenancies governed by the Act

> "...any tenancy where the property comprised in the tenancy is, or includes premises which are, occupied by the tenant and are so occupied for the purposes of a business carried on by him or for those and other purposes (section 23)."

If a tenancy falls within this definition the protected tenancy regime of the Rent Act 1977 and the assured tenancy regime of the Housing Act 1988 will be excluded (RA 1977, s.24(3) and Housing Act 1988, s.1 and sched. 1 para. 4).

(a) Any tenancy

Most fixed term or periodic tenancies, save in the exceptional cases referred to below, will be covered by section 23 including a tenancy granted under Part II of the 1954 Act itself.

A tenancy at will, whether arising by implication of law or expressly will not be within section 23 (*Wheeler v. Mercer* [1957] A.C. 416 (implied tenancy at will); *Hagee Ltd v. AB Erikson & Larson* [1976] Q.B. 209 and *Cardiothoracic Institute v. Shrewdcrest Ltd* [1976] 3 All E.R. 633 (express tenancies). See also *Javad v. Acquil* [1991] 1 All E.R. 243).

It follows from section 23 that a genuine licence to occupy premises for business purposes will not be protected by Part II of the Landlord and Tenant Act 1954. (Reference should be made to Chapter 1 for a discussion of the lease/licence distinction in the context of business premises).

(b) Premises

The reference to "premises" in section 23 does not mean that the subject matter of the tenancy has to be a building or other structure. In *Bracey v. Read* [1963] Ch. 88 a tenancy of open land used as gallops for the exercise and training of racehorses was held to be within the Act (but see also *University of Reading v. Johnson-Houghton* [1985] 2 E.G.L.R. 113).

(c) Which are occupied by the tenant

The issue of whether premises are *occupied by the tenant* (for business purposes) has proved to be a difficult one in cases where the tenant is permitting others to carry out some activity, business or otherwise, on the premises. The matter was considered by the House of Lords in *Graysim Holdings Ltd v. P&O Property Holdings Ltd* [1996] A.C. 329.

The premises in question comprised a market which was let to the tenant. In turn the tenant had let the individual units in the market to sub-tenants who each had exclusive possession of his or her unit, although the tenant had employed a market superintendent with an office on the site to look after the bin room and lavatories, etc.

The House of Lords held that whether the tenant can still be said to be in occupation in such circumstances is one of fact and degree. On the facts of the case the retention of common parts and a management role by the tenant was insufficient to amount to business occupation on his part of either the common parts or the whole property. Thus the only business user was that of the sub-tenants. As Lord Nicholls observed (at p.343) "intermediate landlords, not themselves in occupation are not within the class of persons the Act was seeking to protect." (See also *Trans-Britannia Properties Ltd v. Darby Properties Ltd* [1986] 1 E.G.L.R. 151, CA). Landlords will no doubt have breathed a sigh of relief at this reversal by the House of Lords of the decision to the contrary by the Court of Appeal. The prospect of paying compensation for loss of statutory rights to tenants and sub-tenants in such a case will not have been a welcome one.

It is however possible to argue, in appropriate circumstances, that a tenant who has sub-let premises has still retained such a degree of control over the use of the premises that the tenant can be said to be "occupying" them himself for the purposes of his business.

This argument succeeded in *Groveside Properties Ltd v. Westminster Medical School* (1984) 47 P.& C.R. 507 where a tenancy of a flat was granted to the Medical School. The flat comprised four study rooms to be occupied individually by medical students along with a kitchen, bathroom, lavatories and sitting room the use of which was shared by the occupiers.

Because of the substantial degree of control which the Medical School exercised over the use of the premises by the students, it was held that as head tenant the school occupied the flat for the purposes of its business and therefore the tenancy was governed by Part II of the Landlord and Tenant Act 1954. The same result was reached in *Linden v. DHSS* [1986] 1 All E.R. 691 where a tenancy of a house was granted to the Department of Health and Social Security who converted it into self contained flats which were then occupied by NHS hospital employees. The Department was held to have retained a sufficient degree of management as to amount to occupation on its part for the purposes of a Government Department. (Contrast *Chapman v. Freeman* [1978] 3 All E.R. 878 where the tenant of a cottage used it for the purpose of accommodating employees who worked at his nearby hotel. This activity was not carried out for the purposes of his hotel business but simply for its convenience. Thus his tenancy was not a business tenancy). Reference should also be made to *Lee Verhulst (Investments) Ltd v. Harwood Trust* [1973] 1 Q.B. 204 where the tenant of a building let out self contained apartments on furnished sub-tenancies but retained rights of control by way of the provision of services in respect of the common parts and the flats themselves to which the head tenant had rights of entry in order to provide the relevant services such as cleaning of the flats and changing of towels and bed linen. The tenant was held to be in occupation of the whole for business purposes.

If the tenant chooses no longer to occupy the premises the protection of Part II will be lost if that absence is sufficient to break "the thread of continuity" (see *Aspinall Finance Ltd v. Viscount Chelsea* [1989] 09 E.G. 77; *Demetriou v. Poolaction Ltd* [1991] 1 E.G.L.R. 100, CA). But it would appear that if the absence is caused by circumstances beyond the tenant's control, such as fire damage, occupation will not be deemed to have been relinquished by the tenant's absence provided he had a realisable intention to return (see *I & H Caplan Ltd v. Caplan (No. 2)* [1963] 1 W.L.R. 1247 (tenant had left pending resolution of 1954 Act proceedings); *Morrison Holdings Ltd v. Manders Property (Wolverhampton) Ltd* [1976] 1 W.L.R. 533 (tenants moved out following a fire); *Hancock & Willis v. GMS Syndicate Ltd* (1983) 265 E.G. 473, CA).

In some circumstances occupation by one person will be treated as equivalent to that of another. Thus occupation by a beneficiary will be treated as that of the trustee tenant (LTA 1954, s.41(1)) and a company tenant can be in occupation through the medium of business user by another company in the same group of companies as the tenant company (LTA 1954, s.42(2)). But occupation by a company set up by the tenant will not be occupation by the tenant even if the tenant is the sole shareholder and in complete control of the company which is a separate legal entity (*Cristina v. Selear* [1985] 2 E.G.L.R. 128 and *Nozari-Zadeh v. Pearl Assurance plc* (1987) 2 E.G.L.R. 91). Because of the obvious difficulties created by this result the Law Commission has recommended that this rule be relaxed to cater for such circumstances (Law Com. 208 paras 2.12–2.13).

(d) For the purposes of a business

Business is widely defined as a trade, profession or employment and any activity carried on by a body of persons whether corporate or unincorporate (section 23(2)).

This clearly covers a wide range of activities whether profit making or not. In *Lee Verhulst (Investments) Ltd v. Harwood Trust* (above) the business was that of sub-letting serviced flats whereas in *Groveside Properties Ltd v. Westminster Medical School* (above) the provision of accommodation for medical students, was in furtherance of the Medical School's educational purposes which was a sufficient "activity" within section 23. It is therefore necessary to draw a distinction between (a) a sub-letting of the whole whereby the tenant is no longer in occupation and (b) a sub-letting of individual units within the premises with retention of a significant degree of control by the head tenant. In the case of the former the tenant will no longer be protected (see *Bagettes v. GP Estates Co. Ltd* [1956] Ch. 290). In the latter case the tenant will remain in "occupation" for business purposes (see above).

The term "activity" is wide and encompassed a lawn tennis club operated by an unincorporated society which was held to be carrying on an activity in *Addiscombe Garden Estates Ltd v. Crabbe* [1958] 1 Q.B. 513.

It will be noted that for the 1954 Act to apply there is no requirement that the initial letting be expressly for business purposes. Thus a tenancy of premises let for residential purposes could come within Part II of the Landlord and Tenant Act 1954 if the premises are subsequently occupied by the tenant for business purposes. But the Act will not apply where the tenancy prohibits business use and the tenant's user is in breach of covenant, unless that breach has been consented to by the immediate landlord or his predecessor in title or the immediate landlord has acquiesced in the breach (section 23(4) and *Chapman v. Freeman* (above)). There is a trap here for the unwary if a sub-tenancy, of premises with a covenant in the head tenancy restricting user to residential purposes, is granted without a similar restriction on business user in that sub-tenancy. The sub-tenant will be able to claim the benefit of the Act even though the business user by the sub-tenant constitutes a breach of covenant by the head tenant (*D'Silva v. Lister House Development Ltd.* [1971] Ch. 17).

In practice most difficulty over the application of section 23 is likely to be encountered in determining whether in marginal cases a particular activity can be said to be a "business use" or, if it is, whether that use is of minimal significance. This is a question of fact. If the activity is not a business use or amounts to a business use of minimal significance then Part II of the 1954 Act is inapplicable.

In *Lewis v. Weldcrest* [1978] 1 W.L.R. 1107 a tenant who sub-let rooms to lodgers on a bed and breakfast basis for little or no profit was not reaping any commercial advantage and therefore was not occupying the premises partly for business purposes. Similarly in *Gurton v. Parrott et al* (1990) 23 H.L.R. 418, CA the tenant, as a hobby, ran a business, of kennelling, grooming and breeding of dogs, from her home for a number of years. This was incidental to the main residential purpose of the tenancy and insufficient to attract the application of Part II of the Landlord and Tenant Act 1954 (see also *Wright v. Mortimer* (1996) 28 H.L.R. 719, CA and *Methodist Secondary Schools Trust Deed v. O'Leary* [1993] 1 E.G.L.R. 105).

There can be a thin line between marginal and significant user as illustrated by the two contrasting cases of *Royal Life Saving Society v. Page* and *Cheryl Investments Ltd v. Saldanha* [1978] 1 W.L.R. 1329. In *Page* it was held that the 1954 Act did not apply to a maisonette occupied as his home by a doctor who (with the landlord's permission) saw the occasional patient there. The doctor, who had consulting rooms in Harley Street was principally employed as medical adviser to the store Selfridges where he worked five days a week. By contrast it was held in *Cheryl Investments v. Saldanha* [1978] 1 W.L.R. 1329 that a tenant's use of his rented flat, in pursuance of his business as an importer, was of a sufficient degree as to amount to a significant purpose of his occupation and hence the tenancy attracted the application of Part II of the 1954 Act.

The importance of the need for occupation by the tenant for business purposes is emphasised by the definition for the purposes of the Act of "the holding" which is defined as:

"the property comprised in the tenancy, there being excluded any part thereof which is occupied neither by the tenant nor by a person employed by the tenant and so employed for the purposes of a business by reason of which the tenancy is one to which [Part II] applies (section 23(3))."

3. The holding

The significance of this definition, as we shall see, is that a claim for a new tenancy under the Act can only be made in respect of "the holding" and not any part of the property which has been sub-let, unless the tenant can be said to remain in occupation of the whole (see above).

4. Exclusions

Section 43 excludes the application of Part II in a number of cases; they are:

(1) a tenancy of an agricultural holding (section 43(1)(a))
(2) a mining lease (section 43(1)(b))
(3) a service tenancy (section 43(2))
(4) a tenancy for a fixed term of not more than 6 months unless there is an option to renew beyond that time or the tenant or his predecessor in the business has been in occupation for more than 12 months (section 43(3)).

Tenancies of licensed premises were formerly excluded but have been included since the Landlord and Tenant (Licensed Premises) Act 1990.

It is also possible to exclude the provisions of the Act dealing with continuation and renewal of the tenancy (*viz* ss. 24–28, see below) by an agreement between landlord and tenant which is contained in or endorsed on the lease and has been sanctioned by the county court (section 38(4) added by Law of Property Act 1969, s.5). It would seem that such agreements are invariably endorsed because the court has no evidence on which to refuse the request (see *Hagee (London) Ltd v. AB Erikson v. Larson* (above) at page 215 *per* Denning L.J.). Any other agreement that the Act shall not apply would be void under section 38(1) (see p.94 above).

B. SECURITY OF TENURE

1. Statutory continuation

The scheme of the Landlord and Tenant Act 1954 is that a tenancy governed by Part II will continue beyond its normal end date unless and until it is determined in accordance with the Act (section 24(1)). (See Chapter 7 p.166 for the effect on an original tenant's contractual liability during the extension). The tenant can then seek a new tenancy if he so wishes (under the procedure examined below). This will be either on his own initiative (section 26) or in response to a landlord's termination notice (section 25). But if the parties agree a new term the current tenancy will not continue beyond the agreed date of commencement of the new term and Part II will then cease to apply to the former term: section 28). It follows that effluxion of time or exercise of a break clause or (in the case of a periodic tenancy) service of a notice to quit by the landlord will not prevent the tenancy continuing by statute.

2. Termination by the tenant

Section 24 does not prevent a tenancy from being determined by a tenant's notice to quit, or a surrender (provided that the tenant has been in occupation for at least a month at the time of surrender or giving of the notice). Nor does it prevent the landlord at any time from forfeiting the tenancy or a superior tenancy for breach of covenant by the tenant (section 24(2)). Reference should be made to Chapter 6 above for termination by surrender or a tenant's notice to quit. It should be noted that an agreement to surrender, as opposed to an actual surrender, will be void as contrary to section 38(1) (*Tarjomani v. Panther Securities Ltd* (1982) 46 P.& C.R. 32).

It follows that without special provision a tenant who wished to bring the tenancy to an end at the expiry of the fixed term (the term date) would be unable to do so without surrendering the tenancy. Accordingly it is provided that, as long as he has been in occupation for at least a month, a tenant under a fixed term tenancy can prevent the tenancy being continued by serving a notice on his landlord (or in the case of a sub-tenancy his immediate landlord), not later than three months before the tenancy would come to an end by effluxion of time apart from the Act. The notice must state that the tenant does not desire the tenancy to continue (LTA 1954, s.27(1)). Similarly a fixed term tenancy which has already been continued by section 24 can be ended on any quarter day (see p.128 above) by a tenant's notice which is for not less than three months. The notice can be given after the term date of the fixed term has passed or before that date (section 27(2)). It has now been settled, by the Court of Appeal, that where the tenant ceases to occupy the premises for business purposes before the term date a section 27 notice is not required to prevent the fixed term arising and continuing. The Act ceases to apply once the tenant has abandoned occupation, because the requirements of section 23(1) (above) are then no longer satisfied and therefore the tenancy can expire by effluxion of time (*Esselte AB & British Sugar plc v. Pearl Assurance plc* [1997] 1 W.L.R. 891 following *Morrison Holdings Ltd v. Manders Property (Wolverhampton) Ltd* (above) and not following *Long Acre Securities Ltd v. Electro Acoustic Industries Ltd* [1990] 1 E.G.L.R. 91). In *Esselte* the tenant had actually served a section 27(2) notice ending on a quarter day following the term date. It was held that the tenancy expired on the earlier term date and therefore the landlord was not entitled to rent after that date.

However, it would seem to be reasonably clear that if the tenancy has been continued beyond the fixed term date when the tenant abandons occupation a section 27(2) notice would still be required from the tenant if he wished to terminate the extended term (see section 24(3)(a)).

3. Request for a new tenancy by the tenant

It has been noted above that if a continuation tenancy has begun, by virtue of section 24, the tenant may request a new tenancy by one of two routes. Strict time limits apply under both procedures and failure to observe them will be fatal to the validity of a notice although it is possible for one party to waive the need for strict compliance by the other (*Kammins Ballrooms Co. Ltd v. Zenith Investments (Torquay) Ltd* [1971] A.C. 850). For service of notices reference should be made to the Landlord and Tenant Act 1927 s.23(1) which is applied to the 1954 Act by LTA 1954, s.66(4). LTA 1927, s.23(1) provides, without prejudice to other methods of service (such as the ordinary post), that notice is to be taken as served if served personally or by registered post or recorded delivery.

When considering this procedure it is necessary to bear in mind that for the purpose of many of the notice procedures in the Landlord and Tenant Act 1954 a distinction is drawn between "the immediate landlord" and "the landlord". In some cases, such as service of a section 27 notice (above) or service of a notice to quit by the landlord, the relevant person will be the immediate landlord. But in other cases (*e.g.* sections 25, 26 and 28 (below)) the relevant person is "the landlord" as defined. Before examining this definition it is worth observing that if the tenant holds directly of the freeholder that person is the relevant landlord for the purposes of the Act in all cases and therefore there would be no need to distinguish between the immediate landlord and "the landlord". But it is a little more complicated where there are intermediate landlords between the tenant in question and the freeholder. The matter is governed by section 44 and Schedule 6 (which refers to "the landlord", as defined by section 44, as the "competent landlord)".

Section 44 in effect provides that the landlord (*i.e.* "the competent landlord"), in relation to a tenancy, is the owner of the reversion on the tenancy (whether immediate or not) which is either (a) the fee simple or (b) a tenancy which will not come to an end within 14 months provided that (i) it is not itself in reversion on such an interest or (ii) that a notice has not been given which will bring it to an end either within that time or any extended period (by virtue of section 36(2) or section 64). In other words, in order to discover who is the competent landlord in the case of a sub-tenancy, it is necessary to proceed up the chain from the tenancy until a person with an interest within (a) or (b) above is identified. That person will be the "competent landlord".

An example should make this clear. If ST is a sub-tenant of T, who is a tenant of the freeholder F, the competent landlord of ST will be T unless T's tenancy is due to expire in less than 14 months, in which case it will be F. But if ST was a sub-tenant only of part of the premises which were let to T then T would remain the competent landlord because his tenancy will continue under section 24 unless F has served a section 25 notice to terminate that tenancy, in which case F will be the competent landlord of ST. (In the case where T has sub-let the whole property his tenancy will not continue because he is no longer occupying it for the purposes of a business).

The first, and, in practice, by far the most usual route to a new tenancy, is by way of a tenant's response to a section 25 notice served by the landlord.

4. Termination by the landlord by a section 25 notice

The landlord can terminate a tenancy to which Part II applies by serving a notice (in statutory form or a form to like effect) on the tenant. To be valid the notice must comply with a number of requirements. Failure to comply with any or all of these requirements will invalidate the notice, although there is nothing to prevent the landlord who discovers his error from serving a new and valid notice (*Smith v. Draper* (1990) 60 P.& C.R. 252). The requirements for a section 25 notice are set out below:

(1) The notice must specify the date at which the tenancy is to come to an end (section 25(1)).

(2) The notice must be given not less than six and not more than 12 months before the specified date of termination (section 25(2)).

(3) In the case of a periodic tenancy the date specified in the section 25 notice must not be earlier than the date on which the tenancy could have been determined apart from the Act (section 25(3)(a)). This will depend on the rules governing the determination of tenancies by notice to quit which are examined in Chapter 6 above. If the notice to quit required under the terms of the tenancy was more than six months then the reference to 12 months in section 25(2) above is altered to the contractual notice period plus six months (section 25(3)(b)). Thus if a periodic tenancy required 12

months notice to quit then a section 25 notice in respect of that tenancy would need to be served not less than six and not more than 18 months before the termination date.

(4) In the case of a fixed term tenancy the specified date must not be earlier than the date on which the tenancy would have expired by effluxion of time (section 25(3),(4)). However, where the tenancy contains a break clause it is common for the landlord to serve a break notice and a section 25 notice at the same time. There is ample authority to the effect that the same notice can be used for both purposes but care will need to be taken that the notice complies with both the contractual requirements concerning the break clause and with section 25 (see *e.g. Scholl Manufacturing Co Ltd v. Clifton (Slim-Line) Ltd* [1967] Ch. 41 and *Aberdeen Steak Houses Group Ltd v. Crown Estate Commissioners* [1997] 31 E.G. 101). If the notice is effective for the purposes of the break clause but does not comply with section 25 the tenancy will continue beyond the break date by virtue of section 24 above (*Castle Laundry (London) Ltd v. Read* [1955] 1 Q.B. 586).

(5) If there are joint landlords all of them must be named in the section 25 notice (*Pearson v. Alyeo* [1990] 1 E.G.L.R. 114).

(6) The common law rule that a notice to quit must relate to the whole of the property let by the tenancy also applies to a section 25 notice (*Moss v. Mobil Oil Co Ltd* [1988] 06 E.G. 109, CA) although there is some uncertainty as to whether the rule prevents a landlord of part from serving a section 25 notice in relation to that part. The point was left open by the Court of Appeal in *Neville Long & Co (Boards) Ltd v. Firmenich & Co* (1983) 268 E.G. 572, CA. In *M & P Enterprises (London) Ltd v. Norfolk Square Hotels Ltd* [1994] 1 E.G.L.R. 129 the reversions to several buildings let on one tenancy were, following severance, owned by four different landlords. It was held that when each landlord served a section 25 notice in relation to his building this was not effective to end the single tenancy.

(7) The notice must require the tenant, within two months of the giving of the section 25 notice, to notify the landlord in writing as to whether or not the tenant is willing to give up possession of the property at the termination date (section 25(5)).

(8) The notice must state whether the landlord would oppose an application by the tenant under the Act for a new tenancy and if so state the ground(s) under section 30 (below) on which he would do so (section 25(6)).

Failure to comply

It seems that in practice section 25 notices are frequently defective. Where the landlord has not used the prescribed form or a form substantially to the like effect the notice will be invalid irrespective of whether the tenant was or was not actually misled (*Sun Alliance and London Assurance Ltd v. Hayman* [1975] 1 W.L.R. 177, CA and *Tegerdine v. Brooks* (1977) 36 P.& C.R. 261. This was confirmed recently by the Court of Appeal in *Sabella Ltd v. Montgomery and Others* [1998] 09 E.G. 153, CA where a notice was (in the light of earlier authority) materially defective and therefore invalid. (In so far as the earlier authority of *Morris v. Patel* [1987] 1 E.G.L.R. 75 might have suggested to the contrary it was to be treated as wrong).

Thus a crucial issue is whether a non statutory form is "substantially to like effect". In *Sun Alliance and London Assurance Ltd. v. Hayman* (above) use of an out of date form was not fatal to the validity of the notice. It was not materially different from the current prescribed form. But if the omissions or differences are actually irrelevant to the particular tenant the form can still be valid. Thus where the notice was not in the exact prescribed form in that it did not, *inter alia*, contain notes relevant to the landlord's opposition to a new tenancy, this did not matter because the landlord had stated that he was not opposing such a tenancy (*Tegerdine v. Brooks* (above)). Hence the defect was not material in that particular case.

Whether or not a reasonable tenant would have been misled or prejudiced by a defect is relevant to the issue of the materiality of that defect. Obvious clerical errors which are not misleading will be ignored. (See *Germax Securities Ltd v. Spiegal* (1979) 37 P.& C.R. 204 where the reference in a section 25 notice to 1976 was obviously intended to be to 1977). In one case a failure to sign the form was cured by an accompanying letter which contained the landlord's signature (*Stidolph v. American School in London Educational Trust* (1969) 113 S.J. 689, CA). But a notice which named as the landlord the actual landlord's parent company was held to be invalid in *Yamaha-Kemble Music (UK) Ltd v. ARC Properties Ltd* [1990] 1 E.G.L.R. 261.

If the tenant is aware of a defect in the section 25 notice but nevertheless waives that defect he will not be able to impugn the validity of the notice (*Smith v. Draper* [1990] 2 E.G.L.R. 69 and *Morrow v. Nadeem* [1987] 1 All E.R. 237).

If the landlord is opposed to the grant of a new tenancy, a failure to state the ground(s) of opposition relied on will be fatal to the validity of the section 25 notice (*Barclays Bank Ltd v. Ascott* [1961] 1 W.L.R. 717).

Once a tenant has been served with a section 25 notice he has two months in which to respond in writing stating whether or not he is willing to give up possession (section 29(2)). If he is not so willing the tenant must make an application to court for a new tenancy. The application must be made not less than two nor more than four months from the date that the landlords's notice was given (section 29(3)). Failure to comply with these strict time limits will mean that the tenant has lost his right to seek a new tenancy unless the landlord is estopped by having made a representation that the tenant will be granted a new tenancy which the tenant has relied on to his detriment (*JT Developments Ltd v. Quinn* [1991] 2 E.G.L.R. 257). These strict time limits have often left solicitors liable in negligence to their tenant clients. The requirement for a counter notice has been criticised by the Law Commission who recommended its abolition (Law Com. 208 para. 2.39).

5. Tenant's request for a new tenancy by service of section 26 notice

(a) Introduction

In the absence of a section 25 notice from the landlord (see above), the tenant can take the initiative and seek a new tenancy by serving a section 26 notice (section 26(1),(4)). This is the second and less well used route which can lead to a new tenancy. It is less well used because tenants will rarely want the present tenancy to come to an end particularly if rents have risen since the rent was fixed or last reviewed. On the other hand if the tenant anticipates a section 25 notice he may serve a section 26 notice as a pre-emptive strike which will prolong his present tenancy longer than would be the case were a section 25 notice to be served (see below).

It should be noted that, unlike the section 25 procedure, the section 26 route is only available to a tenant whose tenancy is for a term of years certain which was granted either for a term of more than one year, or for a term of more than one year and then from year to year (section 26(1)). It can be served whether the contractual fixed term is still subsisting or has been extended by section 24 (above).

As in the case of a landlord's section 25 notice, the section 26 procedure is governed by strict time limits. Thus the notice must state the date when the new tenancy is to commence and this must not be more than twelve, or less than six months after the making of the request.

Furthermore the specified date must not be earlier than the date on which, apart from the Act, the current tenancy would have ended by effluxion of time (or could be brought to an end by a notice to quit given by the tenant) (section 26(2)). (Hence if the tenant serves a notice six months before his fixed term tenancy will expire specifying a commencement date of 12 months later than the date of the notice he will prolong his tenancy by six months. But see the interim rent provisions below which if operated will affect the rent to be paid during the continuation tenancy).

(b) Requirements of section 26 notice

The section 26 notice must be in the prescribed form and set out the tenant's proposals as to (a) the property to be comprised in the new tenancy (which must be the whole or part of the property comprised in the current tenancy) (b) the rent to be payable under the new tenancy and (c) the other terms of the new tenancy (section 26(3)). Failure to do so will render the notice invalid in the absence of waiver of the defect by the landlord. (See *Bristol Cars Ltd v. RKH (Hotels) Ltd* (1979) 251 E.G. 1279, CA where the date specified in the tenant's notice was not only earlier than six months ahead but also earlier than the contractual term date. However, the landlords were estopped because they did not take the invalidity point until after they had begun negotiations for a new tenancy and applied for an interim rent (see below)).

(c) Limitations

A section 26 notice cannot be served if the tenant has already served a notice to quit or, as the case may be, a section 27 notice electing to terminate the tenancy (see above). Furthermore, just as a section 26 notice cannot be served if the landlord has already served a section 25 notice (see above), the landlord is similarly prevented from serving a valid section 25 notice once the tenant has served a section 26 notice (section 26(4)). A valid section 26 notice, once served, will also prevent the tenant subsequently serving a notice to quit or a section 27 notice (section 26(4)). These bars are necessary of course to keep the different statutory procedures apart from each other.

(d) Effect of section 26 notice

As noted above, a section 26 notice will terminate the tenancy as from immediately before the date specified in the request for the beginning of a new tenancy (section 26(5)).

Once the section 26 notice is served, the landlord has two months within which he can give notice to the tenant that he will oppose an application to the court for the grant of a new tenancy. This notice must specify the ground(s) of opposition (in section 30(1)) on which he intends to rely (section 26(6)). If within four months of the tenant's request the new tenancy has not been granted the tenant must apply to the court for a new tenancy (section 29(3)). If he does not he will lose his rights under Part II. It must be remembered that time is of the essence in the case of the notice procedure. See, for example, *Railtrack v. Gojra* [1998] 08 E.G. 158 where the tenant failed to apply in time. The case was unusual in that because of this failure the tenants sought to argue that their section 26 notice was invalid! The notice had been served on the British Railways Board as landlord on a date when Railtrack had taken over the former's operations. Nevertheless it was held that the service was effective because the former landlord was Railtrack's duly authorised agent for the receipt of notices. Failure to observe the strict time limits is particularly disastrous for a tenant. If he does not apply for a new tenancy within the four-month period he will not be able to serve a new notice and start again because the tenancy will end on the date specified in the original notice (see section 26(5) above; *Stile Properties Ltd v. Gooch* [1980] 1 W.L.R. 62, CA; *Polyviou v. Seeley* [1980] 1 W.L.R. 55, CA).

(e) Section 26 notice and break clauses

Section 26 raised a conundrum in the case of *Garston v. Scottish Widows Fund* [1998] 3 All E.R. 596, CA which is an excellent illustration of the war of tactics waged by commercial landlords and tenants over the issue of termination of leases and lease renewal. The plaintiffs were partners in a firm of London solicitors who had been granted a 20-year tenancy of office accommodation with a right to determine the tenancy at the end of the tenth year of the term by exercising a break option (see p.119 above) giving not less than six months notice. The tenancy had been entered into at an economic high point since when there had been a severe recession in the London commercial property market. The rental value of the property had declined dramatically and thus the tenants were anxious to end the term prematurely. To that end they served a notice exercising the break clause. At the same time the tenants served a section 26 notice requesting a new tenancy. The clear aim was to end the current high rent tenancy and obtain a new tenancy under the Act at a (much lower) current market rent. But was this possible? The outcome of the case was clearly going to be of interest to far more tenants than the plaintiffs in this particular case. Unfortunately for the tenants, Rattee J. (relying on the law at that time) ruled that the break notice was invalid. The tenancy had been granted on July 10, 1985 but was expressed to operate from June 24, 1985. Thus the end of the tenth year of the term was in fact June 23, 1995 and not July 9, 1995 as mistakenly stated in the tenant's break notice. The tenant's argument then turned to the section 26 issue. As noted above, section 26(2) states that a section 26 notice can specify a commencement date for a new tenancy which must not be "earlier than the date on which the current tenancy can end by effluxion of time *or could be brought to an end by notice to quit given by the tenant*." (italics supplied) whilst section 26(5) says that a valid section 26 notice will terminate the tenancy immediately before the date specified in the notice. The tenants argued that because a notice to quit is defined (in section 69(1)) as including a notice under a break clause, the italicised words of the section 26(2) proviso applied and that the break date was therefore the relevant date for the purposes of the section 26 notice. Because the date specified in the section 26 notice for the commencement of the new tenancy was not earlier than the break date it was argued that the section 26 notice was valid and (in accordance with section 26(5)) operated to break the tenancy. This daring argument failed. Rattee J. ruled that the first limb of the proviso governed fixed terms (whether or not the tenancy contained a break clause) and the second limb periodic tenancies. Thus in the present case the section 26 notice was invalid because the date specified for commencement of the new tenancy was earlier than "the current tenancy would come to an end by effluxion of time" which was the contractual term date. When the matter came before the Court of Appeal the decision of the House of Lords in *Mannai Investment Co Ltd v. Eagle Star Life Assurance Co Ltd* (see p.121 above) meant that the tenant succeeded on the issue of the validity of the break clause. Hence the Court of Appeal did not have to consider the section 26 issue because the 1954 Act became irrelevant. However, no doubt to the relief of landlords, the Court endorsed the ruling of Rattee J. on the point and sensibly held that it was not the purpose of section 26 to allow a tenant to choose to terminate a tenancy prematurely and then argue for a new tenancy on more favourable terms.

6. Interim rent

A landlord who has served a section 25 notice, or received a section 26 notice, is permitted to apply to the court for determination of a rent which it would be reasonable for the tenant to pay during the statutory continuation (section 24A). This power to determine an interim rent was introduced by the Law of Property Act 1969, section 3 because of the unfairness that would otherwise result to landlords where there was a delay in the granting of the new tenancy. Without the possibility of an interim rent the continuation tenancy would be at the old rent which would encourage tenants to prevaricate in order to prolong the old tenancy at the passing rent where rental levels are rising. The Law Commission has recommended that the tenant should have a similar right to protect him against a falling rental market (Law Com. No. 208 para. 2.63). The interim rent is to be determined on the basis of a hypothetical yearly tenancy (see section 24A(3) and section 34) but regard is also to be had to the rent currently payable. This may mean that a lower rent than the current market rent is determined where the latter is significantly higher than the current rent. Some landlords seek to avoid these problems by providing for a contractual rent review on the termination of the contractual term. The interim rent is payable from whichever is the later of either (a) the date when proceedings for determination of an interim rent were begun or (b) the date of any section 25 or section 26 notice that has been served (section 24A(3)).

7. Landlord's opposition to a new tenancy

We saw above that whether a section 25 notice has been served by the landlord or a section 26 notice has been served by the tenant, the landlord can oppose a new tenancy on one or more of the grounds set out in section 30. He must specify the ground(s) relied on in the section 25 notice or, as the case may be, in his response to a section 26 notice from the tenant.

In the case of grounds (a) (b) and (c) the relevant time for determining whether the ground is satisfied is the date of the court hearing but it has been suggested that the court may also take into account the circumstances at the time of service of the landlord's section 25 notice or as the case may be the tenant's section 26 notice (*Betty's Cafes Ltd v. Phillips Furnishing Stores Ltd* [1959] A.C. 20). As an alternative to relying on the first three grounds the landlord might consider forfeiting the tenancy for breach of covenant. If successful he would thereby forestall any claim to a new tenancy under the Landlord and Tenant Act 1954 (see above). But until forfeiture is complete the tenant will not be precluded from taking advantage of the 1954 Act (see *Meadows v. Clerical, Medical and General Life Assurance Society* [1981] Ch. 70).

Grounds of opposition

The grounds on which the landlord is permitted to oppose a new tenancy are set out in section 30(1) and are examined below.

(a) That the tenant ought not to be granted a new tenancy in view of the state of repair of the holding, being a state resulting from the tenant, failure to comply with his repairing and maintenance obligations if any.

This ground vests a wide discretion in the judge who will consider all the circumstances including the seriousness of the breach, the tenant's willingness to remedy the faults and the reasons for the tenant's non-compliance with his obligations (*Lyons v. Central Commercial Properties Ltd* [1958] 1 W.L.R. 869).

(b) That the tenant ought not to be granted a new tenancy in view of his persistent delay in paying rent which has become due.

As in the case of ground (a) the court has a wide discretion and can take into account the amount of rent unpaid, the period of delay and the reasons for delay or non-payment, along with the likely prospects of the tenant continuing to comply with his obligations were a new tenancy to be granted (see *Hurstfell v. Leicester Square Property Co* [1988] 37 E.G. 109).

(c) That the tenant ought not to be granted a new tenancy in view of other substantial breaches by him of his obligations under the current tenancy or for any other reason connected with the tenant's use or management of the holding

It will be observed that only substantial breaches of covenant are to be considered under the first limb of this ground and that the court can look at the tenant's conduct throughout the tenancy (see *Eichner v. Midland Bank Executor and Trustee Co Ltd* [1970] 1 W.L.R. 1120, CA where it was considered permissible in a ground (c) case for the judge to take into account matters such as the tenant's history of paying rent and ability to pay the rent in the future). The second limb of this ground makes it clear that the conduct complained of might not be a breach of covenant but a breach of the general law such as planning controls as in *Turner and Bell v. Searles (Stanford-le-Hope) Ltd* (1977) 33 P.& C.R. 208 where the use to which the tenant had put the property was in breach of an enforcement notice under the Town and Country Planning Act 1971 and as such amounted to a criminal offence.

(d) That the landlord has offered and is willing to provide or secure the provision of suitable alternative accommodation for the tenant

A number of conditions apply to his ground.

(1) The terms on which the alternative accommodation is available must be reasonable having regard to the terms of the current tenancy and to all other relevant circumstances.

(2) The accommodation and the time at which it will be available must be suitable for the tenant's requirements, including the requirement to preserve goodwill, having regard to the nature and class of his business and to the situation and extent of, and facilities afforded by the holding.

If this ground is established there is no residual discretion in the court. (Contrast the parallel ground in the Rent Act 1977, s.98 and Part IV sched. 15. see p.285 above). In the county court case of *Chaplin Ltd v. Regent Capital Holdings Ltd* [1994] 1 E.G.L.R. 249 it was held that (a) the landlord need not make the offer before the service of the notice but that once made the offer must not be withdrawn and (b) that the requirements as to reasonableness must be met at the date of the court hearing.

(e) Where the current tenancy is a sub-tenancy of part of a larger holding of which the landlord requires possession in order to dispose of or let the whole at a substantially higher rent than the aggregate rent he could obtain for the separate lettings of the individual parts

The court also has a discretion in respect of this little used ground which is limited to use by a landlord against a sub-tenant of part of a larger property also owned by the landlord. It follows that it is only of relevance where the intermediate tenancy is to end soon and where the intermediate tenant would have no right to remain. If it were otherwise the intermediate tenant would be the "competent landlord" (see p.386 above).

(f) That on the termination of the current tenancy the landlord intends to demolish or reconstruct the premises comprised in the holding or a substantial part of those premises or to carry out substantial work of construction on the holding or part thereof and that he could not reasonably do so without obtaining possession of the holding

Along with the following ground this is one of the grounds of opposition to a new tenancy most frequently relied upon in practice by landlords. As such it has spawned a large body of case law.

The landlord's intention, which must be established at the date of the hearing, must be a firm intention. This means that the landlord must have sufficiently advanced plans which he has a reasonable prospect of achieving. But this should be contrasted with the position in a case where a break clause permitted the landlord to break the lease by giving notice of the landlord's "desire" to carry out works of demolition or reconstruction. It was sufficient for this purpose for the landlord to establish a "wish" to demolish or reconstruct rather than a firm "intention" (*Aberdeen Steak House Group Ltd v. Crown Estates Commissioners* [1997] 31 E.G. 101).

The leading case on para. (f) and the need for intention is the decision of the House of Lords in *Betty's Cafes Ltd v. Phillips Furnishing Stores Ltd* above). The tenants served a section 26 notice requesting a new tenancy and the landlord served a counter notice in which they relied on section 30(1)(f) stating that they intended to reconstruct the premises. Although no resolution to carry out the relevant works had been passed by the landlord company's board at the time of service of the counter notice, a resolution to spend £20,000 on works, within a year of recovering possession, was passed during the hearing of the tenant's application. It was held that this was sufficient to satisfy the ground. The landlord's motive for recovering possession (*e.g.* to sell or grant a new lease to somebody else, or indeed to occupy himself) was held to be immaterial (see further *Fishers v. Taylors Furnishing Stores Ltd* [1956] 2 Q.B. 78, CA; *Turner v. Wandsworth Borough Council* [1994] 1 E.G.L.R. 134).

In so concluding, the House of Lords considered what was meant by "intends" in this context. They were content to solve this issue by adopting the judgment delivered by Asquith L.J. (as he then was) in *Cunliffe v. Goodman* [1950] 2 K.B. 237, 253, CA (a decision on section 18 of the Landlord and Tenant Act 1927 (see p.68 above) where he stated that "intention"

"to my mind connotes a state of affairs which the party 'intending'—I will call him X—does more than merely contemplate: it connotes a state of affairs which, on the contrary, he decides, so far as in him lies, to bring about, and which, in point of possibility, he has a reasonable prospect of being able to bring about, by his own act of volition."

He later said that the project must have "moved out of the zone of contemplation— out of the sphere of the tentative, the provisional and the exploratory—into the valley of decision. (p.259)"

This meaning of intention was also adopted in *Fishers v. Taylors Furnishing Stores Ltd* (above) where Denning L.J. (as he then was) referred to the need for the landlord to establish "a firm and settled intention not likely to be changed." If, as in that case, the premises are, in the words of Denning L.J. in another case "old and worn out or ripe for development, [and] the proposed work is obviously desirable, plans and arrangements are well in hand, and the landlord has the present means and ability to carry out the work" it is likely that the landlord's intention will be readily satisfied (*Reohorn v. Barry Corporation* [1956] 1 W.L.R. 845, 849, CA). By contrast the court will not be so readily satisfied "when the premises are comparatively new or the desirability of the project is open to doubt, when there are many difficulties still to be surmounted, such as the preparation and approval of plans or the obtaining of finance, or when as in the past the landlord has fluctuated in his mind as to what to do with the premises." (*ibid*). The Court of Appeal did not find the necessary intention to exist in *Reohorn* where the tenant of a car park sought to obtain a new tenancy from the landlord corporation who opposed the tenant's application relying on section 30(1)(f). The council argued that they intended to facilitate a comprehensive redevelopment of the area including the car park by a development company. But this was not enough.

"In the present case the premises are ripe for development and the proposed work is obviously desirable: but the difficulty is to be satisfied that the corporation have the present means and ability to carry out the work. 'Intention' connotes an ability to carry it into effect. A man cannot properly be said to 'intend' to do a work of reconstruction when he has not got the means to carry it out. He may *hope* to do so: he will not have the *intention* to do so. In this case the corporation contemplate turning this land into a splendid estate by the sea. They are exploring the possibilities of it; they are discussing the ways and means, in the shape of a building lease; but that is as far as they have got. Their ability to do the work, or to cause it to be done, is, I think, open to question. (*ibid*)."

The question of whether there is a reasonable prospect of a project coming to fruition is one of fact. Although planning permission might be needed for a scheme it is not fatal to a successful claim under para. (f) that it has not yet been obtained if a reasonable landlord would believe that there is a reasonable prospect that it will be forthcoming if the landlord recovers possession (*Gregson v. Cyril Lord* [1963] 1 W.L.R. 41 approved of by the House of Lords in *Westminster City Council v. British Waterways Board* [1985] A.C. 676 HL; see also *Cadogan v. McCarthy & Stone Developments Ltd* [1996] E.G.C.S. 94). It would clearly make sense, and increase the landlord's prospects of success, for him to travel as far along the road of planning as possible. If the landlord is a company a resolution of the board should be obtained (see *Espresso Coffee Machine Co Ltd v. Guardian Assurance Co Ltd* [1959] 1 W.L.R. 250).

The landlord does not have to show that he intends to do the work himself. It will suffice that it is done by an agent or a developer under a building lease provided the landlord maintains overall control (see, *e.g. Reohorn v. Barry Corporation* (above); *Gilmour Caterers Ltd v. St Bartholomews Hospital Board of Governors* [1956] 1 Q.B. 387).

Ground (f) draws a distinction between (a) work which amounts to demolition or reconstruction of *the holding* or a substantial part of it and (b) work which is a substantial work of construction on *the holding* or a substantial part thereof. Thus works on another part of the premises or other premises not leased to the tenant will not suffice. (See also *Barth v. Pritchard* [1990] 1 E.G.L.R. 109 where Stocker L.J. was of the view that the proposed works, considered as a whole, could not amount to "construction" if none of the items considered separately could be so regarded).

Reconstruct means re-build. (*Percy E. Cadle & Co. Ltd v. Jacmarch Properties Ltd* [1957] 1 Q.B. 323 where putting in an internal staircase was considered to be a matter of improvement rather than reconstruction). In *Romulus Trading Co Ltd v. Henry Smith's Charity Trustees* [1990] 2 E.G.L.R. 75, CA it was held by the Court of Appeal that for works to amount to substantial "reconstruction" they had to be works of rebuilding which involved a substantial interference with the structure of the building, which, for this purpose, was not necessarily confined to outside or other load bearing walls. (per Farquharson L.J. at page 77).

Finally para. (f) requires the landlord to establish that the landlord could not reasonably do the works, etc, in question without obtaining possession of the holding. In *Heath v. Drown* [1973] A.C. 498 the House of Lords held that this means legal possession and not physical possession. In other words if there are provisions in the tenancy which permit the landlord to enter and carry out the necessary works he cannot say that he requires legal possession (see *Price v. Esso Petroleum* [1980] 2 E.G.L.R. 58). But it has also been held that the landlord will require legal possession if what he proposes goes beyond what he is permitted to do by exercise of any right of entry in the tenancy or under any right of entry he would have in the new tenancy if granted. (*Little Park Service Station Ltd v. Regent Oil Co Ltd* [1967] 2 Q.B. 655 where the tenancy contained adequate rights of entry as in *Heath v. Drown* (above). But see now section 31A(1)(a), below). It has also been held that if the end result would result in premises which are inconsistent with the terms of the existing tenancy it cannot be said that the landlord will not require legal possession. This occurred in *Leathwoods Ltd v. Total Oil (G.B.) Ltd* (1984) 270

E.G. 1083 where the landlord intended to renovate premises which as currently occupied by the tenant were used as a petrol filling station and for the sale and repair of cars. The landlord planned to construct a much larger filling station and to remove the facilities for repairs or sales. The landlord required legal possession to do this because otherwise they would be in derogation of their grant if the tenant were permitted to remain after the new works because they would no longer be able to carry on their former business.

The need for possession for the purposes of ground (f), must be considered alongside the Landlord and Tenant Act 1954, section 31A (which was added by the Law of Property Act 1969, s.7(1)).

Section 31A comes into play once the landlord has established that he legally requires possession in accordance with para. (f) above (see *Romulus Trading Co Ltd v. Henry Smith's Charity Trustees* (above)). It provides that the court shall not hold that the landlord cannot reasonably carry out the works, etc., without obtaining possession if either:

    (a)   the tenant agrees to the inclusion in the new tenancy of terms giving the landlord access and other facilities for carrying out the intended work provided that this would be sufficient to enable the work to be carried out without possession being obtained and without interfering to a substantial extent or for a substantial time with the tenant's use of the premises for the purposes of his business (section 31A(1)(a)) or

    (b)   the tenant is willing to accept a tenancy of an economically separable part of the holding and either (a) above is satisfied in respect of that part or possession of the remainder of the holding would be reasonably sufficient to enable the landlord to carry out the intended work (section 31A(1)(b)). For this purpose the court will not modify the landlord's plans or question whether the landlord's intentions are reasonable provided they are bona fide. (*Decca Navigator Co. Ltd v. Greater London Council* [1974] 1 W.L.R. 748).

Paragraph (a) will surmount the obstacle which hitherto existed where there is no adequate right of entry in the current tenancy (see above). But the proviso might present a tenant with difficulties. If, notwithstanding the new terms, the tenant's use of the premises will still be interfered with to a substantial extent or for a substantial time he will not be able to rely on section 31A. Whether this would be the case is a matter of fact and degree (*Price v. Esso Petroleum Ltd* (1980) 255 E.G. 243). It has been held that the interference must be both substantial **and** for a substantial period of time (*Cerex Jewels Ltd v. Peachey Property Corporation Ltd* [1986] 2 E.G.L.R. 65, CA where works which would have taken not more than two weeks did not satisfy this requirement. But compare *Redfern v. Reeves* (1978) 37 P.& C.R. 364 (one or two months) and *Blackburn v. Hussain* [1988] 1 E.G.L.R. 77 (eight weeks) where in each case the likely interference was considered to be substantial).

(g) That on the termination of the current tenancy the landlord intends to occupy the holding for the purposes, or partly for the purposes, of a business to be carried on by him therein, or as his residence

As in the case of ground (f) the landlord must establish the necessary intention at the time of the hearing. The landlord need not intend to occupy personally. Occupation can be through an agent or manager (see *Skeet v. Powell-Sheddon* [1988] 2 E.G.L.R. 112, CA where the proposed manager was the tenant's husband who was to manage the use of the premises as a hotel). In *Parkes v. Westminster Roman Catholic Diocese Trustee* (1978) 36 P.& C.R. 22 the landlord trustees could occupy through a parish priest. But there must be occupation through somebody.

An intention to sub-let without retaining any form of control over the property is insufficient (*Jones v. Jenkins* [1986] 1 E.G.L.R. 113). An intention will suffice if the intended business user is by another company in the same group as the landlord (company) tenant (section 42(3)(a)). A difficulty with para. (g) for the tenant is that the landlord's intention to occupy might be for a limited period only. In *Willis v. Association of Universities of the British Commonwealth* [1965] 1 Q.B. 140 at 150 Lord Denning M.R. suggested that as short a period as six months might suffice.

A landlord who intends to carry out works of demolition or reconstruction should also combine this ground with a claim under para. (f) (*Fishers v. Taylors Furnishing Stores Ltd* (above)).

Section 30(1)(g) must be read with section 30(2) which introduces an important qualification whereby ground (g) cannot be relied upon where the landlord's interest was bought or created within the five-year period before the end of the current tenancy and at all times since the date of creation or acquisition the holding has been comprised within a tenancy governed by section 23(1) (above) *viz*; a business tenancy within Part II of the Act. But this "five-year rule" does not apply if the landlord's interest was purchased or created before the grant of the current tenancy (*Northcote Laundry Ltd v. Frederick Dornelly Ltd* [1968] 1 W.L.R. 562). Transfers within a group of companies are ignored for this purpose: section 42(3)(b).

8. Landlord successfully opposes a new tenancy

If the landlord successfully opposes a new tenancy by establishing one or more of the grounds of opposition in section 30(1) the court cannot grant a new tenancy (section 31(1)). The current tenancy will then come to an end three months after the date when the application is finally disposed of (section 64).

A special rule as to timing applies in the case of grounds (d), (e) and (f) in section 30(1). If the court is not satisfied that the ground relied on is made out at that time but that it is satisfied that it will be made out within a period of not more than a year the court must make a declaration to that effect stating the date on which it is believed that the requirements will be satisfied. The tenant then has 14 days to apply to the court for an order that the tenancy shall terminate on that later date rather than on the actual date of termination. If he does not it will be as if the landlord had successfully opposed the new tenancy.

9. Compensation for disturbance

Section 37 deals with the question of compensation for disturbance where the tenant is unable to obtain a new tenancy. It operates:

(a) where the court is precluded from granting a new tenancy because the landlord has successfully established ground (e) (f) or (g) of section 30(1) and has not relied on any other ground.

(b) where no ground other than grounds (e) (f) or (g) were relied upon in the landlord's section 25 notice or in his counter notice to the tenant's section 26 notice and either no application is made under section 24 for a new tenancy or such an application has been withdrawn (section 37(1)).

The amount of compensation to which the tenant is entitled, for the loss of premises which are occupied solely for the purposes of a business, is either the rateable value or twice the rateable value of the holding (section 37(2),(3) and S.I. 1990 No. 363).

(1)   Compensation of twice the rateable value is payable where there has been 14 years continuous business user of the holding or the premises comprised in it under the same business. This business user need not have been by the current tenant provided there has been continuity of business user under the same business throughout by the tenant and any previous tenant. The 14-year period is that before the date of termination which will either be the date specified in a landlord's section 25 notice or the date specified in a tenant's section 26 request as the day from which the new tenancy is to begin (section 37(7)). In *Bacchiocchi v. Academic Agency Ltd* [1998] 2 All E.R. 241, CA a tenant who closed the business for cleaning and left 12 days before the end of the term was not disentitled to double compensation. The extent of the holding is determined as at the date of the section 25 or section 26 notice (*Edicron v. William Whiteley Ltd* [1984] 1 W.L.R. 59) whilst the date for assessing compensation is when the tenant leaves (*Cardshops Ltd v. John Lewis Properties Ltd* [1983] Q.B. 161).

(2)   In any other case the compensation payable will be the rateable value.

The parties are free to negotiate the compensation between themselves if they so wish once the right to compensation has accrued (section 38(2)). Indeed they can agree before then to exclude or limit the right as they think fit and many tenancies so provide (section 38(3)). But this freedom to exclude or limit compensation is subject to the important proviso that such an agreement will not be valid if the premises have been occupied for the purposes of the business of the occupier for five years before the date on which the tenant is to leave. This occupation can have been by the present tenant or a previous tenant or tenants provided there has been continuity of business user under the same business throughout the relevant period (*ibid*).

10. Landlord does not, or fails to, oppose a new tenancy

If the landlord either does not oppose a new tenancy, or is unsuccessful in his opposition, the tenant will be entitled to a new tenancy on the terms and conditions to be decided by the court in accordance with sections 32–35 (section 29(1)). Alternatively the parties can choose to make their own private agreement (section 28). The problem with section 29 is that the tenant will lose the right to a new tenancy unless he has applied to the court within the appropriate time limits (see above). This is a great waste of time and resources because most renewals are in practice settled by agreement. The Law Commission has recommended that the parties be free to extend the time limits to avoid unnecessary precautionary applications to the court (Law Com. No. 208. para. 2.59).

11. Grant of a new tenancy by the court

(a) The holding

In default of agreement between the parties as to the property to be comprised in the new tenancy, the court will designate that property by reference to the circumstances existing at the date of the order (section 32(1)). Thus the tenancy will normally be of "the holding" (*i.e.* that part of the premises let which is occupied by the tenant for the purposes of a business, etc., see p.384 above). It will thus exclude any part of the premises which the tenant does not personally so occupy, such as where he has sub-let part. This general rule is qualified in two instances. The first is where, in accordance with section 31A(1) above, the tenant is willing to accept a tenancy of an economically separable part of the existing holding to enable the landlord to carry out proposed works etc thereby preventing successful reliance by the landlord on the section 30(1)(f) ground of opposition to a new tenancy (section 32(1A). In such a case the order will necessarily be for a new tenancy of that separate part. The second is where there are other premises comprised in the current tenancy as well as the holding and the landlord requires the tenant to take a new tenancy of the whole (section 32(2)).

Any ancillary rights (such as easements over adjoining land) which are included in the current tenancy and which are enjoyed by the tenant at the time of the application to the court can also be carried over into the new tenancy, unless the parties agree otherwise, or in default of such agreement, determined by the court (section 32(3)). There would seem to be no good reason why the grant of the new tenancy should not also convert informal rights currently enjoyed *de facto* with the landlord's permission into easements (in accordance with LPA 1925, s.62 and the principle in *Goldberg v. Edwards* [1950] Ch. 247). However, in *G Orlik (Meat Products) Ltd v. Thanet Building Society* (1974) 29 P.&C.R. 126, the tenant, who had been allowed to park on adjoining land of the landlord by permission of the current landlord's predecessor in title, was not allowed to have such a right inserted in the new tenancy. He did not at any time have any right to park there as against the *current* landlord.

(b) Duration of the new tenancy

In the absence of agreement between the parties as to the length of the new term the court has a discretion to determine what it considers to be a reasonable length in all the circumstances up to a maximum of 14 years (section 33). (The Law Commission has recommended that the maximum should be marginally increased to 15 years although it is difficult to see the purpose of this somewhat slight proposal. See Law Com. No. 208 para. 2.76). The court's discretion is wide and amongst the factors which it will take into account are (a) the length of the current term (b) the length of time over which the tenant has held over under the current tenancy and (c) the comparative hardship as between landlord and tenant.

The courts have also used section 33 to deal with circumstances where the landlord has failed to make out a ground of opposition under paragraph (f) or (g) of section 30(1). As we have seen above the landlord may fail to establish the requirements of ground (f) because his plans for redevelopment are at an insufficiently advanced stage. A ground (g) plea may fail because of the "five-year rule". In such cases although the court is bound to order a new tenancy the court may decide that it would be appropriate to order a shorter term than would otherwise have been the case. (See *Reohorn v. Barry Corporation* (above) (para. (f)) and *Upsons Ltd v. E Robins Ltd* [1956] 1 Q.B. 131 (para. (g)). Alternatively the court might order a longer term with appropriate break dates (see *e.g.*, *McCombie v. Grand Junction Co. Ltd* [1962] 1 W.L.R. 581; *J.H.Edwards & Sons Ltd v. Central London Commercial Estates Ltd* (1983) 271 E.G. 697; *National Car Parks Ltd v. Paternoster Consortium Ltd* [1990] 15 E.G. 53).

(c) Terms of the new tenancy other than rent

The terms of the new tenancy, other than as to rent, are to be agreed by the parties but in default of agreement they may be determined by the court which is required to have regard to the terms of the current tenancy and to all relevant circumstances (section 35(1)).

It is specifically provided that one of those circumstances includes a reference to the operation of the Landlord and Tenant (Covenants) Act 1995 (s.35(2)). It will be recalled that a tenancy granted on or after January 1, 1996 (unless in pursuance of a court order made before that date) will be a "new tenancy" for the purposes of the Act (LTCA 1995 s.1(2)). As such the tenancy will therefore be governed by the new privity rules contained in that Act with regard to the enforceability of covenants in the tenancy after assignment. The most important of these rules are (a) the abolition of the privity of contract principle, (b) the possibility of the landlord seeking an authorised guarantee agreement from an assignor and (c) the landlord's right to specify the circumstances in which he can be deemed to be reasonably withholding consent to an assignment (see Chapters 4 and 7 above). Landlords can be expected to request that the new rights be reflected in a "new tenancy". If so this would certainly have an effect on the rent obtainable under that tenancy (see below). (See further R. Bunce and P. Williams, "*Lease renewals after the 1995 Act*" (1996) 15 E.G. 96).

The terms of the current tenancy are clearly an important factor when considering the form of the new tenancy. But this will not enable the benefit of an option to buy the freehold to be carried over if by the terms of the original tenancy this had to be exercised during the original term (*Kirkwood v. Johnson* (1979) 38 P.&C.R. 392). On the other hand a break clause in the current tenancy will almost certainly be replicated in the new tenancy (*Leslie & Godwin Investments Ltd v. Prudential Insurance Co Ltd* (1987) 283 E.G. 1565). Indeed such a clause might well now be considered appropriate in any event in accordance with modern practice. This would almost certainly be a legitimate exercise of the court's discretion. In *Cairnplace Ltd v. C.B.L.C. (Property Investments) Co Ltd* [1984] 1 W.L.R. 696 the court ordered that the tenant provide a surety to guarantee performance of his obligations under the new tenancy. Such a requirement is commonplace in modern business tenancies.

The leading case on the extent of the court's discretion is *O'May v. City of London Real Property Co. Ltd* [1983] 2 A.C. 726 which confirmed that the starting point is clearly the terms of the current tenancy. If any party wishes to propose a change to those terms the onus of adducing good reasons is clearly on that party. Furthermore the court will not accede to such a request unless the proposed change is fair and reasonable. The court will clearly be hesitant to order the insertion of terms which give the landlord an advantage which he did not have under the original tenancy. Thus in *O'May* the landlords had granted to the tenants a five-year tenancy of premises in a modern office block. Under the terms of the tenancy the landlord was obliged to maintain the common parts, etc. Although the landlord was willing to grant a new tenancy he proposed that it should contain provision for the landlord to provide services and to maintain and repair the building but that the tenant should contribute to the costs by way of a service charge. He also proposed a consequential small reduction in the rent payable. The landlord's objective was to create a "clear lease" thus making his reversion more marketable. (It was estimated that the value of the reversion would be enhanced by between one and two million pounds if there were a clear lease). The tenant refused to agree to the proposed variation. The House of Lords held that the landlord had not established a good reason why the tenancy should be varied in this way. Lord Hailsham said the proposed change should be fair and reasonable and:

> "..should take into account, amongst other things, the comparatively weak position of a sitting tenant requiring renewal, particularly in conditions of scarcity, and the general purpose of the Act which is to protect the business interests of the tenant so far as they affected by the approaching termination of the current lease, in particular as regards his security of tenure [1983] 2 A.C. 726 at 740)."

The court held that it was not fair and reasonable for the landlord to shift to the tenant the financial risks and burden (through the proposed new service charge) of the fluctuating costs of repair and maintenance of the building despite the proposed modest rent reduction. On the same principles a landlord was not permitted to narrow the user clause in a new tenancy so as to prevent a tenant selling second-hand clothes when under the current tenancy he had been selling new and second-hand clothes (*Gold v. Brighton Corporation* [1956] 1 W.L.R. 1291. See also *Charles Clements (London) Ltd v. Rank City Wall Ltd* (1978) 246 E.G. 739 where an attempt by the landlord to relax the current user covenant in the new tenancy, in order to raise the rental value of the premises, was rejected by the court. The converse occurred in *Aldwych Club Ltd v. Copthall Property Co Ltd* (1962) 185 E.G. 219, where the tenant unsuccessfully sought a more stringent user covenant in an attempt to reduce the rental value.

The *O'May* decision can cause some problems in practice because, as we have seen above, clear leases of the kind rejected in that case subsequently became commonplace in the commercial property market and it may well be that it would be reasonable in all the circumstances for such provision to be made in a particular case on lease renewal under the 1954 Act. (The Law Commission has suggested that this matter should be made clear by statute Law Com. No. 208 para. 4.56).

(d) The rent under the new tenancy

The rent under the new tenancy will be the amount agreed by the parties or in the absence of agreement as determined by the court. By section 34(1) the rent is that which, having regard to the tenancy (other than those relating to rent), the holding might reasonably be expected to be let for in the open market by a willing lessor, disregarding the following matters.

(1) Any effect on rent of the fact that the tenant or his predecessors in title have been in occupation of the holding.

(2) Any goodwill attached to the holding by reason of the carrying on there of the tenant's business whether by the tenant or a predecessor in that business.

(3) Any effect on rent of certain improvements. This means an improvement which was carried out by a person who was at the time the tenant but only if the following conditions are satisfied:

(i) that it was carried out other than in pursuance of an obligation to the immediate landlord; and

(ii) that it was either carried out during the current tenancy or not more than 21 years before the application for the new tenancy was made provided that the holding or the relevant part affected by the improvement has at all times since the improvement was made been held on a business tenancy within section 23 and that at the termination of each of those tenancies the tenant did not quit (section 33(1),(2)).

(4) In the case of a holding comprising licensed premises any addition to its value attributable to the licence if it appears to the court that the benefit of the licence belongs to the tenant.

The court is specifically empowered, at its discretion, to include a rent review clause in the new tenancy. This is standard practice in tenancies other than short tenancies. The clause may be an upwards or downwards review clause (see, *e.g. Janes (Gowns) Ltd v. Harlow Development Corpn* (1979) 253 E.G. 799; *Amarjee v. Barrowfen Properties Ltd* [1993] 2 E.G.L.R. 133, CC; *Fourbouys plc v. Newport Borough Council* [1994] 1 E.G.L.R. 13, CC).

The rent to be paid under the new tenancy is described by Hill and Redman as "the most frequent source of dispute under the operation of the Act." As in the case of other terms of the new tenancy, one of the circumstances to be taken into account when determining the rent is the effect of the Landlord and Tenant (Covenants) Act 1995 (s.33(4)) (see Chapters 4 and 7 above).

In practice the matter is determined in most cases by the use of expert evidence given by experienced surveyors as to the level of rents for comparable properties or if there are none by extrapolation from their knowledge of rental levels and increases generally in the area (see *W.J Barton Ltd v. Long Acre Securities Ltd* [1982] 1 W.L.R. 398; *Newey & Eyre Ltd v. J. Curtis & Son Ltd* (1984) 271 E.G. 891 and *National Car Parks v. Colebrook Estates Ltd* (1982) 266 E.G. 810).

INDEX